The Moral Life

Jane Eddy 229
222

The Moral Life

An Introductory Reader
in Ethics and Literature

LOUIS P. POJMAN

New York   Oxford
OXFORD UNIVERSITY PRESS
2000

Oxford University Press

Oxford New York
Athens Auckland Bangkok Bogotá Buenos Aires Calcutta
Cape Town Chennai Dar es Salaam Delhi Florence Hong Kong Istanbul
Karachi Kuala Lumpur Madrid Melbourne Mexico City Mumbai
Nairobi Paris São Paulo Singapore Taipei Tokyo Toronto Warsaw

and associated companies in
Berlin Ibadan

Copyright © 2000 by Oxford University Press, Inc.

Published by Oxford University Press, Inc.,
198 Madison Avenue, New York, New York, 10016
http://www.oup-usa.org

Oxford is a registered trademark of Oxford University Press

Library of Congress Cataloging-in-Publication Data

Pojman, Louis P.
    The moral life : an introductory reader in ethics and literature /
Louis P. Pojman.
        p.   cm.
    Includes bibliographical references.
    ISBN 0-19-512844-3 (pbk. : alk. paper)
    1. Ethics.   I. Title.
BJ1025.P67   1999
170—dc21   98-46486
                                                              CIP

Printing (last digit): 9 8 7 6 5 4 3

Printed in the United States of America
on acid-free paper

Dedicated to
my colleagues in the English department
United States Military Academy
West Point

●

Where Philosophy and English
cross-fertilize each other
in a magnificent manner

CONTENTS

PREFACE

This is a book integrating literature with philosophy, while also covering both classical and contemporary ethical theory and applied topics. Literature often highlights moral ideas, focusing on particular people in their dilemmas, awakening our imagination to new possibilities, and enabling us to understand the moral life in fresh and creative ways. Good literature compels us to rethink and revise our everyday assumptions. It sets before us powerful particularities, which serve both as reinforcers and counterexamples to our sweeping principles. Harriet Beecher Stowe's *Uncle Tom's Cabin* challenged the assumptions of ante-bellum America and created great sympathy for the abolitionist cause. Arthur Koestler's *Darkness at Noon* and George Orwell's *Animal Farm* and *1984* brought clearly home to millions the dangers of totalitarianism. Dostoevski's *Crime and Punishment* made us aware of the haunting voice of conscience that could overturn our best rationalization. William Golding's *Lord of the Flies* is like a picture worth a thousand arguments on why we need morality. William Styron's *Sophie's Choice* faces us with the tragedy of moral choice when all options are unacceptable. Aldous Huxley's *Brave New World* highlights the paradox of freedom and welfare better than any political philosophy book I've ever read. Victor Hugo's bishop of Digne encountering Jean Valjean is a more eloquent statement on the virtuous person than anything ever published in professional journals on virtue ethics. Tolstoy's short stories on greed and love leave their indelible marks on our souls. And so it goes. Good literature is the contemporary equivalent of the parables of the New Testament. It makes the abstract concrete, brings it home to the heart, and forces us to think with innovative imagination.

Yet, acknowledging the element of truth in Kant's rejection of the empirical and the need for examples in ethics, particularity often is one-sided and passion-ridden. If it leaves us merely with gut reactions to a particular tragedy, it tends toward bias and irrationality. One needs cool-headed philosophical analysis to play a sturdy role in sorting out the ambiguities and ambivalences in literature, to abstract from particulars and universalize principles, to generate wide-ranging intellectual theories. To paraphrase Kant, the passionate imagination of literature is blind without the cool head of philosophy, but the cool head of philosophy is sterile and as frigid as an iceberg without the passions of life, conveyed in literature.

I have endeavored to join forces, to unite literature and philosophy in the service of ethical understanding. Most sections of this work open with literary pieces.

This work is divided into four parts:

I. *The Nature of Morality.* The central problems: What is morality? What is it for? What is its scope and force? I use Golding's *Lord of the Flies,* Melville's *Billy Budd,* and Styron's *Sophie's Choice* to highlight central themes, followed by philosophical essays that delve more systematically into the nature of morality, the nature of good and evil, and, relating to the scope and force of morality, moral relativism and objectivism. One might wonder why the latter issue comes in so soon, but there may be no issue more in dispute among young people today than this topic. Hence its prominence.

II. *Moral Theories.* The three classic ethical theories: utilitarianism, deontological ethics, and virtue ethics. Following the chapter on virtue ethics, I have included essays on particular virtues and vices, such as Tolstoy's "How Much Land Does a Man Need?" and "Where Love Is, There Is God," Kant's "Jealousy, Malice, and Ingratitude," Helen Keller's "Three Days to See," and Vice Admiral Stockdale's "The World of Epictetus."

III. *Moral Issues.* Why be moral? What is the meaning of life? What is important about freedom, autonomy, and self-respect? I have included Plato's classic discussion of "The Ring of Gyges," James Rachels' exposition of ethical egoism, followed by my critique of ethical egoism, and writings by Epicurus, Epictetus, Camus, Frankl, Buddha, Nozick, Sartre, Martin Luther King, Jr., and Thomas Hill.

IV. *Applied Ethics.* Contemporary issues such as sex, love, and marriage; abortion; substance abuse; animal rights; and the environment. I have chosen issues that relate primarily to personal, rather than social, morality.

There are fifteen chapters and eighty-six articles in all. Short introductions open each part and chapter. Each reading is introduced with an abstract and most essays conclude with questions for further reflection.

Many people have helped with this project. Robert Miller, Philosophy Editor at Oxford University Press, first proposed the idea of this anthology and gave enormous support to it. My colleagues in the English Department (an umbrella department for philosophy at West Point—we have seventeen philosophers in the English Department, which must be a record—plus a lot of English faculty who are addictive philosophers). This book is dedicated to all the members of my department, who are as collegial, honorable, and unpretentious colleagues as any I have had the pleasure of working with. Captain Jowell Parks and Lieutenant Colonels Janice Hudley, Mike Owens, Al Bishop, and Mike Burke all made excellent suggestions along the way. Colonel Peter Stromberg, our head, has supported my work with wonderful generosity. Mylan Engel contributed an original essay on vegetarianism for this volume. Robert Audi, Margarita Levin, Robert van Wyk, Bonnie Steinbock, and several anonymous reviewers offered good advice, as did my wife, Trudy, who has been my deepest friend and inspiration for over thirty years.

United States Military Academy   *L. P. P.*
West Point, N.Y.
January 1999

The Moral Life

Introduction

On the Nature of Morality

Morality is about good and evil, and right and wrong action. What exactly are these? It is not always easy to say. Various religions and philosophies differ. What is the good? Religious people identify it with God, the source of all being and value. Plato thought the good was a transcendent, indefinable mystery, the source of all being and value. It is the absolute truth, higher even than God and discoverable by reason and intuition. Plato's follower, the Cambridge philosopher G. E. Moore, modified Plato's formula, omitting the transcendent dimension. The good, he thought, was a nonnatural, indefinable property like the color yellow. It was not the source of all reality, only of morality and aesthetic reality. On the other hand, Jeremy Bentham (chapter 4), William James, and Richard Taylor (chapter 2) deny there is anything mysterious or transcendent about goodness. They hold that the good is a definable, natural property. It refers to pleasure or the object of desire—*good* is a functional term which refers to the satisfaction of our desires, the pleasure we feel when satisfied. Variations on this basic hedonism appear in the literature; the human good for Mill consists not just in any kind of pleasure but in certain qualities of pleasure—a deep sense of well-being or happiness spread over a lifetime, not necessarily a life of ecstatic rapture, "but moments of such, in an existence made up of few and transitory pains, many and various pleasures, with a decided predominance of the active over the passive, and having as the foundation of the whole, not to expect more from life than it is capable of bestowing."[1]

[1]John Stuart Mill, *Utilitarianism* (1863, chapter 2). Mill elaborates on his functional hedonism: "Happiness is a life in which exist free action (includ-

For Nietzsche (chapter 2) goodness has nothing to do with pleasure or happiness ("Only the Englishman wants that") but power, the sense of dominating, of being in control, of being the alpha male in the pack. Goodness derives from the will to power that we all deeply crave. As such it is hierarchical and inegalitarian. But the envious mediocre masses detest this natural good, and so are determined to crush it. Morality, according to Nietzsche, is the herd's attempt to institutionalize mediocrity and protect the sheep from the more excellent wolves. The priests, both religious and secular moralizers, invent the soft moral virtues (pity, patience, peace, kindness, forgiveness, and tolerance) in order to protect themselves from their betters. Helping the worst off, redeeming the worthless, forgiving the criminal, maintaining the lives of sick bodies and diseased souls—the criminals, the stupid, and the mediocre. The ideas of good and evil must be understood in the clash between the superior overmen, and the priests who represent the masses. Right and wrong action, then, become a kind of politically correct ideology which, ironically, proves the Nietzschean point of the will to power. For the moralists invent good and evil in order to empower themselves and their clientele against their superior enemy.

Where does the truth lie in these matters? One thing everyone engaged in the debate recognizes: morality is both personal and social. It is personal in that it has to do with how we should live our lives, what we should strive to become. It is social in that it recognizes that we are not hermits or gods, independent beings with no need for each other. We are centers of conscious striving, desire, who have wills of our own but have to adjust the pursuit of our goals in the light of other people's desires and interests. How to reconcile and adjust these twin forces, the personal and the social, is the central domain of ethics. It is the central concern of this anthology. Many works of ethics emphasize the broader areas of social policy or social ethics: just-war theory, economic relations, punishment, political arrangements, and institutional justice. There is a place for that. But what I want us to focus on in this work is the more personal dimension of ethics: its raison d'être, its funda-

---

ing meaningful work), loving relations, and moral character, and in which the individual is not plagued by guilt and anxiety but is blessed with peace and satisfaction."

mental purposes. We want to build from the ground up, for unless we get our foundations firmly laid, our structure will be in danger of capsizing. We will first study the nature of morality, beginning with a sizable selection from William Golding's moral allegory, *Lord of the Flies*. After a commentary, we will examine the philosophical analogue to Golding's work, Thomas Hobbes's *Leviathan*, written three hundred years earlier. After this we raise one of the most crucial questions about morality: is it universally valid or only relative to individual choice or one's culture?

In Part II we progress to the three classic moral theories: *utilitarianism*, which aims at maximizing good consequences, usually defined in terms of pleasure or happiness; *deontological ethics*, which focuses on the individual act (its inherent rightness or wrongness) and the individual (his or her inherent dignity or value); and *virtue ethics*, which focuses on character, the kind of qualities we should inculcate, the kind of people we should become. But all of these theories recognize the role of virtue and vice—morally significant character traits. So in the fourth chapter of Part II we examine several classic virtues and vices.

In Part III we consider theoretical issues that are implicit in our study of the nature of morality and moral theories, enlarging on what was said earlier. If the first two parts constituted the foundations and formal structure of moral theory, Part III deals with the materials in our building. First we examine the idea of the self in relation to others. Sometimes we can flout moral rules when it is in our perceived interest to do so. Should we do so? Why should we be moral whenever we can enhance personal gain by disregarding morality's requirements? This problem is related to the second—what really is important about life, what, if anything, gives it meaning? Or is it merely "a tale told by an idiot, full of sound and fury, signifying nothing"? Here we look at various worldviews about the nature and destiny of humanity: Epicureanism, Stoicism, Theism, Buddhism, Existentialism, and others. In chapter 10 we examine the importance of freedom and autonomy.

Finally, in Part IV we examine seven practical moral issues. Continuing our metaphor of the house, these constitute the inner dynamics, the plumbing, electricity, and furniture. In chapter 11 we examine the meaning of human sexuality in relation to love and marriage. What does morality permit and forbid? Why is adultery wrong? Is monogamous marriage really a moral good? Should we need licenses to have children? Chapter 12 analyzes the difficult problem of abortion. In chapter 13 we consider the use and abuse of drugs and alcohol. Chapter 14 deals with our duties to animals and takes up the issue of vegetarianism. Chapter 15 considers our duty to the environment.

I have generally included readings which take opposing stands on the issues at hand, though sometimes I have simply included a reading to stimulate thinking, say on LaFollette's claim that the government should require people to obtain a license to have children or Engel's claim that moral people already hold beliefs that commit them to being vegetarians. The main purpose of this work is to help you think through the difficult and exciting personal dimensions of what morality is about. Hence the use of literature to supplement philosophical analysis.

Literature particularizes general problems, brings them home to us, enlivening the imagination so that we see and feel nuances that are vital to resolving difficult moral issues, possibilities that we might not have considered in our abstract thinking about moral dilemmas. But it is no substitute for philosophical analysis, so while many chapters begin with a literary work, the philosophical essays are where most of the necessary argument takes place.

Part I

The Nature
of Morality
Good and Evil

In this part of our work we consider three fundamental questions relating to morality: What is the purpose of morality? What are good and evil? Is morality essentially relative or are there objective moral truths? We begin each chapter with a literary selection and then go on to provide a philosophical analysis. Let us look briefly at the first of these questions.

What is the purpose of morality? What is morality for? It seems to have many purposes. These include enabling us to reach our goals in socially acceptable ways, enabling us to resolve conflicts of interests fairly, developing certain kinds of positive character, promoting human happiness, enabling society to survive. You can probably think of others. But just as a picture is worth a thousand words, a good story may do more to illuminate the purpose of morality than a thousand disquisitions on the subject. So we begin our book with a sizable selection from William Golding's *Lord of the Flies,* a modern allegory on the nature and purpose of morality. A group of British private school boys are marooned on an island; detached from the constraints of civilization, they turn into savages. Whether or not human nature is as depraved as Golding makes it out to be, the significance of the book lies in the fact that it illuminates the need for and purpose of ethical codes. After Golding's novel, I give an analysis on its meaning for our understanding of morality. This is followed by a selection from Thomas Hobbes's classic work *Leviathan* (1651), which, in seventeenth-century prose, poignantly sets forth a similar message to Golding's.

These three chapters center on the foundational problems of moral philosophy. It is imperative that we think clearly about them before we tackle normative theories and applied ethics. Let us turn now to one of the great moral allegories of our time, William Golding's *Lord of the Flies*.

CHAPTER 1

What Is the Purpose of Morality?

Lord of the Flies
A Moral Allegory

WILLIAM GOLDING

William Golding is considered one of the most profoundly insightful writers of our age. His works explore the human condition and the need for moral consciousness. In this work, published in 1954, Golding describes a situation in which the veneer of civilization is stripped away from children and a primordial evil emerges out of the depths of the human heart.

An indeterminate number of schoolboys, ranging in age from six to twelve, are cast adrift on an uninhabited island in the Pacific, after being evacuated from England during the next world war. They are forced to create their own social system. All begins well, as Ralph is democratically chosen leader of the group and appropriate rules are agreed upon: keep the fire going, use proper sanitation, obey proper authority and orderly procedures in the assembly. Bereft of modern technology, they must reinvent simple tools or use tools for innovative purposes: eyeglasses to focus the sun's light to start a fire, sticks for spears. They construct shelters and build a fire on the top of the mountain in order to signal their presence to passing ships. They miss simple conveniences: scissors to cut their long, knotty hair, toothbrushes, sanitary facilities, and clothes.

For a while the constraints of civilized society prevent total chaos. While the youngest children, "littluns," are frightened and homesick, the older boys entertain them. They seem ready to make the best out of their fate, and recognize the necessity of substantive and procedural rules. Only he who has the white conch, the symbol of authority, may speak at an assembly, and the democratically chosen leader is invested with limited powers. Even the sadistic Roger, while taunting little Henry by throwing stones near him, manages to keep the stones from harming the child.

Here, invisible yet strong, was the taboo of the old life. Round the squatting child was the protection of parents and school and policemen and the law. Roger's arm was conditioned by a civilization that knew nothing of him and was in ruins. (p. 78)

After some initial euphoria at being liberated from the adult world of constraints into an exciting world of fun in the sun, the children come up against the usual banes of social existence: filth, competition for power and status, neglect of social responsibility, failure of public policy, and escalating violence. Two boys, Ralph, the son of a naval officer, and Jack, the head choirboy, vie for leadership and a bitter rivalry emerges between them. As a compromise, a division of labor ensues in which Jack's choirboy hunters refuse to help Ralph and a few others in constructing shelters. Piggy, the bespectacled asthmatic, acts as the wise and rational counselor, and Simon, an epileptic, is portrayed as possessing special spiritual insight, but these qualities, rationality and spirituality, are tested by the Lord of the Flies. Freeloading soon becomes a common phenomenon as the majority of children leave their tasks to play on the beach. Sanitation becomes a problem, as the diarrheal children defecate all over the beach. Neglect of the fire causes it to burn out, which, in turn, results in failure to be rescued by a passing ship. We enter the novel as Jack returns with his choirboy hunters, having slain their first pig, only to be reprimanded by Ralph for not tending the fire.

The hunters were more silent now, but at this they buzzed again. Ralph flung back his hair. One arm pointed at the empty horizon. His voice was loud and savage, and struck them into silence.

"There was a ship."

Jack, faced at once with too many awful implications, ducked away from them. He laid a hand on the pig and drew his knife. Ralph brought his arm down, fist clenched, and his voice shook.

"There was a ship. Out there. You said you'd keep the fire going and you let it out!" He took a step towards Jack who turned and faced him.

"They might have seen us. We might have gone home—"

This was too bitter for Piggy, who forgot his timidity in the agony of his loss. He began to cry out, shrilly:

"You and your blood, Jack Merridew! You and your hunting! We might have gone home——"

Ralph pushed Piggy on one side.

"I was chief; and you were going to do what I said. You talk. But you can't even build huts—then you go off hunting and let out the fire——"

He turned away, silent for a moment. Then his voice came again on a peak of feeling.

"There was a ship——"

One of the smaller hunters began to wail. The dismal truth was filtering through to everybody. Jack went very red as he hacked and pulled at the pig.

"The job was too much. We needed everyone."

Ralph turned.

"You could have had everyone when the shelters were finished. But you had to hunt—"

"We needed meat."

Jack stood up as he said this, the bloodied knife in his hand. The two boys faced each other. There was the brilliant world of hunting, tactics, fierce exhilaration, skill; and there was the world of longing and baffled common-sense. Jack transferred the knife to his left hand and smudged blood over his forehead as he pushed down the plastered hair.

Piggy began again.

"You didn't ought to have let that fire out. You said you'd keep the smoke going——"

This from Piggy, and the wails of agreement from some of the hunters drove Jack to violence. The bolting look came into his blue eyes. He took a step, and able at last to hit someone, stuck his fist into Piggy's stomach. Piggy sat down with a grunt. Jack stood over him. His voice was vicious with humiliation.

"You would, would you? Fatty!"

Ralph made a step forward and Jack smacked Piggy's head. Piggy's glasses flew off and tinkled on the rocks. Piggy cried out in terror:

"My specs!"

He went crouching and feeling over the rocks but Simon, who got there first, found them for him. Passions beat about Simon on the mountain-top with awful wings.

"One side's broken."

Piggy grabbed and put on the glasses. He looked malevolently at Jack.

"I got to have them specs. Now I only got one eye. Jus' you wait——"

Jack made a move towards Piggy who scrambled away till a great rock lay between them. He thrust his head over the top and glared at Jack through his one flashing glass.

"Now I only got one eye. Just you wait——"

Jack mimicked the whine and scramble.

"Jus' you wait—yah!"

Piggy and the parody were so funny that the hunters began to laugh. Jack felt encouraged. He went on scrambling and the laughter rose to a gale of hysteria. Unwillingly Ralph felt his lips twitch; he was angry with himself for giving way.

He muttered.

"That was a dirty trick."

Jack broke out of his gyration and stood facing Ralph. His words came in a shout.

"All right, all right!"

He looked at Piggy, at the hunters, at Ralph.

"I'm sorry. About the fire, I mean. There. I——"

He drew himself up.

"—I apologize."

The buzz from the hunters was one of admiration at this handsome behaviour. Clearly they were of the opinion that Jack had done the decent thing, had put himself in the right by his generous apology and Ralph, obscurely, in the wrong. They waited for an appropriately decent answer.

Yet Ralph's throat refused to pass one. He resented, as an addition to Jack's misbehaviour, this verbal trick. The fire was dead, the ship was gone. Could they not see? Anger instead of decency passed his throat.

"That was a dirty trick."

They were silent on the mountain-top while the opaque look appeared in Jack's eyes and passed away.

Ralph's final word was an ungracious mutter.

"All right. Light the fire."

With some positive action before them, a little of the tension died. Ralph said no more, did nothing, stood looking down at the ashes round his feet. Jack was loud and active. He gave orders, sang, whistled, threw remarks at the silent Ralph—remarks that did not need an answer, and therefore could not invite a snub; and still Ralph was silent. No one, not even Jack, would ask him to move and in the end they had to build the fire three yards away and in a place not really as convenient. So Ralph asserted his chieftainship and could not have chosen a better way if he had thought for days. Against this weapon, so indefinable and so effective, Jack was powerless and raged without knowing why. By the time the pile was built, they were on different sides of a high barrier.

When they had dealt with the fire another crisis arose. Jack had no means of lighting it. Then to his surprise, Ralph went to Piggy and took the glasses from him. Not even Ralph knew how a link between him and Jack had been snapped and fastened elsewhere.

"I'll bring 'em back."

"I'll come too."

Piggy stood behind him, islanded in a sea of meaningless colour, while Ralph knelt and focused the glossy spot. Instantly the fire was alight Piggy held out his hands and grabbed the glasses back.

Before these fantastically attractive flowers of violet and red and yellow, unkindness melted away. They became a circle of boys round a camp fire and even Piggy and Ralph were half-drawn in. Soon some of the boys were rushing down the slope for more wood while Jack hacked the pig. They tried holding the whole carcass on a stake over the fire, but the stake burnt more quickly than the pig roasted. In the end they skewered bits of meat on branches and held them in the flames: and even then almost as much boy was roasted as meat.

Ralph dribbled. He meant to refuse meat but his past diet of fruit and nuts, with an odd crab or fish, gave him too little resistance. He accepted a piece of half-raw meat and gnawed it like a wolf.

Piggy spoke, also dribbling.

"Aren't I having none?"

Jack had meant to leave him in doubt, as an assertion of power; but Piggy by advertising his omission made more cruelty necessary.

"You didn't hunt."

"No more did Ralph," said Piggy wetly, "nor Simon." He amplified. "There isn't more than a ha'porth of meat in a crab."

Ralph stirred uneasily. Simon, sitting between the twins and Piggy, wiped his mouth and shoved his piece of meat over the rocks to Piggy, who grabbed it. The twins giggled and Simon lowered his face in shame.

Then Jack leapt to his feet, slashed off a great hunk of meat, and flung it down at Simon's feet.

"Eat! Damn you!"

He glared at Simon.

"Take it!"

He spun on his heel, centre of a bewildered circle of boys.

"I got you meat!"

Numberless and inexpressible frustrations combined to make his rage elemental and awe-inspiring.

"I painted my face—I stole up. Now you eat—all of you—and I——"

Slowly the silence on the mountain-top deepened till the click of the fire and the soft hiss of roasting meat could be heard clearly. Jack looked round for understanding but found only respect. Ralph stood among the ashes of the signal fire, his hands full of meat, saying nothing.

Then at last Maurice broke the silence. He changed the subject to the only one that could bring the majority of them together.

"Where did you find the pig?"

Roger pointed down the unfriendly side.

"They were there—by the sea."

Jack, recovering, could not bear to have his story told. He broke in quickly.

"We spread round. I crept, on hands and knees. The spears fell out because they hadn't barbs on. The pig ran away and made an awful noise——"

"It turned back and ran into the circle, bleeding——"

All the boys were talking at once, relieved and excited.

"We closed in——"

The first blow had paralysed its hind quarters, so then the circle could close in and beat and beat—

"I cut the pig's throat——"

The twins, still sharing their identical grin, jumped up and ran round each other. Then the rest joined in, making pig-dying noises and shouting.

"One for his nob!"

"Give him a fourpenny one!"

Then Maurice pretended to be the pig and ran squealing into the centre, and the hunters, circling still, pretended to beat him. As they danced, they sang.

"*Kill the pig. Cut her throat. Bash her in.*"

Ralph watched them, envious and resentful. Not till they flagged and the chant died away, did he speak.

"I'm calling an assembly."

One by one, they halted, and stood watching him.

"With the conch. I'm calling a meeting even if we have to go on into the dark. Down on the platform. When I blow it. Now."

He turned away and walked off, down the mountain.

[Things degenerate. The fire, the symbol of hope, is left unattended, and the conch, the symbol of orderly governance, is disdained by Jack's group. With the diminished symbols, Ralph's authority, and the rational procedures he stands for, become undermined. Frightened little Percival reports that he has seen the beast, a preternatural creature who bodes no good. Piggy dismisses such talk as superstitious and assures the group that life follows scientific laws that exclude the preternatural. Ghosts and beasts can't exist. Why not?

"'Cos things wouldn't make sense. Houses an' streets, an' TV—they wouldn't work."

But Simon thinks differently. "Maybe there is a beast."

The assembly cried out savagely and Ralph stood up in amazement. "You, Simon? You believe in this?"

. . . "What I mean is . . . maybe it's only us."

"Nuts" [responded] Piggy shocked out of decorum . . .

Simon became inarticulate in his effort to express mankind's essential illness.

Eventually Jack succeeds in winning all but five of the boys to his cause. Only Simon, Piggy, and the twins, Sam and Eric ("Samneric"), remain with Ralph in his project of keeping the fire burning and living by the rule of law, though Simon has gone off on a venture. The crowd has joined Jack and his hunters. Jack rules by charismatic might, livening their spirits with pig hunts and orgies, but treating the littluns cruelly. Needing a magnifying glass to start their fire for the pig roast, three hunters, Jack, Roger, and Maurice, steal into Ralph and Piggy's shelter, attack Ralph and Piggy, and steal Piggy's glasses. We enter (chapter 11) where Ralph and his friends are grieving the loss of the glasses and the fire. Piggy, com-

plains that without his glasses he can't see, and demands that they confront Jack with his crime. He speaks:]

"I got the conch. I'm going to that Jack Merridew an' tell him, I am."

"You'll get hurt."

"What can he do more than he has? I'll tell him what's what. You let me carry the conch, Ralph. I'll show him the one thing he hasn't got."

Piggy paused for a moment and peered round at the dim figures. The shape of the old assembly, trodden in the grass, listened to him.

"I'm going to him with this conch in my hands. I'm going to hold it out. Look, I'm goin' to say, you're stronger than I am and you haven't got asthma. You can see, I'm goin' to say, and with both eyes. But I don't ask for my glasses back, not as a favour. I don't ask you to be a sport, I'll say, not because you're strong, but because what's right's right. Give me my glasses, I'm going to say—you got to!"

Piggy ended, flushed and trembling. He pushed the conch quickly into Ralph's hands as though in a hurry to be rid of it and wiped the tears from his eyes. The green light was gentle about them and the conch lay at Ralph's feet, fragile and white. A single drop of water that had escaped Piggy's fingers now flashed on the delicate curve like a star.

At last Ralph sat up straight and drew back his hair.

"All right. I mean—you can try if you like. We'll go with you."

"He'll be painted," said Sam, timidly. "You know how he'll be——"

"—he won't think much of us——"

"—if he gets waxy we've had it——"

Ralph scowled at Sam. Dimly he remembered something that Simon had said to him once, by the rocks.

"Don't be silly," he said. And then he added quickly, "Let's go."

He held out the conch to Piggy who flushed, this time with pride.

"You must carry it."

"When we're ready I'll carry it——"

Piggy sought in his mind for words to convey his passionate willingness to carry the conch against all odds.

"—I don't mind. I'll be glad, Ralph, only I'll have to be led."

Ralph put the conch back on the shining log.

"We better eat and then get ready."

They made their way to the devastated fruit trees. Piggy was helped to his food and found some by touch. While they ate, Ralph thought of the afternoon.

"We'll be like we were. We'll wash——"

Sam gulped down a mouthful and protested.

"But we bathe every day!"

Ralph looked at the filthy objects before him and sighed.

"We ought to comb our hair. Only it's too long."

"I've got both socks left in the shelter," said Eric, "so we could pull them over our heads like caps, sort of."

"We could find some stuff," said Piggy, "and tie your hair back."

"Like a girl!"

"No. 'Course not."

"Then we must go as we are," said Ralph, "and they won't be any better."

Eric made a detaining gesture.

"But they'll be painted! You know how it is——"

The others nodded. They understood only too well the liberation into savagery that the concealing paint brought.

"Well, we won't be painted," said Ralph, "because we aren't savages."

Samneric looked at each other.

"All the same——"

Ralph shouted.

"No paint!" . . .

They set off along the beach in formation. Ralph went first, limping a little, his spear carried over one shoulder. He saw things partially through the tremble of the heat haze over the flashing sands, and his own long hair and injuries. Behind him came the twins, worried now for a while but full of unquenchable vitality. They said little but trailed the butts of their wooden spears; for Piggy had found, that looking down, shielding his tired sight from the sun, he could just see these moving along the sand. He walked between the trailing butts, therefore, the conch held carefully between his two hands. The boys made a compact little group that moved over the beach, four plate-like shadows dancing and mingling beneath them. There was no sign left of the storm, and the beach was swept clean like a blade that has been scoured. The sky and the mountain were at an immense distance, shimmering in the heat; and the reef was lifted by mirage, floating in a kind of silver pool half-way up the sky.

They passed the place where the tribe had danced. The charred sticks still lay on the rocks where the rain had quenched them but the sand by the water was smooth again. They passed this in silence. No one doubted that the tribe would be found at the Castle Rock and when they came in sight of it they stopped with one accord. The densest tangle on the island, a mass of twisted stems, black and green and impenetrable, lay on their left and tall grass swayed before them. Now Ralph went forward.

Here was the crushed grass where they had all lain when he had gone to prospect. There was the neck of land, the ledge skirting the rock, up there were the red pinnacles.

Sam touched his arm.

"Smoke."

There was a tiny smudge of smoke wavering into the air on the other side of the rock.

"Some fire—I don't think."

Ralph turned.

"What are we hiding for?"

He stepped through the screen of grass on to the little open space that led to the narrow neck.

"You two follow behind. I'll go first, then Piggy a pace behind me. Keep your spears ready."

Piggy peered anxiously into the luminous veil that hung between him and the world.

"Is it safe? Ain't there a cliff? I can hear the sea."

"You keep right close to me."

Ralph moved forward on to the neck. He kicked a stone and it bounded into the water. Then the sea sucked down, revealing a red, weedy square forty feet beneath Ralph's left arm.

"Am I safe?" quavered Piggy. "I feel awful——"

High above them from the pinnacles came a sudden shout and then an imitation war-cry that was answered by a dozen voices from behind the rock.

"Give me the conch and stay still."

"Halt! Who goes there?"

Ralph bent back his head and glimpsed Roger's dark face at the top.

"You can see who I am!" he shouted. "Stop being silly!"

He put the conch to his lips and began to blow. Savages appeared, painted out of recognition, edging round the ledge towards the neck. They carried spears and disposed themselves to defend the entrance. Ralph went on blowing and ignored Piggy's terrors.

Roger was shouting.

"You mind out—see?"

At length Ralph took his lips away and paused to get his breath back. His first words were a gasp, but audible.

"—calling an assembly."

The savages guarding the neck muttered among themselves but made no motion. Ralph walked forwards a couple of steps. A voice whispered urgently behind him.

"Don't leave me, Ralph."

"You kneel down," said Ralph sideways, "and wait till I come back."

He stood half-way along the neck and gazed at the savages intently. Freed by the paint, they had tied their hair back and were more comfortable than he was. Ralph made a resolution to tie his own back afterwards. Indeed he felt like telling them to wait and doing it there and then; but that was impossible. The savages sniggered a bit and one gestured at Ralph with his spear. High above, Roger took his hands off the lever and leaned out to see what was going on. The boys on the neck stood in a pool of their own shadow, diminished to shaggy heads. Piggy crouched, his back shapeless as a sack.

"I'm calling an assembly."

Silence.

Roger took up a small stone and flung it between the twins, aiming to miss. They started and Sam only just kept his footing. Some source of power began to pulse in Roger's body.

Ralph spoke again, loudly.

"I'm calling an assembly."

He ran his eye over them.

"Where's Jack?"

The group of boys stirred and consulted. A painted face spoke with the voice of Robert.

"He's hunting. And he said we weren't to let you in."

"I've come to see about the fire," said Ralph, "and about Piggy's specs."

The group in front of him shifted and laughter shivered outwards from among them, light, excited laughter that went echoing among the tall rocks.

A voice spoke from behind Ralph.

"What do you want?"

The twins made a bolt past Ralph and got between him and the entry. He turned quickly. Jack, identifiable by personality and red hair, was advancing from the forest. A hunter crouched on either side. All three were masked in black and green. Behind them on the grass the headless and paunched body of a sow lay where they had dropped it.

Piggy wailed.

"Ralph! Don't leave me!"

With ludicrous care he embraced the rock, pressing himself to it above the sucking sea. The sniggering of the savages became a loud derisive jeer.

Jack shouted above the noise.

"You go away, Ralph. You keep to your end. This is my end and my tribe. You leave me alone."

The jeering died away.

"You pinched Piggy's specs," said Ralph, breathlessly. "You've got to give them back."

"Got to? Who says?"

Ralph's temper blazed out.

"I say! You voted for me for Chief. Didn't you hear the conch? You played a dirty trick—we'd have given you fire if you'd asked for it——"

The blood was flowing in his cheeks and the bunged-up eye throbbed.

"You could have had fire whenever you wanted. But you didn't. You came sneaking up like a thief and stole Piggy's glasses!"

"Say that again!"

"Thief! Thief!"

Piggy screamed.

"Ralph! Mind me!"

Jack made a rush and stabbed at Ralph's chest with his spear. Ralph sensed the position of the weapon from the glimpse he caught of Jack's arm and put the thrust aside with his own butt. Then he brought the end round and caught Jack a stinger across the ear. They were chest to chest, breathing fiercely, pushing and glaring.

"Who's a thief?"

"You are!"

Jack wrenched free and swung at Ralph with his spear. By common consent they were using the spears as sabres now, no longer daring the lethal points. The blow struck Ralph's spear and slid down, to fall agonizingly on his fingers. Then they were apart once more, their positions reversed, Jack towards the Castle Rock and Ralph on the outside towards the island.

Both boys were breathing very heavily.

"Come on then——"

"Come on——"

Truculently they squared up to each other but kept just out of fighting distance.

"You come on and see what you get!"

"You come on——"

Piggy clutching the ground was trying to attract Ralph's attention. Ralph moved, bent down, kept a wary eye on Jack.

"Ralph—remember what we came for. The fire. My specs."

Ralph nodded. He relaxed his fighting muscles, stood easily and grounded the butt of his spear. Jack watched him inscrutably through his paint. Ralph glanced up at the pinnacles, then towards the group of savages.

"Listen. We've come to say this. First you've got to give back Piggy's specs. If he hasn't got them he can't see. You aren't playing the game——"

The tribe of painted savages giggled and Ralph's mind faltered. He pushed his hair up and gazed at the green and black mask before him, trying to remember what Jack looked like.

Piggy whispered.

"And the fire."

"Oh yes. Then about the fire. I say this again. I've been saying it ever since we dropped in."

He held out his spear and pointed at the savages.

"Your only hope is keeping a signal fire going as long as there's light to see. Then maybe a ship 'll notice the smoke and come and rescue us and take us home. But without that smoke we've got to wait till some ship comes by accident. We might wait years; till we were old——"

The shivering, silvery, unreal laughter of the savages sprayed out and echoed away. A gust of rage shook Ralph. His voice cracked.

"Don't you understand, you painted fools? Sam, Eric, Piggy and me—we aren't enough. We tried to keep the fire going, but we couldn't. And then you, playing at hunting. . . . "

He pointed past them to where the trickle of smoke dispersed in the pearly air.

"Look at that! Call that a signal fire? That's a cooking fire. Now you'll eat and there'll be no smoke. Don't you understand? There may be a ship out there—"

He paused, defeated by the silence and the painted anonymity of the group guarding the entry. The chief opened a pink mouth and addressed Samneric who were between him and his tribe.

"You two. Get back."

No one answered him. The twins, puzzled, looked at each other; while Piggy, reassured by the cessation of violence, stood up carefully. Jack glanced back at Ralph and then at the twins.

"Grab them!"

No one moved. Jack shouted angrily.

"I said 'grab them'!"

The painted group moved round Samneric nervously and unhandily. Once more the silvery laughter scattered.

Samneric protested out of the heart of civilization.

"Oh, I say!"

"—honestly!"

Their spears were taken from them.

"Tie them up!"

Ralph cried out hopelessly against the black and green mask.

"Jack!"

"Go on. Tie them."

Now the painted group felt the otherness of Samneric, felt the power in their own hands. They felled the twins clumsily and excitedly. Jack was inspired. He knew that Ralph would attempt a rescue. He struck in a humming circle behind him and Ralph only just parried the blow. Beyond them the tribe and the twins were a loud and writhing heap. Piggy crouched again. Then the twins lay, astonished, and the tribe stood round them. Jack turned to Ralph and spoke between his teeth.

"See? They do what I want."

There was silence again. The twins lay, inexpertly tied up, and the tribe watched Ralph to see what he would do. He numbered them through his fringe, glimpsed the ineffectual smoke.

His temper broke. He screamed at Jack.

"You're a beast and a swine and a bloody, bloody thief!"

He charged.

Jack, knowing this was the crisis, charged too. They met with a jolt and bounced apart. Jack swung with his fist at Ralph and caught him on the ear. Ralph hit Jack in the stomach and made him grunt.

Then they were facing each other again, panting and furious, but unnerved by each other's ferocity. They became aware of the noise that was the background to this fight, the steady shrill cheering of the tribe behind them.

Piggy's voice penetrated to Ralph.

"Let me speak."

He was standing in the dust of the fight, and as the tribe saw his intention the shrill cheer changed to a steady booing.

Piggy held up the conch and the booing sagged a little, then came up again to strength.

"I got the conch!"

He shouted.

"I tell you, I got the conch!"

Surprisingly, there was silence now; the tribe were curious to hear what amusing thing he might have to say.

Silence and pause; but in the silence a curious air-noise, close by Ralph's head. He gave it half his attention—and there it was again; a faint "Zup!" Someone was throwing stones: Roger was dropping them, his one hand still on the lever. Below him, Ralph was a shock of hair and Piggy a bag of fat.

"I got this to say. You're acting like a crowd of kids."

The booing rose and died again as Piggy lifted the white, magic shell.

"Which is better—to be a pack of painted niggers like you are, or to be sensible like Ralph is?"

A great clamour rose among the savages. Piggy shouted again.

"Which is better—to have rules and agree, or to hunt and kill?"

Again the clamour and again—"Zup!"

Ralph shouted against the noise.

"Which is better, law and rescue, or hunting and breaking things up?"

Now Jack was yelling too and Ralph could no longer make himself heard. Jack had backed right against the tribe and they were a solid mass of menace that bristled with spears. The intention of a charge was forming among them; they were working up to it and the neck would be swept clear. Ralph stood facing them, a little to one side, his spear ready. By him stood Piggy still holding out the talisman, the fragile, shining beauty of the shell. The storm of sound beat at them, an incantation of hatred. High overhead, Roger, with a sense of delirious abandonment, leaned all his weight on the lever.

Ralph heard the great rock long before he saw it. He was aware of a jolt in the earth that came to him through the soles of his feet, and the breaking sound of stones at the top of the cliff. Then the monstrous red thing bounded across the neck and he flung himself flat while the tribe shrieked.

The rock struck Piggy a glancing blow from chin to knee: the conch exploded into a thousand white fragments and ceased to exist. Piggy, saying nothing, with no time for even a grunt, travelled through the air sideways from the rock, turning over as he went. The rock bounded twice and was lost in the forest. Piggy fell forty feet and landed on his back across that square, red rock in the sea. His head opened and stuff came out and turned red. Piggy's arms and legs twitched a bit, like a pig's after it has been killed. Then the sea breathed again in a long, slow sigh, the water boiled white and pink over the rock; and when it went, sucking back again, the body of Piggy was gone.

This time the silence was complete. Ralph's lips formed a word but no sound came.

Suddenly Jack bounded out from the tribe and began screaming wildly.

"See? See? That's what you'll get! I meant that! There isn't a tribe for you any more! The conch is gone—"

He ran forward, stooping.

"I'm Chief!"

Viciously, with full intention, he hurled his spear at Ralph. The point tore the skin and flesh over Ralph's ribs, then sheared off and fell in the water. Ralph stumbled, feeling not pain but panic, and the tribe, screaming now like the Chief, began to advance. Another spear, a bent one that would not fly straight, went past his face and one fell from on high where Roger was. The twins lay hidden behind the tribe and the anonymous devils' faces swarmed across the neck. Ralph turned and ran. A great noise as of sea-gulls rose behind him. He obeyed an instinct that he did not know he possessed and swerved over the open space so that the spears went wide. He saw the headless body of the sow and jumped in time. Then he was crashing through foliage and small boughs and was hidden by the forest.

The Chief stopped by the pig, turned and held up his hands.

"Back! Back to the fort!"

Presently the tribe returned noisily to the neck where Roger joined them.

The Chief spoke to him angrily.

"Why aren't you on watch?"

Roger looked at him gravely.

"I just came down——"

The hangman's horror clung round him. The Chief said no more to him but looked down at Samneric.

"You got to join the tribe."

"You lemme go——"

"—and me."

The Chief snatched one of the few spears that were left and poked Sam in the ribs.

"What d'you mean by it, eh?" said the Chief fiercely. "What d'you mean by coming with spears? What d'you mean by not joining my tribe?"

The prodding became rhythmic. Sam yelled.

"That's not the way."

Roger edged past the Chief, only just avoiding pushing him with his shoulder. The yelling ceased, and Samneric lay looking up in quiet terror. Roger advanced upon them as one wielding a nameless authority.

CRY OF THE HUNTERS

Ralph lay in a covert, wondering about his wounds. The bruised flesh was inches in diameter over his right ribs, with a swollen and bloody scar where the spear had hit him. His hair was full of dirt and tapped like the tendrils of a creeper. All over he was scratched and bruised from his flight through the forest. By the time his breathing was normal again, he had worked out that bathing these injuries would have to wait. How could you listen for naked feet if you were splashing in water? How could you be safe by the little stream or on the open beach?

Ralph listened. He was not really far from the Castle Rock, and during the first panic he had thought he heard sounds of pursuit. But the hunters had only sneaked into the fringes of the greenery, retrieving spears perhaps, and then had rushed back to the sunny rock as if terrified of the darkness under the leaves. He had even glimpsed one of them, striped brown, black, and red, and had judged that it was Bill. But really, thought Ralph, this was not Bill.

This was a savage whose image refused to blend with that ancient picture of a boy in shorts and shirt.

The afternoon died away; the circular spots of sunlight moved steadily over green fronds and brown fibre but no sound came from behind the Rock. At last Ralph wormed out of the ferns and sneaked forward to the edge of that impenetrable thicket that fronted the neck of land. He peered with elaborate caution between branches at the edge and could see Robert sitting on guard at the top of the cliff. He held a spear in his left hand and was tossing up a pebble and catching it again with the right. Behind him a column of smoke rose thickly, so that Ralph's nostrils flared and his mouth dribbled. He wiped his nose and mouth with the back of his hand and for the first time since the morning felt hungry. The tribe must be sitting round the gutted pig, watching the fat ooze and burn among the ashes. They would be intent.

Another figure, an unrecognizable one, appeared by Robert and gave him something, then turned and went back behind the rock. Robert laid his spear on the rock beside him and began to gnaw between his raised hands. So the feast was beginning and the watchman had been given his portion.

Ralph saw that for the time being he was safe. He limped away through the fruit trees, drawn by the thought of the poor food yet bitter when he remembered the feast. Feast to-day, and then tomorrow. . . .

He argued unconvincingly that they would let him alone; perhaps even make an outlaw of him. But then the fatal unreasoning knowledge came to him again. The breaking of the conch and the deaths of Piggy and Simon lay over the island like a vapour. These painted savages would go further and further. Then there was that indefinable connection between himself and Jack; who therefore would never let him alone; never.

He paused, sun-flecked, holding up a bough, prepared to duck under it. A spasm of terror set him shaking and he cried aloud.

"No. They're not as bad as that. It was an accident."

He ducked under the bough, ran clumsily, then stopped and listened.

He came to the smashed acres of fruit and ate greedily. He saw two littluns and, not having any idea of his own appearance, wondered why they screamed and ran.

When he had eaten he went towards the beach. The sunlight

was slanting now into the palms by the wrecked shelter. There was the platform and the pool. The best thing to do was to ignore this leaden feeling about the heart and rely on their common sense, their daylight sanity. Now that the tribe had eaten, the thing to do was to try again. And anyway, he couldn't stay here all night in an empty shelter by the deserted platform. His flesh crept and he shivered in the evening sun. No fire; no smoke; no rescue.

[Jack launches a murderous manhunt for Ralph, who hides in the forest. After a time, he hears "a curious trickling sound and then a louder crepitation as if someone were unwrapping great sheets of cellophane." Smoke was flowing through the branches "in white and yellow wisps." Jack had started a forest fire in order to smoke Ralph out into the open. What could he do? He was beginning to panic. He might find a place away from the fire and climb a tree or he could try to burst their line. A third idea was to find a hiding place somewhere and hope his pursuers would pass by him.]

A nearer cry stood him on his feet and immediately he was away again, running fast among thorns and brambles. Suddenly he blundered into the open, found himself again in that open space—and there was the fathom-wide grin of the skull, no longer ridiculing a deep blue patch of sky but jeering up into a blanket of smoke. Then Ralph was running beneath trees, with the grumble of the forest explained. They had smoked him out and set the island on fire.

Hide was better than a tree because you had a chance of breaking the line if you were discovered.

Hide, then.

He wondered if a pig would agree, and grimaced at nothing. Find the deepest thicket, the darkest hole on the island, and creep in. Now, as he ran, he peered about him. Bars and splashes of sunlight flitted over him and sweat made glistening streaks on his dirty body. The cries were far now, and faint.

At last he found what seemed to him the right place, though the decision was desperate. Here, bushes and a wild tangle of creeper made a mat that kept out all the light of the sun. Beneath it was a space, perhaps a foot high, though it was pierced everywhere by parallel and rising stems. If you wormed into the middle of that you would be five yards from the edge, and hidden, unless the savage chose to lie down and look for you; and even then, you would be in darkness—and if the worst happened and he saw you, then you had a chance to burst out at him, fling the whole line out of step and double back.

Cautiously, his stick trailing behind him, Ralph wormed between the rising stems. When he reached the middle of the mat he lay and listened.

The fire was a big one and the drum-roll that he had thought was left so far behind was nearer. Couldn't a fire out-run a galloping horse? He could see the sun-splashed ground over an area of perhaps fifty yards from where he lay: and as he watched, the sunlight in every patch blinked at him. This was so like the curtain that flapped in his brain that for a moment he thought the blinking was inside him. But then the patches blinked more rapidly, dulled and went out, so that he saw that a great heaviness of smoke lay between the island and the sun.

If anyone peered under the bushes and chanced to glimpse human flesh it might be Samneric who would pretend not to see and say nothing. He laid his cheek against the chocolate-coloured earth, licked his dry lips and closed his eyes. Under the thicket, the earth was vibrating very slightly; or perhaps there was a sound beneath the obvious thunder of the fire and scribbled ululations that was too low to hear.

Someone cried out. Ralph jerked his cheek off the earth and looked into the dulled light. They must be near now, he thought, and his chest began to thump. Hide, break the line, climb a tree—which was the best after all? The trouble was you only had one chance.

Now the fire was nearer; those volleying shots were great limbs, trunks even, bursting. The fools! The fools! The fire must be almost at the fruit trees—what would they eat to-morrow?

Ralph stirred restlessly in his narrow bed. One chanced nothing! What could they do? Beat him? So what? Kill him? A stick sharpened at both ends.

The cries, suddenly nearer, jerked him up. He could see a striped savage moving hastily out of a green tangle, and coming towards the mat where he hid, a savage who carried a spear. Ralph gripped his fingers into the earth. Be ready now, in case.

Ralph fumbled to hold his spear so that it was point foremost; and now he saw that the stick was sharpened at both ends.

The savage stopped fifteen yards away and uttered his cry.

Perhaps he can hear my heart over the noises of the fire. Don't scream. Get ready.

The savage moved forward so that you could only see him from the waist down. That was the butt of his spear. Now you could see him from the knee down. Don't scream.

A herd of pigs came squealing out of the greenery behind the savage and rushed away into the forest. Birds were screaming, mice shrieking, and a little hopping thing came under the mat and cowered.

Five yards away the savage stopped, standing right by the thicket, and cried out. Ralph drew his feet up and crouched. The stake was in his hands, the stake sharpened at both ends, the stake that vibrated so wildly, that grew long, short, light, heavy, light again.

The ululation spread from shore to shore. The savage knelt down by the edge of the thicket, and there were lights flickering in the forest behind him. You could see a knee disturb the mould. Now the other. Two hands. A spear.

A face.

The savage peered into the obscurity beneath the thicket. You could tell that he saw light on this side and on that, but not in the middle—there. In the middle was a blob of dark and the savage wrinkled up his face, trying to decipher the darkness.

The seconds lengthened. Ralph was looking straight into the savage's eyes.

Don't scream.

You'll get back.

Now he's seen you. He's making sure. A stick sharpened.

Ralph screamed, a scream of fright and anger and desperation. His legs straightened, the screams became continuous and foaming. He shot forward, burst the thicket, was in the open, screaming, snarling, bloody. He swung the stake and the savage tumbled over; but there were others coming towards him, crying out. He swerved as a spear flew past and then was silent, running. All at once the lights flickering ahead of him merged together, the roar of the forest rose to thunder and a tall bush directly in his path burst into a great fan-shaped flame. He swung to the right, running desperately fast, with the heat beating on his left side and the fire racing forward like a tide. The ululation rose behind him and spread along, a series of short sharp cries, the sighting call. A brown figure showed up at his right and fell away. They were all running, all crying out madly. He could hear them crashing in the undergrowth and on the left was the hot, bright thunder of the fire. He forgot his wounds, his hunger and thirst, and became fear; hopeless fear on flying feet, rushing through the forest towards the open beach. Spots jumped before his eyes and turned into red circles that expanded quickly till they passed out of sight. Below him, someone's legs were getting tired and the desperate ululation advanced like a jagged fringe of menace and was almost overhead.

He stumbled over a root and the cry that pursued him rose even higher. He saw a shelter burst into flames and the fire flapped at his right shoulder and there was the glitter of water. Then he was down, rolling over and over in the warm sand, crouching with arm up to ward off, trying to cry for mercy.

He staggered to his feet, tensed for more terrors, and looked up at a huge peaked cap. It was a white-topped cap, and above the green shade of the peak was a crown, an anchor, gold foliage. He saw white drill, epaulettes, a revolver, a row of gilt buttons down the front of a uniform.

A naval officer stood on the sand, looking down at Ralph in wary astonishment. On the beach behind him was a cutter, her bows hauled up and held by two ratings. In the stern-sheets another rating held a sub-machine gun.

The ululation faltered and died away.

The officer looked at Ralph doubtfully for a moment, then took his hand away from the butt of the revolver.

"Hullo."

Squirming a little, conscious of his filthy appearance, Ralph answered shyly.

"Hullo."

The officer nodded, as if a question had been answered.

"Are there any adults—any grown-ups with you?"

Dumbly, Ralph shook his head. He turned a half-pace on the sand. A semicircle of little boys, their bodies streaked with coloured clay, sharp sticks in their hands, were standing on the beach making no noise at all.

"Fun and games," said the officer.

The fire reached the coco-nut palms by the beach and swallowed them noisily. A flame, seemingly detached, swung like an acrobat and licked up the palm heads on the platform. The sky was black.

The officer grinned cheerfully at Ralph.

"We saw your smoke. What have you been doing? Having a war or something?"

Ralph nodded.

The officer inspected the little scarecrow in front of him. The kid needed a bath, a hair-cut, a nose-wipe and a good deal of ointment.

"Nobody killed, I hope? Any dead bodies?"

"Only two. And they've gone."

The officer leaned down and looked closely at Ralph.

"Two? Killed?"

Ralph nodded again. Behind him, the whole island was shuddering with flame. The officer knew, as a rule, when people were telling the truth. He whistled softly.

Other boys were appearing now, tiny tots some of them, brown, with the distended bellies of small savages. One of them came close to the officer and looked up.

"I'm, I'm——"

But there was no more to come. Percival Wemys Madison sought in his head for an incantation that had faded clean away.

The officer turned back to Ralph.

"We'll take you off. How many of you are there?"

Ralph shook his head. The officer looked past him to the group of painted boys.

"Who's boss here?"

"I am," said Ralph loudly.

A little boy who wore the remains of an extraordinary black cap on his red hair and who carried the remains of a pair of spectacles at his waist, started forward, then changed his mind and stood still.

"We saw your smoke. And you don't know how many of you there are?"

"No, sir."

"I should have thought," said the officer as he visualized the search before him, "I should have thought that a pack of British boys—you're all British aren't you?—would have been able to put up a better show than that—I mean——"

"It was like that at first," said Ralph, "before things——"

He stopped.

"We were together then——"

The officer nodded helpfully.

"I know. Jolly good show. Like the Coral Island."

Ralph looked at him dumbly. For a moment he had a fleeting picture of the strange glamour that had once invested the beaches. But the island was scorched up like dead wood—Simon was dead—and Jack had. . . . The tears began to flow and sobs shook him. He gave himself up to them now for the first time on the island; great, shuddering spasms of grief that seemed to wrench his whole body. His voice rose under the black smoke before the burning wreckage of the island; and infected by that emotion, the other little boys began to shake and sob too. And in the middle of them, with filthy body, matted hair, and unwiped nose, Ralph wept for the end of innocence, the darkness of man's heart, and the fall through the air of the true, wise friend called Piggy.

The officer, surrounded by these noises, was moved and a little embarrassed. He turned away to give them time to pull themselves together; and waited, allowing his eyes to rest on the trim cruiser in the distance.

For Further Reflection

1. What is the main idea about morality that you get out of this selection from *Lord of the Flies?*

2. Piggy tells Ralph that he is going to Jack to order him to return his glasses. "I don't ask for my glasses back as a favor . . . but because what's right's right. Give me my glasses. . . . You got to." What is Piggy presupposing about the situation and about the significance of morality? What is Jack's response? How does he further respond upon being called a thief? Why is he infuriated by that charge?

3. Compare Ralph's understanding of morality with Piggy's and Jack's. How do they exhibit different moral positions?

4. What, if anything, is the significance of the conch and how do you interpret its destruction?

On the Nature and Purpose of Morality
Reflections on William Golding's
Lord of the Flies

LOUIS P. POJMAN

Louis P. Pojman is professor of philosophy at the United
States Military Academy and the editor of this volume. In
this essay he analyzes Golding's novel in terms of the nature
and purpose of morality. He relates it to Hobbes's account
in the *Leviathan* (see the next reading) and identifies the
larger purposes of morality.

> Which is better—to have rules and agree, or to hunt
> and kill?
> —Piggy[1]

> Morality is more honored in the breach than in the
> observance.
> —Thomas Hobbes

Why exactly do we need moral codes? What function do they play
in our lives and in society in general? William Golding's classic
novel *Lord of the Flies* (1954), a modern moral allegory, abridged
in the previous reading, may provide us with a clue to the answer
to these questions.

Golding's allegory is a response to a Victorian British children's
classic, *The Coral Island* (1858), by Robert Ballantyne, in which
three teenage boys are shipwrecked on an unidentified Pacific
island. Ralph Rover, the fifteen-year-old narrator, Jack Martin, and
the creative and wise Peterkin Gay. These boys prove to be ideal
Englishmen and live in uninterrupted harmony, a utopia, until they
encounter cannibals who capture them. But just when the cannibals are about to boil them for dinner, missionaries arrive who con-

---

This essay was written specifically for this volume. Copyright © 2000
Louis P. Pojman.
[1]William Golding, *Lord of the Flies* (New York: G. P. Putnam, 1959), p. 222.

vert the cannibals and liberate them from heathen darkness and the boys from the dark cauldron. The book was written as a refutation of the prevailing Calvinist and Puritan doctrine of original sin, which holds that human nature is ineluctably perverse. In *The Coral Island,* human nature is essentially good.

Since then, two traumatic, cataclysmic world wars have disabused us of such Pollyanna-like humanism and the age of innocence. Golding transforms Ralph Rover into Ralph, the commonsensical, decent, and likable leader; Jack Martin into the rapacious and Dionysian Jack Merridew, redheaded rival of Ralph, who demands the position of leadership because he is head choirboy and can sing C-sharp; and creative and wise Peterkin into two persons, Simon, the clairvoyant, mystical epileptic, and Piggy, the asthmatic, myopic philosopher, the conscience of Ralph.

Lord of the Flies is the antithesis of *The Coral Island.* It portrays the very opposite of the Victorian utopia, a dystopia, a virtual hell. Jack overthrows Ralph as the leader, and with him, humane rules. The unbridled lust for excitement leads to the great orgiastic pig-kills, the sodomizing of a female pig, and finally, at its nadir, to the thirst for human blood. They turn into savages, sadistically hunting, "Kill the beast! Cut its throat! Spill its blood!" In their Dionysian frenzy, Simon is mistaken for the beast and killed. Piggy has his glasses stolen with impunity and is sadistically murdered. Ralph, who resists the depravity to the end, is hunted like a pig and is about to be destroyed when the British navy, seeing the smoke of the burning jungle, comes to the rescue.

What is Golding trying to tell us? He comments on his work:

> The theme is an attempt to trace the defects of society back to the defects of human nature. The moral is that the shape of a society must depend on the ethical nature of the individual and not only any political system however apparently logical or respectable. The whole book is symbolic in nature except the rescue in the end where adult life appears, dignified and capable, but in reality enmeshed in the same evil as the symbolic life of the children on the island. The officer, having interrupted a manhunt [of Ralph], prepares to take the children off the island in a cruiser which will presently be hunting its enemy in the same implacable way. And who will rescue the adult and his cruiser?[2]

---

[2]Op. cit. E. L. Epstein, "Notes on *Lord of the Flies,*" p. 250–51.

Civilization's power is weak and vulnerable to atavistic, volcanic passions. The sensitive Simon, the symbol of religious consciousness (as in "Simon Peter," the first disciple of Jesus), who prophesies that Ralph will be saved and is the first to discover and fight against the "ancient, inescapable recognition" of the beast in us, is slaughtered by the group in a wild frenzy. Only Piggy and Ralph, mere observers of the orgiastic homicide, feel vicarious pangs of guilt at this atrocity.

The incarnation of philosophy and culture—poor, fat, nearsighted Piggy, with his broken spectacles and asthma—becomes ever more pathetic as the chaos increases. The nadir of his ridiculous position is reached after the rebels, led by Jack, steal his spectacles in order to harness the sun's rays for starting fires. After Ralph, the emblem of not too bright but morally good civilized leadership, fails to persuade Jack to return the glasses, Piggy asserts his moral right to them:

> You're stronger than I am and you haven't got asthma. You can see. . . . But I don't ask for my glasses back, not as a favour. I don't ask you to be a sport . . . not because you're strong, but because what's right's right. Give me my glasses. . . . You got to. (p. 211)

Piggy might as well have addressed the fire itself, for in this state of anarchy moral discourse is a foreign tongue that only incites the worst elements to greater immorality. Roger, Jack's sadistic lieutenant, perched on a cliff above, finally liberated from the constraints which held back his arm from harming little Henry, responds to moral reasoning by dislodging a huge rock from a cliff that hits Piggy and flings him to his death forty feet below.

The title *Lord of the Flies* comes from a translation of the Greek *Beelzebub,* which is a name for the devil. The boys are frightened by shadowy figures which they imagine to be a supernatural beast, but, as the prophetic Simon points out, "Maybe [the beast] is only us." We need no external devil to bring about evil. We have found the devil and, in the words of Pogo, "he is us." Ubiquitous, ever waiting for a moment to strike out, he emerges from the depths of the subconscious whenever there is a conflict of interest or a moment of moral lassitude. As E. L. Epstein says, "The tenets of civilization, the moral and social codes, the Ego, the intelligence itself, form only a veneer over this white-hot power, this uncontrollable force, 'the fury and the mire of human veins.'"[3]

[3]Op. cit., p. 252.

Beelzebub's ascendancy proceeds through fear, hysteria, violence, and death. A delegation starts out hunting pigs for meat. The hunters quickly find themselves enjoying the excitement, the violence, the bloody destruction of the pig, the symbol of the beast. In order to drown the incipient shame over bloodthirstiness, and take on a persona more compatible with their deed, the children paint themselves with colored mud. Their lusting for the kill takes on all the powerful overtones of an orgiastic sexual ritual, including ritual, sadistic sodomy, as they lunge the wooden spear up the rectum of the female pig. Liberated from their social selves, they kill without remorse whoever gets in their way. The death of Simon and Piggy (the symbols of the religious and the philosophical, the two great fences blocking the descent to hell) and the final orgiastic hunt with the "spear sharpened at both ends" signal for Ralph the depths of evil in the human heart.

Ironically, it is the British navy that finally comes to the rescue and saves Ralph (civilization) just when all seems lost. But the symbol of the navy is a Janus-faced omen. On the one hand it may symbolize the fact that a military defense is, unfortunately, sometimes needed to save civilization from the barbarians (Hilter's Nazis or Jack and Roger's allies), but on the other hand it symbolizes the quest for blood and vengeance latent in contemporary civilization. The children's world is really only a stage lower than the adult world whence they come, and that shallow civilization could very well regress to tooth and claw if it were scratched too sharply. The children were saved by the adults, but who will save the adults, who put so much emphasis in military enterprises and weapons systems—in the euphemistic name of "defense"? To quote Epstein:

> The officer, having interrupted a man-hunt, prepares to take the children off the island in a cruiser which will presently be hunting its enemy in the same implacable way. And who will rescue the adult and his cruiser?[4]

The fundamental ambiguity of human existence is seen in every section of the book, poignantly mirroring the human condition. Even Piggy's spectacles, the sole example of modern technology on the island, become a bane for the island as Jack uses them to

---

[4]Op. cit., p. 251.

ignite a forest fire that will smoke out their prey, Ralph, and that ends up burning down the entire forest and destroying the island's animal life. The spectacles are a symbol both of our penchant for misusing technology to vitiate the environment and of our ability to create weapons that will lead to global suicide.

Golding is trying to place his finger on a defect of human nature. What exactly is that defect? An older theological term for it is *original sin,* a certain tendency to assert one's ego against God and the social good. One need not be a theist with a concept of sin to accept this message: human nature has a tendency to selfishness, to a desperate egotism, which, in appropriate circumstances, is all too willing to harm others unjustly. Cut off from the sanctions of adult civilization, these preteens lack the resources to sustain the institutions that would mitigate the damage of unbridled egoism.

Ask yourself, What could make the difference between the dystopia of *Lord of the Flies* and the utopia of *Coral Island.* Could you rewrite Golding's book in order to achieve an opposite ending? I had a conversation with a Bucknell University philosophy student, Coleen Zoller, who said that she thinks *Lord of the Flies* is a very male book, illustrating the worst kind of male behavior. "Women would typically act differently. They would stress cooperation and caring for one another. The process would be quite different." Do you think this is true? Can you imagine different young people acting better?

WHY DO WE NEED MORALITY?: HOBBES'S ACCOUNT

Why do we need morality? What is its nature and purpose? What does it do for us that no other social arrangement does? There are many philosophical replies to these questions, but a classic reply, one relevant to the situation of *Lord of the Flies,* is that given by the English philosopher Thomas Hobbes (1588–1679) in his book *Leviathan* (1651). Hobbes believed that human beings always act out of perceived self-interest, that is, they invariably seek gratification and avoid harm. His argument goes like this:

Nature has made us basically equal in physical and mental abilities, so that while one person may be somewhat stronger or have a higher IQ than another, each has the ability to harm, even kill, the other, if not alone, then in confederacy with others. Furthermore, we all want to attain our goals, including sufficient food, shelter, security, power, wealth, and other scarce resources. These two facts, equality of ability to harm and desire to attain our goals, lead to an unstable state.

> From this equality of ability arises equality of hope in the attaining of our ends. And therefore if any two people desire the same thing, which nevertheless they cannot both enjoy, they become enemies; and in the way to their end, which is principally their own preservation and sometimes their enjoyment only, endeavor to destroy, or subdue one another. And from hence it comes to pass, that where an invader hath no more to fear, than another man's single power; if one plant, sow, build, or possess a convenient seat, others may probably be expected to come prepared with forces united, to dispossess, and deprive him, not only of the fruit of his labor, but also of his life or liberty. And the invader again is in the like danger of another.[5]

Given this state of insecurity, people have reason to fear one another. Hobbes calls this a "state of nature," one in which there are no common ways of life, no laws or moral rules which are enforced, no justice or injustice, for these concepts lack application. There are no reliable expectations about other people's behavior—except that they will follow their own inclinations and perceived interests, tending to be arbitrary, violent, and capricious.

> Hereby it is manifest, that during the time men live without a common power to keep them all in awe, they are in that condition which is called war; and such a war, as is for *every man, against every man*. For war consists not in battle only or in the act of fighting; but in a tract of time, wherein the will to contend in battle is sufficiently known: and therefore the notion of *time,* is to be considered in the nature of war; as it is in the nature of weather. For as the nature of foul weather lies not in the shower or two of rain, but in an inclination thereto of many days together; so the nature of war consists not in actual fighting, but in the known disposition thereto, during all the time there is no disposition to the contrary.

[5]Thomas Hobbes, *Leviathan* (1651), chapter 13.

The consequence of the state of nature, this war of all against all, is described thusly:

> In such a condition, there is no place for industry; because the fruit thereof is uncertain: and consequently no cultivating of the earth; no navigation, nor use of the comfortable buildings; no instruments of moving, and removing, such things as require much force; no knowledge of the face of the earth; no account of time; no arts; no literature; no society; and which is worst of all, continual fear, and danger of violent death; and the life of man solitary, poor, nasty, brutish and short.

But this state of nature, or more exactly, state of anarchy and chaos, is in no one's interest. We can all do better if we compromise, give up some of our natural liberty—to do as we please—so that we will all be more likely to get what we want: security, happiness, power, prosperity, and peace. So rational egoists that we are, according to Hobbes, we exchange some of our liberty for a *social contract* or *covenant,* wherein a ruler and rules are set over us, which we are to obey, since they are enforced by a mighty ruler, the State, the *Leviathan.* Only within this contract does morality arise and do justice, and injustice come into being. Where there is no enforceable law, there is neither right nor wrong, justice nor injustice.

So morality is a form of social control. We all opt for an enforceable set of rules which *if almost all of us obey almost all of the time almost all will be better off almost all of the time.* A select few, conceivably, might be better off in the state of nature, but the vast majority will be better off in a situation of security and mutual cooperation. It may turn out that some people cheat, renege on their contract, but so long as the adherence is widespread by most of us most of the time, we will all flourish.

Hobbes didn't claim that a pure state of nature ever existed or that humanity ever really formally entered into such a contract, though he notes that among nations such a state actually exists, so that a "cold war" keeps us all in fear. Rather, Hobbes is offering an explanation of the function of morality. He is answering the question, Why do we need morality. Why? Because without it existence would be an unbearable hell in which life was "solitary, poor, nasty, brutish and short."

THE PURPOSES OF MORALITY

What is the role of morality in human existence? What are little boys and girls and big men and women made of that requires ethical consciousness? Ralph answers these questions at the end of *Lord of the Flies*.

> And in the middle of [the children], with filthy body, matted hair, and unwiped nose, Ralph wept for the end of innocence, the darkness of man's heart, and the fall through the air of the true, wise friend called Piggy. (p. 248)

In this wise modern moral allegory, we catch a glimpse of some of the purposes of morality. Rules formed over the ages and internalized within us hold us back and hopefully defeat the "Lord of the Flies" in society, whether he be inherent in us individually or an emergent property of corporate existence. The moral code restrains even the sadistic Rogers of society from evil until untoward social conditions open up the sluice gates of sadism and random violence. Morality is the force that enables Piggy and Ralph to maintain a modicum of order within their dwindling society, first motivating them to compromise with Jack and then keeping things in a wider perspective.

In Golding's allegory, morality is "honored more in the breach than in the observance," for we see the consequences of not having rules and principles and virtuous character. As Piggy says, "Which is better—to have rules and agree, or to hunt and kill [each other]?" Morality consists of a set of rules which if followed by nearly everyone will promote the flourishing of nearly everyone. These rules restrict our freedom but only in order to promote greater freedom and well-being. More specifically morality seems to have these five purposes:

1. To keep society from falling apart.
2. To ameliorate human suffering.
3. To promote human flourishing.
4. To resolve conflicts of interest in just and orderly ways.
5. To assign praise and blame, reward the good and punish the guilty.

Let us elaborate these purposes. Imagine what society would be if everyone or nearly everyone did whatever he or she pleased, disregarding basic moral rules. I would make a promise to you to help you with your philosophy homework tomorrow if you fix my car today. You believe me. So you fix my car, but you are deeply angry when I laugh at you on the morrow when I drive away to the beach instead of helping you with your homework. Or you loan me money but I run off with it. Or I lie to you or harm you when it is in my interest or even kill you when I feel the urge.

In such a society parents would abandon or abuse their children and spouses betray each other whenever it was convenient. The very notion of a *spouse* would be meaningless, since it connotes commitment, loyalty, fidelity, all of which are *moral* notions. No one would have an incentive to cooperate or help anyone else because reciprocity (a moral principle) would not be recognized. Great suffering would go largely unameliorated and, certainly, people would not be very happy. We would not flourish or reach our highest potential. Under such circumstances society would break down. Even thieves must adhere to moral rules with each other, if they have any hope of robbing others.

I recently visited the former USSR countries Kazakhstan and Russia, which are undergoing a difficult transition from communism to democracy (which hopefully will be resolved favorably). In this transition, with the state's power considerably withdrawn, crime is on the increase and distrust is prevalent. At night I had to navigate my way up the staircases in our apartment building in complete darkness. I inquired as to why there were no light bulbs in the stairwells, only to be told that the residents stole them, believing that if they did not take them, their neighbors would. Without a dominant authority, the former Communist authorities, the social contract has eroded and everyone must struggle alone in the darkness.

We need moral rules to guide our actions in ways that light up our paths and prevent and reduce suffering, that enhance human (and animal, for that matter) well-being, that allow us to resolve our conflicts of interests according to recognizably fair rules, and to assign responsibility for actions, so that we can praise and blame, reward and punish people according to how their actions reflect moral principles.

Even though these five purposes are related, they are not identical, and different moral theories emphasize different purposes and in different ways. Utilitarianism stresses human flourishing and the amelioration of suffering, whereas contractual systems rooted in rational self-interest accent the role of resolving conflicts of interest. A complete moral theory would include a place for each of these purposes. Such a system has the goal of internalizing the rules that promote these principles in each moral person's life, producing the virtuous person, someone who is "a jewel that shines in [morality's] own light," to paraphrase Kant. It is fair to say that morality is a necessary condition for happiness. Whether it is also a sufficient condition for happiness is more controversial, a question we shall consider in Part III. The goal of morality is to create happy and virtuous people, the kind that create flourishing communities. That's why it is the most important subject on earth.

For Further Reflection

1. What, according to Pojman, is the main message of *Lord of the Flies?* Do you agree? Explain.

2. How does Pojman relate Golding's novel to Hobbes's account of morality?

3. Discuss Pojman's five purposes of morality. Do you agree morality has all of these purposes? If not, explain. Can you think of other purposes it has?

On the State of Nature

THOMAS HOBBES

Thomas Hobbes (1588–1679), the greatest English political philosopher, set forth the classic version of the idea that morality and politics arise out of a social contract. He was born on Good Friday, April 5, 1588, in Westbury, England, the son of an eccentric vicar. On the day of his birth the Spanish Armada, the greatest naval fleet the world had then

---

From Thomas Hobbes, *Leviathan,* 1651.

seen, was spotted off the coast of southern England. The chronicler John Aubrey reports that Hobbes's mother, only seven months pregnant, startled by the news, fell into labor and delivered him. Hobbes wrote of this experience, "Unbeknownst to my mother at that time she gave birth to twins, myself and fear. And fear has been my constant companion throughout life." Hobbes's lifetime was filled with the dangers of war, the invading Spanish Armada, the religious wars of Europe, the Civil War in England. His political philosophy may be read as a cure against the fear and insecurity of people desperately in need of peace and tranquility. Hobbes was educated at Oxford University, and lived through an era of political revolutions as a scholar and tutor (to the future Charles II).

Hobbes is known today primarily for his masterpiece in political theory, *Leviathan* (1651), a book written during the English civil wars (1642–1652), sometimes referred to as "the Great Rebellion," which pitted the forces of monarchy (the Royalists) under Charles I against those of Parliament under Oliver Cromwell. Hobbes's work was intended to support the Royalists, as he believed that the monarchy was the best guarantee for orderly and stable government. Yet the Royalists misconstrued his interpretation as supporting the rebels, no doubt because Hobbes rejected the usual grounds for the monarchy, the divine right of kings. For this reason, and because the book conveyed a materialist view of human nature, thought to be dangerous to religion, it was suppressed or violently attacked throughout Hobbes's lifetime.

What are the doctrines his contemporaries found so controversial? First of all, Hobbes breaks from the medieval notion that the state is a natural organism, based on natural devotion and interdependence. He develops a moral and political theory based not on natural affection, but on psychological egoism. Hobbes argues that people are all egoists who always act in their own self-interest, to obtain gratification and avoid harm. However, we cannot obtain any of the basic goods because of the inherent fear of harm and death, the insecurity in an unregulated "state of nature," in which life is "solitary, poor, nasty, brutish and short." We cannot relax our guard, for everyone is constantly in fear of everyone else. In this state of anarchy the prudent person concludes that it really is in all our self-interest to make a contract to keep to a minimal morality of respecting human life, keeping covenants made, and obeying the laws of the society. This minimal morality, which Hobbes refers to as "the laws of nature" is nothing more than a set of maxims of prudence. In order to ensure that we all obey this covenant Hobbes proposes a strong sovereign or "Leviathan" to impose severe penalties on those who disobey the laws, for "covenants without the sword are but words."[1]

OF THE NATURAL CONDITION OF MANKIND AS CONCERNING THEIR FELICITY, AND MISERY

Nature hath made men so equal, in the faculties of the body, and mind; as that though there be found one man sometimes manifestly stronger in body, or of quicker mind than another; yet when all is reckoned together, the difference between man, and man, is not so considerable, as that one man can thereupon claim to himself any benefit, to which another may not pretend, as well as he. For

---

[1]The term *Leviathan* refers to the sea monster (or whale) referred to in the Book of Job:

> Let those curse the day who are skilled to rouse up Leviathan (3:8) . . .
> Can you draw out Leviathan with a fishhook or press down his tongue with a cord?
> Can you put a rope in his nose or pierce his jaw with a hook? . . .
> Will he make a covenant with you to take him for your servant for ever? . . .
> His sneezings flash forth light, and his eyes are like the eyelids of the dawn.
> Out of his mouth go flaming torches; sparks of fire leap forth.
> Out of his nostrils comes forth smoke, as from a boiling pot and burning rushes.
> His breath kindles coals, and flame comes forth from his mouth . . .
> When he raises himself up the mighty are afraid; at the crashing they are beside themselves . . .
> Upon earth there is not his like, a creature without fear.
> He beholds everything that is high; he is king over all the sons of pride. (Job 41)

as to the strength of body, the weakest has strength enough to kill the strongest, either by secret machination, or by confederacy with others, that are in the same danger with himself.

And as to the faculties of the mind, setting aside the arts grounded upon words, and especially that skill of proceeding upon general, and infallible rules, called science; which very few have, and but in few things; as being not a native faculty, born with us; nor attained, as prudence, while we look after somewhat else, I find yet a greater equality amongst men, than that of strength. For prudence, is but experience; which equal time, equally bestows on all men, in those things they equally apply themselves unto. That which may perhaps make such equality incredible, is but a vain conceit of one's own wisdom, which almost all men think they have in a greater degree, than the vulgar; that is, than all men but themselves, and a few others, whom by fame, or for concurring with themselves, they approve. For such is the nature of men, that howsoever they may acknowledge many others to be more witty, or more eloquent, or more learned; yet they will hardly believe there be many so wise as themselves; for they see their own wit at hand, and other men's at a distance. But this proveth rather that men are in that point equal, than unequal. For there is not ordinarily a greater sign of the equal distribution of any thing, than that every man is contented with his share.

From this equality of ability, ariseth equality of hope in the attaining of our ends. And therefore if any two men desire the same thing, which nevertheless they cannot both enjoy, they become enemies; and in the way to their end, which is principally their own conservation, and sometimes their delectation only, endeavour to destroy, or subdue one another. And from hence it comes to pass, that where an invader hath no more to fear, than another man's single power; if one plant, sow, build, or possess a convenient seat, others may probably be expected to come prepared with forces united, to dispossess, and deprive him, not only of the fruit of his labour, but also of his life, or liberty. And the invader again is in the like danger of another.

And from this diffidence of one another, there is no way for any man to secure himself, so reasonable, as anticipation; that is, by force, or wiles, to master the persons of all men he can, so long, till he see no other power great enough to endanger him: and this is no more than his own conservation requireth, and is generally allowed. Also because there be some, that taking pleasure in contemplating their own power in the acts of conquest, which they pursue farther than their security requires; if others, that otherwise would be glad to be at ease within modest bounds, should not by invasion increase their power, they would not be able, long time, by standing only on their defence, to subsist. And by consequence, such augmentation of dominion over men being necessary to a man's conservation, it ought to be allowed him.

Again, men have no pleasure, but on the contrary a great deal of grief, in keeping company, where there is no power able to over-awe them all. For every man looketh that his companion should value him, at the same rate he sets upon himself: and upon all signs of contempt, or undervaluing, naturally endeavours, as far as he dares, (which amongst them that have no common power to keep them in quiet, is far enough to make them destroy each other), to extort a greater value from his contemners, by damage; and from others, by the example.

So that in the nature of man, we find three principal causes of quarrel. First, competition; secondly, diffidence; thirdly, glory.

The first, maketh men invade for gain; the second, for safety; and the third, for reputation. The first use violence, to make themselves masters of other men's persons, wives, children, and cattle; the second, defend them; the third, for trifles, as a word, a smile, a different opinion, and any other sign of undervalue, either direct in their persons, or by reflection in their kindred, their friends, their nation, their profession, or their name.

Hereby it is manifest, that during the time men live without a common power to keep them all in awe, they are in that condition which is called war; and such a war, as is of every man, against every man. For war, consisteth not in battle only, or the act of fighting; but in a tract of time, wherein the will to contend by battle is sufficiently known: and therefore the notion of *time,* is to be considered in the nature of war; as it is in the nature of weather. For as the nature of foul weather, lieth not in the shower or two of rain; but in an inclination thereto of many days together: so the nature of war, consisteth not in actual fighting; but in the known disposition thereto, during all the time there is no assurance to the contrary. All other time is PEACE.

Whatsoever therefore is consequent to a time of war, where every man is enemy to every man; the same is consequent to the time, wherein men live without other security, than what their own strength, and their own invention shall furnish them withal. In such condition, there is no place for industry; because the fruit thereof is uncertain: and consequently no culture of the earth; no navigation, nor use of the commodities that may be imported by sea; no commodious building; no instruments of moving, and removing, such things as require much force; no knowledge of the face of the earth; no account of time; no arts; no letters; no society; and which is worst of all, continual fear, and danger of violent death; and the life of man, solitary, poor, nasty, brutish, and short.

It may seem strange to some man, that has not well weighed these things; that nature should thus dissociate, and render men apt to invade, and destroy one another: and he may therefore, not trusting to this inference, made from the passions, desire perhaps to have the same confirmed by experience. Let him therefore consider with himself, when taking a journey, he arms himself, and seeks to go well accompanied; when going to sleep, he locks his doors; when even in his house he locks his chests; and this when he knows there be laws, and public officers, armed, to revenge all injuries shall be done him; what opinion he has of his fellow-subjects, when he rides armed; of his fellow citizens, when he locks his doors; and of his children, and servants, when he locks his chests. Does he not there as much accuse mankind by his actions, as I do by my words? But neither of us accuse man's nature in it. The desires, and other passions of man, are in themselves no sin. No more are the actions, that proceed from those passions, till they know a law that forbids them: which till laws be made they cannot know: nor can any law be made, till they have agreed upon the person that shall make it.

It may peradventure be thought, there was never such a time, nor condition of war as this; and I believe it was never generally so, over all the world: but there are many places, where they live so now. For the savage people in many places of America, except the government of small families, the concord whereof dependeth on natural lust, have no government at all; and live at this day in that brutish manner, as I said before. Howsoever, it may be perceived what manner of life there would be, where there were no common power to fear, by the manner of life, which men that have formerly lived under a peaceful government, use to degenerate into, in a civil war.

But though there had never been any time, wherein particular men were in a condition of war one against another; yet in all times, kings, and persons of sovereign authority, because of their independency, are in continual jealousies, and in the state and posture of gladiators; having their weapons pointing, and their eyes fixed on one another; that is, their forts, garrisons, and guns upon the frontiers of their kingdoms; and continual spies upon their neighbours; which is a posture of war. But because they uphold thereby, the industry of their subjects; there does not follow from it, that misery, which accompanies the liberty of particular men.

To this war of every man, against every man, this also is consequent; that nothing can be unjust. The notions of right and wrong, justice and injustice have there no place. Where there is no common power, there is no law: where no law, no injustice. Force, and fraud, are in war the two cardinal virtues. Justice, and injustice are none of the faculties neither of the body, nor mind. If they were, they might be in a man that were alone in the world, as well as his senses, and passions. They are qualities, that relate to men in society, not in solitude. It is consequent also to the same condition, that there be no propriety, no dominion, no *mine* and *thine* distinct; but only that to be every man's, that he can get; and for so long, as he can keep it. And thus much for the ill condition, which man by mere nature is actually placed in; though with a possibility to come out of it, consisting partly in the passions, partly in his reason.

The passions that incline men to peace, are fear of death; desire of such things as are necessary to commodious living; and a hope by their industry to obtain them. And reason suggesteth convenient articles of peace, upon which men may be drawn to agreement. These articles, are they, which otherwise are called the Laws of Nature: whereof I shall speak more particularly, in the two following chapters.

OF THE FIRST AND SECOND NATURAL LAWS, AND OF CONTRACTS

The right of nature, which writers commonly call *jus naturale,* is the liberty each man hath, to use his own power, as he will himself, for the preservation of his own nature; that is to say, of his own life; and consequently, of doing any thing, which in his own judgment, and reason, he shall conceive to be the aptest means thereunto.

By LIBERTY, is understood, according to the proper signification of the word, the absence of external impediments: which impediments, may oft take away part of a man's power to do what he would; but cannot hinder him from using the power left him, according as his judgment, and reason shall dictate to him.

A LAW OF NATURE, *lex naturalis,* is a precept or general rule, found out by reason, by which a man is forbidden to do that, which is destructive of his life, or taketh away the means of preserving the same; and to omit that, by which he thinketh it may be best preserved. For though they that speak of this subject, use to confound *jus,* and *lex, right* and *law:* yet they ought to be distinguished; because RIGHT, consisteth in liberty to do, or to forbear; whereas LAW, determineth, and bindeth to one of them: so that law, and right, differ as much, as obligation, and liberty; which in one and the same matter are inconsistent.

And because the condition of man, as hath been declared in the precedent chapter, is a condition of war of every one against every one; in which case every one is governed by his own reason; and there is nothing he can make use of, that may not be a help unto him, in preserving his life against his enemies; it followeth, that in such a condition, every man has a right to every thing; even to one another's body. And therefore, as long as this natural right of every man to every thing endureth, there can be no security to any man, how strong or wise soever he be, of living out the time, which nature ordinarily alloweth men to live. And consequently it is a precept, or general rule of reason, *that every man, ought to endeavour peace, as far as he has hope of obtaining it; and when he cannot obtain it, that he may seek, and use, all helps, and advantages of war.* The first branch of which rule, containeth the first, and fundamental law of nature; which is, *to seek peace, and follow it.* The second, the sum of the right of nature; which is, *by all means we can, to defend ourselves.*

From this fundamental law of nature, by which men are commanded to endeavour peace, is derived this second law; *that a man be willing, when others are so too, as far-forth, as for peace, and defence of himself he shall think it necessary, to lay down this right* *to all things; and be contented with so much liberty against other men, as he would allow other men against himself.* For as long as every man holdeth this right, of doing any thing he liketh; so long are all men in the condition of war. But if other men will not lay down their right, as well as he; then there is no reason for any one, to divest himself of his: for that were to expose himself to prey, which no man is bound to, rather than to dispose himself to peace. This is that law of the Gospel; *whatsoever you require that others should do to you, that do ye to them. And that law of all men, quod tibi fieri non vis, alteri ne feceris.**

To *lay down* a man's *right* to any thing, is to *divest* himself of the *liberty,* of hindering another of the benefit of his own right to the same. For he that renounceth, or passeth away his right, giveth not to any other man a right which he had not before; because there is nothing to which every man had not right by nature: but only standeth out of his way, that he may enjoy his own original right, without hindrance from him; not without hindrance from another. So that the effect which redoundeth to one man, by another man's defect of right, is but so much diminution of impediments to the use of his own right original.

Right is laid aside, either by simply renouncing it; or by transferring it to another. By *simply* RENOUNCING; when he cares not to whom the benefit thereof redoundeth. By TRANSFERRING; when he intendeth the benefit thereof to some certain person, or persons. And when a man hath in either manner abandoned, or granted away his right; then is he said to be OBLIGED, or BOUND, not to hinder those, to whom such right is granted, or abandoned, from the benefit of it: and that he *ought,* and it is his DUTY, not to make void that voluntary act of his own: and that such hindrance is INJUSTICE, and INJURY, as being *sine jure,†* the right being before renounced, or transferred. So that *injury,* or *injustice,* in the controversies of the world, is somewhat like to that, which in the disputations of scholars is called *absurdity.* For as it is there called an absurdity, to contradict what one maintained in the beginning: so in the world, it is called injustice, and injury, voluntarily to undo that, which from

*["What you do not want done to you, do not do to others."—ed. note]
†[That is, without right.—ed. note]

the beginning he had voluntarily done. The way by which a man either simply renounceth, or transferreth his right, is a declaration, or signification, by some voluntary and sufficient sign, or signs, that he doth so renounce, or transfer; or hath so renounced, or transferred the same, to him that accepteth it. And these signs are either words only, or actions only; or, as it happeneth most often, both words, and actions. And the same are the BONDS, by which men are bound, and obliged: bonds, that have their strength, not from their own nature, for nothing is more easily broken than a man's word, but from fear of some evil consequence upon the rupture.

Whensoever a man transferreth his right, or renounceth it; it is either in consideration of some right reciprocally transferred to himself; or for some other good he hopeth for thereby. For it is a voluntary act: and of the voluntary acts of every man, the object is some *good to himself.* And therefore there be some rights, which no man can be understood by any words, or other signs, to have abandoned, or transferred. At first a man cannot lay down the right of resisting them, that assault him by force, to take away his life; because he cannot be understood to aim thereby, at any good to himself. The same may be said of wounds, and chains, and imprisonment; both because there is no benefit consequent to such patience; as there is to the patience of suffering another to be wounded, or imprisoned: as also because a man cannot tell, when he seeth men proceed against him by violence, whether they intend his death or not. And lastly the motive, and end for which this renouncing, and transferring of right is introduced, is nothing else but the security of a man's person, in his life, and in the means of so preserving life, as not to be weary of it. And therefore if a man by words, or other signs, seem to despoil himself of the end, for which those signs were intended; he is not to be understood as if he meant it, or that it was his will; but that he was ignorant of how such words and actions were to be interpreted.

The mutual transferring of right, is that which men call CONTRACT.

There is a difference between transferring of right to the thing; and transferring, or tradition, that is delivery of the thing itself. For the thing may be delivered together with the translation of the right; as in buying and selling with ready-money; or exchange of goods, or lands: and it may be delivered some time after.

Again, one of the contractors, may deliver the thing contracted for on his part, and leave the other to perform his part at some determinate time after, and in the mean time be trusted; and then the contract on his part, is called PACT, or COVENANT: or both parts may contract now, to perform hereafter: in which cases, he that is to perform in time to come, being trusted, his performance is called *keeping of promise,* or faith; and the failing of performance, if it be voluntary, *violation of faith.*

When the transferring of right, is not mutual: but one of the parties transferreth, in hope to gain thereby friendship, or service from another, or from his friends; or in hope to gain the reputation of charity, or magnanimity; or to deliver his mind from the pain of compassion; or in hope of reward in heaven, this is not contract, but GIFT, FREE-GIFT, GRACE: which words signify one and the same thing.

Signs of contract, are either *express,* or *by inference.* Express, are words spoken with understanding of what they signify: and such words are either of the time *present,* or *past;* as, *I give, I grant, I have given, I have granted, I will that this be yours:* or of the future; as, *I will give, I will grant:* which words of the future are called PROMISE.

If a covenant be made, wherein neither of the parties perform presently, but trust one another; in the condition of mere nature, which is a condition of war of every man against every man, upon any reasonable suspicion, it is void: but if there be a common power set over them both, with right and force sufficient to compel performance, it is not void. For he that performeth first, has no assurance the other will perform after; because the bonds of words are too weak to bridle men's ambition, avarice, anger, and other passions, without the fear of some coercive power; which in the condition of mere nature, where all men are equal, and judges of the justness of their own fears, cannot possibly be supposed. And therefore he which performeth first, does but betray himself to his enemy; contrary to the right, he can never abandon, of defending his life, and means of living.

But in a civil estate, where there is a power set up to constrain those that would otherwise violate their faith, that fear is no more reasonable: and for that cause, he which by the covenant is to perform first, is obliged so to do.

The cause of fear, which maketh such a covenant invalid, must be always something arising after the covenant made; as some new fact, or other sign of the will not to perform: else it cannot make the covenant void. For that which could not hinder a man from promising, ought not to be admitted as a hindrance of performing.

OF OTHER LAWS OF NATURE

From that law of nature, by which we are obliged to transfer to another, such rights, as being retained, hinder the peace of mankind, there followeth a third; which is this, *that men perform their covenants made:* without which, covenants are in vain, and but empty words; and the right of all men to all things remaining, we are still in the condition of war.

And in this law of nature, consisteth the fountain and original of JUSTICE. For where no covenant hath preceded, there hath no right been transferred, and every man has right to every thing; and consequently, no action can be unjust. But when a covenant is made, then to break it is *unjust:* and the definition of INJUSTICE, is no other than *the not performance of covenant.* And whatsoever is not unjust, is *just.*

But because covenants of mutual trust, where there is a fear of not performance on either part, as hath been said in the former chapter, are invalid; though the original of justice be the making of covenants; yet injustice actually there can be none, till the cause of such fear be taken away; which while men are in the natural condition of war, cannot be done. Therefore before the names of just, and unjust can have place, there must be some coercive power, to compel men equally to the performance of their covenants, by the terror of some punishment, greater than the benefit they expect by the breach of their covenant; and to make good that propriety, which by mutual contract men acquire, in recompense of the universal right they abandon: and such power there is none before the erection of a commonwealth. And this is also to be gathered out of the ordinary definition of justice in the Schools: for they say, that *justice is the constant will of giving to every man his own,* and therefore where there is no *own,* that is, no propriety, there is no injustice; and where there is no coercive power erected, that is, where there is no commonwealth, there is no propriety; all men having right to all things: therefore where there is no commonwealth, there nothing is unjust. So that the nature of justice, consisteth in keeping of valid covenants:

but the validity of covenants begins not but with the constitution of a civil power, sufficient to compel men to keep them: and then it is also that propriety begins. . . .

For Further Reflection

1. Hobbes wrote, "The utility of morality and civil philosophy is to be estimated, not so much by the commodities we have by knowing these sciences, as by the calamities we receive from not knowing them." What does he mean by this, and does the selection above illustrate it?

2. Is Hobbes's view of human nature accurate? Do we always act out of the motivations of fear and distrust? Are people entirely self-interested egoists? Is psychological egoism, the view that we always do what we perceive to be in our best interest, too bleak and one-sided?

3. Hobbes thought that only an absolute sovereign could establish or ensure peace and civil society. Is he correct? What would his estimation of democracy be? Could democratic society make use of his analysis? How would democrats modify Hobbes's theory?

4. David Hume criticized the idea that contract theories provide a justification of political authority. First of all, there is no evidence of an original contract ever being made and, secondly, even if our ancestors did sign an original contract, why should that give us any reason for obeying the laws of the state? Even as we are not bound by the marriage or business contracts of our ancestors, why should we be obligated by their political contracts?

Further Readings for Chapter 1

Baier, Kurt. *The Moral Point of View.* Ithaca, N.Y.: Cornell University Press, 1958. This influential work sees morality primarily in terms of social control.

Frankena, William K. *Ethics.* 2d ed. Englewood Cliffs, N.J.: Prentice-Hall, 1973. A succinct, reliable guide.

Gert, Bernard. *Morality: A New Justification of the Moral Rules.* 2d ed. Oxford: Oxford University Press, 1988. A clear and comprehensive discussion of the nature of morality.

MacIntyre, Alasdair. *A Short History of Ethics.* New York: Macmillan, 1966. A lucid, if uneven, survey of the history of Western ethics.

Mackie, J. L. *Ethics: Inventing Right and Wrong.* New York: Penguin, 1976. This book takes a very different view of ethics from mine, viewing ethics from a skeptical perspective.

Pojman, Louis. *Ethics: Discovering Right and Wrong.* Belmont, Calif.: Wadsworth Publishing Company, 1999. An objectivist perspective.

Singer, Peter. *The Expanding Circle: Ethics and Sociobiology.* Oxford: Oxford University Press, 1983. A fascinating attempt to relate ethics to sociobiology.

Taylor, Paul. *Principles of Ethics.* Evanston, Ill.: Dickerson, 1975. This work covers many of the same topics as my book, usually from a different perspective. His discussion of the principle of universalizability (pp. 95–105) is especially useful.

Taylor, Richard, *Good and Evil.* Buffalo, N.Y.: Prometheus, 1970. A lively, easy-to-read work that sees the main role of morality to be the resolution of conflicts of interest.

Turnbull, Colin. *The Mountain People.* New York: Simon & Schuster, 1972. An excellent anthropological study of a people living on the edge of morality.

Van Wyk, Robert. *Introduction to Ethics.* New York: St. Martin's Press, 1990. A clearly written recent introduction to the subject.

Warnock, G. J. *The Object of Morality.* London: Methuen, 1971. A clearly written, well-argued analysis of the nature of morality.

CHAPTER 2

Good and Evil

What are Good and Evil? In the general introduction I contrasted two classical notions of the good: Plato's transcendent notion that the good was the source of all being and morality, and the hedonic notion that the good is defined as pleasure (and, by extension, happiness). Plato and religious theories have a common thesis that good is transcendent. It has a source beyond the empirical, in God or in a world of ideas. Similarly, for transcendentalists, the opposite of goodness, evil, is preternatural, inexplicable by ordinary understanding, mysterious. The third-century Manicheans and Zoroastrians believed that good and evil were two independent, equally powerful forces, always in conflict. St. Augustine (354–430), partly in response to the Manicheans, to which he formerly belonged, developed the idea that evil was not a real being, at all, but merely an absence of the good. It is parasitic on the good, a state of deprivation. Others attribute evil to the devil. On the other hand, the hedonist tradition rejects this transcendental approach and identifies the good with pleasure and happiness and evil with pain and suffering, purely empirical experiences. There is nothing mysterious about evil. It is, on the hedonist account, merely a problem of socializing human beings to take others into due consideration.

For many people the hedonist account lacks sufficient explanatory power. Evil is a profound mystery, more perplexing than the nature of Good, for it seems gratuitous. How could a good God permit evil? This is the question raised in our second reading, from Dostoevski's *Brothers Karamazov,* where the cynical philosopher, Ivan, asks his religious brother, Alyosha, how he can explain the problem of evil in the world.

Something bewildering and fascinating does surround evil. We are shocked, even horrified, at the brutalities of the Nazis or Pol

Pot's atrocities. Shakespeare's Iago is one of the most frightening characters in literature, for he seems to carry sadism to an unprecedented height, or, at least, to approach Milton's Satan, who cries out in *Paradise Lost,* "Evil be thou my good." Is this ugly feature, malignity, in all of us to some extent? Is it a primordial force that civilization constantly represses? Or is it simply an outcome of frustrated endeavors, a result of a failed upbringing? Yet we sometimes discover families, where love and consideration are strong, where one child develops into a moral monster. This was apparently the case of a youth in Washington who killed his two parents, both teachers, who, it is reported, gave him enormous love and care. Was he an ornery child from early childhood? Sometimes good children grow up in neglected environments and bad people grow up in good environments. What accounts for this?

We begin this chapter with a selection from Herman Melville's *Billy Budd,* the story of an innocent, beautiful youth, Billy Budd, who becomes entrapped in evil, in the guise of master-at-arms John Claggart. It is Billy's inner nobility that brings out Claggart's venom and leads to the tragedy of the story. Our third reading is from William Styron's *Sophie's Choice,* in which a young Polish mother is forced by a Nazi doctor at Auschwitz to make a terrible life-or-death choice between her children.

The very opposite of the evil of John Claggart and the Nazi doctor are the Protestant Pastor Trocme and the people of Le Chambon, France, who, at enormous personal risk, save the lives of six thousand Jews from the Nazis. Philip Hallie analyzes the situation in our fourth reading. In our fifth reading, the Australian philosopher Stanley Benn analyzes wickedness into four distinct types: selfishness, conscientious wickedness, heteronomous wickedness, and pathological wickedness. Benn gives a purely naturalistic account of evil, defining it as "any object, property or happening about which it is both intelligible and correct to say that it would be a better state of affairs if that object, et cetera, did not exist or occur." Benn's article includes an insightful account of malignity, including Claggart and Iago.

In our sixth reading, the German philosopher Friedrich Nietzsche offers a radically different analysis of good and evil, as constructions of a weak herd morality, fearful of the superior ability of the natural aristocrat, whose master morality transcends what we now call good and evil. It is no accident that Nietzsche names his hero

Zarathustra, the name of the ancient Zoroastrian leader, who believed that good and evil were independent, eternally co-present forces in the universe. Finally, in our last reading, Richard Taylor gives a thoroughly naturalist account of the origin of good and evil, as based on our interests and preferences.

Billy Budd

HERMAN MELVILLE

Herman Melville (1819–1891), the American novelist, wrote *Billy Budd* late in life. It was not published until Melville had been dead more than thirty years. The story takes place in 1797, a time when the British navy was threatened by mutinies, in which its very authority was at stake. It was the custom of naval ships to stop merchant vessels at sea and impress sailors into its service. Such occurred when men from the British man-of-war the HMS *Indomitable* went on board a merchant ship and impressed one sailor into His Majesty's service. The sailor was Billy Budd, a handsome and guileless twenty-one-year-old orphan, known for his affable nature and inability to speak clearly. He was illiterate and stammered, but nevertheless communicated such genuine good will that he was the darling of his mates. When informed by his new masters that he would not be returning home but out to sea, Billy changed his plans cheerfully and devoted himself to his duties as a good citizen and sailor. He soon became immensely popular on board the *Indomitable*.

One man, however, despised Billy. He was John Claggart, master-at-arms. Perhaps Claggart was jealous of Billy's good looks and popularity. We are not told the exact reasons, but Claggart loathed Billy to the point of concocting a fantastic story of mutiny, supposedly instigated by Billy. Claggart went to the captain of the *Indomitable*, Captain Vere, and reported an alleged meeting between Billy and another sailor discussing mutiny. There was such a meeting, only it was instigated by Claggart, and Billy renounced the suggestion of rebellion without hesitation.

Captain Vere was an honorable, fair-minded man of good will, who liked Billy and suspected that Claggart was lying. He warned his master-at-arms that bearing false witness against a fellow sailor at sea merited the death penalty.

From Herman Melville, *Billy Budd*. The manuscript of *Billy Budd* was found among Melville's possessions after he died. It was not published until 1924.

Then he invited Billy into his office and instructed Claggart to face him with the charges. We enter as Billy is being
accused of plotting to mutiny.

With the measured step and calm collected air of an asylum physician approaching in the public hall some patient beginning to show
indications of a coming paroxysm, Claggart deliberately advanced
within short range of Billy, and mesmerically looking him in the
eye, briefly recapitulated the accusation.

Not at first did Billy take it in. When he did the rose-tan of his
cheek looked struck as by white leprosy. He stood like one impaled
and gagged. Meanwhile the accuser's eyes, removing not as yet
from the blue, dilated ones, underwent a phenomenal change, their
wonted rich violet color blurring into a muddy purple. Those lights
of human intelligence losing human expression, icily protruding like
alien eyes of certain uncatalogued creatures of the deep.

The first mesmeric glance was one of surprised fascination; the
last was as the hungry lurch of the torpedo-fish.

"Speak, man!" said Captain Vere to the transfixed one, struck by
his aspect even more than by Claggart's. "Speak! defend yourself."
Which appeal caused but a strange, dumb gesturing and gurgling
in Billy; amazement at such an accusation so suddenly sprung on
inexperienced nonage; this, and it may be horror at the accuser,
serving to bring out his lurking defect, and in this instance for the
time intensifying it into a convulsed tongue-tie; while the intent
head and entire form, straining forward in an agony of ineffectual
eagerness to obey the injunction to speak and defend himself, gave
an expression to the face like that of a condemned vestal priestess
in the moment of being buried alive, and in the first struggle against
suffocation.

Though at the time Captain Vere was quite ignorant of Billy's liability to vocal impediment, he now immediately divined it, since
vividly Billy's aspect recalled to him that of a bright young school-
mate of his whom he had seen struck by much the same startling
impotence in the act of eagerly rising in the class to be foremost in
response to a testing question put to it by the master. Going close
up to the young sailor, and laying a soothing hand on his shoulder,
he said, "There is no hurry, my boy. Take your time, take your time."
Contrary to the effect intended, these words, so fatherly in tone,

doubtless touching Billy's heart to the quick, prompted yet more violent efforts at utterance—efforts soon ending for the time in confirming the paralysis, and bringing to the face an expression which
was as a crucifixion to behold. The next instant, quick as the flame
from a discharged cannon at night, his right arm shot out, and Claggart dropped to the deck. Whether intentionally, or but owing to the
young athlete's superior height, the blow had taken effect full upon
the forehead, so shapely and intellectual-looking a feature in the
master-at-arms; so that the body fell over lengthwise, like a heavy
plank tilted from erectness. A gasp or two, and he lay motionless.

"Fated boy," breathed Captain Vere, in tone so low as to be
almost a whisper. . . .

Who in the rainbow can draw the line where the violet tint ends
and the orange tint begins? Distinctly we see the difference of the
colors, but where exactly does the one first blendingly enter into
the other? So with sanity and insanity. In pronounced cases there
is no question about them. But in some supposed cases, in various degrees supposedly less pronounced, to draw the exact line of
demarcation few will undertake, though for a fee becoming con-
siderate some professional experts will. There is nothing namable
but that some men will, or undertake to, do it for pay.

Whether Captain Vere, as the surgeon professionally and privately surmised, was really the sudden victim of any degree of aberration, every one must determine for himself by such light as this
narrative may afford.

That the unhappy event which has been narrated could not have
happened at a worse juncture was but too true. For it was close
on the heel of the suppressed insurrections, an aftertime very critical to naval authority, demanding from every English sea commander two qualities not readily interfusable—prudence and rigor.
Moreover, there was something crucial in the case.

In the jugglery of circumstances preceding and attending the
event on board the *Indomitable,* and in the light of that martial
code whereby it was formally to be judged, innocence and guilt
personified in Claggart and Budd in effect changed places. In a
legal view the apparent victim of the tragedy was he who had
sought to victimize a man blameless; and the indisputable deed of
the latter, navally regarded, constituted the most heinous of military crimes. Yet more. The essential right and wrong involved in
the matter, the clearer that might be, so much the worse for the

responsibility of a loyal sea commander, inasmuch as he was not authorized to determine the matter on that primitive basis.

Small wonder then that the *Indomitable*'s captain, though in general a man of rapid decision, felt that circumspectness not less than promptitude was necessary. Until he could decide upon his course, and in each detail; and not only so, but until the concluding measure was upon the point of being enacted, he deemed it advisable, in view of all the circumstances, to guard as much as possible against publicity. Here he may or may not have erred. Certain it is, however, that subsequently in the confidential talk of more than one or two gun rooms and cabins he was not a little criticized by some officers, a fact imputed by his friends and vehemently by his cousin Jack Denton to professional jealousy of Starry Vere. Some imaginative ground for invidious comment there was. The maintenance of secrecy in the matter, the confining all knowledge of it for a time to the place where the homicide occurred, the quarterdeck cabin; in these particulars lurked some resemblance to the policy adopted in those tragedies of the palace which have occurred more than once in the capital founded by Peter the Barbarian.

The case indeed was such that fain would the *Indomitable*'s captain have deferred taking any action whatever respecting it further than to keep the foretopman a close prisoner till the ship rejoined the squadron and then submitting the matter to the judgment of his admiral.

But a true military officer is in one particular like a true monk. Not with more of self-abnegation will the latter keep his vows of monastic obedience than the former his vows of allegiance to martial duty.

Feeling that unless quick action was taken on it, the deed of the foretopman, so soon as it should be known on the gun decks, would tend to awaken any slumbering embers of the Nore[1] among the crew, a sense of the urgency of the case overruled in Captain Vere every other consideration. But though a conscientious disciplinarian, he was no lover of authority for mere authority's sake. Very far was he from embracing opportunities for monopolizing to himself the perils of moral responsibility, none at least that could properly be

---

[1]The mutiny on the ship *Nore* shook the British navy's authority and created a spirit of insurrection among its seamen.

referred to an official superior or shared with him by his official equals or even subordinates. So thinking, he was glad it would not be at variance with usage to turn the matter over to a summary court of his own officers, reserving to himself, as the one on whom the ultimate accountability would rest, the right of maintaining a supervision of it, or formally or informally interposing at need. Accordingly a drumhead court was summarily convened, he electing the individuals composing it: the first lieutenant, the captain of marines, and the sailing master.

In associating an officer of marines with the sea lieutenant and the sailing master in a case having to do with a sailor, the commander perhaps deviated from general custom. He was prompted thereto by the circumstance that he took that soldier to be a judicious person, thoughtful, and not altogether incapable of grappling with a difficult case unprecedented in his prior experience. Yet even as to him he was not without some latent misgiving, for withal he was an extremely good-natured man, an enjoyer of his dinner, a sound sleeper, and inclined to obesity—a man who though he would always maintain his manhood in battle might not prove altogether reliable in a moral dilemma involving aught of the tragic. As to the first lieutenant and the sailing master, Captain Vere could not but be aware that though honest natures, of approved gallantry upon occasion, their intelligence was mostly confined to the matter of active seamanship and the fighting demands of their profession.

The court was held in the same cabin where the unfortunate affair had taken place. This cabin, the commander's, embraced the entire area under the poop deck. Aft, and on either side, was a small stateroom, the one now temporarily a jail and the other a dead-house, and a yet smaller compartment, leaving a space between expanding forward into a goodly oblong of length coinciding with the ship's beam. A skylight of moderate dimension was overhead, and at each end of the oblong space were two sashed porthole windows easily convertible back into embrasures for short carronades.

All being quickly in readiness, Billy Budd was arraigned, Captain Vere necessarily appearing as the sole witness in the case, and as such temporarily sinking his rank, though singularly maintaining it in a matter apparently trivial, namely, that he testified from the ship's weather side, with that object having caused the court to sit on the lee side. Concisely he narrated all that had led up to the catastrophe, omitting nothing in Claggart's accusation and deposing as to the manner in which the prisoner had received it. At this testimony the three officers glanced with no little surprise at Billy Budd, the last man they would have suspected either of the mutinous design alleged by Claggart or the undeniable deed he himself had done. The first lieutenant, taking judicial primacy and turning toward the prisoner, said, "Captain Vere has spoken. Is it or is it not as Captain Vere says?"

In response came syllables not so much impeded in the utterance as might have been anticipated. They were these: "Captain Vere tells the truth. It is just as Captain Vere says, but it is not as the master-at-arms said. I have eaten the King's bread and I am true to the King."

"I believe you, my man," said the witness, his voice indicating a suppressed emotion not otherwise betrayed.

"God will bless you for that, your honor!" not without stammering said Billy, and all but broke down. But immediately he was recalled to self-control by another question, to which with the same emotional difficulty of utterance he said, "No, there was no malice between us. I never bore malice against the master-at-arms. I am sorry that he is dead. I did not mean to kill him. Could I have used my tongue I would not have struck him. But he foully lied to my face and in presence of my captain, and I had to say something, and I could only say it with a blow, God help me!"

In the impulsive aboveboard manner of the frank one the court saw confirmed all that was implied in words that just previously had perplexed them, coming as they did from the testifier to the tragedy and promptly following Billy's impassioned disclaimer of mutinous intent—Captain Vere's words, "I believe you, my man."

Next it was asked of him whether he knew of or suspected aught savoring of incipient trouble (meaning mutiny, though the explicit term was avoided) going on in any section of the ship's company.

The reply lingered. This was naturally imputed by the court to the same vocal embarrassment which had retarded or obstructed previous answers. But in main it was otherwise here, the question immediately recalling to Billy's mind the interview with the afterguardsman in the forechains. But an innate repugnance to playing a part at all approaching that of an informer against one's own shipmates—the same erring sense of uninstructed honor which had stood in the way of his reporting the matter at the time, though as a loyal man-of-war's man it was incumbent on him, and failure so to do, if charged against him and proven, would have subjected him to the heaviest of penalties; this, with the blind feeling now his that nothing really was being hatched, prevailed with him. When the answer came it was a negative.

"One question more," said the officer of marines, now first speaking and with a troubled earnestness. "You tell us that what the master-at-arms said against you was a lie. Now why should he have so lied, so maliciously lied, since you declare there was no malice between you?"

At that question, unintentionally touching on a spiritual sphere wholly obscure to Billy's thoughts, he was nonplussed, evincing a confusion indeed that some observers, such as can readily be imagined, would have construed into involuntary evidence of hidden guilt. Nevertheless, he strove some way to answer, but all at once relinquished the vain endeavor, at the same time turning an appealing glance toward Captain Vere as deeming him his best helper and friend. Captain Vere, who had been seated for a time, rose to his feet, addressing the interrogator. "The question you put to him comes naturally enough. But how can he rightly answer it?—or anybody else, unless indeed it be he who lies within there," designating the compartment where lay the corpse. "But the prone one there will not rise to our summons. In effect, though, as it seems to me, the point you make is hardly material. Quite aside from any conceivable motive actuating the master-at-arms, and irrespective of the provocation to the blow, a martial court must needs in the present case confine its attention to the blow's consequence, which consequence justly is to be deemed not otherwise than as the striker's deed."

This utterance, the full significance of which it was not at all likely that Billy took in, nevertheless caused him to turn a wistful interrogative look toward the speaker, a look in its dumb expressiveness not unlike that which a dog of generous breed might turn upon his master, seeking in his face some elucidation of a previous gesture ambiguous to the canine intelligence. Nor was the same utterance without marked effect upon the three officers, more especially the soldier. Couched in it seemed to them a meaning unanticipated, involving a prejudgment on the speaker's part. It served to augment a mental disturbance previously evident enough.

The soldier once more spoke, in a tone of suggestive dubiety addressing at once his associates and Captain Vere: "Nobody is present—none of the ship's company, I mean—who might shed lateral light, if any is to be had, upon what remains mysterious in this matter."

"That is thoughtfully put," said Captain Vere; "I see your drift. Ay, there is a mystery; but, to use a scriptural phrase, it is a 'mystery of iniquity,' a matter for psychologic theologians to discuss. But what has a military court to do with it? Not to add that for us any possible investigation of it is cut off by the lasting tongue-tie of—him—in yonder," again designating the mortuary stateroom. "The prisoner's deed—with that alone we have to do."

To this, and particularly the closing reiteration, the marine soldier, knowing not how aptly to reply, sadly abstained from saying aught. The first lieutenant, who at the outset had not unnaturally assumed primacy in the court, now overrulingly instructed by a glance from Captain Vere, a glance more effective than words, resumed that primacy. Turning to the prisoner, "Budd," he said, and scarce in equable tones, "Budd, if you have aught further to say for yourself, say it now."

Upon this the young sailor turned another quick glance toward Captain Vere; then, as taking a hint from that aspect, a hint confirming his own instinct that silence was now best, replied to the lieutenant, "I have said all, sir."

The marine—the same who had been the sentinel without the cabin door at the time that the foretopman, followed by the master-at-arms, entered it—he, standing by the sailor throughout these judicial proceedings, was now directed to take him back to the after compartment originally assigned to the prisoner and his custodian. As the twain disappeared from view, the three officers, as partially liberated from some inward constraint associated with Billy's mere presence, simultaneously stirred in their seats. They exchanged looks of troubled indecision, yet feeling that decide they must and without long delay. For Captain Vere, he for the time stood—unconsciously with his back toward them, apparently in one of his absent fits—gazing out from a sashed porthole to windward upon the monotonous blank of the twilight sea. But the court's silence continuing, broken only at moments by brief consultations, in low earnest tones, this served to arouse him and energize him. Turning, he to-and-fro paced the cabin athwart; in the returning ascent to windward climbing the slant deck in the ship's lee roll, without knowing it symbolizing thus in his action a mind resolute to surmount difficulties even if against primitive instincts strong as the wind and the sea. Presently he came to a stand before the three. After scanning their faces he stood less as mustering his thoughts for expression than as one only deliberating how best to put them to well-meaning men not intellectually mature, men with whom it was necessary to demonstrate certain principles that were axioms to himself. Similar impatience as to talking is perhaps one reason that deters some minds from addressing any popular assemblies.

When speak he did, something, both in the substance of what he said and his manner of saying it, showed the influence of un-shared studies modifying and tempering the practical training of an active career. This, along with his phraseology, now and then was suggestive of the grounds whereon rested that imputation of a certain pedantry socially alleged against him by certain naval men of wholly practical cast, captains who nevertheless would frankly concede that His Majesty's navy mustered no more efficient officer of their grade than Starry Vere.

What he said was to this effect: "Hitherto I have been but the witness, little more; and I should hardly think now to take another tone, that of your coadjutor for the time, did I not perceive in you—at the crisis too—a troubled hesitancy, proceeding, I doubt not, from the clash of military duty with moral scruple—scruple vitalized by compassion. For the compassion, how can I otherwise than share it? But, mindful of paramount obligations, I strive against scruples that may tend to enervate decision. Not, gentlemen, that I hide from myself that the case is an exceptional one. Speculatively regarded, it well might be referred to a jury of casuists. But for us here, acting not as casuists or moralists, it is a case practical, and under martial law practically to be dealt with.

"But your scruples: do they move as in a dusk? Challenge them. Make them advance and declare themselves. Come now; do they import something like this: If, mindless of palliating circumstances, we are bound to regard the death of the master-at-arms as the prisoner's deed, then does that deed constitute a capital crime whereof the penalty is a mortal one. But in natural justice is nothing but the prisoner's overt act to be considered? How can we adjudge to summary and shameful death a fellow creature innocent before God, and whom we feel to be so?—Does that state it aright? You sign sad assent. Well, I too feel that, the full force of that. It is Nature. But do these buttons that we wear attest that our allegiance is to Nature? No, to the King. Though the ocean, which is inviolate Nature primeval, though this be the element where we move and have our being as sailors, yet as the King's officers lies our duty in a sphere correspondingly natural? So little is that true, that in receiving our commissions we in the most important regards ceased to be natural free agents. When war is declared are we the commissioned fighters previously consulted? We fight at command. If our judgments approve the war, that is but coincidence. So in other particulars. So now. For suppose condemnation to follow these present proceedings. Would it be so much we ourselves that would condemn as it would be martial law operating through us? For that law and the rigor of it, we are not responsible. Our vowed responsibility is in this: That however pitilessly that law may operate in any instances, we nevertheless adhere to it and administer it.

"But the exceptional in the matter moves the hearts within you. Even so too is mine moved. But let not warm hearts betray heads that should be cool. Ashore in a criminal case, will an upright judge allow himself off the bench to be waylaid by some tender kinswoman of the accused seeking to touch him with her tearful plea? Well, the heart here, sometimes the feminine in man, is as that piteous woman, and hard though it be, she must here be ruled out."

He paused, earnestly studying them for a moment; then resumed.

"But something in your aspect seems to urge that it is not solely the heart that moves in you, but also the conscience, the private conscience. But tell me whether or not, occupying the position we do, private conscience should not yield to that imperial one formulated in the mode under which alone we officially proceed?"

Here the three men moved in their seats, less convinced than agitated by the course of an argument troubling but the more the spontaneous conflict within.

Perceiving which, the speaker paused for a moment; then abruptly changing his tone, went on.

"To steady us a bit, let us recur to the facts.—In wartime at sea a man-of-war's man strikes his superior in grade, and the blow kills. Apart from its effect the blow itself is, according to the Articles of War, a capital crime. Furthermore—"

"Ay, sir," emotionally broke in the officer of marines, "in one sense it was. But surely Budd purposed neither mutiny nor homicide."

"Surely not, my good man. And before a court less arbitrary and more merciful than a martial one, that plea would largely extenuate. At the Last Assizes it shall acquit. But how here? We proceed under the law of the Mutiny Act. In feature no child can resemble his father more than that Act resembles in spirit the thing from which it derives—War. In His Majesty's service—in this ship, indeed—there are Englishmen forced to fight for the King against their will. Against their conscience, for aught we know. Though as their fellow creatures some of us may appreciate their position, yet as navy officers what reck we of it? Still less recks the enemy. Our impressed men he would fain cut down in the same swath with our volunteers. As regards the enemy's naval conscripts, some of whom may even share our own abhorrence of the regicidal French Directory, it is the same on our side. War looks but to the frontage, the appearance. And the Mutiny Act, War's child, takes after the father. Budd's intent or non-intent is nothing to the purpose.

"But while, put to it by those anxieties in you which I cannot but respect, I only repeat myself—while thus strangely we prolong proceedings that should be summary—the enemy may be sighted and an engagement result. We must do; and one of two things must we do—condemn or let go."

"Can we not convict and yet mitigate the penalty?" asked the sailing master, here speaking, and falteringly, for the first.

"Gentlemen, were that clearly lawful for us under the circumstances, consider the consequences of such clemency. The people" (meaning the ship's company) "have native sense; most of them are familiar with our naval usage and tradition; and how would they take it? Even could you explain to them—which our official position forbids—they, long molded by arbitrary discipline, have not that kind of intelligent responsiveness that might qualify them to comprehend and discriminate. No, to the people the foretopman's deed, however it be worded in the announcement, will be plain homicide committed in a flagrant act of mutiny. What penalty for that should follow, they know. But it does not follow. *Why?* they will ruminate. You know what sailors are. Will they not revert to the recent outbreak at the Nore? Ay. They know the well-founded alarm—the panic it struck throughout England. Your clement sentence they would account pusillanimous. They would think that we flinch, that we are afraid of them—afraid of practicing a lawful rigor singularly demanded at this juncture, lest it should provoke new troubles. What shame to us such a conjecture on their part, and how deadly to discipline. You see then, whither, prompted by duty and the law, I steadfastly drive. But I beseech you, my friends, do not take me amiss. I feel as you do for this unfortunate boy. But did he know our hearts, I take him to be of that generous nature that he would feel even for us on whom this military necessity so heavy a compulsion is laid."

With that, crossing the deck he resumed his place by the sashed porthole, tacitly leaving the three to come to a decision. On the cabin's opposite side the troubled court sat silent. Loyal lieges, plain and practical, though at bottom they dissented from some points Captain Vere had put to them, they were without the faculty, hardly had the inclination, to gainsay one whom they felt to be an earnest man, one too not less their superior in mind than in naval rank. But it is not improbable that even such of his words as were not without influence over them, less came home to them than his closing appeal to their instinct as sea officers: in the forethought he threw out as to the practical consequences to discipline, considering the unconfirmed tone of the fleet at the time, should a man-of-war's man's violent killing at sea of a superior in grade be allowed to pass for aught else than a capital crime demanding prompt infliction of the penalty. . . .

In brief, Billy Budd was formally convicted and sentenced to be hung at the yardarm in the early morning watch, it being now night. Otherwise, as is customary in such cases, the sentence would forthwith have been carried out. In wartime on the field or in the fleet, a mortal punishment decreed by a drumhead court—on the field sometimes decreed by but a nod from the general—follows without delay on the heel of conviction, without appeal. . . .

The next morning Billy Budd was hanged. His last words were "God bless Captain Vere!"

For Further Reflection

1. Normally we think that one must intend to kill a victim before one can be guilty of murder, as opposed to involuntary manslaughter. But Budd never intended to kill Claggart. Should he have been charged with murder?

2. Why did Captain Vere take the stance he did against Billy? Was he concerned with the deterrent effect an execution would have at a time when mutiny was a serious problem or did he think

he was bound to carry out the letter of the law? What should he have done? Why?

3. Perhaps the most interesting thing about this story is the stark contrast between Claggart and Billy Budd. What are some of the moral lessons we may learn from this contrast and how they encounter one another?

Why Is There Evil?

FYODOR DOSTOEVSKI

Fyodor Dostoevski (1822–1881), the great Russian novelist, was born in Moscow. His revolutionary sympathies and a penchant for gambling managed to keep him in constant danger. Among his famous novels are *Crime and Punishment* (1866) and *The Brothers Karamazov* (1880), from which our reading is taken.

In this scene, the philosophical cynic Ivan Karamazov explains to his devoutly religious brother, Alyosha, a Christian monk, why the problem of evil prevents him from accepting God.

"Well, tell me where to begin, give your orders. The existence of God, eh?"

"Begin where you like. You declared yesterday at father's that there was no God." Alyosha looked searchingly at his brother.

"I said that yesterday at dinner on purpose to tease you and I saw your eyes glow. But now I've no objection to discussing with you, and I say so very seriously. I want to be friends with you, Alyosha,

From Fyodor Dostoevski, *The Brothers Karamazov,* translated by Constance Garnett (London: Heinemann, 1912).

for I have no friends and want to try it. Well, only fancy, perhaps I too accept God," laughed Ivan, "that's a surprise for you, isn't it?"

"Yes of course, if you are not joking now."

"Joking? I was told at the elder's yesterday that I was joking. You know, dear boy, there was an old sinner in the eighteenth century who declared that, if there were no God, he would have to be invented. . . . And man has actually invented God. And what's strange, what would be marvelous, is not that God should really exist; the marvel is that such an idea, the idea of the necessity of God, could enter the head of such a savage, vicious beast as man. So holy it is, so touching, so wise and so great a credit it does to man. As for me, I've long resolved not to think whether man created God or God man. . . . For what are we aiming at now? I am trying to explain as quickly as possible my essential nature, that is what manner of man I am, what I believe in, and for what I hope, that's it, isn't it? And therefore I tell you that I accept God simply. But you must note this: if God exists and if He really did create the world, then, as we all know, He created it according to the geometry of Euclid and the human mind with the conception of only three dimensions in space. Yet there have been and still are geometricians and philosophers, and even some of the most distinguished, who doubt whether the whole universe, or to speak more widely the whole of being, was only created in Euclid's geometry; they even dare to dream that two parallel lines, which according to Euclid can never meet on earth, may meet somewhere in infinity. I have come to the conclusion that, since I can't understand even that, I can't expect to understand about God. I acknowledge humbly that I have no faculty for settling such questions. I have a Euclidian earthly mind, and how could I solve problems that are not of this world? And I advise you never to think about it either, my dear Alyosha, especially about God, whether He exists or not. All such questions are utterly inappropriate for a mind created with an idea of only three dimensions. And so I accept God and am glad to, and what's more I accept His wisdom, His purpose—which are utterly beyond our ken; I believe in the underlying order and the meaning of life; I believe in the eternal harmony in which they say we shall one day be blended. I believe in the Word to Which the universe is striving, and Which Itself was 'with God,' and Which Itself is God and so on, and so on, to infinity. There are all sorts of phrases for it. I seem to be on the right path, don't I? Yet would you believe it, in the final result I don't accept this world of

God's, and, although I know it exists, I don't accept it at all. It's not that I don't accept God, you must understand, it's the world created by Him I don't and cannot accept. Let me make it plain. I believe like a child that suffering will be healed and made up for, that all the humiliating absurdity of human contradictions will vanish like a pitiful mirage, like the despicable fabrication of the impotent and infinitely small Euclidian mind of man, that in the world's finale, at the moment of eternal harmony, something so precious will come to pass that it will suffice for all hearts, for the comforting of all resentments, for the atonement of all the crimes of humanity, of all the blood they've shed; that it will make it not only possible to forgive but to justify all that has happened with men—but though all that may come to pass, I don't accept it. I won't accept it. Even if parallel lines do meet and I see it myself, I shall see it and say that they've met, but still I won't accept it. That's what's at the root of me, Alyosha; that's my creed.

" . . . Do you understand why this infamy must be and is permitted? Without it, I am told, man could not have known good and evil. Why should he know that diabolical good and evil when it costs so much? Why, the whole world of knowledge is not worth that child's prayer to 'dear, Kind God'! I say nothing of the sufferings of grown-up people, they have eaten the apple, damn them, and the devil take them all! But these little ones! I am making you suffer, Alyosha, you are not yourself. I'll leave off if you like."

"Never mind. I want to suffer too," muttered Alyosha.

"One picture, only one more, because it's so curious, so characteristic, and I have only just read it in some collection of Russian antiquities. I've forgotten the name. I must look it up. It was in the darkest days of serfdom at the beginning of the century, and long live the Liberator of the People! There was in those days a general of aristocratic connections, the owner of great estates, one of these men—somewhat exceptional, I believe, even then—who, retiring from the service into a life of leisure, are convinced that they've earned absolute power over the lives of their subjects. There were such men then. So our general, settled on his property of two thousand souls, lives in pomp and domineers over his poor neighbors as though they were dependents and buffoons. He has kennels of hundreds of hounds and nearly a hundred dog-boys—all mounted, and in uniform. One day a serf boy, a little child of eight, threw a stone in play and hurt the paw of the general's favorite hound. 'Why is my favorite dog lame?' He is told that the boy threw a stone that hurt the dog's paw. 'So you did it.' The general looked the child up and down. 'Take him.' He was taken—taken from his mother and kept shut up all night. Early that morning the general comes out on horseback, with the hounds, his dependents, dog-boys, and huntsmen, all mounted around him in full hunting parade. The servants are summoned for their edification, and in front of them all stands the mother of the child. The child is brought from the lockup. It's a gloomy, cold, foggy autumn day, a capital day for hunting. The general orders the child to be undressed; the child is stripped naked. He shivers, numb with terror not daring to cry. . . . 'Make him run,' commands the general. 'Run! run!' shout the dog-boys. The boy runs. . . . 'At him!' yells the general, and he sets the whole pack of hounds on the child. The hounds catch him, and tear him to pieces before his mother's eyes! . . . I believe the general was afterwards declared incapable of administering his estates. Well—what did he deserve? To be shot? to be shot for the satisfaction of our moral feelings? Speak, Alyosha!"

"To be shot," murmured Alyosha, lifting his eyes to Ivan with a pale twisted smile.

"Bravo!" cried Ivan delighted. "If even you say so . . . You're a pretty monk! So there is a little devil sitting in your heart, Alyosha Karamazov!"

"What I said was absurd, but—"

"That's just the point that 'but'!" cried Ivan. "Let me tell you, novice, that the absurd is only too necessary on earth. The world stands on absurdities, and perhaps nothing would have come to pass in it without them. We know what we know!"

"What do you know?"

"I understand nothing," Ivan went on, as though in delirium. "I don't want to understand anything now. I want to stick to the fact. I made up my mind long ago not to understand. If I try to under-stand anything, I shall be false to the fact and I have determined to stick to the fact."

"Why are you trying me?" Alyosha cried, with sudden distress. "Will you say what you mean at last?"

"Of course, I will; that's what I've been leading up to. You are dear to me, I don't want to let you go, and I won't give you up to your Zossima."

Ivan for a minute was silent, his face became all at once very sad.

"Listen! I took the case of the children only to make my case clearer. Of the other tears of humanity with which the earth is soaked from its crust to its center, I will say nothing. I have narrowed my subject on purpose. I am a bug, and I recognize in all humility that I cannot understand why the world is arranged as it is. Men are themselves to blame, I suppose; they were given paradise, they wanted freedom, and stole fire from heaven, though they knew they would become unhappy, so there is no need to pity them. With my pitiful, earthly, Euclidian understanding, all I know is that there is suffering and that there are none guilty; that cause follows effect, simply and directly; that everything flows and finds its level—but that's only Euclidian nonsense, I know that, and I can't consent to live by it! What comfort is it to me that there are none guilty and that cause follows effect simply and directly, and that I know it—I must have justice, or I will destroy myself. And not justice in some remote infinite time and space, but here on earth, and that I could see myself. I have believed in it. I want to see it, and if I am dead by then, let me rise again, for if it all happens without me, it will be too unfair. Surely I haven't suffered, simply that I, my crimes and my sufferings, may manure the soil of the future harmony for somebody else. I want to see with my own eyes the hind lie down with the lion and the victim rise up and embrace his murderer. I want to be there when everyone suddenly understands what it has all been for. All the religions of the world are built on this longing, and I am a believer. But then there are the children, and what am I to do about them? That's a question I can't answer. For the hundredth time I repeat, there are numbers of questions, but I've only taken the children, because in their case what I mean is so unanswerably clear. Listen! If all must suffer to pay for the eternal harmony, what have children to do with it, tell me, please? It's beyond all comprehension why they should suffer, and why they should pay for the harmony. Why should they, too, furnish material to enrich the soil for the harmony of the future? I understand solidarity in sin among men. I understand solidarity in retribution, too; but there can be no such solidarity with children. And if it is really true that they must share responsibility for all their fathers' crimes, such a truth is not of this world and is beyond my comprehension. Some jester will say, perhaps, that the child would have grown up and have sinned, but you see he didn't grow up, he was torn to pieces by the dogs, at eight years old. Oh, Alyosha, I am not blaspheming! I understand, of course, what an upheaval of the universe it will be, when everything in heaven and earth blends in one hymn of praise and everything that lives and has lived cries aloud: 'Thou art just, O Lord, for Thy ways are revealed,' when the mother embraces the fiend who threw her child to the dogs, and all three cry aloud with tears, 'Thou are just, O Lord!' then, of course, the crown of knowledge will be reached and all will be made clear. But what pulls me up here is that I can't accept that harmony. And while I am on earth, I make haste to take my own measures. You see, Alyosha, perhaps it really may happen that if I live to that moment, or rise again to see it, I, too, perhaps, may cry aloud with the rest, looking at the mother embracing the child's torturer, 'Thou art just, O Lord!' but I don't want to cry aloud then. While there is still time, I hasten to protect myself and so I renounce the higher harmony altogether. It's not worth the tears of that one tortured child who beat itself on the breast with its little fist and prayed in its stinking outhouse, with its unexpiated tears to 'dear, kind God'! It's not worth it, because those tears are unatoned for. They must be atoned for, or there can be no harmony. But how? How are you going to atone for them? Is it possible? By their being avenged? But what do I care for avenging them? What do I care for a hell for oppressors? What good can hell do, since those children have already been tortured? And what becomes of harmony, if there is hell? I want to forgive. I want to embrace. I don't want more suffering. And if the sufferings of children go to swell the sum of sufferings which was necessary to pay for truth, then I protest that the truth is not worth such a price. I don't want the mother to embrace the oppressor who threw her son to the dogs! She dare not forgive him! Let her forgive him for herself, if she will, let her forgive the torturer for the immeasurable suffering of her mother's heart. But the sufferings of her tortured child she has no right to forgive; she dare not forgive the torturer, even if the child were to forgive him! And if that is so, if they dare not forgive, what becomes of harmony? Is there in the whole world a being who would have the right to forgive and could forgive? I don't want harmony. From love for humanity I don't want it. I would rather be left with the unavenged suffering. I would rather remain with my unavenged suffering and unsatisfied indignation, *even if I were wrong.* Besides, too high a price is asked for harmony; it's beyond our means to pay so much to enter on it. And so I hasten to give back my entrance ticket, and if I am an honest man I am bound to give it back as soon as possible. And that I am doing. It's not God that I don't accept, Alyosha, only I most respectfully return Him the ticket."

"That's rebellion," murmured Alyosha, looking down.

"Rebellion? I am sorry you call it that," said Ivan earnestly. "One can hardly live in rebellion, and I want to live. Tell me yourself, I challenge you—answer. Imagine that you are creating a fabric of human destiny with the object of making men happy in the end, giving them peace and rest at last, but that it was essential and inevitable to torture to death only one tiny creature—that baby beating its breast with its fist, for instance—and to found that edifice on its unavenged tears, would you consent to be the architect on those conditions? Tell me, and tell the truth."

"No, I wouldn't consent," said Alyosha softly.

For Further Reflection

1. There are three propositions involved in the traditional formulation of the problem of evil:

   God is all-powerful (including being all-knowing).

   God is perfectly good.

   Evil exists.

   These premises seem to be mutually incompatible, for if God is all-good, he will not allow evil if he can help it. And if he is all-powerful, he is able to prevent evil. But evil exists. Hence, the problem of evil. How does Ivan deal with these premises? Is there any way to resolve this problem that makes sense of all the premises?

2. Do you think that the existence of enormous evil, such as Ivan portrays, counts against the existence of God? Explain why or why not.

Sophie's Choice

WILLIAM STYRON

William Styron, the well-known American novelist, received the Pulitzer Prize in 1967 for *The Confessions of Nat Turner*. In this *Sophie's Choice* excerpt he describes a young Polish mother, Sophie, with her two small children, being transported in a crowded train by German soldiers during World War II to Auschwitz, the Nazi concentration camp. There she is examined by a doctor, whom she calls *Jemand von Niemand* (literally, every man of no man), who first tries to seduce her but shortly after offers her a fateful choice. We enter the story with Sophie and her two children, Jan and Eva, on the train.

The name Oświęcim—Auschwitz—which had at first murmured its way through the compartment made [Sophie] weak with fear, but she had no doubt whatever that that was where the train was going. A minuscule sliver of light, catching her eye, drew her attention to a tiny crack in the plywood board across the window, and during the first hour of the journey she was able to see enough by the dawn's glow to tell their direction: south. Due south past the country villages that crowd around Warsaw in place of the usual suburban outskirts, due south past greening fields and copses crowded with birch trees, south in the direction of Cracow. Only Auschwitz, of all their plausible destinations, lay south, and she recalled the despair she felt when with her own eyes she verified where they were going. The reputation of Auschwitz was ominous, vile, terrifying. Although in the Gestapo prison rumors had tended to support Auschwitz as the place where they would eventually be shipped, she had hoped incessantly and prayed for a labor camp in Germany, where so many Poles had been transported and where, according to other rumor, conditions were less brutal, less harsh. But as Auschwitz loomed more and more inevitably and now, on the train, made itself inescapable, Sophie was smothered by the realization that she was victim of punishment by association, retribution through chance concurrence. She kept saying to herself: I don't belong here. If she had not had the misfortune of being taken prisoner at the same time as so many of the Home Army members (a stroke of bad luck further complicated by her connection with Wanda, and their common dwelling place, even though she had not lifted a finger to help the Resistance), she might have been adjudged guilty of the serious crime of meat smuggling but not of the infinitely more grave crime of subversion, and hence might not be headed for a destination so forbiddingly malign. But among other ironies, she realized, was this one: she had not been *judged* guilty of anything, merely interrogated and forgotten. She had then been thrown in haphazardly among these partisans, where she was victim less of any specific retributive justice than of a general rage—a kind of berserk lust for complete domination and oppression which seized the Nazis whenever they scored a win over the Resistance, and which this time had even extended to the several hundred bedraggled Poles ensnared in that last savage roundup.

Certain things about the trip she remembered with utter clarity. The stench, the airlessness, the endless shifting of positions—stand up, sit down, stand up again. At the moment of a sudden stop a box toppling down on her head, not stunning her, not hurting too much, but raising an egg-size bulge at the top of her skull. The view outside the crack, where spring sunlight darkened into drizzling rain: through the film of rain, birch trees still tormented by the past winter's crushing snowfall, bent into shapes of white parabolic arches, strongbows, catapults, beautiful broken skeletons, whips. Lemon dots of forsythia everywhere. Delicate green fields blending into distant forests of spruce and larch and pine. Sunshine again. Jan's books, which he tried to read in the feeble light as he sat on her lap: *The Swiss Family Robinson* in German; Polish editions of *White Fang* and *Penrod and Sam*. Eva's two possessions, which she refused to park in the luggage rack but clutched fiercely as if any moment they might be wrested from her hands: the flute in its leather case and her *mís*—the one-eared, one-eyed teddy bear she had kept since the cradle.

More rain outside, a torrent. Now the odor of vomit, pervasive, unextinguishable, cheesy. Fellow passengers: two frightened convent girls of sixteen or so, sobbing, sleeping, waking to murmur prayers to the Holy Virgin; Wiktor, a black-haired, intense, infuriated young Home Army member already plotting revolt or escape, cease-lessly scribbling messages on slips of paper to be passed to Wanda in another compartment; a fear-maddened shriveled old lady claim-ing to be the niece of Wieniawski, claiming the bundle of parchment she kept pressed close to her to be the original manuscript of his famous *Polonaise,* claiming some kind of immunity, dissolving into tears like the schoolgirls at Wiktor's snarled remark that the Nazis would wipe their asses on the worthless *Polonaise.* Hunger pangs beginning. Nothing at all to eat. Another old woman—quite dead—laid out in the exterior aisle on the spot where her heart attack had felled her, her hands frozen around a crucifix and her chalk-white face already smudged by the boots and shoes of people treading over and around her. Through her crevice once more: Cracow at night, the familiar station, moonlit railroad yards where they lay stranded hour after hour. In the greenish moonglow an extraordinary sight: a German soldier standing in *feldgrau* uniform and with slung rifle, masturbating with steady beat in the half-light of the deserted yard, grinningly exhibiting himself to such curious or indifferent or be-mused prisoners as might be looking through the peepholes. An hour's sleep, then the morning's brightness. Crossing the Vistula, murky and steaming. Two small towns she recognized as the train moved westward through the dusty pollen-gold morning: Skawina, Zator. Eva beginning to cry for the first time, torn by spasms of hunger. Hush, baby. A few more moments' drowse riven by a sun-flooded, splendid, heart-wrenching, manic dream: herself begowned and bediademed, seated at the keyboard before ten thousand on-lookers, yet somehow—astoundingly—flying, *flying,* soaring to de-liverance on the celestial measures of the Emperor Concerto. Eyelids fluttering apart. A slamming, braking stop. Auschwitz.

They waited in the car during most of the rest of the day. At an early moment the generators ceased working; the bulbs went out in the compartment and what remaining light there was cast a milky pallor, filtering through the cracks in the plywood shutters. The dis-tant sound of band music made its way into the compartment. There was a vibration of panic in the car; it was almost palpable, like the prickling of hair all over one's body, and in the near-darkness there came a surge of anxious whispering—hoarse, rising, but as incom-prehensible as the rustle of an army of leaves. The convent girls began to wail in unison, beseeching the Holy Mother. Wiktor loudly

told them to shut up, while at the same instant Sophie took courage
from Wanda's voice, faint from the other end of the car, begging
Resistance members and deportees alike to stay calm, stay quiet.

It must have been early in the afternoon when word came regarding the hundreds upon hundreds of Jews from Malkinia in the forward cars. *All Jews in vans* came a note to Wiktor, a note which he
read aloud in the gloom and which Sophie, too numb with fright to
even clutch Jan and Eva close against her breast for consolation,
immediately translated into: All the Jews have gone to the gas. Sophie
joined with the convent girls in prayer. It was while she was praying
that Eva began to wail loudly. The children had been brave during
the trip, but now the little girl's hunger blossomed into real pain. She
squealed in anguish while Sophie tried to rock and soothe her, but
nothing seemed to work; the child's screams were for a moment more
terrifying to Sophie than the word about the doomed Jews. But soon
they stopped. Oddly, it was Jan who came to the rescue. He had a
way with his sister and now he took over—at first shushing her in
the words of some private language they shared, then pressing next
to her with his book. In the pale light he began reading to her from
the story of Penrod, about little boys' pranks in the leafy Elysian
small-town marrow of America; he was able to laugh and giggle, and
his thin soprano singsong cast a gentle spell, combining with Eva's
exhaustion to lull her to sleep.

Several hours passed. It was late afternoon. Finally another slip
of paper was passed to Wiktor: *AK first car in vans*. This plainly
meant one thing—that, like the Jews, the several hundred Home
Army members in the car just forward had been transported to
Birkenau and the crematoriums. Sophie stared straight ahead, composed her hands in her lap and prepared for death, feeling inexpressible terror but for the first time, too, tasting faintly the blessed
bitter relief of acceptance. The old niece of Wieniawski had fallen
into a comalike stupor, the *Polonaise* in crumpled disarray, rivulets
of drool flowing from the corners of her lips. In trying to recon-
struct that moment a long time later, Sophie wondered whether she
might not then have become unconscious herself, for the next thing
she remembered was her own daylight-dazzled presence outside
on the ramp with Jan and Eva, and coming face to face with Haupt-
sturmführer Fritz Jemand von Niemand, doctor of medicine.

Sophie did not know his name then, nor did she ever see him
again. I have christened him Fritz Jemand von Niemand because it

seems as good a name as any for an SS doctor—for one who appeared to Sophie as if from nowhere and vanished likewise forever from her sight, yet who left a few interesting traces of himself behind. One trace: the recollected impression of relative youth—thirty-five, forty—and the unwelcome good looks of a delicate and disturbing sort. Indeed, traces of Dr. Jemand von Niemand and his appearance and his voice and his manner and other attributes would remain with Sophie forever. The first words he said to her, for example: *"Ich möchte mit dir schlafen."* Which means, as bluntly and as unseductively as possible: "I'd like to get you into bed with me." Dreary loutish words, spoken from an intimidating vantage point, no finesse, no class, callow and cruel, an utterance one might expect from a B-grade movie Nazi *Schweinhund.* But these, according to Sophie, were the words he first said. Ugly talk for a doctor and a gentleman (perhaps even an aristocrat), although he was visibly, indisputably drunk, which might help explain such coarseness. Why Sophie, at first glance, thought he might be an aristocrat—Prussian perhaps, or of Prussian origin—was because of his extremely close resemblance to a Junker officer, a friend of her father's, whom she had seen once as a girl of sixteen or so on a summer visit to Berlin. Very "Nordic"-looking, attractive in a thin-lipped, austere, unbending way, the young officer had treated her frostily during their brief meeting, almost to the point of contempt and boorishness; nonetheless, she could not help but be taken by his arresting handsomeness, by—surprisingly—something not really effeminate but rather silkily feminine about his face in repose. He looked a bit like a militarized Leslie Howard, whom she had had a mild crush on ever since *The Petrified Forest.* Despite the dislike he had inspired in her, and her satisfaction in not having to see this German officer again, she remembered thinking about him later rather disturbingly: If he had been a woman, he would have been a person I think I might have felt drawn to. But now here was his counterpart, almost his replica, standing in his slightly askew SS uniform on the dusty concrete platform at five in the afternoon, flushed with wine or brandy or schnapps and mouthing his unpatrician words in an indolently patrician, Berlin-accented voice: "I'd like to get you into bed with me."

Sophie ignored what he was saying, but as he spoke she glimpsed one of those insignificant but ineffaceable details—another spectral trace of the doctor—that would always spring out in vivid trompe l'oeil from the confused surface of the day: a sprinkling of boiled-

rice grains on the lapel of the SS tunic. There were only four or
five of these; shiny with moisture still, they looked like maggots.
She gave them her dazed scrutiny, and while doing so she realized
for the first time that the piece of music being played just then by
the welcoming prisoners' band—hopelessly off-key and disorgan-
ized, yet flaying her nerves with its erotic sorrow and turgid beat
as it had even in the darkened car—was the Argentine tango "La
Cumparsita." Why had she not been able to name it before? Ba-
dum-*ba*-dum!

"*Du bist eine Polack,*" said the doctor. "*Bist du auch eine Kom-
munistin?*" Sophie placed one arm around Eva's shoulders, the
other arm around Jan's waist, saying nothing. The doctor belched,
then more sharply elaborated: "I know you're a Polack, but are you
also another one of these filthy Communists?" And then in his fog
he turned toward the next prisoners, seeming almost to forget
Sophie.

Why hadn't she played dumb? "*Nicht sprecht Deutsch.*" It could
have saved the moment. There was such a press of people. Had she
not answered in German he might have let the three of them pass
through. But there was the cold fact of her terror, and the terror
caused her to behave unwisely. She knew now what blind and merciful ignorance had prevented very few Jews who arrived here from
knowing, but which her association with Wanda and the others had
caused her to know and to dread with fear beyond utterance: a selection. She and the children were undergoing at this very moment the
ordeal she had heard about—rumored in Warsaw a score of times in
whispers—but which had seemed at once so unbearable and
unlikely to happen to her that she had thrust it out of her mind. But
here she was, and here was the doctor. While over there—just
beyond the roofs of the boxcars recently vacated by the death-bound
Malkinia Jews—was Birkenau, and the doctor could select for its
abyssal doors anyone whom he desired. This thought caused her
such terror that instead of keeping her mouth shut she said, "*Ich bin
polnisch! In Krakow geboren!*" Then she blurted helplessly, "I'm not
Jewish! Or my children—they're not Jewish either." And added,
"They are racially pure. They speak German." Finally she announced,
"I'm a Christian. I'm a devout Catholic."

The doctor turned again. His eyebrows arched and he looked at
Sophie with inebriate, wet, fugitive eyes, unsmiling. He was now
so close to her that she smelled plainly the alcoholic vapor—a ran-

cid fragrance of barley or rye—and she was not strong enough to return his gaze. It was then that she knew she had said something wrong, perhaps fatally wrong. She averted her face for an instant, glancing at an adjoining line of prisoners shambling through the golgotha of their selection, and saw Eva's flute teacher Zaorski at the precise congealed instant of his doom—dispatched to the left and to Birkenau by an almost imperceptible nod of a doctor's head. Now, turning back, she heard Dr. Jemand von Niemand say, "So you're not a Communist. You're a believer."

"*Ja, mein Hauptmann.* I believe in Christ." What folly! She sensed from his manner, his gaze—the new look in his eye of luminous intensity—that everything she was saying, far from helping her, from protecting her, was leading somehow to her swift undoing. She thought: Let me be struck dumb.

The doctor was a little unsteady on his feet. He leaned over for a moment to an enlisted underling with a clipboard and murmured something, meanwhile absorbedly picking his nose. Eva, pressing heavily against Sophie's leg, began to cry. "So you believe in Christ the Redeemer?" the doctor said in a thick-tongued but oddly abstract voice, like that of a lecturer examining the delicately shaded facet of a proposition in logic. Then he said something which for an instant was totally mystifying: "Did He not say, 'Suffer the little children to come unto Me'?" He turned back to her, moving with the twitchy methodicalness of a drunk.

Sophie, with an inanity poised on her tongue and choked with fear, was about to attempt a reply when the doctor said, "You may keep one of your children."

"*Bitte?*" said Sophie.

"You may keep one of your children," he repeated. "The other one will have to go. Which one will you keep?"

"You mean, I have to choose?"

"You're a Polack, not a Yid. That gives you a privilege—a choice."

Her thought processes dwindled, ceased. Then she felt her legs crumple. "I can't choose! I can't choose!" She began to scream. Oh, how she recalled her own screams! Tormented angels never screeched so loudly above hell's pandemonium. "*Ich kann nicht wählen!*" she screamed.

The doctor was aware of unwanted attention. "Shut up!" he ordered. "Hurry now and choose. Choose, goddamnit, or I'll send them both over there. Quick!"

She could not believe any of this. She could not believe that she was now kneeling on the hurtful, abrading concrete, drawing her children toward her so smotheringly tight that she felt that their flesh might be engrafted to hers even through layers of clothes. Her disbelief was total, deranged. It was disbelief reflected in the eyes of the gaunt, waxy-skinned young Rottenführer, the doctor's aide, to whom she inexplicably found herself looking upward in supplication. He appeared stunned, and he returned her gaze with a wide-eyed baffled expression, as if to say: I can't understand this either.

"Don't make me choose," she heard herself plead in a whisper, "I can't choose."

"Send them both over there, then," the doctor said to the aide, "*nach links.*"

"Mama!" She heard Eva's thin but soaring cry at the instant that she thrust the child away from her and rose from the concrete with a clumsy stumbling motion. "Take the baby!" she called out. "Take my little girl!"

At this point the aide—with a careful gentleness that Sophie would try without success to forget—tugged at Eva's hand and led her away into the waiting legion of the damned. She would forever retain a dim impression that the child had continued to look back, beseeching. But because she was now almost completely blinded by salty, thick, copious tears she was spared whatever expression Eva wore, and she was always grateful for that. For in the bleakest honesty of her heart she knew that she would never have been able to tolerate it, driven nearly mad as she was by her last glimpse of that vanishing small form.

For Further Reflection

1. This is a classic moral dilemma in which both options are bad: either *actively* condemn one of your children to death, or by *refusing to choose* have both killed. What should Sophie have done? What would you do? Why?

From Cruelty to Goodness

PHILIP HALLIE

Philip Hallie grew up in Chicago and earned his degrees at Grinnell, Oxford, and Harvard. For many years he was professor of philosophy at Wesleyan University. Among his many works are *The Paradox of Cruelty* (1969) and *Lest Innocent Blood Be Shed* (1979).

In this essay Hallie examines the reality of cruelty, especially institutional cruelty, such as that of slavery and the Nazi treatment of Jews during World War II. Institutionalized cruelty involves the undermining of dignity by perpetrating a false inequality of worth and power. By degrading the victim, the victimizer exalts his own perception of self-worth, but in reality becomes evil. As an example of the kind of goodness necessary to defeat cruelty, Hallie describes the Protestant citizens, especially Pastor Trocme, of the village of Le Chambon, who risked their lives to save six thousand Jews from the Nazis.

I am a student of ethics, of good and evil; but my approach to these two rather melodramatic terms is skeptical. I am in the tradition of the ancient Greek *skeptikoi,* whose name means "inquirers" or "investigators." And what we investigate is relationships among particular facts. What we put into doubt are the intricate webs of high-level abstractions that passed for philosophizing in the ancient world, and that still pass for philosophizing. My approach to good and evil emphasizes not abstract common nouns like "justice," but proper names and verbs. Names and verbs keep us close to the facts better than do our highfalutin common nouns. Names refer to particular people, and verbs connect subjects with predicates *in time,* while common nouns are above all this.

One of the words that is important to me is my own name. For me, philosophy is personal; it is closer to literature and history than it is to the exact sciences, closer to the passions, actions, and com-

Reprinted from "From Cruelty to Goodness" © 1981 The Hastings Center by permission of The Hastings Center.

mon sense of individual persons than to a dispassionate technical science. It has to do with the personal matter of wisdom. And so ethics for me is personal—my story, and not necessarily (though possibly) yours. It concerns particular people at particular times.

But ethics is more than such particulars. It involves abstractions, that is, rules, laws, ideals. When you look at the ethical magnates of history you see in their words and deeds two sorts of ethical rules: negative and positive. The negative rules are scattered throughout the Bible, but Moses brought down from Mount Sinai the main negative ethical rules of the West: Thou shalt not murder; thou shalt not betray. . . . The positive injunctions are similarly spread throughout the Bible. In the first chapter of the book of Isaiah we are told to ". . . defend the fatherless, plead for the widow." The negative ethic forbids certain actions; the positive ethic demands certain actions. To follow the negative ethic is to be decent, to have clean hands. But to follow the positive ethic, to be one's brother's keeper, is to be more than decent—it is to be active, even aggressive. If the negative ethic is one of decency, the positive one is the ethic of riskful, strenuous nobility.

In my early studies of particularized ethical terms, I found myself dwelling upon negative ethics, upon prohibitions. And among the most conspicuous prohibitions I found embodied in history was the prohibition against deliberate harmdoing, against cruelty. "Thou shalt not be cruel" had as much to do with the nightmare of history as did the prohibitions against murder and betrayal. In fact, many of the Ten Commandments—especially those against murder, adultery, stealing, and betrayal—were ways of prohibiting cruelty.

Early in my research it became clear that there are various approaches to cruelty, as the different commandments suggest. For instance, there is the way reflected in the origins of the word "cruel." The Latin *crudus* is related to still older words standing for bloodshed, or raw flesh. According to the etymology of the word, cruelty involves the spilling of blood.

But modern dictionaries give the word a different meaning. They define it as "disposed to giving pain." They emphasize awareness, not simply bloodshed. After all, they seem to say, you cannot be cruel to a dead body. There is no cruelty without consciousness.

And so I found myself studying the kinds of awareness associated with the hurting of human beings. It is certainly true that for millennia in history and literature people have been torturing each other not only with hard weapons but also with hard words.

Still, the word "pain" seemed to be a simplistic and superficial way of describing the many different sorts of cruelty. In Reska Weiss's *Journey Through Hell* (London, 1961) there is a brief passage of one of the deepest cruelties that Nazis perpetrated upon extermination camp inmates. On a march

> Urine and excreta poured down the prisoners' legs, and by nightfall the excrement, which had frozen to our limbs, gave off its stench.

And Weiss goes on to talk not in terms of "pain" or bloodshed, but in other terms:

> . . . We were really no longer human beings in the accepted sense. Not even animals, but putrefying corpses moving on two legs.

There is one factor that the idea of "pain" and the simpler idea of bloodshed do not touch: cruelty, not playful, quotidian teasing or ragging, but cruelty (what the anti-cruelty societies usually call "substantial cruelty") involves the maiming of a person's dignity, the crushing of a person's self-respect. Bloodshed, the idea of pain (which is usually something involving a localizable occurrence, localizable in a tooth, in a head, in short, in the body), these are superficial ideas of cruelty. A whip, bleeding flesh, these are what the journalists of cruelty emphasize, following the etymology and dictionary meaning of the word. But the depths of an understanding of cruelty lie in the depths of an understanding of human dignity and of how you can maim it without bloodshed, and often without localizable bodily pain.

In excremental assault, in the process of keeping camp inmates from wiping themselves or from going to the latrine, and in making them drink water from a toilet bowl full of excreta (and the excreta of the guards at that) localizable pain is nothing. Deep humiliation is everything. We human beings believe in hierarchies, whether we are skeptics or not about human value. There is a hierarchical gap between shit and me. We are even above using the word. We are "above" walking around besmirched with feces. Our dignity, whatever the origins of that dignity may be, does not permit it. In order to be able to want to live, in order to be able to walk erect, we must respect ourselves as beings "higher" than our feces. When we feel that we are not "higher" than dirt or filth, then our lives are maimed at the very center, in the very depths, not merely in some localizable portion of our bodies. And when our lives are so maimed we become things, slaves, instruments. From ancient times until this moment, and as long as there will be human beings on this planet, there are those who know this and will use it, just as the Roman slave owners and the Southern American slave owners knew it when—one time a year—they encouraged the slaves to drink all the alcohol they could drink so that they could get bestially drunk and then even more bestially sick afterwards, under the eyes of their generous owners. The self-hatred, the loss of self-respect that the Saturnalia created in ancient Rome, say, made it possible to continue using the slaves as things, since they themselves came to think of themselves as things, as sub-human tools of the owners and the overseers.

Institutionalized cruelty, I learned, is the subtlest kind of cruelty. In episodic cruelty the victim knows he is being hurt, and his victimizer knows it too. But in a persistent pattern of humiliation that endures for years in a community, both the victim and the victimizer find ways of obscuring the harm that is being done. Blacks come to think of themselves as inferior, even esthetically inferior (black is "dirty"); and Jews come to think of themselves as inferior, even esthetically (dark hair and aquiline noses are "ugly"), so that the way they are being treated is justified by their "actual" inferiority, by the inferiority they themselves feel.

A similar process happens in the minds of the victimizers in institutionalized cruelty. They feel that since they are superior, even esthetically ("to be blonde is to be beautiful"), they deserve to do what they wish, deserve to have these lower creatures under their control. The words of Heinrich Himmler, head of the Nazi SS, in Posen in the year 1943 in a speech to his SS subordinates in a closed session, show how institutionalized cruelty can obscure harmdoing:

> ... the words come so easily. "The Jewish people will be exterminated," says every party member, "of course. It's in our program ... extermination. We'll take care of it." And then they come, these nice 80 million Germans, and every one of them has his decent Jew. Sure the others are swine, but his one is a fine Jew ... Most of you will know what it means to have seen 100 corpses together, or 500 to 1000. To have made one's way through that, and ... to have remained a decent person throughout, that is what has made us hard. That is a page of glory in our history. ...

In this speech he was making a sharp distinction between the program of crushing the Jews and the personal sentiments of individual Germans. The program stretched over years; personal sentiments were momentary. He was pleading for the program, for institutionalized destruction.

But one of the most interesting parts of the speech occurs toward the end of it:

> . . . in sum, we can say that we fulfilled the heaviest of tasks [destroying the Jews] in love to our people. And we suffered no harm in our essence, in our soul, in our character. . . .

Commitment that overrides all sentimentality transforms cruelty and destruction into moral nobility, and commitment is the lifeblood of an institution.

CRUELTY AND THE POWER RELATIONSHIPS

But when I studied all these ways that we have used the word "cruelty," I was nagged by the feeling that I had not penetrated into its inner structure. I was classifying, sorting out symptoms; but symptoms are signals, and what were the symptoms signals *of?* I felt like a person who had been studying cancer by sorting out brief pains from persistent pains, pains in the belly from pains in the head. I was being superficial, and I was not asking the question, "What are the forces behind these kinds of cruelty?" I felt that there were such forces, but as yet I had not touched them.

Then one day I was reading in one of the great autobiographies of western civilization, Frederick Douglass's *Life and Times*. The passage I was reading was about Douglass's thoughts on the origins of slavery. He was asking himself: "How could these whites keep us enslaved?" And he suddenly realized:

> My faculties and powers of body and soul are not my own, but are the property of a fellow-mortal in no sense superior to me, except that he has the physical power to compel me to be owned and controlled by him. By the combined physical force of the community I am his slave—a slave for life.

And then I saw that a disparity in power lay at the center of the dynamism of cruelty. If it was institutional cruelty it was in all likelihood a difference involving both verbal and physical power that kept the cruelty going. The power of the majority and the weakness of a minority were at the center of the institutional cruelty of slavery and of Nazi anti-Semitism. The whites not only outnumbered the blacks in America, but had economic and political ascendancy over them. But just as important as these "physical" powers was the power that words like "nigger" and "slave" gave the white majority. Their language sanctified if it did not create their power ascendancy over the blacks, and one of the most important projects of the slave-holders and their allies was that of seeing to it that the blacks themselves thought of themselves in just these powerless terms. They utilized the language to convince not only the whites but the blacks themselves that blacks were weak in mind, in will power, and in worth. These words were like the excremental assault in the killing camps of the Nazis: they diminished both the respect the victimizers might have for their victims and the respect the victims might have for themselves.

It occurred to me that if a power differential is crucial to the idea of cruelty, then when that power differential is maintained, cruelty will tend to be maintained, and when that power differential is eliminated, cruelty will tend to be eliminated. And this seemed to work. In all kinds of cruelty, violent and polite, episodic and institutional, when the victim arms himself with the appropriate strength, the cruelty diminishes or disappears. When Jews joined the Bush Warriors of France, the Maquis, and became powerful enough to strike at Vichy or the Nazis, they stopped being victims of French and Nazi cruelty. When Frederick Douglass learned to use the language with great skill and expressiveness, and when he learned to use his physical strength against his masters, the power differential between him and his masters diminished, and so did their cruelty to him. In his autobiography he wrote:

> A man without force is without the essential dignity of humanity. Human nature is so constituted that it cannot honor a helpless man, though it can pity him, and even this it cannot do long if signs of power do not arise.

When I looked back at my own childhood in Chicago, I remembered that the physical and mental cruelties that I suffered in the slums of the southwest side when I was about ten years old sharply diminished and finally disappeared when I learned how to defend myself physically and verbally. It is exactly this lesson that Douglass learned while growing up in the cruel institution of slavery.

Cruelty then, whatever else it is, is a kind of power relationship, an imbalance of power wherein the stronger party becomes the victimizer and the weaker becomes the victim. And since many general terms are most swiftly understood in relationship with their opposites (just as "heavy" can be understood most handily in relationship with what we mean by "light") the opposite of cruelty lay in a situation where there is no imbalance of power. The opposite of cruelty, I learned, was freedom from that unbalanced power relationship. Either the victim should get stronger and stand up to the victimizer, and thereby bring about a balance of their powers, or the victim should free himself from the whole relationship by flight.

In pursuing this line of thought, I came to believe that, again, dictionaries are misleading: many of them give "kindness" as the antonym for "cruelty." In studying slavery in America and the concentration camps of central Europe I found that kindness could be the ultimate cruelty, especially when it was given within that unbalanced power relationship. A kind overseer or a kind camp guard can exacerbate cruelty, can remind his victim that there are other relationships than the relationship of cruelty, and can make the victim deeply bitter, especially when he sees the self-satisfied smile of his victimizer. He is being cruelly treated when he is given a penny or a bun after having endured the crushing and grinding of his mental and bodily well-being. As Frederick Douglass put it:

> The kindness of the slave-master only gilded the chain. It detracted nothing from its weight or strength. The thought that men are for other and better uses than slavery throve best under the gentle treatment of a kind master.

No, I learned, the opposite of cruelty is not kindness. The opposite of the cruelty of the overseer in American slavery was not the kindness of that overseer for a moment or for a day. An episodic kindness is not the opposite of an institutionalized cruelty. The opposite of institutionalized cruelty is freedom from the cruel relationship.

It is important to see how perspectival the whole meaning of cruelty is. From the perspective of the SS guard or the southern overseer, a bit of bread, a smile is indeed a diminution of cruelty.

But in the relationship of cruelty, the point of view of the victim-izer is of only minor importance; it is the point of view of the victim that is authoritative. The victim feels the suffering in his own mind and body, whereas the victimizer, like Himmler's "hard" and "decent" Nazi, can be quite unaware of that suffering. The sword does not feel the pain that it inflicts. Do not ask it about suffering.

GOODNESS PERSONIFIED IN LE CHAMBON

All these considerations drove me to write my book *The Paradox of Cruelty*. But with the book behind me, I felt a deep discontent. I saw cruelty as an embodiment, a particular case of evil. But if cruelty is one of the main evils of human history, why is the opposite of cruelty not one of the key goods of human history? Freedom from the cruel relationship, either by escaping it or by redressing the imbalance of power, was not essential to what western philosophers and theologians have thought of as goodness. Escape is a negative affair. Goodness has something positive in it, something triumphantly affirmative.

Hoping for a hint of goodness in the very center of evil, I started looking closely at the so-called "medical experiments" of the Nazis upon children, usually Jewish and Gypsy children, in the death camps. Here were the weakest of the weak. Not only were they despised minorities, but they were, as individuals, still in their non-age. They were dependents. Here the power imbalance between the cruel experimenters and their victims was at its greatest. But instead of seeing light or finding insight by going down into this hell, into the deepest depth of cruelty, I found myself unwillingly becoming part of the world I was studying. I found myself either yearning to be viciously cruel to the victimizers of the children, or I found myself feeling compassion for the children, feeling their despair and pain as they looked up at the men and women in white coats cutting off their fingertips one at a time, or breaking their slender bones, or wounding their internal organs. Either I became a would-be victimizer or one more Jewish victim, and in either case I was not achieving insight, only misery, like so many other students of the Holocaust. And when I was trying to be "objective" about my studies, when I was succeeding at being indifferent to both the victimizers and the victims of these cruel relationships, I became cold; I became another monster who could look upon the maiming of a child with an indifferent eye.

To relieve this unending suffering, from time to time I would turn to the literature of the French resistance to the Nazis. I had been trained by the U.S. Army to understand it. The resistance was a way of trying to redress the power imbalance between Hitler's Fortress Europe and Hitler's victims, and so I saw it as an enemy of cruelty. Still, its methods were often cruel like the methods of most power struggles, and I had little hope of finding goodness here. We soldiers violated the negative ethic forbidding killing in order, we thought, to follow the positive ethic of being our brothers' keepers.

And then one gray April afternoon I found a brief article on the French village of Le Chambon-sur-Lignon. I shall not analyze here the tears of amazement and gladness and release from despair—in short, of joy—that I shed when I first read that story. Tears themselves interest me greatly—but not the tears of melancholy hindsight and existential despair; rather the tears of awe you experience when the realization of an ideal suddenly appears before your very eyes or thunders inside your mind; these tears interest me.

And one of the reasons I wept at first reading about Le Chambon in those brief, inaccurate pages was that at last I had discovered an embodiment of goodness in opposition to cruelty. I had discovered in the flesh and blood of history, in people with definite names in a definite place at a definite time in the nightmare of history, what no classical or religious ethicist could deny was goodness.

The French Protestant village of Le Chambon, located in the Cévennes Mountains of southeastern France, and with a population of about 3,500, saved the lives of about 6,000 people, most of them Jewish children whose parents had been murdered in the killing camps of central Europe. Under a national government which was not only collaborating with the Nazi conquerors of France but frequently trying to outdo the Germans in anti-Semitism in order to please their conquerors, and later under the day-to-day threat of destruction by the German Armed SS, they started to save children in the winter of 1940, the winter after the fall of France, and they continued to do so until the war in France was over. They sheltered the refugees in their own homes and in various houses they established especially for them; and they took many of them across

the terrible mountains to neutral Geneva, Switzerland, in the teeth
of French and German police and military power. The people of
Le Chambon are poor, and the Huguenot faith to which they belong
is a diminishing faith in Catholic and atheist France; but their spiritual power, their capacity to act in unison against the victimizers
who surrounded them, was immense, and more than a match for
the military power of those victimizers.

But for me as an ethicist the heart of the matter was not only
their special power. What interested me was that they obeyed *both*
the negative and the positive injunctions of ethics; they were good
not only in the sense of trying to be their brothers' keepers, protecting the victim, "defending the fatherless," to use the language
of Isaiah; they were also good in the sense that they obeyed the
negative injunctions against killing and betraying. While those
around them—including myself—were murdering in order presumably, to help mankind in some way or other, they murdered
nobody, and betrayed not a single child in those long and dangerous four years. For me as an ethicist they were the embodiment
of unambiguous goodness.

But for me as a student of cruelty they were something more:
they were an embodiment of the opposite of cruelty. And so, somehow, at last, I had found goodness in opposition to cruelty. In
studying their story, and in telling it in *Lest Innocent Blood Be Shed,*
I learned that the opposite of cruelty is not simply freedom from
the cruel relationship; it is *hospitality.* It lies not only in something
negative, an absence of cruelty or of imbalance; it lies in unsenti-
mental, efficacious love. The opposite of the cruelties of the camps
was not the liberation of the camps, the cleaning out of the barracks and the cessation of the horrors. All of this was the *end* of
the cruelty relationship, not the opposite of that relationship. And
it was not even the end of it, because the victims would never forget and would remain in agony as long as they remembered their
humiliation and suffering. No, the opposite of cruelty was not the
liberation of the camps, not freedom; it was the hospitality of the
people of Chambon, and of very few others during the Holocaust.
The opposite of cruelty was the kind of goodness that happened
in Chambon.

Let me explain the difference between liberation and hospitality
by telling you about a letter I received a year ago from a woman

who had been saved by the people of Le Chambon when she was a young girl. She wrote:

> Never was there a question that the Chambonnais would not share all they had with us, meager as it was. One Chambonnais once told me that even if there was less, they still would want more for us.

And she goes on:

> It was indeed a very different attitude from the one in Switzerland, which while saving us also resented us so much.
>
> If today we are not bitter people like most survivors it can only be due to the fact that we met people like the people of Le Chambon, who showed to us simply that life can be different, that there are people who care, that people can live together and even risk their own lives for their fellow man.

The Swiss liberated refugees and removed them from the cruel relationship; the people of Le Chambon did more. They taught them that goodness could conquer cruelty, that loving hospitality could remove them from the cruel relationship. And they taught me this, too.

It is important to emphasize that cruelty is not simply an episodic, momentary matter, especially institutional cruelty like that of Nazism or slavery. As we have seen throughout this essay, not only does it persist while it is being exerted upon the weak; *it can persist in the survivors* after they have escaped the power relationship. The survivors torture themselves, continue to suffer, continue to maim their own lives long after the actual torture is finished. The self-hatred and rage of the blacks and the despair of the native Americans and the Jews who have suffered under institutional crushing and maiming are continuations of original cruelties. And these continuations exist because only a superficial liberation from torture has occurred. The sword has stopped falling on their flesh in the old obvious ways, but the wounds still bleed. I am not saying that the village of Chambon healed these wounds—they go too deep. What I am saying is that the people I have talked to who were once children in Le Chambon have more hope for their species and more respect for themselves as human beings than most other survivors I have met. The enduring hospitality they met in Le Chambon helped them find realistic hope in a world of persisting cruelty.

What was the nature of this hospitality that saved and deeply changed so many lives? It is hard to summarize briefly what the Chambonnais did, and above all how they did it. The morning after a new refugee family came to town they would find on their front door a wreath with *"Bienvenue!"* "Welcome!" painted on a piece of cardboard attached to the wreath. Nobody knew who had brought the wreath; in effect, the whole town had brought it.

It was mainly the women of Chambon who gave so much more than shelter to these, the most hated enemies of the Nazis. There was Madame Barraud, a tiny Alsatian, who cared for the refugee boys in her house with all the love such a tiny body could hold, and who cared for the way they felt day and night. And there were others.

But there was one person without whom Le Chambon could not have become the safest place in Europe for Jews: the Huguenot minister of the village, André Trocmé. Trocmé was a passionately religious man. He was massive, more than six feet tall, blonde, with a quick temper. Once long after the war, while he was lecturing on the main project of his life, the promotion of the idea of non-violence in international relations, one of the members of his audience started to whisper a few words to his neighbor. Trocmé let this go on for a few moments, then interrupted his speech, walked up to the astonished whisperer, raised his massive arm, pointed toward the door, and yelled, "Out! Out! Get out!" And the lecture was on nonviolence.

The center of his thought was the belief that God showed how important man was by becoming Himself a human being, and by becoming a particular sort of human being who was the embodiment of sacrificially generous love. For Trocmé, every human being was like Jesus, had God in him or her, and was just as precious as God Himself. And when Trocmé with the help of the Quakers and others organized his village into the most efficient rescue machine in Europe, he did so not only to save the Jews, but also to save the Nazis and their collaborators. He wanted to keep them from blackening their souls with more evil—he wanted to save them, the victimizers, from evil.

One of the reasons he was successful was that the Huguenots had been themselves persecuted for hundreds of years by the kings of France, and they knew what persecution was. In fact, when the people of Chambon took Jewish children and whole families across the mountains of southeastern France into neutral Switzerland, they often followed pathways that had been taken by Huguenots in their flight from the Dragoons of the French kings.

A particular incident from the story of Le Chambon during the Nazi occupation of France will explain succinctly why he was successful in making the village a village of refuge. But before I relate the story, I must point out that the people of the village did not think of themselves as "successful," let alone as "good." From their point of view, they did not do anything that required elaborate explanation. When I asked them why they helped these dangerous guests, they invariably answered, "What do you mean, 'Why'? Where else could they go? How could you turn them away? What is so special about being ready to help (*prête à servir*)? There was nothing else to do." And some of them laughed in amazement when I told them that I thought they were "good people." They saw no alternative to their actions and to the way they acted, and therefore they saw what they did as necessary, not something to be picked out for praise. Helping these guests was for them as natural as breathing or eating—one does not think of alternatives to these functions; they did not think of alternatives to sheltering people who were endangering not only the lives of their hosts but the lives of all the people of the village.

And now the story. One afternoon a refugee woman knocked on the door of a farmhouse outside the village. The farmers around the village proper were Protestants like most of the others in Chambon, but with one difference: they were mostly "Darbystes," followers of a strange Scot named Darby, who taught their ancestors in the nineteenth century to believe every word of the Bible, and indeed, who had them memorize the Bible. They were literal fundamentalists. The farm-woman opened the door to the refugee and invited her into the kitchen where it was warm. Standing in the middle of the floor the refugee, in heavily accented French, asked for eggs for her children. In those days of very short supplies, people with children often went to the farmers in the "gray market" (neither black nor exactly legal) to get necessary food. This was early in 1941, and the farmers were not yet accustomed to the refugees. The farm-woman looked into the eyes of the shawled refugee and asked, "Are you Jewish?" The woman started to tremble, but she could not lie, even though that question was usually the beginning of the end of life for Jews in Hitler's Fortress Europe. She answered, "Yes."

The woman ran from the kitchen to the staircase nearby, and while the refugee trembled with terror in the kitchen, she called up the stairs, "Husband, children, come down, come down! We have in our house at this very moment a representative of the Chosen People!"

Not all the Protestants in Chambon were Darbyste fundamentalists; but almost all were convinced that people are the children of God, and are as precious as God Himself. Their leaders were Huguenot preachers and their following of the negative and positive commandments of the Bible came in part from their personal generosity and courage, but also in part from the depths of their religious conviction that we are all children of God, and we must take care of each other lovingly. This combined with the ancient and deep historical ties between the Huguenots and the Jews of France and their own centuries of persecution by the Dragoons and Kings of France helped make them what they were, "always ready to help," as the Chambonnais saying goes.

A CHOICE OF PERSPECTIVES

We have come a long way from cruelty to the people of Chambon, just as I have come a long way in my research from concrete evil to concrete goodness. Let me conclude with a point that has been alternately hinted at and stressed in the course of this essay.

A few months after *Lest Innocent Blood Be Shed* was published I received a letter from Massachusetts that opened as follows:

> I have read your book, and I believe that you mushy-minded moralists should be awakened to the facts. Nothing happened in Le Chambon, nothing of any importance whatsoever.
>
> The Holocaust, dear Professor, was like a geological event, like an earthquake. No person could start it; no person could change it; and no person could end it. And no small group of persons could do so either. It was the armies and the nations that performed actions that counted. Individuals did nothing. You sentimentalists have got to learn that the great masses and big political ideas make the difference. Your people and the people they saved simply do not exist.

Now between this position and mine there is an abyss that no amount of shouted arguments or facts can cross. And so I shall not answer this letter with a tightly organized reply. I shall answer it only by telling you that one of the reasons institutional cruelty exists and persists is that people believe that individuals can do nothing, that only vast ideologies and armies can act meaningfully. Every act of institutional cruelty—Nazism, slavery, and all the others— lives not with people in the concrete, but with abstractions that blind people to individuals. Himmler's speech to the SS leadership in 1943 is full of phrases like "exterminating a bacillus," and "The Jewish people will be exterminated." And in that speech he attacks any German who believes in "his decent Jew." Institutional cruelty, like other misleading approaches to ethics, blinds us to the victim's point of view; and when we are blind to that point of view we can countenance and perpetrate cruelty with impunity.

I have told you that I cannot and will not try to refute the let- ter from Massachusetts. I shall only summarize the point of view of this essay with another story.

I was lecturing a few months ago in Minneapolis, and when I fin- ished talking about the Holocaust and the village of Le Chambon, a woman stood up and asked me if the village of Le Chambon was in the Department of Haute-Loire, the high sources of the Loire River. Obviously she was French, with her accent; and all French people know that there are many villages called "Le Chambon" in France, just as any American knows that there are many "Main Streets" in the United States. I said that Le Chambon was indeed in the Haute- Loire.

She said, "Then you have been speaking about the village that saved all three of my children. I want to thank you for writing this book, not only because the story will now be permanent, but also because I shall be able to talk about those terrible days with Amer- icans now, for they will understand those days better than they have. You see, you Americans, though you sometimes cross the oceans, live on an island here as far as war is concerned . . ."

Then she asked to come up and say one sentence. There was not a sound, not even breathing, to be heard in the room. She came to the front of the room and said, "The Holocaust was storm, lightning, thunder, wind, rain, yes. And Le Chambon was the rainbow."

Only from her perspective can you understand the cruelty and the goodness I have been talking about, not from the point of view of the gentleman from Massachusetts. You must choose which perspective is best, and your choice will have much to do with your feelings about the preciousness of life, and not only the preciousness of other people's lives. If the lives of others are precious to you, your life will become more precious to you.

For Further Reflection

1. What does Hallie mean when he says that "philosophy is personal; it is closer to literature and history than it is to the exact sciences"?

2. How does Hallie characterize cruelty? Why does he think that institutionalized cruelty is the worst kind of cruelty?

3. Explain Hallie's notion of power relations and how they bear on the reality of cruelty.

4. Reflect on the story of the people of Le Chambon, who saved thousands of Jews. What were their motives? What lessons can we learn from them?

5. How does Hallie use this story to illustrate the antidote to cruelty? Compare the letter from Massachusetts with the statement of the woman in Minneapolis: "The Holocaust was storm, lightning, thunder, wind, rain, yes. And Le Chambon was the rainbow."

Wickedness

STANLEY BENN

Stanley Benn (1921–1986) was a research fellow in philosophy at the Australian National University, Canberra. He was the author of several important works in social and political

From *Ethics* (1985): 795–809. Reprinted by permission of The University of Chicago Press.

philosophy. In this essay Benn analyzes the concept of wickedness, describing four types: (1) selfishness: the person pursues his or her own good, disregarding the rights and good of others; (2) conscientious wickedness: the person is unconditionally loyal to a person or group, even when it does evil; (3) heteronomous wickedness: the person abdicates personal responsibility for his or her actions. Adolph Eichmann is an example—a Nazi who freely gave up his personal moral moorings in complete obedience to authority. See Stanley Milgram's essay (chapter 10) for an interesting study of this kind of vice. (4) pathological wickedness: the person makes evil his or her highest value, as Satan does in Milton's *Paradise Lost* when he cries, "Evil be thou my good!" This is the worst kind of wickedness because it inverts evil into a value to be sought for its own sake.

EVILS IN NATURE AND EVILS IN PERSONS

When philosophers talk of the problem of evil, they generally mean a problem in theodicy. Anyone who believes in a morally perfect, omniscient, and omnipotent God needs to explain and justify the existence of evils in the world. Unbelievers have no such problem. Nevertheless there are still uses to which the concept of evil can be put. Diseases, deformities, earthquakes and floods that destroy crops and wreck cities—these are, for anyone, too intelligibly evils, instances of what I shall term "evils in nature." I do not confine that term, however, to what we commonly call "natural disasters" but use it to denote any object, property, or happening about which it is both intelligible and correct to say that it would be a better state of affairs if that object et cetera did not exist or occur.

I take evil in nature to be a simple fact. It is a feature of the world that animals and human beings alike suffer pain, that there is ugliness as well as beauty, that there are bereavements and grievous disappointments. These things simply happen and are no less natural evils for their happening to conscious and rational beings. I do not mean, of course, that consciousness of the evil is never a necessary constituent: clearly this must be so in the case of a bereavement or a disappointment, though it is more problematic in cases of evils of ugliness. But bereavements and disappointments, while evils for human beings, are not evils in human beings. I shall make no attempt to say why such things are accounted evil; on the contrary, evil in nature I take for present purposes to be unproblematic, so that I shall not consider that I am begging any questions if I use that concept in explicating evil in human beings.

One kind of evil in human beings is "wickedness"—a word that has fallen undeservedly on bad times with the secularization of moral discourse. Wickedness in human beings is still a new kind of evil in nature, but one which raises special problems because, having in general a capacity for rational action and judgment, wicked people not merely are evil but also do evil, with evil intent. My purpose in this article is to inquire into forms of human wickedness, their relation with other evils in human beings, and their relation to freedom of choice and motivation to evil.

By "wickedness" I mean whatever it is about someone that warrants our calling him a wicked person. It is therefore a different notion from what makes an action an evil deed, for an evil deed may be done by someone who is not wicked but only weak or misguided. Neither is every wrongdoer evil, for one may do wrong with good intentions or even (some would say) because in some situations whatever one did would be wrong. And conversely, someone who was fully conscious and rational but also completely paralyzed and aphasic, who spent his life hating everyone about him, rejoicing in their misfortune, wishing them ill, and reveling in malignant fantasies, would be a wicked person who did no wrong at all. Indispensable, however, to the notion of a wicked person is a cognitive capacity, or at least a capacity to envisage states of affairs in the imagination, conjoined with a set of attitudes toward such states of affairs. G. E. Moore, whose account of evil is in terms not of persons but of "states of things," nevertheless describes the "great positive evils" as "organic unities" constituted by "cognitions of some object, accompanied by some emotion," where "emotion" is roughly equivalent to what I mean by "attitude."[1]

Common, however, to both wickedness in action and wickedness in attitude is an evil maxim, in something like Kant's sense. A person perceives situations, real or imagined, under certain

---

[1]G. E. Moore, *Principia Ethica* (Cambridge: Cambridge University Press, 1903), p. 208.

descriptions and has attitudes in respect of them in accordance with general maxims. If I recognize someone as virtuous and hate him just for being virtuous, I have the maxim, Virtuous people are to be hated. Vandals act on the maxim, Beautiful objects are to be destroyed, racists on the maxim, Blacks are to be despised or hurt, egoists on the maxim, No one's interests but my own are to count. In each case the gerundival form of the maxim specifies a kind of action or attitudinal response, in accordance with what that person takes as a rule of life.

A person may be wicked because the maxims that order his life are, by and large, evil maxims, that is, maxims that no one ought to act on at all. Sometimes this may be seen as a kind of mistake on his part; he may believe to be good what is really evil, and vice versa. And then we may need some way of distinguishing culpable and nonculpable mistakes. But in other instances there is no mistake: a person may act on an evil maxim, knowing it to be so. That is the nature of malignant or Satanic wickedness. These are both problematic issues to which I return.

It is possible, however, for a person to be wicked not because the first-order maxims of his actions are inherently wicked but because they are regulated by some higher-order maxim which systematically excludes consideration of any good which might circumscribe his first-order maxims. An example of such a restrictive higher-order maxim might be, No maxim is to be entertained as a rule of conduct that would circumscribe the duty to obey the orders of superior officers. Selfish wickedness and conscientious wickedness, which I shall consider a little later, are restrictive in much the same way, for whether or not, in either case, the maxims of action are inherently evil, the regulating principle will be found to be excluding in the required sense. These forms of wickedness I shall term "wickednesses of exclusion."

By contrast with those who act on evil first-order maxims, or who so order their first-order maxims as to exclude what ought nevertheless to be taken account of, the merely weak willed and the morally indolent and the people who cannot control their passions are not wicked people, for the maxims they really do acknowledge and on which they would wish to act are good ones. Such people are morally defective, and therefore bad, precisely because their actions fall short of their good intentions. That very incoherence is a mitigating condition, though not, of course, an excusing one.

I shall outline, in most of the remainder of this article, a typology of wickedness, which will shed some light on the difficult moral and philosophical questions of responsibility and culpability and on the possibility of evil actions knowingly performed. The primary distinctions are between self-centered, conscientious, and malignant forms of wickedness. In each case I shall ask how far ignorance, error, or incapacity is necessarily or possibly a feature of the actions and maxims of action under discussion and what difference it could make to the judgment of wickedness.

SELF-CENTERED FORMS OF WICKEDNESS

The least problematic kind of self-centered wicked person is the selfish one, but the category includes as well any person whose maxims are regulated by a higher-order maxim restricting consideration to goods and evils respecting only subjects and groups defined by reference to the agent himself. So a person who devoted himself exclusively to promoting the interests of his family or of his firm or to the aggrandizement of his nation might be wicked in this way if he did so with a ruthless unconcern for whether other people might be entitled or required to act on corresponding maxims of their own. The cruder kind of chauvinist or jingoist—My country, right or wrong—acts on just such a self-centered principle, providing he does not universalize it for citizens of others countries too.

The merely selfish person recognizes his own well-being as a good and acts for the sake of it. That is to say, in being selfish he does not embrace evil as such, under that description. Self-interest is not merely an intelligible motive but also one that many philosophers have thought to be a paradigm of a motive, the motive of self-love. Selfishness is wicked not on account of its end but for what is excludes, for it consists in closing one's eyes and one's heart to any good but a self-centered good. In Kant's view, this is the most characteristic form of human wickedness.

According to Kant, the moral law, as the law of reason, is not merely accessible to any rational being but also, for human beings at least, always one spring of action, necessarily motivating in some degree. So it is not that the selfishly wicked person is motivated by a perverse antagonism to the moral law. Rather, self-love, which is for any rational person a genuine spring, assumes an irrational precedence over the moral law. Accordingly, a wicked person is not one whom the law cannot motivate but rather someone who "reverses the moral order of the springs in adopting them into his maxims: he adopts, indeed, the moral law along with that of self-love; but. . . . he makes the spring of self-love and its inclinations the condition of obedience to the moral law; whereas, on the contrary, the latter ought to be adopted. . . . as the sole spring, being the *supreme condition* of the satisfaction of the former."[2]

The selfish person may, however, be mistaken in his belief that what he intends is really good, even from his own narrow perspective; it may in reality be damaging, even to himself. Someone altogether committed to increasing his own wealth or power—a miser or a megalomaniac—may be wrong to value such things, at any rate as ends instead of as means to other goods. That error is not, however, an excuse for his wickedness since his specific wickedness as a selfish person derives from what is excluded rather than from the end he actually seeks. That, of course, can add to his wickedness. Sadistic wickedness is more shocking, perhaps, than miserliness because the suffering of others, to which the miser or the vain person may be merely indifferent and inattentive, is for the sadist itself the source of the pleasure which makes it seem a good. In taking it to be so, however, the sadist may still be mistaken, even in his own terms, if, for instance, the pleasure is part of a self-destructive rake's progress of personal degradation. There would be no inconsistency, however, in deeming the sadist wicked on account both of the intrinsic evil and of the exclusiveness of his maxim while yet feeling compassion for someone who is destroying himself so worthlessly.

PSYCHOPATHY

In contrast to selfish wickedness, the form of self-centered evil in persons manifested in a psychopathic personality may not count as wickedness at all. This takes the form of a kind of moral imbecil-

---

[2]I. Kant, "Of the Indwelling of the Bad Principle along with the Good, or On the Radical Evil in Human Nature," in *Kant's Theory of Ethics*, trans. T. K. Abbot (London: Longman, Green & Co., 1927), p. 343.

ity. The psychopath, like the selfishly wicked person, acts from self-love. His is capable, at least within limits, of instrumental deliberation, though he may be prone to discount future satisfactions heavily in favor of immediate gratification. So he may be liable to do evil impulsively to satisfy a whim. But the more significant point is that he does not see it as evil, except, perhaps, in a conventional sense: This is something that I know most people do not like being done, so I had better conceal the body. But the kind of considerations that might justify and rationalize conventional disapproval can get no purchase on his understanding. To the extent that the psychopath has, and perceives in himself, the capacity to make decisions which can make a difference to the way things turn out— to the extent that he is capable of forming beliefs taking account of evidence and argument and of acting on those beliefs—he satisfies the minimal conditions for being a rational chooser or, one may say, a natural person.[3] Full rationality does not, however, consist only in the capacity to take account of relevant considerations advanced by others. It includes also the capacity to decenter: to conceive of ways of looking at the world, and at oneself, from someone else's standpoint or from no particular standpoint at all— from the standpoint of anyone. It is this capacity that the psychopath lacks. Whereas the selfish person understands well enough how the well-being of other persons can be a reason for someone's action or forbearance but disregards such reasons, the psychopath is simply unable to see how that could be a reason for him at all. To be asked to take account of such a reason would be, to him, like being asked to have regard to sensibilities of a stone or, perhaps, to the relevance of the color of someone's hair when deciding whether to make off with his wallet. While it would be wrong to say that the psychopath has no view of good and evil (for he knows what he would enjoy and what he would prefer not to suffer), he is incapable of understanding that distinction in any but a self-centered way. So though his maxims never take account of others' interests, it is not because a higher-order maxim excludes them;

---

[3]For a fuller statement of the theory of natural and moral personality on which this article relies, see S. I. Benn, "Freedom, Autonomy, and the Concept of a Person," *Aristotelian Society Proceedings* (1975–76) 76 (1976): 109–30.

it is that first-order maxims embodying them are simply unintelligible to him. Such a person does not act on an evil maxim, knowing it to be evil, nor does he act on a self-centered second-order maxim that excludes relevant first-order maxims since he can hardly be said to have any second-order maxims at all. Such a person cannot be wicked. Nevertheless, he may be both an evil in nature and an instance of evil in a person.

Moral imbecility may well fill us with horror; certainly it is frightening. As much might be said, however, of other evils in nature, such as cancers or leprosy. But there may be something besides to account for our special hostility toward the moral imbecile. It is hard to see him simply as an evil but amoral force, like a man-eating tiger in a Bengal village, for he is defective in a capacity without which people in society could not live together. He seems at once to claim consideration as a fellow person and to disqualify himself from that consideration. Because he satisfies the minimal conditions for a rational chooser, he qualifies for the respect due to a person and is a bearer of rights, but as a moral defective, he is incompetent to bear the corresponding obligations and responsibilities. In assessing his moral status, it is hard not to judge him by the standards appropriate to a person of normal capacities, of which he is a monstrously deformed travesty. Nevertheless, though qualified as a person, he is disqualified from counting as a wicked one. And precisely because he is a person, we are subject to moral constraints in dealing with this evil that do not apply to our dealings with man-eating tigers.

CONSCIENTIOUS WICKEDNESS

The conscientiously wicked person is distinguished from the self-centered one in that the maxims of his actions are seen by him as universally valid and applicable. Unlike the crude chauvinist's complete indifference to other nations' claims, the conscientiously wicked nationalist might hold that his nation's supremacy would be universally valid and overriding good, perhaps because it would be good for all humanity, perhaps because it had some excellence which any rational being would have to recognize as generating an overriding claim. The higher-order maxim by which the conscientiously wicked person lives is not self-centered; rather, it rules that all considerations not directly validated by his primary ideal goal or principle are necessarily subordinate when they conflict with it. So a conscientious Nazi need not always be indifferent to the claims of humanity instantiated in the plight of Jews. Were they anywhere but in Germany, or perhaps anywhere but in Europe, and were they not (as the Nazis claimed) an international conspiracy against the German nation, there would be a case for not exterminating them, perhaps even for manifesting concern for their well-being; but any such considerations were necessarily and totally overridden by the Herrenvolk ideal, which thus, in a Nazi's view, legitimated the Final Solution. Of course, the conscientious Nazi was himself one of the Herrenvolk, but it was not for that self-centered reason that he maintained its exclusive moral priority.

As with self-centered wickedness, conscientious wickedness can arise when the putative ideal is genuinely a good but is pursued with a ruthlessness that excludes other goods which ought to be taken account of. But it is also possible that the putative ideal is itself a monstrous error. In both cases it is alike necessary to build into the analysis criteria of culpability for the misjudgment of values. Suppose, for instance, that Aztec priests truly believed that human sacrifice gave pleasure to the god and that to please the god was good not because that way the harvests would be good (an acceptably valuable if not always an acceptably overriding end) but just as a good in itself and, further, that individual human beings as such were of subordinate concern. But suppose, also, that there was nothing in their moral consciousness with which such beliefs would not cohere. It is hard to see how they could then be called wicked. It is that reservation, however, that their moral consciousness be coherent, that makes their case problematic, where the case of Adolf Hitler is not. We must deplore murderous behavior as evil since slaying human beings is evil in nature, and if it is the result of intentional action, it must count as an evil in persons that they could act like that. But for it to count as a wickedness in persons, they must have within their repertoire some humane principles that the Aztecs (at least the Aztecs of my hypothesis) did not have. That exoneration cannot be extended, however, to tyrants and fanatics nearer home—Adolf Hitler, for instance. The resources of the European moral tradition afforded him ample reasons for treating the sufferings of Jews as of some account even set against the objective of racial purity, itself an end which that tradition provided ample grounds for questioning.

Conscientious wickedness is rarely a case of pursuing an end unaware of attendant consequences as evils; it is more often a case of a single-minded pursuit of an objective which (unlike racial purity) can reasonably be seen as good, but at the cost of a callous insensitivity to evil done by the way. It is not that the person believes the incidental evil to be itself good but rather that, having reason to think it evil, he nevertheless systematically disregards it. It is not that one cannot honestly believe with Robespierre and Saint-Just, that out of a Terror can emerge a Republic of virtue or, with the IRA, that only through indiscriminate violence can a united Ireland arise but that to go through with it one must almost certainly stifle sensibility to the horrors through which one must wade to bring it about. That sensibility, too, is a part of one's moral consciousness, no less than the perceived ideal. For a person whose conception of the moral law has developed within a moral tradition that recognizes indiscriminate murder as evil, such single-mindedness may be possible only if he has a sense of mission so great or an arrogance so overwhelming that he can desensitize himself, school himself to a callous disregard for considerations to which he nevertheless can and ought to attend.

Doing evil that good may come of it, or a greater evil be avoided, is not, however, a sufficient condition for wickedness in a person. Everyone responsible for major political decisions is likely to have been confronted with such difficult and painful choices. The history of atomic warfare is a record of one such dilemma after another. The mark of the wicked person is that such choices are for him neither difficult nor painful since the considerations that would make them so are systematically neutralized. It may, indeed, be a causally necessary condition for making such choices that one make of oneself a wicked person in this sense; in an evil world, perhaps only the wicked are callous enough to do the evil that needs to be done. "Whoever wants to engage in politics at all," wrote Max Weber, ". . . . must know that he is responsible for what may become of himself under the impact of these paradoxes. . . . He lets himself in for the diabolical forces lurking in all violence. . . . Everything that is striven for through political action operating with violent means and following an ethic of responsibility endangers the 'salvation of the soul.' "[4]

---

[4]Max Weber, "Politics as a Vocation," in *From Max Weber,* ed. H. H. Gerth and C. Wright Mills (London: Kegan Paul, Trench, Trubner & Co., 1948), pp. 125–26.

Conscientious wickedness is not so radically different, then, from selfish wickedness. In both cases it is the refusal to acknowledge the moral significance of evils which one nevertheless knows or could reasonably be expected to know as evils that constitutes the person's wickedness.

HETERONOMOUS WICKEDNESS

The kinds of wickedness identified so far are manifested in people whose responses to situations, whether active or merely contemplative, are their own; theirs is the judgment, theirs the act, theirs the wickedness. But if the Nuremberg defendants were arguably like that, Eichmann in Jerusalem pleaded that he simply obeyed orders and could not therefore be responsible for the evils in which he had participated. He had not, he said, felt any hatred of the Jews or any pleasure from their sufferings and destruction. He had committed himself conscientiously to a line of duty, but unlike Hitler and his leading henchmen, he could plausibly disclaim responsibility for having adopted the aims to which his official duties directed him. His defense amounted to the claim that what he did must be seen under the global description of doing his duty, not of pursuing evil, and the former is not itself a description of wickedness, not in any of the terms that I have set out so far. If, then, wickedness in a person requires that he adopt an evil maxim, how was Eichmann wicked? In a perceptive discussion of Hannah Arendt's report of the Eichmann Trial, Barry Clarke has created the category of "heteronomous evil" to cover such a case, and I shall follow him in this, though I shall call it "heteronomous wickedness."[5]

Clarke's argument depends on a distinction between acting spontaneously and acting autonomously. Eichmann not only relied utterly on his superiors for directions for acting in all relevant regards but in joining the Nazi Party and the bureaucracy also opted out

---

[5]Barry Clarke, "Beyond 'The Banality of Evil,'" *British Journal of Political Science* 10 (1980): 417–39 (on Hannah Arendt, *Eichmann in Jerusalem: A Report on the Banality of Evil* [London: Faber & Faber, 1963]).

of critical judgment in all matters affecting his official duties. He had chosen heteronomy, and the evil that he did followed from that decision.[6] Could he be said, then, to have possessed the capacity for free choice that is the mark of a person, the condition for responsibility for oneself, and therefore a necessary condition for one's being a wicked person?

A correct perspective on such an argument must distinguish between the ordinary practical capacity of a normal minimally rational chooser to make decisions (which I have elsewhere called "autarchy"—a self-directing condition) and the capacity to make autonomous judgments.[7] The salient conditions for autarchy were outlined above, in discussing the moral status of the psychopath, who in my view satisfies them while yet lacking moral responsibility. In some people, however, autarchy is impaired, in various degrees ranging from catatonia through autism to compulsions of various kinds. Under hypnosis, a person loses autarchy to a considerable degree; a person acting under posthypnotic suggestion less so. Such people are programmed—and by other people—and are therefore heterarchic. To the extent that one is autistic, compulsive, or heterarchic, one lacks the capacity to decide for oneself, which is the condition for free, responsible action, and to just that extent one lacks the capacity for wickedness. But Eichmann was heteronomous, not heterarchic, and heteronomy is not merely consistent with autarchy—it requires it.

By autonomy I understand a character trait amounting to a capacity to act on principles (i.e., in accordance with a *nomos*) that are one's own because one has made them so by a process of rational reflection on the complex of principles and values that one has assimilated from one's social environment. It is a process in which

---

[6]"Eichmann made two exceptions in his merciless anti-Semitic programme, once when he helped a half-Jewish cousin, and another time when at his uncle's request he helped a Viennese Jewish couple: but his conscience bothered him so much afterwards that he 'confessed his sins' (Eichmann's phrase) to his superiors" (John Kleinig, "Always Let Your Conscience Be Your Guide?" *Interchange* 1 [1967]: 107, referring to the account in Arendt, p. 131).

[7]See my analysis of autarchy and autonomy, heterarchy and heteronomy, set out at greater length in Benn.

one confronts the incoherences and conflicts within that complex and works to resolve them into something like a coherent set of moral attitudes. We do not invent our morality ex nihilo; we make it our own by creatively testing it for consistency. Now Eichmann certainly did nothing like that. On the contrary, he handed over his conscience to the care of the party, the state, and the Fuehrer, thereby imposing on his power of autarchic decision (which remained all the same quite unimpaired) constraints which he thereafter would not look at critically. But, of course, nothing made it impossible for him to do so. He had, as Clarke puts it, elected for heteronomy, and though as time went on it no doubt became increasingly difficult, psychologically speaking, to challenge the system to which he had put himself in thrall, still he had made it so himself; he had willfully made himself the compliant and unreflecting tool of wickedness, which is a perversion of the moral nature of persons as choosers.

I do not mean that one may never accept moral leadership from others or commit oneself to a role in a movement or an organization, nor do I mean that in the performance of the duties of an office one must always do precisely what one would have chosen to do irrespective of the requirements of the office. Social practices and institutions would lose their point if that were the case; they are, after all, ways of coordinating the acts of many people toward common goals and will work as such only if people can rely on one another to do what is expected of them. But this does not entail a duty to suspend all judgment. In accepting the guidance of an authority, we are responsible for satisfying ourselves that the principles for which it stands are ones which in general we can endorse; though its particular injunctions may sometimes puzzle us, we must be prepared to monitor its performance over all.

We have to distinguish, therefore, between a conditional and an absolute heteronomy. A person who chooses a conditional heteronomy may reasonably submit to the guidance of the party or the church, providing he does not surrender the power to judge whether it remains true to the principles that led him to choose just that one as the good one. We resign ourselves absolutely to heteronomy at the risk of becoming, like Eichmann, people of evil will, with a capacity in no way impaired to grasp the evil that we do in obeying wicked orders but willfully disregarding it as evil. As with the conscientiously and the selfishly wicked persons, the heteronomously wicked has become insensitive to certain morally significant states of affairs just because the maxim of his actions and attitudes leaves no place for them in his moral constitution.

WICKEDNESS AND MORAL LUCK

Of course, not every absolutely heteronomous person is necessarily wicked. Someone who submits in this total fashion to the guidance of a saint may be less than admirable as a person; but it would be both perverse and wildly censorious to call him wicked. For that one must be disposed to act, or respond, in accordance with evil maxims or in disregard of good ones. The saint's disciple will do neither. But a person who does evil by reason of having elected to put his moral judgment into the keeping of evil persons or institutions has taken a gamble that, as a morally responsible person, he is not entitled to take—and has lost.

This qualification suggests a more general and far-reaching one, affecting all the categories of wickedness discussed so far. Selfish people, people dedicated solely to their families or to the interests of their firms or their countries, and fanatics conscientiously pursuing a blinkered ideal all have it in them to be wicked people. But if the actions picked out for them by their restrictive second-order maxims happened never to be evil actions, it would be harsh to call such people wicked, even if their first-order maxims were always self-centered or narrowly principled. For, as I suggested earlier, such maxims are not always intrinsically bad. Imagine someone who acted single-mindedly on a maxim of self-interest but whose actions were, by social circumstances, under such close scrutiny that any action that damaged someone else, or any denial of help to someone in need, would invite the penalties of public censure. He would have reasons for taking account of appropriate other-regarding maxims, though they would be reasons encapsulated in a self-interested strategy. Such a person would be morally unworthy, but his social institutions would save him from actualizing the wickedness which was latent in him. The Puritan communities of the seventeenth century maintained strict moral surveillance over their members because they were more concerned with saving people from doing wickedness of which they were capable than with moral worth, which, they believed, few, if any, people possessed, and then only by divine election. But we do not have to accept the doctrine of predestination to believe that what preserves many quite ordinary people from wickedness is the good fortune of their circumstances and that in a Belsen or an Auschwitz they might be capable not merely of the desperate meanness of so many of the inmates but also of the wickedness of very nearly all the guards.

MALIGNITY

In all the forms of wickedness treated so far, the regulative maxim has been directed to something understood by the agent, however perversely, as a good. For some philosophers, as we shall see, this has been held to be a necessary condition for any rational action at all. The kind of wickedness, however, which Coleridge saw instantiated in Iago as "motiveless malignity," and which Milton's Satan epitomizes in "Evil be thou my good," throws doubt on this supposition.

Iago and Satan are, of course, the paradigm instances in literature of the unalloyed wickedness of malignity, of pursuing evil under the aspect of evil. According to Kant, "In order to call a man bad, it should be possible to argue a priori from some actions, or from a single consciously bad action to a bad maxim as its foundation, and from this to a general source in the actor of all particular morally bad maxims, this source again being itself a maxim."[8] But Kant denies that human beings can adopt as a fundamental maxim, informing all rational choices as a kind of perverse moral law, the maxim, Do evil for evil's sake. A "malignant reason," a "bad Rational Will," would require that "antagonism to the law would itself be made a spring of action . . . so that the subject would be made a *devilish* being."[9] Kant believes that human beings cannot be like this yet it is not easy to see why since he believes that devils who are presumably also rational, can be. Perhaps to be a devil is to be irrational in the special way that, while apprehending the moral law, one responds to it, like Satan, antagonistically, finding in it not a spring of action but a spring of counteraction. I

[8]Kant, p. 327.
[9]Ibid., p. 342.

shall consider in a moment whether it is logically possible to make evil one's end, but if it is not, then it must be impossible for devils too. And if the impossibility is not of this kind, I cannot see why human beings may not also be Satanic.

I suggested earlier that the attitudes and actions of a selfishly wicked person are governed by a conception of the good, albeit the good of the agent himself; his wickedness consists in his indifference to other values. A malignant person, by contrast, should take account of the suffering of someone else as a reason for action, irrespective of self-love, just as much as would a benevolent person. But unlike the latter, he would promote it. It is as evil that he rejoices in the suffering and not because he sees it, in some partial or distorted way, as a good, even for himself. He does not think himself better off for it; he is no less disinterested in rejoicing in it than is a benevolent person who rejoices in someone else's good fortune. Just as the prospect of satisfying one's own sexual desire is pleasurable to contemplate, as a good, so, for the malignant person, someone else's suffering is a pleasure to contemplate, but as an evil, apprehended as such. Correspondingly, it is unalloyed wickedness to hate the good, apprehended as good, and because it is good, and to seek its destruction on that account.

The unalloyed wickedness of malignity presents a logical or a psychological problem, not a moral one. The difficulty is not to decide what attitude to adopt toward it; if it exists at all, it is to be totally abhorred. The problem is rather to understand its motivation or, indeed, to decide whether the very description of it is coherent. Is it perhaps that we perceive something as unalloyed wickedness only because we haven't fully understood it?

According to Socrates, a man who knows the good cannot choose to do evil; no one intentionally chooses evil knowing it to be so.[10] Since my account of unalloyed wickedness implicitly denies this claim, it is necessary to consider why Socrates may have made it.

---

[10]See Plato, *Protagoras* 352a–358d. In the *Laws,* Plato asserts: "No wrongdoer is so of deliberation. For no man will ever deliberately admit supreme evil, and least of all in his most precious possessions. But every man's most precious possession, as we said, is his soul; no man, then, we may be sure, will of set purpose receive the supreme evil into this most precious thing and live with it there all his life through" (731c).

But more than that, what account can we give of motivation to evil if the one given by Socrates turns out not to be true?

Socrates' paradox can be made plausible given a certain view of the motives of action. If we suppose that all intentional or voluntary action is undertaken with some aim, it must be supposed that what is aimed at must be desired; and if someone desires it, he must see it as a good thing to bring it about.[11] Accordingly, for Socrates, whoever aims at evil does so in ignorance of its true nature, under the misapprehension of it as good.

The trouble with Socrates' story is that it distorts the nature of true malignity. I said earlier that a malignant person recognizes the suffering of someone else as an evil and rejoices in it just because it is evil and that he would not rejoice in it were it not that he saw it as such. Even more perplexing, on Socrates' account, is the case of self-destructive action prompted by self-hatred. One must go a long and devious way round to find a good that such a person might believe that he was promoting in spiting himself. Clearly if one aims at an outcome then, in a rather weak sense, one must desire it; but it is not, even for the person desiring it, necessarily desirable on that account. For what is desirable is what it is appropriate to desire, and the malignant person desires things very often precisely because they are not appropriate. Consider the case of Claggart, the master-at-arms, in Herman Melville's story *Billy Budd*. Claggart conceives a hatred of "the Handsome Sailor," "who in Claggart's own phrase was 'the sweet and pleasant young fellow,'" and falsely charges him with sedition in order to destroy him.[12] Claggart has no reason to hate Billy if by "reason" we mean reason of interest. There is no apparent good that can come to him, or to anyone else, from the evil that will come about. So far from moving him to act for the sake of something he sees as a good, his hatred moves him to spite and to destroy it.[13]

---

[11] Michael Stocker has examined the claim that it is not possible to desire the bad in "Desiring the Bad: An Essay in Moral Psychology," *Journal of Philosophy* 76 (1979): 738–53.

[12] Herman Melville, *Billy Budd and Other Tales* (New York: New American Library of World Literature, Inc., 1961), chap. 11, p. 35.

[13] See Peter Kivy, "Melville's *Billy* and the Secular Problem of Evil: The Worm in the Bud," *Monist* 63 (1980): 480–93, for a stimulating discussion of the problem of malignity in general and Claggart in particular.

Claggart's reason for hating Billy is precisely his goodness. He can appreciate it only as a reproach, as something that diminishes him, that he must therefore hate and destroy.[14] There is a passage in Schopenhauer that expresses this state of mind most eloquently: "Very bad men bear the stamp of inward suffering in the very expression of the countenance. . . . From this inward torment, which is absolutely and directly essential to them, there finally proceeds that delight in the suffering of others which does not spring from mere egoism, but is disinterested, and which constitutes wickedness proper, rising to the pitch of cruelty. For this the suffering of others is not a means for the attainment of the ends of its own will, but an end in itself."[15] Schopenhauer's explanation is that such wicked persons suffer "an intensity of will" that nothing could assuage. "Every privation" (every frustration of desire) "is infinitely increased by the enjoyment of others, and relieved by the knowledge that others suffer the same privation." Moreover, an "attained end never fulfills the promise of the desired object." From "a manifestation of will reaching the point of extraordinary wickedness, there necessarily springs an excessive inward misery, an eternal unrest, an incurable pain; he seeks indirectly the alleviation which directly is denied him,—seeks to mitigate his own suffering by the sight of the suffering of others, which at the same time he recognises as an expression of his power. The suffering of others now becomes for him an end in itself, and is a spectacle in which he delights; and thus arises the phenomenon of pure cruelty, blood thirstiness, which history exhibits so often in the Neros and Domitians, in the African Deis, in Robespierre, and the like."[16]

Of course, one might say that Coleridge was mistaken and that the malignity of Iago and Claggart, with which Schopenhauer's story accords so well, was not "motiveless" but was motivated by envy or resentment. But these motives are not motives of interest, prompted by a good to be brought about by action. They explain the action only by filling out further the description of what is done by giving

---

[14]Compare Iago, of Cassio: "He hath a daily beauty in his life that makes me ugly" (Othello, 5.1.19–20).

[15]A. Schopenhauer, *The World as Will and Idea,* in *The Philosophy of Schopenhauer,* ed. Irwin Edman (New York: Modern Library, 1928), p. 293.

[16]Ibid., p. 294.

us a better grasp of the organic relation between the state of affairs, the beliefs of the agent, and the attitude that binds us together. Envious and resentful people are not aiming to bring about a good; nor does the good that they recognize appeal to them. On the contrary, it inflames and enrages them.

I have interpreted the Socratic position up to this point as a psychological theory about how an end must be perceived for it to be a motivating cause, and I have tried to rebut this theory by showing that one can grasp the motives of Iago and Claggart without having to convert them into perceived goods, whether goods for the agents themselves or goods that the agents themselves perceived as appropriately desired.[17] Suppose, however, that we take the Socratic claim to be logical rather that psychological. On this interpretation, seeing something as good is to acknowledge that there is the strongest possible practical reason for seeking it, however one may fail in practice through weakness of will. Conversely, to see something as evil would be to recognize that there is a reason not to seek it. So it would be incoherent to adopt Satan's policy of pursuing evil for its own sake since this would be to have as one's reason for action what was logically a reason against action.

Schopenhauer's account of malignity is too plausible, however, for the logical objection to clinch the matter. That objection depends on an assumed nexus between recognizing that there is a reason for

---

[17]Iago makes some pretense that his animosity toward Othello is prompted by a report that the latter had seduced his wife. Supposing him really to have believed that, it is interesting to see how that could change our judgment of Iago. It would still be the case that he knowingly wished an evil on Othello, but not now simply for evil's sake. Revenge, responding to an injury, represents a primitive kind of justice; the maxim of his action would then have been not to do evil for evil's sake but to exact just recompense. And this, presumably, is where a retributivist's defense of punishment must begin since he defends the inflicting of evil not, like the malignant, for evil's sake but in the name of justice. To satisfy one's claim to vengeance is thus not merely an intelligible motive but also one that in some measure redeems malignity, as envy does not. Resentment straddles these two possibilities. Like Claggart and Iago, one can resent being diminished by goodness, which is no injury, but one can also resent a real injury, and someone who wished another ill on that account, though falling short of charity, would be a wicked person only to the extent that his justified grievance made him insensitive to counterconsiderations.

action, having that reason as one's own, and being motivated to act on it. There seem to be two ways, though, in which one could recognize the good (or the desirable) and the evil (the undesirable). Paradigmatically, it is true, to see a state of affairs as desirable is to acknowledge that, by criteria of value and appropriateness that one can acknowledge as one's own, there is a reason for desiring things so. But we can envisage a person imagining very well what it would be like to have such a moral experience, to make the appraisals that most people make, and to see why, indeed, they found desirable the things that they did, given the kind of people that they were. And he could envy them for being as they are while being filled, like Claggart, with resentment and hate for them and the things they love and value just because he knows that there is no possibility that he could be like them, think like them, feel like them, or care like them. Precisely because the good that he sees cannot motivate him, he hates it for its very inaccessibility. He grasps the attraction of the good and knows its opposite as evil, but in an encapsulated way that prevents its being also—for him—a reason for action in the way that it is for them. His acknowledging it as good amounts to seeing that it is a reason, but it is not a reason that he can have or that could be his motive.

The way in which the malignant subject experiences such a rancorous motivation to evil may be set out schematically as follows:

1. Properties $C_1 \ldots C_n$ in a person are virtues (V).
2. Anyone is a good person (G) if and only if he has properties V.
3. For any G, X is a reason for action (e.g., the principle that one should turn the other cheek).
4. I value someone's being a G if and only if I believe I could myself succeed in being a G.
5. I value V if and only if I can be a G.
6. I do not believe I can have X as my reason for action.
7. Therefore I do not believe I could succeed in being a G.
8′. Any properties that I would value if I had them (P), but which I believe I cannot succeed in having, are to be despised (maxim 1).
8″. Any person (S) who succeeds in having P is to be made to suffer for having them (maxim 2).
8‴. Any action that only an S would have a reason for doing

is to be avoided, and the contrary action is to be done
(maxim 3).

9. To despise virtue, to cause good people to suffer, and to
do wrong, that is, to act on maxims 1, 2, and 3, is evil.

10. So evil is to be done (maxim 4).

It might be objected that anyone adopting maxims 1–4 would
do so only in order to assuage a sense of his own inadequacy and
that this amounts to embracing evil only for the sake of a perceived
good. But of course, if one knew that this was what one was
doing—crying "sour grapes"—the strategy would be ineffective. The
malignant could assuage a sense of inadequacy only if he was really
unaware of this aspect of his motivation; otherwise he would know
when he said that he detested virtue that he really admired it. The
explanatory methods of depth psychology consist precisely in constructing scenarios such that the end of every action is an intelligible good or the relief of an intelligible unease. But the putative
unconscious strategies are by no means always successful—the
malignant's rancor is not assuaged, nor does he feel any the less
inadequate when his rival is laid low; for if it is indeed his own
moral failing in comparison with his rival's virtue that dismays him,
acting viciously as a reprisal can only aggravate the sense of inferiority. The method of depth psychology must explain, therefore,
why the good that is the imputed objective is so ineffectually pursued. Meanwhile, whatever the psychiatric explanation, there can
be little doubt that the malignant subject really is hating good and
delighting in evil under precisely these descriptions, without feeling that there is anything logically incoherent in doing so. And
while the phenomenology of rancor may not apply in precisely the
same way to every instance of malignancy, it is enough to suggest
that the nexus between recognition of a reason, having it as one's
own, and being motivated to act on it can be broken.

For Further Reflection

1. What is Benn's definition of evil? How is it related to wickedness? Do you agree with his analysis?

2. Analyze Benn's four types of wickedness. Do they overlap? Do
they help us understand the nature of evil?

3. Examine Benn's concept of malignity. Some philosophers argue that it is not possible knowingly to choose evil as one's goal. What does Benn think about this thesis and how does he treat it? Do you agree with him?

Beyond Good and Evil

FRIEDRICH NIETZSCHE

Friedrich Nietzsche (1844–1900) was a German philosopher and a forerunner of existentialism. Descended through both of his parents from Lutheran ministers, Nietzsche was raised in a devout Christian home and was known as "the little Jesus" by his schoolmates. He studied theology at the University of Bonn and philology at Leipzig, becoming an atheist in the process. At the age of twenty-four he was appointed professor of classical philology at the University of Basel in Switzerland, where he taught for ten years until forced by ill health to retire. Eventually he became mentally ill.

Nietzsche believes that the fundamental creative force that motivates all creation is the will to power. We all seek not happiness but to affirm ourselves, to flourish and dominate. Since we are essentially unequal in ability, intelligence, and imagination, it follows that the fittest will survive and be victorious in the contest with the weaker and the baser. Great beauty inheres in the struggle of noble spirits ascending to a pinnacle on the trunks of lesser beings, including lesser human beings. But this process is hampered by Judeo-Christian morality, which Nietzsche labels "slave morality." Slave morality, which is the invention of jealous priests, envious and resentful of the excellent and the powerful, advocates that we become meek and mild, that we believe the

---

Reprinted from *The Complete Works of Nietzsche,* ed. Oscar Levy, vols. 10 and 11 (New York: T. Foulis, 1910).

lie of all humans having equal worth. He sometimes, as in our reading, refers to this as the ethics of "resentment." The herd resents their superior competitors.

Nietzsche's idea of an inegalitarian, aesthetic ethic assumes the thesis that God is dead. God plays no vital role in our culture—except as a protector of the slave morality, including the idea of equal worth of all persons. If we recognize that there is no rational basis for believing in God, we will see that the whole edifice of slave morality must crumble and with it the notion of equal worth. In its place will arise the morality of the noble person based on the virtues of high courage, disciplined passion, pride, and intelligence, in the pursuit of affirmation and excellence.

We begin this section with Nietzsche's famous description of the madman who announces the death of God; we then turn to selections from *Beyond Good and Evil*.

THE MADMAN AND THE DEATH OF GOD

Have you ever heard of the madman who on a bright morning lighted a lantern and ran to the market-place calling out unceasingly: "I seek God! I seek God!"—As there were many people standing about who did not believe in God, he caused a great deal of amusement. Why! is he lost? said one. Has he strayed away like a child? said another. Or does he keep himself hidden? Is he afraid of us? Has he taken a seavoyage? Has he emigrated?—the people cried out laughingly, all in a hubbub. The insane man jumped into their midst and transfixed them with his glances. "Where is God gone?" he called out. "I mean to tell you! *We have killed him,*—you and I! We are all his murderers! But how have we done it? How were we able to drink up the sea? Who gave us the sponge to wipe away the whole horizon? What did we do when we loosened this earth from its sun? Whither does it now move? Whither do we move? Away from all suns? Do we not dash on unceasingly? Backwards, side-ways, forwards, in all directions? Is there still an above and below? Do we not stray, as through infinite nothingness? Does not empty space breathe upon us? Has it not become colder? Does not night come on continually, darker and darker? Shall we not have to light lanterns in the morning? Do we not hear the noise of the grave-diggers who are burying God? Do we not smell the divine putrefaction?—for even Gods putrefy! God is dead! God remains dead! And we have killed him! How shall we console ourselves, the most murderous of all murderers? The holiest and the mightiest that the world has hitherto possessed, has bled to death under our knife—who will wipe the blood from us? With what water could we cleanse ourselves? What lustrums, what sacred games shall we have to devise? Is not the magnitude of this deed too great for us? Shall we not ourselves have to become Gods, merely to seem worthy of it? There never was a greater event—and on account of it, all who are born after us belong to a higher history than any history hitherto!"—Here the madman was silent and looked again at his hearers; they also were silent and looked at him in surprise. At last he threw his lantern on the ground, so that it broke in pieces and was extinguished. "I come too early," he then said, "I am not yet at the right time. This prodigious event is still on its way, and is travelling—it has not yet reached men's ears. Lightning and thunder need time, the light of the stars needs time, deeds need time, even after they are done, to be seen and heard. This deed is as yet further from them than the furthest star—*and yet they have done it!*"—It is further stated that the madman made his way into different churches on the same day, and there intoned his *Requiem aeternam deo*. When led out and called to account, he always gave the reply: "What are these churches now, if they are not the tombs and monuments of God?"— . . .

WHAT IS NOBLE?

Every elevation of the type "man," has hitherto been the work of an aristocratic society and so it will always be—a society believing in a long scale of gradations of rank and differences of worth among human beings, and requiring slavery in some form or other. Without the *pathos of distance,* such as grows out of the incarnated difference of classes, out of the constant outlooking and downlooking of the ruling caste on subordinates and instruments, and out of their equally constant practice of obeying and commanding, of keeping down and keeping at a distance—that other more mysterious pathos could never have arisen, the longing for an ever new widening of distance within the soul itself, the formation of ever higher, rarer, further, more extended, more comprehensive states, in short, just the elevation of the type "man," the continued "self-surmounting of man," to use a moral formula in a super-moral sense. To be sure, one must not resign oneself to any humanitarian illusions about the history of the origin of an aristocratic society (that is to say, of the preliminary condition for the elevation of the type "man"): the truth is hard. Let us acknowledge unprejudicedly how ever higher civilisation hitherto has *originated!* Men with a still natural nature, barbarians in every terrible sense of the word, men of prey, still in possession of unbroken strength of will and desire for power, threw themselves upon weaker, more moral, more peaceful races (perhaps trading or cattle-rearing communities), or upon old mellow civilisations in which the final vital force was flickering out in brilliant fireworks of wit and depravity. At the commencement, the noble caste was always the barbarian caste: their superiority did not consist first of all in their physical, but in their psychical power—they were more *complete* men (which at every point also implies the same as "more complete beasts").

Corruption—as the indication that anarchy threatens to break out among the instincts, and that the foundation of the emotions, called "life," is convulsed—is something radically different according to the organisation in which it manifests itself. When, for instance, an aristocracy like that of France at the beginning of the Revolution, flung away its privileges with sublime disgust and sacrificed itself to an excess of its moral sentiments, it was corruption:—it was really only the closing act of the corruption which had existed for centuries, by virtue of which that aristocracy had abdicated step by step its lordly prerogatives and lowered itself to a *function* of royalty (in the end even to its decoration and parade-dress). The essential thing, however, in a good and healthy aristocracy is that it should *not* regard itself as a function either of the kingship or the commonwealth, but as the *significance* and highest justification thereof—that it should therefore accept with a good conscience the sacrifice of a legion of individuals, who, *for its sake,* must be suppressed and reduced to imperfect men, to slaves and instruments. Its fundamental belief must be precisely that society is *not* allowed to exist for its own sake, but only as a foundation and scaffolding, by means of which a select class of beings may be able to elevate themselves to their higher duties, and in general to a higher *exis-*

tence: like those sun-seeking climbing plants in Java—they are called *Sipo Matador*—which encircle an oak so long and so often with their arms, until at last, high above it, but supported by it, they can unfold their tops in the open light, and exhibit their happiness.

To refrain mutually from injury, from violence, from exploitation, and put one's will on a par with that of others: this may result in a certain rough sense in good conduct among individuals when the necessary conditions are given (namely, the actual similarity of the individuals in amount of force and degree of worth, and their co-relation within one organisation). As soon, however, as one wished to take this principle more generally, and if possible even as *the fundamental principle of society,* it would immediately disclose what it really is—namely, a Will to the *denial* of life, a principle of dissolution and decay. Here one must think profoundly to the very basis and resist all sentimental weakness: life itself is *essentially* appropriation, injury, conquest of the strange and weak, suppression, severity, obtrusion of peculiar forms, incorporation, and at the least, putting it mildest, exploitation;—but why should one for ever use precisely these words on which for ages a disparaging purpose has been stamped? Even the organisation within which, as was previously supposed, the individuals treat each other as equal—it takes place in every healthy aristocracy—must itself, if it be a living and not a dying organisation, do all that towards other bodies, which the individuals within it refrain from doing to each other: it will have to be the incarnated Will to Power, it will endeavour to grow, to gain ground, attract to itself and acquire ascendency—not owing to any morality or immorality, but because it *lives,* and because life *is* precisely Will to Power. On no point, however, is the ordinary consciousness of Europeans more unwilling to be corrected than on this matter; people now rave everywhere, even under the guise of science, about coming conditions of society in which "the exploiting character" is to be absent:—that sounds to my ears as if they promised to invent a mode of life which should refrain from all organic functions. "Exploitation" does not belong to a depraved, or imperfect and primitive society: it belongs to the *nature* of the living being as a primary organic function; it is a consequence of the intrinsic Will to Power, which is precisely the Will to Life.—Granting that as a theory this is a novelty—as a reality it is the *fundamental fact* of all history: let us be so far honest towards ourselves!

MASTER AND SLAVE MORALITY

In a tour through the many finer and coarser moralities which have hitherto prevailed or still prevail on the earth, I found certain traits recurring regularly together, and connected with one another, until finally two primary types revealed themselves to me, and a radical distinction was brought to light. There is *master-morality* and *slave-morality;*—I would at once add, however, that in all higher and mixed civilisations, there are also attempts at the reconciliation of the two moralities; but one finds still oftener the confusion and mutual misunderstanding of them, indeed, sometimes their close juxtaposition—even in the same man, within one soul. The distinctions of moral values have either originated in a ruling caste, pleasantly conscious of being different from the ruled—or among the ruled class, the slaves and dependents of all sorts. In the first case, when it is the rulers who determine the conception "good," it is the exalted, proud disposition which is regarded as the distinguishing feature, and that which determines the order of rank. The noble type of man separates from himself the beings in whom the opposite of this exalted, proud disposition displays itself: he despises them. Let it at once be noted that in this first kind of morality the antithesis "good" and "bad" means practically the same as "noble" and "despicable";—the antithesis "good" and "*evil*" is of a different origin. The cowardly, the timid, the insignificant, and those thinking merely of narrow utility are despised; moreover, also, the distrustful, with their constrained glances, the self-abasing, the dog-like kind of men who let themselves be abused, the mendicant flatterers, and above all the liars:—it is a fundamental belief of all aristocrats that the common people are untruthful. "We truthful ones"—the nobility in ancient Greece called themselves. It is obvious that everywhere the designations of moral value were at first applied to *men,* and were only derivatively and at a later period applied to *actions;* it is a gross mistake, therefore, when historians of morals start with questions like, "Why have sympathetic actions been praised?" The noble type of man regards *himself* as a determiner of values; he does not require to be approved of; he passes the judgment: "What is injurious to me is injurious in itself"; he knows that it is he himself only who confers honour on things; he is a *creator of values.* He honours whatever he recognises in himself: such morality is self-glorification. In the foreground there is the feeling of plenitude, of power, which seeks to overflow, the happiness of high tension, the consciousness of a wealth which would fain give and bestow:—the noble man also helps the unfortunate, but not—or scarcely—out of pity, but rather from an impulse generated by the superabundance of power. The noble man honours in himself the powerful one, him also who has power over himself, who knows how to speak and how to keep silence, who takes pleasure in subjecting himself to severity and hardness, and has reverence for all that is severe and hard. "Wotan placed a hard heart in my breast," says an old Scandinavian Saga: it is thus rightly expressed from the soul of a proud Viking. Such a type of man is even proud of *not* being made for sympathy; the hero of the Saga therefore adds warningly: "He who has not a hard heart when young, will never have one." The noble and brave who think thus are the furthest removed from the morality which sees precisely in sympathy, or in acting for the good of others, or in *désintéressement,* the characteristic of the moral; faith in oneself, pride in oneself, a radical enmity and irony towards "selflessness," belong as definitely to noble morality, as do a careless scorn and precaution in presence of sympathy and the "warm heart."—It is the powerful who *know* how to honour, it is their art, their domain for invention. The profound reverence for age and for tradition—all law rests on this double reverence—the belief and prejudice in favour of ancestors and unfavourable to newcomers, is typical in the morality of the powerful; and if, reversely, men of "modern ideas" believe almost instinctively in "progress" and the "future," and are more and more lacking in respect for old age, the ignoble origin of these "ideas" has complacently betrayed itself thereby. A morality of the ruling class, however, is more especially foreign and irritating to present-day taste in the sternness of its principle that one has duties only to one's equals; that one may act towards beings of a lower rank, towards all that is foreign, just as seems good to one, or "as the heart desires," and in any case "beyond good and evil": it is here that sympathy and similar sentiments can have a place. The ability and obligation to exercise prolonged gratitude and prolonged revenge—both only within the circle of equals—artfulness in retaliation, *raffinement* of the idea in friendship, a certain necessity to have enemies (as outlets for the emotions of envy, quarrelsomeness, arrogance—in fact, in order to be a good *friend*): all these are typical characteristics of the noble morality, which, as has been pointed out, is not the morality of "modern ideas," and is therefore at present difficult to realise and also to unearth and disclose.—It is otherwise with the second type of morality, *slave-morality*. Supposing that the abused, the oppressed, the suffering, the unemancipated, the weary, and those uncertain of themselves, should moralise, what will be the common element in their moral estimates? Probably a pessimistic suspicion with regard to the entire situation of man will find expression, perhaps a condemnation of man, together with his situation. The slave has an unfavourable eye for the virtues of the powerful; he has a scepticism and distrust, a *refinement* of distrust of everything "good" that is there honoured—he would fain persuade himself that the very happiness there is not genuine. On the other hand, *those* qualities which serve to alleviate the existence of sufferers are brought into prominence and flooded with light; it is here that sympathy, the kind, helping hand, the warm heart, patience, diligence, humility, and friendliness attain to honour; for here these are the most useful qualities, and almost the only means of supporting the burden of existence. Slave-morality is essentially the morality of utility. Here is the seat of the origin of the famous antithesis "good" and "evil":—power and dangerousness are assumed to reside in the evil, a certain dreadfulness, subtlety, and strength, which do not admit of being despised. According to slave-morality, therefore, the "evil" man arouses fear; according to master-morality, it is precisely the "good" man who arouses fear and seeks to arouse it, while the bad man is regarded as the despicable being. The contrast attains its maximum when, in accordance with the logical consequences of slave-morality, a shade of depreciation—it may be slight and well-intentioned—at last attaches itself to the "good" man of this morality; because, according to the servile mode of thought, the good man must in any case be the *safe* man: he is good-natured, easily deceived, perhaps a little stupid, *un bonhomme.* Everywhere that slave-morality gains the ascendency, language shows a tendency to approximate the significations of the words "good" and "stupid."—A last fundamental difference: the desire for *freedom,* the instinct for happiness and the refinements of the feeling of liberty belong as necessarily to slave-morals and morality, as artifice and enthusiasm in reverence and devotion are the regular symptoms of an aristocratic mode of thinking and estimating.— Hence we can understand without further detail why love *as a passion*—it is our European specialty—must absolutely be of noble origin; as is well known, its invention is due to the Provençal poet-cavaliers, those brilliant, ingenious men of the *"gai saber,"* to whom Europe owes so much, and almost owes itself. . . .

There is an *instinct for rank,* which more than anything else is already the sign of a *high* rank; there is a *delight* in the *nuances* of reverence which leads one to infer noble origin and habits. The refinement, goodness, and loftiness of a soul are put to a perilous test when something passes by that is of the highest rank, but is not yet protected by the awe of authority from obtrusive touches and incivilities: something that goes its way like a living touchstone, undistinguished, undiscovered, and tentative, perhaps voluntarily veiled and disguised. He whose task and practice it is to investigate souls, will avail himself of many varieties of this very art to determine the ultimate value of a soul, the unalterable, innate order of rank to which it belongs: he will test it by its *instinct for reverence. Différence engendre haine* [Difference engenders hate.—ED.]: the vulgarity of many a nature spurts up suddenly like dirty water, when any holy vessel, any jewel from closed shrines, any book bearing the marks of great destiny, is brought before it; while on the other hand, there is an involuntary silence, a hesitation of the eye, a cessation of all gestures, by which it is indicated that a soul *feels* the nearness of what is worthiest of respect. . . .

The revolt of the slaves in morals begins in the very principle of *resentment* becoming creative and giving birth to values—a resentment experienced by creatures who, deprived as they are of the proper outlet of action, are forced to find their compensation in an imaginary revenge. While every aristocratic morality springs from a triumphant affirmation of its own demands, the slave-morality says "no" from the very outset to what is "outside itself," "different from itself," and "not itself": and this "no" is its creative deed. This reversal of the valuing standpoint—this *inevitable* gravitation to the objective instead of back to the subjective—is typical of "resentment": the slave-morality requires as the condition of its existence an external and objective world, to employ physiological terminology, it requires objective stimuli to be capable of action at all—its action is fundamentally a reaction. The contrary is the case when we come to the aristocrat's system of values: it acts and grows spontaneously, it merely seeks its antithesis in order to pronounce a more grateful and exultant "yes" to its own self;—its negative conception, "low," "vulgar," "bad," is merely a pale late-born foil in comparison with its positive and fundamental conception (saturated as it is with life and passion), of "we aristocrats, we good ones, we beautiful ones, we happy ones."

When the aristocratic morality goes astray and commits sacrilege on reality, this is limited to that particular sphere with which it is *not* sufficiently acquainted—a sphere, in fact, from the real knowledge of which it disdainfully defends itself. It misjudges, in some cases, the sphere which it despises, the sphere of the common vulgar man and the low people: on the other hand, due weight should be given to the consideration that in any case the mood of contempt, of disdain, of superciliousness, even on the supposition that it *falsely* portrays the object of its contempt, will always be far removed from that degree of falsity which will always characterise the attacks—in effigy, of course—of the vindictive hatred and revengefulness of the weak in onslaughts on their enemies. In point of fact, there is in contempt too strong an admixture of nonchalance, of casualness, of boredom, of impatience, even of personal exultation, for it to be capable of distorting its victim into a real caricature or a real monstrosity. Attention again should be paid to the almost benevolent *nuances* which, for instance, the Greek nobility imports into all the words by which it distinguishes the common people from itself; note how continuously a kind of pity, care, and consideration imparts its honeyed *flavour,* until at last almost all the words which are applied to the vulgar man survive finally as expressions for "unhappy," "worthy of pity" . . . —and how, conversely, "bad," "low," "unhappy" have never ceased to ring in the Greek ear with a tone in which "unhappy" is the predominant note: this is a heritage of the old noble aristocratic morality, which remains true to itself even in contempt. . . . The "well-born" simply *felt* themselves the "happy"; they did not have to manufacture their happiness artificially through looking at their enemies, or in cases to talk and lie themselves into happiness (as is the custom with all resentful men); and similarly, complete men as they were, exuberant with strength, and consequently *necessarily* energetic, they were too wise to dissociate happiness from action—activity becomes in their minds necessarily counted as happiness (that is the etymology of εὖ πράττειν—all in sharp contrast to the "happiness" of the weak and the oppressed, with their festering venom and malignity, among whom happiness appears essentially as a narcotic, a deadening, a quietude, a peace, a "Sabbath," an enervation of the mind and relaxation of the limbs—in short, a purely *passive* phenomenon. While the aristocratic man lived in confidence and openness with himself γεν-ναῖος, "noble-born," emphasises the nuance "sincere," and perhaps also "naïf"), the resentful man, on the other hand, is neither sincere nor naïf, nor honest and candid with himself. His soul *squints;* his mind loves hidden crannies, tortuous paths and backdoors, everything secret appeals to him as *his* world, *his* safety, *his* balm; he is past master in silence, in not forgetting, in waiting, in provisional self-depreciation and self-abasement. A race of such *resentful* men will of necessity eventually prove more *prudent* than any aristocratic race, it will honour prudence on quite a distinct scale, as, in fact, a paramount condition of existence, while prudence among aristocratic men is apt to be tinged with a delicate flavour of luxury and refinement; so among them it plays nothing like so integral a part as that complete certainty of function of the governing *unconscious* instincts, or as indeed a certain lack of prudence, such as a vehement and valiant charge, whether against danger or the enemy, or as those ecstatic bursts of rage, love, reverence, gratitude, by which at all times noble souls have recognised each other. When the resentment of the aristocratic man manifests itself, it fulfils and exhausts itself in an immediate reaction, and consequently instills no *venom:* on the other hand, it never manifests itself at all in countless instances, when in the case of the feeble and weak it would be inevitable. An inability to take seriously for any length of time their enemies, their disasters, their *misdeeds*— that is the sign of the full strong natures who possess a superfluity of moulding plastic force, that heals completely and produces forgetfulness: a good example of this in the modern world is Mirabeau, who had no memory for any insults and meannesses which were practised on him, and who was only incapable of forgiving because he forgot. Such a man indeed shakes off with a shrug many a worm which would have buried itself in another; it is only in characters like these that we see the possibility (supposing, of course, that there is such a possibility in the world) of the real "*love* of one's enemies." What respect for his enemies is found, forsooth, in an aristocratic man—and such a reverence is already a bridge to love! He insists on having his enemy to himself as his distinction. He tolerates no other enemy but a man in whose character there is nothing to despise and *much* to honour! On the other hand, imagine the "enemy" as the resentful man conceives him—and it is here exactly that we see his work, his creativeness; he has conceived "the evil enemy," the "evil one," and indeed that is the root idea from which he now evolves as a contrasting and corresponding figure a "good one," himself—his very self!

The method of this man is quite contrary to that of the aristocratic man, who conceives the root idea "good" spontaneously and straight away, that is to say, out of himself, and from that material then creates for himself a concept of "bad"! This "bad" of aristocratic origin and that "evil" out of the cauldron of unsatisfied hatred—the former an imitation, an "extra," an additional nuance; the latter, on the other hand, the original, the beginning, the essential act in the conception of a slave-morality—these two words "bad" and "evil," how great a difference do they mark, in spite of the fact that they have an identical contrary in the idea "good." But the idea "good" is *not* the same: much rather let the question be asked, "Who is really evil according to the meaning of the morality of resentment?" In all sternness let it be answered thus:—*just* the good man of the other morality, just the aristocrat, the powerful one, the one who rules, but who is distorted by the venomous eye of resentfulness, into a new colour, a new signification, a new appearance. This particular point we would be the last to deny: the man who learnt to know those "good" ones only as enemies, learnt at the same time not to know them only as *"evil enemies,"* and the same men who . . . were kept so rigorously in bounds through convention, respect, custom, and gratitude, though much more through mutual vigilance and jealousy, . . . these men who in their relations with each other find so many new ways of manifesting consideration, self-control, delicacy, loyalty, pride, and friendship, these men are in reference to what is outside their circle (where the foreign element, a *foreign* country, begins), not much better than beasts of prey, which have been let loose. They enjoy there freedom from all social control, they feel that in the wilderness they can give vent with impunity to that tension which is produced by enclosure and imprisonment in the peace of society, they *revert* to the innocence of the beast-of-prey conscience, like jubilant monsters, who perhaps come from a ghostly bout of murder, arson, rape, and torture, with bravado and a moral equanimity, as though merely some wild student's prank had been played, perfectly convinced that the poets have now an ample theme to sing and celebrate. It is impossible not to recognise at the core of all these aristocratic races the beast of prey; the magnificent *blonde brute,* avidly rampant for spoil and victory; this hidden core needed an outlet from time to time, the beast must get loose again, must return into the wilderness—the Roman, Arabic, German, and Japanese nobility, the Homeric heroes, the Scandinavian Vikings, are all alike in this need. It is the aristocratic races who have left the idea "Barbarian" on all the tracks in which they have marched; nay, a consciousness of this very barbarianism, and even a pride in it, manifests itself even in their highest civilisation (for example, when Pericles says to his Athenians in that celebrated funeral oration, "Our audacity has forced a way over every land and sea, rearing everywhere imperishable memorials of itself for *good* and for *evil*"). This audacity of aristocratic races, mad, absurd, and spasmodic as may be its expression; the incalculable and fantastic nature of their enterprises, . . . their nonchalance and contempt for safety, body, life, and comfort, their awful joy and intense delight in all destruction, in all the ecstasies of victory and cruelty,—all these features become crystallised, for those who suffered thereby in the picture of the "barbarian," of the "evil enemy," perhaps of the "Goth" and of the "Vandal." The profound, icy mistrust which the German provokes, as soon as he arrives at power—even at the present time—is always still an aftermath of that inextinguishable horror with which for whole centuries Europe has regarded the wrath of the blonde Teuton beast. . . .

. . . One may be perfectly justified in being always afraid of the blonde beast that lies at the core of all aristocratic races, and in being on one's guard: but who would not a hundred times prefer to be afraid, when one at the same time admires, than to be immune from fear, at the cost of being perpetually obsessed with the loathsome spectacle of the distorted, the dwarfed, the stunted, the envenomed? And is that not our fate? What produces to-day our repulsion towards "man"?—for we *suffer* from "man," there is no doubt about it. It is not fear; it is rather that we have nothing more to fear from men; it is that the worm "man" is in the foreground and pullulates; it is that the "tame man," the wretched mediocre and unedifying creature, has learnt to consider himself a goal and a pinnacle, an inner meaning, an historic principle, a "higher man"; yes, it is that he has a certain right so to consider himself, in so far as he feels that in contrast to that excess of deformity, disease, exhaustion, and effeteness whose odour is beginning to pollute present-day Europe, he at any rate has achieved a relative success, he at any rate still says "yes" to life.

GOODNESS AND THE WILL TO POWER

What is good?—All that enhances the feeling of power, the Will to Power, and the power itself in man. What is bad?—All that proceeds from weakness. What is happiness?—The feeling that power is increasing—that resistance has been overcome.

Not contentment, but more power; not peace at any price but war; not virtue, but competence (virtue in the Renaissance sense, *virtu,* free from all moralistic acid). The first principle of our humanism: The weak and the failures shall perish. They ought even to be helped to perish.

What is more harmful than any vice?—Practical sympathy and pity for all the failures and all the weak: Christianity.

Christianity is the religion of pity. Pity opposes the noble passions which heighten our vitality. It has a depressing effect, depriving us of strength. As we multiply the instances of pity we gradually lose our strength of nobility. Pity makes suffering contagious and under certain conditions it may cause a total loss of life and vitality out of all proportion to the magnitude of the cause. . . . Pity is the practice of nihilism.

For Further Reflection

1. What do you make of the parable of God's death? What is its significance for ethics?

2. A good exercise for getting a grip on the radicality of Nietzsche's ethics is to read Jesus's Sermon on the Mount (chapter 7) after reading Nietzsche. Discuss the contrast.

3. Compare Nietzsche's ethics with Aristotle's ethics of virtue (chapter 6). What are the similarities and differences? How might Aristotle respond to the charge that his ethics are really a "gentleman's" version of Nietzsche's more shocking ideas?

On the Origin of Good and Evil

RICHARD TAYLOR

Richard Taylor taught philosophy at Brown University, Rochester University, and Union College. In this essay he argues that morality, especially good and evil, is not a transcendental but a naturalistic reality, something that originates in the fact that we are *conative* beings (having desires and felt needs). If we had no desires, no values would exist—no good and evil, which are functional terms, referring to our goals and interests. Right and wrong emerge in social situations, as rules for behavior. They are based on common goals and interests. The rules and practices that either promote cooperation toward meeting our desires or resolve interpersonal conflict are *right* rules and practices, and those rules and practices that hinder cooperation and conflict resolution are *wrong* ones.

It has, as we have seen, been fairly characteristic of moral philosophers to begin with an assumed dichotomy between what *is* and what *ought* to be. Having turned their backs on the former as having little relevance to philosophical ethics, they have proclaimed the content of the latter as the unique realm of ethics. Some, in fact, have declared it a fallacy even to attempt to derive any philosophy of what ought to be from what in fact is, which pretty much amounts to declaring that facts can have little bearing upon ethics. One result of this is that moral philosophy has all too often resembled declamation. The advocates for the various and conflicting programs have had little to appeal to other than their own intuitions of things, these being sometimes baptized as the deliverances of "practical reason" and the like.

I am now going to remove this distinction between *is* and *ought*. More precisely, I shall show that all moral distinctions, beginning with the basic distinction between good and evil, are based entirely on certain facts and, in particular, on facts concerning human nature.

From Richard Taylor, *Good and Evil* (Amherst, NY: Prometheus Books). Copyright © 1984. Reprinted by permission of the publisher.

It is because men are the kind of beings they are—namely, what I have called conative beings—that the distinction between good and evil arises in the first place. Once this has been seen, we can see what good and evil in fact are. This basic distinction then having been made clear—and having been based not on intuitions and sentiments or abstract reasoning but on a certain conception of human nature—we can derive the further distinctions between moral right and wrong and give a fairly clear content to the idea of the common good.

MEN AS CONATIVE BEINGS

Men are rational or cognitive beings, but to say this is very far from stating the whole truth about them. So far as ethics is concerned, it leaves entirely out of account the most important fact about men, that they are desiderative or conative beings as well. I have already explained what this means, but it needs to be briefly reiterated here, as it is crucial to establishing the distinction between good and evil.

To describe men as conative is not to say anything at all abstruse or metaphysical, as this bit of terminology might suggest. It is only to call attention to a fact of human nature with which everyone is perfectly familiar: men have needs, desires, and goals; they pursue ends; they have certain wants and generally go about trying to satisfy them in various ways. Psychologists, metaphysicians, and others might have conflicting theories concerning how this fact is to be understood and explained, but the fact itself is hardly open to any question. It is more obvious that men are, in the sense just explained, conative beings, than that they are rational ones. There are men whom one might genuinely doubt to be rational, but it is doubtful whether anyone has ever seen a living man whom he suspected had no needs, desires, or wants. Such a man would be totally inactive and resemble a statue more than a man.

Thus, when a man is seen doing anything, it can generally be asked why he is doing it, what he is doing it for, or what he is trying to accomplish. This need not suggest that his behavior is not caused in the usual ways, although some might want to maintain this. What it does mean is that there is some point to what he is doing, some outcome that he intends. It implies nothing more.

For example, a man is seen operating a typewriter. Why is he doing that? Perhaps he is writing a letter, or an editorial, or something of that sort. In short, he has some purpose, and his typewriting activity is his means to fulfilling it. Or a man is seen running. What for? Perhaps to get to a store before it closes, or to catch a bus. Again, he has some purpose and is trying to fulfill it by running. Or once more, a man is seen walking toward a pump with an empty bucket. What for? Presumably, to fill the bucket (a goal) to enable himself to drink, wash, and so on (further purposes or goals).

I have used these exceedingly commonplace examples of human activity to illustrate three points. The first is that voluntary or deliberate human activity is generally interpreted as goal-directed. When we ask why a man is doing whatever it is that he is doing, we are usually seeking some explanation in terms of what he is trying to accomplish by that activity. This presupposes something about men that is universally taken for granted: men have goals and purposes and wants and desires, and they generally act in ways they consider appropriate to fulfilling them. It presupposes, in fact, that they are conative beings or, as I shall sometimes express it, that they are beings having desires and wants.

The second point is that, in speaking of a man's goals or purposes, one need not be referring to some *ultimate* goal, or even to any that is very important. The goal of one's activity might be exceedingly trivial and of only momentary significance, as in the foregoing examples. It could hardly be one's ultimate goal, or the goal of one's lifetime, to fill a bucket with water or to catch a bus. Yet, that might be precisely what his goal is then and there. Of course most men do have larger, more long-range goals. A man will spend years struggling, for example, in pursuit of some objective important to him, such as a degree in medicine, or perhaps fame as an author. Some men do devote the better part of their lives to ends having that kind of personal importance. In speaking of human behavior as goal-directed, however, I do not have this sort of thing primarily in mind, even though I include it. What I am calling attention to is much simpler and more commonplace. The conative aspect of human nature is as well exhibited by a man munching an apple or swatting a fly as it is by someone devoting his lifetime to a great ambition.

And the third point is that reason appears to enter into men's purposeful activity primarily to devise the means to attain the ends and has little to do with ends themselves. Thus, if a man wants to fill a bucket with water, it is in the clearest sense rational that he should carry it to the pump, as the most elementary reason or intelligence

indicates that this is the appropriate means to that end. Merely wishing that pail might become filled, or trying to find some way to bring
the pump to the pail, would be unreasonable, precisely in the sense
that these are not means that give much promise of working. There
is not, however, any reason for filling the pail in the first place. There
is, to be sure, some further purpose that can thus be fulfilled—the
purpose of drinking, for example, or of washing—but this only indicates that filling the pail, which is his immediate purpose, is in turn
a means to still some further purpose. It is, for example, neither
rational nor irrational that one should want to drink; it is merely an
expression of fact that he is thirsty. In the same sense, it is neither
rational nor irrational that a man should want to swat a fly, or catch
a bus, or become a physician, or attain fame as an author. These are
simply statements of this or that man's aims or goals, both trivial and
great, and they have nothing to do with reason. How they are to be
reached, on the other hand, has a great deal to do with reason, for
in general, one can set about trying to accomplish whatever it is he
wants to accomplish in either an intelligent and rational way or otherwise. To say he is pursuing his goals in an intelligent way is only
to say, as an inference from experience, that the means he adopts
has some promise of succeeding.

CONATION AS THE PRECONDITION
OF GOOD AND EVIL

With these rather commonplace observations in mind, let us now
ask what conditions are necessary in order that any distinction
between good and evil and between right and wrong can be made.
That is, what must be presupposed in saying of something that it
is good, or that it is bad, or in saying of an action that it is morally
right or morally wrong?

Unthinking men have a tendency to assume that some things are
just naturally good and others bad, and some actions right and some
wrong, and that we need only to discover which are which. Even
some of the most thoughtful philosophers, as we have seen, have
started out with the same assumption. Thus, it is supposed that men
are born into a world in which these distinctions already hold. Many
have insisted that these distinctions cannot either have been contrived by men, or have awaited man's invention of laws, conven-

tions, and customs. Ever so many things are man-made, including laws and moral customs; however, it is often thought that we cannot suppose the ultimate distinctions between good and evil or right and wrong to be such, for this would render all ethics, all justice, and all morality entirely relative. Indeed, most philosophers have thought that the problem of the moralist is simply to discover the true nature of goodness and rightness; they have disagreed not on whether such things exist independently of men, but on what *is* truly good, and what is truly right.

But now let us note that the basic distinction between good and evil could not even theoretically be drawn in a world that we imagined to be devoid of all life. That is, if we suppose the world to be exactly as it is, except that it contains not one living thing, it seems clear that nothing in it would be good and nothing bad. It would just be a dead world, turning through space with a lifeless atmosphere. Having deprived our imagined world of all life, we can modify it in numberless ways, but by no such modification can we ever produce the slightest hint of good or evil in it until we introduce at least one living being capable of reacting in one way or another to the world as that being finds it. Thus, we can imagine on the one hand that it is filled with things satisfying, lovely, and beautiful—with sunrises and sunsets, pleasing sights and sounds and fragrant odors, and with all things that beings like ourselves would find necessary and agreeable to life. Or we can imagine the opposite—a world that is dark and cold, filled with nauseous smells and barren of anything that would redeem such bleak aspects. But so long as we suppose that neither of these worlds does contain any being like ourselves, or any sentient being whatever, then neither world is *better* or *worse* than the other. Each is simply a world of facts, neutral with respect to good or evil, and destined to remain so until we suppose at least one onlooker capable of some sort of reaction to such facts.

Next we note that, if we begin to add inhabitants to this world who are, like ourselves, more or less rational, intelligent, and capable of perception but who, unlike ourselves, have no needs, purposes, or desires, the distinction between good and evil still does not arise. Imagine, for example, a whole colony of machinelike beings, living together and interacting in various ways. These beings, we can suppose, can perceive what is going on around them, distinguish between true and false, and make various inferences; but they are machinelike in that nothing matters to them, nothing makes any difference so far as their needs and purposes are concerned, because they have no needs or purposes, they do not care about anything. If it is raining, they observe that it is raining, but they seek no shelter, for they have no interest in being dry. If it is bitterly cold, then again they note this fact, but make no attempt to warm themselves because they care not whether they are warm or cold. If one of these beings observes another moving with great speed and force toward itself, it infers that a collision is impending, but makes no attempt to step aside, because it has no purpose that would be frustrated by such a collision. It has not even the desire to perpetuate its own existence, because it has no desires whatever. Having then been run down and broken by the onrushing being, losing a few limbs perhaps, it simply notes that this has happened, but it does not retaliate, because it had no interest in preserving any of its limbs or other parts anyway; and so on.

Such beings are, to be sure, difficult to imagine, for if we suppose them to be capable of perceiving, then we seem to imagine them to be living things, and it is difficult to imagine *any* living thing having no interests or purposes whatever, not even an interest in self-preservation. But of course we need not imagine that they are living things; we can instead suppose that they are enormously complicated machines, if that makes it easier. And then we need only suppose that they share with certain living things, such as ourselves, the capacity to perceive what is going on and to draw certain conclusions from what they perceive, but that they do *not* share with other living things, such as ourselves, any interest in what is going on. They are, in short, possessed of some degree of intelligence, but of no will whatever.

Now I think it is clear that a world inhabited by such beings would still be a world devoid of any good or evil. Like the first world we imagined, which did not even contain any beings of the most elementary intelligence, this one might contain anything we care to put into it without there arising the least semblance of good or of evil—until we imagine it to contain at least one being having some need, interest, or purpose. It would not matter to the beings just described whether their world was one filled with sunlight, warmth, and beauty, or dark and cold and filled with nauseous smells, because nothing would matter to them. They could tell the difference between sunlight and darkness, between warmth and cold, but they could in no way tell the difference between good and bad. Such a distinction would in fact have no meaning to them, and if they found their world dark, smelly, and cold they would have no basis for pronouncing it bad, simply because they would have no preference for any other kind of world.

THE EMERGENCE OF GOOD AND EVIL

Thus far, then, there is no good and no evil; there is nothing but bare facts of this kind or that.

But now let us suppose a world, much like our own, except that it contains throughout its vastness just one sentient being, a being who, like ourselves, cannot only perceive what is contained in the world around him and make certain inferences, but one to whom what he finds makes a difference. Suddenly, with the introduction of just one such being, certain things in the world do acquire the aspect of good and evil. Those things are good that this one being finds satisfying to his needs and desires, and those bad to which he reacts in the opposite way. Things in the world are not merely perceived by this being, but perceived as holding promise or threat to whatever interests him. Thus, the things that nourish and give warmth and enhance life are deemed good, and those that frustrate and threaten are deemed bad. The distinction between good and evil in a world containing only one living being possessed of needs and wants arises, then, only in relation to those needs and wants, and in no way existed in their absence. In the most general terms, those things are good that satisfy this being's actual wants, those that frustrate them are bad.

Now, with this picture still before us, let us note two things that are highly significant for the problems before us. The first is that the judgments of this solitary being concerning good and evil are as *absolute* as any judgment can be. Such a being is, indeed, the measure of all things: of good things as good and of bad things as bad. Whatever this being finds and declares to be good *is* good, and what he similarly finds to be evil, *is* evil. No distinction can be made, in terms of this being, between what is merely good *for him* and what is good *absolutely*. Whatever is good for him is good absolutely; there is no higher standard of goodness. For what could it be? If good and evil in this world arise only in relation to this being's wants and needs, then what could it possibly mean to say that something satisfies these but is nevertheless bad, or that something frustrates them but is nevertheless good? There simply is nothing else, apart from these wants and needs, in terms of which good and evil can possibly be measured, or even exist.

The second thing to note is that, even though good and evil have emerged with the appearance in this world of a single living being having wants and needs, no moral obligation has similarly arisen. The distinction between moral *right* and *wrong* has not yet come into the picture at all. That such a being should find something useful and agreeable and subsequently seize it, or find something threatening and shun it, is neither right nor wrong. Whatever he finds and wants is his for the taking, by a kind of natural right that is nothing but the absence of any natural wrong, and he cannot possibly have an obligation to undertake what would injure him, or even so much as make him the least uncomfortable. Although he can in this moral solitude create good and evil for himself, merely by his own declaration of what he finds things to be, he can in no way inflict them. For who could be his beneficiary or victim, besides himself? To whom could he owe any obligation to do anything? And by what standard, other than good and evil themselves, over which he is the sole judge, could any action of his be deemed right or wrong? He could, to be sure, fail to act in his own best interest, or even injure himself through neglect or stupidity, for which he would be accountable to no one. It would be as inappropriate to ascribe any moral responsibility to this solitary being as to the merest insect crawling through the grass.

Our next step, then, is to add another being like ourselves, another conative being with his own feelings, wants, and interests, and to suppose that the two who now inhabit our world have some interaction with each other. No new distinction between good and evil is introduced with the introduction of this new inhabitant, for that distinction emerged, complete and perfect, as soon as we assumed the existence of but one such inhabitant. With this small plurality of beings, it remains just what it was before. The first inhabitant deemed those things good that he found agreeable to his needs and purposes, and those things bad that threatened the opposite, and in this judgment he was absolutely correct. For him, the good and evil of things consisted of precisely such promise and threat to his interests. Such, accordingly, will it also be for our second sentient and goal-directed inhabitant. Those things will be good for him that promise fulfillment of his aims, whether grand or trifling, and those that threaten the opposite will be bad. In this judgment he, too, cannot err. For this will be precisely what the distinction between good and evil will mean to him, as it is what it means to the first; it will be the condition, and the only condition, of such a distinction being drawn by either of them. And we are not, it should be noted, here supposing any power of reasoning in either of our two beings. We do not suppose them to be appraising the various features of their common environment in terms of what they promise or threaten, and then *inferring* from such features that they have the moral qualities of good or evil. We do not even assume these two beings to be rational, though the picture is not altered in case they are. We only assume them to be sentient beings with needs, or in other words, beings who desire and shun, and can feel it when their needs are fulfilled, and when they are not.

THE EMERGENCE OF RIGHT AND WRONG

There was, we noted, no place for such ethical notions as right and wrong or for moral obligation, so long as we imagined a world containing only one purposeful and sentient being, although the presence of such a being was enough to produce good and evil. With the introduction of a multiplicity of such beings, however, we have supplied the foundation for these additional notions, for they are based on the fact that the aims or purposes of such beings can conflict. Thus, two or more such beings can covet the same thing. In that case each will deem it a good, but it can easily arise that not both can possess it, that its possession by one will mean deprivation for the other. The result is a conflict of wills, which can lead to a mutual aggression in which each stands to lose more than the thing for which they are contending is worth to either of them. Such a situation can produce a threat to life itself, for example, and without life all good and evil are reduced to zero.

There is, moreover, another side to the coin. For just as the wills of two purposeful beings can conflict, in the manner just suggested, so also can they coincide in a very significant way. That is, situations can arise in which each of two such beings needs the help of the other in order to attain what it wants, or to ward off some evil. They may, for example, be threatened by some force, animate or inanimate, that the strength of neither is sufficient to overcome, but from which their combined strength offers some hope of safety. Or again, each may find that he possesses in excess of his own needs something that the other requires. One, for example, may possess an excess of food, of which the other has none, while the latter one possesses an excess of the requirements for shelter, entirely lacking to the former. The possibility of mutual giving and taking thus presents itself, wherein each can benefit greatly at small cost to himself. Or again, two such beings may have some common end, such as the begetting of children, for which some sort of cooperation is needed by the very nature of things, and so on.

The supposition of a multiplicity of beings, each with its own needs and purposes, presents, in short, numberless possibilities for (1) conflict, and (2) cooperation. Possibilities of the first kind are loaded with the threat of evil, and those of the second kind with the promise of good, still thinking of good and evil in the sense already adduced—namely, as that which satisfies or fulfills, and that which frustrates felt needs and goals.

RIGHT AND WRONG AS RELATIVE TO RULES

If needs are to be satisfied and goals fulfilled, however, then situations of conflict and, particularly, situations of cooperation must be resolved in the context of *rules,* using the notion of rules in an extremely broad sense that encompasses any regular and predictable behavior. Thus, it becomes a "rule" that two or more such beings, faced with a common threat, shall abstain from attacking each other until that threat is overcome. It becomes another rule that they shall meet the threat together by combining their resources, inasmuch as acting in accordance with such rules will enable each to avoid what appears as an evil. When two such beings each covet the same thing, and not both can possess it, it may become a rule that it remains with him who first possessed it. The underlying basis for such a rule is that, if it is disregarded, the coveted thing may end up in the hands of neither, and that evils even greater than this, such as mutual injury or even death, may follow instead. When each of two such beings possesses an excess of what is sought by the other, a rule of trading becomes obviously advantageous to both. Through such behavior, the good of each is enhanced at no significant cost. The alternative is combat, in which each would be faced with the possibility of total loss.

Now it should be clear from this that by rules I do not mean rational principles of conduct, in the sense that it would require any powers of reason to discover them, much less do I mean principles that are set forth in any coherent writing or speech. They need not be things that are formulated at all. Rules, in the sense that I am now considering them, are nothing but practices or ways of behaving that are more or less regular and that can, therefore, be expected. They are, on the other hand, rational in this sense: such behavior offers promise, to those who behave in the manner in question, of avoiding evil and attaining good. Mutual aggression, for example, always presents the threat of great and unpredictable evil to each aggressor, and the possibility of such evil is almost certain to outweigh any possibility of good. To the extent, therefore, that some good can be ensured by a certain mode of behavior or, as I am using the term, by action in accordance with a rule, and that such behavior will remove the threat of evil contained in any situation of combat, then action in accordance with the rule is better than combat. In that sense, but only in that sense, it is more rational.

Suppose, for example, that among a certain people the practice arises that men, on approaching one another, extend a forearm with the palm of the hand open and exposed to view, each thus indicating that he is unarmed. The gesture is recognized and acknowledged by each then grasping the other's open hand, that is, by shaking hands. Now here, clearly, is a rule, as I am using the term, even though it does not need to be formulated or embodied in any code. It is simply a regular mode of behavior. It has as its obvious purpose the avoidance of evil and the advancement of good and is in that sense, but that sense only, rational. It would be most treacherously violated by one who, extending his open hand of friendship, assaulted his greeter with a weapon concealed in his other hand. The treachery of this would consist in using the rule to promote the very evil the rule was meant to avoid.

THE WORLD AS IT IS

We have been imagining, then, a world, at first lifeless and barren, that gradually becomes occupied with beings having needs, feelings, and purposes. Until the appearance of the first such being, that world contains no hint of good or evil, but both arise the moment he comes into the picture. With the multiplication of such beings, the possibilities of further goods and evils arise with the appearance of situations of cooperation and conflict. Good is increased and enhanced by the former and evil by the latter. Cooperation, however, and the safe resolution of conflict obviously require certain regular modes of behavior, or what I have called rules. These notions having been made tolerably clear, we can now refine and elaborate on the imaginary picture with which we began until it begins to resemble the world of men in which we actually live.

Thus, we can suppose that the multiplicity of sentient and purposeful beings by which our imaginary world is inhabited are men like ourselves, for we, too, are sentient and purposeful beings. We can suppose that those modes of behavior required for cooperation and the resolution of conflict situations become actual precepts, conveyed by one generation to the next, and that the most important of them come to be rules embodied in traditional literature for which men have a certain awe. They are, thus, passed from generation to generation, like the Ten Commandments of scripture. Others come to assume the form of written laws, and various practical means are hit on for securing, as nearly as possible, the adherence to them on the part of all. Groupings of men are formed for the attainment of the maximum of good for some or all and the minimization of evil. Thus do societies arise, by their common adherence to rules that become more elaborate as the societies themselves become larger and more complex. The behavior required by such rules rises, by some degree or other, to that level we call civilized conduct; but the basic principle of those rules remains exactly what it was from the outset: the minimization of conflict and its consequent evil, and the maximization of cooperation and its consequent good.

All this is, of course, but a sketch, and a very superficial one, but no more is really needed for our present purpose, which is to explain good and evil and moral right and wrong.

How, then, do moral right and wrong arise? The answer is fairly obvious in the light of what has been said. Right is simply the adherence to rule, and wrong is violation of it. The notions of right and wrong absolutely presuppose the existence of rules, at least in the broad sense of rule with which we began. That two beings should fight and injure each other in their contest for something that each covets, and thereby, perhaps, each lose the good he wanted to seize, is clearly an evil to both. But in the absence of a rule of behavior—that is, some anticipated behavior to the contrary—no wrong has been done; only an evil has been produced. Given such a rule, however—for example, given the simple and rudimentary expectation that the thing in question shall be his who first took it—then a wrong is committed by the one who attempts to divest the holder of that good. The wrong comes into being with the violation of the rule, and in no way existed ahead of the rule. The same is, of course, true of right. If, for example, we presuppose no expectation that a good may be enjoyed in peace by whoever first seizes it, then, if another nevertheless, in the absence of any such rule, abstains from seizing that good from its first possessor, this potential aggressor has clearly fostered a good, simply by eschewing an evil. But he has in no way done "the right thing," for the notion of *right* conduct can have no meaning in the absence of some sort of rule. If one is tempted to say that this would-be aggressor has done something morally right, then one will find that all he means is that he has produced an effect that was good. That is something entirely different. One also may be reading into a situation, in which, by hypothesis, there is no rule to which to adhere, certain rules of right and wrong that one has learned to respect.

For Further Reflection

1. Examine Taylor's theory of good and evil and right and wrong. First, note that he claims that humans are basically conative beings—moved by will and desire—rather than rational beings. Do you agree with this? What role does he think reason plays in life?

2. Outline the four stages in the thought process, from a universe with no conscious beings to his final stage. Where do good and evil enter in? Where do right and wrong enter in? How are the two categories related to each other? Do you agree with Taylor's analysis? Explain your answer.

3. What, according to Taylor, is the purpose of rules? Give an example of a rule to illustrate his point. Do you find his analysis convincing? Explain your answer.

4. Are some rules better than others?

Further Readings for Chapter 2

Hallie, Philip P. *Cruelty*. Middletown, Conn.: Wesleyan University Press, 1982.

Kekes, John. "The Reflexivity of Evil," *Social Philosophy and Policy,* vol. 15, no. 1 (1998).

Midgley, Mary. *Wickedness: A Philosophical Essay*. Boston: Routledge and Kegan Paul, 1984.

Milo, Ronald. *Immorality*. Princeton: Princeton University Press, 1984.

Milo, Ronald. "Virtue, Knowledge and Wickedness," *Social Philosophy and Policy,* vol. 15, no. 1 (1998).

Nietzsche, Frederich. *Beyond Good and Evil,* trans. R. J. Hollingdale. Penguin, 1990.

Taylor, Richard. *Good and Evil*. Buffalo, N.Y.: Prometheus, 1970.

CHAPTER 3

Is Everything Relative?

Is morality essentially relative or are there objective moral truths? This question haunts contemporary society. On the one hand, anthropologists have uncovered a multitudinous array of variegated cultural codes and moral practices. Who are we to judge another culture? Tolerance would seem to require that we allow for a plethora of practices and ways of expressing morality. We've been taught that multicultural diversity is a good in its own right, so we should be accepting of difference. On the other hand, some actions seem wrong in principle (torturing or killing the innocent, breaking promises, lying, and destroying other people's property) and some actions seem morally good (helping people who are in need, keeping contracts, cooperating for mutual benefit, and promoting justice). How do we reconcile these opposing insights?

The readings in this chapter inquire into the strengths and weaknesses of moral relativism, the theory that the validity of moral principles is dependent on cultural or subjective acceptance. Our first reading is an ancient observation of the Greek historian Herodotus on how different cultures project their customs onto the heavens, identifying them with eternal verities. Our second reading is a defense of relativism by the cultural anthropologist Ruth Benedict, who develops the theme set forth by Herodotus. Cultural norms are the colored glasses through which we view all our world. In our third reading, I critique moral relativism and defend its opposite, moral objectivism. I argue, that while some things are relative, there are universal moral truths, valid for all people at all times. In our fourth reading, "Judge Not?," Jean Bethke Elshtain questions the dictum which is at the heart of relativism. And, finally, Henrik Ibsen illustrates the philosophy of moral objectivism in the person of Dr. Stockmann, who defies his culture in the name of truth.

Custom Is King

HERODOTUS

Herodotus (485–430 B.C.), a Greek and the first Western historian, in this brief passage from his *Histories* illustrates cultural relativism and may suggest that ethical relativism is the correct view ("culture is king").

Thus it appears certain to me, by a great variety of proofs, that Cambyses was raving mad; he would not else have set himself to make a mock of holy rites and long-established usages. For if one were to offer men to choose out of all the customs in the world such as seemed to them the best, they would examine the whole number, and end by preferring their own; so convinced are they that their own usages far surpass those of all others. Unless, therefore, a man was mad, it is not likely that he would make sport of such matters. That people have this feeling about their laws may be seen by very many proofs: among others, by the following. Darius, after he had got the kingdom, called into his presence certain Greeks who were at hand, and asked—"What he should pay them to eat the bodies of their fathers when they died?" To which they answered, that there was no sum that would tempt them to do such a thing. He then sent for certain Indians, of the race called Callatians, men who eat their fathers, and asked them, while the Greeks stood by, and knew by the help of an interpreter all that was said— "What he should give them to burn the bodies of their fathers at their decease?" The Indians exclaimed aloud, and bade him forbear such language. Such is men's wont herein; and Pindar was right, in my judgment, when he said, "Custom is the king o'er all."

From Herodotus, *The Histories of Herodotus,* translated by George Rawlinson (New York: Appleton, 1859).

The Case for Moral Relativism

RUTH BENEDICT

Ruth Benedict (1887–1948), an American anthropologist, taught at Columbia University and is best known for her book *Patterns of Culture* (1934). Benedict sets forth a theory of moral relativism in which moral principles are based on the common beliefs and practices of social systems. Since these systems or cultures can vary, so can morality. Like a work of art, the social system chooses which theme of its repertoire of basic tendencies to emphasize and then goes about to create a more or less comprehensive system of mores to support those tendencies. What is considered normal or abnormal behavior will depend on the choices of these social systems, or what Benedict calls the "idea-practice pattern of the culture."

In this selection Benedict assembles a varied array of cultural data from her research of tribal behavior on an island in northwest Melanesia from which she draws her conclusions that moral relativism is the correct view of morality.

Modern social anthropology has become more and more a study of the varieties and common elements of cultural environment and the consequences of these in human behavior. For such a study of diverse social orders primitive peoples fortunately provide a laboratory not yet entirely vitiated by the spread of a standardized worldwide civilization. Dyaks and Hopis, Fijians and Yakuts are significant for psychological and sociological study because only among these simpler peoples has there been sufficient isolation to give opportunity for the development of localized social forms. In the higher cultures the standardization of custom and belief over a couple of continents has given a false sense of the inevitability of the particular forms that have gained currency, and we need to turn to a wider survey in order to check the conclusions we hastily base

From "Anthropology and the Abnormal," by Ruth Benedict, in *The Journal of General Psychology* 10 (1934): 59–82, a publication of the Helen Dwight Reid Educational Foundation.

upon this near-universality of familiar customs. Most of the simpler cultures did not gain the wide currency of the one which, out of our experience, we identify with human nature, but this was for various historical reasons, and certainly not for any that gives us as its carriers a monopoly of social good or of social sanity. Modern civilization, from this point of view, becomes not a necessary pinnacle of human achievement but one entry in a long series of possible adjustments.

These adjustments, whether they are in mannerisms like the ways of showing anger, or joy, or grief in any society, or in major human drives like those of sex, prove to be far more variable than experience in any one culture would suggest. In certain fields, such as that of religion or of formal marriage arrangements, these wide limits of variability are well known and can be fairly described. In others it is not yet possible to give a generalized account, but that does not absolve us of the task of indicating the significance of the work that has been done and of the problems that have arisen.

One of these problems relates to the customary modern normal-abnormal categories and our conclusions regarding them. In how far are such categories culturally determined, or in how far can we with assurance regard them as absolute? In how far can we regard inability to function socially as diagnostic of abnormality, or in how far is it necessary to regard this as a function of the culture?

As a matter of fact, one of the most striking facts that emerge from a study of widely varying cultures is the ease with which our abnormals function in other cultures. It does not matter what kind of "abnormality" we choose for illustration, those which indicate extreme instability, or those which are more in the nature of character traits like sadism or delusions of grandeur or of persecution, there are well-described cultures in which these abnormals function at ease and with honor, and apparently without danger or difficulty to the society. . . .

The most notorious of these is trance and catalepsy. Even a very mild mystic is aberrant in our culture. But most peoples have regarded even extreme psychic manifestations not only as normal and desirable, but even as characteristic of highly valued and gifted individuals. This was true even in our own cultural background in that period when Catholicism made the ecstatic experience the mark of sainthood. It is hard for us, born and brought up in a culture that makes no use of the experience, to realize how important a role it may play and how many individuals are capable of it, once it has been given an honorable place in any society. . . .

Cataleptic and trance phenomena are, of course, only one illustration of the fact that those whom we regard as abnormals may function adequately in other cultures. Many of our culturally discarded traits are selected for elaboration in different societies. Homosexuality is an excellent example, for in this case our attention is not constantly diverted, as in the consideration of trance, to the interruption of routine activity which it implies. Homosexuality poses the problem very simply. A tendency toward this trait in our culture exposes an individual to all the conflicts to which all aberrants are always exposed, and we tend to identify the consequences of this conflict with homosexuality. But these consequences are obviously local and cultural. Homosexuals in many societies are not incompetent, but they may be such if the culture asks adjustments of them that would strain any man's vitality. Wherever homosexuality has been given an honorable place in any society, those to whom it is congenial have filled adequately the honorable roles society assigns to them. Plato's *Republic* is, of course, the most convincing statement of such a reading of homosexuality. It is presented as one of the major means to the good life, and it was generally so regarded in Greece at that time.

The cultural attitude toward homosexuals has not always been on such a high ethical plane, but it has been very varied. Among many American Indian tribes there exists the institution of the berdache, as the French called them. These men-women were men who at puberty or thereafter took the dress and the occupations of women. Sometimes they married other men and lived with them. Sometimes they were men with no inversion, persons of weak sexual endowment who chose this role to avoid the jeers of the women. The berdaches were never regarded as of first-rate supernatural power, as similar men-women were in Siberia, but rather as leaders in women's occupations, good healers in certain diseases, or, among certain tribes, as the genial organizers of social affairs. In any case, they were socially placed. They were not left exposed to the conflicts that visit the deviant who is excluded from participation in the recognized patterns of his society.

The most spectacular illustrations of the extent to which normality may be culturally defined are those cultures where an abnormality of our culture is the cornerstone of their social structure. It is not possible to do justice to these possibilities in a short discussion. A recent study of an island of northwest Melanesia by Fortune describes a society built upon traits which we regard as beyond the border of paranoia. In this tribe the exogamic groups look upon each other as prime manipulators of black magic, so that one marries always into an enemy group which remains for life one's deadly and unappeasable foes. They look upon a good garden crop as a confession of theft, for everyone is engaged in making magic to induce into his garden the productiveness of his neighbors'; therefore no secrecy in the island is so rigidly insisted upon as the secrecy of a man's harvesting of his yams. Their polite phrase at the acceptance of a gift is, "And if you now poison me, how shall I repay you this present?" Their preoccupation with poisoning is constant; no woman ever leaves her cooking pot for a moment untended. Even the great affinal economic exchanges that are characteristic of this Melanesian culture area are quite altered in Dobu since they are incompatible with this fear and distrust that pervades the culture. They go farther and people the whole world outside their own quarters with such malignant spirits that all-night feasts and ceremonials simply do not occur here. They have even rigorous religiously enforced customs that forbid the sharing of seed even in one family group. Anyone else's food is deadly poison to you, so that communality of stores is out of the question. For some months before harvest the whole society is on the verge of starvation, but if one falls to the temptation and eats up one's seed yams, one is an outcast and a beachcomber for life. There is no coming back. It involves, as a matter of course, divorce and the breaking of all social ties.

Now in this society where no one may work with another and no one may share with another, Fortune describes the individual who was regarded by all his fellows as crazy. He was not one of those who periodically ran amok and, beside himself and frothing at the mouth, fell with a knife upon anyone he could reach. Such behavior they did not regard as putting anyone outside the pale. They did not even put the individuals who were known to be liable to these attacks under any kind of control. They merely fled when they saw the attack coming on and kept out of the way. "He would be all right tomorrow." But there was one man of sunny, kindly disposition who liked work and liked to be helpful. The compulsion was too strong for him to repress it in favor of the opposite tendencies of his culture. Men and women never spoke of him without laughing; he was silly and simple and definitely crazy. Nevertheless, to the ethnologist used to a culture that has, in Christianity, made his type the model of all virtue, he seemed a pleasant fellow. . . .

. . . Among the Kwakiutl it did not matter whether a relative had died in bed of disease, or by the hand of an enemy, in either case death was an affront to be wiped out by the death of another person. The fact that one had been caused to mourn was proof that one had been put upon. A chief's sister and her daughter had gone up to Victoria, and either because they drank bad whiskey or because their boat capsized they never came back. The chief called together his warriors, "Now I ask you, tribes, who shall wail? Shall I do it or shall another?" The spokesman answered, of course, "Not you, Chief. Let some other of the tribes." Immediately they set up the war pole to announce their intention of wiping out the injury, and gathered a war party. They set out, and found seven men and two children asleep and killed them. "Then they felt good when they arrived at Sebaa in the evening."

The point which is of interest to us is that in our society those who on that occasion would feel good when they arrived at Sebaa that evening would be the definitely abnormal. There would be some, even in our society, but it is not a recognized and approved mood under the circumstances. On the Northwest Coast those are favored and fortunate to whom that mood under those circumstances is congenial, and those to whom it is repugnant are unlucky. This latter minority can register in their own culture only by doing violence to their congenial responses and acquiring others that are difficult for them. The person, for instance, who, like a Plains Indian whose wife has been taken from him, is too proud to fight, can deal with the Northwest Coast civilization only by ignoring its strongest bents. If he cannot achieve it, he is the deviant in that culture, their instance of abnormality.

This head-hunting that takes place on the Northwest Coast after a death is no matter of blood revenge or of organized vengeance. There is no effort to tie up the subsequent killing with any responsibility on the part of the victim for the death of the person who is being mourned. A chief whose son has died goes visiting wherever his fancy dictates, and he says to his host, "My prince has died today, and you go with him." Then he kills him. In this, according to their interpretation, he acts nobly because he has not been downed. He has thrust back in return. The whole procedure is meaningless without the fundamental paranoid reading of bereavement. Death, like all the other untoward accidents of existence, confounds man's pride and can only be handled in the category of insults.

Behavior honored upon the Northwest Coast is one which is recognized as abnormal in our civilization, and yet it is sufficiently close to the attitudes of our own culture to be intelligible to us and to have a definite vocabulary with which we may discuss it. The megalomaniac paranoid trend is a definite danger in our society. It is encouraged by some of our major preoccupations, and it confronts us with a choice of two possible attitudes. One is to brand it as abnormal and reprehensible, and is the attitude we have chosen in our civilization. The other is to make it an essential attribute of ideal man, and this is the solution in the culture of the Northwest Coast.

These illustrations, which it has been possible to indicate only in the briefest manner, force upon us the fact that normality is culturally defined. An adult shaped to the drives and standards of either of these cultures, if he were transported into our civilization, would fall into our categories of abnormality. He would be faced with the psychic dilemmas of the socially unavailable. In his own culture, however, he is the pillar of society, the end result of socially inculcated mores, and the problem of personal instability in his case simply does not arise.

No one civilization can possibly utilize in its mores the whole potential range of human behavior. Just as there are great numbers of possible phonetic articulations, and the possibility of language depends on a selection and standardization of a few of these in order that speech communication may be possible at all, so the possibility of organized behavior of every sort, from the fashions of local dress and houses to the dicta of a people's ethics and religion, depends upon a similar selection among the possible behavior traits. In the field of recognized economic obligations or sex taboos this selection is as nonrational and subconscious a process as it is in the field of phonetics. It is a process which goes on in the group for long periods of time and is historically conditioned by innumerable accidents of isolation or of contact of peoples. In any comprehensive study of psychology, the selection that different cultures have made in the course of history within the great circumference of potential behavior is of great significance.

Every society, beginning with some slight inclination in one direction or another, carries its preference farther and farther, integrating itself more and more completely upon its chosen basis, and discarding those types of behavior that are uncongenial. Most of those organizations of personality that seem to us most uncontrovertibly abnormal have been used by different civilizations in the very foundations of their institutional life. Conversely the most valued traits of our normal individuals have been looked on in differently organized cultures as aberrant. Normality, in short, within a very wide range, is culturally defined. It is primarily a term for the socially elaborated segment of human behavior in any culture; and abnormality, a term for the segment that that particular civilization does not use. The very eyes with which we see the problem are conditioned by the long traditional habits of our own society.

It is a point that has been made more often in relation to ethics than in relation to psychiatry. We do not any longer make the mistake of deriving the morality of our locality and decade directly from the inevitable constitution of human nature. We do not elevate it to the dignity of a first principle. We recognize that morality differs in every society, and is a convenient term for socially approved habits. Mankind has always preferred to say, "It is morally good," rather than "It is habitual," and the fact of this preference is matter enough for a critical science of ethics. But historically the two phrases are synonymous.

The concept of the normal is properly a variant of the concept of the good. It is that which society has approved. A normal action is one which falls well within the limits of expected behavior for a particular society. Its variability among different peoples is essentially a function of the variability of the behavior patterns that different societies have created for themselves, and can never be wholly divorced from a consideration of culturally institutionalized types of behavior.

Each culture is a more or less elaborate working-out of the potentialities of the segment it has chosen. In so far as a civilization is well integrated and consistent within itself, it will tend to carry farther and farther, according to its nature, its initial impulse toward a particular type of action, and from the point of view of any other culture those elaborations will include more and more extreme and aberrant traits.

Each of these traits, in proportion as it reinforces the chosen behavior patterns of that culture, is for that culture normal. Those individuals to whom it is congenial either congenitally, or as the result of childhood sets, are accorded prestige in that culture, and are not visited with the social contempt or disapproval which their traits would call down upon them in a society that was differently organized. On the other hand, those individuals whose character- istics are not congenial to the selected type of human behavior in that community are the deviants, no matter how valued their per- sonality traits may be in a contrasted civilization.

The Dobuan who is not easily susceptible to fear of treachery, who enjoys work and likes to be helpful, is their neurotic and re- garded as silly. On the Northwest Coast the person who finds it difficult to read life in terms of an insult contest will be the person upon whom fall all the difficulties of the culturally unprovided for. The person who does not find it easy to humiliate a neighbor, nor to see humiliation in his own experience, who is genial and lov- ing, may, of course, find some unstandardized way of achieving satisfactions in his society, but not in the major patterned responses that his culture requires of him. If he is born to play an important role in a family with many hereditary privileges, he can succeed only by doing violence to his whole personality. If he does not succeed, he has betrayed his culture; that is, he is abnormal.

I have spoken of individuals as having sets toward certain types of behavior, and of these sets as running sometimes counter to the types of behavior which are institutionalized in the culture to which they belong. From all that we know of contrasting cultures it seems clear that differences of temperament occur in every society. The matter has never been made the subject of investigation, but from the available material it would appear that these temperament types are very likely of universal recurrence. That is, there is an ascertain- able range of human behavior that is found wherever a sufficiently large series of individuals is observed. But the proportion in which behavior types stand to one another in different societies is not uni- versal. The vast majority of individuals in any group are shaped to the fashion of that culture. In other words, most individuals are plas- tic to the moulding force of the society into which they are born. In a society that values trance, as in India, they will have supernormal experience. In a society that institutionalizes homosexuality, they will be homosexual. In a society that sets the gathering of possessions as the chief human objective, they will amass property. The deviants, whatever the type of behavior the culture has institutionalized, will remain few in number, and there seems no more difficulty in moulding the vast malleable majority to the "normality" of what we consider an aberrant trait, such as delusions of reference, than to the normality of such accepted behavior patterns as acquisitiveness. The small proportion of the number of the deviants in any culture is not a function of the sure instinct with which that society has built itself upon the fundamental sanities, but of the universal fact that, happily, the majority of mankind quite readily take any shape that is presented to them. . . .

For Further Reflection

1. Is Benedict correct in saying that our culture is "but one entry in a long series of possible adjustments"? What are the implications of this statement?

2. Can we separate the descriptive (or fact-stating) aspect of anthropological study from the prescriptive (evaluative) aspect of evaluating cultures? Are there some independent criteria by which we can say that some cultures are better than others? Can you think how this project might be begun?

3. What are the implications of Benedict's claim that morality is simply whatever a culture deems normal behavior? Is this a satisfactory equation? Can you apply it to the institution of slavery or the Nazi policy of anti-Semitism?

4. What is the significance of Benedict's statement, "The very eyes with which we see the problem are conditioned by the long traditional habits of our own society"? Can we apply the conceptual relativism embodied in this statement to her own position?

The Case Against Moral Relativism

LOUIS P. POJMAN

In this article Pojman analyzes the structure of ethical relativism as constituted by two theses: the diversity thesis and the dependency thesis. Then he examines two types of ethical relativism: subjectivism and conventionalism, arguing that both types have serious problems. Next he indicates a way of taking into account the insights of relativism while maintaining an objectivist position. Pojman outlines two objectivist arguments and concludes by suggesting some reasons why people have been misled by relativist arguments.

"WHO'S TO JUDGE WHAT'S RIGHT OR WRONG?"

> Like many people, I have always been instinctively a moral relativist. As far back as I can remember . . . it has always seemed to be obvious that the dictates of morality arise from some sort of convention or understanding among people, that different people arrive at different understandings, and that there are no basic moral demands that apply to everyone. This seemed so obvious to me I assumed it was everyone's instinctive view, or at least everyone who gave the matter any thought in this day and age.
>
> —Gilbert Harman[1]

Ethical relativism is the doctrine that the moral rightness and wrongness of actions vary from society to society and that there are not absolute universal moral standards on all men at all times. Accordingly, it holds that whether or not

---

[1]Gilbert Harman, "Is There a Single True Morality?" in *Morality, Reason and Truth*, eds. David Copp and David Zimmerman (Rowman & Allenheld, 1984).

it is right for an individual to act in a certain way depends
on or is relative to the society to which he belongs.

—John Ladd[2]

Gilbert Harman's intuitions about the self-evidence of ethical relativism contrast strikingly with Plato's or Kant's equal certainty about
the truth of objectivism, the doctrine that universally valid or true
ethical principles exist.[3] "Two things fill the soul with ever new and
increasing wonder and reverence the oftener and more fervently
reflection ponders on it: the starry heavens above and the moral
law within," wrote Kant. On the basis of polls taken in my ethics
and introduction to philosophy classes over the past several years,
Harman's views may signal a shift in contemporary society's moral
understanding. The polls show a two-to-one ratio in favor of moral
relativism over moral absolutism, with fewer than five percent of
the respondents recognizing that a third position between these two
polar opposites might exist. Of course, I'm not suggesting that all
of these students had a clear understanding of what relativism
entails, for many who said they were relativists also contended in
the same polls that abortion except to save the mother's life is
always wrong, that capital punishment is always wrong, or that suicide is never morally permissible.

Among my university colleagues, a growing number also seem to
embrace moral relativism. Recently one of my nonphilosopher colleagues voted to turn down a doctoral dissertation proposal because
the student assumed an objectivist position in ethics. (Ironically, I

---

[2]John Ladd, *Ethical Relativism* (Wadsworth, 1973).

[3]Lest I be misunderstood, in this essay I will generally be speaking about the
validity rather than the truth of moral principles. Validity holds that they are
proper guides to action, whereas truth presupposes something more. It presupposes Moral Realism, the theory that moral principles have special ontological status (see Part IX). Although this may be true, not all objectivists
agree. R. M. Hare, for instance, argues that moral principles, while valid, do
not have truth value. They are like imperatives which have practical application but cannot be said to be true. Also, I am mainly concerned with the
status of *principles*, not theories themselves. There may be a plurality of
valid moral theories, all containing the same objective principles. I am grateful to Edward Sherline for drawing this distinction to my attention.

found in this same colleague's work rhetorical treatment of individual liberty that raised it to the level of a non-negotiable absolute). But irony and inconsistency aside, many relativists are aware of the tension between their own subjective positions and their metatheory that entails relativism. I confess that I too am tempted by the allurements of this view and find some forms of it plausible and worthy of serious examination. However, I also find it deeply troubling.

In this essay I will examine the central notions of ethical relativism and look at the implications that seem to follow from it. Then I will present the outline of a very modest objectivism, one that takes into account many of the insights of relativism and yet stands as a viable option to it.

1. An Analysis of Relativism

Let us examine the theses contained in John Ladd's succinct statement on ethical (conventional) relativism that appears at the beginning of this essay. If we analyze it, we derive the following argument:

1. Moral rightness and wrongness of actions vary from society to society, so there are no universal moral standards held by all societies.
2. Whether or not it is right for individuals to act in a certain way depends on (or is relative to) the society to which they belong.
3. Therefore, there are no absolute or objective moral standards that apply to all people everywhere.

1. The first thesis, which may be called the *diversity thesis,* is simply a description that acknowledges the fact that moral rules differ from society to society. The Spartans of ancient Greece and the Dobu of New Guinea believe that stealing is morally right, but we believe it is wrong. The Roman father had the power of life and death (*just vitae necisque*) over his children, whereas we condemn parents for abusing their children. A tribe in East Africa once threw deformed infants to the hippopotamuses, and in ancient Greece and Rome infants were regularly exposed, while we abhor infanticide. Ruth Benedict describes a tribe in Melanesia that views cooperation and kindness as vices, whereas we see them as virtues. While in ancient Greece, Rome, China and Korea parricide was condemned as "the most execrable of crimes," among Northern Indians aged persons,

persons who were no longer capable of walking, were left alone to starve. Among the California Gallinomero, when fathers became feeble, a burden to their sons, "the poor old wretch is not infrequently thrown down on his back and securely held while a stick is placed across his throat, and two of them seat themselves on the ends of it until he ceases to breathe."[4] Sexual practices vary over time and place. Some cultures permit homosexual behavior, while others condemn it. Some cultures practice polygamy, while others view it as immoral. Some cultures condone while others condemn premarital sex. Some cultures accept cannibalism, while the very idea revolts us. Some West African tribes perform clitoridectomies on girls, whereas we deplore such practices. Cultural relativism is well documented, and "custom is the king o'er all." There may or may not be moral principles that are held in common by every society, but if there are any, they seem to be few at best. Certainly it would be very difficult to derive any single "true" morality by observing various societies' moral standards.

2. The second thesis, *the dependency thesis,* asserts that individual acts are right or wrong depending on the nature of the society from which they emanate. Morality does not occur in a vacuum, and what is considered morally right or wrong must be seen in a context that depends on the goals, wants, beliefs, history, and environment of the society in question. As William G. Sumner says,

> We learn the morals as unconsciously as we learn to walk and hear and breathe, and [we] never know any reason why the [morals] are what they are. The justification of them is that when we wake to consciousness of life we find them facts which already hold us in the bonds of tradition, custom, and habit.[5]

Trying to see things from an independent, noncultural point of view would be like taking out our eyes in order to examine their contours and qualities. There is no "innocent eye." We are simply culturally determined beings.

We could, of course, distinguish between a weak and a strong thesis of dependency, for the nonrelativist can accept a certain

---

[4]Reported by the anthropologist Powers, *Tribes of California,* p. 178. Quoted in E. Westermarck, *Origin and Development of Moral Ideals* (London, 1906), p. 386. This work is a mine of examples of cultural diversity.
[5]W. G. Sumner, *Folkways* (Ginn & Co., 1906), p. 76.

degree of relativity in the way moral principles are *applied* in various cultures, depending on beliefs, history, and environment. For example, Jewish men express reverence for God by covering their heads when entering places of worship, whereas Christian men uncover their heads when entering places of worship. Westerners shake hands upon greeting each other, whereas Hindus place their hands together and point them toward the person to be greeted. Both sides adhere to principles of reverence and respect but apply them differently. But the ethical relativist must maintain a stronger thesis, one that insists that the moral principles themselves are products of the cultures and may vary from society to society. The ethical relativist contends that even beyond environmental factors and differences in beliefs, a fundamental disagreement exists among societies. One way for the relativist to support this thesis is by appealing to an indeterminacy of translation thesis, which maintains that there is a conceptual relativity among language groups so that we cannot even translate into our language the worldviews of a culture with a radically different language.

In a sense we all live in radically different worlds. But the relativist wants to go further and maintain that there is something conventional about *any* morality, so that every morality really depends on a level of social acceptance. Not only do various societies adhere to different moral systems, but the very same society could (and often does) change its moral views over place and time. For example, the majority of people in the southern United States now view slavery as immoral, whereas one hundred and forty years ago they did not. Our society's views on divorce, sexuality, abortion, and assisted suicide have changed somewhat as well—and they are still changing.

3. The conclusion that there are no absolute or objective moral standards binding on all people follows from the first two propositions. Combining cultural relativism (*the diversity thesis*) with *the dependency thesis* yields ethical relativism in its classic form. If there are different moral principles from culture to culture and if all morality is rooted in culture, then it follows that there are no universal moral principles that are valid (or true) for all cultures and peoples at all times.

2. Subjectivism

Some people think that this conclusion is still too tame, and they maintain that morality is dependent not on the society but rather on the individual. As my students sometimes maintain, "Morality is in the eye of the beholder." They treat morality like taste or aesthetic judgments—person relative. This form of moral subjectivism has the sorry consequence that it makes morality a very useless concept, for, on its premises, little or no interpersonal criticism or judgment is logically possible. Suppose that you are repulsed by observing John torturing a child. You cannot condemn him if one of his principles is "torture little children for the fun of it." The only basis for judging him wrong might be that he was a hypocrite who condemned others for torturing. But suppose that another of his principles is that hypocrisy is morally permissible (for him); thus we cannot condemn him for condemning others for doing what he does.

On the basis of subjectivism Adolf Hitler and the serial murderer Ted Bundy could be considered as moral as Gandhi, so long as each lived by his own standards, whatever those might be. Witness the following paraphrase of a tape-recorded conversation between Ted Bundy and one of his victims in which Bundy justifies his murder:

> Then I learned that all moral judgments are "value judgments," that all value judgments are subjective, and that none can be proved to be either 'right' or 'wrong.' I even read somewhere that the Chief Justice of the United States had written that the American Constitution expressed nothing more than collective value judgments. Believe it or not, I figured out for myself—what apparently the Chief Justice couldn't figure out for himself—that if the rationality of one value judgment was zero, multiplying it by millions would not make it one whit more rational. Nor is there any 'reason' to obey the law for anyone, like myself, who has the boldness and daring—the strength of character—to throw off its shackles. . . . I discovered that to become truly free, truly unfettered, I had to become truly uninhibited. And I quickly discovered that the greatest obstacle to my freedom, the greatest block and limitation to it, consists in the insupportable 'value judgment' that I was bound to respect the rights of others. I asked myself, who were these 'others'? Other human beings, with human rights? Why is it more wrong to kill a human animal than any other animal, a pig or a sheep or a steer? Is your life more to you than a hog's life to a hog? Why should I be willing to sacrifice my pleasure more for the one than for the other? Surely you would not, in this age of scientific enlightenment, declare that God or nature has marked some pleasures as 'moral' or 'good' and others as 'immoral' or 'bad'? In any case, let me assure you, my dear young lady, that there is absolutely no comparison between the pleasure I might take in eating ham and the pleasure I anticipate in raping and murdering you.

That is the honest conclusion to which my education has led me—
after the most conscientious examination of my spontaneous and
uninhibited self.[6]

Notions of good and bad, or right and wrong, cease to have
interpersonal evaluative meaning. We might be revulsed by the
views of Ted Bundy, but that is just a matter of taste. A student
might not like it when her teacher gives her an F on a test paper,
while he gives another student an A for a similar paper, but there
is no way to criticize him for injustice, because justice is not one
of his chosen principles.

Absurd consequences follow from subjectivism. If it is correct,
then morality reduces to aesthetic tastes about which there can be
neither argument nor interpersonal judgment. Although many students say they espouse subjectivism, there is evidence that it conflicts with other of their moral views. They typically condemn Hitler
as an evil man for his genocidal policies. A contradiction seems to
exist between subjectivism and the very concept of morality, which
it is supposed to characterize, for morality has to do with *proper* resolution of interpersonal conflict and the amelioration of the human
predicament (both deontological and teleological systems do this,
but in different ways—see chapters 5 and 4 of this anthology). Whatever else it does, morality has a minimal aim of preventing a Hobbesian state of nature (see chapter 1), wherein life is "solitary, poor,
nasty, brutish, and short." But if so, subjectivism is no help at all, for
it rests neither on social agreement of principle (as the conventionalist maintains) nor on an objectively independent set of norms that
bind all people for the common good. If there were only one person on earth, there would be no occasion for morality, because there
wouldn't be any interpersonal conflicts to resolve or others whose
suffering he or she would have a duty to ameliorate. Subjectivism
implicitly assumes something of this solipsism, an atomism in which
isolated individuals make up separate universes.

Subjectivism treats individuals like billiard balls on a societal pool
table where they meet only in radical collisions, each aimed at his or
her own goal and striving to do in the others before they themselves

---

[6]This is a paraphrased and rewritten statement of Ted Bundy by Harry V.
Jaffa, *Homosexuality and the Natural Law* (Claremont, CA: The Claremont
Institute of the Study of Statesmanship and Political Philosophy, 1990), 3–4.

are done in. This atomistic view of personality is belied by the facts that we develop in families and mutually dependent communities in which we share a common language, common institutions, and similar rituals and habits, and that we often feel one another's joys and sorrows. As John Donne wrote, "No man is an island, entire of itself; every man is a piece of the continent."

Radical individualistic ethical relativism is incoherent. If so, it follows that the only plausible view of ethical relativism must be one that grounds morality in the group or culture. This form is called *conventionalism.*

3. Conventionalism

Conventional ethical relativism, the view that there are no objective moral principles but that all valid moral principles are justified (or are made true) by virtue of their cultural acceptance, recognizes the social nature of morality. That is precisely its power and virtue. It does not seem subject to the same absurd consequences which plague subjectivism. Recognizing the importance of our social environment in generating customs and beliefs, many people suppose that ethical relativism is the correct metaethical theory. Furthermore, they are drawn to it for its liberal philosophical stance. It seems to be an enlightened response to the sin of ethnocentricity, and it seems to entail or strongly imply an attitude of tolerance toward other cultures. Anthropologist Ruth Benedict says, that in recognizing ethical relativity, "We shall arrive at a more realistic social faith, accepting as grounds of hope and as new bases for tolerance the coexisting and equally valid patterns of life which mankind has created for itself from the raw materials of existence."[7] The most famous of those holding this position is the anthropologist Melville Herskovits, who argues even more explicitly than Benedict that ethical relativism entails intercultural tolerance.

1. If morality is relative to its culture, then there is no independent basis for criticizing the morality of any other culture but one's own.
2. If there is no independent way of criticizing any other culture, we ought to be *tolerant* of the moralities of other cultures.

[7]Ruth Benedict, *Patterns of Culture* (New American Library, 1934), p. 257.

3. Morality is relative to its culture. Therefore,

4. We ought to be *tolerant* of the moralities of other cultures.[8]

Tolerance is certainly a virtue, but is this a good argument for it? I think not. If morality simply is relative to each culture, then if the culture in question does not have a principle of tolerance, its members have no obligation to be tolerant. Herskovits seems to be treating the *principle of tolerance* as the one exception to his relativism. He seems to be treating it as an absolute moral principle. But from a relativistic point of view there is no more reason to be tolerant than to be intolerant and neither stance is objectively morally better than the other.

Not only do relativists fail to offer a basis for criticizing those who are intolerant, but they cannot rationally criticize anyone who espouses what they might regard as a heinous principle. If, as seems to be the case, valid criticism supposes an objective or impartial standard, relativists cannot morally criticize anyone outside their own culture. Adolf Hitler's genocidal actions, so long as they are culturally accepted, are as morally legitimate as Mother Teresa's works of mercy. If Conventional Relativism is accepted, racism, genocide of unpopular minorities, oppression of the poor, slavery, and even the advocacy of war for its own sake are as equally moral as their opposites. And if a subculture decided that starting a nuclear war was somehow morally acceptable, we could not morally criticize these people. Any actual morality, whatever its content, is as valid as every other, and more valid than ideal moralities—since the latter aren't adhered to by any culture.

There are other disturbing consequences of ethical relativism. It seems to entail that reformers are always (morally) wrong since they go against the tide of cultural standards. William Wilberforce was wrong in the eighteenth century to oppose slavery; the British were immoral in opposing *suttee* in India (the burning of widows, which is now illegal in India). The early Christians were wrong in refusing to serve in the Roman army or to bow down to Caesar, since the majority in the Roman Empire believed that these two acts were moral duties. In fact, Jesus himself was immoral in breaking the law of His day by healing on the Sabbath day and by advo-

---

[8]Melville Herskovits, *Cultural Relativism* (Random House, 1972).

cating the principles of the Sermon on the Mount, since it is clear that few in His time (or in ours) accepted them.

Yet we normally feel just the opposite, that the reformer is a courageous innovator who is right, who has the truth, against the mindless majority. Sometimes the individual must stand alone with the truth, risking social censure and persecution. As Dr. Stockman says in Ibsen's *Enemy of the People,* after he loses the battle to declare his town's profitable but polluted tourist spa unsanitary, "The most dangerous enemy of the truth and freedom among us—is the compact majority. Yes, the damned, compact and liberal majority. The majority has *might*—unfortunately—but *right* it is not. Right—are I and a few others." Yet if relativism is correct, the opposite is necessarily the case. Truth is with the crowd and error with the individual.

Similarly, conventional ethical relativism entails disturbing judgments about the law. Our normal view is that we have a prima facie duty to obey the law, because law, in general, promotes the human good. According to most objective systems, this obligation is not absolute but relative to the particular law's relation to a wider moral order. Civil disobedience is warranted in some cases where the law seems to be in serious conflict with morality. However, if moral relativism is true, then neither law nor civil disobedience has a firm foundation. On the one hand, from the side of the society at large, civil disobedience will be morally wrong, so long as the majority culture agrees with the law in question. On the other hand, if you belong to the relevant subculture which doesn't recognize the particular law in question (because it is unjust from your point of view), disobedience will be morally mandated. The Ku Klux Klan, which believes that Jews, Catholics and Blacks are evil or undeserving of high regard, are, given conventionalism, morally permitted or required to break the laws which protect these endangered groups. Why should I obey a law that my group doesn't recognize as valid?

To sum up, unless we have an independent moral basis for law, it is hard to see why we have any general duty to obey it; and unless we recognize the priority of a universal moral law, we have no firm basis to justify our acts of civil disobedience against "unjust laws." Both the validity of law and morally motivated disobedience of unjust laws are annulled in favor of a power struggle.

There is an even more basic problem with the notion that morality is dependent on cultural acceptance for its validity. The problem is that the notion of a *culture* or *society* is notoriously difficult to define. This is especially so in a pluralistic society like our own where the notion seems to be vague with unclear boundary lines. One person may belong to several societies (subcultures) with different value emphases and arrangements of principles. A person may belong to the nation as a single society with certain values of patriotism, honor, courage, laws (including some which are controversial but have majority acceptance, such as the current law on abortion). But he or she may also belong to a church which opposes some of the laws of the State. He may also be an integral member of a socially mixed community where different principles hold sway, and he may belong to clubs and a family where still other rules are adhered to. Relativism would seem to tell us that where he is a member of societies with conflicting moralities he must be judged both wrong and not-wrong whatever he does. For example, if Mary is a U.S. citizen and a member of the Roman Catholic Church, she is wrong (qua Catholic) if she chooses to have an abortion and not-wrong (qua citizen of the U.S.A.) if she acts against the teaching of the Church on abortion. As a member of a racist university fraternity, KKK, John has no obligation to treat his fellow Black student as an equal, but as a member of the university community itself (where the principle of equal rights is accepted) he does have the obligation; but as a member of the surrounding community (which may reject the principle of equal rights) he again has no such obligation; but then again as a member of the nation at large (which accepts the principle) he is obligated to treat his fellow with respect. What is the morally right thing for John to do? The question no longer makes much sense in this moral Babel. It has lost its action-guiding function.

Perhaps the relativist would adhere to a principle which says that in such cases the individual may choose which group to belong to as primary. If Mary chooses to have an abortion, she is choosing to belong to the general society relative to that principle. And John must likewise choose among groups. The trouble with this option is that it seems to lead back to counter-intuitive results. If Murder Mike of Murder, Incorporated, feels like killing Bank President Ortcutt and wants to feel good about it, he identifies with the Murder, Incorporated society rather than the general public morality. Does this justify the killing? In fact, couldn't one justify anything simply by forming a small subculture that approved of it? Ted Bundy would be morally pure in raping and killing innocents simply by virtue of forming a little coterie. How large must the group be in order to be a legitimate subculture or society? Does it need ten or fifteen people? How about just three?

Come to think about it, why can't my burglary partner and I found our own society with a morality of its own? Of course, if my partner dies, I could still claim that I was acting from an originally social set of norms. But why can't I dispense with the interpersonal agreements altogether and invent my own morality—since morality, on this view, is only an invention anyway? Conventionalist relativism seems to reduce to subjectivism. And subjectivism leads, as we have seen, to moral solipsism, to the demise of morality altogether.

Should one object that this is an instance of the *Slippery Slope Fallacy*,[9] let that person give an alternative analysis of what constitutes a viable social basis for generating valid (or true) moral principles. Perhaps we might agree (for the sake of argument, at least) that the very nature of morality entails two people making an agreement. This move saves the conventionalist from moral solipsism, but it still permits almost any principle at all to count as moral. And what's more, those principles can be thrown out and their contraries substituted for them as the need arises. If two or three people decide that they will make cheating on exams morally acceptable for themselves, via forming a fraternity "Cheaters Anonymous" at their university, then cheating becomes moral. Why not? Why not rape, as well?

However, I don't think you can stop the move from conventionalism to subjectivism. The essential force of the validity of the chosen moral principle is that it is dependent on *choice*. The conventionalist holds that it is the choice of the group, but why should I accept the group's silly choice, when my own is better (for me)? Why should anyone give such august authority to a culture of society? If this is all morality comes to, why not reject it altogether—even though one might want to adhere to its directives when others are looking in order to escape sanctions?

4. *A Critique of Ethical Relativism*

However, while we may fear the demise of morality, as we have known it, this in itself may not be a good reason for rejecting relativism. That is, for judging it false. Alas, truth may not always be edifying. But the consequences of this position are sufficiently alarming to prompt us to look carefully for some weakness in the rela-

---

[9]The fallacy of objecting to a proposition on the erroneous grounds that, if accepted, it will lead to a chain of states of affairs which are absurd or unacceptable.

tivist's argument. So let us examine the premises and conclusion listed at the beginning of this essay as the three theses of relativism.

1. *The Diversity Thesis*. What is considered morally right and wrong varies from society to society, so that there are no moral principles accepted by all societies.
2. *The Dependency Thesis*. All moral principles derive their validity from cultural acceptance.
3. *Ethical Relativism*. Therefore, there are no universally valid moral principles, objective standards which apply to all people everywhere and at all times.

Does any one of these seem problematic? Let us consider the first thesis, the diversity thesis, which we have also called cultural relativism. Perhaps there is not as much diversity as anthropologists like Sumner and Benedict suppose. One can also see great similarities between the moral codes of various cultures. E. O. Wilson has identified over a score of common features,[10] and before him Clyde Kluckhohn has noted much significant common ground between cultures.

> Every culture has a concept of murder, distinguishing this from execution, killing in war, and other "justifiable homicides." The notions of incest and other regulations upon sexual behavior, the prohibitions upon untruth under defined circumstances, of restitution and reciprocity, of mutual obligations between parents and children—these and many other moral concepts are altogether universal.[11]

Colin Turnbull's description of the sadistic, semidisplaced, disintegrating Ik in Northern Uganda supports the view that a people without principles of kindness, loyalty, and cooperation will degenerate into a Hobbesian state of nature.[12] But he has also produced evidence that underneath the surface of this dying society, there is a deeper moral code from a time when the tribe flourished, which occasionally surfaces and shows its nobler face.

On the other hand, there is enormous cultural diversity and many

---

[10]E. O. Wilson, *On Human Nature* (Bantam Books, 1979), pp. 22–23.

[11]Clyde Kluckhohn, "Ethical Relativity: Sic et Non," *Journal of Philosophy*, LII (1955).

[12]Colin Turnbull, *The Mountain People* (New York: Simon & Schuster, 1972).

societies have radically different moral codes. Cultural relativism seems to be a fact, but, even if it is, it does not by itself establish the truth of ethical relativism. Cultural diversity in itself is neutral between theories. For the objectivist could concede complete cultural relativism, but still defend a form of universalism; for he or she could argue that some cultures simply lack correct moral principles.

On the other hand, a denial of complete cultural relativism (i.e., an admission of some universal principles) does not disprove ethical relativism. For even if we did find one or more universal principles, this would not prove that they had any objective status. We could still *imagine* a culture that was an exception to the rule and be unable to criticize it. So the first premise doesn't by itself imply ethical relativism and its denial doesn't disprove ethical relativism.

We turn to the crucial second thesis, the dependency thesis. Morality does not occur in a vacuum, but rather what is considered morally right or wrong must be seen in a context, depending on the goals, wants, beliefs, history, and environment of the society in question. We distinguished a *weak* and a *strong* thesis of dependency. The weak thesis says that the application of principles depends on the particular cultural predicament, whereas the strong thesis affirms that the principles themselves depend on that predicament. The nonrelativist can accept a certain relativity in the way moral principles are *applied* in various cultures, depending on beliefs, history, and environment. For example, a raw environment with scarce natural resources may justify the Eskimos' brand of euthanasia to the objectivist, who in another environment would consistently reject that practice. The members of a tribe in the Sudan throw their deformed children into the river because of their belief that such infants *belong* to the hippopotamus, the god of the river. We believe that they have a false belief about this, but the point is that the same principles of respect for property and respect for human life are operative in these contrary practices. They differ with us only in belief, not in substantive moral principle. This is an illustration of how nonmoral beliefs (e.g., deformed children belong to the hippopotamus) when applied to common moral principles (e.g., give to each his due) generate different actions in different cultures. In our own culture the difference in the nonmoral belief about the status of a fetus generates opposite moral prescriptions. The major difference between pro-choicers and pro-lifers is not whether we should kill persons but whether fetuses are really persons. It is a debate about the facts of the matter, not the principle of killing innocent persons.

So the fact that moral principles are weakly dependent doesn't show that ethical relativism is valid. In spite of this weak dependency on nonmoral factors, there could still be a set of general moral norms applicable to all cultures and even recognized in most, which are disregarded at a culture's own expense.

What the relativist needs is a strong thesis of dependency, that somehow all principles are essentially cultural inventions. But why should we choose to view morality this way? Is there anything to recommend the strong thesis over the weak thesis of dependency? The relativist may argue that in fact we don't have an obvious impartial standard from which to judge. "Who's to say which culture is right and which is wrong?" But this seems to be dubious. We can reason and perform thought experiments in order to make a case for one system over another. We may not be able to *know* with certainty that our moral beliefs are closer to the truth than those of another culture or those of others within our own culture, but we may be *justified* in believing that they are. If we can be closer to the truth regarding factual or scientific matters, why can't we be closer to the truth on moral matters? Why can't a culture be simply confused or wrong about its moral perceptions? Why can't we say that the society like the Ik which sees nothing wrong with enjoying watching its own children fall into fires is less moral in that regard than the culture that cherishes children and grants them protection and equal rights? To take such a stand is not to commit the fallacy of ethnocentrism, for we are seeking to derive principles through critical reason, not simply uncritical acceptance of one's own mores.

Many relativists embrace relativism as a default position. Objectivism makes no sense to them. I think this is Ladd and Harman's position, as the latter's quotation at the beginning of this article seems to indicate. Objectivism has insuperable problems, so the answer must be relativism. The only positive argument I know for the strong dependency thesis upon which ethical relativism rests is that of the indeterminacy of translation thesis. This theory, set forth by B. L. Whorf and W. V. Quine,[13] holds that languages are often so funda-

---

[13]See Benjamin Whorf, *Language, Thought and Reality* (MIT Press, 1956); and W. V. Quine, *Word and Object* (MIT Press, 1960), and *Ontological Relativity* (Columbia University Press, 1969).

mentally different from one another that we cannot accurately translate concepts from one to another. But this thesis, while relatively true even within a language (each of us has an idiolect), seems falsified by experience. We do learn foreign languages and learn to translate across linguistic frameworks. For example, people from a myriad of language groups come to the United States and learn English and communicate perfectly well. Rather than a complete hiatus, the interplay between these other cultures eventually enriches the English language with new concepts (for example, *forte/foible, taboo,* and *coup de grâce*), even as English has enriched (or "corrupted" as the French might argue) other languages. Even if it turns out that there is some indeterminacy of translation between language users, we should not infer from this that no translation or communication is possible. It seems reasonable to believe that general moral principles are precisely those things that can be communicated transculturally. The kind of common features that Kluckhohn and Wilson advance—duties of restitution and reciprocity, regulations on sexual behavior, obligations of parents to children, a no-unnecessary-harm principle, and a sense that the good should flourish and the guilty be punished—these and others constitute a common human experience, a common set of values within a common human predicament of struggling to survive and flourish in a world of scarce resources.[14] So it is possible to communicate cross-culturally and find that we agree on many of the important things in life. If this is so,

---

[14]David Hume gave the classic expression to this idea of a common human nature when he wrote:

> It is universally acknowledged that there is a great uniformity among the actions of men, in all nations and ages, and that human nature remains still the same, in its principles and operations. The same events follow from the same causes. Ambition, avarice, self-love, vanity, friendship, generosity, public spirit; these passions, mixed in various degrees, and distributed through society, have been, from the beginning of the world, and still are, the source of all the actions and enterprises which have ever been observed among mankind. Would you know the sentiments, inclinations, and course of life of the Greeks and Romans? Study well the temper and actions of the French and English: you cannot be much mistaken in transferring to the former most of the observations which you have made with regard to the latter. Mankind are so much the same, in all times and places, that history informs us of nothing new or strange in that particular. Its chief use is only to discover the constant and universal principles of human nature, by show-

then the indeterminacy of translation thesis, upon which relativism rests, must itself be relativized to the point where it is no objection to objective morality.

5. The Case for Moral Objectivism

If nonrelativists are to make their case, they will have to offer a better explanation of cultural diversity and why we should nevertheless adhere to moral objectivism. One way of doing this is to appeal to a divine law, and human sin, which causes deviation from that law. Although I think that human greed, selfishness, pride, self-deception and other maladies have a great deal to do with moral differences and that religion may lend great support to morality, I don't think that a religious justification is necessary for the validity of moral principles. In any case, in this section I shall outline a modest nonreligious objectivism, first by appealing to our intuitions and secondly by giving a naturalist account of morality that transcends individual cultures.

First, I must make it clear that I am distinguishing moral *absolutism* from moral *objectivism*. The absolutist believes that there are nonoverideable moral principles which ought never to be violated. Kant's system, or one version of it, is a good example. One ought never to break a promise, no matter what. Act utilitarianism also seems absolutist, for the principle, Do that act that has the most promise of yielding the most utility, is nonoverrideable. An objectivist need not posit any nonoverrideable principles, at least not in

---

ing men in all varieties of circumstances and situations, and furnishing us with materials, from which we may form our observations, and become acquainted with the regular springs of human action and behavior. These records of wars, intrigues, factions, and revolutions, are so many collections of experiments by which the politician or moral philosopher fixes the principles of his science; in the same manner as the physician or natural philosopher becomes acquainted with the nature of plants, minerals, and other external objects, by the experiments which he forms concerning them. Nor are the earth, water, and other elements examined by Aristotle and Hippocrates more like to those which at present lie under our observation than the men described by Polybius and Tacitus are to those who now govern the world. *Essays, Moral, Political and Literary* (Longman, Green, 1875).

unqualified general form, and so need not be an absolutist. As Renford Bambrough put it,

> To suggest that there is a *right* answer to a moral problem is at once to be accused of or credited with a belief in moral absolutes. But it is no more necessary to believe in moral absolutes in order to believe in moral objectivity than it is to believe in the existence of absolute space or absolute time in order to believe in the objectivity of temporal and spatial relations and of judgments about them.[15]

On the objectivist's account moral principles are what William Ross refers to as *prima facie* principles, valid rules of action which should generally be adhered to, but which may be overridden by another moral principle in cases of moral conflict. For example, while a principle of justice may generally outweigh a principle of benevolence, there are times when enormous good could be done by sacrificing a small amount of justice, so that an objectivist would be inclined to act according to the principle of benevolence. There may be some absolute or nonoverrideable principles, but there need not be many or any for objectivism to be true.[16]

If we can establish or show that it is reasonable to believe that there is at least one objective moral principle which is binding on all people everywhere in some ideal sense, we shall have shown that relativism is probably false and that a limited objectivism is true. Actually, I believe that there are many qualified general ethical principles which are binding on all rational beings, but one will suffice to refute relativism. The principle I've chosen is the following:

A. It is morally wrong to torture people for the fun of it.

I claim that this principle is binding on all rational agents, so that if some agent, S, rejects A, we should not let that affect our intuition that A is a true principle but rather try to explain S's behavior as perverse, ignorant, or irrational instead. For example, suppose Adolf Hitler doesn't accept A. Should that affect our confi-

[15]Renford Bambrough, *Moral Skepticism and Moral Knowledge* (London: Routledge & Kegan Paul, 1979), p. 33.
[16]William Ross, *The Right and the Good* (Oxford University Press, 1930), p. 18f.

dence in the truth of A? Is it not more reasonable to infer that Adolf is morally deficient, morally blind, ignorant, or irrational than to suppose that his noncompliance is evidence against the truth of A?

Suppose further that there is a tribe of Hitlerites somewhere who enjoy torturing people. The whole culture accepts torturing others for the fun of it. Suppose that Mother Teresa or Gandhi tries unsuccessfully to convince them that they should stop torturing people altogether, and they respond by torturing the reformers. Should this affect our confidence in A? Would it not be more reasonable to look for some explanation of Hitlerite behavior? For example, we might hypothesize that this tribe lacked a developed sense of sympathetic imagination which is necessary for the moral life. Or we might theorize that this tribe was on a lower evolutionary level than most *Homo sapiens.* Or we might simply conclude that the tribe was closer to a Hobbesian state of nature than most societies, and as such probably would not survive. But we need not know the correct answer as to why the tribe was in such bad shape in order to maintain our confidence in A as a moral principle. If A is a basic or core belief for us, we will be more likely to doubt the Hitlerites' sanity or ability to think morally than to doubt the validity of A.

We can perhaps produce other candidates for membership in our minimally basic objective moral set. For example:

1. Do not kill innocent people.
2. Do not cause unnecessary pain or suffering.
3. Do not cheat or steal.
4. Keep your promises and honor your contracts.
5. Do not deprive another person of his or her freedom.
6. Do justice, treating equals equally and unequals unequally.
7. Tell the truth.
8. Help other people, at least when the cost to oneself is minimal.
9. Reciprocate (show gratitude for services rendered).
10. Obey just laws.

These ten principles are examples of the *core morality,* principles necessary for the good life. They are not arbitrary, for we can give reasons why they are necessary to social cohesion and human flourishing. Principles like the Golden Rule, not killing innocent people, treating equals equally, truth telling, promise keeping, and the like

are central to the fluid progression of social interaction and the resolution of conflicts of which ethics are about (at least minimal morality is, even though there may be more to morality than simply these
kinds of concerns). For example, language itself depends on a general and implicit commitment to the principle of truth telling. Accuracy of expression is a primitive form of truthfulness. Hence, every
time we use words correctly we are telling the truth. Without this
behavior, language wouldn't be possible. Likewise, without the recognition of a rule of promise keeping, contracts are of no avail and
cooperation is less likely to occur. And without the protection of life
and liberty, we could not secure our other goals.

A moral code or theory would be adequate if it contained a requisite set of these objective principles or the core morality, but there
could be more than one adequate moral code or theory which contained different rankings of these principles and other principles
consistent with *core morality*. That is, there may be a certain relativity to secondary principles (whether to opt for monogamy rather
than polygamy, whether to include a principle of high altruism in
the set of moral duties, whether to allocate more resources to medical care than to environmental concerns, whether to institute a law
to drive on the left side of the road or the right side of the road,
and so forth), but in every morality a certain core will remain,
though applied somewhat differently because of differences in environment, belief, tradition, and the like.

The core moral rules are analogous to the set of vitamins necessary for a healthy diet. We need an adequate amount of each vitamin—some humans more of one than another—but in prescribing a
nutritional diet we don't have to set forth recipes, specific foods,
place settings, or culinary habits. Gourmets will meet the requirements differently than ascetics and vegetarians, but the basic nutrients may be had by all without rigid regimentation or an absolute set
of recipes.

Stated more positively, an objectivist who bases his or her moral
system on a common human nature with common needs and desires
might argue for objectivism somewhat in this manner:

1. Human nature is relatively similar in essential respects, having a common set of needs and interests.
2. Moral principles are functions of human needs and interests,
   instituted by reason in order to promote the most signifi-

cant interests and needs of rational beings (and perhaps others).

3. Some moral principles will promote human interests and meet human needs better than others.

4. Those principles which will meet essential needs and promote the most significant interests of humans in optimal ways can be said to be objectively valid moral principles.

5. Therefore, since there is a common human nature, there is an objectively valid set of moral principles, applicable to all humanity.

This argument assumes that there is a common human nature. In a sense, I accept a *strong dependency thesis*—morality *depends* on human nature and the needs and interests of humans in general, but not on any specific cultural choice. There is only one large human framework to which moral principles are relative.[17] I have considered the evidence for this claim toward the end of Section 4, but the relativist may object. I cannot defend it any further in this paper, but suppose we content ourselves with a less controversial first premise, stating that some principles will tend to promote the most significant interests of persons. The revised argument would go like this:

1. Objectively valid moral principles are those adherence to which meets the needs and promotes the most significant interests of persons.

2. Some principles are such that adherence to them meets the needs and promotes the most significant interests of persons.

3. Therefore, there are some objectively valid moral principles.

Either argument would satisfy objectivism, but the former makes it clearer that it is our common human nature that generates the

---

[17]In his essay "Moral Relativism" in *Moral Relativism and Moral Objectivity* (Blackwell, 1996) by Gilbert Harman and Judith Jarvis Thomson, Harman defines moral relativism as the claim that "There is no single true morality. There are many different moral frameworks, none of which is more correct than the others." (p. 5) I hold that morality has a function of serving the needs and interests of human beings, so that some frameworks do this better than others. Essentially, all adequate theories will contain the principles I have identified in this essay.

common principles.[18] However, as I mentioned, some philosophers might not like to be tied down to the concept of a common human nature, in which case the second version of the argument may be used. It has the advantage that even if it turned out that we did have somewhat different natures or that other creatures in the universe had somewhat different natures, some of the basic moral principles would still survive.

If this argument succeeds, there are ideal moralities (and not simply adequate ones). Of course, there could still be more than one ideal morality, from which presumably an ideal observer would choose under optimal conditions. The ideal observer may conclude that out of an infinite set of moralities two, three, or more combinations would tie for first place. One would expect that these would be similar, but there is every reason to believe that all of these would contain the set of core principles.

Of course, we don't know what an ideal observer would choose, but we can imagine that the conditions under which such an observer would choose would be conditions of maximal knowledge about the consequences of action-types and impartiality, second-order qualities which ensure that agents have the best chance of making the best decisions. If this is so, then the more we learn to judge impartially and the more we know about possible forms of life, the better chance we have to approximate an ideal moral system. And if there is the possibility of approximating ideal moral systems with an objective core and other objective components, then ethical relativism is certainly false. We can confidently dismiss it as an aberration and get on with the job of working out better moral systems.

Let me make the same point by appealing to your intuitions in another way. Imagine that you have been miraculously transported to the dark kingdom of hell, and there you get a glimpse of the sufferings of the damned. What is their punishment? Well, they have eternal back itches which ebb and flow constantly. But they cannot scratch their backs, for their arms are paralyzed in a frontal position, so they writhe with itchiness throughout eternity. But just

---

[18]I owe the reformulation of the argument to Bruce Russell. Edward Sherline has objected (in correspondence) that assuming a common human nature in the first argument begs the question against the relativist. You may be the judge.

as you are beginning to feel the itch in your own back, you are suddenly transported to heaven. What do you see in the kingdom of the blessed? Well, you see people with eternal back itches, who cannot scratch their own backs. But they are all smiling instead of writhing. Why? Because everyone has his or her arms stretched out to scratch someone else's back, and, so arranged in one big circle, a hell is turned into a heaven of ecstasy.

If we can imagine some states of affairs or cultures that are better than others in a way that depends on human action, we can ask what are those character traits that make them so. In our story people in heaven, but not in hell, cooperate for the amelioration of suffering and the production of pleasure. These are very primitive goods, not sufficient for a full-blown morality, but they give us a hint as to the objectivity of morality. Moral goodness has something to do with the ameliorating of suffering, the resolution of conflict, and the promotion of human flourishing. If our heaven is really better than the eternal itchiness of hell, then whatever makes it so is constitutively related to moral rightness.

6. *An Explanation of the Attraction of Ethical Relativism*

Why, then, is there such a strong inclination toward ethical relativism? I think that there are four reasons, which haven't been adequately emphasized. One is the fact that the options are usually presented as though absolutism and relativism were the only alternatives, so conventionalism wins out against an implausible competitor. At the beginning of this paper I referred to a student questionnaire that I have been giving for twenty years. It reads as follows: "Are there any ethical absolutes, moral duties binding on all persons at all times, or are moral duties relative to culture? Is there any alternative to these two positions?" Fewer than five percent suggest a third position and very few of them identify objectivism. Granted, it takes a little philosophical sophistication to make the crucial distinctions, and it is precisely for lack of this sophistication or reflection that relativism has procured its enormous prestige. But, as Ross and others have shown and as I have argued in this paper, one can have an objective morality without being absolutist.

The second reason for an inclination toward ethical relativism is the confusion of moral objectivism with moral realism. A realist is a person who holds that moral values have independent existence, if only as emergent properties. The anti-realist claims that they do not have independent existence. But objectivism is compatible with either of these views. All it calls for is deep intersubjective agreement among humans because of a common nature and common goals and needs.

An example of a philosopher who confuses objectivity with realism is the late J. L. Mackie, who rejects objectivism because there are no good arguments for the independent existence of moral values. He admits, however, that there is a great deal of intersubjectivity in ethics. "There could be agreement in valuing even if valuing is just something people do, even if this activity is not further validated. Subjective agreement would give intersubjective values, but intersubjectivity is not objectivity."[19] But Mackie fails to note that there are two kinds of intersubjectivity, and that one of them gives all that the objectivist wants for a moral theory. Consider the following situations of intersubjective agreement:

Set A

A1. All the children in first grade at School S would agree that playing in the mud is preferable to learning arithmetic.

A2. All the youth in the district would rather take drugs than go to school.

A3. All the people in Jonestown, British Guiana, agree that the Rev. Jones is a prophet from God, and they love him dearly.

A4. Almost all the people in community C voted for George Bush.

Set B

B1. All the thirsty desire water to quench their thirst.

B2. All humans (and animals) prefer pleasure to pain.

B3. Almost all people agree that living in society is more satisfying than living as hermits alone.

The naturalist contrasts these two sets of intersubjective agreements and says that the first set is accidental, not part of what it means to be a person, whereas the agreements in the second set

---

[19]J. L. Mackie, *Ethics: Inventing Right and Wrong* (Penguin, 1977), p. 22.

are basic to being a person, basic to our nature. Agreement on the essence of morality, the core set, is the kind of intersubjective agreement more like the second kind, not the first. It is part of the essence of a human in community, part of what it means to flourish as a person, to agree and adhere to the moral code.

The third reason is that our recent sensitivity to cultural relativism and the evils of ethnocentrism, which have plagued the relations of Europeans and Americans with those of other cultures, has made us conscious of the frailty of many aspects of our moral repertoire, so that there is a tendency to wonder "Who's to judge what's really right or wrong?" However, the move from a reasonable cultural relativism, which rightly causes us to rethink our moral systems, to an ethical relativism, which causes us to give up the heart of morality altogether, is an instance of the fallacy of confusing factual or descriptive statements with normative ones. Cultural relativism doesn't entail ethical relativism. The very reason that we are against ethnocentricism constitutes the same basis for our being for an objective moral system: that impartial reason draws us to it.

We may well agree that cultures differ and that we ought to be cautious in condemning what we don't understand, but this in no way need imply that there are not better and worse ways of living. We can understand and excuse, to some degree at least, those who differ from our best notions of morality, without abdicating the notion that cultures without principles of justice or promise keeping or protection of the innocent are morally poorer for these omissions.

A fourth reason which has driven some to moral nihilism and others to relativism is the decline of religion in Western society. As one of Dostoevsky's characters has said, "If God is dead, all things are permitted." The person who has lost religious faith feels a deep vacuum and understandably confuses it with a moral vacuum, or he or she finally resigns to a form of secular conventionalism. Such people reason that if there is no God to guarantee the validity of the moral order, there must not be a universal moral order. There is just radical cultural diversity and death at the end. But even if there turns out to be no God and no immortality, we still will want to live happy, meaningful lives during our fourscore years on earth. If this is true, then it matters by which principles we live, and those which win out in the test of time will be objectively valid principles.

In conclusion I have argued (1) that cultural relativism (the fact that there are cultural differences regarding moral principles) does not entail ethical relativism (the thesis that there are no objectively valid universal moral principles); (2) that the dependency thesis (that morality derives its legitimacy from individual cultural acceptance) is mistaken; and (3) that there are universal moral principles based on a common human nature and a need to solve conflicts of interest and flourish.

So "Who's to judge what's right or wrong?" We are. We are to do so on the basis of the best reasoning we can bring forth, and with sympathy and understanding.[20]

For Further Reflection

1. Is Pojman correct in thinking most American students tend to be moral relativists? If he is, why is this? What is the attraction of relativism? If he's not correct, explain your answer.

2. Explain the difference between subjective ethical relativism and conventionalism.

3. Sometimes people argue that since there are no universal moral truths, each culture's morality is as good as every other, so we ought not to interfere in its practices. Assess this argument.

4. Does moral relativism have a bad effect on society? Reread the tape-recorded conversation between serial murderer Ted Bundy and one of his victims (pages 165–166) in which Bundy attempts to justify the murder of his victim on the basis of the idea that all moral values are subjective. Analyze Bundy's discussion. How would the relativist respond to Bundy's claim that relativism justifies rape and murder? What do you think? Why?

[20]Bruce Russell, Morton Winston, Edward Sherline, and an anonymous reviewer made important criticisms on earlier versions of this article, issuing in this revision.

Judge Not?

JEAN BETHKE ELSHTAIN

Jean Bethke Elshtain, who was born in Germany, is Laura Spelman Rockefeller professor of social and political ethics at the University of Chicago. She is the author of several works in social ethics, including *Democracy on Trial*. In this essay she examines the platitude that we should not judge other people and gives reasons for thinking that we are not only permitted to make moral judgments but have an obligation to do so.

We are a society awash in exculpatory strategies. We've devised lots of fascinating ways to let ourselves or others off the hook: all one need do is think of recent, well-publicized trials to appreciate the truth of this. We Americans are at present being bombarded with sensationalistic tales of victimization and equally sensationalistic proclamations of immunity from responsibility. Alternately bemused and troubled by the Oprah Winfreyization of American life, I sometimes think of my grandmother.

Dear Grandma (may she rest in peace) knew how to judge. She was tough as nails on people she found despicable or merely wanting. She chewed them out in her low German dialect (being a Volga German, *hochdeutsch* was not her tongue), and we grandchildren could figure out a thing or two. We knew when she was describing someone as "swinish" or "dirty," these being ways to characterize those who stole from others, beat their wives or their livestock, or abused their children. (Women, of course, could be abusers, too.) We missed a good bit of her assessments, though, as it was the policy of my grandmother, my mother, and Aunts Mary and Martha not to teach us *plattdeutsch*. When Grandma was really on a roll and wanted nothing less than to condemn someone to perdition, her favorite judging word was "Russki." Hearing it sent a frisson through our tender flesh and bones. The last time I heard her say this I was

Reprinted from Jean Bethke Elshtain, "Judge Not?" *First Things* (October 1994) with permission of the Institute on Religion & Public Life, New York, N.Y.

forty-three or forty-four years old and it still frightened me, not quite out of my wits, but I remained convinced, as I had been since the age of five or six when I had acquired some inkling of what was at stake, that that person was doomed, no two ways about it.

"Russki" was her shorthand judgment on the garden-variety cheat, the ordinary bum, the farmer who shortchanged his hired hands, or the mother who kept her kids in dirty clothes, let their noses run, and never washed their hair. Why "Russki" as a term of judgment? That was historic overdetermination. It was the Russians who had begun to undermine the historic immunities of the Volga German communities. Under Tsar Nicholas, on the throne when my grandparents' families emigrated to the New Country from what my grandmother always called the Old Country, their sons were being drafted into the Russian Army; and they were so fearful that they hid their Bibles (Luther's German translation) in secret places.

I suppose my grandmother would be a good candidate for sensitivity training. She is beyond the reach of the enthusiasts of pop psychology with its quivering "non-judgmentalism," having died at the age of ninety-four two years ago, but it gives me a shiver of another sort (one of delight) to imagine a confrontation between Grandma and a "facilitator," eyes agleam with programmed goodness, saying things like, "Now, Mrs. Lind, *why* do you feel that way?" Or: "Don't you think that's a little harsh? Have you considered how hurtful such words can be?" Probably the facilitator would want to take a good look at my mother, and, in addition to Aunts Mary and Martha, Uncle Bill and Uncle Ted, too, no doubt damaged beyond repair, having been reared by such a no-nonsense judger. Good luck! I doubt they would have the slightest inkling of what she was going on about. There was no room in the family idiom for evasions of responsibility and you would find yourself the subject of an assessment of a rather decisive sort if you tried one.

No doubt from time to time my grandmother and her children rushed to judgment. I know my sisters and brothers and I sometimes wished Mom wouldn't embarrass us in public by being so, well, *decisive* in her assessment of things—more than once delivered up in front of those being assessed, too. I recall wanting to seek the nearest exit on more than one occasion. But then I thought, even at the time, better this than someone agreeable and eternally smiling, like my nemesis, the mother of Judy Belcher (not her real name), who was a "pal" to her daughter. They "talked about everything," especially "boyfriends" and "fashion," and they liked to "have fun together." I found this pretty disgusting. I still do. Judging seems to run in the family.

But to say this is not to say much. For what is at stake is the capacity to make judgments as an ethical issue of the gravest sort, and along with it, the discernment of what it means to judge well. In other words, we need a clear sense of why judging is important and what is involved in the activity of judging, and we need a way to distinguish between rash judging—not judging well—and the kind of judging that lies at the heart of what it means to be a self-respecting human subject in a community of other equally self-respecting subjects.

Judging has been in bad odor for quite some time in American culture. It is equated with being punitive, or with insensitivity, or with various "phobias" and "isms." It is the mark of antiquated ways of thinking, feeling, and willing. Better, no doubt, to be something called "open-minded," a trait thought to be characteristic of sensitive and supportive persons. A young woman well known to me reports that she and her fellow teachers at one of the elite New York public high schools were enjoined not to make students "feel bad" by being too decisive in their assessments of student work and effort. I breathed a sigh of recognition when she told me this; it is the sort of thing one hears in the higher reaches of the academy, too. In fact, this attitude is everywhere, even on bumper stickers. At least some of the readers of this essay will have sighted a bumper sticker that reads: "A Mind Is Like a Parachute. It Works Best When It Is Open." Yes, indeed, one wants to counter, the more open—meaning the more porous and thin—the better. A rather more convenient way of being in the world than being called upon to discriminate in the old—best—sense of the word. An open mind of the sort celebrated by the bumper sticker may signify an empty head, a person incapable of those acts of discernment we call "judging," one who is, in fact, driven to see in such acts mere prejudice.

But prejudice and judgment are two very different human possibilities; indeed, the more we proliferate prejudices, free from the scrutiny of that discernment we aim to evade, the less capable we are, over time, of making judgments. An example or two, in line with Kant's insistence that "Examples are the go-cart of judgments," may suffice. When I first began university teaching, in 1973, I taught a course called "Feminist Politics and Theory." I taught it for several years until I decided the tumult was too much to put up with semester after semester. One problem I encountered went like this. I had designed the course as a sustained exercise in assessing, and critically contrasting, competing feminist accounts of culture and politics. I asked my students to engage certain questions that presupposed their capacity for judgment: What sort of picture of the human condition is presented by this theorist? Could her prescription for change be implemented? How? What would the world look like if it were? And so on. But I ran into trouble straight-off for, in the eyes of many of my students, what I was supposed to be doing was condemning that big booming abstraction, Patriarchy, for fifty minutes three times a week. I was supposed to embrace, not criticize, feminist doctrines—all of them—even though the ideas of the radical separatist feminists scarcely comported with those of liberal feminists on many issues. Needless to say, the Marxist feminists and the eco-feminists didn't see eye-to-eye on lots of things either.

Students sometimes showed up in my office bereft and troubled. One told me she had been a feminist since she was fourteen and didn't need to hear feminism criticized. Another told me she was so "upset" by my criticism of the text of a feminist who proposed test-tube reproduction and a world run by beneficent cyber-engineers, and so "shocked" at my insistence that she respond to a series of questions asking her to sift, discriminate, and assess this text and others, that she had complained to, and sought refuge in, a support group at the women's center. Yet another refused to write a paper contrasting Freud's essays on female development with what the psychoanalytic feminists were doing with Freud because "Freud was a cancer-ridden, cigar-smoking misogynist." This expression of prejudice was not an authentic moment of judging, of course, not least because the student had refused to read the assigned texts. She was repeating a prejudice, not forming a judgment.

A teacher quickly wearies of this sort of thing because it undermines the presuppositions that guide and help to constitute the pedagogical enterprise, one of the most important of these suppositions being that students are capable of weighing alternatives with a generosity of spirit and quality of discernment that makes their subsequent judgments at least plausible if not unassailable. I have always been fond of a pithy sentence in a letter Freud wrote to his fiancee, Martha: "A human being must be able to pull himself together to form a judgment, otherwise he turns into what we Viennese call a *guten*

Potschen [doormat]." Apart from being stepped on, what is the problem with persons as doormats? Precisely this: they have sloughed off that which is theirs to do—to enter a community of judging, meaning that one can see error and try to put it right, one can distinguish the more from the less important, one can appropriately name phenomena and act accordingly. As an example of the latter, think of the distinction to be marked between "misfortune" and an "injustice" and what we are enjoined to do whether we confront one or the other. Now Freud was not urging Martha to be cruel or incapable of compassion or forgiveness; rather, he was urging her to stiffen her spine a bit, to stand up for herself, and not to shrink from acts of assessment and discernment.

Judging involves calling things by their real names, embracing the difficult recognition that what Hannah Arendt called "an enormously enlarged empathy" does not in itself suffice to sustain the capacity for that critical thinking we call judging. Arendt had little use for those who treated adults as if they were children by spoon-feeding them palatable "truths" rather than the harder truths of life and politics. If we over-assimilate our situation to that of others, and pretend that we are "at one" with them, we may lose the point at which we leave off and they begin. We are then in danger of losing the faculty of judgment that, for Arendt, consists in "thinking the particular" and through this concrete act reaching for more general conclusions and truths.

Why is judging—what Arendt called the preeminent political faculty—at a nadir among us? Surely much of the explanation lies in the triumph of the ideology of victimization coupled with self-esteem mania. The two are, of course, closely linked. Examples are so numerous it is hard to pick and choose. Take one from the public schools. By now most discerning citizens are familiar with the study showing that American schoolchildren scored much lower on math accomplishment tests than did their counterparts from several other societies—even while these same Americans were the ones who "felt best" about their math ability. Here the emphasis on "feeling good" by contrast to concrete accomplishment results in students being incapable of an accurate discernment of where they really stand on their math ability. Here is a second story, this from the literary front. My son is an aspiring poet and he finds increasingly depressing the many moments, whether in class or out, when a poem that is weak in execution and flat in evocative power is embraced as something "real" and important because it speaks about the poet's own undigested experiences, which by definition can never be assessed and criticized. In other words, the self-referential prejudices of our time swamp a cooler set of criticisms and judgments, and wind up making a triumph of something rather petty. In the process, the work of those young men and women who really struggle with form and language and getting it right is trivialized, their accomplishments discounted. In some circles, if you carefully and precisely criticize a weak poem, you may face censure because the poem and its author's psyche or identity are at one; thus, you find yourself in the position of criticizing her (or his) life, given the utter collapse of one into the other, when what you really want to do is to explain why you think this isn't a very good poem.

The culture of victimization, then, and the triumph of pop-psych notions of "self-esteem," in contrast to a self capable of discernment and judging well, seems a pretty clear source of our discontents in this matter. Of course, any decent person is concerned about victims, and there are *real* victims in our less than perfect world. But that is not the issue. An ideology of victimization (of the feminist sort) casts women as victims of male oppression from the very beginning of time; indeed, female victimization has taken on foundational status. But this victim ideology diverts attention from concrete and specific instances of female victimization in favor of pushing a relentless worldview structured around such dichotomies as victim/victimizer, guilty/innocent, tainted/pure. The female victim, construed as innocent, remains somehow free from sin. Remember Arendt's insistence, following Kant, that judging "is the faculty of thinking the particular." An ideology of victimization—with its harsh and exaggerated polemicism—actually hurts the cause of women's rights, for it provides grounds for callous or sexist individuals to deprecate the claims of actual victims.

Victimization ideology is little more than a politics of resentment, given the growing body of evidence demonstrating that women, though they often have been victims of injustice, have played a variety of active roles throughout history and in every culture. Of course, who didn't know that? It is quite incredible that one must make this point against those who, in the name of feminism, promote the generic prejudice that women are victims *simpliciter.* Our world is filled with noisy forces urging us to refrain from judging precisely in the name of justice. This dangerous nonsense is in evidence in every issue of any daily newspaper anywhere. The jurors in the Reginald Denny beating case decided not to convict because the thugs who smashed a man's face to an unrecognizable pulp and exulted for the cameras as if they had just made the winning touchdown at a Superbowl Game were in the grip of a "mob psychology" and could not, therefore, be judged for their specific acts of wanton, and repeated, violence. The Menendez brothers were "victims" who, although they blasted their parents numerous times with a shotgun, were not to be held accountable. We cannot judge them given what they "went through," as one juror put it.

Take another case, one worth looking at in some detail. A woman in Nashville, Tennessee, starved her infant son to death. Turned into a robot, so it was claimed, she was unable to feed the infant even though the husband was away at work all day. Her defense was based on her having been abused by this husband even though when he got home from work, the two of them would dress up and go out on the town, frequenting sleazy bars, looking for men and women for three-way sex. Meanwhile, a baby is starving to death. Of this terrible story, victimization doctrine holds that as a victim of abuse herself, the woman, by definition, could not in turn be victimizing another. We cannot judge her actions because she is oppressed. According to her lawyers, who are now mounting an appeal, the jury that found her guilty has victimized her twice. But one who looks at victimization as a concrete and specific act would argue that, although it is terrible to be abused, for a twenty-three-year old woman with a range of options open to her (she might have given the infant to her mother to care for, as she had done with an older child) to starve an infant to death is more terrible yet. Surely, to make that assessment is not an act prompted by a harsh desire for revenge. It flows, rather, from a recognition that we are able to distinguish real victims from rhetorical ones, evil acts and crimes from less serious misdeeds.

As the lawyers for this woman said, the woman cannot be "held accountable," and to do so is a "male deal . . . or a society deal, but some people just don't get it." Now, we are told, the perpetrator is a victim twice or even thrice—of that amorphous entity, society, of her husband, and of the jury that found her guilty. The woman's mother has stepped in, proclaiming that she, too, is a "victim" for she "lost a grandson." Notice the language: she "lost" the grandson, as if he had been misplaced, not knowingly, over a six-week period, starved to death as he lay, immobile, listless, no longer able to cry, in his own waste in a filthy crib in a locked room as his parents played out their fantasies with male and female prostitutes. This is nigh unbelievable, but there it is. Even if this awful case gets turned back on appeal, we—all of us—are in danger of being worn down by arguments of this sort; hence, the more likely it is that, at some future point, we will have forgotten what it means to hold *this* person accountable in *this* situation for *this* particular horrible deed.

Let's pursue this just a bit further, depressing as it is, because the elimination of the possibility of judgment, the evacuation of the very capacity of judging would spell the end of the human subject as a self-respecting accountable being. Judging is a sign, a mark, of our respect for the dignity of others and ourselves. We are surrounded by various strategies of exculpation—ways to evade responsibility for a situation or an outcome should one happen to be a member of an "oppressed" or "victimized" group. In a recent book, *The Alchemy of Race and Rights,* the author, Patricia Williams, plays the victim card to achieve both ends simultaneously. Acknowledging that the Tawana Brawley accusations in the now-notorious 1988 scandal were part of a hoax, Williams suggests that that doesn't really matter. For Brawley was a victim of "some unspeakable crime." "No matter how she got there. No matter who did it to her—and even if she did it to herself." That is, even if Brawley injured herself, "her condition was clearly the expression of some crime against her, some tremendous violence, some great violation that challenges comprehension." Brawley was the victim of a "meta-rape," and this secures both her victim status and legitimates the power plays of those who cynically manipulated the situation. These latter escape judgment; and Brawley cannot be judged either. But the "society" that somehow "did" this to her on a "meta" level becomes responsible given the prejudice that in a "racist" society all African Americans are victims of the dominant "metanarrative." Consider the alternative view of black possibility and responsibility noted by Stephen Carter:

> We must never lose the capacity for judgment, especially the capacity to judge ourselves and our people. . . . Standards of morality matter no less than standards of excellence. There are black people who commit heinous crimes, and not all of them are driven by hunger and neglect. . . . We are not automatons. To understand all may indeed be to forgive all, but no civilization can survive when the capacity for understanding is allowed to supersede the capacity for

judgment. Otherwise, at the end of the line lies a pile of garbage: Hitler wasn't evil, just insane.

"When the capacity for understanding is allowed to supersede the capacity for judgment"—let the words linger for a moment. Then conjure with the teaching of Jesus: "Judge not that ye be not judged," this, of course, from the Sermon on the Mount. These, too, are words I grew up with. And I pondered them, wondering if my mother's "judgmental" attitude was compatible with Jesus' injunction. We were also told: "There but for the grace of God go I." We were told to "walk around in the other guy's shoes" before we judged severely or before we judged at all. Squaring this with Grandma's dismissive "Russki" was no easy matter. I sometimes repaired to Lincoln, one of my childhood heroes. I especially loved the magnificent Second Inaugural, "With malice toward none, with charity for all . . ." Those words I could square with judgment. Malice and judgment: the punitive and the fair are not the same. Lincoln had, after all, insisted that the nations were under God's judgment, and our terrible Civil War, the war he was prosecuting in terms of "unconditional surrender," was our punishment for chattel slavery. Lincoln was no value-free, laid-back kind of guy: compassion with judgment, this framed his life and work. "Judge not" is, then, not an injunction to spineless acceptance but a caution against peremptory legalisms that leave no space for acts of compassion and witness.

I have also found helpful the discussion of the lively British philosopher, Mary Midgley. In her book *Can't We Make Moral Judgments?* Midgley notes our contemporary search for a nonjudgmental politics and quotes all those people who cry, in effect, "But surely it's always wrong to make moral judgments." We are not permitted to make anyone uncomfortable, to be "insensitive." Yet moral judgment of "some kind," says Midgley, "is a necessary element to our thinking." Judging involves our whole nature—it isn't just icing on the cake of self-identity. Judging makes it possible for us to "find our way through a whole forest of possibilities."

Midgley argues that Jesus was taking aim at sweeping condemnations and vindictiveness: he was not trashing the "whole faculty of judgment." Indeed, Jesus is making the "subtle point that while we cannot possibly avoid judging, we can see to it that we judge fairly, as we would expect others to do to us." This is part and parcel, then, of justice as fairness, as a discernment about a particular case and person and deed. Subjectivism in such matters—of the "I'm okay, you're okay," variety—is a cop-out, a way to stop forming and expressing moral judgments altogether. This strange suspension of specific moments of judgment goes hand-in-glove, of course, with an often violent rhetoric of condemnation of whole categories of persons, past and present—that all-purpose villain, the Dead White European Male, comes to mind.

Perhaps this is the point at which we might recall Tocqueville's warnings about "What Sort of Despotism Democratic Nations Have to Fear," for Tocqueville's worst-case scenario has quite a bit to do with judging or, better put, no longer being able to distinguish the better from the worse, the excellent from the mediocre, slavishness from self-responsibility. Democratic despotism, according to Tocqueville, would have a "different character" from the tyranny of the Old World. "It would be more widespread and milder; it would degrade men rather than torment them." Thus, Tocqueville sees citizens withdrawing into themselves, circling around one another in pursuit of "the petty and banal pleasures with which they glut their souls." The exercise of genuine free choice becomes rarer, the activity of free will occurs "within a narrower compass, and little by little robs each citizen of the proper use of his own faculties." The words Tocqueville uses to describe this state of things are "hinder . . . restrain . . . enervate . . . stultify." Losing over time the "faculty of thinking, feeling, and acting for themselves," these citizens "slowly fall below the level of humanity." Tocqueville nowhere talks about collapse of the faculty of judgment in a specific sense but that, surely, is much of what is at stake. Judging is central to, indeed constitutive of, both our self-identity *and* our sociality: it helps us to disentangle, analyze, separate, discern and, in so doing, puts us smack dab in a world of others—not apart, not above, not below, but *among*.

Told that, if we are "powerful" we cannot judge others but can only be judged, and on the other hand that if we are "powerless" we can judge totally but cannot be judged—since the "powerful" by definition "don't get it"—we fall into an intellectual laziness that is itself ethically corrupt and corrupting. As Midgley notes, Jesus' message was: do not stone people, do not cast them out, do not write them off. His target was punitive self-righteousness. With such self-righteousness now a major cottage industry, are we in the danger zone imagined by Tocqueville? That is the question to which sober reflection on judging leads us—or at least where it should.

For Further Reflection

1. Why does judging have a bad odor in American culture?

2. Examine Elshtain's reasons for being judgmental, and for thinking nonjudgmentalism is "dangerous nonsense." Are they convincing? Explain your answer.

The Enemy of the People

HENRIK IBSEN

Henrik Ibsen (1828–1906), a Norwegian, is considered one of the greatest dramatists of all time. He was influenced by the Danish existentialist Søren Kierkegaard, who held that truth is unpopular and lonely. Kierkegaard wanted inscribed on his tombstone the epitaph THE INDIVIDUAL, signifying the idea of individual integrity in the face of the corrupt masses. Several of Ibsen's plays convey this idea, including the one excerpted here.

Our story takes place in a small Norwegian town that has become prosperous thanks to its baths, which bring people from miles around to seek their healing powers. Dr. Thomas Stockmann, the medical officer in charge of overseeing the baths, is also credited with founding them. His brother Peter is the mayor of the town. Noticing that during the previous summer visitors to the baths contracted

From *The Best Known Works of Henrik Ibsen* (New York: Blue Ribbon Books, 1928).

typhus, Stockmann sends water samples to the university. He has just received the university report stating that the water is dangerously polluted. Dr. Stockmann prepares an article on the problem, which the liberal editor Hovstad is delighted to print in the progressive newspaper the *People's Messenger*. Aslaksen, the printer, and leader of the skilled workers' guild, is also strongly behind Stockmann in his endeavor to reveal the truth, seeing it as a means to undermine the power of the old guard and capitalists. However, when these established powers get wind of Stockmann's news, they exert their influence, first by informing the town that in order to redesign the piping system, the town will have to tax the people for some twenty thousand pounds and the baths will have to be closed for two years. The message is clear: cleaning up the polluted baths will have a severe economic cost.

Suddenly, the liberals switch sides. Peter, the mayor, warns his brother against publishing the article. Hovstad squirms and reneges on his promise to publish the exposé. Aslaksen pleads for moderation. Even Stockmann's wife, Katherine, pleads with him to drop the matter. Only his daughter, Petra, stands squarely behind him. We enter with Peter discussing the report with Stockmann.

PETER.   Was it necessary to make all these investigations behind my back?

DR. STO.   Yes, because until I was absolutely certain about it—

PETER.   Then you mean that you are absolutely certain now?

DR. STO.   Surely you are convinced of that.

PETER.   Is it your intention to bring this document before the Baths Committee as a sort of official communication?

DR. STO.   Certainly. Something must be done in the matter—and that quickly.

PETER.   As usual, you employ violent expressions in your report. You say, amongst other things, that what we offer visitors in our Baths is a permanent supply of poison.

DR. STO.   Well, can you describe it any other way, Peter? Just think—water that is poisonous, whether you drink it or bathe in it! And this we offer to the poor sick folk who come to us trustfully and pay us at an exorbitant rate to be made well again!

PETER.   And your reasoning leads you to this conclusion, that we must build a sewer to draw off the alleged impurities from Mölledal and must relay the water-conduits.

DR. STO.   Yes. Do you see any other way out of it? I don't.

PETER.   I made a pretext this morning to go and see the town engineer, and, as if only half seriously, broached the subject of these proposals as a thing we might perhaps have to take under consideration some time later on.

DR. STO.   Some time later on!

PETER.   He smiled at what he considered to be my extravagance, naturally. Have you taken the trouble to consider what your proposed alterations would cost? According to the information I obtained, the expenses would probably mount up to fifteen or twenty thousand pounds.

DR. STO.   Would it cost so much?

PETER.   Yes; and the worst part of it would be that the work would take at least two years.

DR. STO.   Two years? Two whole years?

PETER.   At least. And what are we to with the Baths in the meantime? Close them? Indeed we should be obliged to. And do you suppose any one would come near the place after it had got about that the water was dangerous?

DR. STO.   Yes, but, Peter, that is what it is.

PETER.   And all this at this juncture—just as the Baths are beginning to be known. There are other towns in the neighborhood with qualifications to attract visitors for bathing purposes. Don't you suppose they would immediately strain every nerve to divert the entire stream of strangers to themselves? Unquestionably they would; and then where should we be? We should probably have to abandon the whole thing, which has cost us so much money—and then you would have ruined your native town.

DR. STO.   I—should have ruined—!

PETER.   It is simply and solely through the Baths that the town has before it any future worth mentioning. You know that just as well as I.

DR. STO.   But what do you think ought to be done, then?

PETER.   Your report has not convinced me that the condition of the water at the Baths is as bad as you represent it to be.

DR. STO.   I tell you it is even worse!—or at all events it will be in summer, when the warm weather comes.

PETER.　As I said, I believe you exaggerate the matter considerably. A capable physician ought to know what measures to take—he ought to be capable of preventing injurious influences or of remedying them if they become obviously persistent.

DR. STO.　Well? What more?

PETER.　The water supply for the Baths is now an established fact, and in consequence must be treated as such. But probably the Committee, at its discretion, will not be disinclined to consider the question of how far it might be possible to introduce certain improvements consistently with a reasonable expenditure.

DR. STO.　And do you suppose that I will have anything to do with such a piece of trickery as that?

PETER.　Trickery!!

DR. STO.　Yes, it would be a trick—a fraud, a lie, a downright crime towards the public, towards the whole community!

PETER.　I have not, as I remarked before, been able to convince myself that there is actually any imminent danger.

DR. STO.　You have! It is impossible that you should not be convinced. I know I have represented the facts absolutely truthfully and fairly. And you know it very well, Peter, only you won't acknowledge it. It was owing to your action that both the Baths and the water-conduits were built where they are; and that is what you won't acknowledge—that damnable blunder of yours. Pooh!—do you suppose I don't see through you?

PETER.　And even if that were true? If I perhaps guard my reputation somewhat anxiously, it is in the interests of the town. Without moral authority I am powerless to direct public affairs as seems, to my judgment, to be best for the common good. And on that account—and for various other reasons too—it appears to me to be a matter of importance that your report should not be delivered to the Committee. In the interests of the public, you must withhold it. Then, later on, I will raise the question and we will do our best, privately; but nothing of this unfortunate affair—not a single word of it—must come to the ears of the public.

DR. STO.　I am afraid you will not be able to prevent that now, my dear Peter.

PETER.　It must and shall be prevented.

DR. STO.　It is no use, I tell you. There are too many people that know about it.

PETER.　That know about it? Who? Surely you don't mean those fellows on the "People's Messenger"?

DR. STO.　Yes, they know. The liberal-minded independent press is going to see that you do your duty.

PETER [*after a short pause*].　You are an extraordinarily independent man, Thomas. Have you given no thought to the consequences this may have for yourself?

DR. STO.　Consequences?—for me?

PETER.　For you and yours, yes.

DR. STO.　What the deuce do you mean?

PETER.　I believe I have always behaved in a brotherly way to you—have always been ready to oblige or to help you?

DR. STO.　Yes, you have, and I am grateful to you for it.

PETER.　There is no need. Indeed, to some extent I was forced to do so—for my own sake. I always hoped that, if I helped to improve your financial position, I should be able to keep some check on you.

DR. STO.　What!! Then it was only for your own sake—!

PETER.　Up to a certain point, yes. It is painful for a man in an official position to have his nearest relative compromising himself time after time.

DR. STO.　And do you consider that I do that?

PETER.　Yes, unfortunately, you do, without even being aware of it. You have a restless, pugnacious, rebellious disposition. And then there is that disastrous propensity of yours to want to write about every sort of possible and impossible thing. The moment an idea comes into your head, you must needs go and write a newspaper article or a whole pamphlet about it.

DR. STO.　Well, but is it not the duty of a citizen to let the public share in any new ideas he may have?

PETER.　Oh, the public doesn't require any new ideas. The public is best served by the good, old-established ideas it already has.

DR. STO.　And that is your honest opinion?

PETER.　Yes, and for once I must talk frankly to you. Hitherto I have tried to avoid doing so, because I know how irritable you are; but now I must tell you the truth, Thomas. You have no conception what an amount of harm you do yourself by your impetuosity. You complain of the authorities, you even complain of the government—you are always pulling them to pieces; you insist that you have been neglected and persecuted. But what else can such a cantankerous man as you expect?

DR. STO. What next? Cantankerous, am I?

PETER. Yes, Thomas, you are an extremely cantankerous man to work with—I know that to my cost. You disregard everything that you ought to have consideration for. You seem completely to forget that it is me you have to thank for your appointment here as medical officer to the Baths.—

DR. STO. I was entitled to it as a matter of course!—I and nobody else! I was the first person to see that the town could be made into a flourishing wateringplace, and I was the only one who saw it at that time. I had to fight single-handed in support of the idea for many years; and I wrote and wrote—

PETER. Undoubtedly. But things were not ripe for the scheme then—though, of course, you could not judge of that in your out-of-the-way corner up north. But as soon as the opportune moment came I—and the others—took the matter into our hands—

DR. STO. Yes, and made this mess of all my beautiful plan. It is pretty obvious now what clever fellows you were!

PETER. To my mind the whole thing only seems to mean that you are seeking another outlet for your combativeness. You want to pick a quarrel with your superiors—an old habit of yours. You cannot put up with any authority over you. You look askance at anyone who occupies a superior official position; you regard him as a personal enemy, and then any stick is good enough to beat him with. But now I have called your attention to the fact that the town's interests are at stake—and, incidentally, my own too. And therefore I must tell you, Thomas, that you will find me inexorable with regard to what I am about to require you to do.

DR. STO. And what is that?

PETER. As you have been so indiscreet as to speak of this delicate matter to outsiders, despite the fact that you ought to have treated it as entirely official and confidential, it is obviously impossible to hush it up now. All sorts of rumours will get about directly, and everybody who has a grudge against us will take care to embellish these rumours. So it will be necessary for you to refute them publicly.

DR. STO. I! How? I don't understand.

PETER. What we shall expect is that, after making further investigations, you will come to the conclusion that the matter is not by any means as dangerous or as critical as you imagined in the first instance.

DR. STO. Oho!—so that is what you expect!

PETER. And, what is more, we shall expect you to make public profession of your confidence in the Committee and in their readiness to consider fully and conscientiously what steps may be necessary to remedy any possible defects.

DR. STO. But you will never be able to do that by patching and tinkering at it—never! Take my word for it, Peter; I mean what I say, as deliberately and emphatically as possible.

PETER. As an officer under the Committee, you have no right to any individual opinion.

DR. STO. [*amazed*]. No right?

PETER. In your official capacity, no. As a private person, it is quite another matter. But as a subordinate member of the staff of the Baths, you have no right to express any opinion which runs contrary to that of your superiors.

DR. STO. This is too much! I, a doctor, a man of science, have no right to—!

PETER. The matter in hand is not simply a scientific one. It is a complicated matter, and has its economic as well as its technical side.

DR. STO. I don't care what it is! I intend to be free to express my opinion on any subject under the sun.

PETER. As you please—but not on any subject concerning the Baths. That we forbid.

DR. STO. [*shouting*]. You forbid—! You! A pack of—

PETER. *I* forbid it—I, your chief; and if I forbid it, you have to obey.

DR. STO. [*controlling himself*]. Peter—if you were not my brother—

PETRA [*throwing open the door*]. Father, you shan't stand this!

MRS. STO. [*coming in after her*]. Petra, Petra!

PETER. Oh, so you have been eavesdropping.

MRS. STO. You were talking so loud, we couldn't help—

PETRA. Yes, I was listening.

PETER. Well, after all, I am very glad—

DR. STO. [*going up to him*].   You were saying something about forbidding and obeying?

PETER.   You obliged me to take that tone with you.

DR. STO.   And so I am to give myself the lie, publicly?

PETER.   We consider it absolutely necessary that you should make
some public statement as I have asked for.

DR. STO.   And if I do not—obey?

PETER.   Then we shall publish a statement ourselves to reassure the
public.

DR. STO.   Very well; but in that case I shall use my pen against
you. I stick to what I have said; I will show that I am right and
that you are wrong. And what will you do then?

PETER.   Then I shall not be able to prevent your being dismissed.

DR. STO.   What—?

PETRA.   Father—dismissed!

MRS. STO.   Dismissed!

PETER.   Dismissed from the staff of the Baths. I shall be obliged to
propose that you shall immediately be given notice, and shall
not be allowed any further participation in the Baths' affairs.

DR. STO.   You would dare to do that!

PETER.   It is you that are playing the daring game.

PETRA.   Uncle, that is a shameful way to treat a man like father!

MRS. STO.   Do hold your tongue, Petra!

PETER [*looking at* PETRA].   Oh, so we volunteer our opinions already,
do we? Of course. [*To* MRS. STOCKMANN.] Katherine, I imagine you
are the most sensible person in this house. Use any influence
you may have over your husband, and make him see what this
will entail for his family as well as—

DR. STO.   My family is my own concern and nobody else's!

PETER.   —for his own family, as I was saying, as well as for the
town he lives in.

DR. STO.   It is I who have the real good of the town at heart! I
want to lay bare the defects that sooner or later must come to
the light of day. I will show whether I love my native town.

PETER.   You, who in your blind obstinacy want to cut off the most
important source of the town's welfare?

DR. STO.   The source is poisoned, man! Are you mad? We are making our living by retailing filth and corruption! The whole of our
flourishing municipal life derives its sustenance from a lie!

PETER.   All imagination—or something even worse. The man who can throw out such offensive insinuations about his native town must be an enemy to our community.

DR. STO. [*going up to him*].   Do you dare to—!

MRS. STO. [*throwing herself between them*].   Thomas!

PETRA [*catching her father by the arm*].   Don't lose your temper, father!

PETER.   I will not expose myself to violence. Now you have had a warning; so reflect on what you owe to yourself and your family. Good-bye. [*Goes out.*]

DR. STO. [*walking up and down*].   Am I to put up with such treatment as this? In my own house, Katherine! What do you think of that!

MRS. STO.   Indeed it is both shameful and absurd Thomas—

PETRA.   If only I could give uncle a piece of my mind—

DR. STO.   It is my own fault. I ought to have flown out at him long ago!—shown my teeth!—bitten! To hear him call me an enemy to our community! Me! I shall not take that lying down, upon my soul!

MRS. STO.   But, dear Thomas, your brother has power on his side—

DR. STO.   Yes, but I have right on mine, I tell you.

MRS. STO.   Oh! yes, right—right. What is the use of having right on your side if you have not got might?

PETRA.   Oh, mother!—how can you say such a thing!

DR. STO.   Do you imagine that in a free country it is no use having right on your side? You are absurd, Katherine. Besides, haven't I got the liberal-minded, independent press to lead the way, and the compact majority behind me? That is might enough, I should think!

MRS. STO.   But, good heavens, Thomas, you don't mean to—?

DR. STO.   Don't mean to what?

MRS. STO.   To set yourself up in opposition to your brother.

DR. STO.   In God's name, what else do you suppose I should do but take my stand on right and truth?

PETRA.   Yes, I was just going to say that.

MRS. STO.   But it won't do you any earthly good. If they won't do it, they won't.

DR. STO.   Oho, Katherine! Just give me time, and you will see how I will carry the war into their camp.

Mrs. Sto. Yes, you carry the war into their camp, and you get your dismissal—that is what you will do.

Dr. Sto. In any case I shall have done my duty towards the public—towards the community. I, who am called its enemy!

Mrs. Sto. But towards your family, Thomas? Towards your own home! Do you think that is doing your duty towards those you have to provide for?

Petra. Ah, don't think always first of us, mother.

Mrs. Sto. Oh, it is easy for you to talk; you are able to shift for yourself, if need be. But remember the boys, Thomas; and think a little too of yourself, and of me—

Dr. Sto. I think you are out of your senses, Katherine! If I were to be such a miserable coward as to go on my knees to Peter and his damned crew, do you suppose I should ever know an hour's peace of mind all my life afterwards?

Mrs. Sto. I don't know anything about that; but God preserve us from the peace of mind we shall have, all the same, if you go on defying him! You will find yourself again without the means of subsistence, with no income to count upon. I should think we had had enough of that in the old days. Remember that, Thomas; think what that means.

Dr. Sto. [collecting himself with a struggle and clenching his fists]. And this is what this slavery can bring upon a free, honourable man! Isn't it horrible, Katherine?

Mrs. Sto. Yes, it is sinful to treat you so, it is perfectly true. But, good heavens, one has to put up with so much injustice in this world.—There are the boys, Thomas! Look at them! What is to become of them? Oh, no, no, you can never have the heart—. [Ejlif and Morten have come in while she was speaking, with their school books in their hands].

Dr. Sto. The boys—! [Recovers himself suddenly.] No, even if the whole world goes to pieces, I will never bow my neck to this yoke! [Goes towards his room.]

Mrs. Sto. [following him]. Thomas—what are you going to do!

Dr. Sto. [at his door]. I mean to have the right to look my sons in the face when they are grown men. [Goes into his room.]

Mrs. Sto. [bursting into tears]. God help us all!

Petra. Father is splendid! He will not give in.

[The boys look on in amazement; Petra signs to them not to speak! . . .

[Stockmann is outraged at the moral cowardice of the "progressives." Leaving the Baths polluted in this way will put the unwitting visitors, seeking health, in grave danger. He tries to rent a hall, but the town leaders are united against him. Finally, an old sea captain, Horster, opens his hall to him to reveal his findings. A crowd gathers, including Hovstad and his brother Peter. After an attempt to muzzle him fails, Dr. Stockmann speaks.]

ASL. [*ringing his bell*].   Dr. Stockmann will address the meeting.

DR. STO.   I should like to have seen anyone, a few days ago, dare to attempt to silence me as has been done to-night! I would have defended my sacred rights as a man, like a lion! But now it is all one to me; I have something of even weightier importance to say to you.

[*The crowd presses nearer to him,* MORTEN KIIL *conspicuous among them.*]

DR. STO. [*continuing*].   I have thought and pondered a great deal, these last few days—pondered over such a variety of things that in the end my head seemed too full to hold them—

PETER [*with a cough*].   Ahem!

DR. STO.   —but I got them clear in my mind at last, and then I saw the whole situation lucidly. And that is why I am standing here to-night. I have a great revelation to make to you, my fellow-citizens! I will impart to you a discovery of a far wider scope than the trifling matter that our water-supply is poisoned and our medicinal Baths are standing on pestiferous soil.

A NUMBER OF VOICES [*shouting*].   Don't talk about the Baths! We won't hear you! None of that!

DR. STO.   I have already told you that what I want to speak about is the great discovery I have made lately—the discovery that all the sources of our moral life are poisoned and that the whole fabric of our civic community is founded on the pestiferous soil of falsehood.

VOICES OF DISCONCERTED CITIZENS.   What is that he says?

PETER.   Such an insinuation—!

ASL. [*with his hand on his bell*].   I call upon the speaker to moderate his language.

DR. STO.   I have always loved my native town as a man only can love the home of his youthful days. I was not old when I went away from here; and exile, longing and memories cast as it were an additional halo over both the town and its inhabitants. [*Some clapping and applause.*] And there I stayed, for many years, in a horrible hole far away up north. When I came into contact with some of the people that lived scattered about among the rocks, I often thought it would of been more service to the poor half-starved creatures if a veterinary doctor had been sent up there, instead of a man like me. [*Murmurs among the crowd.*]

BILL. [*laying down his pen*]. I'm damned if I have ever heard—!

HOV. It is an insult to a respectable population!

DR. STO. Wait a bit! I do not think anyone will charge me with having forgotten my native town up there. I was like one of the eider-ducks brooding on its nest, and what I hatched was—the plans for these Baths. [*Applause and protests.*] And then when fate at last decreed for me the great happiness of coming home again—I assure you, gentlemen, I thought I had nothing more in the world to wish for. Or rather, there was one thing I wished for—eagerly, untiringly, ardently—and that was to be able to be of service to my native town and the good of the community.

PETER [*looking at the ceiling*]. You chose a strange way of doing it—ahem!

DR. STO. And so, with my eyes blinded to the real facts, I revelled in happiness. But yesterday morning—no, to be precise, it was yesterday afternoon—the eyes of my mind were opened wide, and the first thing I realised was the colossal stupidity of the authorities—. [*Uproar, shouts and laughter.* MRS. STOCKMANN *coughs persistently.*]

PETER. Mr. Chairman!

ASL. [*ringing his bell*]. By virtue of my authority—!

DR. STO. It is a petty thing to catch me up on a word, Mr. Aslasken. What I mean is only that I got scent of the unbelievable pig-gishness our leading men had been responsible for down at the Baths. I can't stand leading men at any price!—I have had enough of such people in my time. They are like billy-goats in a young plantation; they do mischief everywhere. They stand in a free man's way, whichever way he turns, and what I should like best would be to see them exterminated like any other vermin—. [*Uproar.*]

PETER. Mr. Chairman, can we allow such expressions to pass?

AsL. [*with his hand on his bell*].   Doctor—!

Dr. Sto.   I cannot understand how it is that I have only now acquired a clear conception of what these gentry are, when I had almost daily before my eyes in this town such an excellent specimen of them—my brother Peter—slow-witted and hidebound in prejudice—. [*Laughter, uproar and hisses.* Mrs. Stockmann *sits coughing assiduously.* Aslaksen *rings his bell violently.*]

The Drunken Man [*who has got in again*].   Is it me he is talking about? My name's Petersen, all right—but devil take me if I—

Angry Voices.   Turn out that drunken man! Turn him out. [*He is turned out again.*]

Peter.   Who was that person?

1st Citizen.   I don't know who he is, Mr. Mayor.

2nd Citizen.   He doesn't belong here.

3rd Citizen.   I expect he is a navvy from over at [*the rest is inaudible*].

AsL.   He had obviously had too much beer.—Proceed, Doctor, but please strive to be moderate in your language.

Dr. Sto.   Very well, gentlemen, I will say no more about our leading men. And if anyone imagines, from what I have just said, that my object is to attack these people this evening, he is wrong—absolutely wide of the mark. For I cherish the comforting conviction that these parasites—all these venerable relics of a dying school of thought—are most admirably paving the way for their own extinction; they need no doctor's help to hasten their end. Nor is it folk of that kind who constitute the most pressing danger to the community. It is not they who are most instrumental in poisoning the sources of our moral life and directing the ground on which we stand. It is not they who are the most dangerous enemies of truth and freedom amongst us.

Shouts from all sides.   Who then? Who is it? Name! Name!

Dr. Sto.   You may depend upon it I shall name them! That is precisely the great discovery I made yesterday. [*Raises his voice.*] The most dangerous enemy to truth and freedom amongst us is the compact majority—yes, the damned compact Liberal majority—that is it! Now you know; [*Tremendous uproar. Most of the crowd are shouting, stamping and hissing. Some of the older men among them exchange stolen glances and seem to be enjoying themselves.* Mrs. Stockmann *gets up, looking anxious.* Ejlif *and* Morten *advance threateningly upon some schoolboys who are*

playing pranks. ASLAKSEN *rings his bell and begs for silence.* HOV-
STAD *and* BILLING *both talk at once, but are inaudible. At last quiet
is restored.*]

ASL.   As chairman, I call upon the speaker to withdraw the ill-
considered expressions he has just used.

DR. STO.   Never, Mr. Aslaksen! It is the majority in our community
that denies me my freedom and seeks to prevent my speaking
the truth.

HOV.   The majority always has right on its side.

BILL.   And truth too, by God!

DR. STO.   The majority *never* has right on its side. Never, I say! That
is one of these social lies against which an independent, intelligent man must wage war. Who is it that constitute the majority
of the population in a country? Is it the clever folk or the stupid? I don't imagine you will dispute the fact that at present the
stupid people are in an absolutely overwhelming majority all the
world over. But, good Lord!—you can never pretend that it is
right that the stupid folk should govern the clever ones! [*Up-roar
and cries.*] Oh. yes—you can shout me down, I know! but you
cannot answer me. The majority has *might* on its side—unfortunately; but *right* it has *not.* I am in the right—I and a few other
scattered individuals. The minority is always in the right. [*Renewed uproar.*]

HOV.   Aha!—so Dr. Stockmann has become an aristocrat since the
day before yesterday!

DR. STO.   I have already said that I don't intend to waste a word
on the puny, narrow-chested, short-winded crew whom we are
leaving astern. Pulsating life no longer concerns itself with them.
I am thinking of the few, the scattered few amongst us, who
have absorbed new and vigorous truths. Such men stand, as it
were, at the outposts, so far ahead that the compact majority has
not yet been able to come up with them; and there they are
fighting for truths that are too newly-born into the world of consciousness to have any considerable number of people on their
side as yet.

HOV.   So the Doctor is a revolutionary now!

DR. STO.   Good heavens—of course I am, Mr. Hovstad! I propose
to raise a revolution against the lie that the majority has the
monopoly of the truth. What sort of truths are they that the majority usually supports? They are truths that are of such advanced

age that they are beginning to break up. And if a truth is as old as that, it is also in a fair way to become a lie, gentlemen. [*Laughter and mocking cries.*] Yes, believe me or not, as you like; but truths are by no means as long-lived as Methuselah—as some folk imagine. A normally constituted truth lives, let us say, as a rule seventeen or eighteen, or at most twenty years; seldom longer. But truths as aged as that are always worn frightfully thin, and nevertheless it is only then that the majority recognises them and recommends them to the community as wholesome moral nourishment. There is no great nutritive value in that sort of fare, I can assure you; and, as a doctor, I ought to know. These "majority truths" are like last year's cured meat—like rancid, tainted ham; and they are the origin of the moral scurvy that is rampant in our communities.

ASL.   It appears to me that the speaker is wandering a long way from his subject.

PETER.   I quite agree with the Chairman.

DR. STO.   Have you gone clean out of your senses, Peter? I am sticking as closely to my subject as I can; for my subject is precisely this, that it is the masses, the majority—this infernal compact majority—that poisons the sources of our moral life and infects the ground we stand on.

HOV.   And all this because the great, broad-minded majority of the people is prudent enough to show deference only to well-ascertained and well-approved truths?

DR. STO.   Ah, my good Mr. Hovstad, don't talk nonsense about well-ascertained truths! The truths of which the masses now approve are the very truths that the fighters at the outposts held to in the days of our grandfathers. We fighters at the outposts nowadays no longer approve of them; and I do not believe there is any other well-ascertained truth except this, that no community can live a healthy life if it is nourished only on such old marrowless truths.

HOV.   But instead of standing there using vague generalities, it would be interesting if you would tell us what these old marrowless truths are, that we are nourished on.

[*Applause from many quarters.*]

DR. STO.   Oh, I could give you a whole string of such abominations; but to begin with I will confine myself to one well-approved truth, which at bottom is a foul lie, but upon which nevertheless Mr. Hovstad and the "People's Messenger" and all the "Messenger's" supporters are nourished.

Hov.   And that is—?

Dr. Sto.   That is, the doctrine you have inherited from your fore-fathers and proclaim thoughtlessly far and wide—the doctrine that the public, the crowd, the masses, are the essential part of the population—that they constitute the People—that the common folk, the ignorant and incomplete element in the community, have the same right to pronounce judgment and to approve, to direct and to govern, as the isolated, intellectually superior personalities in it.

Bill.   Well, damn me if ever I—

Hov. [*at the same time, shouting out.*]   Fellow-citizens, take good note of that!

A number of voices [*angrily*].   Oho!—we are not the People! Only the superior folk are to govern, are they!

A Workman.   Turn the fellow out, for talking such rubbish!

Another.   Out with him!

Another [*calling out*].   Blow your horn, Evensen!

[*A horn is blown loudly, amidst hisses and an angry uproar.*]

Dr. Sto. [*when the noise has somewhat abated*].   Be reasonable! Can't you stand hearing the voice of truth for once? I don't in the least expect you to agree with me all at once; but I must say I did expect Mr. Hovstad to admit I was right, when he had recovered his composure a little. He claims to be a freethinker—

Voices [*in murmurs of astonishment*].   Freethinker, did he say? Is Hovstad a freethinker?

Hov. [*shouting*].   Prove it, Dr. Stockmann! When have I said so in print?

Dr. Sto. [*reflecting*].   No, confound it, you are right!—you have never had the courage to. Well, I won't put you in a hole, Mr. Hovstad. Let us say it is I that am the freethinker, then. I am going to prove to you, scientifically, that the "People's Messenger" leads you by the nose in a shameful manner when it tells you that you—that the common people, the crowd, the masses, are the real essence of the People. That is only a newspaper lie, I tell you! The common people are nothing more than the raw material of which a People is made. [*Groans, laughter and uproar.*] Well, isn't that the case? Isn't there an enormous difference between a well-bred and an ill-bred strain of animals?

Take, for instance, a common barn-door hen. What sort of eating do you get from a shrivelled up old scrag of a fowl like that? Not much, do you! And what sort of eggs does it lay? A fairly good crow or a raven can lay pretty nearly as good an egg. But take a well-bred Spanish or Japanese hen, or a good pheasant or a turkey—then you will see the difference. Or take the case of dogs, with whom we humans are on such intimate terms. Think first of an ordinary common cur—I mean one of the horrible, coarse-haired, low-bred curs that do nothing but run about the streets and befoul the walls of the houses. Compare one of these curs with a poodle whose sires for many generations have been bred in a gentleman's house, where they have had the best of food and had the opportunity of hearing soft voices and music. Do you not think that the poodle's brain is developed to quite a different degree from that of the cur? Of course it is. It is puppies of well-bred poodles like that, that showmen train to do incredibly clever tricks—things that a common cur could never learn to do even if it stood on its head. [*Uproar and mocking cries.*]

A CITIZEN [*calls out*].   Are you going to make out we are dogs, now?

ANOTHER CITIZEN.   We are not animals, Doctor!

DR. STO.   Yes, but, bless my soul, we *are,* my friend! It is true we are the finest animals anyone could wish for; but, even amongst us, exceptionally fine animals are rare. There is a tremendous difference between poodle-men and cur-men. And the amusing part of it is, that Mr. Hovstad quite agrees with me as long as it is a question of four-footed animals—

HOV.   Yes, it is true enough as far as they are concerned.

DR. STO.   Very well. But as soon as I extend the principle and apply it to two-legged animals, Mr. Hovstad stops short. He no longer dares to think independently, or to pursue his ideas to their logical conclusion; so he turns the whole theory upside down and proclaims in the "People's Messenger" that it is the barn-door hens and street curs that are the finest specimens in the menagerie. But that is always the way, as long as a man retains the traces of common origin and has not worked his way up to intellectual distinction.

HOV.   I lay no claim to any sort of distinction. I am the son of humble countryfolk, and I am proud that the stock I come from is rooted deep among the common people he insults.

Voices. Bravo, Hovstad! Bravo! Bravo!

Dr. Sto. The kind of common people I mean are not only to be found low down in the social scale; they crawl and swarm all around us—even in the highest social positions. You have only to look at your own fine, distinguished Mayor! My brother Peter is every bit as plebeian as anyone that walks in two shoes—[*laughter and hisses*].

Peter. I protest against personal allusions of this kind.

Dr. Sto. [*imperturbably*]. —and that, not because he is, like myself, descended from some old rascal of a pirate from Pomerania or thereabouts—because that is who we are descended from—

Peter. An absurd legend. I deny it!

Dr. Sto. —but because he thinks what his superiors think and holds the same opinions as they. People who do that are, intellectually speaking, common people; and that is why my magnificent brother Peter is in reality so very far from any distinction—and consequently also so far from being liberal-minded.

Peter. Mr. Chairman—!

Hov. So it is only the distinguished men that are liberal-minded in this country? We are learning something quite new! [*Laughter.*]

Dr. Sto. Yes, that is part of my new discovery too. And another part of it is that broad-mindedness is almost precisely the same thing as morality. That is why I maintain that it is absolutely inexcusable in the "People's Messenger" to proclaim, day in and day out, the false doctrine that it is the masses, the crowd, the compact majority, that have the monopoly of broad-mindedness and morality—and that vice and corruption and every kind of intellectual depravity are the result of culture, just as the filth that is draining into our Baths is the result of the tanneries up at Mölledal! [*Uproar and interruptions.* Dr. Stockmann *is undisturbed, and goes on, carried away by his ardour, with a smile.*] And yet this same "People's Messenger" can go on preaching that the masses ought to be elevated to higher conditions of life! But, bless my soul, if the "Messenger's" teaching is to be depended upon, this very raising up the masses would mean nothing more or less than setting them straightway upon the paths of depravity! Happily the theory that culture demoralises is only an old falsehood that our forefathers believed in and we have inherited. No, it is ignorance, poverty, ugly conditions of life, that do the devil's work! In a house which does not get aired and swept every day—my wife Katherine maintains that the floor ought to be scrubbed as well, but that is a debatable question—in such a house, let me tell you, people will lose within two or three years the power of thinking or acting in a moral manner. Lack of oxygen weakens the conscience. And there must be a plentiful lack of oxygen in very many houses in this town, I should think, judging from the fact that the whole compact majority can be unconscientious enough to wish to build the town's prosperity on a quagmire of falsehood and deceit.

ASL. We cannot allow such a grave accusation to be flung at a citizen community.

A CITIZEN. I move that the Chairman direct the speaker to sit down.

VOICES [*angrily*]. Hear, hear! Quite right! Make him sit down!

DR. STO. [*losing his self-control*]. Then I will go and shout the truth at every street corner! I will write it in other towns' newspapers! The whole country shall know what is going on here.

HOV. It almost seems as if Dr. Stockmann's intentions were to ruin the town.

DR. STO. Yes, my native town is so dear to me that I would rather ruin it than see it flourishing upon a lie.

ASL. This is really serious. [*Uproar and cat-calls.* MRS. STOCKMANN *coughs, but to no purpose; her husband does not listen to her any longer.*]

HOV. [*shouting above the din.*] A man must be a public enemy to wish to ruin a whole community!

DR. STO. [*with growing fervour*]. What does the destruction of a community matter, I tell you! All who live by lies ought to be exterminated like vermin! You will end by infecting the whole country; you will bring about such a state of things that the whole country will deserve to be ruined. And if things come to that pass, I shall say from the bottom of my heart: Let the whole country perish, let all these people be exterminated!

VOICES FROM THE CROWD. That is talking like an out-and-out enemy of the people!

BILL. There sounded the voice of the people, by all that's holy!

THE WHOLE CROWD [*shouting*]. Yes, yes! He is an enemy of the people! He hates his country! He hates his own people!

ASL. Both as a citizen and as an individual, I am profoundly disturbed by what we have had to listen to. Dr. Stockmann has shown himself in a light I should never have dreamed of. I am unhappily obliged to subscribe to the opinion which I have just heard my estimable fellow-citizens utter; and I propose that we should give expression to that opinion in a resolution. I propose a resolution as follows: "This meeting declares that it considers Dr. Thomas Stockmann, Medical Officer of the Baths, to be an enemy of the people." [*A storm of cheers and applause. A number of men surround the* Doctor *and hiss him.* Mrs. Stockmann *and* Petra *have got up from their seats.* Morten *and* Ejlif *are fighting the other schoolboys for hissing; some of their elders separate them.*]

Dr. Sto. [*to the men who are hissing him*].   Oh, you fools! I tell you that—

Asl. [*ringing his bell*].   We cannot hear you now, Doctor. A formal vote is about to be taken; but, out of regard for personal feelings, it shall be by ballot and not verbal. Have you any clean paper, Mr. Billing?

Bill.   I have both blue and white here.

Asl. [*going to him*].   That will do nicely; we shall get on more quickly that way. Cut it up into small strips—yes, that's it. [*To the meeting.*] Blue means no; white means yes. I will come round myself and collect votes. [Peter Stockmann *leaves the hall.* Aslaksen *and one or two others go around the room with the slips of paper in their hats.*]

1st Citizen [*to* Hovstad].   I say, what has come to the Doctor? What are we to think of it?

Hov.   Oh, you know how headstrong he is.

2nd Citizen [*to* Billing].   Billing, you go to their house—have you ever noticed if the fellow drinks?

Bill.   Well I'm hanged if I know what to say. There are always spirits on the table when you go.

3rd Citizen.   I rather think he goes quite off his head sometimes.

1st Citizen.   I wonder if there is any madness in his family?

Bill.   I shouldn't wonder if there were.

4th Citizen.   No, it is nothing more than sheer malice; he wants to get even with somebody for something or other.

Bill.   Well certainly he suggested a rise in his salary on one occasion lately, and did not get it.

The Citizens [*together*].   Ah!—then it is easy to understand how it is!

THE DRUNKEN MAN [*who has got amongst the audience again*].   I want a blue one, I do! And I want a white one too!

VOICES.   It's that drunken chap again! Turn him out!

MORTEN KIIL [*going up to* DR. STOCKMANN.]   Well, Stockmann, do you see what these monkey tricks of yours lead to?

DR. STO.   I have done my duty.

MORTEN KIIL.   What was that you said about the tanneries at Mölledal?

DR. STO.   You heard well enough. I said they were the source of all the filth.

MORTEN KIIL.   My tannery too?

DR. STO.   Unfortunately your tannery is by far the worst.

MORTEN KIIL.   Are you going to put that in the papers?

DR. STO.   I shall conceal nothing.

MORTEN KIIL.   That may cost you dear, Stockmann. [*Goes out.*]

A STOUT MAN [*going up to* CAPTAIN HORSTER, *without taking any notice of the ladies.*]   Well, Captain, so you lend your house to enemies of the people?

HORS.   I imagine I can do what I like with my own possessions, Mr. Vik.

THE STOUT MAN.   Then you can have no objection to my doing the same with mine.

HORS.   What do you mean, sir?

THE STOUT MAN.   You shall hear from me in the morning. [*Turns his back on him and moves off.*]

PETRA.   Was that not your owner, Captain Horster?

HORS.   Yes, that was Mr. Vik the ship-owner.

ASL. [*with the voting-papers in his hands, gets up on to the platform and rings his bell.*]   Gentlemen, allow me to announce the result. By the votes of every one here except one person—

A YOUNG MAN.   That is the drunk chap!

ASL.   By the votes of every one here except a tipsy man, this meeting of citizens declares Dr. Thomas Stockmann to be an enemy of the people. [*Shouts and applause.*] Three cheers for our ancient and honourable citizen community! [*Renewed applause.*] Three cheers for our able and energetic Mayor, who has so loyally suppressed the promptings of family feeling! [*Cheers.*] The meeting is dissolved. [*Gets down.*]

BILL.   Three cheers for the Chairman!

THE WHOLE CROWD.   Three cheers for Aslaksen! Hurrah!

DR. STO.   My hat and coat, Petra! Captain, have you room on your ship for passengers to the New World?

HORS.   For you and yours we will make room, Doctor. . . .

[*Horn-blowing, hisses, and wild cries.* DR. STOCKMANN *goes out through the hall with his family,* HORSTER *elbowing a way for them.*]

THE WHOLE CROWD [*howling after as they go.*]   Enemy of the People! Enemy of the People!

BILL. [*as he puts his papers together*].   Well, I'm damned if I go and drink toddy with the Stockmanns tonight!

[*The crowd press towards the exit. The uproar continues outside; shouts of "Enemy of the People!" are heard from without.*] . . .

[Dr. Stockmann is declared an enemy of the people and is ostracized by the community. He tells Katherine, "You should never wear your best trousers when you go out to fight for freedom and truth. It is not that I care so much about the trousers, you know; you can always sew them up again for me. But that the common herd should dare to make this attack on me, as if they were my equals—that is what I cannot, for the life of me, swallow!"

He is fired from his post and informed that his patients have been instructed to boycott him. His two sons are attacked at school and Petra is fired from her teaching position. His wife wants the family to move away from this town, and his brother, Peter, agrees. But Dr. Stockmann refuses to leave. He will open up a school and serve the poor. He will fight the battle to its finish.]

For Further Reflection

1. What is the key conflict in this play? How well does Dr. Stockmann deal with it?

2. What virtues and vices are exemplified in this play? Assess the various characters, especially Dr. Stockmann. Do you agree with Aslaksen that he should be more moderate? Or is Stockmann a man of rare courage and integrity?

3. What would you do in this situation? Should he leave town as his wife and brother advise?

4. What are the implications of Dr. Stockmann's actions for the issue of moral relativism?

5. Is the problem portrayed in this play relevant today? If so, what are we doing about it? Explain your answer.

6. How important is it to proclaim the truth even when it may have social repercussions?

Further Readings for Chapter 3

Brink, David. *Moral Realism and the Foundation of Ethics.* Cambridge: Cambridge University Press, 1989.

Fishkin, James. *Beyond Subjective Morality.* New Haven: Yale University, 1984.

Harman, Gilbert. "Moral Relativism Defended." *Philosophical Review* 84 (1975).

Ladd, John, ed. *Ethical Relativism.* Belmont, Calif.: Wadsworth Publishing Company, 1973. A good collection of basic readings.

Westermarck, Edward. *Ethical Relativity.* Atlantic Highlands, N.J.: Humanities Press, 1960.

Williams, Bernard. *Morality.* New York: Harper Torchbooks, 1972.

Wong, David. *Moral Relativity.* Berkeley and Los Angeles: University of California Press, 1985.

Part II

Moral Theories
and Moral Character

Suppose you are on an island with a dying millionaire. As he lies dying, he entreats you for one final favor: "I've dedicated my whole life to baseball and have gotten endless pleasure, and some pain, rooting for the New York Yankees for fifty years. Now that I am dying, I want to give all my assets, $6 million, to the Yankees. Would you take this money [he indicates a box containing the money in large bills] back to New York and give it to the New York Yankees' owner, George Steinbrenner, so that he can buy better players?" You agree to carry out his wish, at which point a huge smile of relief and gratitude breaks out on his face as he expires in your arms. After returning to New York, you see a newspaper advertisement placed by the World Hunger Relief Organization (whose integrity you do not doubt) pleading for $6 million to be used to save 100,000 people dying of starvation in East Africa. Not only will the $6 million save their lives, but it will be used to purchase small technology and the kinds of fertilizers necessary to build a sustainable economy. You reconsider your promise to the dying Yankees fan in the light of this consideration. What should you do with the money?

What is the right thing to do in this kind of situation? Consider some traditional moral principles and see if they help you come to a decision. One principle often given to guide action is "Let your conscience be your guide." I recall this principle with fondness, for it was the one my father taught me at an early age, and it still echoes in my mind. But does it help here? No. Since conscience is primarily a function of our upbringing, people's consciences will speak to them in different ways according to how they were brought up. Depending on their upbringing, some people feel no qualms about terrorist acts, whereas others feel the torments of conscience over stepping on a gnat. Suppose your conscience tells you to give the money to the Yankees and my conscience tells me to give the money to the World Hunger Relief Organization. How can we ever discuss the matter? If conscience is the end of the matter, we're left mute.

Another principle urged on us is "Do whatever is most loving." St. Augustine (354–430) said, "Love God and do whatever you want." Love is surely a wonderful value, but is it enough to guide our actions where there is a conflict of interest? "Love is blind," it has been said, "but reason, like marriage, is an eye opener." Whom should I love in the case of the disbursement of the millionaire's money? The millionaire or the starving people? It's not clear how love alone will settle anything. In fact, it is not obvious that we must always do what is most loving. Should we always treat our enemies in loving ways? Or is it morally acceptable to hate those who have purposefully and unjustly harmed us, our loved ones, and other innocent people? Should the survivors of Auschwitz love Adolf Hitler? We will deal with these questions later. Here we must be content to notice that love alone does not solve difficult moral issues.

A third principle often given to guide us in moral actions is the Golden Rule: "Do unto others as you would have them do unto you." We will look more closely at this principle in chapter 5, but for the moment we should note that it has problems. First of all, it cannot be taken literally. Suppose I love to hear loud rock music. I would love you to play it loud for me, so I reason that I should play it loud for you—even though I know that you hate it. So the rule must be modified: "Do unto others as you would have them do unto you if you were in their shoes." But this still has problems. If I were in the shoes of Sirhan Sirhan (the assassin of Robert Kennedy), I'd want to be released from the penitentiary, but it's not clear that he should be. If I put myself in a sex-starved person's shoes, I'd want the next available person to have sex with me, but it's not obvious that I need to comply with that want.

Similarly, the Golden Rule doesn't tell me to whom to give the millionaire's money.

Conscience, love, the Golden Rule are all worthy rules of thumb to help us through life. They work for most of us most of the time over ordinary moral situations. But in more complicated cases, especially where there are legitimate conflicts of interests, they are limited.

A more promising strategy for solving dilemmas is that of following definite moral rules. Suppose you decide to give the millionaire's money to the Yankees in order to keep your promise or because to do otherwise would be stealing. The principle you followed would be "Always keep your promise" and/or "Thou shalt not steal" (the Eighth Commandment). Principles are important in life. All learning involves understanding a set of rules. As Oxford University philosopher R. M. Hare says,

> To learn to do anything is never to learn to do an individual act; it is always to learn to do acts of a certain kind in a certain kind of situation; and this is to learn a principle. . . . Without principles we could not learn anything whatever from our elders. . . . Every generation would have to start from scratch and teach itself. But . . . self-teaching, like all other teaching, is the teaching of principles.[1]

If you decide to act on the principle of promise-keeping or not stealing in the case of the millionaire's money, then you adhere to a type of moral theory called *deontology.*

If, on the other hand, you decide to give the money to the World Hunger Relief Organization in order to save an enormous number of lives and restore economic solvency to the region, you side with a type of theory called *teleology* or *teleological ethics.*

Traditionally, two major types of ethical systems have dominated the field. In one, the locus of value is the act or kind of act, and in the other, the locus of value is the outcome or consequences of the act. The former type of theory is called deontological (from the Greek *deon,* meaning "duty," and *logos* meaning "logic"), and the latter is called teleological (from the Greek *teleos,* meaning "having reached one's end" or "finished"). Whereas teleological systems see the ultimate criterion of morality in some nonmoral value that results from acts, deontological systems see certain features in the act itself as having intrinsic value. For example, a teleologist would judge whether lying was morally right or wrong by the consequences it produced, but a deontologist would see something intrinsically wrong in the very act of lying. In the next chapter we will con-

---

[1]R. M. Hare, *The Language of Morals* (Oxford University Press, 1952), p. 60.

sider the dominant version of teleological ethics, utilitarianism. In chapter 5, we'll examine Immanuel Kant's ethics as the major form of deontological ethics. Then in chapter 6 we shall examine a third theory, virtue ethics, that holds that what is important is moral character—virtue, not (primarily) rules. It rejects the emphasis on rules set forth in these first two theories. But before we turn to this alternative, let us say a few words about teleological ethics, especially utilitarianism.

As we mentioned earlier, a teleologist is a person whose ethical decision-making aims solely at maximizing nonmoral goods such as pleasure, happiness, welfare, and the amelioration of suffering. That is, the standard of right or wrong action for the teleologist is the comparative consequences of the available actions. The act that produces the best consequences is right. Whereas the deontologist is concerned only with the rightness of the act itself, the teleologist asserts that there is no such thing as an act having intrinsic worth. Whereas for the deontologist there is something intrinsically bad about lying, for the teleologist the only thing wrong with lying is the bad consequences it produces. If you can reasonably calculate that a lie will do even slightly more good than telling the truth, you have an obligation to lie. We will examine a deontological account of lying in Charles Fried's article in chapter 5.

CHAPTER 4

Utilitarianism

Utilitarianism is a consequentialist theory which aims at maximizing happiness or "utility." The founders, Jeremy Bentham (1748–1832) and John Stuart Mill (1806–1873), were humanist reformers, who believed that the letter of the law was often a serious impediment to social progress. "The greatest happiness for the greatest number" was their motto. Morality should serve humanity, not vice versa. They were active in promoting penal reform, animal welfare, and women's rights. According to their theory, we should punish criminals not for retributive (or backward-looking) reasons, but simply to prevent their further crimes and to deter others (forward-looking reasons). The classic version of utilitarianism, called *act utilitarianism,* states that an act is right to the extent that it promotes the most overall happiness. So before you do anything, you ought to consider if other acts might better promote utility. If there are, you have a duty to do them. For example, you should give the money you promised to give to the New York Yankees (in our opening thought-experiment) to the starving people if you think more good will come of it. The atomic bombing of Hiroshima and Nagasaki during World War II was justified on utilitarian grounds. A more moderate version of utilitarianism is called *rule utilitarianism,* which holds that we must choose a set of rules that promise to result in the greatest overall happiness, and follow them even when a given instance is unlikely to result in the greatest happiness for the most people.

A common criticism of utilitarianism is that it fails to take human rights seriously. Bentham thought all rights were legal rather than moral. He said that human rights were nonsense and inalienable rights "nonsense on stilts." What is important is responsibility, not rights. We are to take responsibility both for what we do and for what we allow to happen. A discussion of utilitarianism and justice will occur in some of our selections.

We turn first to a famous incident that occurred on the open seas in which Seaman Holmes was confronted with a dilemma of having his longboat sink or throwing passengers overboard. After this, we consider Bentham's classical exposition of utilitarianism and then Kai Nielsen's modern defense. Then we examine Bernard Williams's critique of utilitarianism and Ursula Le Guin's short story about a town whose utilitarian happiness was predicated on the suffering of a child. Finally, we examine Aldous Huxley's dialogue between the utilitarian social engineer of the brave new world, Mustapha Mond, and the savage, who chooses freedom over happiness.

We turn first to a moral dilemma which brings out utilitarian calculations: the case of Seaman Holmes and the longboat of the *William Brown*.

Seaman Holmes and the Longboat of the William Brown, Reported by John William Wallace

The American ship *William Brown* left Liverpool on March 13, 1841, bound for Philadelphia. She had on board (besides a heavy cargo) 17 of a crew and 65 passengers. About 10 o'clock on the night of April 19, when distant 250 miles southwest of Cape Race, Newfoundland, the vessel struck an iceberg, and began to sink rapidly. The long-boat and the jolly-boat were cleared away and lowered. The captain, the second mate, 7 of the crew, and 1 passenger got into the jolly-boat. The first-mate, 8 seamen, including Holmes, and 32 passengers (41 in all) got into the long-boat. This was about twice as many passengers as the boat was made to hold. The remaining 31 passengers were forced to stay with the sinking ship and soon perished. On the following morning (Tuesday) the captain, being about to part company with the long-boat, gave its crew several directions, and, among other counsel, advised them to obey all the orders of the first-mate, as they would obey his, the captain's. The crew promised that they would do so.

The long-boat was believed to be in generally good condition, but it turned out that she had a leak. The passengers had buckets and bailed so that the vessel remained afloat. However, the captain and mate reported that "a very little irregularity in the stowage would have capsized the long-boat" and "if she had struck any piece of ice she would inevitably have gone down. There was great peril of ice for any boat."

Having survived for 24 hours, on Tuesday night heavy rain fell, and the boat began to sink lower into the sea. The first-mate concluded that the men must be thrown overboard to save the boat. He ordered the crew to throw the male passengers overboard. They

---

United States v. Holmes (case no. 15,383), Circuit Court E. d. Pennsylvania, April 22, 1842. Reported by John William Wallace.

hesitated. The first-mate repeated the order. "Men, you must go to work, or we shall all perish." They then went to work; and threw out 14 male passengers. Two sisters of one of the men voluntarily dove into the sea. Two married men and a boy were spared, as well as the women. The long-boat stayed afloat. The next morning Holmes discovered a ship in the distance and drew its attention to the long-boat, so that everyone on board was saved.

After the ship reached Philadelphia, the first-mate and most of the seamen, aware of the impending trial, disappeared. Holmes alone was present to be tried for manslaughter. The judge instructed the jury that the law of the sea required that passengers must always be saved in preference to seamen except those indispensable for operating the boat. If, after sacrificing the lives of the expendable sailors, passengers still must be sacrificed, lots must be drawn, assuming there is time to do so.

The survivors testified that Holmes acquitted himself heroically and compassionately during this ordeal. As the boat was about to pull away from the wreck, Holmes, hearing the desperate cry of a mother for her little daughter, who had been left behind, dashed back at the risk of his life, found the girl, and carried her in his arms to the long-boat.

The jury found Holmes guilty of manslaughter but recommended mercy. He was sentenced to six months' imprisonment at hard labor, in addition to the nine months he had already served in prison while waiting for the trial.

For Further Reflection

1. Discuss the various aspects of this case. What are the salient features? What should the first mate have done? What should Holmes have done? What would you have done in Holmes's place? Do you agree with the law that passengers' lives should be preferred to seamen's? Why or why not?

Classical Utilitarianism

JEREMY BENTHAM

Jeremy Bentham (1748–1832) was a British utilitarian and legal reformer. In this essay from *An Introduction to the Principles of Morals and Legislation,* he argues that pleasure is the only intrinsic value and pain the only intrinsic evil. All other goods and evils are derived from these two qualities. Moral rightness and wrongness are defined in his hedonistic utilitarian approach according to their consequences in producing pleasure and pain.

OF THE PRINCIPLE OF UTILITY

I. Nature has placed mankind under the governance of two sovereign masters, *pain* and *pleasure.* It is for them alone to point out what we ought to do, as well as to determine what we shall do. On the one hand the standard of right and wrong, on the other the chain of causes and effects, are fastened to their throne. They govern us in all we do, in all we say, in all we think: every effort we can make to throw off our subjection, will serve but to demonstrate and confirm it. In words a man may pretend to abjure their empire: but in reality he will remain subject to it all the while. The *principle of utility* recognizes this subjection, and assumes it for the foundation of that system, the object of which is to rear the fabric of felicity by the hands of reason and of law. Systems which attempt to question it, deal in sounds instead of sense, in caprice instead of reason, in darkness instead of light.

But enough of metaphor and declamation: it is not by such means that moral science is to be improved.

II. The principle of utility is the foundation of the present work: it will be proper therefore at the outset to give an explicit and determinate account of what is meant by it. By the principle of utility is meant that principle which approves or disapproves of every action whatsoever, according to the tendency which it appears to

---

Excerpted from *An Introduction to the Principles of Morals and Legislation* (1789).

have to augment or diminish the happiness of the party whose interest is in question: or, what is the same thing in other words, to promote or to oppose that happiness. I say of every action whatsoever; and therefore not only of every action of a private individual, but of every measure of government.

III. By utility is meant that property in any object, whereby it tends to produce benefit, advantage, pleasure, good, or happiness, (all this in the present case comes to the same thing) or (what comes again to the same thing) to prevent the happening of mischief, pain, evil, or unhappiness to the party whose interest is considered: if that party be the community in general, then the happiness of the community: if a particular individual, then the happiness of that individual.

VALUE OF A LOT OF PLEASURE OR PAIN, HOW TO BE MEASURED

I. Pleasures then, and the avoidance of pains, are the ends which the legislator has in view: it behoves him therefore to understand their *value*. Pleasures and pains are the *instruments* he has to work with; it behoves him therefore to understand their force, which is again, in other words, their value.

II. To a person considered *by himself,* the value of a pleasure or pain considered *by itself,* will be greater or less, according to the four following circumstances:

1. Its intensity.
2. Its *duration.*
3. Its *certainty* or *uncertainty.*
4. Its *propinquity* or *remoteness.*

III. These are the circumstances which are to be considered in estimating a pleasure or a pain considered each of them by itself. But when the value of any pleasure or pain is considered for the purpose of estimating the tendency of any *act* by which it is produced, there are two other circumstances to be taken into the account; these are,

5. Its *fecundity,* or the chance it has of being followed by sensations of the *same* kind: that is, pleasures, if it be a pleasure: pains, if it be a pain.

6. Its *purity,* or the chance it has of *not* being followed by sensations of the *opposite* kind: that is, pains, if it be a pleasure: pleasures, if it be a pain.

These two last, however, are in strictness scarcely to be deemed properties of the pleasure or the pain itself; they are not, therefore, in strictness to be taken into the account of the value of that pleasure or that pain. They are in strictness to be deemed properties only of the act, or other event, by which such pleasure or pain has been produced; and accordingly are only to be taken into the account of the tendency of such act or such event.

IV. To a *number* of persons, with reference of each of whom the value of a pleasure or a pain is considered, it will be greater or less, according to seven circumstances: to wit, the six preceding ones; *viz.*

1. Its *intensity.*
2. Its *duration.*
3. Its *certainty* or *uncertainty.*
4. Its *propinquity* or *remoteness.*
5. Its *fecundity.*
6. Its *purity.*

And one other; to wit:

7. Its *extent;* that is, the number of persons to whom it *extends;* or (in other words) who are affected by it.

V. To take an exact account then of the general tendency of any act, by which the interests of a community are affected, proceed as follows. Begin with any one person of those whose interests seem most immediately to be affected by it: and take an account,

1. Of the value of each distinguishable pleasure which appears to be produced by it in the first instance.

2. Of the value of each *pain* which appears to be produced by it in the *first* instance.

3. Of the value of each pleasure which appears to be produced by it *after* the first. This constitutes the *fecundity* of the first *pleasure* and the *impurity* of the first *pain.*

4. Of the value of each *pain* which appears to be produced by it after the first. This constitutes the *fecundity* of the first *pain,* and the *impurity* of the first pleasure.

5. Sum up all the values of all the *pleasures* on the one side, and those of all the pains on the other. The balance, if it be on the side of pleasure, will give the *good* tendency of the act upon the whole, with respect to the interests of that *individual* person; if on the side of pain, the *bad* tendency of it upon the whole.

6. Take an account of the *number* of persons whose interests appear to be concerned; and repeat the above process with respect to each. *Sum up* the numbers expressive of the degrees of *good* tendency, which the act has, with respect to each individual, in regard to whom the tendency of it is *good* upon the whole: do this again with respect to each individual, in regard to whom the tendency of it is *bad* upon the whole. Take the *balance;* which, if on the side of *pleasure,* will give the general *good tendency* of the act, with respect to the total number or community of individuals concerned; if on the side of pain, the general *evil tendency,* with respect to the same community.

VI. It is not to be expected that this process should be strictly pursued previously to every moral judgment, or to every legislative or judicial operation. It may, however, be always kept in view: and as near as the process actually pursued on these occasions approaches to it, so near will such process approach to the character of an exact one.

VII. The same process is alike applicable to pleasure and pain, in whatever shape they appear: and by whatever denomination they are distinguished: to pleasure, whether it be called *good* (which is properly the cause or instrument of pleasure) or *profit* (which is distant pleasure, or the cause or instrument of distant pleasure), or *convenience,* or *advantage, benefit, emolument, happiness,* and so forth: to pain, whether it be called *evil,* (which corresponds to *good*) or *mischief,* or *inconvenience,* or *disadvantage,* or *loss,* or *unhappiness,* and so forth.

VIII. Nor is this a novel and unwarranted, any more than it is a useless, theory. In all this there is nothing but what the practice of mankind, wheresoever they have a clear view of their own interest, is perfectly conformable to. An article of property, an estate in land, for instance, is valuable, on what account? On account of the pleasures of all kinds which it enables a man to produce, and what comes to the same thing the pains of all kinds which it enables him to avert. But the value of such an article of property is universally understood to rise or fall according to the length or shortness of the time which a man had in it: the certainty or uncertainty of its coming into possession: and the nearness or remoteness of the time at which, if at all, it is to come into possession. As to the *intensity* of the pleasures which a man may derive from it, this is never thought of, because it depends upon the use which each particular person may come to make of it; which cannot be estimated till the particular pleasures he may come to derive from it, or the particular pains he may come to exclude by means of it, are brought to view. For the same reason, neither does he think of the *fecundity* or *purity* of those pleasures.

Thus much for pleasure and pain, happiness and unhappiness, in *general*. . . .

XVII. Under the Gentoo and Mahometan religions, the interests of the rest of the animal creation seem to have met with some attention. Why have they not, universally, with as much as those of human creatures, allowance made for the difference in point of sensibility? Because the laws that are have been the work of mutual fear; a sentiment which the less rational animals have not had the same means as man has of turning to account. Why **ought** they not? No reason can be given. If the being eaten were all, there is very good reason why we should be suffered to eat such of them as we like to eat: we are the better for it, and they are never the worse. They have none of those long-protracted anticipations of future misery which we have. The death they suffer in our hands commonly is, and always may be, a speedier, and by that means a less painful one, than that which would await them in the inevitable course of nature. If the being killed were all, there is very good reason why we should be suffered to kill such as molest us: we should be the worse for their living, and they are never the worse for being dead. But is there any reason why we should be suffered to torment them? Not any that I can see. Are there any why we should **not** be suffered to torment them? Yes, several. The day has been, I grieve to say in many places it is not yet past, in which the greater part of the species, under the denomination of slaves, have been treated by the law exactly upon the same footing, as, in England for example, the inferior races of animals are

still. The day may come, when the rest of the animal creation may
acquire those rights which never could have been withholden from
them but by the hand of tyranny. The French have already discovered that the blackness of the skin is no reason why a human
being should be abandoned without redress to the caprice of a tor-
mentor. It may come one day to be recognized, that the number
of the legs, the villosity of the skin, or the termination of the **os**
sacrum, are reasons equally insufficient for abandoning a sensitive
being to the same fate. What else is it that should trace the insuperable line? Is it the faculty of reason, or, perhaps, the faculty of
discourse? But a full-grown horse or dog is beyond comparison a
more rational, as well as a more conversable animal, than an infant
of a day, or a week, or even a month, old. But suppose the case
were otherwise, what would it avail? The question is not, Can they
reason? nor, Can they *talk?* but, Can they **suffer**?

For Further Reflection

1. Analyze Bentham's utilitarianism. Do you agree with him that
   "pain and pleasure" are our "two sovereign masters"? What does
   he mean by *pain* and *pleasure?* Note that *pleasure* is an ambiguous word. It can mean "sensuous titillation" or "satisfaction."
   Which does Bentham mean? Which concept does he need for
   his theory?

2. In his own time Bentham was criticized for setting forth a "pig
   philosophy," since his "simplistic" notions of motivation by pain
   and pleasure are more suited to pigs than humans. Do you
   agree with this judgment?

3. Bentham's utilitarianism requires that we perform a hedonic calculus, summing up all the prospective pleasures likely to result
   from an act and subtracting the pains. Go over his process and
   note the difficulties of doing this.

4. Reread the last paragraph regarding the criterion of suffering
   as the basis for moral consideration. What are the implications
   of this principle for ethics? For our relations with animals?

A Defense of Utilitarianism

KAI NIELSEN

Kai Nielsen, until his recent retirement, was professor of philosophy at Calgary University. He has written important works in the philosophy of religion and in political theory, as well as in ethics. This essay is a clear example of act utilitarianism, the doctrine that we ought to evaluate each act on its own merits, those merits consisting in whether the act maximizes utility. Nielsen sets forth his theory as a credible alternative to moral conservativism or deontological ethics, which maintains that there are "moral principles, prescribing determinate actions, with which it would always be wrong not to act in accordance no matter what the consequences." He argues, to the contrary, that it is the consequences that determine the moral worth of an action.

Nielsen's arguments in favor of utilitarianism partly depend on the notion of negative responsibility. That is, we are responsible not only for the consequences of our actions, but also for the consequences of our *nonactions*.

I

It is sometimes claimed that any consequentialist view of ethics has monstrous implications which make such a conception of morality untenable. What we must do—so the claim goes—is reject all forms of consequentialism and accept what has been labeled 'conservatism' or 'moral absolutism.' By 'conservatism' is meant, here, a normative ethical theory which maintains that there is a privileged moral principle or cluster of moral principles, prescribing determinate actions, with which it would always be wrong not to act in accordance no matter what the consequences. A key example of such a principle is the claim that it is always wrong to kill an innocent human, whatever the consequences of not doing so.

From *Ethics* 82 (1972): 113–124. Reprinted by permission of The University of Chicago Press.

I will argue that such moral conservatism is itself unjustified and, indeed, has morally unacceptable consequences, while consequentialism does not have implications which are morally monstrous and does not contain evident moral mistakes.

A consequentialist maintains that actions, rules, policies, practices, and moral principles are ultimately to be judged by certain consequences: to wit (for a very influential kind of consequentialism), by whether doing them more than, or at least as much as doing anything else, or acting in accordance with them more than or at least as much as acting in accordance with alternative policies, practices, rules or principles, tends, on the whole, and for *everyone* involved, to maximize satisfaction and minimize dissatisfaction. The states of affairs to be sought are those which maximize these things to the greatest extent possible for all mankind. But while this all sounds very humane and humanitarian, when its implications are thought through, it has been forcefully argued, it will be seen actually to have inhumane and morally intolerable implications. Circumstances could arise in which one holding such a view would have to assert that one was justified in punishing, killing, torturing, or deliberately harming the innocent, and such a consequence is, morally speaking, unacceptable.[1] As Anscombe has put it, anyone who "really thinks, *in advance,* that it is open to question whether such an action as procuring the judicial execution of the innocent should be quite excluded from consideration—I do not want to argue with him; he shows a corrupt mind."[2]

At the risk of being thought to exhibit a corrupt mind and a shallow consequentialist morality, I should like to argue that things are not as simple and straightforward as Anscombe seems to believe.

Surely, every moral man must be appalled at the judicial execution of the innocent or at the punishment, torture, and killing of the innocent. Indeed, being appalled by such behavior partially defines what it is to be a moral agent. And a consequentialist has

[1] Alan Donagan, "Is There a Credible Form of Utilitarianism?" and H. J. McCloskey, "A Non-Utilitarian Approach to Punishment," both in Michael D. Bayles, ed. *Contemporary Utilitarianism* (Garden City, N.Y.: Doubleday, 1968).

[2] Elizabeth Anscombe, "Modern Moral Philosophy," *Philosophy 23* (January 1957): 16–17.

very good utilitarian grounds for being so appalled, namely, that it is always wrong to inflict pain for its own sake. But this does not get to the core considerations which divide a conservative position such as Anscombe's from a consequentialist view. There are a series of tough cases that need to be taken to heart and their implications thought through by any reflective person, be he a conservative or a consequentialist. By doing this, we can get to the heart of the issue between conservatism and consequentialism. Consider this clash between conservatism and consequentialism arising over the problem of a 'just war.'

> If we deliberately bomb civilian targets, we do not pretend that civilians are combatants in any simple fashion, but argue that this bombing will terminate hostilities more quickly, and will minimize all around suffering. It is hard to see how any brand of utilitarian will escape Miss Anscombe's objections. We are certainly killing the innocent . . . we are not killing them for the sake of killing them, but to save the lives of other innocent persons. Utilitarians, I think, grit their teeth and put up with this as part of the logic of total war; Miss Anscombe and anyone who thinks like her surely has to either redescribe the situation to ascribe guilt to the civilians or else she has to refuse to accept this sort of military tactics as simply wrong.[3]

It is indeed true that we cannot but feel the force of Anscombe's objections here. But is it the case that anyone shows a corrupt mind if he defends such bombing when, horrible as it is, it will quite definitely lessen appreciably the total amount of suffering and death in the long run, and if he is sufficiently nonevasive not to rationalize such a bombing of civilians into a situation in which all the putatively innocent people—children and all—are somehow in some measure judged guilty? Must such a man exhibit a corrupt moral sense if he refuses to hold that such military tactics are never morally justified? Must this be the monstrous view of a fanatical man devoid of any proper moral awareness? It is difficult for me to believe that this must be so.

Consider the quite parallel actions of guerrilla fighters and terrorists in wars of national liberation. In certain almost unavoidable

---

[3]Alan Ryan, "Review of Jan Narveson's *Morality and Utility,*" *Philosophical Books 9,* no. 3 (October 1958): 14.

circumstances, they must deliberately kill the innocent. We need to see some cases in detail here to get the necessary contextual background, and for this reason the motion picture *The Battle of Algiers* can be taken as a convenient point of reference. There we saw Algerian women—gentle, kindly women with children of their own and plainly people of moral sensitivity—with evident heaviness of heart, plant bombs which they had every good reason to believe would kill innocent people, including children; and we also saw a French general, also a human being of moral fiber and integrity, order the torture of Arab terrorists and threaten the bombing of houses in which terrorists were concealed but which also contained innocent people, including children. There are indeed many people involved in such activities who are cruel, sadistic beasts, or simply morally indifferent or, in important ways, morally uncomprehending. But the characters I have referred to from *The Battle of Algiers* were not of that stamp. They were plainly moral agents of a high degree of sensitivity, and yet they deliberately killed or were prepared to kill the innocent. And, with inessential variations, this is a recurrent phenomenon of human living in extreme situations. Such cases are by no means desert-island or esoteric cases.

It is indeed arguable whether such actions are always morally wrong—whether anyone should ever act as the Arab women or French general acted. But what could not be reasonably maintained, *pace* Anscombe, by any stretch of the imagination, is that the characters I described from *The Battle of Algiers* exhibited corrupt minds. Possibly morally mistaken, yes; guilty of moral corruption, no.

Dropping the charge of moral corruption but sticking with the moral issue about what actions are right, is it not the case that my consequentialist position logically forces me to conclude that under some circumstances—where the good to be achieved is great enough—I must not only countenance but actually advocate such violence toward the innocent? But is it not always, no matter what the circumstances or consequences, wrong to countenance, advocate, or engage in such violence? To answer such a question affirmatively is to commit oneself to the kind of moral absolutism or conservatism which Anscombe advocates. But, given the alternatives, should not one be such a conservative or at least hold that certain deontological principles must never be overridden?

I will take, so to speak, the papal bull by the horns and answer that there are circumstances when such violence must be reluctantly assented to or even taken to be something that one, morally speaking, must do. But, *pace* Anscombe, this very much needs arguing, and I shall argue it; but first I would like to set out some further but simpler cases which have a similar bearing. They are, by contrast, artificial cases. I use them because, in their greater simplicity, by contrast with my above examples, there are fewer variables to control and I can more conveniently make the essential conceptual and moral points. But, if my argument is correct for these simpler cases, the line of reasoning employed is intended to be applicable to those more complex cases as well.

II

Consider the following cases embedded in their exemplary tales:

1. The Case of the Innocent Fat Man

Consider the story (well known to philosophers) of the fat man stuck in the mouth of a cave on a coast. He was leading a group of people out of the cave when he got stuck in the mouth of the cave and in a very short time high tide will be upon them, and unless he is promptly unstuck, they all will be drowned except the fat man, whose head is out of the cave. But, fortunately or unfortunately, someone has with him a stick of dynamite. The short of the matter is, either they use the dynamite and blast the poor innocent fat man out of the mouth of the cave or everyone else drowns. Either one life or many lives. Our conservative presumably would take the attitude that it is all in God's hands and say that he ought never to blast the fat man out, for it is always wrong to kill the innocent. Must or should a moral man come to that conclusion? I shall argue that he should not.

My first exemplary tale was designed to show that our normal, immediate, rather absolutistic, moral reactions need to be questioned along with such principles as 'The direct intention of the death of an innocent person is never justifiable.' I have hinted (and later shall argue) that we should *beware* of our moral outrage here—our naturally conservative and unreflective moral reactions—for here the consequentialist has a strong case for what I shall call 'moral radicalism.'

But, before turning to a defense of that, I want to tell another story taken from Philippa Foot but used for my own purposes.[4] This tale, I shall argue, has a different import than our previous tale. Here our unrehearsed, commonsense moral reactions will stand up under moral scrutiny. But, I shall also argue when I consider them in Section III, that our commonsense moral reactions here, initial expectations to the contrary notwithstanding, can be shown to be justified on consequentialist grounds. The thrust of my argument for this case is that we are not justified in opting for a theistic and/or deontological absolutism or in rejecting consequentialism.

2. The Magistrate and the Threatening Mob

A magistrate or judge is faced with a very real threat from a large and uncontrollable mob of rioters demanding a culprit for a crime. Unless the criminal is produced, promptly tried, and executed, they will take their own bloody revenge on a much smaller and quite vulnerable section of the community (a kind of frenzied pogrom). The judge knows that the real culprit is unknown and that the authorities do not even have a good clue as to who he may be. But he also knows that there is within easy reach a disreputable, thoroughly disliked, and useless man, who, though innocent, could easily be blamed so that the mob would be quite convinced that he was guilty and would be pacified if he were promptly executed. Recognizing that he can prevent the occurrence of extensive carnage only by framing some innocent person, the magistrate has him framed, goes through the mockery of a trial, and has him executed. Most of us regard such a framing and execution of such a man in such circumstances as totally unacceptable.[5] There are some who would say that it is categorically wrong—morally inexcusable—*whatever the circumstances.* Indeed, such a case remains a problem for the consequentialist, but here again, I shall argue, one can

[4]Philippa Foot, "The Problem of Abortion and the Doctrine of the Double Effect," *Oxford Review,* no. 5 (1967): 5–15.
[5]Later, I shall show that there are desert-island circumstances—i.e., highly improbable situations—in which such judicial railroading might be a moral necessity. But I also show what little force desert-island cases have in the articulation and defense of a normative ethical theory.

consistently remain a consequentialist and continue to accept commonsense moral convictions about such matters.

My storytelling is at an end. The job is to see what the stories imply. We must try to determine whether thinking through their implications should lead a clear-headed and morally sensitive man to abandon consequentialism and to adopt some form of theistic absolutism and/or deontological absolutism. I shall argue that it does not.

III

I shall consider the last case first because there are good reasons why the consequentialist should stick with commonsense moral convictions for such cases. I shall start by giving my rationale for that claim. If the magistrate were a tough-minded but morally conscientious consequentialist, he could still, on straightforward consequentialist grounds, refuse to frame and execute the innocent man, even knowing that this would unleash the mob and cause much suffering and many deaths. The rationale for his particular moral stand would be that, by so framing and then executing such an innocent man, he would, in the long run, cause still more suffering through the resultant corrupting effect on the institution of justice. That is, in a case involving such extensive general interest in the issue—without that, there would be no problem about preventing the carnage or call for such extreme measures—knowledge that the man was framed, that the law had prostituted itself, would, surely, eventually leak out. This would encourage mob action in other circumstances, would lead to an increased skepticism about the incorruptibility or even the reliability of the judicial process, and would set a dangerous precedent for less clearheaded or less scrupulously humane magistrates. Given such a potential for the corruption of justice, a utilitarian or consequentialist judge or magistrate could, on good utilitarian or consequentialist grounds, argue that it was morally wrong to frame an innocent man. If the mob must rampage if such a sacrificial lamb is not provided, then the mob must rampage.

Must a utilitarian or consequentialist come to such a conclusion? The answer is no. It is the conclusion which is, as things stand, the most reasonable conclusion, but that he *must* come to it is far too strong a claim. A consequentialist could *consistently*—I did not say successfully—argue that, in taking the above tough-minded utilitarian position, we have overestimated the corrupting effects of such judicial railroading. His circumstance was an extreme one: a situation not often to be repeated even if, instead of acting as he did, he had set a precedent by such an act of judicial murder. A utilitarian rather more skeptical than most utilitarians about the claims of commonsense morality might reason that the lesser evil here is the judicial murder of an innocent man, vile as it is. He would persist in his moral iconoclasm by standing on the consequentialist rock that the lesser evil is always to be preferred to the greater evil.

The short of it is that utilitarians could disagree, as other consequentialists could disagree, about what is morally required of us in that case. The disagreement here between utilitarians or consequentialists of the same type is not one concerning fundamental moral principles but a disagreement about the empirical facts, about what course of action would in the long run produce the least suffering and the most happiness for *everyone* involved.[6]

However, considering the effect advocating the deliberate judicial killing of an innocent man would have on the reliance people put on commonsense moral beliefs of such a ubiquitous sort as the belief that the innocent must not be harmed, a utilitarian who defended the centrality of commonsense moral beliefs would indeed have a strong utilitarian case here. But the most crucial thing to recognize is that, to regard such judicial bowing to such a threatening mob as unqualifiedly wrong, as morally intolerable, one need not reject utilitarianism and accept some form of theistic or deontological absolutism.

It has been argued, however, that, in taking such a stance, I still have not squarely faced the moral conservative's central objection to the judicial railroading of the innocent. I allow, as a consequentialist, that there could be circumstances, at least as far as logical possibilities are concerned, in which such a railroading would be justified but that, as things actually go, it is not and probably never in fact will be justified. But the conservative's point is that

---

[6]'Everyone' here is used distributively, i.e., I am talking about the interests of each and every one. In that sense, everyone's interests need to be considered.

in *no circumstances, either actual or conceivable, would it be justified*. No matter what the consequences, it is unqualifiedly unjustified. To say, as I do, that the situations in which it might be justified are desert-island, esoteric cases which do not occur in life, is not to the point, for, as Alan Donagan argues, "Moral theory is *a priori,* as clear-headed utilitarians like Henry Sidgwick recognized. It is, as Leibniz would say, 'true of all possible words.' "[7] Thus, to argue as I have and as others have that the counterexamples directed against the consequentialists appeal to conditions which are never in fact fulfilled or are unlikely to be fulfilled is beside the point.[8] Whether "a moral theory is true or false depends on whether its implications for all possible worlds are true. Hence, whether utilitarianism (or consequentialism) is true or false cannot depend on how the actual world is."[9] It is possible to specify logically conceivable situations in which consequentialism would have implications which are monstrous—for example, certain beneficial judicial murders of the innocent (whether they are even remotely likely to obtain is irrelevant)—hence consequentialism must be false.

We should not take such a short way with consequentialists, for what is true in Donagan's claim about moral theory's being a priori will not refute or even render implausible consequentialism, and what would undermine it in such a claim about the a priori nature of moral theory and presumably moral claims is not true.

To say that moral theory is a priori is probably correct if that means that categorical moral claims—fundamental moral statements—cannot be deduced from empirical statements or nonmoral theological statements, such that it is a contradiction to assert the empirical and/or nonmoral theological statements and deny the categorical moral claims or vice versa.[10] In that fundamental sense, it is reasonable and, I believe, justifiable to maintain that moral the-

---

[7]Donagan, *op. cit.,* p. 189.

[8]T. L. S. Sprigge argues in such a manner in his "A Utilitarian Reply to Dr. McCloskey" in Michael D. Bayles, ed. *Contemporary Utilitarianism* (Garden City, N.Y.: Doubleday, 1968).

[9]Donagan, *op. cit.,* p. 194.

[10]There is considerable recent literature about whether it is possible to derive moral claims from nonmoral claims. See W. D. Hudson, ed., *The Is-Ought Question: A Collection of Papers on the Central Problem in Moral Philosophy* (New York: St. Martin's Press, 1969).

ory is autonomous and a priori. It is also a priori in the sense that moral statements are not themselves a kind of empirical statement. That is, if I assert 'One ought never to torture any sentient creature' or 'One ought never to kill an innocent man,' I am not trying to predict or describe what people do or are likely to do but am asserting what they are *to do*. It is also true that, if a moral statement is true, it holds for all possible worlds *in which situations are exactly the sort characterized in the statement*. If it is true for one, it is true for all. You cannot consistently say that A ought to do B in situation Y and deny that someone exactly like A in a situation exactly like Y ought to do B.

In these ways, moral claims and indeed moral theory are a priori. But it is also evident that none of these ways will touch the consequentialist or utilitarian arguments. After all, the consequentialist need not be, and typically has not been, an ethical naturalist—he need not think moral claims are derivable from factual claims or that moral claims are a subspecies of empirical statement and he could accept—indeed, he must accept—what is an important truism anyway, that you cannot consistently say that A ought to do B in situation Y and deny that someone exactly like A in a situation exactly like Y ought to do B. But he could and should deny that moral claims are a priori in the sense that rational men must or even will make them without regard for the context, the situation, in which they are made. We say people ought not to drive way over the speed limit, or speed on icy roads, or throw knives at each other. But, if human beings had a kind of metallic exoskeleton and would not be hurt, disfigured, or seriously inconvenienced by knives sticking in them or by automobile crashes, we would not—so evidently at least—have good grounds for saying such speeding or knife throwing is wrong. It would not be so obvious that it was unreasonable and immoral to do these things if these conditions obtained.

In the very way we choose to describe the situation when we make ethical remarks, it is important in making this choice that we know what the world is like and what human beings are like. Our understanding of the situation, our understanding of human nature and motivation cannot but affect our structuring of the moral case. The consequentialist is saying that, as the world goes, there are good grounds for holding that judicial killings are morally intolerable, though he would have to admit that if the world (including human beings) were very different, such killings could be something that ought to be done. But, in holding this, he is not committed to denying the universalizability of moral judgments, for, where he would reverse or qualify the moral judgment, the situation must be different. He is only committed to claiming that, where the situation is the same or relevantly similar and the persons are relevantly similar, they must, if they are to act morally, do the same thing. However, he is claiming both (1) that, as things stand, judicial killing of the innocent is always wrong and (2) that it is an irrational moral judgment to assert of reasonably determinate actions (e.g., killing an innocent man) that they are unjustifiable and morally unacceptable on all *possible* worlds, whatever the situation and whatever the consequences.

Donagan's claims about the a priori nature of moral theories do not show such a consequentialist claim to be mistaken or even give us the slightest reason for thinking that it is mistaken. What is brutal and vile, for example, throwing a knife at a human being just for the fun of it, would not be so, if human beings were invulnerable to harm from such a direction because they had a metallic exoskeleton. Similarly, what is, as things are, morally intolerable, for example, the judicial killing of the innocent, need not be morally intolerable in all conceivable circumstances.

Such considerations support the utilitarian or consequentialist skeptical of simply taking the claims of our commonsense morality as a rock-bottom ground of appeal for moral theorizing. Yet it may also well be the case—given our extensive cruelty any way—that, if we ever start sanctioning such behavior, an even greater callousness toward life than the very extensive callousness extant now will, as a matter of fact, develop. Given a normative ethical theory which sanctions, *under certain circumstances,* such judicial murders, there may occur an undermining of our moral disapproval of killing and our absolutely essential moral principle that all human beings, great and small, are deserving of respect. This is surely enough, together with the not unimportant weight of even our unrehearsed moral feelings, to give strong utilitarian weight *here* to the dictates of our commonsense morality. Yet, I think I have also said enough to show that someone who questions their 'unquestionableness' in such a context does not thereby exhibit a 'corrupt mind' and that it is an open question whether he must be conceptually confused or morally mistaken over this matter.

IV

So far, I have tried to show with reference to the case of the magistrate and the threatening mob how consequentialists can reasonably square their normative ethical theories with an important range of commonsense moral convictions. Now, I wish by reference to the case of the innocent fat man to establish that there is at least a serious question concerning whether such fundamental commonsense moral convictions should always function as 'moral facts' or a kind of moral ground to test the adequacy of normative ethical theories or positions. I want to establish that careful attention to such cases shows that we are not justified in taking the principles embodied in our commonsense moral reasoning about such cases as normative for all moral decisions. That a normative ethical theory is incompatible with some of our 'moral intuitions' (moral feelings or convictions) does not refute the normative ethical theory. What I will try to do here is to establish that this case, no more than the case examined in Section III, gives us adequate grounds for abandoning consequentialism and for adopting moral conservativism.

Forget the levity of the example and consider the case of the innocent fat man. If there really is no other way of unsticking our fat man and if plainly, without blasting him out, everyone in the cave will drown, then, innocent or not, he should be blasted out. This indeed overrides the principle that the innocent should never be deliberately killed, but it does not reveal a callousness toward life, for the people involved are caught in a desperate situation in which, if such extreme action is not taken, many lives will be lost and far greater misery will obtain. Moreover, the people who do such a horrible thing or acquiesce in the doing of it are not likely to be rendered more callous about human life and human suffering as a result. Its occurrence will haunt them for the rest of their lives and is as likely as not to make them more rather than less morally sensitive. It is not even correct to say that such a desperate act shows a lack of respect for persons. We are not treating the fat man merely as a means. The fat man's person—his interests and rights—are not ignored. Killing him is something which is undertaken with the greatest reluctance. It is only when it is quite certain that there is no other way to save the lives of the others that such a violent course of action is justifiably undertaken.

Alan Donagan, arguing rather as Anscombe argues, maintains that "to use any innocent man ill for the sake of some public good is directly to degrade him to being a mere means" and to do this is of course to violate a principle essential to morality, that is, that human beings should never merely be treated as means but should be treated as ends in themselves (as persons worthy of respect.)[11] But, as my above remarks show, it need not be the case, and in the above situation it is not the case, that in killing such an innocent man we are treating him *merely* as a means. The action is universalizable, all alternative actions which would save his life are duly considered, the blasting out is done only as a last and desperate resort with the minimum of harshness and indifference to his suffering and the like. It indeed sounds ironical to talk this way, given what is done to him. But if such a terrible situation were to arise, there would always be more or less humane ways of going about one's grim task. And in acting in the more humane ways toward the fat man, as we do what we must do and would have done to ourselves were the roles reversed, we show a respect for his person.[12]

In so treating the fat man—not just to further the public good but to prevent the certain death of a whole group of people (that is, to prevent an even greater evil than his being killed in this way)—the claims of justice are not overridden either, for each individual involved, if he is reasoning correctly, should realize that if he were so stuck rather than the fat man, he should in such situations be blasted out. Thus, there is no question of being unfair. Surely we must choose between evils here, but is there anything more reasonable, more morally appropriate, than choosing the lesser evil when doing or allowing some evil cannot be avoided? That is, where there is no avoiding both and where our actions can determine whether a greater or lesser evil obtains, should we not plainly always opt for the lesser evil? And is it not obviously a

---

[11]Donagan, *op. cit.,* pp. 199–200.

[12]Again, I am not asserting that we would have enough fortitude to assent to it were the roles actually reversed. I am making a conceptual remark about what as moral beings we must try to do and not a psychological observation about what we can do.

greater evil that all those other innocent people should suffer and die than that the fat man should suffer and die? Blowing up the fat man is indeed monstrous. But letting him remain stuck while the whole group drowns is still more monstrous.

The consequentialist is on strong moral ground here, and, if his reflective moral convictions do not square either with certain unrehearsed or with certain reflective particular moral convictions of human beings, so much the worse for such commonsense moral convictions. One could even usefully and relevantly adapt here—though for a quite different purpose—an argument of Donagan's. Consequentialism of the kind I have been arguing for provides so persuasive "a theoretical basis for common morality that when it contradicts some moral intuition, it is natural to suspect that intuition, not theory, is corrupt."[13] Given the comprehensiveness, plausibility, and overall rationality of consequentialism, it is not unreasonable to override even a deeply felt moral conviction if it does not square with such a theory, though, if it made no sense or overrode the bulk of or even a great many of our considered moral convictions, that would be another matter indeed.

Anticonsequentialists often point to the inhumanity of people who will sanction such killing of the innocent, but cannot the compliment be returned by speaking of the even greater inhumanity, conjoined with evasiveness, of those who will allow even more death and far greater misery and then excuse themselves on the ground that they did not intend the death and misery but merely forbore to prevent it? In such a context, such reasoning and such forbearing to prevent seems to me to constitute a moral evasion. I say it is evasive because rather than steeling himself to do what in normal circumstances would be a horrible and vile act but in this circumstance is a harsh moral necessity, he allows, when he has the power to prevent it, a situation which is still many times worse. He tries to keep his 'moral purity' and avoid 'dirty hands' at the price of utter moral failure and what Kierkegaard called 'double-mindedness.' It is understandable that people should act in this morally evasive way but this does not make it right.

My consequentialist reasoning about such cases as the case of the innocent fat man is very often resisted on the grounds that it

[13]Donagan, *op. cit.*, p. 198.

starts a very dangerous precedent. People rationalize wildly and irrationally in their own favor in such situations. To avoid such rationalization, we must stubbornly stick to our deontological principles and recognize as well that very frequently, if people will put their wits to work or just endure, such admittedly monstrous actions done to prevent still greater evils will turn out to be unnecessary.

The general moral principles surrounding bans on killing the innocent are strong and play such a crucial role in the ever-floundering effort to humanize the savage mind—savage as a primitive and savage again as a contemporary in industrial society—that it is of the utmost social utility, it can be argued, that such bans against killing the innocent not be called into question in any practical manner by consequentialist reasoning.

However, in arguing in this way, the moral conservative has plainly shifted his ground, and he is himself arguing on consequentialist grounds that we must treat certain nonconsequentialist moral principles as absolute (as principles which can never *in fact,* from a reasonable moral point of view, be overridden, for it would be just too disastrous to do so).[14] But now he is on my home court, and my reply is that there is no good evidence at all that in the circumstances I characterized, overriding these deontological principles would have this disastrous effect. I am aware that a bad precedent could be set. Such judgments must not be made for more doubtful cases. But my telling my two stories in some detail, and my contrasting them, was done in order to make evident the type of situation, with its attendant rationale, in which the overriding of those deontological principles can be seen clearly to be justified and the situations in which this does obtain and why. My point was to specify the situations in which we ought to override our commonsense moral convictions about those matters, and the contexts in which we are not so justified or at least in which it is not clear which course of action is justified.[15]

---

[14]Jonathan Bennett, "Whatever the Consequences" *Analysis* 26 (1966), has shown that this is a very common equivocation for the conservative and makes, when unnoticed, his position seem more plausible than it actually is.

[15]I have spoken, conceding this to the Christian absolutist for the sake of the discussion, as if (1) it is fairly evident what our commonsense moral con-

If people are able to be sufficiently clear-headed about these matters, they can see that there are relevant differences between the two sorts of cases. But I was also carefully guarding against extending such 'moral radicalism'—if such it should be called—to other and more doubtful cases. Unless solid empirical evidence can be given that such a 'moral radicalism' would—if it were to gain a toehold in the community—overflow destructively and inhumanely into the other doubtful and positively unjustifiable situations, nothing has been said to undermine the correctness of my consequentialist defense of 'moral radicalism' in the contexts in which I defended it.

For Further Reflection

1. Analyze Nielsen's arguments for utilitarianism. What are their strengths and weaknesses?

2. Does it make sense to use utilitarian reasoning in deciding how to fight a war? How would a deontologist and a utilitarian differ in deciding on the morality of dropping the A-bomb on Hiroshima during World War II?

3. Consider the two examples given in this article: the fat man in the cave and the judge and the threatening mob. What is the morally right thing to do in these cases? Does utilitarianism have a better answer than deontological ethics to this question?

4. What is negative responsibility? What are its implications? What are some problems with it?

---

victions are here and (2) that they are deontological principles taken to hold no matter what the consequences. But that either (1) or (2) is clearly so seems to me very much open to question.

Against Utilitarianism

BERNARD WILLIAMS

Bernard Williams holds a joint appointment as professor of philosophy at both Oxford University and the University of California at Berkeley. In this selection he argues that utilitarianism is a bad moral theory because it violates moral integrity, itself a deep moral ideal. That is, utilitarians frequently require us to reject conscience and our personal ideals in favor of the "lesser of evils." It is the concept of *negative responsibility* (discussed in Nielsen's article) that is the prime culprit in this degenerate process. Because, according to utilitarianism, we are responsible for evil if we knowingly let it happen when we could do something about it, the utilitarian requires us to do lesser evils—even when they require us to violate moral principles and do great harm. Williams offers two examples of how utilitarianism infringes on our integrity.

It is because consequentialism attaches value ultimately to states of affairs, and its concern is with what states of affairs the world contains, that it essentially involves the notion of *negative responsibility*: that if I am ever responsible for anything, then I must be just as much responsible for things that I allow or fail to prevent, as I am for things that I myself, in the more everyday restricted sense, bring about. Those things also must enter my deliberations, as a responsible moral agent, on the same footing. What matters is what states of affairs the world contains, and so what matters with respect to a given action is what comes about if it is done, and what comes about if it is not done, and those are questions not intrinsically affected by the nature of the causal linkage, in particular by whether the outcome is partly produced by other agents.

The strong doctrine of negative responsibility flows directly from consequentialism's assignment of ultimate value to states of affairs.

Reprinted with permission from *Utilitarianism: For and Against,* edited by J. J. C. Smart and Bernard Williams (Cambridge University Press, 1973).

Looked at from another point of view, it can be seen also as a special application of something that is favoured in many moral outlooks not themselves consequentialist—something which, indeed, some thinkers have been disposed to regard as the essence of morality itself: a principle of impartiality. Such a principle will claim that there can be no relevant difference from a moral point of view which consists just in the fact, not further explicable in general terms, that benefits or harms accrue to one person rather than to another—'it's me' can never in itself be a morally comprehensible reason. [By] this principle, familiar with regard to the reception of harms and benefits, we can see consequentialism as extending to their production: from the moral point of view, there is no comprehensible difference which consists just in my bringing about a certain outcome rather than someone else's producing it. That the doctrine of negative responsibility represents in this way the extreme of impartiality, and abstracts from the identity of the agent, leaving just a locus of causal intervention in the world—that fact is not merely a surface paradox. It helps to explain why consequentialism can seem to some to express a more serious attitude than nonconsequentialist views, why part of its appeal is to a certain kind of high-mindedness. Indeed, that is part of what is wrong with it.

Let us look more concretely at two examples, to see what utilitarianism might say about them, what we might say about utilitarianism and, most importantly of all, what would be implied by certain ways of thinking about the situations. . . .

(1) George, who has just taken his Ph.D. in chemistry, finds it extremely difficult to get a job. He is not very robust in health, which cuts down the number of jobs he might be able to do satisfactorily. His wife has to go out to work to keep them, which itself causes a great deal of strain, since they have small children and there are severe problems about looking after them. The results of all this, especially on the children, are damaging. An older chemist, who knows about this situation, says that he can get George a decently paid job in a certain laboratory, which pursues research into chemical and biological warfare. George says that he cannot accept this, since he is opposed to chemical and biological warfare. The older man replies that he is not too keen on it himself, come to that, but after all George's refusal is not going to make the job or the laboratory go away; what is more, he happens to know that if George refuses the job, it will certainly go to a contemporary of George's

who is not inhibited by any such scruples and is likely if appointed to push along the research with greater zeal than George would. Indeed, it is not merely concern for George and his family, but (to speak frankly and in confidence) some alarm about this other man's excess of zeal, which has led the older man to offer to use his influence to get George the job. . . . George's wife, to whom he is deeply attached, has views (the details of which need not concern us) from which it follows that at least there is nothing particularly wrong with research into CBW. What should he do?

(2) Jim finds himself in the central square of a small South American town. Tied up against the wall are a row of twenty Indians, most terrified, a few defiant, in front of them several armed men in uniform. A heavy man in a sweat-stained khaki shirt turns out to be the captain in charge and, after a good deal of questioning of Jim which establishes that he got there by accident while on a botanical expedition, explains that the Indians are a random group of the inhabitants who, after recent acts of protest against the government, are just about to be killed to remind other possible protestors of the advantages of not protesting. However, since Jim is an honoured visitor from another land, the captain is happy to offer him a guest's privilege of killing one of the Indians himself. If Jim accepts, then as a special mark of the occasion, the other Indians will be let off. Of course, if Jim refuses, then there is no special occasion, and Pedro here will do what he was about to do when Jim arrived, and kill them all. Jim, with some desperate recollection of schoolboy fiction, wonders whether if he got hold of a gun, he could hold the captain, Pedro and the rest of the soldiers to threat, but it is quite clear from the set-up that nothing of that kind is going to work: any attempt at that sort of thing will mean that all the Indians will be killed, and himself. The men against the wall, and the other villagers, understand the situation, and are obviously begging him to accept. What should he do?

To these dilemmas, it seems to me that utilitarianism replies, in the first case, that George should accept the job, and in the second, that Jim should kill the Indian. Not only does utilitarianism give these answers but, if the situations are essentially as described and there are no further special factors, it regards them, it seems to me, as *obviously* the right answers. But many of us would certainly wonder whether, in (1), that could possibly be the right answer at all; and in the case of (2), even one who came to think that perhaps that was the answer, might well wonder whether it was obviously the answer. Nor is it just a question of the rightness or obviousness of these answers. It is also a question of what sort of considerations come into finding the answer. A feature of utilitarianism is that it cuts out a kind of consideration which for some others makes a difference to what they feel about such cases: a consideration involving the idea, as we might first and very simply put it, that each of us is specially responsible for what *he* does, rather than for what other people do. This is an idea closely connected with the value of integrity. It is often suspected that utilitarianism, at least in its direct forms, makes integrity as a value more or less unintelligible. I shall try to show that this suspicion is correct. Of course, even if that is correct, it would not necessarily follow that we should reject utilitarianism; perhaps, as utilitarians sometimes suggest, we should just forget about integrity, in favour of such things as a concern for the general good. However, if I am right, we cannot merely do that, since the reason why utilitarianism cannot understand integrity is that it cannot coherently describe the relations between a man's projects and his actions.

TWO KINDS OF REMOTER EFFECT

A lot of what we have to say about this question will be about the relations between my projects and other people's projects. But before we get on to that, we should first ask whether we are assuming too hastily what the utilitarian answers to the dilemmas will be. In terms of more dire effects of the possible decisions, there does not indeed seem much doubt about the answer in either case; but it might be said that in terms of more remote or less evident effects counterweights might be found to enter the utilitarian scales. Thus the effect on George of a decision to take the job might be invoked, or its effect on others who might know of his decision. The possibility of there being more beneficent labours in the future from which he might be barred or disqualified, might be mentioned; and so forth. Such effects—in particular, possible effects on the agent's character, and effects on the public at large—are often invoked by utilitarian writers dealing with problems about lying or promise-breaking, and some similar considerations might be invoked here.

There is one very general remark that is worth making about arguments of this sort. The certainty that attaches to these hypotheses about possible effects is usually pretty low; in some cases, indeed, the hypothesis invoked is so implausible that it would scarcely pass if it were not being used to deliver the respectable moral answer, as in the standard fantasy that one of the effects of one's telling a particular lie is to weaken the disposition of the world at large to tell the truth. The demands on the certainty or probability of these beliefs as beliefs about particular actions are much milder than they would be on beliefs favouring the unconventional course. It may be said that this is as it should be, since the presumption must be in favour of the conventional course: but that scarcely seems a *utilitarian* answer, unless utilitarianism has already taken off in the direction of not applying the consequences to the particular act at all.

Leaving aside that very general point, I want to consider now two types of effect that are often invoked by utilitarians, and which might be invoked in connection with these imaginary cases. The attitude or tone involved in invoking these effects may sometimes seem peculiar; but that sort of peculiarity soon becomes familiar in utilitarian discussions, and indeed it can be something of an achievement to retain a sense of it.

First, there is the psychological effect on the agent. Our descriptions of these situations have not so far taken account of how George or Jim will be after they have taken the one course or the other; and it might be said that if they take the course which seemed at first the utilitarian one, the effects on them will be in fact bad enough and extensive enough to cancel out the initial utilitarian advantages of that course. Now there is one version of this effect in which, for a utilitarian, some confusion must be involved, namely that in which the agent feels bad, his subsequent conduct and relations are crippled and so on, *because he thinks that he has done the wrong thing*— for if the balance of outcomes was as it appeared to be *before* invoking this effect, then he has not (from the utilitarian point of view) done the wrong thing. So that version of the effect, for a rational and utilitarian agent, could not possibly make any difference to the assessment of right and wrong. However, perhaps he is not a thoroughly rational agent, and is disposed to have bad feelings, whichever he decided to do. Now such feelings, which are from a strictly utilitarian point of view irrational—nothing, a utilitarian can point out, is advanced by having them—cannot, consistently, have any great weight in a utilitarian calculation. I shall consider in a moment an argument to suggest that they should have no weight at all in it. But short of that, the utilitarian could reasonably say that such feelings should not be encouraged, even if we accept their existence, and that to give them a lot of weight is to encourage them. Or, at the very best, even if they are straightforwardly and without any discount to be put into the calculation, their weight must be small: they are after all (and at best) one man's feelings.

That consideration might seem to have particular force in Jim's case. In George's case, his feelings represent a larger proportion of what is to be weighed, and are more commensurate in character with other items in the calculation. In Jim's case, however, his feelings might seem to be of very little weight compared with other things that are at stake. There is a powerful and recognizable appeal that can be made on this point: as that a refusal by Jim to do what he has been invited to do would be a kind of self-indulgent squeamishness. That is an appeal which can be made by other than utilitarians— indeed, there are some uses of it which cannot be consistently made by utilitarians, as when it essentially involves the idea that there is something dishonourable about such self-indulgence. But in some versions it is a familiar, and it must be said a powerful, weapon of utilitarianism. One must be clear, though, about what it can and cannot accomplish. The most it can do, so far as I can see, is to invite one to consider how seriously, and for what reasons, one feels that what one is invited to do is (in these circumstances) wrong, and in particular, to consider that question from the utilitarian point of view. When the agent is not seeing the situation from a utilitarian point of view, the appeal cannot force him to do so; and if he does come round to seeing it from a utilitarian point of view, there is virtually nothing left for the appeal to do. If he does not see it from a utilitarian point of view, he will not see his resistance to the invitation, and the unpleasant feelings he associates with accepting it, *just* as disagreeable experiences of his; they figure rather as emotional expressions of a thought that to accept would be wrong. He may be asked, as by the appeal, to consider whether he is right, and indeed whether he is fully serious, in thinking that. But the assertion of the appeal, that he is being self-indulgently squeamish, will not itself answer that question, or even help to answer it, since it essentially tells him to regard his feelings just as unpleasant experiences of his, and he cannot, by doing that, answer the question they pose when they are precisely not so regarded, but are regarded as indications of what he thinks is right and wrong. If he does come round fully to the utilitarian point of view then of course he will regard these feelings just as unpleasant experiences of his. And once Jim—at least— has come to see them in that light, there is nothing left for the appeal to do, since *of course* his feelings, so regarded, are of virtually no weight at all in relation to the other things at stake. The 'squeamishness' appeal is not an argument which adds in a hitherto neglected consideration. Rather, it is an invitation to consider the situation, and one's own feelings, from a utilitarian point of view.

The reason why the squeamishness appeal can be very unsettling, and one can be unnerved by the suggestion of self-indulgence in going against utilitarian considerations, is not that we are utilitarians who are uncertain what utilitarian value to attach to our moral feelings, but that we are partially at least not utilitarians, and cannot regard our moral feelings merely as objects of utilitarian value. Because our moral relation to the world is partly given by such feelings, and by a sense of what we can or cannot 'live with,' to come to regard those feelings from a purely utilitarian point of view, that is to say, as happenings outside one's moral self, is to lose a sense of one's moral identity; to lose, in the most literal way, one's integrity. At this point utilitarianism alienates one from one's moral feelings; we shall see a little later how, more basically, it alienates one from one's actions as well. . . .

INTEGRITY

The [two] situations have in common that if the agent does not do a certain disagreeable thing, someone else will, and in Jim's situation at least the result, the state of affairs after the other man has acted, if he does, will be worse than after Jim has acted, if Jim does. The same, on a smaller scale, is true of George's case. I have already suggested that it is inherent in consequentialism that it offers a strong doctrine of negative responsibility. If I know that if I do X, O_1 will eventuate, and if I refrain from doing X, O_2 will, and that O_2 is worse than O_1, then I am responsible for O_2 if I refrain voluntarily from doing X. 'You could have prevented it,' as will be said, and truly, to Jim, if he refuses, by the relatives of the other Indians.

In the present cases, the situation of O_2 includes another agent bringing about results worse than O_1. So far as O_2 has been identified up to this point—merely as the worse outcome which will eventuate if I refrain from doing X—we might equally have said that what that other brings about is O_2; but that would be to under-describe the situation. For what occurs if Jim refrains from action is not solely twenty Indians dead, but *Pedro's killing twenty Indians,* and that is not a result which Pedro brings about, though the death of the Indians is. We can say: what one does is not included in the outcome of what one does, while what another does can be included in the outcome of what one does. For that to be so, as the terms are now being used, only a very weak condition has to be satisfied: for Pedro's killing the Indians to be the outcome of Jim's refusal, it only has to be causally true that if Jim had not refused, Pedro would not have done it.

That may be enough for us to speak, in some sense, of Jim's responsibility for that outcome, if it occurs; but it is certainly not enough, it is worth noticing, for us to speak of Jim's *making* those things happen. For granted this way of their coming about, he could have made them happen only by making Pedro shoot, and there is no acceptable sense in which his refusal makes Pedro shoot. If the captain had said on Jim's refusal, 'you leave me with no alternative,' he would have been lying, like most who use that phrase. While the deaths, and the killing, may be the outcome of Jim's refusal, it is misleading to think, in such a case, of Jim having an *effect* on the world through the medium (as it happens) of Pedro's acts; for this is to leave Pedro out of the picture in his essential role of one who has intentions and projects, projects for realizing which Jim's refusal would leave an opportunity. Instead of thinking in terms of supposed effects of Jim's projects on Pedro, it is more revealing to think in terms of the effects of Pedro's projects on Jim's decision.

Utilitarianism would do well then to acknowledge the evident fact that among the things that make people happy is not only making other people happy, but being taken up or involved in any of a vast range of projects, or—if we waive the evangelical and moralizing associations of the word—commitments. One can be committed to such things as a person, a cause, an institution, a career, one's own genius, or the pursuit of danger.

Now none of these is itself the *pursuit of happiness:* by an exceedingly ancient platitude, it is not at all clear that there could be anything which was just that, or at least anything that had the slightest chance of being successful. Happiness, rather, requires being involved in, or at least content with, something else. It is not impossible for utilitarianism to accept that point: it does not have to be saddled with a naive and absurd philosophy of mind about the relation between desire and happiness. What it does have to say is that if such commitments are worthwhile, then pursuing the projects that flow from them, and realizing some of those projects, will make the person for whom they are worthwhile, happy. It may be that to claim that is still wrong: it may well be that a commitment can make sense to a man (can make sense of his life) without his supposing that it will make him *happy*. But that is not the present point; let us grant to utilitarianism that all worthwhile human projects must conduce, one way or another, to happiness. The point is that even if that is true, it does not follow, nor could it possibly be true, that those projects are themselves projects of pursuing happiness. One has to believe in, or at least want, or quite minimally, be content with, other things, for there to be anywhere that happiness can come from.

Utilitarianism, then, should be willing to agree that its general aim of maximizing happiness does not imply that what everyone is doing is just pursuing happiness. On the contrary, people have to be pursuing other things. What those other things may be, utilitarianism, sticking to its professed empirical stance, should be prepared just to find out. No doubt some possible projects it will want to discourage, on the grounds that their being pursued involves a negative balance of happiness to others: though even there, the unblinking accountant's eye of the strict utilitarian will have something to put in the positive column, the satisfactions of the destructive agent. Beyond that, there will be a vast variety of generally beneficent or at least harmless projects; and some no doubt, will take the form not just of tastes or fancies, but of what I have called 'commitments.' It may even be that the utilitarian researcher will find that many of those with commitments, who have really identified themselves with objects outside themselves, who are thoroughly involved with other persons, or institutions, or activities or causes, are actually happier than those whose projects and wants are not like that. If so, that is an important piece of utilitarian empirical lore.

When I say 'happier' here, I have in mind the sort of consideration which any utilitarian would be committed to accepting: as for instance that such people are less likely to have a breakdown or commit suicide. Of course that is not all that is actually involved, but the point in this argument is to use to the maximum degree utilitarian notions, in order to locate a breaking point in utilitarian thought. In appealing to this strictly utilitarian notion, I am being more consistent with utilitarianism than Smart is. In his struggles with the problem of the brain-electrode man, Smart commends the idea that 'happy' is a partly evaluative term, in the sense that we call 'happiness' those kinds of satisfaction which, as things are, we approve of. But *by what standard* is this surplus element of approval supposed, from a utilitarian point of view, to be allocated? There is no source for it, on a strictly utilitarian view, except further degrees of satisfaction, but there are none of those available, or the problem would not arise. Nor does it help to appeal to the fact that we dislike in prospect things which we like when we get there, for from a utilitarian point of view it would seem that the original dislike was merely irrational or based on an error. Smart's argument at this point seems to be embarrassed by a well-known utilitarian uneasiness, which comes from a feeling that it is not respectable to ignore the 'deep,' while not having anywhere left in human life to locate it.

Let us now go back to the agent as utilitarian, and his higher-order project of maximizing desirable outcomes. At this level, he is committed only to that: what the outcome will actually consist of will depend entirely on the facts, on what persons with what projects and what potential satisfactions there are within calculable reach of the causal levers near which he finds himself. His own substantial projects and commitments come into it, but only as one lot among others—they potentially provide one set of satisfactions among those which he may be able to assist from where he happens to be. He is the agent of the satisfaction system who happens to be at a particular point at a particular time: in Jim's case, our man in South America. His own decisions as a utilitarian agent are a function of all the satisfactions which he can effect from where he is: and this means that the projects of others, to an indeterminately great extent, determine his decision.

This may be so either positively or negatively. It will be so positively if agents within the causal field of his decision have projects which are at any rate harmless and so should be assisted. It will equally be so, but negatively, if there is an agent within the causal field whose projects are harmful, and have to be frustrated to maximize desirable outcomes. So it is with Jim and the soldier Pedro.

On the utilitarian view, the undesirable projects of other people as much determine, in this negative way, one's decisions as the desirable ones do positively: if those people were not there, or had different projects, the causal nexus would be different, and it is the actual state of the causal nexus which determines the decision. The determination to an indefinite degree of my decisions by other people's projects is just another aspect of my unlimited responsibility to act for the best in a causal framework formed to a considerable extent by their projects.

The decision so determined is, for utilitarianism, the right decision. But what if it conflicts with some project of mine? This, the utilitarian will say, has already been dealt with: the satisfaction to you of fulfilling your project, and any satisfactions to others of your so doing, have already been through the calculating device and have been found inadequate. Now in the case of many sorts of projects, that is a perfectly reasonable sort of answer. But in the case of projects of the sort I have called 'commitments,' those with which one is more deeply and extensively involved and identified, this cannot just by itself be an adequate answer, and there may be no adequate answer at all. For, to take the extreme sort of case, how can a man, as a utilitarian agent, come to regard as one satisfaction among others, and a dispensable one, a project or attitude round which he has built his life, just because someone else's projects have so structured the causal scene that that is how the utilitarian sum comes out?

The point here is not, as utilitarians may hasten to say, that if the project or attitude is that central to his life, then to abandon it will be very disagreeable to him and great loss of utility will be involved. I have already argued in section 4 that it is not like that; on the contrary, once he is prepared to look at it like that, the argument in any serious case is over anyway. The point is that he is identified with his actions as flowing from projects and attitudes which in some cases he takes seriously at the deepest level, as what his life is about (or, in some cases, this section of his life—seriousness is not necessarily the same as persistence). It is absurd to demand of such a man, when the sums come in from the utility network which the projects of others have in part determined, that he should just step aside from his own project and decision and acknowledge the decision which utilitarian calculation requires. It is to alienate him in a real sense from his actions and the source of his action in his own convictions. It is to make him into a channel between the input of everyone's projects, including his own, and an output of optimistic decision; but this is to neglect the extent to which *his* actions and *his* decisions have to be seen as the actions and decisions which flow from the projects and attitudes with which he is most closely identified. It is thus, in the most literal sense, an attack on his integrity.

These sorts of considerations do not in themselves give solutions to practical dilemmas such as those provided by our examples; but I hope they help to provide other ways of thinking about them. In fact, it is not hard to see that in George's case, viewed from this perspective, the utilitarian solution would be wrong. Jim's case is different, and harder. But if (as I suppose) the utilitarian is probably right in this case, that is not to be found out just by asking the utilitarian's questions. Discussions of it—and I am not going to try to carry it further here—will have to take seriously the distinction between my killing someone, and its coming about because of what I do that someone else kills them: a distinction based, not so much on the distinction between action and inaction, as on the distinction between my projects and someone else's projects. At least it will have to start by taking that seriously, as utilitarianism does not; but then it will have to build out from there by asking why that distinction seems to have less, or a different, force in this case than it has in George's. One question here would be how far one's powerful objection to killing people just is, in fact, an application of a powerful objection to their being killed. Another dimension of that is the issue of how much it matters that the people at risk are actual, and there, as opposed to hypothetical, or future, or merely elsewhere.

There are many other considerations that could come into such a question, but the immediate point of all this is to draw one particular contrast with utilitarianism: that to reach a grounded decision in such a case should not be regarded as a matter of just discounting one's reactions, impulses and deeply held projects in the face of the pattern of utilities, nor yet merely adding them in—but in the first instance of trying to understand them.

Of course, time and circumstances are unlikely to make a grounded decision, in Jim's case at least, possible. It might not even be decent. Instead of thinking in a rational and systematic way either about utilities or about the value of human life, the relevance of the people at risk being present, and so forth, the presence of the people at risk may just have its effect. The significance of the immediate should not be underestimated. Philosophers, not only utilitarian ones, repeatedly urge one to view the world *sub specie aeternitatis,* but for most human purposes that is not a good *species* to view it under. If we are not agents of the universal satisfaction system, we are not primarily janitors of any system of values, even our own: very often, we just act, as a possibly confused result of the situation in which we are engaged. That, I suspect, is very often an exceedingly good thing.

For Further Reflection

1. Why does Williams reject the utilitarian notion of negative responsibility?

2. What is Williams's main objection to *consequentialism* (his term for utilitarianism)? Examine the cases of George and Jim. What do you think is the right thing to do in these cases? What are Williams's answers? Do you agree with his reasoning?

3. What does Williams mean by *integrity?* What role does this notion play in his argument? Some have criticized Williams for unjustifiably exalting integrity too highly. They say, if my feelings of integrity conflict with making hard but rationally supported choices, we ought to overcome those feelings and do what is right. Here is an illustration. I have given my whole life to support political party X, which had admirable goals and did much good. But the party has been irremediably morally corrupted and now is harming people. Still my sense of integrity is tied up in all the good the party once stood for. I reason that it would be a good thing to destroy the party, for the good of humanity, and I have the opportunity to do so. But my sense of integrity prevents me from easily doing this. I deeply identify with party X. Although this may be a hard decision, many ethicists would argue that we must overcome our squeamishness and do the right thing: destroy party X, so that its present evil will be ineffectual. How would Williams deal with this case? How would you?

The Ones Who Walk
Away from Omelas

URSULA LE GUIN

Ursula Le Guin is the author of many novels and short story collections, including *The Wind's Twelve Quarters,* from which this short story is taken. The story is about an ideal utilitarian, utopian society that is dependent on one significant suffering. Le Guin credits a passage from the philosopher William James as the point of departure for this story. James wrote:

> Or if the hypothesis were offered us of a world in which Messr. Fourier's and Bellamy's and Morris's utopias should all be outdone, and millions kept permanently happy on the one simple condition that a certain lost soul on the far-off edge of things should lead a life of lonely torment, what except a special and independent sort of emotion can it be which would make us immediately feel, even though an impulse arose within us to clutch at the happiness so offered, how hideous a thing would be its enjoyment when deliberately accepted as the fruit of such a bargain?

With a clamor of bells that set the swallows soaring, the Festival of Summer came to the city Omelas, bright-towered by the sea. The rigging of the boats in harbor sparkled with flags. In the streets between houses with red roofs and painted walls, between old moss-grown gardens and under avenues of trees, past great parks and public buildings, processions moved. Some were decorous: old people in long stiff robes of mauve and grey, grave master workmen, quiet, merry women carrying their babies and chatting as they walked. In other streets the music beat faster, a shimmering of gong and tambourine, and the people went dancing, the procession was a dance. Children dodged in and out, their high calls rising like the swallows' crossing flights over the music and the singing. All the processions wound towards the north side of the city, where on the great water-meadow called the Green Fields boys and girls, naked in the bright air, with mud-stained feet and ankles and long, lithe arms, exercised their restive horses before the race. The horses wore no gear at all but a halter without bit. Their manes were braided with streamers of silver, gold, and green. They flared their nostrils and pranced and boasted to one another; they were vastly excited, the horse being the only animal who has adopted our ceremonies as his own. Far off to the north and west the mountains stood up half encircling Omelas on her bay. The air of morning was so clear that the snow still crowning the Eighteen Peaks burned with white-gold fire across the miles of sunlit air, under the dark blue of the sky. There was just enough wind to make the banners that marked the racecourse snap and flutter now and then. In the silence of the broad green meadows one could hear the music winding through the city streets, farther and nearer and ever approaching, a cheerful faint sweetness of the air that from time to time trembled and gathered together and broke out into the great joyous clanging of the bells.

Joyous! How is one to tell about joy? How describe the citizens of Omelas?

They were not simple folk, you see, though they were happy. But we do not say the words of cheer much any more. All smiles have become archaic. Given a description such as this one tends to make certain assumptions. Given a description such as this one tends to look next for the King, mounted on a splendid stallion and surrounded by his noble knights, or perhaps in a golden litter borne by great-muscled slaves. But there was no king. They did not use swords, or keep slaves. They were not barbarians. I do not know the rules and laws of their society, but I suspect that they were singularly few. As they did without monarchy and slavery, so they also got on without the stock exchange, the advertisement, the secret police, and the bomb. Yet I repeat that these were not simple folk, not dulcet shepherds, noble savages, bland utopians. They were not less complex than us. The trouble is that we have a bad habit, encouraged by pedants and sophisticates, of considering happiness as something rather stupid. Only pain is intellectual, only evil interesting. This is the treason of the artist: a refusal to admit the banality of evil and the terrible boredom of pain. If you can't lick 'em, join 'em. If it hurts, repeat it. But to praise despair is to condemn delight, to embrace violence is to lose hold of everything else. We have almost lost hold; we can no longer describe a happy man, nor make any celebration of joy. How can I tell you about the people of Omelas? They were not naïve and happy children—though their children were, in fact, happy. They were mature, intelligent, passionate adults whose lives were not wretched. O miracle! but I wish I could describe it better. I wish I could convince you. Omelas sounds in my words like a city in a fairy tale, long ago and far away, once upon a time. Perhaps it would be best if you imagined it as your own fancy bids, assuming it will rise to the occasion, for certainly I cannot suit you all. For instance, how about technology? I think that there would be no cars or helicopters in and above the streets; this follows from the fact that the people of Omelas are happy people. Happiness is based on a just discrimination of what is necessary, what is neither necessary nor destructive, and what is destructive. In the middle category, however—that of the unnecessary but undestructive, that of comfort, luxury, exuberance, etc.—they could perfectly well have central heating, subway trains, washing machines, and all kinds of marvelous devices not yet invented here, floating light-sources, fuelless power, a cure for the common cold. Or they could have none of that: it doesn't matter. As you like it. I incline to think that people from towns up and down the coast have been coming in to Omelas during the last days before the Festival on very fast little trains and double-decked trams, and that the train station of Omelas is actually the handsomest building in town, though plainer than the magnificent Farmers' Market. But even granted trains, I fear that Omelas so far strikes some of you as goody-goody. Smiles, bells, parades, horses, bleh. If so, please add an orgy. If an orgy would help, don't hesitate. Let us not, however, have temples from which issue beautiful nude priests and priestesses already half in ecstasy and ready to copulate with any man or woman, lover or stranger, who desires union with the deep godhead of the blood, although that was my first idea. But really it would be better not to have any temples in Omelas—at least, not manned temples. Religion yes, clergy no. Surely the beautiful nudes can just wander about, offering themselves like divine soufflés to the hunger of the needy and the rapture of the flesh. Let them join the processions. Let tambourines be struck above the copulations, and the glory of desire be proclaimed upon the gongs, and (a not unimportant point) let the offspring of these delightful rituals be beloved and looked after by all. One thing I know there is none of in Omelas is guilt. But what else should there be? I thought at first there were no drugs, but that is puritanical. For those who like it, the faint insistent sweetness of *drooz* may perfume the ways of the city, *drooz* which first brings a great lightness and brilliance to the mind and limbs, and then after some hours a dreamy languor, and wonderful visions at last of the very arcana and inmost secrets of the Universe, as well as exciting the pleasure of sex beyond all belief; and it is not habit-forming. For more modest tastes I think there ought to be beer. What else, what else belongs in the joyous city? The sense of victory, surely, the celebration of courage. But as we did without clergy, let us do without soldiers. The joy built upon successful slaughter is not the right kind of joy; it will not do; it is fearful and it is trivial. A boundless and generous contentment, a magnanimous triumph felt not against some outer enemy but in communion with the finest and fairest in the souls of all men everywhere and the splendor of the world's summer: this is what swells the hearts of the people of Omelas, and the victory they celebrate is that of life. I really don't think many of them need to take *drooz*.

Most of the processions have reached the Green Fields by now. A marvelous smell of cooking goes forth from the red and blue tents of the provisioners. The faces of small children are amiably sticky; in the benign grey beard of a man a couple of crumbs of rich pastry are entangled. The youths and girls have mounted their horses and are beginning to group around the starting line of the course. An old woman, small, fat, and laughing, is passing out flowers from a basket, and tall young men wear her flowers in their shining hair. A child of nine or ten sits at the edge of the crowd, alone, playing on a wooden flute. People pause to listen, and they smile, but they do not speak to him, for he never ceases playing and never sees them, his dark eyes wholly rapt in the sweet, thin magic of the tune.

He finishes, and slowly lowers his hands holding the wooden flute.

As if that little private silence were the signal, all at once a trumpet sounds from the pavilion near the starting line: imperious, melancholy, piercing. The horses rear on their slender legs, and some of them neigh in answer. Sober-faced, the young riders stroke the horses' necks and soothe them, whispering, "Quiet, quiet, there my beauty, my hope. . . ." They begin to form in rank along the starting line. The crowds along the racecourse are like a field of grass and flowers in the wind. The Festival of Summer has begun.

Do you believe? Do you accept the festival, the city, the joy? No? Then let me describe one more thing.

In a basement under one of the beautiful public buildings of Omelas, or perhaps in the cellar of one of its spacious private homes, there is a room. It has one locked door, and no window. A little light seeps in dustily between cracks in the boards, secondhand from a cobwebbed window somewhere across the cellar. In one corner of the little room a couple of mops, with stiff, clotted, foul-smelling heads, stand near a rusty bucket. The floor is dirt, a little damp to the touch, as cellar dirt usually is. The room is about three paces long and two wide: a mere broom closet or disused tool room. In the room a child is sitting. It could be a boy or a girl. It looks about six, but actually is nearly ten. It is feeble-minded. Perhaps it was born defective, or perhaps it has become imbecile through fear, malnutrition, and neglect. It picks its nose and occasionally fumbles vaguely with its toes or genitals, as it sits hunched in the corner farthest from the bucket and the two mops. It is afraid of the mops. It finds them horrible. It shuts its eyes, but it knows the mops are still standing there; and the door is locked; and nobody will come. The door is always locked; and nobody ever comes, except that sometimes—the child has no understanding of time or interval—sometimes the door rattles terribly and opens, and a person, or several people, are there. One of them may come in and kick the child to make it stand up. The others never come close, but peer in at it with frightened, disgusted eyes. The food bowl and the water jug are hastily filled, the door is locked, the eyes disappear. The people at the door never say anything, but the child, who has not always lived in the tool room, and can remember sunlight and its mother's voice, sometimes speaks. "I will be good," it says. "Please let me out. I will be good!" They never answer. The child used to scream for help at night, and cry a good deal, but now it only makes a kind of whining, "eh-haa, eh-haa," and it speaks less and less often. It is so thin there are no calves to its legs; its belly protrudes; it lives on a half-bowl of corn meal and grease a day. It is naked. Its buttocks and thighs are a mass of festered sores, as it sits in its own excrement continually.

They all know it is there, all the people of Omelas. Some of them have come to see it, others are content merely to know it is there. They all know that it has to be there. Some of them understand why, and some do not, but they all understand that their happiness, the beauty of their city, the tenderness of their friendships, the health of their children, the wisdom of their scholars, the skill of their makers, even the abundance of their harvest and the kindly weathers of their skies, depend wholly on this child's abominable misery.

This is usually explained to children when they are between eight and twelve, whenever they seem capable of understanding; and most of those who come to see the child are young people, though often enough an adult comes, or comes back, to see the child. No matter how well the matter has been explained to them, these young spectators are always shocked and sickened at the sight. They feel disgust, which they had thought themselves superior to. They feel anger, outrage, impotence, despite all the explanations. They would like to do something for the child. But there is nothing they can do. If the child were brought up into the sunlight out of that vile place, if it were cleaned and fed and comforted, that would be a good thing, indeed; but if it were done, in that day and hour all the prosperity and beauty and delight of Omelas would wither and be destroyed. Those are the terms. To exchange all the goodness and grace of every life in Omelas for that single, small improvement: to throw away the happiness of thousands for the chance of the happiness of one: that would be to let guilt within the walls indeed.

The terms are strict and absolute; there may not even be a kind word spoken to the child.

Often the young people go home in tears, or in a tearless rage, when they have seen the child and faced this terrible paradox. They may brood over it for weeks or years. But as time goes on they begin to realize that even if the child could be released, it would not get much good of its freedom: a little vague pleasure of warmth and food, no doubt, but little more. It is too degraded and imbecile to know any real joy. It has been afraid too long ever to be free of fear. Its habits are too uncouth for it to respond to humane treatment. Indeed, after so long it would probably be wretched without walls about it to protect it, and darkness for its eyes, and its own excrement to sit in. Their tears at the bitter injustice dry when they begin to perceive the terrible justice of reality, and to accept it. Yet it is their tears and anger, the trying of their generosity and the acceptance of their helplessness, which are perhaps the true source of the splendor of their lives. Theirs is no vapid, irresponsible happiness. They know that they, like the child, are not free. They know compassion. It is the existence of the child, and their knowledge of its existence, that makes possible the nobility of their architecture, the poignancy of their music, the profundity of their science. It is because of the child that they are so gentle with children. They know that if the wretched one were not there snivelling in the dark, the other one, the flute-player, could make no joyful music as the young riders line up in their beauty for the race in the sunlight of the first morning of summer.

Now do you believe in them? Are they not more credible? But there is one more thing to tell, and this is quite incredible.

At times one of the adolescent girls or boys who go to see the child does not go home to weep or rage, does not, in fact, go home at all. Sometimes also a man or woman much older falls silent for a day or two, and then leaves home. These people go out into the street, and walk down the street alone. They keep walking, and walk straight out of the city of Omelas, through the beautiful gates. They keep walking across the farmlands of Omelas. Each one goes alone, youth or girl, man or woman. Night falls; the traveler must pass down village streets, between the houses with yellow-lit windows, and on out into the darkness of the fields. Each alone, they go west or north, towards the mountains. They go on. They leave Omelas, they walk ahead into the darkness, and they do not come back. The place they go towards is a place even less imaginable to most of us than the city of happiness. I cannot describe it at all. It is possible that it does not exist. But they seem to know where they are going, the ones who walk away from Omelas.

For Further Reflection

1. Discuss how this short story applies to the debate over utilitarianism. Would you walk away from Omelas (Salem spelled backward plus O for Oregon)? Explain your answer.

2. Do we already live in a world like Omelas, only not a utopia? Is our happiness predicated on the suffering of poorer nations from whom we get cheap goods?

The Utilitarian Social Engineer and the Savage (*from* Brave New World)

ALDOUS HUXLEY

Aldous Huxley (1894–1963) was one of the great prophetic English writers of the twentieth century. In his classic futuristic novel, *Brave New World* (which takes place several hundred years after Ford invented the automobile—the beginning of the technological era), the "year of our Ford" (A.F.) replaces "the year of our Lord" (A.D.) as the prime chronological designator. Sexuality is divorced from procreation. Sexual intercourse—"feelies"—is recreational, occurs promiscuously and daily. Children are genetically manufactured by the "Bokanovsky Process" in state hatcheries according to eugenic principles (Alpha Plus intellectuals, Beta and Delta workers . . . Epsilon Minus morons) to fill various state functions. Individualism, especially personal commitments like those of family loyalty, are viewed as repugnant, giving way to the social motto "Community, Identity, Stability." This separation of sex from procreation typically struck people as the most implausible feature of Huxley's 1932 fantasy. But today it is close to a possibility. We have the technological knowledge to be able to produce or manufacture babies with specific genomes. Science fiction may become science.

In the following excerpt we meet the controller of the Brave New World utopia, Mustapha Mond, the utilitarian social engineer, who explains to his troublesome guests, John "the Savage," so named because he was brought up in "uncivilized primitive" American Indian culture, and the two Alpha dissidents, Helmholtz Watson and Bernard Marx, why individual freedom and happiness are incompatible. Mond himself fully understands that social and personal happiness means sacrificing some valuable things, such as personal freedom, Shakespeare, the search for truth, science, and religion; but the quest for truth and beauty lead to social unrest, sickness, old age, and sadness. These constitute the tragedy of freedom. Hence personal freedom has to be reduced to a vanishing point. The motto of *Brave New World* could well be "The Greatest Happiness for the Greatest Number."

John "the Savage" has been brought to the utopia of the Brave New World. While he is in the Hospital for the Dying, where his mother, Linda, has just died, he sees the Delta workers deadening their minds on drugs (*soma*) and impersonal sex. He desperately tries to liberate low-caste Deltas from their bondage to mindless hedonism. We enter the story as the 162 menial workers at the hospital are about to receive their *soma* ration.

The menial staff of the Park Lane Hospital for the Dying consisted of one hundred and sixty-two Deltas divided into two Bokanovsky Groups of eighty-four red-headed female and seventy-eight dark dolychocephalic male twins, respectively. At six, when their working day was over, the two Groups assembled in the vestibule of the Hospital and were served by the Deputy Sub-Bursar with their *soma* ration.

From the lift the Savage stepped out into the midst of them. But his mind was elsewhere—with death, with his grief, and his remorse; mechanically, without consciousness of what he was doing, he began to shoulder his way through the crowd.

"Who are you pushing? Where do you think you're going?"

High, low, from a multitude of separate throats, only two voices squeaked or growled. Repeated indefinitely, as though by a train of mirrors, two faces, one a hairless and freckled moon haloed in orange, the other a thin, beaked bird-mask, stubbly with two days' beard, turned angrily towards him. Their words and, in his ribs, the sharp nudging of elbows, broke through his unawareness. He woke once more to external reality, looked round him, knew what he saw—knew it, with a sinking sense of horror and disgust, for the recurrent delirium of his days and nights, the nightmare of swarming indistinguishable sameness. Twins, twins. . . . Like maggots they had swarmed defilingly over the mystery of Linda's death. Maggots again, but larger, full grown, they now crawled across his grief and his repentance. He halted and, with bewildered and horrified eyes, stared round him at the khaki mob, in the midst of which, over-topping it by a full head, he stood. "How many goodly creatures are there here!" The singing words mocked him derisively. "How beauteous mankind is! O brave new world . . ."

"*Soma* distribution!" shouted a loud voice. "In good order, please. Hurry up there."

A door had been opened, a table and chair carried into the vestibule. The voice was that of a jaunty young Alpha, who had entered carrying a black iron cash-box. A murmur of satisfaction went up from the expectant twins. They forgot all about the Savage. Their attention was now focused on the black cash-box, which the young man had placed on the table, and was now in process of unlocking. The lid was lifted.

"Oo-oh!" said all the hundred and sixty-two simultaneously, as though they were looking at fireworks.

The young man took out a handful of tiny pill-boxes. "Now," he said peremptorily, "step forward, please. One at a time, and no shoving."

One at a time, with no shoving, the twins stepped forward. First two males, then a female, then another male, then three females, then . . .

The Savage stood looking on. "O brave new world, O brave new world . . ." In his mind the singing words seemed to change their tone. They had mocked him through his misery and remorse, mocked him with how hideous a note of cynical derision! Fiendishly laughing, they had insisted on the low squalor, the nauseous ugli-ness of the nightmare. Now, suddenly, they trumpeted a call to arms. "O brave new world!" Miranda was proclaiming the possi-bility of loveliness, the possibility of transforming even the night-mare into something fine and noble. "O brave new world!" It was a challenge, a command.

"No shoving there now!" shouted the Deputy Sub-Bursar in a fury. He slammed down the lid of his cash-box. "I shall stop the distribution unless I have good behaviour."

The Deltas muttered, jostled one another a little, and then were still. The threat had been effective. Deprivation of *soma*—appalling thought!

"That's better," said the young man, and reopened his cash-box.

Linda had been a slave, Linda had died; others should live in free-dom, and the world be made beautiful. A reparation, a duty. And suddenly it was luminously clear to the Savage what he must do; it was as though a shutter had been opened, a curtain drawn back.

"Now," said the Deputy Sub-Bursar.

Another khaki female stepped forward.

"Stop!" called the Savage in a loud and ringing voice. "Stop!"

He pushed his way to the table; the Deltas stared at him with astonishment.

"Ford!" said the Deputy Sub-Bursar, below his breath. "It's the Savage." He felt scared.

"Listen, I beg of you," cried the Savage earnestly. "Lend me your ears . . ." He had never spoken in public before, and found it very difficult to express what he wanted to say. "Don't take that horrible stuff. It's poison, it's poison."

"I say, Mr. Savage," said the Deputy Sub-Bursar, smiling propitiatingly. "Would you mind letting me . . . "

"Poison to soul as well as body."

"Yes, but let me get on with my distribution, won't you? There's a good fellow." With the cautious tenderness of one who strokes a notoriously vicious animal, he patted the Savage's arm. "Just let me . . ."

"Never!" cried the Savage.

"But look here, old man . . ."

"Throw it all away, that horrible poison."

The words "Throw it all away" pierced through the enfolding layers of incomprehension to the quick of the Delta's consciousness. An angry murmur went up from the crowd.

"I come to bring you freedom," said the Savage, turning back towards the twins. "I come . . ."

The Deputy Sub-Bursar heard no more; he had slipped out of the vestibule and was looking up a number in the telephone book.

"Not in his own rooms," Bernard summed up. "Not in mine, not in yours. Not at the Aphroditæum; not at the Centre or the College. Where can he have got to?"

Helmholtz shrugged his shoulders. They had come back from their work expecting to find the Savage waiting for them at one or other of the usual meeting-places, and there was no sign of the fellow. Which was annoying, as they had meant to nip across to Biarritz in Helmholtz's four-seater sporticopter. They'd be late for dinner if he didn't come soon.

"We'll give him five more minutes, said Helmholtz. "If he doesn't turn up by then we'll . . ."

The ringing of the telephone bell interrupted him. He picked up the receiver. "Hullo. Speaking." Then, after a long interval of listening, "Ford in Flivver!" he swore. "I'll come at once."

"What is it?" Bernard asked

"A fellow I know at the Park Lane Hospital," said Helmholtz. "The Savage is there. Seems to have gone mad. Anyhow, it's urgent. Will you come with me?"

Together they hurried along the corridor to the lifts.

"But do you like being slaves?" the Savage was saying as they entered the Hospital. His face was flushed, his eyes bright with ardour and indignation. "Do you like being babies? Yes, babies. Mewling and puking, he added, exasperated by their bestial stupidity into throwing insults at those he had come to save. The insults bounced off their carapace of thick stupidity; they stared at him with a blank expression of dull and sullen resentment in their eyes. "Yes, puking!" he fairly shouted. Grief and remorse, compassion and duty—all were forgotten now and, as it were, absorbed into an intense overpowering hatred of these less than human monsters. "Don't you want to be free and men? Don't you even understand what manhood and freedom are?" Rage was making him fluent; the words came easily, in a rush. "Don't you?" he repeated, but got no answer to his question. "Very well then," he went on grimly. "I'll teach you; I'll *make* you be free whether you want to or not." And pushing open a window that looked on to the inner court of the Hospital, he began to throw the little pill-boxes of *soma* tablets in handfuls out into the area.

For a moment the khaki mob was silent, petrified, at the spectacle of this wanton sacrilege, with amazement and horror.

"He's mad," whispered Bernard, staring with wide open eyes. "They'll kill him. They'll . . ." A great shout suddenly went up from the mob; a wave of movement drove it menacingly towards the Savage. "Ford help him!" said Bernard, and averted his eyes.

"Ford helps those who help themselves." And with a laugh, actually a laugh of exultation, Helmholtz Watson pushed his way through the crowd.

"Free, free!" the Savage shouted, and with one hand continued to throw the *soma* into the area while, with the other, he punched the indistinguishable faces of his assailants. "Free!" And suddenly there was Helmholtz at his side—"Good old Helmholtz!"—also punching—"Men at last!"—and in the interval also throwing the poison out by handfuls through the open window. "Yes, men! men!" and there was no more poison left. He picked up the cash-box and showed them its black emptiness. "You're free!"

Howling, the Deltas charged with a redoubled fury.

Hesitant on the fringes of the battle. "They're done for," said Bernard and, urged by a sudden impulse, ran forward to help them; then thought better of it and halted; then, ashamed, stepped forward again; then again thought better of it, and was standing in an agony of humiliated indecision—thinking that *they* might be killed if he didn't help them, and that *he* might be killed if he did—when (Ford be praised!), goggle-eyed and swine-snouted in their gas-masks, in ran the police.

Bernard dashed to meet them. He waved his arms; and it was action, he was doing something. He shouted "Help!" several times, more and more loudly so as to give himself the illusion of helping. "Help! *Help!* Help!"

The policemen pushed him out of the way and got on with their work. Three men with spraying machines buckled to their shoulders pumped thick clouds of *soma* vapour into the air. Two more were busy round the portable Synthetic Music Box. Carrying water pistols charged with a powerful anæsthetic, four others had pushed their way into the crowd and were methodically laying out, squirt by squirt, the more ferocious of the fighters.

"Quick, quick!" yelled Bernard. "They'll be killed if you don't hurry. They'll . . . Oh!" Annoyed by his chatter, one of the policemen had given him a shot from his water pistol. Bernard stood for a second or two wambling unsteadily on legs that seemed to have lost their bones, their tendons, their muscles, to have become mere sticks of jelly, and at last not even jelly—water: he tumbled in a heap on the floor.

Suddenly, from out of the Synthetic Music Box a Voice began to speak. The Voice of Reason, the Voice of Good Feeling. The sound-track roll was unwinding itself in Synthetic Anti-Riot Speech Number Two (Medium Strength). Straight from the depths of a non-existent heart, "My friends, my friends!" said the Voice so pathetically, with a note of such infinitely tender reproach that, behind their gas masks, even the policemen's eyes were momentarily dimmed with tears, "what is the meaning of this? Why aren't you all being happy and good together? Happy and good," the Voice repeated. "At peace, at peace." It trembled, sank into a whisper and momentarily expired. "Oh, I do want you to be happy," it began, with a yearning earnestness. "I do so want you to be good! Please, please be good and . . ."

Two minutes later the Voice and the *soma* vapour had produced their effect. In tears, the Deltas were kissing and hugging one another—half a dozen twins at a time in a comprehensive embrace. Even Helmholtz and the Savage were almost crying. A fresh supply of pill-boxes was brought in from the Bursary; a new distribution was hastily made and, to the sound of the Voice's richly affectionate, baritone valedictions, the twins dispersed, blubbering as though their hearts would break. "Good-bye, my dearest, dearest friends, Ford keep you! Good-bye, my dearest, dearest friends, Ford keep you. Good-bye my dearest, dearest . . ."

When the last of the Deltas had gone the policeman switched off the current. The angelic Voice fell silent.

"Will you come quietly?" asked the Sergeant, "or must we anæsthetize?" He pointed his water pistol menacingly.

"Oh, we'll come quietly," the Savage answered, dabbing alternately a cut lip, a scratched neck, and a bitten left hand. . . .

The room into which the three were ushered was the Controller's study.

"His fordship will be down in a moment." The Gamma butler left them to themselves.

Helmholtz laughed aloud.

"It's more like a caffeine-solution party than a trial," he said, and let himself fall into the most luxurious of the pneumatic arm-chairs. "Cheer up, Bernard," he added, catching sight of his friend's green unhappy face. But Bernard would not be cheered; without answering, without even looking at Helmholtz, he went and sat down on the most uncomfortable chair in the room, carefully chosen in the obscure hope of somehow deprecating the wrath of the higher powers.

The Savage meanwhile wandered restlessly round the room, peering with a vague superficial inquisitiveness at the books in the shelves, at the sound-track rolls and reading machine bobbins in their numbered pigeon-holes. On the table under the window lay a massive volume bound in limp black leather-surrogate, and stamped with large golden T's. He picked it up and opened it. MY LIFE AND WORK, BY OUR FORD. The book had been published at Detroit by the Society for the Propagation of Fordian Knowledge. Idly he turned the pages, read a sentence here, a paragraph there, and had just come to the conclusion that the book didn't interest him, when the door opened, and the Resident World Controller for Western Europe walked briskly into the room.

Mustapha Mond shook hands with all three of them; but it was to the Savage that he addressed himself. "So you don't much like civilization, Mr. Savage," he said.

The Savage looked at him. He had been prepared to lie, to bluster, to remain sullenly unresponsive; but, reassured by the good-humoured intelligence of the Controller's face, he decided to tell the truth, straightforwardly. "No." He shook his head.

Bernard started and looked horrified. What would the Controller think? To be labelled as the friend of a man who said that he didn't like civilization—said it openly and, of all people, to the Controller—it was terrible. "But, John," he began. A look from Mustapha Mond reduced him to an abject silence.

"Of course," the Savage went on to admit, "there are some very nice things. All that music in the air, for instance . . ."

"Sometimes a thousand twangling instruments will hum about my ears and sometimes voices."

The Savage's face lit up with a sudden pleasure. "Have you read it too?" he asked. "I thought nobody knew about that book here, in England."

"Almost nobody. I'm one of the very few. It's prohibited, you see. But as I make the laws here, I can also break them. With impunity, Mr. Marx," he added, turning to Bernard. "Which I'm afraid you *can't* do."

Bernard sank into a yet more hopeless misery.

"But why is it prohibited?" asked the Savage. In the excitement of meeting a man who had read Shakespeare he had momentarily forgotten everything else.

The Controller shrugged his shoulders. "Because it's old; that's the chief reason. We haven't any use for old things here."

"Even when they're beautiful?"

"Particularly when they're beautiful. Beauty's attractive, and we don't want people to be attracted by old things. We want them to like the new ones."

"But the new ones are so stupid and horrible. Those plays, where there's nothing but helicopters flying about and you *feel* the people kissing." He made a grimace. "Goats and monkeys!" Only in Othello's words could he find an adequate vehicle for his contempt and hatred.

"Nice tame animals, anyhow," the Controller murmured parenthetically.

"Why don't you let them see *Othello* instead?"

"I've told you; it's old. Besides, they couldn't understand it."

Yes, that was true. He remembered how Helmholtz had laughed at *Romeo and Juliet*. "Well then," he said, after a pause, "something new that's like *Othello,* and that they could understand."

"That's what we've all been wanting to write," said Helmholtz, breaking a long silence.

"And it's what you never will write," said the Controller. "Because, if it were really like *Othello* nobody could understand it, however new it might be. And if were new, it couldn't possibly be like *Othello.*"

"Why not?"

"Yes, why not?" Helmholtz repeated. He too was forgetting the unpleasant realities of the situation. Green with anxiety and apprehension, only Bernard remembered them; the others ignored him. "Why not?"

"Because our world is not the same as Othello's world. You can't make flivvers without steel—and you can't make tragedies without social instability. The world's stable now. People are happy; they get what they want, and they never want what they can't get. They're well off; they're safe; they're never ill; they're not afraid of death; they're blissfully ignorant of passion and old age; they're plagued with no mothers or fathers; they've got no wives, or children, or lovers to feel strongly about; they're so conditioned that they practically can't help behaving as they ought to behave. And if anything should go wrong, there's *soma.* Which you go and chuck out of the window in the name of liberty, Mr. Savage. *Liberty!*" He laughed. "Expecting Deltas to know what liberty is! And now expecting them to understand *Othello!* My good boy!"

The Savage was silent for a little. "All the same," he insisted obstinately, "*Othello's* good, *Othello's* better than those feelies."

"Of course it is," the Controller agreed. "But that's the price we have to pay for stability. You've got to choose between happiness and what people used to call high art. We've sacrificed the high art. We have the feelies and the scent organ instead."

"But they don't mean anything."

"They mean themselves; they mean a lot of agreeable sensations to the audience."

"But they're . . . they're told by an idiot."

The Controller laughed. "You're not being very polite to your friend, Mr. Watson. One of our most distinguished Emotional Engineers . . ."

"But he's right," said Helmholtz gloomily. "Because it *is* idiotic. Writing when there's nothing to say . . ."

"Precisely. But that requires the most enormous ingenuity. You're making flivvers out of the absolute minimum of steel—works of art out of practically nothing but pure sensation."

The Savage shook his head. "It all seems to me quite horrible."

"Of course it does. Actual happiness always looks pretty squalid in comparison with the over-compensations for misery. And, of course, stability isn't nearly so spectacular as instability. And being contented has none of the glamour of a good fight against misfortune, none of the picturesqueness of a struggle with temptation, or a fatal overthrow by passion or doubt. Happiness is never grand."

"I suppose not," said the Savage after a silence. "But need it be quite so bad as those twins?" He passed his hand over his eyes as though he were trying to wipe away the remembered image of those long rows of identical midgets at the assembling tables, those queued-up twin-herds at the entrance to the Brentford monorail station, those human maggots swarming round Linda's bed of death, the endlessly repeated face of his assailants. He looked at his bandaged left hand and shuddered. "Horrible!"

"But how useful! I see you don't like our Bokanovsky Groups; but, I assure you, they're the foundation on which everything else is built. They're the gyroscope that stabilizes the rocket plane of state on its unswerving course." The deep voice thrillingly vibrated; the gesticulating hand implied all space and the onrush of the irresistible machine. Mustapha Mond's oratory was almost up to synthetic standards.

"I was wondering," said the Savage, "why you had them at all—seeing that you can get whatever you want out of those bottles. Why don't you make everybody an Alpha Double Plus while you're about it?"

Mustapha Mond laughed. "Because we have no wish to have our throats cut," he answered. "We believe in happiness and stability. A society of Alphas couldn't fail to be unstable and miserable. Imagine a factory staffed by Alphas—that is to say by separate and unrelated individuals of good heredity and conditioned so as to be capable (within limits) of making a free choice and assuming responsibilities. Imagine it!" he repeated.

The Savage tried to imagine it, not very successfully.

"It's an absurdity. An Alpha-decanted, Alpha-conditioned man would go mad if he had to do Epsilon Semi-Moron work—go mad, or start smashing things up. Alphas can be completely socialized—but only on condition that you make them do Alpha work. Only an Epsilon can be expected to make Epsilon sacrifices, for the good reason that for him they aren't sacrifices; they're the line of least resistance. His conditioning has laid down rails along which he's got to run. He can't help himself; he's foredoomed. Even after decanting, he's still inside a bottle—an invisible bottle of infantile and embryonic fixations. Each one of us, of course," the Controller meditatively continued, "goes through life inside a bottle. But if we happen to be Alphas, our bottles are, relatively speaking, enormous. We should suffer acutely if we were confined in a narrower space. You cannot pour upper-caste champagne-surrogate into lower-caste bottles. It's obvious theoretically. But it has also been proved in actual practice. The result of the Cyprus experiment was convincing."

"What was that?" asked the Savage.

Mustapha Mond smiled. "Well, you can call it an experiment in rebottling if you like. It began in A.F. 473. The Controllers had the island of Cyprus cleared of all its existing inhabitants and recolonized with a specially prepared batch of twenty-two thousand Alphas. All agricultural and industrial equipment was handed over to them and they were left to manage their own affairs. The result exactly fulfilled all the theoretical predictions. The land wasn't properly worked; there were strikes in all the factories; the laws were set at naught, orders disobeyed; all the people detailed for a spell of low-grade work were perpetually intriguing for high-grade jobs, and all the people with high-grade jobs were counter-intriguing at all costs to stay where they were. Within six years they were having a first-class civil war. When nineteen out of the twenty-two thousand had been killed, the survivors unanimously petitioned the World Controllers to resume the government of the island. Which they did. And that was the end of the only society of Alphas that the world has ever seen."

The Savage sighed, profoundly.

"The optimum population," said Mustapha Mond, "is modelled on the iceberg—eight-ninths below the water line, one-ninth above."

"And they're happy below the water line?"

"Happier than above it. Happier than your friend here, for example." He pointed.

"In spite of that awful work?"

"Awful? *They* don't find it so. On the contrary, they like it. It's light, it's childishly simple. No strain on the mind or the muscles. Seven and a half hours of mild, unexhausting labour, and then the *soma* ration and games and unrestricted copulation and the feelies. What more can they ask for? True," he added, "they might ask for shorter hours. And of course we could give them shorter hours. Technically, it would be perfectly simple to reduce all lower-caste working hours to three or four a day. But would they be any the happier for that? No, they wouldn't. The experiment was tried, more than a century and a half ago. The whole of Ireland was put on to the four-hour day. What was the result? Unrest and a large increase in the consumption of *soma;* that was all. Those three and a half hours of extra leisure were so far from being a source of happiness, that people felt constrained to take a holiday from them. The Inventions Office is stuffed with plans for labour-saving processes. Thousands of them." Mustapha Mond made a lavish gesture. "And why don't we put them into execution? For the sake of the labourers; it would be sheer cruelty to afflict them with excessive leisure. It's the same with agriculture. We could synthesize every morsel of food, if we wanted to. But we don't. We prefer to keep a third of the population on the land. For their own sakes—because it takes *longer* to get food out of the land than out of a factory. Besides, we have our stability to think of. We don't want to change. Every change is a menace to stability. That's another reason why we're so chary of applying new inventions. Every discovery in pure science is potentially subversive; even science must sometimes be treated as a possible enemy. Yes, even science."

Science? The Savage frowned. He knew the word. But what it exactly signified he could not say. Shakespeare and the old men of the pueblo had never mentioned science, and from Linda he had only gathered the vaguest hints: science was something you made helicopters with, something that caused you to laugh at the Corn Dances, something that prevented you from being wrinkled and losing your teeth. He made a desperate effort to take the Controller's meaning.

"Yes," Mustapha Mond was saying, "that's another item in the cost of stability. It isn't only art that's incompatible with happiness; it's also science. Science is dangerous; we have to keep it most carefully chained and muzzled."

"What?" said Helmholtz, in astonishment. "But we're always saying that science is everything. It's a hypnopædic platitude."

"Three times a week between thirteen and seventeen," put in Bernard.

"And all the science propaganda we do at the College . . ."

"Yes; but what sort of science?" asked Mustapha Mond sarcastically. "You've had no scientific training, so you can't judge. I was a pretty good physicist in my time. Too good—good enough to realize that all our science is just a cookery book, with an orthodox theory of cooking that nobody's allowed to question, and a list of recipes that mustn't be added to except by special permission from the head cook. I'm the head cook now. But I was an inquisitive young scullion once. I started doing a bit of cooking on my own. Unorthodox cooking, illicit cooking. A bit of real science, in fact." He was silent.

"What happened?" asked Helmholtz Watson.

The Controller sighed. "Very nearly what's going to happen to you young men. I was on the point of being sent to an island."

The words galvanized Bernard into violent and unseemly activity. "Send *me* to an island?" He jumped up, ran across the room, and stood gesticulating in front of the Controller. "You can't send *me*. I haven't done anything. It was the others. I swear it was the others." He pointed accusingly to Helmholtz and the Savage. "Oh, please don't send me to Iceland. I promise I'll do what I ought to do. Give me another chance. Please give me another chance." The tears began to flow. "I tell you, it's their fault," he sobbed. "And not to Iceland. Oh please, your fordship, please . . ." And in a paroxysm of abjection he threw himself on his knees before the Controller. Mustapha Mond tried to make him get up; but Bernard persisted in his grovelling; the stream of words poured out inexhaustibly. In the end the Controller had to ring for his fourth secretary.

"Bring three men," he ordered, "and take Mr. Marx into a bedroom. Give him a good *soma* vaporization and then put him to bed and leave him."

The fourth secretary went out and returned with three green-uniformed twin footmen. Still shouting and sobbing, Bernard was carried out.

"One would think he was going to have his throat cut," said the Controller, as the door closed. "Whereas, if he had the smallest sense, he'd understand that his punishment is really a reward. He's being sent to an island. That's to say, he's being sent to a place where he'll meet the most interesting set of men and women to be found anywhere in the world. All the people who, for one reason or another, have got too self-consciously individual to fit into community-life. All the people who aren't satisfied with orthodoxy, who've got independent ideas of their own. Every one, in a word, who's any one. I almost envy you, Mr. Watson."

Helmholtz laughed. "Then why aren't you on an island yourself?"

"Because, finally, I preferred this," the Controller answered. "I was given the choice: to be sent to an island, where I could have got on with my pure science, or to be taken on to the Controllers' Council with the prospect of succeeding in due course to an actual Controllership. I chose this and let the science go." After a little silence, "Sometimes," he added, "I rather regret the science. Happiness is a hard master—particularly other people's happiness. A much harder master, if one isn't conditioned to accept it unquestioningly, than truth." He sighed, fell silent again, then continued in a brisker tone, "Well, duty's duty. One can't consult one's own preference. I'm interested in truth, I like science. But truth's a menace, science is a public danger. As dangerous as it's been beneficent. It has given us the stablest equilibrium in history. China's was hopelessly insecure by comparison; even the primitive matriarchies weren't steadier than we are. Thanks, I repeat, to science. But we can't allow science to undo its own good work. That's why we so carefully limit the scope of its researches—that's why I almost got sent to an island. We don't allow it to deal with any but the most immediate problems of the moment. All other enquiries are most sedulously discouraged. It's curious," he went on after a little pause, "to read what people in the time of Our Ford used to write about scientific progress. They seemed to have imagined that it could be allowed to go on indefinitely, regardless of everything else. Knowledge was the highest good, truth the supreme value; all the rest was secondary and subordinate. True, ideas were beginning to change even then. Our Ford himself did a great deal to shift the emphasis from truth and beauty to comfort and happiness. Mass production demanded the shift. Universal happiness keeps the wheels steadily turning; truth and beauty can't. And, of course, whenever the masses seized political power, then it was happiness rather than truth and beauty that mattered. Still, in spite of everything, unrestricted scientific research was still permitted. People still went on talking about truth and beauty as though they were the sovereign goods. Right up to the time of the Nine Years' War. *That* made them change their tune all right. What's the point of truth or beauty or knowledge when the anthrax bombs are popping all around you? That was when science first began to be controlled— after the Nine Years' War. People were ready to have even their appetites controlled then. Anything for a quiet life. We've gone on controlling ever since. It hasn't been very good for truth, of course. But it's been very good for happiness. One can't have something for nothing. Happiness has got to be paid for. You're paying for it, Mr. Watson—paying because you happen to be too much interested in beauty. I was too much interested in truth; I paid too."

"But *you* didn't go to an island," said the Savage, breaking a long silence.

The Controller smiled. "That's how I paid. By choosing to serve happiness. Other people's—not mine. It's lucky," he added, after a pause, "that there are such a lot of islands in the world. I don't know what we should do without them. Put you all in the lethal chamber, I suppose. By the way, Mr. Watson, would you like a tropical climate? The Marquesas, for example; or Samoa? Or something rather more bracing?"

Helmholtz rose from his pneumatic chair. "I should like a thoroughly bad climate," he answered. "I believe one would write better if the climate were bad. If there were a lot of wind and storms, for example . . ."

The Controller nodded his approbation. "I like your spirit, Mr. Watson. I like it very much indeed. As much as I officially disapprove of it." He smiled. "What about the Falkland Islands?"

"Yes, I think that will do," Helmholtz answered. "And now, if you don't mind, I'll go and see how poor Bernard's getting on."

"Art, science—you seem to have paid a fairly high price for your happiness," said the Savage, when they were alone. "Anything else?"

"Well, religion, of course," replied the Controller. "There used to be something called God—before the Nine Years' War. But I was forgetting; you know all about God, I suppose."

"Well . . ." The Savage hesitated. He would have liked to say something about solitude, about night, about the mesa lying pale under the moon, about the precipice, the plunge into shadowy darkness, about death. He would have liked to speak; but there were no words. Not even in Shakespeare.

The Controller, meanwhile, had crossed to the other side of the room and was unlocking a large safe set into the wall between the bookshelves. The heavy door swung open. Rummaging in the darkness within, "It's a subject," he said, "that has always had a great interest for me." He pulled out a thick black volume. "You've never read this, for example."

The Savage took it. "*The Holy Bible, containing the Old and New Testaments,*" he read aloud from the title-page.

"Nor this." It was a small book and had lost its cover.

"*The Imitation of Christ.*"

"Nor this." He handed out another volume.

"*The Varieties of Religious Experience.* By William James."

"And I've got plenty more," Mustapha Mond continued, resuming his seat. "A whole collection of pornographic old books. God in the safe and Ford on the shelves." He pointed with a laugh to his avowed library—to the shelves of books, the rack full of reading-machine bobbins and sound-track rolls.

"But if you know about God, why don't you tell them?" asked the Savage indignantly. "Why don't you give them these books about God?"

"For the same reason as we don't give them *Othello:* they're old; they're about God hundreds of years ago. Not about God now."

"But God doesn't change."

"Men do, though."

"What difference does that make?"

"All the difference in the world," said Mustapha Mond. He got up again and walked to the safe. "There was a man called Cardinal Newman," he said. "A cardinal," he exclaimed parenthetically, "was a kind of Arch-Community-Songster."

"'I Pandulph, of fair Milan, cardinal.' I've read about them in Shakespeare."

"Of course you have. Well, as I was saying, there was a man called Cardinal Newman. Ah, here's the book." He pulled it out.

"And while I'm about it I'll take this one too. It's by a man called Maine de Biran. He was a philosopher, if you know what that was."

"A man who dreams of fewer things than there are in heaven and earth," said the Savage promptly.

"Quite so. I'll read you one of the things he *did* dream of in a moment. Meanwhile, listen to what this old Arch-Community-Song-ster said." He opened the book at the place marked by a slip of paper and began to read. "'We are not our own any more than what we possess is our own. We did not make ourselves, we cannot be supreme over ourselves. We are not our own masters. We are God's property. Is it not our happiness thus to view the matter? Is it any happiness or any comfort, to consider that we *are* our own? It may be thought so by the young and prosperous. These may think it a great thing to have everything, as they suppose, their own way—to depend on no one—to have to think of nothing out of sight, to be without the irksomeness of continual acknowledgment, continual prayer, continual reference of what they do to the will of another. But as time goes on, they, as all men, will find that independence was not made for man—that it is an unnatural state—will do for a while, but will not carry us on safely to the end . . .'" Mustapha Mond paused, put down the first book and, picking up the other, turned over the pages. "Take this, for example," he said, and in his deep voice once more began to read: "'A man grows old; he feels in himself that radical sense of weakness, of listlessness, of discomfort, which accompanies the advance of age; and, feeling thus, imagines himself merely sick, lulling his fears with the notion that this dis-tressing condition is due to some particular cause, from which, as from an illness, he hopes to recover. Vain imaginings! That sickness is old age; and a horrible disease it is. They say that it is the fear of death and of what comes after death that makes men turn to religion as they advance in years. But my own experience has given me the conviction that, quite apart from any such terrors or imaginings, the religious sentiment tends to develop as we grow older; to develop because, as the passions grow calm, as the fancy and sensibilities are less excited and less excitable, our reason becomes less troubled in its working, less obscured by the images, desires and distractions, in which it used to be absorbed; whereupon God emerges as from behind a cloud; our soul feels, sees, turns towards the source of all light; turns naturally and inevitably; for now that all that gave to the world of sensations its life and charms has begun to leak away from us, now that phenomenal existence is no more bolstered up by impressions from within or from without, we feel the need to lean on something that abides, something that will never play us false— a reality, an absolute and everlasting truth. Yes; we inevitably turn to God; for this religious sentiment is of its nature so pure, so delightful to the soul that experiences it, that it makes up to us for all our other losses.'" Mustapha Mond shut the book and leaned back in his chair. "One of the numerous things in heaven and earth that these philosophers didn't dream about was this" (he waved his hand), "us, the modern world. 'You can only be independent of God while you've got youth and prosperity; independence won't take you safely to the end.' Well, we've now got youth and prosperity right up to the end. What follows? Evidently, that we can be independent of God. 'The religious sentiment will compensate us for all our losses.' But there aren't any losses for us to compensate; religious sentiment is superfluous. And why should we go hunting for a substitute for youthful desires, when youthful desires never fail? A substitute for distractions, when we go on enjoying all the old fooleries to the very last? What need have we of repose when our minds and bodies continue to delight in activity? of consolation, when we have *soma?* of something immovable, when there is the social order?"

"Then you think there is no God?"

"No, I think there quite probably is one."

"Then why? . . ."

Mustapha Mond checked him. "But he manifests himself in different ways to different men. In premodern times he manifested himself as the being that's described in these books. Now . . ."

"How does he manifest himself now?" asked the Savage.

"Well, he manifests himself as an absence; as though he weren't there at all."

"That's your fault."

"Call it the fault of civilization. God isn't compatible with machinery and scientific medicine and universal happiness. You must make your choice. Our civilization has chosen machinery and medicine and happiness. That's why I have to keep these books locked up in the safe. They're smut. People would be shocked it . . ."

The Savage interrupted him. "But isn't it *natural* to feel there's a God?"

"You might as well ask if it's natural to do up one's trousers with zippers," said the Controller sarcastically. "You remind me of another of those old fellows called Bradley. He defined philosophy as the finding of bad reason for what one believes by instinct. As if one believed anything by instinct! One believes things because one has been conditioned to believe them. Finding bad reasons for what one believes for other bad reasons—that's philosophy. People believe in God because they've been conditioned to believe in God."

"But all the same," insisted the Savage, "it is natural to believe in God when you're alone—quite alone, in the night, thinking about death . . ."

"But people never are alone now," said Mustapha Mond. "We make them hate solitude; and we arrange their lives so that it's almost impossible for them ever to have it."

The Savage nodded gloomily. At Malpais he had suffered because they had shut him out from the communal activities of the pueblo, in civilized London he was suffering because he could never escape from those communal activities, never be quietly alone.

"Do you remember that bit in *King Lear?*" said the Savage at last. "'The gods are just and of our pleasant vices make instruments to plague us; the dark and vicious place where thee he got cost him his eyes,' and Edmund answers—you remember, he's wounded, he's dying—'Thou hast spoken right; 'tis true. The wheel has come full circle; I am here.' What about that now? Doesn't there seem to be a God managing things, punishing, rewarding?"

"Well, does there?" questioned the Controller in his turn. "You can indulge in any number of pleasant vices with a freemartin and run no risks of having your eyes put out by your son's mistress. 'The wheel has come full circle; I am here.' But where would Edmund be nowadays? Sitting in a pneumatic chair, with his arm round a girl's waist, sucking away at his sex-hormone chewing-gum and looking at the feelies. The gods are just. No doubt. But their code of law is dictated, in the last resort, by the people who organize society; Providence takes its cue from men."

"Are you sure?" asked the Savage. "Are you quite sure that the Edmund in that pneumatic chair hasn't been just as heavily punished as the Edmund who's wounded and bleeding to death? The gods are just. Haven't they used his pleasant vices as an instrument to degrade him?"

"Degrade him from what position? As a happy, hard-working, goods-consuming citizen he's perfect. Of course, if you choose some other standard than ours, then perhaps you might say he was degraded. But you've got to stick to one set of postulates. You can't play Electro-magnetic Golf according to the rules of Centrifugal Bumble-puppy."

"But value dwells not in particular will," said the Savage. "It holds his estimate and dignity as well wherein 'tis precious of itself as in the prizer."

"Come, come," protested Mustapha Mond, "that's going rather far, isn't it?"

"If you allowed yourselves to think of God, you wouldn't allow yourselves to be degraded by pleasant vices. You'd have a reason for bearing things patiently, for doing things with courage. I've seen it with the Indians."

"I'm sure you have," said Mustapha Mond. "But then we aren't Indians. There isn't any need for a civilized man to bear anything that's seriously unpleasant. And as for doing things—Ford forbid that he should get the idea into his head. It would upset the whole social order if men started doing things on their own."

"What about self-denial, then? If you had a God, you'd have a reason for self-denial."

"But industrial civilization is only possible when there's no self-denial. Self-indulgence up to the very limits imposed by hygiene and economics. Otherwise the wheels stop turning."

"You'd have a reason for chastity!" said the Savage, blushing a little as he spoke the words.

"But chastity means passion, chastity means neurasthenia. And passion and neurasthenia mean instability. And instability means the end of civilization. You can't have a lasting civilization without plenty of pleasant vices."

"But God's the reason for everything noble and fine and heroic. If you had a God . . ."

"My dear young friend," said Mustapha Mond, "civilization has absolutely no need of nobility or heroism. These things are symptoms of political inefficiency. In a properly organized society like ours, nobody has any opportunities for being noble or heroic. Conditions have got to be thoroughly unstable before the occasion can arise. Where there are wars, where there are divided allegiances, where there are temptations to be resisted, objects of love to be fought for or defended—there, obviously, nobility and heroism have some sense. But there aren't any wars nowadays. The greatest care is taken to prevent you from loving any one too much. There's no such thing as a divided allegiance; you're so conditioned that you can't help doing what you ought to do. And what you ought to do is on the whole so pleasant, so many of the natural impulses are allowed free play, that there really aren't any temptations to resist. And if ever, by some unlucky chance, anything unpleasant should somehow happen, why, there's always *soma* to give you a holiday from the facts. And there's always *soma* to calm your anger, to reconcile you to your enemies, to make you patient and long-suffering. In the past you could only accomplish these things by making a great effort and after years of hard moral training. Now, you swallow two or three half-gramme tablets, and there you are. Anybody can be virtuous now. You can carry at least half your mortality about in a bottle. Christianity without tears—that's what *soma* is."

"But the tears are necessary. Don't you remember what Othello said? 'If after every tempest came such calms, may the winds blow till they have wakened death.' There's a story one of the old Indians used to tell us, about the Girl of Mátaski. The young men who wanted to marry her had to do a morning's hoeing in her garden. It seemed easy; but there were flies and mosquitoes, magic ones. Most of the young men simply couldn't stand the biting and stinging. But the one that could—he got the girl."

"Charming! But in civilized countries," said the Controller, "you can have girls without hoeing for them; and there aren't any flies or mosquitoes to sting you. We got rid of them all centuries ago."

The Savage nodded, frowning. "You got rid of them. Yes, that's just like you. Getting rid of everything unpleasant instead of learning to put up with it. Whether 'tis better in the mind to suffer the slings and arrows of outrageous fortune, or to take arms against a sea of troubles and by opposing end them . . . But you don't do either. Neither suffer nor oppose. You just abolish the slings and arrows. It's too easy." . . .

"What you need," the Savage went on, "is something *with* tears for a change. Nothing costs enough here."

("Twelve and a half million dollars," Henry Foster had protested when the Savage told him that. "Twelve and a half million—that's what the new Conditioning Centre cost. Not a cent less.")

"Exposing what is mortal and unsure to all that fortune, death and danger dare, even for an eggshell. Isn't there something in that?" he asked, looking up at Mustapha Mond. "Quite apart from God—though of course God would be a reason for it. Isn't there something in living dangerously?"

"There's a great deal in it," the Controller replied. "Men and women must have their adrenals stimulated from time to time."

"What?" questioned the Savage, uncomprehending.

"It's one of the conditions of perfect health. That's why we've made the V.P.S. treatments compulsory."

"V.P.S.?"

"Violent Passion Surrogate. Regularly once a month. We flood the whole system with adrenin. It's the complete physiological equivalent of fear and rage. All the tonic effects of murdering Desdemona and being murdered by Othello, without any of the inconveniences."

"But I like the inconveniences."

"We don't," said the Controller. "We prefer to do things comfortably."

"But I don't want comfort. I want God, I want poetry, I want real danger, I want freedom, I want goodness. I want sin."

"In fact," said Mustapha Mond, "you're claiming the right to be unhappy."

"All right then," said the Savage defiantly, "I'm claiming the right to be unhappy."

"Not to mention the right to grow old and ugly and impotent; the right to have syphilis and cancer; the right to have too little to eat; the right to be lousy; the right to live in constant apprehension of what may happen tomorrow; the right to catch typhoid; the right to be tortured by unspeakable pains of every kind." There was a long silence.

"I claim them all," said the Savage at last.

Mustapha Mond shrugged his shoulders. "You're welcome," he said.

For Further Reflection

1. In *Brave New World* Huxley starkly contrasts freedom and high culture with happiness. Is his description of the tension between these two values accurate or is it a caricature? Explain your answer.

2. Following up on the first question, is Huxley's satire on utilitarianism insightful, or is it really aimed at a straw man? Note Huxley himself criticized his work as offering the Savage "only

two alternatives, an insane life in Utopia, or the life of a primitive in an Indian village, a life more human in some respects, but in other hardly less queer and abnormal. At the time the book was written this idea, that human beings are given free will in order to choose between insanity, on the one hand, and lunacy on the other, was one that I found amusing and regarded as quite possibly true. . . . Today I feel no wish to demonstrate that sanity is impossible. On the contrary, though I remain no less sadly certain than in the past that sanity is a rather rare phenomenon, I am convinced that it can be achieved and would like to see more of it." (Preface to *Brave New World,* 1946 edition) Do you agree with this reflection of Huxley's, that the truth is in the middle—between complete, unregulated freedom of will and social stability wherein we can find happiness?

3. What, if any, are the lessons of Huxley's novel for our age?

Further Readings for Chapter 4

Bentham, Jeremy. *Introduction to the Principles of Morals and Legislation.* Edited by W. Harrison. Oxford: Oxford University Press, 1948.

Hardin, Russell. *Morality within the Limits of Reason.* Chicago: University of Chicago Press, 1988. A cogent contemporary defense of utilitarianism.

Hare, R. M. *Moral Thinking.* Oxford: Oxford University Press, 1981.

Mill, John Stuart. *Utilitarianism.* Indianapolis: Bobbs-Merrill, 1957.

Quinton, Anthony. *Utilitarian Ethics.* New York: Macmillan, 1973. A clear exposition of classical utilitarianism.

Smart, J. J. C., and Bernard Williams. *Utilitarianism For and Against.* Cambridge: Cambridge University Press, 1973. A classic debate on the subject.

CHAPTER 5

Deontological Ethics

We have already outlined the basic ideas of deontological ethics in the introduction to this part. Deontologists distinguish themselves from consequentialists, like utilitarians, by holding that rightness and wrongness of acts are determined by the intrinsic quality of the act itself or the kind of act it is, not by its consequences. So, recurring to the example in the last chapter, a deontologist would tend to give the millionaire's money to the owner of the New York Yankees, according to the millionaire's request, not to the world hunger organization. There are two classic versions of deontological ethics: Kant's categorical imperative and Ross's intuitionism. Both are featured in this chapter. As you will see from the second reading, Immanuel Kant, the great eighteenth-century German philosopher, held that we may test the moral status of our acts by asking whether we could will the maxim (or principle) of that act to be a universal law of nature. If we can so universalize the principle, the act passes the test of what is morally permissible. If we cannot, then the act is immoral. Kant argued that we cannot will that lying or promise-breaking be universal laws, so that they must be seen as immoral. For Kant, such moral principles are absolute. They have no exceptions.

The second kind of deontological ethics is that of W. D. Ross, the Oxford philosopher, who in our third reading sets forth an intuitionist morality. If we consult our conscience, we will hit upon obvious moral principles. W. D. Ross, unlike Kant, is not an absolutist. Moral principles have *prima facie* or conditional bindingness. They are valid principles, having universal application, but they may not always win out in the end. Another, more stringent, duty may override the normal duty. So, while I should generally tell the

truth, I may be obligated to lie, if by so doing I may save an innocent person's life.

We look at Ambrose Bierce's short story "A Horseman in the
Sky" as an example of deontological thinking. We examine William
Whately's critique of the Golden Rule as a moral principle, Charles
Fried's penetrating deontological analysis of lying as morally wrong,
and Thomas Nagel's provocative essay "Moral Luck," which suggests that much, if not most, of our moral status is a product of
sheer luck. And in chapter 6 Bernard Mayo will also criticize deontological ethics. But first we look at a brief selection from Søren
Kierkegaard's *Either/Or* on the nature of duty.

On Duty

SØREN KIERKEGAARD

Søren Kierkegaard (1813–1855), widely regarded as the
father of existentialism, thought that each human life had a
special purpose, and that by living within the light we had,
we would be guided to higher self-realization, ultimately discovering our relationship with God. He thought that the first
great leap in awareness was the realization of the ethical
dimension in life, when the "aesthete," the young hedonist,
who has hitherto lived for self-gratification, suddenly
becomes aware of something eternal within—duty. In a way,
our sense of duty is an indication of our immortality—or at
least our participation in something eternal, for we sense that
the ethical within us has eternal value and it, in turn, points
to our having such value. In this passage from *Either/Or II*
(that is, either the aesthetic-hedonic way or the ethical),
through his pseudonym, Judge William, Kierkegaard first
describes the importance of choosing the ethical way of life
over the aesthetic and then goes on to describe his first conscious realization of the ethical dimension, when, as a five-
year-old, he was given a homework assignment.

Judge William is rebuking a young aesthete for persisting in a hedonic way of life.

You have chosen the aesthetic, but an aesthetic choice is not choice.
The act of choosing is essentially a proper and stringent expression
of the ethical. Whenever one really makes a conscious choice, it
involves the ethical. That is, the only absolute either/or is the choice
between good and evil, and this is precisely the ethical. The aesthetic
choice is either entirely immediate, a giving in to one's emotions, and
to that extent no choice at all, or else it is the kind of choice that is
temporary and diverse. When a person deliberates aesthetically upon
a number of life's perplexities, he does not easily get a single
either/or, but a whole multiplicity, because the defining factor in the
choice is not ethically emphasized, and because when one does not

From Søren Kierkegaard, *Enten/Eller II* (Copenhagen: Gyldendalske
Boghandels Forlag, 1902). Translated by Louis P. Pojman.

choose absolutely one chooses only for the moment, and so can choose something different the next moment. The ethical choice is therefore, in one sense, much easier, simpler, but in another sense, infinitely more difficult. He who would define his life task ethically has ordinarily not so considerable a selection to choose from. On the other hand, the act of choice has far more importance for him. In making a choice it is not so much a question of choosing the right as of the energy, the sincerity, the passion with which one chooses. Thereby the personality announces its inner infinity, and thereby, in turn, the person realizes his true self. Therefore, even if a person were to choose the particular wrong, he will nonetheless discover, exactly because of the energy with which he chose, that he had chosen the wrong. For since the choice is being made with the whole inwardness of his personality, his entire nature is purified and he himself brought into immediate relation to the eternal Power whose omnipresence interpenetrates the whole of existence. . . .

My choice, my either/or, does not initially denote the choice between good and evil. Rather it denotes the choice whereby one chooses good and evil/or excludes them. . . . He who chooses the ethical, chooses the good, but here the good is entirely abstract, only its being is realized, and hence he could choose evil. . . . In the ethical the person defines himself by a new set of categories, good and evil, and so, on one level, the aesthetic is absolutely excluded, but on another level, a relative one, subservient to the ethical, it is incorporated. The whole aesthetic dimension returns, but as relative to the ethical. . . .

The ethical thesis is that every person has a particular calling. This, in turn, is a consequence of the fact that a rational order exists in the world in which every person, if he will, may find his place in such a manner that he expresses at the same time the universal-human and the individual.

He who understands himself ethically is at once in possession of an absolute difference, i.e., that between good and evil, and if in himself he finds more of the evil than of the good, this does not mean that the evil is what is to come forth, but it means that the evil is to be suppressed and the good allowed to emerge.

The ethical way is the way of duty, and duty may be defined not as a burden imposed from without, but as an inner necessity. This is how to understand duty, not as a multitude of obligations which have an external source, but as an expression of one's inmost nature.

The ethical is the universal and, hence, it is abstract. As a complete abstraction it is always prohibitive, appearing as law. But when the self realizes the ethical as part of his innermost being, it becomes to the highest degree positive. Only when the individual himself is the universal is it possible to realize the ethical. This is the secret of conscience, it is the secret which the individual life shares with itself, that it is at once an individual life and at the same time the universal. He makes himself the universal person, not by stripping himself of his concreteness but by clothing himself with the universal, by permeating his concreteness with the universal. The task of the ethical person is to transform himself into the universal person, while still retaining his individuality.

What is important is not the multifariousness of duty but its energy, its intensity. The main thing is not whether one can count off on one's fingers how many duties one has, but that a person has once felt the intensity of duty in such a way that the consciousness of it is for him the assurance of the eternal validity of his being.

Let me illustrate these points with an example, one from my earliest childhood. When I was five years old I was sent to school. It is natural that such events make deep impressions upon a child, but the question is, what kind of an impression? Children are curious and their curiosity is often confused about the significance of their experiences. This may well have been the case with me. I showed up at school, met my teacher, and then was given as my homework assignment for the following day the first ten lines of Balle's *Lesson Book,* which I soon memorized. Every other impression was then obliterated from my soul. My assignment alone dominated my soul. As a child, I had a very good memory, so I soon learned my lines. My sister had heard me recite them several times and confirmed that I knew them. I went to bed, but before falling asleep, I recited them once more. I fell asleep determined on reviewing my lesson the following morning. I awoke early, at five o'clock, got dressed, took up my book, and read it again.

At this moment this event so marks my soul that it seems as though it only happened yesterday. To me it was as if heaven and earth might collapse if I failed to learn my lesson, but, on the other hand, as if, even if heaven and earth were to collapse, this would not exempt me from carrying out my assignment, of learning my lesson. At that age I didn't understand much about the nature of duties. I knew only about one duty, that of learning my lesson, and yet I can trace my whole ethical perspective of life to this impression.

For Further Reflection

1. What does Kierkegaard mean by the transition from the aesthetic to the ethical stage of life? What constitutes each stage? How does the progression from the aesthetic to the ethical way transform the individual? Do you agree with his analysis?
2. What does Kierkegaard mean by the universal dimension in the ethical? How does it function in the ideal life?
3. Can you relate to Kierkegaard's experience of learning his grammar book? What are its implications for morality in general?

The Moral Law

IMMANUEL KANT

Immanuel Kant (1724–1804) was born into a deeply pietistic Lutheran family in Königsberg, Germany, and lived in that town his entire life. At sixteen he entered the University of Königsberg, where he later taught philosophy. He is considered the greatest philosopher of the Enlightenment. Among his works are *Critique of Pure Reason* (1781), *Prolegomena to Any Future Metaphysic* (1785), and *Foundations of the Metaphysic of Morals* (1785), from which the present selection is taken.

In this classic work Kant rejects such ethical theories as the theory of moral sentiments, set forth by the eighteenth-century Scottish moralists Francis Hutcheson and David Hume, in which morality is naturalistic, contingent, and hypothetical. The moral sentiment view is contingent in that it is based on human nature and, in particular, on our feelings or sentiments. Had we been created differently, we would have a different nature and, hence, different moral duties. Morality in this view consists of hypothetical imperatives in that they depend on our desires for their realiza-

---

Reprinted from *The Foundations of the Metaphysic of Morals,* Translated by T. K. Abbott (this translation first published in 1873).

tion. For example, we should obey the law because we want a peaceful, orderly society. We should seek peace because it is necessary for personal happiness. The naturalistic ethicists were typically utilitarians who sought to maximize human happiness.

Kant rejects this naturalistic, utilitarian account of ethics. Ethics is not *contingent* but *absolute,* and its duties or imperatives are not *hypothetical* but *categorical* (nonconditional). Ethics is based not on feeling but on reason. It is because we are rational beings that we are valuable and capable of discovering moral laws binding on all persons at all times. As such, our moral duties are not dependent on feelings but on reason. They are unconditional, universally valid, and necessary, regardless of the possible consequences or opposition to our inclinations.

This is Kant's first formulation of his *categorical imperative:* "Act only on that maxim whereby you can at the same time will that it would become a universal law." This imperative is given as the criterion (or second-order principle) by which to judge all other principles. If we can consistently will that everyone do some type of action, then the categorical imperative enjoins that type of action. If we cannot consistently will that everyone do some type of action, then that type of action is morally wrong. Kant argues, for example, that we cannot consistently will that everyone make false promises, for the very institution of promising entails or depends on general adherence to keeping the promise or intending to do so.

Kant offers a second formulation of the categorical imperative: "So act as to treat humanity, whether in your own person or in that of any other, in every case as an end and never as merely a means only." Each person by virtue of his or her reason has dignity and profound worth, which entail that he or she must never be exploited, manipulated, or merely used as a means to our idea of what is for the general good.

PREFACE

As my concern here is with moral philosophy, I limit the question suggested to this: Whether it is not of the utmost necessity to construct a pure moral philosophy, perfectly cleared of everything which is only empirical, and which belongs to anthropology? for that such a philosophy must be possible is evident from the common idea of duty and of the moral laws. Everyone must admit that if a law is to have moral force, *i.e.* to be the basis of an obligation, it must carry with it absolute necessity; that, for example, the precept, "Thou shall not lie," is not valid for men alone, as if other rational beings had no need to observe it; and so with all the other moral laws properly so called; that, therefore, the basis of obligation must not be sought in the nature of man, or in the circumstances in the world in which he is placed, but *a priori* simply in the conception of pure reason; and although any other precept which is founded on principles of mere experience may be in certain respects universal, yet in as far as it rests even in the least degree on an empirical basis, perhaps only as to a motive, such a precept, while it may be a practical rule, can never be called a moral law. . . .

THE GOOD WILL

Nothing can possibly be conceived in the world, or even out of it, which can be called good, without qualification, except a Good Will. Intelligence, wit, judgment, and the other *talents* of the mind, however they may be named, or courage, resolution, perseverance, as qualities of temperament, are undoubtedly good and desirable in many respects; but these gifts of nature may also become extremely bad and mischievous if the will which is to make use of them, and which, therefore, constitutes what is called *character,* is not good. It is the same with the *gifts of fortune.* Power, riches, honour, even health, and the general well-being and contentment with one's conditions which is called *happiness,* inspire pride, and often presumption, if there is not a good will to correct the influence of these on the mind, and with this also to rectify the whole principle of acting, and adapt it to its end. The sight of a being who is not adorned with a single feature of a pure and good will, enjoying unbroken prosperity, can never give pleasure to an imperial rational spectator. Thus a good will appears to constitute the indispensable condition even of being worthy of happiness.

There are even some qualities which are of service to this good will itself, and may facilitate its action, yet which have no intrinsic unconditional value, but always presuppose a good will, and this qualifies the esteem that we justly have for them, and does not permit us to regard them as absolutely good. Moderation in the affections and passions, self-control, and calm deliberation are not only good in many respects, but even seem to constitute part of the intrinsic worth of the person; but they are far from deserving to be called good without qualification, although they have been so unconditionally praised by the ancients. For without the principles of a good will, they may become extremely bad; and the coolness of a villain not only makes him far more dangerous, but also directly makes him more abominable in our eyes than he would have been without it.

A good will is good not because of what it performs or effects, not by its aptness for the attainment of some proposed end, but simply by virtue of the volition, that is, it is good in itself, and considered by itself to be esteemed much higher than all that can be brought about by it in favour of any inclination, nay, even of the sum-total of all inclinations. Even if it should happen that, owing to special disfavour of fortune, or the niggardly provision of a stepmotherly nature, this will should wholly lack power to accomplish its purpose, if with its greatest efforts it should yet achieve nothing, and there should remain only the good will (not, to be sure, a mere wish, but the summoning of all means in our power), then, like a jewel, it would still shine by its own light, as a thing which has its whole value in itself. Its usefulness or fruitlessness can neither add to nor take away anything from this value. It would be, as it were, only the setting to enable us to handle it the more conveniently in common commerce, or to attract to it the attention of those who are not yet connoisseurs, but not to recommend it to true connoisseurs, or to determine its value.

WHY REASON WAS MADE TO GUIDE THE WILL

There is, however, something so strange in this idea of the absolute value of the mere will, in which no account is taken of its utility, that notwithstanding the thorough assent of even common reason to the idea, yet a suspicion must arise that it may perhaps really be the product of mere high-blown fancy, and that we may have misunderstood the purpose of nature in assigning reason as the governor of our will. Therefore we will examine this idea from this point of view.

In the physical constitution of an organized being, that is, a being adapted suitably to the purposes of life, we assume it as a fundamental principle that no organ for any purpose will be found but what is also the fittest and best adapted for that purpose. Now in a being which has reason and a will, if the proper object of nature were its *conservatism,* its *welfare,* in a word, its *happiness,* then nature would have hit upon a very bad arrangement in selecting the reason of the creature to carry out this purpose. For all the actions which the creature has to perform with a view to this purpose, and the whole rule of its conduct, would be far more surely prescribed to it by instinct, and that end would have been attained thereby much more certainly than it ever can be by reason. Should reason have been communicated to this favoured creature over and above, it must only have served it to contemplate the happy constitution of its nature, to admire it, to congratulate itself thereon, and to feel thankful for it to the beneficent cause, but not that it should subject its desires to that weak and delusive guidance, and meddle bunglingly with the purpose of nature. In a word, nature would have taken care that reason should not break forth into *practical exercise,* nor have the presumption, with its weak insight, to think out for itself the plan of happiness, and of the means of attaining it. Nature would not only have taken on herself the choice of the ends, but also of the means, and with wise foresight would have entrusted both to instinct.

And, in fact, we find that the more a cultivated reason applies itself with deliberate purpose to the enjoyment of life and happiness, so much the more does the man fail of true satisfaction. And from this circumstance there arises in many, if they are candid enough to confess it, a certain degree of *misology,* that is, hatred of reason, especially in the case of those who are most experienced in the use of it, because after calculating all the advantages they derive, I do not say from the invention of all the arts of common luxury, but even from the sciences (which seem to them to be after all only a luxury of the understanding), they find that they have, in fact, only brought more trouble on their shoulders, rather than gained in happiness; and they end by envying, rather than despising, the more common stamp of men who keep closer to the guidance of mere instinct, and do not allow their reason much influence on their conduct. And this we must admit, that the judgment of those who would very much lower the lofty eulogies of the advantages which reason gives us in regard to the happiness and satisfaction of life, or who would even reduce them below zero, is by no means morose or ungrateful to the goodness with which the world is governed, but that there lies at the root of these judgments the idea that our existence has a different and far nobler end, for which, and not for happiness, reason is properly intended, and which must, therefore, be regarded as the supreme condition to which the private ends of man must, for the most part, be postponed.

For as reason is not competent to guide the will with certainty in regard to its objects and the satisfaction of all our wants (which it to some extent even multiplies), this being an end to which an implanted instinct would have led with much greater certainty; and since, nevertheless, reason is imparted to us as a practical faculty, *i.e.* as one which is to have influence on the *will,* therefore, admitting that nature generally in the distribution of her capacities has adapted the means to the end, its true destination must be to produce a *will,* not merely good as a *means* to something else, but *good in itself,* for which reason was absolutely necessary. This will then, though not indeed the sole and complete good, must be the supreme good and the condition of every other, even of the desire of happiness. Under these circumstances, there is nothing inconsistent with the wisdom of nature in the fact that the cultivation of the reason, which is requisite for the first and unconditional purpose, does in many ways interfere, at least in this life, with the attainment of the second, which is always conditional, namely, happiness. Nay, it may even reduce it to nothing, without nature thereby failing in her purpose. For reason recognizes the establishment of a good will as its highest practical destination, and in attaining this purpose is capable only of a satisfaction of its own proper kind, namely, that from the attainment of an end, which end again is determined by reason only, notwithstanding that this may involve many a disappointment to the ends of inclination.

THE FIRST PROPOSITION OF MORALITY

[An action must be done from a sense of duty, if it is to have moral worth]

We have then to develop the notion of a will which deserves to be highly esteemed for itself, and is good without a view to anything further, a notion which exists already in the sound natural understanding, requiring rather to be cleared up than to be taught, and which in estimating the value of our actions always takes the first place, and constitutes the condition of all the rest. In order to do this, we will take the notion of duty, which includes that of a good will, although implying certain subjective restrictions and hindrances. These, however, far from concealing it, or rendering it unrecognizable, rather bring it out by contrast, and make it shine forth so much the brighter.

I omit here all actions which are already recognized as inconsistent with duty although they may be useful for this or that purpose, for with these the question whether they are done *from duty* cannot arise at all, since they even conflict with it. I also set aside those actions which really conform to duty, but to which men have *no* direct *inclination,* performing them because they are impelled thereto by some other inclination. For in this case we can readily distinguish whether the action which agrees with duty is done *from duty,* or from a selfish view. It is much harder to make this distinction when the action accords with duty, and the subject has besides a *direct* inclination to it. For example, it is always a matter of duty that a dealer should not overcharge an inexperienced purchaser; and wherever there is much commerce the prudent tradesman does not overcharge, but keeps a fixed price for everyone, so that a child buys of him as well as any other. Men are thus *honestly* served; but this is not enough to make us believe that the tradesman has so acted from duty and from principles of honesty: his own advantage required it; it is out of the question in this case to suppose that he might besides have a direct inclination in favour of the buyers, so that, as it were, from love he should give no advantage to one over another. Accordingly the action was done neither from duty nor from direct inclination, but merely with a selfish view.

On the other hand, it is a duty to maintain one's life; and, in addition, everyone has also a direct inclination to do so. But on this account the often anxious care which most men take for it has no intrinsic worth, and their maxim has no moral import. They preserve their life *as duty requires,* no doubt, but not *because duty requires.* On the other hand, if adversity and hopeless sorrow have completely taken away the relish for life; if the unfortunate one, strong in mind, indignant at his fate rather than desponding or dejected, wishes for death, and yet preserves his life without loving it—not from inclination or fear, but from duty—then his maxim has a moral worth.

To be beneficent when we can is a duty; and besides this, there are many minds so sympathetically constituted that, without any other motive of vanity or self-interest, they find a pleasure in spreading joy around them, and can take delight in the satisfaction of others so far as it is their own work. But I maintain that in such a case an action of this kind, however proper, however amiable it may be, has nevertheless no true moral worth, but is on a level with other inclinations, *e.g.* the inclination to honour, which, if it is happily directed to that which is in fact of public utility and accordant with duty, and consequently honourable, deserves praise and encouragement, but not esteem. For the maxim lacks the moral import, namely, that such actions be done *from duty,* not from inclination. Put the case that the mind of that philanthropist was clouded by sorrow of his own, extinguishing all sympathy with the lot of others, and that while he still has the power to benefit others in distress, he is not touched by their trouble because he is absorbed with his own; and now suppose that he tears himself out of this dead insensibility, and performs the action without any inclination to it, but simply from duty, then first has his action its genuine moral worth. Further still; if nature has put little sympathy in the heart of this or that man; if he, supposed to be an upright man, is by temperament cold and indifferent to the sufferings of others, perhaps because in respect of his own he is provided with the special gift of patience and fortitude, and supposes, or even requires, that others should have the same—and such a man would certainly not be the meanest product of nature—but if nature had not specially framed him for a philanthropist, would he not still find in himself a source from whence to give himself a far higher worth than that of a good-natured temperament could be? Unquestionably. It is just in this that the moral worth of the character is brought out which is incomparably the highest of all, namely, that he is beneficent, not from inclination, but from duty.

To secure one's own happiness is a duty, at least indirectly; for discontent with one's condition, under a pressure of many anxieties and amidst unsatisfied wants, might easily become a great

temptation to transgression of duty. But here again, without looking to duty, all men have already the strongest and most intimate
inclination to happiness, because it is just in this idea that all inclinations are combined in one total. But the precept of happiness is
often of such a sort that it greatly interferes with some inclinations,
and yet a man cannot form any definite and certain conception of
the sum of satisfaction of all of them which is called happiness. It
is not then to be wondered at that a single inclination, definite both
as to what it promises and as to the time within which it can be
gratified, is often able to overcome such a fluctuating idea, and that
a gouty patient, for instance, can choose to enjoy what he likes,
and to suffer what he may, since, according to his calculation, on
this occasion at least, he has [only] not sacrificed the enjoyment of
the present moment to a possibly mistaken expectation of a happiness which is supposed to be found in health. But even in this
case, if the general desire for happiness did not influence his will,
and supposing that in his particular case health was not a necessary element in this calculation, there yet remains in this, as in all
other cases, this law, namely, that he should promote his happiness not from inclination but from duty, and by this would his conduct first acquire true moral worth.

It is in this manner, undoubtedly, that we are to understand those
passages of Scripture also in which we are commanded to love our
neighbour, even our enemy. For love, as an affection, cannot be
commanded, but beneficence for duty's sake may; even though we
are not impelled to it by any inclination—nay, are even repelled
by a natural and unconquerable aversion. This is *practical* love,
and not *pathological**—a love which is seated in the will, and not
in the propensions of sense—in principles of action and not of tender sympathy; and it is this love alone which can be commanded.

THE SECOND PROPOSITION OF MORALITY

The second proposition is: That an action done from duty derives
its moral worth, *not from the purpose* which is to be attained by it,
but from the maxim by which it is determined, and therefore does
not depend on the realization of the object of the action, but merely

*Passional or emotional

on the *principle of volition* by which the action has taken place, without regard to any object of desire. It is clear from what precedes that the purposes which we may have in view in our actions, or their effects regarded as ends and springs of the will, cannot give to actions any unconditional or moral worth. In what, then, can their worth lie, if it is not to consist in the will and in reference to its expected effect? It cannot lie anywhere but in the *principle of the will* without regard to the ends which can be attained by the action. For the will stands between its *a priori principle,* which is formal, and its *a posteriori* spring, which is material, as between two roads, and as it must be determined by something, it follows that it must be determined by the formal principle of volition when an action is done from duty, in which case every material principle has been withdrawn from it.

THE THIRD PROPOSITION OF MORALITY

The third proposition, which is a consequence of the two preceding, I would express thus: *Duty is the necessity of acting from respect for the law.* I may have *inclination* for an object as the effect of my proposed action, but I cannot have *respect* for it, just for this reason, that it is an effect and not an energy of will. Similarly, I cannot have respect for inclination, whether my own or another's; I can at most, if my own, approve it; if another's, sometimes even love it; *i.e.* look on it as favourable to my own interest. It is only what is connected with my will as a principle, by no means as an effect—what does not subserve my inclination, but overpowers it, or at least in case of choice excludes it from its calculation—in other words, simply the law of itself, which can be an object of respect, and hence a command. Now an action done from duty must wholly exclude the influence of inclination, and with it every object of the will, so that nothing remains which can determine the will except objectively the *law,* and subjectively *pure respect* for this practical law, and consequently the maxim that I should follow this law even to the thwarting of all my inclinations.

Thus the moral worth of an action does not lie in the effect expected from it, nor in any principle of action which requires to borrow its motive from this expected effect. For all these effects— agreeableness of one's condition, and even the promotion of the happiness of others—could have been also brought about by other causes, so that for this there would have been no need of the will of a rational being; whereas it is in this alone that the supreme and unconditional good can be found. The pre-eminent good which we call moral can therefore consist in nothing else than *the conception of law* in itself, *which certainly is only possible in a rational being*, in so far as this conception, and not the expected effect, determines the will. This is a good which is already present in the person who acts accordingly, and we have not to wait for it to appear first in the result.

THE SUPREME PRINCIPLE OF MORALITY: THE CATEGORICAL IMPERATIVE

But what sort of law can that be, the conception of which must determine the will, even without paying any regard to the effect expected from it, in order that this will may be called good absolutely and without qualification? As I have deprived the will of every impulse which could arise to it from obedience to any law, there remains nothing but the universal conformity of its actions to law in general, which alone is to serve the will as a principle, *i.e.* I am never to act otherwise than so *that I could also will that my maxim should become a universal law.* Here, now, it is the simple conformity to law in general, without assuming any particular law applicable to certain actions, that serves the will as its principle, and must so serve it, if duty is not to be a vain delusion and a chimerical notion. The common reason of men in its practical judgments perfectly coincides with this, and always has in view the principle here suggested. Let the question be, for example: May I when in distress make a promise with the intention not to keep it? I readily distinguish here between the two significations which the question may have: Whether it is prudent, or whether it is right, to make a false promise? The former may undoubtedly often be the case. I see clearly indeed that it is not enough to extricate myself from a present difficulty by means of this subterfuge, but it must be well considered whether there may not hereafter spring from this lie much greater inconvenience than that from which I now free myself, and as, with all my supposed *cunning,* the consequences cannot be so easily foreseen but that credit once lost may be much more injurious to me than any mischief which

I seek to avoid at present, it should be considered whether it would
not be more *prudent* to act herein according to a universal maxim,
and to make it a habit to promise nothing except with the intention
of keeping it. But it is soon clear to me that such a maxim will still
only be based on the fear of consequences. Now it is a wholly different thing to be truthful from duty, and to be so from apprehension of injurious consequences. In the first case, the very notion of
the action already implies a law for me; in the second case, I must
first look about elsewhere to see what results may be combined with
it which would affect myself. For to deviate from the principle of duty
is beyond all doubt wicked; but to be unfaithful to my maxim of prudence may often be very advantageous to me, although to abide by
it is certainly safer. The shortest way, however, and an unerring one,
to discover the answer to this question whether a lying promise is
consistent with duty, is to ask myself, Should I be content that my
maxim (to extricate myself from difficulty by a false promise) should
hold good as a universal law, for myself as well as for others? and
should I be able to say to myself, "Every one may make a deceitful
promise when he finds himself in a difficulty from which he cannot
otherwise extricate himself"? Then I presently become aware that
while I can will the lie, I can by no means will that lying should be
a universal law. For with such a law there would be no promises at
all, since it would be in vain to allege my intention in regard to my
future actions to those who would not believe this allegation, or if
they over-hastily did so, would pay me back in my own coin. Hence
my maxim, as soon as it should be made a universal law, would necessarily destroy itself.

I do not, therefore, need any far-reaching penetration to discern
what I have to do in order that my will may be morally good. Inexperienced in the course of the world, incapable of being prepared
for all its contingencies, I only ask myself: Canst thou also will that
thy maxim should be a universal law? If not, then it must be rejected,
and that not because of a disadvantage accruing from myself or
even to others, but because it cannot enter as a principle into a
possible universal legislation, and reason extorts from me immediate respect for such legislation. I do not indeed as yet *discern* on
what this respect is based (this the philosopher may inquire), but
at least I understand this, that it is an estimation of the worth which
far outweighs all worth of what is recommended by inclination,
and that the necessity of acting from *pure* respect for the practical

law is what constitutes duty, to which every other motive must give place, because it is the condition of a will being good *in itself,* and the worth of such a will is above everything.

Thus, then, without quitting the moral knowledge of common human reason, we have arrived at its principle. And although, no doubt, common men do not conceive it in such an abstract and universal form, yet they always have it really before their eyes, and use it as the standard of their decision. . . .

Nor could anything be more fatal to morality than that we should wish to derive it from examples. For every example of it that is set before me must be first itself tested by principles of morality, whether it is worthy to serve as an original example, *i.e.* as a pattern, but by no means can it authoritatively furnish the conception of morality. Even the Holy One of the Gospels must first be compared with our ideal of moral perfection before we can recognize Him as such; and so He says of Himself, "Why call ye Me [whom you see] good; none is good [the model of good] but God only [whom ye do not see]." But whence have we the conception of God as the supreme good? Simply from the *idea* of moral perfection, which reason frames *a priori,* and connects inseparably with the notion of a free will. Imitation finds no place at all in morality, and examples serve only for encouragement, *i.e.* they put beyond doubt the feasibility of what the law commands, they make visible that which the practical rule expresses more generally, but they can never authorize us to set aside the true original which lies in reason, and to guide ourselves by examples.

From what has been said, it is clear that all moral conceptions have their seat and origin completely *a priori* in the reason, and that, moreover, in the commonest reason just as truly as in that which is in the highest degree speculative; that they cannot be obtained by abstraction from any empirical, and therefore merely contingent knowledge; that it is just this purity of their origin that makes them worthy to serve as our supreme practical principle, and that just in proportion as we add anything empirical, we detract from their genuine influence, and from the absolute value of actions; that it is not only of the greatest necessity, in a purely speculative point of view, but is also of the greatest practical importance, to derive these notions and laws from pure reason, to present them pure and unmixed, and even to determine the compass of this practical or pure rational knowledge, *i.e.* to determine the whole faculty of pure practical reason; and, in doing so, we must not make its principles dependent on the particular nature of human reason, though in speculative philosophy this may be permitted, or may even at times be necessary; but since moral laws ought to hold good for every rational creature, we must derive them from the general concept of a rational being. In this way, although for its *application* to man morality has need of anthropology, yet, in the first instance, we must treat it independently as pure philosophy, *i.e.* as metaphysic, complete in itself (a thing which in such distinct branches of science is easily done); knowing well that unless we are in possession of this, it would not only be vain to determine the moral element of duty in right actions for purposes of speculative criticism, but it would be impossible to base morals on their genuine principles, even for common practical purposes, especially of moral instruction, so as to produce pure moral dispositions, and to engraft them on men's minds to the promotion of the greatest possible good in the world. . . .

THE RATIONAL GROUND
OF THE CATEGORICAL IMPERATIVE

. . . [T]he question, how the imperative of *morality* is possible, is undoubtedly one, the only one, demanding a solution, as this is not at all hypothetical, and the objective necessity which it presents cannot rest on any hypothesis, as is the case with the hypothetical imperatives. Only here we must never leave out of consideration that we *cannot* make out *by any example,* in other words empirically, whether there is such an imperative at all; but it is rather to be feared that all those which seem to be categorical may yet be at bottom hypothetical. For instance, when the precept is: Thou shalt not promise deceitfully; and it is assumed that the necessity of this is not a mere counsel to avoid some other evil, so that it should mean: Thou shalt not make a lying promise, lest if it become known thou shouldst destroy thy credit, but that an action of this kind must be regarded as evil in itself, so that the imperative of the prohibition is categorical; then we cannot show with certainty in any example that the will was determined merely by the law, without any other spring of action, although it may appear to be so. For it is always possible that fear of disgrace, perhaps also obscure dread of other dangers, may have a secret influence on the will. Who can prove by experience the nonexistence of a cause when all that experience tells us is that we do not perceive it? But in such a case the so-called moral imperative, which as such appears to be categorical and unconditional, would in reality be only a pragmatic precept, drawing our attention to our own interests, and merely teaching us to take these into consideration.

We shall therefore have to investigate *a priori* the possibility of a categorical imperative, as we have not in this case the advantage of its reality being given in experience, so that [the elucidation of] its possibility should be requisite only for its explanation, not for its establishment. In the meantime it may be discerned beforehand that the categorical imperative alone has the purport of a practical law: all the rest may indeed be called *principles* of the will but not laws, since whatever is only necessary for the attainment of some arbitrary purpose may be considered as in itself contingent, and we can at any time be free from the precept if we give up the purpose: on the contrary, the unconditional command leaves the will no liberty to choose the opposite; consequently it alone carries with it that necessity which we require in a law.

Secondly, in the case of this categorical imperative or law of morality, the difficulty (of discerning its possibility) is a very profound one. It is an *a priori* synthetical practical proposition; and as there is so much difficulty in discerning the possibility of speculative propositions of this kind, it may readily be supposed that the difficulty will be no less with the practical.

FIRST FORMULATION OF THE CATEGORICAL IMPERATIVE: UNIVERSAL LAW

In this problem we will first inquire whether the mere conception of a categorical imperative may not perhaps supply us also with the formula of it, containing the proposition which alone can be a categorical imperative; for even if we know the tenor of such an absolute command, yet how it is possible will require further special and laborious study, which we postpone to the last section.

When I conceive a hypothetical imperative, in general I do not know beforehand what it will contain until I am given the condition. But when I conceive a categorical imperative, I know at once what it contains. For as the imperative contains besides the law only the necessity that the maxims shall conform to this law, while the law contains no conditions restricting it, there remains nothing but the general statement that the maxim of the action should conform to a universal law, and it is this conformity alone that the imperative properly represents as necessary.

There is therefore but one categorical imperative, namely, this: *Act only on that maxim whereby thou canst at the same time will that it should become a universal law.*

Now if all imperatives of duty can be deduced from this one imperative as from their principle, then, although it should remain undecided whether what is called duty is not merely a vain notion, yet at least we shall be able to show what we understand by it and what this notion means.

Since the universality of the law according to which effects are produced constitutes what is properly called *nature* in the most general sense (as to form), that is the existence of things so far as it is determined by general laws, the imperative of duty may be expressed thus: *Act as if the maxim of thy action were to become by thy will a universal law of nature.*

FOUR ILLUSTRATIONS

We will now enumerate a few duties, adopting the usual division of them into duties to ourselves and to others, and into perfect and imperfect duties.

1. A man reduced to despair by a series of misfortunes feels wearied of life, but is still so far in possession of his reason that he can ask himself whether it would not be contrary to his duty to himself to take his own life. Now he inquires whether the maxim of his action could become a universal law of nature. His maxim is: From self-love I adopt it as a principle to shorten my life when its longer duration is likely to bring more evil than satisfaction. It is asked then simply whether this principle founded on self-love can become a universal law of nature. Now we see at once that a system of nature of which it should be a law to destroy life by means of the very feeling whose special nature it is to impel to the improvement of life would contradict itself, and therefore could not exist as a system of nature; hence that maxim cannot possibly exist as a universal law of nature, and consequently would be wholly inconsistent with the supreme principle of all duty.

2. Another finds himself forced by necessity to borrow money. He knows that he will not be able to repay it, but sees also that nothing will be lent to him, unless he promises stoutly to repay it in a definite time. He desires to make this promise, but he has still so much conscience as to ask himself: Is it not unlawful and inconsistent with duty to get out of a difficulty in this way? Suppose, however, that he resolves to do so, then the maxim of his action would be expressed thus: When I think myself in want of money, I will borrow money and promise to repay it, although I know that I never can do so. Now this principle of self-love or of one's own advantage may perhaps be consistent with my whole future welfare; but the question is, Is it right? I change then the suggestion of self-love into a universal law, and state the question thus: How would it be if my maxim were a universal law? Then I see at once that it could never hold as a universal law of nature, but would necessarily contradict itself. For supposing it to be a universal law that everyone when he thinks himself in a difficulty should be able to promise whatever he pleases, with the purpose of not keeping his promise, the promise itself would become impossible, as well as the end that one might have in view in it, since no one would consider that anything was promised to him, but would ridicule all such statements as vain pretenses.

3. A third finds in himself a talent which with the help of some culture might make him a useful man in many respects. But he finds himself in comfortable circumstances, and prefers to indulge in pleasure rather than to take pains in enlarging and improving his happy natural capacities. He asks, however, whether his maxim of neglect of his natural gifts, besides agreeing with his inclination to indulgence, agrees also with what is called duty. He sees then that a system of nature could indeed subsist with such a universal law although men (like the South Sea islanders) should let their talents rest, and resolve to devote their lives merely to idleness, amusement, and propagation of their species—in a word, to enjoyment; but he cannot possibly *will* that this should be a universal law of nature, or be implanted in us as such by a natural instinct. For, as a rational being, he necessarily wills that his faculties be developed, since they serve him, and have been given him, for all sorts of possible purposes.

4. A fourth, who is in prosperity, while he sees that others have to contend with great wretchedness and that he could help them, thinks: What concern is it of mine? Let everyone be as happy as

Heaven pleases, or as he can make himself; I will take nothing from him nor even envy him, only I do not wish to contribute anything to his welfare or to his assistance in distress! Now no doubt if such a mode of thinking were a universal law, the human race might very well subsist, and doubtless even better than in a state in which everyone talks of sympathy and good-will, or even takes care occasionally to put it into practice, but, on the other side, also cheats when he can, betrays the rights of men, or otherwise violates them. But although it is possible that a universal law of nature might exist in accordance with that maxim, it is impossible to *will* that such a principle should have the universal validity of a law of nature. For a will which resolved this would contradict itself, inasmuch as many cases might occur in which one would have need of the love and sympathy of others, and in which, by such a law of nature, sprung from his own will, he would deprive himself of all hope of the aid he desires.

These are a few of the many actual duties, or at least what we regard as such, which obviously fall into two classes on the one principle that we have laid down. We must be *able to will* that a maxim of our action should be a universal law. This is the canon of the moral appreciation of the action generally. Some actions are of such a character that their maxim cannot without contradiction be even *conceived* as a universal law of nature, far from it being possible that we should *will* that it *should* be so. In others this intrinsic impossibility is not found, but still it is impossible to *will* that their maxim should be raised to the universality of a law of nature, since such a will would contradict itself. It is easily seen that the former violate strict or rigorous (inflexible) duty; the latter only laxer (meritorious) duty. Thus it has been completely shown by these examples how all duties depend as regards the nature of the obligation (not the object of the action) on the same principle.

SECOND FORMULATION OF THE CATEGORICAL IMPERATIVE: HUMANITY AS AN END IN ITSELF

... Now I say: man and generally any rational being *exists* as an end in himself, *not merely as a means* to be arbitrarily used by this or that will, but in all his actions, whether they concern himself or other rational beings, must be always regarded at the same time as an end. All objects of the inclinations have only a conditional worth; for if the inclinations and the wants founded on them did not exist, then their object would be without value. But the inclinations themselves being sources of want are so far from having an absolute worth for which they should be desired, that, on the contrary, it must be the universal wish of every rational being to be wholly free from them. Thus the worth of any object which is *to be acquired* by our action is always conditional. Beings whose existence depends not on our will but on nature's, have nevertheless, if they are nonrational beings, only a relative value as means, and are therefore called *things;* rational beings, on the contrary, are called *persons,* because their very nature points them out as ends in themselves, that is as something which must not be used merely as means, and so far therefore restricts freedom of action (and is an object of respect). These, therefore, are not merely subjective ends whose existence has a worth *for us* as an effect of our action, but *objective ends,* that is things whose existence is an end in itself: an end moreover for which no other can be substituted, which they should subserve *merely* as means, for otherwise nothing whatever would possess *absolute worth;* but if all worth were conditioned and therefore contingent, then there would be no supreme practical principle of reason whatever.

If then there is a supreme practical principle or, in respect of the human will, a categorical imperative, it must be one which, being drawn from the conception of that which is necessarily an end for everyone because it is *an end in itself,* constitutes an *objective* principle of will, and can therefore serve as a universal practical law. The foundation of this principle is: *rational nature exists as an end in itself.* Man necessarily conceives his own existence as being so: so far then this is a *subjective* principle of human actions. But every other rational being regards its existence similarly, just on the same rational principle that holds for me: so that it is at the same time an objective principle, from which as a supreme practical law all laws of the will must be capable of being deduced. Accordingly the practical imperative will be as follows: *So act as to treat humanity, whether in thine own person or in that of any other, in every case as an end withal, never as means only.* . . .

. . . Looking back now on all previous attempts to discover the principle of morality, we need not wonder why they all failed. It was seen that man was bound to laws by duty, but it was not observed that the laws to which he is subject are *only those of his own giving,* though at the same time they are *universal,* and that he is only bound to act in conformity with his own will; a will, however, which is designed by nature to give universal laws. For when one has conceived man only as subject to a law (no matter what), then this law required some interest, either by way of attraction or constraint, since it did not originate as a law from *his own* will, but his will was according to a law obliged by *something else* to act in a certain manner. Now by this necessary consequence all the labour spent in finding a supreme principle of *duty* was irrevocably lost. For men never elicited duty, but only a necessity of acting from a certain interest. Whether this interest was private or otherwise, in any case the imperative must be conditional, and could not by any means be capable of being a moral command. I will therefore call this the principle of *Autonomy* of the will, in contrast with every other which I accordingly reckon as *Heteronomy.*

THE KINGDOM OF ENDS

The conception of every rational being as one which must consider itself as giving in all the maxims of its will universal laws, so as to judge itself and its actions from this point of view—this conception leads to another which depends on it and is very fruitful, that of a *kingdom of ends.*

By a *kingdom* I understand the union of different rational beings in a system by common laws. Now since it is by laws that ends are determined as regards their universal validity, hence, if we abstract from the personal differences of rational beings, and likewise from all the content of their private ends, we shall be able to conceive all ends combined in a systematic whole (including both rational beings as ends in themselves, and also the special ends which each may propose to himself), that is to say, we can conceive a kingdom of ends, which on the preceding principles is possible.

For all rational beings come under the *law* that each of them must treat itself and all others *never merely as means,* but in every case *at the same time as ends in themselves.* Hence results a systematic union of rational beings by common objective laws, *i.e.,* a kingdom which may be called a kingdom of ends, since what these laws have in view is just the relation of these beings to one another as ends and means. . . .

For Further Reflection

1. Is Kant's philosophy merely a development of the Golden Rule: "Do unto others what you would have them do unto you"? If it is equivalent, does it make Kant's system more intuitively plausible? But does it also lead to problems with what Kant thought to be the implications of his system? For example, on the basis of the Golden Rule one might endorse certain instances of euthanasia, but Kant's discussion of suicide seems to rule this out.

2. Kant's ethics is called deontological (from the Greek word for "duty") because he believes that the value of an act is in the act itself rather than in its consequences (as teleologists hold). Deontological ethics has been criticized as being too rigid. Do you think that this is true? Should the notion of consequences be taken into consideration?

3. How would Kant deal with moral conflicts? When two universal principles conflict, how would Kant resolve the dilemma?

4. Kant's categorical imperative has also been criticized for being more wide open than he realized, for it doesn't limit what could be universalized. How would Kant respond to these counterexamples: (1) Everyone should tie his right shoe before his left shoe; (2) All retarded or senile people should be executed by the government (adding, if I should become retarded or senile, I should also undergo this fate).

Intuitionism

W. D. ROSS

Sir William D. Ross (1877–1971) was provost of Oriel College, Oxford University. His book *The Right and the Good* (1930), from which the present selection is taken, is a classic treatise in ethical intuitionism. Ross argues against utilitarianism (both hedonistic utilitarianism and Moore's ideal utilitarianism), asserting that optimal consequences have nothing to do with moral rightness or wrongness. We have intuitive knowledge of rightness and wrongness in terms of action-guiding principles, such as to keep promises made, to promote justice, to show gratitude for benefits rendered, and to refrain from harming others. Unlike Kant's principles, however, these principles are not absolutes, that is, duties that must never be overridden by more binding moral duties. Moral principles are *prima facie* duties. That is, while their intrinsic value is not dependent on circumstances, their application is. They can be overridden by other *prima facie* duties. Essentially, these principles are the outcomes of generations of reflection on our duty, and their holistic schema has been internalized within us, so that ultimately, as Aristotle said, the "decision lies in the perception."

. . . A . . . theory has been put forward by Professor Moore that what makes actions right is that they are productive of more *good* than could have been produced by any other action open to the agent.

This theory is in fact the culmination of all the attempts to base rightness on productivity of some sort of result. The first form this attempt takes is the attempt to base rightness on conduciveness to the advantage or pleasure of the agent. This theory comes to grief over the fact, which stares us in the face, that a great part of duty consists in an observance of the rights and a furtherance of the interests of others, whatever the cost to ourselves may be. Plato and others may be right in holding that a regard for the rights of others never in the long run involves a loss of happiness for the agent, that 'the just life profits a man.' But this, even if true, is irrelevant to the rightness of the act. As soon as a man does an action *because* he thinks he will promote his own interests thereby, he is acting not from a sense of its rightness but from self-interest.

To the egoistic theory hedonistic utilitarianism supplies a much-needed amendment. It points out correctly that the fact that a certain pleasure will be enjoyed by the agent is no reason why he *ought* to bring it into being, rather than an equal or greater pleasure to be enjoyed by another, though, human nature being what it is, it makes it not unlikely that he *will* try to bring it into being. But hedonistic utilitarianism in its turn needs a correction. On reflection it seems clear that pleasure is not the only thing in life that we think good in itself, that for instance we think the possession of a good character, or an intelligent understanding of the world, as good or better. A great advance is made by the substitution of 'productive of the greatest good' for 'productive of the greatest pleasure.'

Not only is this theory more attractive than hedonistic utilitarianism, but its logical relation to that theory is such that the latter could not be true unless *it* were true, while it might be true though hedonistic utilitarianism were not. It is in fact one of the logical bases of hedonistic utilitarianism. For the view that what produces the maximum pleasure is right has for its bases the views (1) that what produces the maximum good is right, and (2) that pleasure is the only thing good in itself. If they were not assuming that what produces the maximum *good* is right, the utilitarians' attempt to show that pleasure is the only thing good in itself, which is in fact the point they take most pains to establish, would have been quite irrelevant to their attempt to prove that only what produces the maximum *pleasure* is right. If, therefore, it can be shown that productivity of the maximum good is not what makes all right actions right, we shall *a fortiori* have refuted hedonistic utilitarianism.

When a plain man fulfills a promise because he thinks he ought to do so, it seems clear that he does so with no thought of its total consequences, still less with any opinion that these are likely to be the best possible. He thinks in fact much more of the past than of the future. What makes him think it right to act in a certain way is the fact that he has promised to do so—that and, usually, nothing more. That his act will produce the best possible consequences is not his reason for calling it right. What lends colour to the theory we are examining, then, is not the actions (which form probably a great majority of our actions) in which some such reflection as 'I have promised' is the only reason we give ourselves for thinking a certain action right, but the exceptional cases in which the consequences of fulfilling a promise (for instance) would be so disastrous to others that we judge it right not to do so. It must of course be admitted that such cases exist. If I have promised to meet a friend at a particular time for some trivial purpose, I should certainly think myself justified in breaking my engagement if by doing so I could prevent a serious accident or bring relief to the victims of one. And the supporters of the view we are examining hold that my thinking so is due to my thinking that I shall bring more good into existence by the one action than by the other. A different account may, however, be given of the matter, an account which will, I believe, show itself to be the true one. It may be said that besides the duty of fulfilling promises, I have and recognize a duty of relieving distress, and that when I think it right to do the latter at the cost of not doing the former, it is not because I think I shall produce more good thereby but because I think it the duty which is in the circumstances more of a duty. This account surely corresponds much more closely with what we really think in such a situation. If, so far as I can see, I could bring equal amounts of good into being by fulfilling my promise and by helping someone to whom I had made no promise, I should not hesitate to regard the former as my duty. Yet on the view that what is right is right because it is productive of the most good I should not so regard it.

There are two theories, each in its way simple, that offer a solution of such cases of conscience. One is the view of Kant, that there are certain duties of perfect obligation, such as those of fulfilling promises, of paying debts, of telling the truth, which admit of no exception whatever in favour of duties of imperfect obligation, such as that of relieving distress. The other is the view of, for instance, Professor Moore and Dr. Rashdall, that there is only the duty of producing good, and that all 'conflicts of duties' should be resolved by asking 'By which action will most good be produced?' But it is more important that our theory fit the facts than that it be simple, and the account we have given above corresponds (it seems to me) better than either of the simpler theories with what we really think, viz. that normally promise-keeping, for example, should come before benevolence, but that when and only when the good to be produced by the benevolent act is very great and the promise comparatively trivial, the act of benevolence becomes our duty.

In fact the theory of 'ideal utilitarianism' if I may for brevity refer so to the theory of Professor Moore, seems to simplify unduly our relations to our fellows It says, in effect, that the only morally significant relation in which my neighbours stand to me is that of being possible beneficiaries by my action. They do stand in this relation to me, and this relation is morally significant. But they may also stand to me in the relation of promisee to promiser, of creditor to debtor, of wife to husband, of child to parent, of friend to friend, of fellow countryman to fellow countryman, and the like; and each of these relations is the foundation of a *prima facie* duty which is more or less incumbent on me according to the circumstances of the case. When I am in a situation, as perhaps I always am, in which more than one of these *prima facie* duties is incumbent on me, what I have to do is to study the situation as fully as I can until I form the considered opinion (it is never more) that in the circumstances one of them is more incumbent than any other; then I am bound to think that to do this *prima facie* duty is my duty *sans phrase* in the situation.

I suggest *'prima facie* duty' or 'conditional duty' as a brief way of referring to the characteristic (quite distinct from that of being a duty proper) which an act has, in virtue of being of a certain kind (e.g., the keeping of a promise), of being an act which would be a duty proper if it were not at the same time of another kind which is morally significant. Whether an act is a duty proper or actual duty depends on *all* the morally significant kinds it is an instance of. The phrase *'prima facie* duty' must be apologized for, since (1) it suggests that what we are speaking of is a certain kind of duty, whereas it is in fact not a duty but something related in a special way to duty. Strictly speaking, we want not a phrase in which duty is qualified by an adjective, but a separate noun. (2) *'Prima' facie* suggests that one is speaking only of an appearance which a moral situation presents at first sight, and which may turn out to be illusory; whereas what I am speaking of is an objective fact involved in the nature of the situation, or more strictly in an element of its nature, though not, as duty proper does, arising from its *whole* nature. I can, however, think of no term which fully meets the case. 'Claim' has been suggested by Professor Prichard. The word 'claim' has the advantage of being quite a familiar one in this connexion,

and it seems to cover much of the ground. It would be quite natural to say, 'a person to whom I have made a promise has a claim
on me,' and also, 'a person whose distress I could relieve (at the
cost of breaking the promise) has a claim on me.' But (1) while
'claim' is appropriate from *their* point of view, we want a word to
express the corresponding fact from the agent's point of view—the
fact of his being subject to claims that can be made against him;
and ordinary language provides us with no such correlative to
'claim.' And (2) (what is more important) 'claim' seems inevitably
to suggest two persons, one of whom might make a claim on the
other; and while this covers the ground of social duty, it is inappropriate in the case of that important part of duty which is the
duty of cultivating a certain kind of character in oneself. It would
be artificial, I think, and at any rate metaphorical, to say that one's
character has a claim on oneself.

There is nothing arbitrary about these *prima facie* duties. Each
rests on a definite circumstance which cannot seriously be held to
be without moral significance. Of *prima facie* duties I suggest, without claiming completeness or finality for it, the following division.

(1) Some duties rest on previous acts of my own. These duties
seem to include two kinds, (*a*) those resting on a promise or what
may fairly be called an implicit promise, such as the implicit undertaking not to tell lies which seems to be implied in the act of entering into conversation (at any rate by civilized men), or of writing
books that purport to be history and not fiction. These may be called
the duties of fidelity. (*b*) Those resting on a previous wrongful act.
These may be called the duties of reparation. (2) Some rest on previous acts of other men, i.e. services done by them to me. These may
be loosely described as the duties of gratitude. (3) Some rest on the
fact or possibility of a distribution of pleasure or happiness (or of the
means thereto) which is not in accordance with the merit of the persons concerned; in such cases there arises a duty to upset or prevent
such a distribution. These are the duties of justice. (4) Some rest on
the mere fact that there are other beings in the world whose condition we can make better in respect of virtue, or of intelligence, or of
pleasure. These are the duties of beneficence. (5) Some rest on the
fact that we can improve our own condition in respect of virtue or
of intelligence. These are the duties of self-improvement. (6) I think
that we should distinguish from (4) the duties that may be summed
up under the title of 'not injuring others.' No doubt to injure others

is incidentally to fail to do them good; but it seems to me clear that non-maleficence is apprehended as a duty distinct from that of beneficence, and as a duty of a more stringent character. It will be noticed that this alone among the types of duty has been stated in a negative way. An attempt might no doubt be made to state this duty, like the others, in a positive way. It might be said that it is really the duty to prevent ourselves from acting either from an inclination to harm others or from an inclination to seek our own pleasure, in doing which we should incidentally harm them. But on reflection it seems clear that the primary duty here is the duty not to harm others, this being a duty whether or not we have an inclination that if followed would lead to our harming them; and that when we have such an inclination the primary duty not to harm others gives rise to a consequential duty to resist the inclination. The recognition of this duty of non-maleficence is the first step on the way to the recognition of the duty of beneficence; and that accounts for the prominence of the commands 'thou shalt not kill,' 'thou shalt not commit adultery,' 'thou shalt not steal,' 'thou shalt not bear false witness,' in so early a code as the Decalogue. But even when we have come to recognize the duty of beneficence, it appears to me that the duty of non-maleficence is recognized as a distinct one, and as *prima facie* more binding. We should not in general consider it justifiable to kill one person in order to keep another alive, or to steal from one in order to give alms to another.

The essential defect of the 'ideal utilitarian' theory is that it ignores, or at least does not do full justice to, the highly personal character of duty. If the only duty is to produce the maximum of good, the question who is to have the good—whether it is myself, or my benefactor, or a person to whom I have made a promise to confer that good on him, or a mere fellow man to whom I stand in no such special relation—should make no difference to my having a duty to produce that good. But we are all in fact sure that it makes a vast difference.

One or two other comments must be made on this provisional list of the divisions of duty. (1) The nomenclature is not strictly correct. For by 'fidelity' or 'gratitude' we mean, strictly, certain states of motivation; and, as I have urged, it is not our duty to have certain motives, but to do certain acts. By 'fidelity,' for instance, is meant, strictly, the disposition to fulfil promises and implicit promises *because we have made them*. We have no general word to cover the actual fulfilment of promises and implicit promises *irre-spective of motive;* and I use 'fidelity,' loosely but perhaps conve-niently, to fill this gap. So too I use 'gratitude' for the returning of services, irrespective of motive. The term 'justice' is not so much confined, in ordinary usage, to a certain state of motivation, for we should often talk of a man as acting justly even when we did not think his motive was the wish to do what was just simply for the sake of doing so. Less apology is therefore needed for our use of 'justice' in this sense. And I have used the word 'beneficence' rather than 'benevolence,' in order to emphasize the fact that it is our duty to do certain things, and not to do them from certain motives.

(2) If the objection be made that this catalogue of the main types of duty is an unsystematic one resting on no logical principle, it may be replied, first, that it makes no claim to being ultimate. It is a *prima facie* classification of the duties which reflection on our moral con-victions seems actually to reveal. And if these convictions are, as I would claim that they are, of the nature of knowledge, and if I have not misstated them, the list will be a list of authentic conditional duties, correct as far as it goes though not necessarily complete. The list of *goods* put forward by the rival theory is reached by exactly the same method—the only sound one in the circumstances—viz. that of direct reflection on what we really think. Loyalty to the facts is worth more than a symmetrical architectonic or a hastily reached sim-plicity. If further reflection discovers a perfect logical basis for this or for a better classification, so much the better.

(3) It may, again, be objected that our theory that there are these various and often conflicting types of *prima facie* duty leaves us with no principle upon which to discern what is our actual duty in particular circumstances. But this objection is not one which the rival theory is in a position to bring forward. For when we have to choose between the production of two heterogeneous goods, say knowledge and pleasure, the 'ideal utilitarian' theory can only fall back on an opinion, for which no logical basis can be offered, that one of the goods is the greater; and this is no better than a similar opinion that one of two duties is the more urgent. And again, when we consider the infinite variety of the effects of our actions in a way of pleasure, it must surely be admitted that the claim which *hedonism* sometimes makes, that it offers a readily applicable criterion of right conduct, is quite illusory.

I am unwilling, however, to content myself with an *argumen-tum ad hominem,* and I would contend that in principle there is no reason to anticipate that every act that is our duty is so for one and the same reason. Why should two sets of circumstances, or one set of circumstances, *not* possess different characteristics, any one of which makes a certain act our *prima facie* duty? When I ask what it is that makes me in certain cases sure that I have a *prima facie* duty to do so and so, I find that it lies in the fact that I have made a promise; when I ask the same question in another case, I find the answer lies in the fact that I have done a wrong. And if on reflection I find (as I think I do) that neither of these reasons is reducible to the other, I must not on any *a priori* ground assume that such a reduction is possible.

It is necessary to say something by way of clearing up the relation between *prima facie* duties and the actual or absolute duty to do one particular act in particular circumstances. If, as almost all moralists except Kant are agreed and as most plain men think, it is sometimes right to tell a lie or to break a promise, it must be maintained that there is a difference between *prima facie* duty and actual or absolute duty. When we think ourselves justified in breaking, and indeed morally obliged to break, a promise in order to relieve someone's distress, we do not for a moment cease to recognize a *prima facie* duty to keep our promise, and this leads us to feel, not indeed shame or repentance, but certainly compunction, for behaving as we do; we recognize, further, that it is our duty to make up somehow to the promise for the breaking of the promise. We have to distinguish from the characteristic of being our duty that of tending to be our duty. Any act that we do contains various elements in virtue of which it falls under various categories. In virtue of being the breaking of a promise, for instance, it tends to be wrong; in virtue of being an instance of relieving distress it tends to be right. Tendency to be one's duty may be called a parti-resultant attribute, i.e. one which belongs to an act in virtue of some one component in its nature. *Being* one's duty is a toti-resultant attribute, one which belongs to an act in virtue of its whole nature and of nothing less than this.

Something should be said of the relation between our apprehension of the *prima facie* rightness of certain types of acts and our mental attitude toward particular acts. It is proper to use the word 'apprehension' in the former case and not in the latter. That an act, *qua* fulfilling a promise, or *qua* effecting a just distribution of good, or *qua* returning services rendered, or *qua* promoting the good of others, or *qua* promoting the virtue or insight of the agent, is *prima facie* right, is self-evident; not in the sense that it is evident from the beginning of our lives, or as soon as we attend to the proposition for the first time, but in the sense that when we have reached sufficient mental maturity and have given sufficient attention to the proposition it is evident without any need of proof, or of evidence beyond itself. It is self-evident, just as a mathematical axiom, or the validity of a form of inference, is evident. The moral order expressed in these propositions is just as much part of the fundamental nature of the universe (and, we may add, of any possible universe in which there were moral agents at all) as is the spatial or numerical structure expressed in the axioms of geometry or arithmetic. In our confidence that these propositions are true there is involved the same trust in our reason that is involved in our confidence in mathematics; and we should have no justification for trusting it in the latter sphere and distrusting it in the former. In both cases we are dealing with propositions that cannot be proved, but that just as certainly need no proof.

Supposing it to be agreed, as I think on reflection it must, that no one *means* by 'right' just 'productive of the best possible consequences,' or 'optimific,' the attributes 'right' and 'optimific' might stand in either of two kinds of relation to each other. (1) They might be so related that we could apprehend *a priori,* either immediately or deductively, that any act that is optimific is right and any act that is right is optimific, as we can apprehend that any triangle that is equilateral is equiangular and *vice versa.* Professor Moore's view is, I think, that the coextensiveness of 'right' and 'optimific' is apprehended immediately. He rejects the possibility of any proof of it. Or (2) the two attributes might be such that the question whether they are invariably connected had to be answered by means of an inductive inquiry. Now at first sight it might seem as if the constant connexion of the two attributes could be immediately apprehended. It might seem absurd to suggest that it could be right for anyone to do an act which would produce consequences less good than those which would be produced by some other act in his power. Yet a little thought will convince us that this is not absurd. The type of case in which it is easiest to see that this is so is, perhaps, that in which one has made a promise. In such a case we all think that *prima facie* it is our duty to fulfil the promise irrespective of the precise goodness of the total consequences. And though we do not think it is necessarily our actual or absolute duty to do so, we are far from thinking that any, even the slightest, gain in the value of the total consequences will necessarily justify us in doing something else instead. Suppose, to simplify the case by abstraction, that the fulfilment of a promise to A would produce 1,000 units of good for him, but that by doing some other act I could produce 1,001 units of good for B, to whom I have made no promise, the other consequences of the two acts being of equal value; should we really think it self-evident that it was our duty to do the second act and not the first? I think not. We should, I fancy, hold that only a much greater disparity of value between the total consequences would justify us in failing to discharge our *prima facie* duty to A. After all, a promise is a promise, and is not to be treated so lightly as the theory we are examining would imply. What, exactly, a promise is, is not so easy to determine, but we are surely agreed that it constitutes a serious moral limitation to our freedom of action. To produce the 1,001 units of good for B rather than fulfil our promise to A would be to take, not perhaps our duty as philanthropists too seriously, but certainly our duty as makers of promises too lightly.

Or consider another phase of the same problem. If I have promised to confer on A a particular benefit containing 1,000 units of good, is it self-evident that if by doing some different act I could produce 1,001 units of good for A himself (the other consequences of the two acts being supposed equal in value), it would be right for me to do so? Again, I think not. Apart from my general *prima facie* duty to do A what goal I can, I have another *prima facie* duty to do him the particular service I have promised to do him, and this is not to be set aside in consequence of a disparity of good of the order of 1,001 to 1,000, though a much greater disparity might justify me in so doing.

Or again, suppose that A is a very good and B a very bad man, should I then, even when I have made no promise, think it self-evidently right to produce 1,001 units of good for B rather than 1,000 for A? Surely not. I should be sensible of a *prima facie* duty of justice, i.e. of producing a distribution of goods in proportion to merit, which is not outweighed by such a slight disparity in the total goods to be produced.

Such instances—and they might easily be added to—make it clear that there is no self-evident connexion between the attributes 'right'

and 'optimific.' The theory we are examining has a certain attractiveness when applied to our decision that a particular act is our duty
(though I have tried to show that it does not agree with our actual
moral judgements even here). But it is not even plausible when
applied to our recognition of *prima facie* duty. For if it were self-
evident that the right coincides with the optimific, it should be
self-evident that what is *prima facie* right is *prima facie* optimific. But
whereas we are certain that keeping a promise is *prima facie* right,
we are not certain that it is *prima facie* optimific (though we are perhaps certain that it is *prima facie* bonific). Our certainty that it is *prima
facie* right depends not on its consequences but on its being the fulfilment of a promise. The theory we are examining involves too much
difference between the evident ground of our conviction about *prima
facie* duty and the alleged ground of our conviction about actual
duty.

The coextensiveness of the right and the optimific is, then, not
self-evident. And I can see no way of proving it deductively; nor, so
far as I know, has anyone tried to do so. There remains the question
whether it can be established inductively. Such an inquiry, to be conclusive, would have to be very thorough and extensive. We should
have to take a large variety of the acts which we, to the best of our
ability, judge to be right. We should have to trace as far as possible
their consequences, not only for the persons directly affected but also
for those indirectly affected, and to these no limit can be set. To make
our inquiry thoroughly conclusive, we should have to do what we
cannot do, viz. trace these consequences into an unending future.
And even to make it reasonably conclusive, we should have to trace
them far into the future. It is clear that the most we could possibly
say is that a large variety of typical acts that are judged right appear,
so far as we can trace their consequences, to produce more good
than any other acts possible to the agents in the circumstances. And
such a result falls far short of proving the constant connexion of the
two attributes. But it is surely clear that no inductive inquiry justifying even this result has ever been carried through. The advocates of
utilitarian systems have been so much persuaded either of the identity or of the self-evident connexion of the attributes 'right' and 'optimific' (or 'felicific') that they have not attempted even such an inductive inquiry as is possible. And in view of the enormous complexity
of the task and the inevitable inconclusiveness of the result, it is
worth no one's while to make the attempt. What, after all, would be

gained by it? If, as I have tried to show, for an act to be right and to be optimific are not the same thing, and an act's being optimific is not even the ground of its being right, then if we could ask ourselves (though the question is really unmeaning) which we ought to do, right acts because they are right or optimific acts because they are optimific, our answer must be 'the former.' If they are optimific as well as right, that is interesting but not morally important; if not, we still ought to do them (which is only another way of saying that they *are* the right acts), and the question whether they are optimific has no importance for moral theory.

There is one direction in which a fairly serious attempt has been made to show the connexion of the attributes 'right' and 'optimific.' One of the most evident facts of our moral consciousness is the sense which we have of the sanctity of promises, a sense which does not, on the face of it, involve the thought that one will be bringing more good into existence by fulfilling the promise than by breaking it. It is plain, I think, that in our normal thought we consider that the fact that we have made a promise is in itself sufficient to create a duty of keeping it, the sense of duty resting on remembrance of the past promise and not on thoughts of the future consequences of its fulfilment. Utilitarianism tries to show that this is not so, that the sanctity of promises rests on the good consequences of the fulfilment of them and the bad consequences of their nonfulfilment. It does so in this way: it points out that when you break a promise you not only fail to confer a certain advantage on your promise but you diminish his confidence, and indirectly the confidence of others, in the fulfilment of promises. You thus strike a blow at one of the devices that have been found most useful in the relations between man and man—the device on which, for example, the whole system of commercial credit rests—and you tend to bring about a state of things wherein each man, being entirely unable to rely on the keeping of promises by others, will have to do everything for himself, to the enormous impoverishment of human well-being.

To put the matter otherwise, utilitarians say that when a promise ought to be kept it is because the total good to be produced by keeping it is greater than the total good to be produced by breaking it, the former including as its main element the maintenance and strengthening of general mutual confidence, and the latter being greatly diminished by a weakening of this confidence. They say, in fact, that the case I put some pages back never arises—the case in which by fulfilling a promise I shall bring into being 1,000 units of good for my promisee, and by breaking it 1,001 units of good for someone else, the other effects of the two acts being of equal value. The other effects, they say, never are of equal value. By keeping my promise I am helping to strengthen the system of mutual confidence; by breaking it I am helping to weaken this; so that really the first act produces $1,000 + x$ units of good, and the second $1,001 - y$ units, and the difference between $+x$ and $-y$ is enough to outweigh the slight superiority in the immediate effects of the second act. In answer to this it may be pointed out that there must be *some* amount of good that exceeds the difference between $+x$ and $-y$ (i.e. exceeds $x + y$); say, $x + y + z$. Let us suppose the *immediate* good effects of the second act to be assessed not at 1,001 but at $1,000 + x + y + z$. Then its *net* good effects are $1,000 + x + z$, i.e. greater than those of the fulfilment of the promise; and the utilitarian is bound to say forthwith that the promise should be broken. Now, we may ask whether that is really the way we think about promises. Do we really think that the production of the slightest balance of good, no matter who will enjoy it, by the breach of a promise frees us from the obligation to keep our promise? We need not doubt that a system by which promises are made and kept is one that has great advantages for the general well-being. But that is not the whole truth. To make a promise is not merely to adapt an ingenious device for promoting the general well-being; it is to put oneself in a new relation to one person in particular, a relation which creates a specifically new *prima facie* duty to him, not reducible to the duty of promoting the general well-being of society. By all means let us try to foresee the net good effects of keeping one's promise and the net good effects of breaking it, but even if we assess the first at $1,000 + x$ and the second at $1,000 + x + z$, the question still remains whether it is not our duty to fulfil the promise. It may be suspected, too, that the effect of a single keeping or breaking of a promise in strengthening or weakening the fabric of mutual confidence is greatly exaggerated by the theory we are examining. And if we suppose two men dying together alone, do we think that the duty of one to fulfil before he dies a promise he has made to the other would be extinguished by the fact that neither act would have any effect on the general confidence? Anyone who holds this may be suspected of not having reflected on what a promise is.

I conclude that the attributes 'right' and 'optimific' are not identical, and that we do not know either by intuition, by deduction, or by induction that they coincide in their application, still less that the latter is the foundation of the former. It must be added, however, that if we are ever under no special obligation such as that of fidelity to a promisee or of gratitude to a benefactor, we ought to do what will produce most good; and that even when we are under a special obligation the tendency of acts to promote general good is one of the main factors in determining whether they are right.

In what has preceded, a good deal of use has been made of 'what we really think' about moral questions; a certain theory has been rejected because it does not agree with what we really think. It might be said that this is in principle wrong; that we should not be content to expound what our present moral consciousness tells us but should aim at a criticism of our existing moral consciousness in the light of theory. Now I do not doubt that the moral consciousness of men has in detail undergone a good deal of modification as regards the things we think right, at the hands of moral theory. But if we are told, for instance, that we should give up our view that there is a special oblig- atoriness attaching to the keeping of promises because it is self- evident that the only duty is to produce as much good as possible, we have to ask ourselves whether we really, when we reflect, *are* convinced that this is self-evident, and whether we really *can* get rid of our view that promise-keeping has a bindingness independent of productiveness of maximum good. In my own experience I find that I cannot, in spite of a very genuine attempt to do so; and I venture to think that most people will find the same, and that just because they cannot lose the sense of special obligation, they cannot accept as self-evident, or even as true, the theory which would require them to do so. In fact it seems, on reflection, self-evident that a promise, simply as such, is something that *prima facie* ought to be kept, and it does *not,* on reflection, seem self-evident that production of max- imum good is the only thing that makes an act obligatory. And to ask us to give up at the bidding of a theory our actual apprehension of what is right and what is wrong seems like asking people to repu- diate their actual experience of beauty, at the bidding of a theory which says 'only that which satisfies such and such conditions can be beautiful.' If what I have called our actual apprehension is (as I would maintain that it is) truly an apprehension, i.e. an instance of knowledge, the request is nothing less than absurd.

I would maintain, in fact, that what we are apt to describe as 'what we think' about moral questions contains a considerable amount that we do not think but know, and that this forms the standard by reference to which the truth of any moral theory has to be tested, instead of having itself to be tested by reference to any theory. I hope that I have in what precedes indicated what in my view these elements of knowledge are that are involved in our ordinary moral consciousness.

It would be a mistake to found a natural science on 'what we really think,' i.e. on what reasonably thoughtful and well-educated people think about the subjects of the science before they have studied them scientifically. For such opinions are interpretations, and often misinterpretations, of sense-experience; and the man of science must appeal from these to sense-experience itself, which furnishes his real data. In ethics no such appeal is possible. We have no more direct way of access to the facts about rightness and goodness and about what things are right or good, than by thinking about them; the moral convictions of thoughtful and well-educated people are the data of ethics just as sense-perceptions are the data of a natural science. Just as some of the latter have to be rejected as illusory, so have some of the former; but as the latter are rejected only when they are in conflict with other more accurate sense-perceptions, the former are rejected only when they are in conflict with other convictions which stand better the test of reflection. The existing body of moral convictions of the best people is the cumulative product of the moral reflection of many generations, which has developed an extremely delicate power of appreciation of moral distinctions; and this the theorist cannot afford to treat with anything other than the greatest respect. The verdicts of the moral consciousness of the best people are the foundation on which he must build; though he must first compare them with one another and eliminate any contradictions they may contain.

For Further Reflection

1. What is Ross's argument against all types of utilitarianism?

2. Ross is both an intuitionist and a pluralist. He thinks we can acquire knowledge of the correct moral principles by consulting our deepest intuitions and he thinks that by so doing we will discover a plurality of principles, not reducible to a single

principle, as utilitarians claim. First of all, do you agree with Ross that we can discover the true principles by consulting our intuitions? And second, do you agree that the principles are, in the last analysis, irreducible to one overarching principle? What are the objections to these positions? Suppose you and I consult our intuitions and come to different conclusions. How can we adjudicate the conflict?

3. What does Ross mean by *prima facie* duty? How does this notion separate his theory from Kant's?

The Golden Rule

Several philosophers and religions have set forth a version of the Golden Rule:

"What you do not want done to yourself, do not do unto others." (Confucius, sixth century B.C.)

"In happiness and suffering, in joy and grief, we should regard all creatures as we regard our own self, and should therefore refrain from inflicting upon others such injury as would appear undesirable to us if inflicted upon ourselves." (Jainism, fifth century B.C.)

"Do nothing to others which if done to you would cause you pain." (Hinduism, third century B.C.)

"What is hateful to you, do not do to your fellow man." (Hillel, Jewish scholar, first century B.C.)

"All things whatsover you would that men should do unto you, do you even so to them." (Jesus, first century A.D.)

"Do not do unto others what you would not have them do unto you." (common negative formula)

"Do unto others as you would have them do unto you." (common positive formula)

"Do unto others as *they* would have you do unto them." (inverted Golden Rule, mentioned by Marcus Singer).[1]

For Further Reflection

1. Compare the various formulations of the Golden Rule. What are the differences? Is there a common thread that runs through all of them?

2. Do you think the Golden Rule is a sufficient rule for all of morality?

A Critique of the Golden Rule

RICHARD WHATELY

Richard Whately (1787–1863), English philosopher and logician, and Archbishop of Dublin, was educated and taught at Oxford University. He is best known for his *Elements of Logic*.

Whately argues that the Golden Rule is not a self-sufficient moral principle but presupposes a background of moral principles.

I. THE GOLDEN RULE

That invaluable rule of our Lord's, "To do to others as we would have them do to us," will serve to explain, when rightly understood, the true character of moral instruction. If you were to understand that precept as designed to convey to us the first notions of right and wrong, and to be your sole guide as to what you ought to do and to avoid in your dealings with your neighbor, you would be greatly perplexed. For you would find that a literal compliance with the precept would be sometimes *absurd,* sometimes *wrong,* and sometimes *impossible.*

[1]See Marcus Singer, "The Golden Rule," *Philosophy,* vol. 38 (October 1963). From Richard Whately, *Introductory Lessons on Morals* (1855).

And probably it is through making this mistake that men in general apply the rule so much seldomer than they ought. For the real occasions for its use occur to all of us every day.

Supposing any one should regard this golden rule as designed to answer the purpose of a complete system of morality, and to teach us the difference of right and wrong; then, if he had let his land to a farmer, he might consider that the farmer would be glad to be excused paying any rent for it, since he would himself, if he were the farmer, prefer having the land rent-free; and that, therefore, the rule of doing as he would be done by requires him to give up all his property. So also a shopkeeper might, on the same principle, think that the rule required him to part with his goods under prime cost, or to give them away, and thus to ruin himself. Now such a procedure would be *absurd*.

Again, supposing a jailer who was intrusted with the safe custody of a prisoner should think himself bound to let the man escape, because he himself, if he were a prisoner, would be glad to obtain freedom, he would be guilty of a breach of trust. Such an application of the rule, therefore, would be morally *wrong*.

And again, if you had to decide between two parties who were pleading their cause before you, you might consider that *each* of them wished for a decision in his *own* favor. And how, then, you might ask, would it be possible to apply the rule? since in deciding *for* the one party you could not but decide *against* the other. A literal compliance with the rule, therefore, would be, in such a case, *impossible*.

II. APPLICATION OF THE GOLDEN RULE

Now, if you were to put such cases as these before any sensible man, he would at once say that you are to consider, not what you might *wish* in each case, but what you would regard as *fair, right, just, reasonable,* if you were in another person's place. If you were a farmer, although you might feel that you would be very glad to have the land rent-free—that is, to become the owner of it—you would not consider that you had any just claim to it, and that you could *fairly expect* the landlord to make you a present of his property. But you would think it reasonable that, if you suffered some great and unexpected loss, from an inundation or any such calamity, he should make an abatement of the rent. And this is what a good landlord generally thinks it right to do, in compliance with the golden rule.

So, also, if you had a cause to be tried, though of course you would *wish* the decision to be in your favor, you would be sensible that all you could *reasonably expect* of the judge would be that he should lay aside all prejudice, and attend impartially and carefully to the evidence, and decide according to the best of his ability. And this—which is what *each* part may fairly claim—is what an upright judge will do. And the like holds good in all the other cases.

III.   DESIGN OF THE GOLDEN RULE

You have seen, then, that the golden rule was far from being designed to impart to men the first notions of justice. On the contrary, it *presupposes* that knowledge; and if we had *no* such notions, we could not properly apply the rule. But the real design of it is to put us on our guard against the danger of being blinded by self-interest. A person who has a good general notion of what is just may often be tempted to act unfairly or unkindly towards his neighbors, when his own interest or gratification is concerned and to overlook the rightful claims of others. When David was guilty of an enormous sin in taking his neighbor's wife, and procuring the death of the husband, he was thinking only of his own gratification, quite forgetful of duty, till his slumbering conscience was roused by the prophet Nathan. On hearing the tale of "the poor man's lamb," his general abhorrence of injustice and cruelty caused him to feel vehement indignation against the supposed offender; but he did not apply his principles to his own case, till the prophet startled him by saying, "Thou art the man!"

And we, if we will make a practice of applying the golden rule, may have a kind of prophet always at hand, to remind us how, and when, to act on our principles of right. We have only to consider, "What should I think were I in the other's place, and he were to do so and so to me? How should I require him to treat me? What could I in fairness claim from him? . . .

For Further Reflection

1. How strong are Whately's arguments? Are they convincing? Can the Golden Rule be suitably set forth, so as to accommodate Whately's criticisms?

2. Consider this counterexample to the Golden Rule: Mrs. Jones feels neglected and wants her husband to talk to her, but Mr. Jones, after a hard day at the office, desperately wants peace and quiet. The criticism states that applying the Golden Rule would yield the following unsatisfactory results: Mrs. Jones would start talking to Mr. Jones, thus making him miserable, while Mr. Jones would remain silent, because that's how he would want Mrs. Jones to treat him. Both are miserable. Is this a fair criticism of the Golden Rule?

A Horseman in the Sky

AMBROSE BIERCE

Ambrose Bierce (1842–?1914) was a journalist who fought in the Civil War. He was famous for his sardonically humorous essays, including *The Devil's Dictionary* (1906). He disappeared into Mexico in 1913 and was presumed dead shortly thereafter.

In this Civil War story Carter Druse, a young Virginian, decides to join the Union Army. He announces this decision to his father, who, though disappointed, instructs him, whatever happens, to do what he conceives to be his duty. The story begins with Carter asleep at his post.

I

One sunny afternoon in the autumn of the year 1861 a soldier lay in a clump of laurel by the side of a road in western Virginia. He lay at full length upon his stomach, his feet resting upon the toes, his head upon the left forearm. His extended right hand loosely grasped his rifle. But for the somewhat methodical disposition of

---

Reprinted from Ambrose Bierce, *Civil War Stories*.

his limbs and a slight rhythmic movement of the cartridge-box at the back of his belt he might have been thought to be dead. He was asleep at his post of duty. But if detected he would be dead shortly afterward, death being the just and legal penalty of his crime.

The clump of laurel in which the criminal lay was in the angle of a road which after ascending southward a steep acclivity to that point turned sharply to the west, running along the summit for perhaps one hundred yards. There it turned southward again and went zigzagging downward through the forest. At the salient of that second angle was a large flat rock, jutting out northward, overlooking the deep valley from which the road ascended. The rock capped a high cliff; a stone dropped from its outer edge would have fallen sheer downward one thousand feet to the tops of the pines. The angle where the soldier lay was on another spur of the same cliff. Had he been awake he would have commanded a view, not only of the short arm of the road and the jutting rock, but of the entire profile of the cliff below it. It might well have made him giddy to look.

The country was wooded everywhere except at the bottom of the valley to the northward, where there was a small natural meadow, through which flowed a stream scarcely visible from the valley's rim. This open ground looked hardly larger than an ordinary door-yard, but was really several acres in extent. Its green was more vivid than that of the inclosing forest. Away beyond it rose a line of giant cliffs similar to those upon which we are supposed to stand in our survey of the savage scene, and through which the road had somehow made its climb to the summit. The configuration of the valley, indeed, was such that from this point of observation it seemed entirely shut in, and one could but have wondered how the road which found a way out of it had found a way into it, and whence came and whither went the waters of the stream that parted the meadow more than a thousand feet below.

No country is so wild and difficult but men will make it a theatre of war; concealed in the forest at the bottom of that military rat-trap, in which half a hundred men in possession of the exits might have starved an army to submission, lay five regiments of Federal infantry. They had marched all the previous day and night and were resting. At nightfall they would take to the road again, climb to the place where their unfaithful sentinel now slept, and descending the other slope of the ridge fall upon a camp of the enemy at about midnight. Their hope was to surprise it, for the road led to the rear of it. In case of failure, their position would be perilous in the extreme; and fail they surely would should accident or vigilance apprise the enemy of the movement.

II

The sleeping sentinel in the clump of laurel was a young Virginian named Carter Druse. He was the son of wealthy parents, an only child, and had known such ease and cultivation and high living as wealth and taste were able to command in the mountain country of western Virginia. His home was but a few miles from where he now lay. One morning he had risen from the breakfast-table and said, quietly but gravely: "Father, a Union regiment has arrived at Grafton. I am going to join it."

The father lifted his leonine head, looked at the son a moment in silence, and replied: "Well, go, sir, and whatever may occur do what you conceive to be your duty. Virginia, to which you are a traitor, must get on without you. Should we both live to the end of the war, we will speak further of the matter. Your mother, as the physician has informed you, is in a most critical condition; at the best she cannot be with us longer than a few weeks, but that time is precious. It would be better not to disturb her."

So Carter Druse, bowing reverently to his father, who returned the salute with a stately courtesy that masked a breaking heart, left the home of his childhood to go soldiering. By conscience and courage, by deeds of devotion and daring, he soon commended himself to his fellows and his officers; and it was to these qualities and to some knowledge of the country that he owed his selection for his present perilous duty at the extreme outpost. Nevertheless, fatigue had been stronger than resolution and he had fallen asleep. What good or bad angel came in a dream to rouse him from his state of crime, who shall say? Without a movement, without a sound, in the profound silence and the languor of the late afternoon, some invisible messenger of fate touched with unsealing finger the eyes of his consciousness—whispered into the ear of his spirit the mysterious awakening word which no human lips ever have spoken, no human memory ever has recalled. He quietly raised his forehead from his arm and looked between the masking stems of the laurels, instinctively closing his right hand about the stock of his rifle.

His first feeling was a keen artistic delight. On a colossal pedestal, the cliff—motionless at the extreme edge of the capping rock and sharply outlined against the sky—was an equestrian statue of impressive dignity. The figure of the man sat on the figure of the horse, straight and soldierly, but with the repose of a Grecian god carved in the marble which limits the suggestion of activity. The gray costume harmonized with its aërial background; the metal of accoutrement and caparison was softened and subdued by the shadow; the animal's skin had no points of high light. A carbine strikingly foreshortened lay across the pommel of the saddle, kept in place by the right hand grasping it at the "grip"; the left hand, holding the bridle rein, was invisible. In silhouette against the sky the profile of the horse was cut with the sharpness of a cameo; it looked across the heights of air to the confronting cliffs beyond. The face of the rider, turned slightly away, showed only an outline of temple and beard; he was looking downward to the bottom of the valley. Magnified by its lift against the sky and by the soldier's testifying sense of the formidableness of a near enemy the group appeared of heroic, almost colossal, size.

For an instant Druse had a strange, half-defined feeling that he had slept to the end of the war and was looking upon a noble work of art reared upon that eminence to commemorate the deeds of an heroic past of which he had been an inglorious part. The feeling was dispelled by a slight movement of the group: the horse, without moving its feet, had drawn its body slightly backward from the verge; the man remained immobile as before. Broad awake and keenly alive to the significance of the situation, Druse now brought the butt of his rifle against his cheek by cautiously pushing the barrel forward through the bushes, cocked the piece, and glancing through the sights covered a vital spot of the horseman's breast. A touch upon the trigger and all would have been well with Carter Druse. At that instant the horseman turned his head and looked in the direction of his concealed foeman—seemed to look into his very face, into his eyes, into his brave, compassionate heart.

Is it then so terrible to kill an enemy in war—an enemy who has surprised a secret vital to the safety of one's self and comrades—an enemy more formidable for his knowledge than all his army for its numbers? Carter Druse grew pale; he shook in every limb, turned faint, and saw the statuesque group before him as black figures, rising, falling, moving unsteadily in arcs of circles in a fiery sky. His hand fell away from his weapon, his head slowly dropped until his face rested on the leaves in which he lay. This courageous gentleman and hardy soldier was near swooning from intensity of emotion.

It was not for long; in another moment his face was raised from earth, his hands resumed their places on the rifle, his forefinger sought the trigger; mind, heart, and eyes were clear, conscience and reason sound. He could not hope to capture that enemy; to alarm him would but send him dashing to his camp with his fatal news. The duty of the soldier was plain: the man must be shot dead from ambush—without warning, without a moment's spiritual preparation, with never so much as an unspoken prayer, he must be sent to his account. But no—there is a hope; he may have discovered nothing—perhaps he is but admiring the sublimity of the landscape. If permitted, he may turn and ride carelessly away in the direction whence he came. Surely it will be possible to judge at the instant of his withdrawing whether he knows. It may well be that his fixity of attention—Druse turned his head and looked through the deeps of air downward, as from the surface to the bottom of a translucent sea. He saw creeping across the green meadow a sinuous line of figures of men and horses—some foolish commander was permitting the soldiers of his escort to water their beasts in the open, in plain view from a dozen summits!

Druse withdrew his eyes from the valley and fixed them again upon the group of man and horse in the sky, and again it was through the sights of his rifle. But this time his aim was at the horse. In his memory, as if they were a divine mandate, rang the words of his father at their parting: "Whatever may occur, do what you conceive to be your duty." He was calm now. His teeth were firmly but not rigidly closed; his nerves were as tranquil as a sleeping babe's—not a tremor affected any muscle of his body; his breathing, until suspended in the act of taking aim, was regular and slow. Duty had conquered; the spirit had said to the body: "Peace, be still." He fired.

III

An officer of the Federal force, who in a spirit of adventure or in quest of knowledge had left the hidden *bivouac* in the valley, and with aimless feet had made his way to the lower edge of a small open space near the foot of the cliff, was considering what he had to gain by pushing his exploration further. At a distance of a quarter-mile before him, but apparently at a stone's throw, rose from its fringe of pines the gigantic face of rock, towering to so great a height above him that it made him giddy to look up to where its edge cut a sharp, rugged line against the sky. It presented a clean, vertical profile against a background of blue sky to a point half the way down, and of distant hills, hardly less blue, thence to the tops of the trees at its base. Lifting his eyes to the dizzy altitude of its summit the officer saw an astonishing sight—a man on horseback riding down into the valley through the air!

Straight upright sat the rider, in military fashion, with a firm seat in the saddle, a strong clutch upon the rein to hold his charger from too impetuous a plunge. From his bare head his long hair streamed upward, waving like a plume. His hands were concealed in the cloud of the horse's lifted mane. The animal's body was as level as if every hoofstroke encountered the resistant earth. Its motions were those of a wild gallop, but even as the officer looked they ceased, with all the legs thrown sharply forward as in the act of alighting from a leap. But this was a flight!

Filled with amazement and terror by this apparition of a horseman in the sky—half believing himself the chosen scribe of some new Apocalypse, the officer was overcome by the intensity of his emotions; his legs failed him and he fell. Almost the same instant he heard a crashing sound in the trees—a sound that died without an echo—and all was still.

The officer rose to his feet, trembling. The familiar sensation of an abraded shin recalled his dazed faculties. Pulling himself together he ran rapidly obliquely away from the cliff to a point distant from its foot; thereabout he expected to find his man; and thereabout he naturally failed. In the fleeting instant of his vision his imagination had been so wrought upon by the apparent grace and ease and intention of the marvelous performance that it did not occur to him that the line of march of aërial cavalry is directly downward, and that he could find the objects of his search at the very foot of the cliff. A half-hour later he returned to camp.

This officer was a wise man; he knew better than to tell an incredible truth. He said nothing of what he had seen. But when the commander asked him if in his scout he had learned anything of advantage to the expedition he answered:

"Yes, sir; there is no road leading down into this valley from the southward."

The commander, knowing better, smiled.

IV

After firing his shot, Private Carter Druse reloaded his rifle and resumed his watch. Ten minutes had hardly passed when a Federal sergeant crept cautiously to him on hands and knees. Druse neither turned his head nor looked at him, but lay without motion or sign of recognition.

"Did you fire?" the sergeant whispered.

"Yes."

"At what?"

"A horse. It was standing on yonder rock—pretty far out. You see it is no longer there. It went over the cliff."

The man's face was white, but he showed no other sign of emotion. Having answered, he turned away his eyes and said no more. The sergeant did not understand.

"See here, Druse," he said, after a moment's silence, "it's no use making a mystery. I order you to report. Was there anybody on the horse?"

"Yes."

"Well?"

"My father."

The sergeant rose to his feet and walked away. "Good God!" he said.

For Further Reflection

1. What was Carter Druse's duty in this situation? Was it different from what he thought it to be? What should he have done? What would you have done?

2. How does this story bear upon deontological ethics? Compare it with Kierkegaard's notion of duty at the beginning of this chapter and Kant's and Ross's notions that follow.

3. What would a utilitarian have done in these circumstances?

The Evil of Lying

CHARLES FRIED

Charles Fried is a professor of law at Harvard University. In this selection from his book *Right and Wrong* he argues that lying is wrong even if it sometimes has good results. However, all things considered, sometimes special other duties override our duty not to lie. Fried defines lying earlier in the book this way: "A person lies when he asserts a proposition he believes to be false." It could turn out that the lie is in fact true, such as when I want to deceive you and tell you that your friend has betrayed you—and it turns out, unbeknownst to me, that he really has. Lying is intentional and bad because it fails to respect truth. But it is not only bad, it is morally wrong, since it violates respect for persons.

The evil of lying is as hard to pin down as it is strongly felt. Is lying wrong or is it merely something bad? If it is bad, why is it bad—is it bad in itself or because of some tendency associated with it? Compare lying to physical harm. Harm is a state of the world and so it can only be classified as bad; the wrong I argued for was the *intentional doing* of harm. Lying, on the other hand, can be wrong, since it is an action. But the fact that lying is an action does not mean that it *must* be wrong rather than bad. It might be that the action of lying should be judged as just another state of the world—a time-extended state, to be sure, but there is no problem about that—and as such it would count as a negative element in any set of circumstances in which it occurred. Furthermore, if lying is judged to be bad it can be bad in itself, like something ugly or painful, or it can be bad only because of its tendency to produce results that are bad in themselves.

If lying were bad, not wrong, this would mean only that, other things being equal, we should avoid lies. And if lying were bad not in itself but merely because of its tendencies, we would have to avoid lies only when those tendencies were in fact likely to be realized. In either case lying would be permissible to produce a

Reprinted by permission of the publishers from *Right and Wrong* by Charles Fried, Cambridge, Mass.: Harvard University Press, Copyright © 1978 by the President and Fellows of Harvard College.

net benefit, including the prevention of more or worse lies. By contrast the categorical norm "Do not lie" does not evaluate states of affairs but is addressed to moral agents, forbidding lies. Now if lying is wrong it is also bad in itself, for the category of the intrinsically bad is weaker and more inclusive than the category of the wrong. And accordingly, many states of the world are intrinsically bad (such as destruction of valuable property) but intentional acts bringing them about are not necessarily wrong.

Bentham plainly believed that lying is neither wrong nor even intrinsically bad: "Falsehood, take it by itself, consider it as not being accompanied by any other material circumstances, nor therefore productive of any material effects, can never, upon the principle of utility, constitute any offense at all." By contrast, Kant and Augustine argued at length that lying is wrong. Indeed, they held that lying is not only wrong *unless* excused or justified in defined ways (which is my view) but that lying is always wrong. Augustine sees lying as a kind of defilement, the liar being tainted by the lie, quite apart from any consequences of the lie. Kant's views are more complex. He argues at one point that lying undermines confidence and trust among men generally: "Although by making a false statement I do no wrong to him who unjustly compels me to speak, yet I do wrong to men in general . . . I cause that declarations in general find no credit, and hence all rights founded on contract should lose their force; and this is a wrong to mankind." This would seem to be a consequentialist argument, according to which lying is bad only insofar as it produces these bad results. But elsewhere he makes plain that he believes these bad consequences to be necessarily, perhaps even conceptually linked to lying. In this more rigoristic vein, he asserts that lying is a perversion of one's uniquely human capacities irrespective of any consequences of the lie, and thus lying is not only intrinsically bad but wrong.

Finally, a number of writers have taken what looks like an intermediate position: the evil of lying is indeed identified with its consequences, but the connection between lying and those consequences, while not a necessary connection, is close and persistent, and the consequences themselves are pervasive and profound. Consider this passage from a recent work by G. F. Warnock:

> I do not necessarily do you any harm at all by deed or word if I induce
> you to believe what is not in fact the case; I may even do you good,

possibly by way, for example, of consolation or flattery. Nevertheless, though deception is not thus necessarily directly damaging it is easy to see how crucially important it is that the natural inclination to have recourse to it should be counteracted. It is, one might say, not the implanting of false beliefs that is damaging, but rather the generation of the suspicion that they may be being implanted. For this under- mines trust; and, to the extent that trust is undermined, all coopera- tive undertakings, in which what one person can do or has reason to do is dependent on what others have done, are doing, or are going to do, must tend to break down. . . . There is no sense in my asking you for your opinion on some point, if I do not suppose that your answer will actually express your opinion (verbal communication is doubtless the most important of all our co-operative undertakings). (*The Object of Morality* [London: Methuen, 1971], p. 84.)

Warnock does not quite say that truth-telling is good in itself or that lying is wrong, yet the moral quality of truth-telling and lying is not so simply instrumental as it is, for instance, for Bentham. Rather, truth-telling seems to bear a fundamental, pervasive rela- tion to the human enterprise, just as lying appears to be funda- mentally subversive of that enterprise. What exactly is the nature of this relation? How does truth-telling bear to human goods a rela- tion which is more than instrumental but less than necessary?

The very definition of lying makes plain that consequences are crucial, for lying is intentional and the intent is an intent to pro- duce a consequence: false belief. But how can I then resist the con- sequentialist analysis of lying? Lying is an attempt to produce a cer- tain effect on another, and if that effect (consequence) is not bad, how can lying be wrong? I shall have to argue, therefore, that to lie is to intend to produce an effect which always has something bad about it, an effect moreover of the special sort that it is wrong to produce it intentionally. To lay that groundwork for my argu- ment about lying, I must consider first the moral value of truth.

TRUTH AND RATIONALITY

A statement is true when the world is the way the statement says it is. Utilitarians insist (as in the quotation from Bentham above) that truth, like everything else, has value just exactly as it produces value—pleasure, pain, the satisfaction or frustration of desire. And of course it is easy to show that truth (like keeping faith, not harming the innocent, respecting rights) does not always lead to the net satisfactions of desire, to the production of utility. It may *tend* to do so, but that tendency explains only why we should discriminate between occasions when truth does and when it does not have value—an old story. It is an old story, for truth—like justice, respect, and self-respect—has a value which consequentialist analyses (utilitarian or any other) do not capture. Truth, like respect, is a foundational value.

The morality of right and wrong does not count the satisfaction of desire as the overriding value. Rather, the integrity of persons, as agents and as the objects of the intentional agency of others, has priority over the attainment of the goals which agents choose to attain. I have sought to show how respect for physical integrity is related to respect for the person. The person, I argued, is not just a locus of potential pleasure and pain but an entity with determinate characteristics. The person is, among other things, necessarily an incorporated, a physical, not an abstract entity. In relation to truth we touch another necessary aspect of moral personality: the capacity for judgment, and thus for choice. It is that aspect which Kant used to ground his moral theory, arguing that freedom and rationality are the basis for moral personality. John Rawls makes the same point, arguing that "moral personality and not the capacity for pleasure and pain . . . [is] the fundamental aspect of the self . . . The essential unity of the self is . . . provided by the concept of right." The concept of the self is prior to the goods which the self chooses, and these goods gather their moral significance from the fact that they have been chosen by moral beings—beings capable of understanding and acting on moral principles.

In this view freedom and rationality are complementary capacities, or aspects of the same capacity, which is moral capacity. A man is free insofar as he is able to act on a judgment because he perceives it to be correct; he is free insofar as he may be moved to action by the judgments his reason offers to him. This is the very opposite of the Humean conception of reason as the slave of the passions. There is no slavery here. The man who follows the steps of a mathematical argument to its conclusion because he judges them to be correct is free indeed. To the extent that we choose our ends we are free; and as to objectively valuable ends which we choose because we see their value, we are still free.

Now, rational judgment is true judgment, and so the moral capacity for rational choice implies the capacity to recognize the matter on which choice is to act and to recognize the kind of result our choices will produce. This applies to judgments about other selves and to judgments in which one locates himself as a person among persons, a self among selves. These judgments are not just arbitrary suppositions: *they are judged to be true of the world*. For consider what the self would be like if these judgments were not supposed to be true. Maybe one might be content to be happy in the manner of the fool of Athens who believed all the ships in the harbor to be his. But what of our perceptions of other people? Would we be content to have those whom we love and trust the mere figments of our imaginations? The foundational values of freedom and rationality imply the foundational value of truth, for the rational man is the one who judges aright, that is, truly. Truth is not the same as judgment, as rationality; it is rather the proper subject of judgment. If we did not seek to judge truly, and if we did not believe we could judge truly, the act of judgment would not be what we know it to be at all.

Judgment and thus truth are *part* of a structure which as a whole makes up the concept of self. A person's relation to his body and the fact of being an incorporated self are another part of that structure. These two parts are related. The bodily senses provide matter for judgments of truth, and the body includes the physical organs of judgment.

THE WRONG OF LYING

So our capacity for judgment is foundational and truth is the proper object of that capacity, but how do we get to the badness of lying, much less its categorical wrongness? The crucial step to be supplied has to do not with the value of truth but with the evil of lying. We must show that to lie to someone is to injure him in a way that particularly touches his moral personality. From that, the passage is indeed easy to the conclusion that to inflict such injury intentionally (remember that all lying is by hypothesis intentional) is not only bad but wrong. It is this first, crucial step which is difficult. After all, a person's capacity for true judgment is not necessarily impaired by inducing in him a particular false belief. Nor would it seem that a person suffers a greater injury in respect to that capacity when he is induced to believe a falsity than when we intentionally prevent him from discovering the truth, yet only in the first case do we lie. Do we really do injury to a person's moral personality when we persuade him falsely that it rained yesterday in Bangkok—a fact in which he has no interest? And do we do him more injury than when we fail to answer his request for yesterday's football scores, in which he is mildly interested? Must we not calculate the injury by the *other* harm it does: disappointed expectations, lost property, missed opportunities, physical harm? In this view, lying would be a way of injuring a person in his various substantive interests—a way of stealing from him, hurting his feelings, perhaps poisoning him—but then the evil of lying would be purely instrumental, not wrong at all.

All truth, however irrelevant or trivial, has value, even though we may cheerfully ignore most truths, forget them, erase them as encumbrances from our memories. The value of every truth is shown just in the judgment that the only thing we must not do is falsify truth. Truths are like other people's property, which we can care nothing about but may not use for our own purposes. It is as if the truth were not ours (even truth we have discovered and which is known only to us), and so we may not exercise an unlimited dominion over it. Our relations to other people have a similar structure: we may perhaps have no duty to them, we may be free to put them out of our minds to make room for others whom we care about more, but we may not harm them. And so we may not falsify truth. But enough of metaphors—what does it mean to say that the truth is not ours?

The capacity for true judgment is the capacity to arrive at judgments which are in fact true of the world as it exists apart from our desires, our choices, our values. It is the world presented to us by true judgments—including true judgments about ourselves—which we then make the subject of our choices, our valuation. Now, if we treat the truth as our own, it must be according to desire or valuation. But for rational beings these activities are supposed to depend on truth; we are supposed to desire and choose according to the world as it is. To choose that something not to be the case when it is in fact the case is very nearly self-contradictory—for choice is not *of* truth but *on the basis of* truth. To deliberate about whether to believe a truth (not whether it is indeed true—another story altogether) is like deciding whether to cheat at solitaire. All this is obvious. In fact I suppose one cannot even coherently talk about choosing to believe something one believes to be false. And this holds equally for all truths—big and little, useful, and down-right inconvenient. But we do and must calculate *about* (and not just *with*) truths all the time as we decide what truths to acquire, what to forget. We decide all the time not to pursue some inquiry because it is not worth it. Such calculations surely must go forward on the basis of what truths are useful, given one's plans and desires. Even when we pursue truth for its own sake, we distinguish between interesting and boring truths.

Considering what truth to acquire or retain differs, however, from deliberately acquiring false beliefs. All truths are acquired as propositions correctly (truly) corresponding to the world, and in this respect, all truths are equal. A lie, however, has the form and occupies the role of truth in that it too purports to be a proposition about the world; only the world does not correspond to it. So the choice of a lie is not like a choice among truths, for the choice of a lie is a choice to affirm as the basis for judgment a proposition which does not correspond to the world. So, when I say that truth is foundational, that truth precedes choice, what I mean is *not* that this or that truth is foundational but that judging according to the facts is foundational to judging at all. A scientist may deliberate about which subject to study and, having chosen his subject, about the data worth acquiring, but he cannot even deliberate as a scientist about whether to acquire false data. Clearly, then, there is something funny (wrong?) about lying to oneself, but how do we go from there to the proposition that it is wrong to lie to someone else? After all, much of the peculiarity about lying to oneself consists in the fact that it seems not so much bad as downright self-contradictory, logically impossible, but that does not support the judgment that it is wrong to lie to another. I cannot marry myself, but that hardly makes it wrong to marry someone else.

Let us imagine a case in which you come as close as you can to lying to yourself: You arrange some operation, some fiddling with your brain that has no effect other than to cause you to believe a proposition you know to be false and also to forget entirely the prior history of how you came to believe that proposition. It seems to me that you do indeed harm yourself in such an operation. This is because a free and rational person wishes to have a certain relation to reality: as nearly perfect as possible. He wishes to build his conception of himself and the world and his conception of the good on the basis of truth. Now if he affirms that the truth is available for fiddling in order to accommodate either his picture of the world or his conception of the good, then this affirms that reality is dependent on what one wants, rather than what one wants being fundamentally constrained by what there is. Rationality is the respect for this fundamental constraint of truth. This is just another way of saying that the truth is prior to our plans and prospects and must be respected whatever our plans might be. What if the truth we "destroy" by this operation is a very trivial and irrelevant truth— the state of the weather in Bangkok on some particular day? There is still an injury to self, because the fiddler must have some purpose in his fiddling. If it is a substantive purpose, then the truth is in fact relevant to that purpose, and my argument holds. If it is just to show it can be done, then he is only trying to show he can do violence to his rationality—a kind of moral blasphemy. Well, what if it is a very *little* truth? Why, then, it is a very little injury he does himself—but that does not undermine my point.

Now, when I lie to you, I do to you what you cannot actually do to yourself—brain-fiddling being only an approximation. The nature of the injury I would do to myself, if I could, explains why lying to you is to do you harm, indeed why it is wrong. The lie is an injury because it produces an effect (or seeks to) which a person as a moral agent should not wish to have produced in him, and thus it is as much an injury as any other effect which a moral agent would not wish to have produced upon his person. To be sure, some people may want to be lied to. That is a special problem; they are like people who want to suffer (not just are willing to risk) physical injury. In general, then, I do not want you to lie to me in the same way that as a rational man I would not lie to myself if I could. But why does this make lying wrong and not merely bad?

Lying is wrong because when I lie I set up a relation which is essentially exploitative. It violates the principle of respect, for I must affirm that the mind of another person is available to me in a way in which I cannot agree my mind would be available to him—for if I do so agree, then I would not expect my lie to be believed. When I lie, I am like a counterfeiter: I do not want the market flooded with counterfeit currency; I do not want to get back my own counterfeit bill. Moreover, in lying to you, I affirm such an unfairly unilateral principle in respect to an interest and capacity which is crucial, as crucial as physical integrity: your freedom and your rationality. When I do intentional physical harm, I say that your body, your person, is available for my purposes. When I lie, I lay claim to your mind.

Lying violates respect and is wrong, as is any breach of trust. Every lie is a broken promise, and the only reason this seems strained is that in lying the promise is made and broken at the same moment. Every lie necessarily implies—as does every assertion—an assurance, a warranty of its truth. The fact that the breach accompanies the making should, however, only strengthen the conclusion that this is wrong. If promise-breaking is wrong, then a lie must be wrong, since there cannot be the supervening factor of changed circumstances which may excuse breaches of promises to perform in the future.

The final one of the convergent strands that make up the wrong of lying is the shared, communal nature of language. This is what I think Kant had in mind when he argued that a lie does wrong "to men in general." If whether people stood behind their statements depended wholly on the particular circumstances of the utterance, then the whole point of communication would be undermined. For every utterance would simply be the occasion for an analysis of the total circumstances (speaker's and hearer's) in order to determine what, if anything, to make of the utterance. And though we do often wonder and calculate whether a person is telling the truth, we do so from a baseline, a presumption that people do stand behind their statements. After all, the speaker surely depends on such a baseline. He wants us to think that he is telling the truth. Speech is a paradigm of communication, and all human relations are based on some form of communication. Our very ability to think, to conceptualize, is related to speech. Speech allows the social to penetrate the intimately personal. Perhaps that is why Kant's dicta seem to vacillate between two positions: lying as a social offense, and lying as an offense against oneself; the requirement of an intent to deceive another, and the insistence that the essence of the wrong is not injury to another but to humanity. Every lie violates the basic commitment to truth which stands behind the social fact of language.

I have already argued that bodily integrity bears a necessary relation to moral integrity, so that an attack upon bodily integrity is wrong, not just bad. The intimate *and* social nature of truth make the argument about lying stronger. For not only is the target aspect of the victim crucial to him as a moral agent but, by lying, we attack that target by a means which itself offends his moral nature; the means of attack are social means which can be said to belong as much to the victim as to his assailant. There is not only the attack at his moral vitals, but an attack with a weapon which belongs to him. Lying is, thus, a kind of treachery. (*Kind of* treachery? Why not treachery pure and simple?) It is as if we not only robbed a man of his treasure but in doing so used his own servants or family as our agents. That speech is our *common* property, that it belongs to the liar, his victim and all of us makes the matter if anything far worse.

So this is why lying is not only bad (a hurt), but wrong, why lying is wrong apart from or in addition to any other injury it does, and why lying seems at once an offense against the victim and against mankind in general, an offense against the liar himself, and against the abstract entity, truth. Whom do you injure when you pass a counterfeit bill?

What about little pointless lies? Do I really mean they are wrong? Well, yes, even a little lie is wrong, *if* it is a true piece of communication, an assertion of its own truth and not just a conventional way of asserting nothing at all or something else (as in the case of polite or diplomatic formulas). A little lie is a little wrong, but it is still something you must not do.

For Further Reflection

1. Evaluate Fried's argument against lying. Why is it always wrong—even if only a little wrong? Is his argument sound? Explain.

2. Fried makes several comparisons of lying with other acts: stealing, injuring, counterfeiting, promise-breaking, and violating the social fact of language. Are these good analogies?

3. Fried says lying is exploitative. Is this always the case? Can you think of cases where one lies not to exploit but to help another?

Moral Luck

THOMAS NAGEL

Thomas Nagel is professor of philosophy at New York University and the author of several works in moral and political philosophy. In this selection Nagel challenges the Kantian way of viewing morality, which assumes that we are all equal rational participants in the moral enterprise, each having the same opportunity to be moral. Nagel suggests that this view is simplistic and fails to take into account the manner in which external factors impinge upon us. They introduce the idea of moral luck, which he defines thus: "Where a significant aspect of what someone does depends on factors beyond his control, yet we continue to treat him in that respect as an object of moral judgment, it can be called moral luck."

Four types of moral luck are considered: constitutive luck, circumstantial luck, consequential luck in which consequences retrospectively justify an otherwise immoral act (or fail to justify an otherwise moral act), and consequential luck in which the consequences affect the type of blame or remorse (or moral praise).

Kant believed that good or bad luck should influence neither our moral judgment of a person and his actions, nor his moral assessment of himself.

> The good will is not good because of what it effects or accomplishes or because of its adequacy to achieve some proposed end; it is good only because of its willing, i.e., it is good of itself. And, regarded for itself, it is to be esteemed incomparably higher than anything which could be brought about by it in favor of any inclination or even of the sum total of all inclinations. Even if it should happen that, by a particular unfortunate fate or by the niggardly provision of a stepmotherly nature, this will should be wholly lacking in power to accomplish its purpose, and if even the greatest effort should not

From *Mortal Questions* (Cambridge University Press, 1979). Reprinted by permission of Cambridge University Press. Notes omitted.

avail it to achieve anything of its end, and if there remained only the good will (not as a mere wish but as the summoning of all the means in our power), it would sparkle like a jewel in its own right, as something that had its full worth in itself. Usefulness or fruitlessness can neither diminish nor augment this worth.

He would presumably have said the same thing about a bad will: whether it accomplishes its evil purposes is morally irrelevant. And a course of action that would be condemned if it had a bad outcome cannot be vindicated if by luck it turns out well. There cannot be moral risk. This view seems to be wrong, but it arises in response to a fundamental problem about moral responsibility to which we possess no satisfactory solution.

The problem develops out of the ordinary conditions of moral judgment. Prior to reflection it is intuitively plausible that people cannot be morally assessed for what is not their fault, or for what is due to factors beyond their control. Such judgment is different from the evaluation of something as a good or bad thing, or state of affairs. The latter may be present in addition to moral judgment, but when we blame someone for his actions we are not merely saying it is bad that they happened, or bad that he exists: we are judging *him,* saying he is bad, which is different from his being a bad thing. This kind of judgment takes only a certain kind of object. Without being able to explain exactly why, we feel that the appropriateness of moral assessment is easily undermined by the discovery that the act or attribute, no matter how good or bad, is not under the person's control. While other evaluations remain, this one seems to lose its footing. So a clear absence of control, produced by involuntary movement, physical force, or ignorance of the circumstances, excuses what is done from moral judgment. But what we do depends in many more ways than these on what is not under our control—what is not produced by a good or a bad will in Kant's phrase. And external influences in this broader range are not usually thought to excuse what is done from moral judgment, positive or negative.

Let me give a few examples, beginning with the type of case Kant has in mind. Whether we succeed or fail in what we try to do nearly always depends to some extent on factors beyond our control. This is true of murder, altruism, revolution, the sacrifice of certain interests for the sake of others—almost any morally important act. What has been done, and what is morally judged, is partly determined by external factors. However jewel-like the good will may be in its own right, there is a morally significant difference between rescuing someone from a burning building and dropping him from a twelfth-story window while trying to rescue him. Similarly, there is a morally significant difference between reckless driving and manslaughter. But whether a reckless driver hits a pedestrian depends on the presence of the pedestrian at the point where he recklessly passes a red light. What we do is also limited by the opportunities and choices with which we are faced, and these are largely determined by factors beyond our control. Someone who was an officer in a concentration camp might have led a quiet and harmless life if the Nazis had never come to power in Germany. And someone who led a quiet and harmless life in Argentina might have become an officer in a concentration camp if he had not left Germany for business reasons in 1930.

I shall say more later about these and other examples. I introduce them here to illustrate a general point. Where a significant aspect of what someone does depends on factors beyond his control, yet we continue to treat him in that respect as an object of moral judgment, it can be called moral luck. Such luck can be good or bad. And the problem posed by this phenomenon, which led Kant to deny its possibility, is that the broad range of external influences here identified seems on close examination to undermine moral assessment as surely as does the narrower range of familiar excusing conditions. If the condition of control is consistently applied, it threatens to erode most of the moral assessments we find it natural to make. The things for which people are morally judged are determined in more ways than we at first realize by what is beyond their control. And when the seemingly natural requirement of fault or responsibility is applied in light of these facts, it leaves few pre-reflective moral judgments intact. Ultimately, nothing or almost nothing about what a person does seems to be under his control.

Why not conclude, then, that the condition of control is false—that it is an initially plausible hypothesis refuted by clear counterexamples? One could in that case look instead for a more refined condition which picked out the *kinds* of lack of control that really undermine certain moral judgments, without yielding the unacceptable conclusion derived from the broader condition, that most or all ordinary moral judgments are illegitimate.

What rules out this escape is that we are dealing not with a theoretical conjecture but with a philosophical problem. The condition of control does not suggest itself merely as a generalization from certain clear cases. It seems *correct* in the further cases to which it is extended beyond the original set. When we undermine moral assessment by considering new ways in which control is absent, we are not just discovering what *would* follow given the general hypothesis, but are actually being persuaded that in itself the absence of control is relevant in these cases too. The erosion of moral judgment emerges not as the absurd consequence of an over-simple theory, but as a natural consequence of the ordinary idea of moral assessment, when it is applied in view of a more complete and precise account of the facts. It would therefore be a mistake to argue from the unacceptablity of the conclusions to the need for a different account of the conditions of moral responsibility. The view that moral luck is paradoxical is not a *mistake,* ethical or logical, but a perception of one of the ways in which the intuitively acceptable conditions of moral judgment threaten to undermine it all. . . .

[Here Nagel begins his discussion of the four types of moral luck:

1. Luck in the way one's action and projects turn out.
2. Luck in how one is determined by antecedent circumstances.
3. Constitutive luck—"the kind of person you are, where this is not just a question of what you deliberately do, but of your inclinations, capacities, and temperament."
4. Circumstantial luck—if circumstances had been different, the judgment of your act would have been assessed differently.]

Let us first consider luck, good and bad, in the way things turn out. Kant, in the above-quoted passage, has one example of this in mind, but the category covers a wide range. It includes the truck driver who accidentally runs over a child, the artist who abandons his wife and five children to devote himself to painting, and other cases in which the possibilities of success and failure are even greater. The driver, if he is entirely without fault, will feel terrible about his role in the event, but will not have to reproach himself. Therefore this example of agent-regent is not yet a case of *moral* bad luck. However, if the driver was guilty of even a minor degree of negligence—failing to have his brakes checked recently, for example—then if that negligence contributes to the death of the child, he will not merely feel terrible. He will blame himself for the death. And what makes this an example of moral luck is that he would have to blame himself only slightly for the negligence itself if no situation arose which required him to brake suddenly and violently to avoid hitting a child. Yet the *negligence* is the same in both cases, and the driver has no control over whether a child will run into his path.

The same is true at higher levels of negligence. If someone has had too much to drink and his car swerves onto the sidewalk, he can count himself morally lucky if there are no pedestrians in his path. If there were, he would be to blame for their deaths, and would probably be prosecuted for manslaughter. But if he hurts no one, although his recklessness is exactly the same, he is guilty of a far less serious legal offense and will certainly reproach himself and be reproached by others much less severely. To take another legal example, the penalty for attempted murder is less than that for successful murder—however similar the intentions and motives of the assailant may be in the two cases. His degree of culpability can depend, it would seem, on whether the victim happened to be wearing a bullet-proof vest, or whether a bird flew into the path of the bullet—matters beyond his control.

Finally, there are cases of decision under uncertainty—common in public and in private life. Anna Karenina goes off with Vronsky, Gauguin leaves his family, Chamberlain signs the Munich Agreement, the Decembrists persuade the troops under their command to revolt against the czar, the American colonies declare their independence from Britain, you introduce two people in an attempt at matchmaking. It is tempting in all such cases to feel that some decision must be possible, in the light of what is known at the time, which will make reproach unsuitable no matter how things turn out. But this is not true; when someone acts in such ways he takes his life, or his moral position, into his hands, because how things turn out determines what he has done. It is possible *also* to assess the decision from the point of view of what could be known at the time, but this is not the end of the story. If the Decembrists had succeeded in overthrowing Nicholas I in 1825 and establishing a constitutional regime, they would be heroes. As it is, not only did they fail and pay for it, but they bore some responsibility for the terrible punishments meted out to the troops who had been persuaded to follow them. If the American Revolution had been a bloody failure resulting in greater repression, then Jefferson, Franklin, and Washington would still have made a noble attempt, and might not even have regretted it on their way to the scaffold, but they would also have had to blame themselves for what they had helped to bring on their compatriots. (Perhaps peaceful efforts at reform would eventually have succeeded.) If Hitler had not overrun Europe and exterminated millions, but instead had died of a heart attack after occupying the Sudetenland, Chamberlain's action at Munich would still have utterly betrayed the Czechs, but it would not be the great moral disaster that has made his name a household word.

In many cases of difficult choice the outcome cannot be foreseen with certainty. One kind of assessment of the choice is possible in advance, but another kind must await the outcome, because the outcome determines what has been done. The same degree of culpability or estimability in intention, motive, or concern is compatible with a wide range of judgments, positive or negative, depending on what happened beyond the point of decision. The *mens rea* which could have existed in the absence of any consequences does not exhaust the grounds of moral judgment. Actual results influence culpability or esteem in a large class of unquestionably ethical cases ranging from negligence through political choice.

That these are genuine moral judgments rather than expressions of temporary attitude is evident from the fact that one can say *in advance* how the moral verdict will depend on the results. If one negligently leaves the bath running with the baby in it, one will realize, as one bounds up the stairs toward the bathroom, that if the baby has drowned one has done something awful, whereas if it has not one has merely been careless. Someone who launches a violent revolution against an authoritarian regime knows that if he fails he will be responsible for much suffering that is in vain, but if he succeeds he will be justified by the outcome. I do not mean that *any* action can be retroactively justified by history. Certain things are so bad in themselves, or so risky, that no results can make them all right. Nevertheless, when moral judgment does depend on the outcome, it is objective and timeless and not dependent on a change of standpoint produced by success or failure. The judgment after the fact follows from an hypothetical judgment that can be made beforehand, and it can be made as easily by someone else as by the agent.

From the point of view which makes responsibility dependent on control, all this seems absurd. How is it possible to be more or less culpable depending on whether a child gets into the path of one's car, or a bird into the path of one's bullet? Perhaps it is true that what is done depends on more than the agent's state of mind or intention. The problem then is, why is it not irrational to base moral assessment on what people do, in this broad sense? It amounts to holding them responsible for the contributions of fate as well as for their own—provided they have made some contribution to begin with. If we look at cases of negligence or attempt, the pattern seems to be that overall culpability corresponds to the product of mental or intentional fault and the seriousness of the outcome. Cases of decision under uncertainty are less easily explained in this way, for it seems that the overall judgment can even shift from positive to negative depending on the outcome. But here too it seems rational to subtract the effects of occurrences subsequent to the choice, that were merely possible at the time, and concentrate moral assessment on the actual decision in light of the probabilities. If the object of moral judgment is the *person,* then to hold him accountable for what he has done in the broader sense is akin to strict liability, which may have its legal uses but seems irrational as a moral position.

The result of such a line of thought is to pare down each act to its morally essential core, an inner act of pure will assessed by motive and intention. Adam Smith advocates such a position in *The Theory of Moral Sentiments,* but notes that it runs contrary to our actual judgments.

> But how well soever we may seem to be persuaded of the truth of this equitable maxim, when we consider it after this manner, in abstract, yet when we come to particular cases, the actual consequences which happen to proceed from any action, have a very great effect upon our sentiments concerning its merit or demerit, and almost always either enhance or diminish our sense of both. Scarce, in any one instance, perhaps, will our sentiments be found, after examination, to be entirely regulated by this rule, which we all acknowledge ought entirely to regulate them.

Joel Feinberg points out further that restricting the domain of moral responsibility to the inner world will not immunize it to luck. Factors beyond the agent's control, like a coughing fit, can interfere with his decisions as surely as they can with the path of a bullet from his gun. Nevertheless the tendency to cut down the scope of moral assessment is pervasive, and does not limit itself to the influence of effects. It attempts to isolate the will from the other direction, so to speak, by separating out constitutive luck. Let us consider that next.

Kant was particularly insistent on the moral irrelevance of qualities of temperament and personality that are not under the control of the will. Such qualities as sympathy or coldness might provide the background against which obedience to moral requirements is more or less difficult, but they could not be objects of moral assessment themselves, and might well interfere with confident assessment of its proper object—the determination of the will by the motive of duty. This rules out moral judgment of many of the virtues and vices, which are states of character that influence choice but are certainly not exhausted by dispositions to act deliberately in certain ways. A person may be greedy, envious, cowardly, cold, ungenerous, unkind, vain, or conceited, but *behave* perfectly by a monumental effort of will. To possess these vices is to be unable to help having certain feelings under certain circumstances, and to have strong spontaneous impulses to act badly. Even if one controls the impulses, one still has the vice. An envious person hates the greater success of others. He can be morally condemned as envious even if he congratulates them cordially and does nothing to denigrate or spoil their success. Conceit, likewise, need not be displayed. It is fully present in someone who cannot help dwelling with secret satisfaction on the superiority of his own achievements, talents, beauty, intelligence, or virtue. To some extent such a quality may be the product of earlier choices; to some extent it may be amenable to change by current actions. But it is largely a matter of constitutive bad fortune. Yet people are morally condemned for such qualities, and esteemed for others equally beyond control of the will: they are assessed for what they are *like*.

To Kant this seems incoherent because virtue is enjoined on everyone and therefore must in principle be possible for everyone. It may be easier for some than for others, but it must be possible to achieve it by making the right choices, against whatever temperamental background. One may want to have a generous spirit, or regret not having one, but it makes no sense to condemn oneself or anyone else for a quality which is not within the control of the will. Condemnation implies that you should not be like that, not that it is unfortunate that you are.

Nevertheless, Kant's conclusion remains intuitively unacceptable. We may be persuaded that these moral judgments are irrational, but they reappear involuntarily as soon as the argument is over. This is the pattern throughout the subject.

The third category to consider is luck in one's circumstances, and I shall mention it briefly. The things we are called upon to do, the moral tests we face, are importantly determined by factors beyond our control. It may be true of someone that in a dangerous situation he would behave in a cowardly or heroic fashion, but if the situation never arises, he will never have the chance to distinguish or disgrace himself in this way, and his moral record will be different.

A conspicuous example of this is political. Ordinary citizens of Nazi Germany had an opportunity to behave heroically by opposing the regime. They also had an opportunity to behave badly, and most of them are culpable for having failed this test. But it is a test to which the citizens of other countries were not subjected, with the result that even if they, or some of them, would have behaved as badly as the Germans in like circumstances, they simply did not and therefore are not similarly culpable. Here again one is morally at the mercy of fate, and it may seem irrational upon reflection, but our ordinary moral attitudes would be unrecognizable without it. We judge people for what they actually do or fail to do, not just for what they would have done if circumstances had been different.

This form of moral determination by the actual is also paradoxical, but we can begin to see how deep in the concept of responsibility the paradox is embedded. A person can be morally responsible only for what he does; but what he does results from a great deal that he does not do; therefore he is not morally responsible for what he is and is not responsible for. (This is not a contradiction, but it is a paradox.)

It should be obvious that there is a connection between these problems about responsibility and control and an even more familiar problem, that of freedom of the will. That is the last type of moral luck I want to take up, though I can do no more within the scope of this essay than indicate its connection with the other types.

If one cannot be responsible for consequences of one's acts due to factors beyond one's control, or for antecedents of one's acts that are properties of temperament not subject to one's will, or for the circumstances that pose one's moral choices, then how can one be responsible even for the stripped-down acts of the will itself, if *they* are the product of antecedent circumstances outside of the will's control?

The area of genuine agency, and therefore of legitimate moral judgment, seems to shrink under this scrutiny to an extensionless point. Everything seems to result from the combined influence of factors, antecedent and posterior to action, that are not within the agent's control. Since he cannot be responsible for them, he cannot be responsible for their results—though it may remain possible to take up the aesthetic or other evaluative analogues of the moral attitudes that are thus displaced.

It is also possible, of course, to brazen it out and refuse to accept the results, which indeed seem unacceptable as soon as we stop thinking about the arguments. Admittedly, if certain surrounding circumstances had been different, then no unfortunate consequences would have followed from a wicked intention, and no seriously culpable act would have been performed; but since the circumstances were *not* different, and the agent *in fact* succeeded in perpetrating a particularly cruel murder, *that* is what he did, and that is what he is responsible for. Similarly, we may admit that if certain antecedent circumstances had been different, the agent would never have developed into the sort of person who would do such a thing; but since he *did* develop (as the inevitable result of those antecedent circumstances) into the sort of swine he is, and into the person who committed such a murder, *that* is what he is blamable for. In both cases one is responsible for what one actually does—even if what one actually does depends in important ways on what is not within one's control. This [compatibilist] account of our moral judgments would leave room for the ordinary conditions of responsibility—the absence of coercion, ignorance, or involuntary movement—as part of the determination of what someone has done—but it is understood not to exclude the influence of a great deal that he has not done.

The only thing wrong with this solution is its failure to explain how skeptical problems arise. For they arise not from the imposition of an arbitrary external requirement, but from the nature of moral judgment itself. Something in the ordinary idea of what someone does must explain how it can seem necessary to subtract from it anything that merely happens—even though the ultimate consequence of such subtraction is that nothing remains. And something in the ordinary idea of knowledge must explain why it seems to be undermined by any influences on belief not within the control of the subject—so that knowledge seems impossible without an impossible foundation in autonomous reason. But let us leave epistemology aside and concentrate on action, character, and moral assessment.

The problem arises, I believe, because the self which acts and is the object of moral judgment is threatened with dissolution by the absorption of its acts and impulses into the class of events. Moral judgment of a person is judgment not of what happens to him, but of him. It does not say merely that a certain event or state of affairs is fortunate or unfortunate or even terrible. It is not an evaluation of a state of the world, or of an individual as part of the world. We are not thinking just that it would be better if he were different, or did not exist, or had not done some of the things he has done. We are judging *him,* rather than his existence or characteristics. The effect of concentrating on the influence of what is not under his control is to make this responsible self seem to disappear, swallowed up by the order of mere events.

What, however, do we have in mind that a person must *be* to be the object of these moral attitudes? While the concept of agency is easily undermined, it is very difficult to give it a positive characterization. That is familiar from the literature on Free Will.

I believe that in a sense the problem has no solution, because something in the idea of agency is incompatible with actions being events, or people being things. But as the external determinants of what someone has done are gradually exposed, in their effect on consequences, character, and choice itself, it becomes gradually clear that actions are events and people things. Eventually nothing remains which can be ascribed to the responsible self, and we are left with nothing but a portion of the larger sequences of events, which can be deplored or celebrated, but not blamed or praised.

Though I cannot define the idea of the active self that is thus undermined, it is possible to say something about its sources. There is a close connection between our feelings about ourselves and our feelings about others. Guilt and indignation, shame and contempt, pride and admiration are internal and external sides of the same moral attitudes. We are unable to view ourselves simply as portions of the world, and from inside we have a rough idea of the boundary between what is us and what is not, what we do and what happens to us, what is our personality and what is an accidental handicap. We apply the same essentially internal conception of the self to others. About ourselves we feel pride, shame, guilt, remorse—and agent-regret. We do not regard our actions and our characters merely as fortunate or unfortunate episodes—though they may also be that. We cannot *simply* take an external evaluative view of ourselves—of what we most essentially are and what we do. And this remains true even when we have seen that we are not responsible for our own existence, or our nature, or the choices we have to make, or the circumstances that give our acts the consequences they have. Those acts remain ours and we remain ourselves, despite the persuasiveness of the reasons that seem to argue us out of existence.

It is this internal view that we extend to others in moral judgment—when we judge *them* rather than their desirability or utility. We extend to others the refusal to limit ourselves to external evaluation, and we accord to them selves like our own. But in both cases this comes up against the brutal inclusion of humans and everything about them in a world from which they cannot be separated and of which they are nothing but contents. The external view forces itself on us at the same time that we resist it. One way this occurs is through the gradual erosion of what we do by the subtraction of what happens.

The inclusion of consequences in the conception of what we have done is an acknowledgment that we are parts of the world, but the paradoxical character of moral luck which emerges from this acknowledgment shows that we are unable to operate with such a view, for it leaves us with no one to be. The same thing is revealed in the appearance that determinism obliterates responsibility. Once we see an aspect of what we or someone else does as something that happens, we lose our grip on the idea that it has been done and that we can judge the doer and not just the happening. This explains why the absence of determinism is no more hospitable to the concept of agency than is its presence—a point that has been noticed often. Either way the act is viewed externally, as part of the course of events.

The problem of moral luck cannot be understood without an account of the internal conception of agency and its special connection with the moral attitudes as opposed to other types of value. I do not have such an account. The degree to which the problem has a solution can be determined only by seeing whether in some degree the incompatibility between this conception and the various ways in which we do not control what we do is only apparent. I have nothing to offer on that topic either. But it is not enough to say merely that our basic moral attitudes toward ourselves and others are determined by what is actual; for they are also threatened by the sources of that actuality, and by the external view of action which forces itself on us when we see how everything we do belongs to a world that we have not created.

For Further Reflection

1. What is Nagel's criticism of Kant? Why does he think that Kant's notion of the good will as the sole determinant of moral goodness is simplistic?

2. Go over the types of moral luck that Nagel discusses. Are his arguments cogent and persuasive? It might help to examine the main examples. Take the German who becomes a Nazi officer who does great evil, but who in different, more peaceful circumstances would have been an average citizen with no great moral culpability. Is Nagel correct to say that the officer just had bad moral luck? Or can more be said about this assessment that would make sense of the Kantian idea of moral goodness?

3. Why does Nagel think that our notion of moral responsibility is deeply problematic, even incoherent?

4. Nagel believes that the free-will determinist debate is paradoxical. If we are determined by antecedent circumstances, then we are not responsible for what we do; but if we are not determined by these conditions, then everything seems arbitrary—free will seems to presuppose the very causal structure that it attacks. Does this make sense? Do you believe that you have free will? Explain your answer.

5. Do you believe there is moral luck or can we, in principle, make genuine moral judgments about people and their actions?

Further Readings for Chapter 5

Acton, Harry. *Kant's Moral Philosophy*. New York: Macmillan, 1970.

Broad, C. D. *Five Types of Ethical Theory*. London: Routledge and Kegan Paul, 1930.

Donagan, Alan. *The Theory of Morality*. Chicago: University of Chicago Press, 1977.

Feldman, Fred. *Introductory Ethics*. Englewood Cliffs, N.J.: Prentice-Hall, 1978. Chapters 7 and 8. A clear and critical exposition.

Harris, C. E. *Applying Moral Theories*. Belmont, Calif.: Wadsworth, 1986. Chapter 7. An excellent exposition of contemporary deontological theories, especially of Gewirth's work.

Kant, Immanuel. *Critique of Practical Reason*. Translated by Lewis White Beck. Indianapolis: Bobbs-Merrill, 1956.

———. *Grounding for the Metaphysics of Morals*. Translated by James Ellington. Indianapolis: Hackett Publishing Company, 1981.

———. *Lectures on Ethics*. Translated by Louis Infield. Indianapolis: Hackett Publishing Company, 1963.

Raphael, D. D. *Moral Philosophy*. Oxford: Oxford University Press, 1981. Chapter 6.

Ross, W. D. *Kant's Ethical Theory*. Oxford: Clarendon Press, 1954.

———. *The Right and the Good*. Oxford: Oxford University Press, 1930.

Ward, Keith. *The Development of Kant's Views of Ethics*. Oxford: Blackwell's, 1972.

Wolff, Robert P. *The Autonomy of Reason: A Commentary on Kant's Groundwork of the Metaphysics of Morals*. New York: Harper & Row, 1973.

Virtue Ethics

John hears that 100,000 people are starving in Ethiopia. He feels deep sorrow about this and sends $100 of his hard-earned money to a famine relief project in that country. Joan hears the same news but doesn't feel anything. However, out of a sense of duty she also sends $100 of her hard-earned money to the relief project.

Jack and Jill each have opportunity to embezzle a million dollars from the bank at which they work. Jill never even considers embezzling; the possibility is not even an option for her. Jack wrestles valiantly with the temptation, almost succumbs to it, but through a grand effort of the will finally succeeds in resisting the temptation.

Who in each case is more moral?

Whereas most ethical theories have been either duty-oriented or action-oriented, that is, either deontological or teleological (utilitarian), there is a third tradition which goes back to Plato and, especially, Aristotle, and which receives support in the writings of the Epicureans, the Stoics, Jesus, and the early Christian church. I refer to *virtue ethics* (sometimes called *aretaic ethics* after the Greek word *arete,* "excellence" or "virtue"). Rather than seeing the heart of ethics in action or duties, virtue ethics centers in the heart and personality of the agent—in his or her character. Whereas, the action-based ethics emphasizes *doing,* virtue ethics emphasizes *being*—being a certain kind of person who will no doubt manifest his or her being in actions or nonactions. For traditional duty-based ethics, the question is "What should I do?" For the virtue ethicist, the question is "What sort of person should I become?"

Virtue ethics seeks to produce excellent persons, who act well out of spontaneous goodness and serve as examples to inspire others. It seeks to create people like Moses, Confucius, Socrates, Jesus, Buddha, Albert Schweitzer, Mohandas Gandhi, and Mother Teresa—

people who light up our moral landscape as jewels who shine in their own light.

We begin our study with one of the most poignant examples of virtue, Victor Hugo's good bishop of Digne in *Les Misérables*. Then we examine a classic passage on the virtues by Aristotle and, after that, a modern interpretation by Bernard Mayo. This is followed by Nathaniel Hawthorne's short story "The Great Stone Face," a story that greatly inspired me as a teenager. Our fifth reading is William Frankena's critique of virtue ethics, in which Frankena argues that while the virtues are important, whatever is valid about virtue ethics should be subordinate to a deontological system. Finally, we examine Jonathan Bennett's "The Conscience of Huckleberry Finn," which argues that sometimes it is better to follow one's heart than one's moral principles.

The Bishop and the Candlesticks

VICTOR HUGO

The French writer Victor Hugo (1802–1885) was one of the greatest novelists of the nineteenth century. His most famous works are *The Hunchback of Notre Dame* and *Les Misérables,* from which this selection is taken.

In this selection we meet Jean Valjean, a forty-six-year-old ex-convict, who, in the year our story opens, 1815, has just been released from the galleys where he was imprisoned for nineteen years.* His original sentence was five years for stealing a loaf of bread to feed his family, but his repeated attempts to escape his cruel prison added fourteen more years to his sentence. Originally a poor but morally uncorrupted laborer, Jean becomes a hardened criminal in the galleys. Now he is released and after four days of weary walking has just entered the French town of Digne. Here is Hugo's description of him:

> A slouched leather cap half hid his face, bronzed by the sun and wind, and dripping with sweat. His shaggy breast was seen through the coarse yellow shirt which at the neck was fastened by a small silver anchor; he wore a cravat twisted like a rope; coarse blue trousers, worn and shabby, white on one knee and with holes in the other; and an old, ragged, gray blouse patched on one side with a piece of green cloth sewed with twine; upon his back was a well-filled knapsack, strongly buckled and quite new. In his hand he carried an enormous knotted stick; his stockingless feet were in hobnailed shoes; his hair was cropped and his beard long. The sweat and heat, his long walk, and the dust added an indescribable meanness to his tattered appearance.

Jean has very little money (109 francs) and knows no one. Famished and exhausted, he seeks food and shelter in the town inns, but is recognized as an unkempt ex-convict and everyone turns him away. Dogs are loosed on

---

Translated from Victor Hugo, *Les Misérables,* 1863.
*"The galleys" refers to a large, low medieval ship propelled by sails and oars. Prisoners were chained to their seats and required to row the ship.

him and, barely escaping their jaws, he is heard to comment, "I am not even a dog." He shivers in the Alpine evening cold. Eventually, an old woman takes pity on him and points him to a house. He knocks on the door.

Unbeknownst to Jean, he has knocked on the door of the bishop of Digne, Monseigneur Charles François-Bienvenu Myriel, also known as M. Bienvenu. The good bishop is dedicated to simple living and helping the poor. His allowance from the state is 3,000 francs a year, but he gives away 2,800 of these francs to the poor. He is known for his humility, kindness, and good works.

His servant, Mme. Magliore, has just entered the house and relates to the bishop and his sister, who lives in the same house, that a terrible looking ex-convict is in town and has been turned out of all the inns. "Indeed," says the bishop. "Yes," replies the frightened Mme. Magliore. "Something will happen in this town tonight." Just then there is a violent knock on the door. The bishop says, "Come in."

THE HEROISM OF PASSIVE OBEDIENCE

The door opened.

It opened quickly, quite wide, as if pushed by someone boldly and with energy.

A man entered.

That man we know already; it was the traveler we have seen wandering about in search of a lodging.

He came in, took one step, and paused, leaving the door open behind him. He had his knapsack on his back, his stick in his hand, and a rough, hard, tired, and fierce look in his eyes, as seen by the firelight. He was hideous. It was an apparition of ill-omen.

Mme. Magliore had not even the strength to scream. She stood trembling with her mouth open.

Mdlle. Baptistine turned, saw the man enter, and started out half alarmed; then, slowly turning back again toward the fire, she looked at her brother, and her face resumed its usual calmness and serenity.

The bishop looked upon the man with a tranquil eye.

As he was opening his mouth to speak, doubtless to ask the

stranger what he wanted, the man, leaning with both hands on his club, glanced from one to another in turn, and, without waiting for the bishop to speak, said, in a loud voice:

"See here! My name is Jean Valjean. I am a convict; I have been nineteen years in the galleys. Four days ago I was set free, and started for Pontarlier, which is my destination; during these four days I have walked from Toulon. To-day I have walked twelve leagues. When I reached this place this evening I went to an inn, and they sent me away on account of my yellow passport, which I had shown at the mayor's office, as was necessary. I went to another inn; they said: 'Get out!' It was the same with one as with another; nobody would have me. I went to the prison and the turnkey would not let me in. I crept into a dog-kennel, the dog bit me, and drove me away as if he had been a man; you would have said that he knew who I was. I went into the fields to sleep beneath the stars; there were no stars. I thought it would rain, and there was no good God to stop the drops, so I came back to the town to get the shelter of some doorway. There in the square I laid down upon a stone; a good woman showed me your house, and said: 'Knock there!' I have knocked. What is this place? Are you an inn? I have money; my savings, 109 francs and 15 sous, which I have earned in the galleys by my work for nineteen years. I will pay. What do I care? I have money. I am very tired—twelve leagues on foot—and I am so hungry. Can I stay?"

"Mme. Magloire," said the bishop, "put on another plate."

The man took three steps and came near the lamp which stood on the table. "Stop," he exclaimed; as if he had not been understood; "not that, did you understand me? I am a galley slave—a convict—I am just from the galleys." He drew from his pocket a large sheet of yellow paper, which he unfolded. "There is my passport, yellow, as you see. That is enough to have me kicked out wherever I go. Will you read it? I know how to read, I do. I learned in the galleys. There is a school there for those who care for it. See, here is what they have put in my passport: 'Jean Valjean, a liberated convict, native of——,' you don't care for that, 'has been nineteen years in the galleys; five years for burglary; fourteen years for having attempted four times to escape. This man is very dangerous.' There you have it! Everybody has thrust me out; will you receive me? Is this an inn? Can you give me something to eat and a place to sleep? Have you a stable?"

"Mme. Magloire," said the bishop, "put some sheets on the bed in the alcove."

We have already described the kind of obedience yielded by these two women.

Mme. Magloire went out to fulfill her orders.

The bishop turned to the man:

"Monsieur, sit down and warm yourself; we are going to take supper presently, and your bed will be made ready while you sup."

At last the man quite understood; his face, the expression of which till then had been gloomy and hard, now expressed stupefaction, doubt and joy, and became absolutely wonderful. He began to stutter like a madman.

"True? What? You will keep me? you won't drive me away—a convict? You call me monsieur and don't say, 'Get out, dog!' as everybody else does. I thought that you would send me away, so I told first off who I am. Oh! the fine woman who sent me here; I shall have a supper! a bed like other people, with mattress and sheets—a bed! It is nineteen years that I have not slept on a bed. You are really willing that I should stay? You are good people! Besides, I have money; I will pay well. I beg your pardon, M. Innkeeper, what is your name? I will pay all you say. You are a fine man. You are an innkeeper, ain't you?"

"I am a priest who lives here," said the bishop.

"A priest," said the man. "Oh, noble priest! Then you do not ask any money? You are the curé, ain't you—the curé of this big church? Yes, that's it. How stupid I am, I didn't notice your cap."

While speaking he had deposited his knapsack and stick in the corner, replaced his passport in his pocket and sat down. Mdlle. Baptistine looked at him pleasantly. He continued:

"You are humane, M. l'Curé; you don't despise me. A good priest is a good thing. Then you don't want me to pay you?"

"No," said the bishop, "keep your money. How much have you? You said 109 francs, I think."

"And 15 sous," added the man.

"One hundred and nine francs and fifteen sous. And how long did it take you to earn that?"

"Nineteen years."

"Nineteen years!"

The bishop sighed deeply.

The man continued: "I have all my money yet. In four days I have spent only 25 sous which I earned by unloading wagons at Grasse. As you are an abbé I must tell you we have an almoner in the galleys. And then one day I saw a bishop; monseigneur, they called him. It was the Bishop of Majore from Marseilles. He is the curé who is over the curés. You see—beg pardon, how I bungle saying it, but for me it is so far off; you know what we are. He said mass in the center of the place on an altar; he had a pointed gold thing on his head that shone in the sun; it was noon. We were drawn up in line on three sides with cannons, and matches lighted before us. We could not see him well. He spoke to us, but he was not near enough, we did not understand him. That is what a bishop is."

While he was talking the bishop shut the door, which he had left wide open.

Mme. Magloire brought in a plate and set it on the table.

"Mme. Magloire," said the bishop, "put this plate as near the fire as you can." Then turning toward his guest, he added: "The night wind is raw in the Alps; you must be cold, monsieur."

Every time he said the word monsieur with his gently solemn and heartily hospitable voice the man's countenance lighted up. Monsieur to a convict is a glass of water to a man dying of thirst at sea. Ignominy thirsts for respect.

"The lamp," said the bishop, "gives a very poor light."

Mme. Magloire understood him, and, going to his bedchamber, took from the mantel the two silver candlesticks, lighted the candles and placed them on the table.

"M. l'Curé," said the man, "you are good; you don't despise me. You take me into your house; you light your candles for me, and I haven't hid from you where I come from, and how miserable I am."

The bishop, who was sitting near him, touched his hand gently and said: "You need not tell me who you are. This is not my house; it is the house of Christ. It does not ask any comer whether he has a name, but whether he has an affliction. You are suffering; you are hungry and thirsty; be welcome. And do not thank me; do not tell me that I take you into my house. This is the home of no man except him who needs an asylum. I tell you, who are a traveler, that you are more at home here than I; whatever is here is yours. What need have I to know your name? Besides, before you told me, I knew it."

The man opened his eyes in astonishment.

"Really? You knew my name?"

"Yes," answered the bishop, "your name is my brother."

"Stop, stop, M. l'Curé," exclaimed the man, "I was famished when I came in, but you are so kind that now I don't know what I am; that is all gone."

The bishop looked at him again and said:

"You have seen much suffering?"

"Oh, the red blouse, the ball and chain, the plank to sleep on, the heat, the cold, the galley's screw, the lash, the double chain for nothing, the dungeon for a word—even when sick in bed, the chain. The dogs, the dogs are happier! nineteen years! and I am 46, and now a yellow passport. That is all."

"Yes," answered the bishop, "you have left a place of suffering. But listen, there will be more joy in heaven over the tears of a repentant sinner than over the white robes of 100 good men. If you are leaving that sorrowful place with hate and anger against men, you are worthy of compassion; if you leave it with good-will, gentleness and peace, you are better than any of us."

Meantime Mme. Magloire had served up supper; it consisted of soup made of water, oil, bread, and salt, a little pork, a scrap of mutton, a few figs, a green cheese, and a large loaf of rye bread. She had, without asking, added to the usual dinner of the bishop a bottle of fine old Mauves wine.

The bishop's countenance was lighted up with this expression of pleasure, peculiar to hospitable natures. "To supper!" he said, briskly, as was his habit when he had a guest. He seated the man at his right. Mdlle. Baptistine, perfectly quiet and natural, took her place at his left.

The bishop said the blessing and then served the soup himself according to his usual custom. The man fell to eating greedily.

Suddenly the bishop said: "It seems to me something is lacking on the table."

The fact was that Mme. Magloire had set out only the three plates which were necessary. Now it was the custom of the house when the bishop had any one to supper to set all six of the silver plates on the table, an innocent display. This graceful appearance of luxury was a sort of child-likeness which was full of charm in this gentle but austere household, which elevated poverty to dignity.

Mme. Magloire understood the remark; without a word she went out, and a moment afterward the three plates for which the bishop had asked were shining on the cloth symmetrically arranged before each of the three diners.

SOME ACCOUNT OF THE DAIRIES OF PONTARLIER

Now, in order to give an idea of what passed at this table, we cannot do better than to transcribe here a passage in a letter from Mdlle. Baptistine to Mme. de Boischevron, in which the conversation between the convict and the bishop is related with charming minuteness:

"This man paid no attention to any one. He ate with the voracity of a starving man. After supper, however, he said:

"'M. l'Curé, all this is too good for me, but I must say that the wagoners, who wouldn't have me eat with them, live better than you.'

"Between us, the remark shocked me a little. My brother answered:

"'They are more fatigued than I am.'

"'No,' responded this man; 'they have more money. You are poor, I can see. Perhaps you are not a curé even? Are you only a curé? Ah! if God is just, you will deserve to be a curé.'

"'God is more than just,' said my brother.

"A moment after he added:

"'M. Jean Valjean, you are going to Pontarlier?'

"'A compulsory journey.'

"I am pretty sure that is the expression the man used. Then he continued:

"'I must be on the road to-morrow morning by day-break. It is a hard journey. If the nights are cold the days are warm.'

"'You are going,' said my brother, 'to a fine country. During the revolution, when my family was ruined, I took refuge at first in Franche-Comté, and supported myself there for some time by the labor of my hands. There I found plenty of work, and had only to make my choice. There are paper-mills, tanneries, distilleries, oil factories, large clock-making establishments, steel manufactories, copper foundries, at least twenty iron foundries, four of which, at Lods, Châtillion, Audincourt, and Beure, are very large.'

"I think I am not mistaken, and that these are the names that my brother mentioned. Then he broke off and addressed me:

"'Dear sister, have we not relatives in that part of the country?'

"I answered:

"'We had; among others, M. Lucenet, who was captain of the gates at Pontarlier under the old régime.'

"'Yes,' replied my brother, 'but in '93 no one had relatives; every one depended upon his hands. I labored. They have in the region of Pontarlier where you are going, M. Valjean, a business which is quite patriarchal and very charming, sister.'

[The bishop engages Jean in a friendly conversation about dairies.]

". . . One thing struck me. This man was what I have told you. Well, my brother during the supper and during the entire evening, with the exception of a few words about Jesus when he entered, did not say a word which could recall to this man who he himself was, nor indicate to him who my brother was. It was apparently a fine occasion to get in a little sermon and set up the bishop above the convict in order to make an impression upon his mind. It would, perhaps, have appeared to some to be a duty, having this unhappy man in hand, to feed the mind at the same time with the body, and to administer reproof, seasoned with morality and advice, or at least a little pity, accompanied by an exhortation to conduct himself better in future. My brother asked him neither his country nor his history; for his crime lay in his history, and my brother seemed to avoid everything which could recall it to him. At one time as my brother was speaking of the mountaineers of Pontarlier who have a pleasant labor near heaven and who, he added, are happy because they are innocent, he stopped short, fearing there might have been in this word which had escaped him something which could wound the feelings of this man. Upon reflection, I think I understand what was passing in my brother's mind. He thought doubtless, that this man, who called himself Jean Valjean, had his wretchedness too constantly before his mind; that it was best not to distress him by referring to it, and to make him think, if it were only for a moment, that he was a common person like any one else by treating him thus in the ordinary way. Is not this really understanding charity? Is there not, dear madame, something truly evangelical in this delicacy which abstains from sermonizing, moralizing and making allusions, and is not the wisest sympathy when a man has a suffering point not to touch upon it at all? It seems to me that this was my brother's inmost thought. At any rate, all I can say is, if he had all these ideas he did not show them even to me; he was, from beginning to end, the same as on other evenings, and he took supper with this Jean Valjean with the same air and manner that he would have supped with M. Gédéon, the provost, or with the curé of the parish." . . .

TRANQUILLITY

After having said good-night to his sister, Mgr. Bienvenu took one of the silver candlesticks from the table, handed the other to his guest, and said to him:

"Monsieur, I will show you to your room."

The man followed him.

As may have been understood from what has been said before, the house was so arranged that one could reach the alcove in the oratory only by passing through the bishop's sleeping-chamber. Just as they were passing through this room Mme. Magloire was putting up the silver in the cupboard at the head of the bed. It was the last thing she did every night before going to bed.

The bishop left his guest in the alcove before a clean, white bed. The man set down the candlestick upon a small table.

"Come," said the bishop, "a good night's rest to you; to-morrow morning, before you go, you shall have a cup of warm milk from our cows."

"Thank you, M. l'Abbé," said the man.

Scarcely had he pronounced these words of peace when suddenly he made a singular motion which would have chilled the two good women of the house with horror had they witnessed it. Even now it is hard for us to understand what impulse he obeyed at that moment. Did he intend to give a warning or to throw out a menace? Or was he simply obeying a sort of instinctive impulse, obscure even to himself? He turned abruptly toward the old man, crossed his arms, and, casting a wild look upon his host, exclaimed in a harsh voice:

"Ah, now, indeed! You lodge me in your house as near to you as that!"

He checked himself and added with a laugh, in which there was something horrible:

"Have you reflected upon it? Who tells you that I am not a murderer?"

The bishop responded:

"God will take care of that."

Then, with gravity, moving his lips like one praying or talking to himself, he raised two fingers of his right hand and blessed the man, who, however, did not bow; and, without turning his head or looking behind him, went into his chamber.

When the alcove was occupied a heavy serge curtain was drawn in the oratory, concealing the altar. Before this curtain the bishop knelt as he passed out and offered a short prayer.

A moment afterward he was walking in the garden, surrendering mind and soul to a dreamy contemplation of these grand and mysterious works of God which night makes visible to the eye.

As to the man, he was so completely exhausted that he did not even avail himself of the clean white sheets; he blew out the candle with his nostril, after the manner of convicts, and fell on the bed, dressed as he was, into a sound sleep.

Midnight struck as the bishop came back to his chamber.

A few moments afterward all in the little house slept. . . .

THE MAN AWAKES

As the cathedral clock struck two, Jean Valjean awoke.

What awakened him was, too good a bed. For nearly twenty years he had not slept in a bed, and, although he had not undressed, the sensation was too novel not to disturb his sleep.

He had slept something more than four hours. His fatigue had passed away. He was not accustomed to give many hours to repose.

He opened his eyes and looked for a moment into the obscurity about him, then he closed them to go to sleep again.

When many diverse sensations have disturbed the day, when the mind is preoccupied, we can fall asleep once, but not a second time. Sleep comes at first much more readily than it comes again. Such was the case with Jean Valjean. He could not get to sleep again, and so he began to think.

He was in one of those moods in which the ideas we have in our minds are perturbed. There was a kind of vague ebb and flow in his brain. His oldest and his latest memories floated about pell mell, and crossed each other confusedly, losing their own shapes, swelling beyond measure, then disappearing all at once, as if in a muddy and troubled stream. Many thoughts came to him, but there was one which continually presented itself, and which drove away all others. What that thought was we shall tell directly. He had noticed the six silver plates and the large ladle that Mme. Magloire had put on the table.

Those six silver plates took possession of him. There they were within a few steps. At the very moment that he passed through the middle room to reach the one he was now in, the old servant was placing them in a little cupboard at the head of the bed. He had marked that cupboard well; on the right, coming from the dining-room. They were solid, and old silver. With the big ladle they would bring, at least, 200 francs; double what he had got for nineteen years' labor. True; he would have got more if the *government* had not *robbed* him.

His mind wavered a whole hour and a long one, in fluctuation and in struggle. The clock struck three. He opened his eyes, rose up hastily in bed, reached out his arm and felt his knapsack, which he had put into the corner of the alcove, then he thrust out his legs and placed his feet on the floor and found himself, he knew not how, seated on his bed.

He remained for some time lost in thought in that attitude, which would have had a rather ominous look had any one seen him there in the dusk—he only awake in the slumbering house. All at once he stooped down, took off his shoes and put them softly upon the mat in front of the bed, then he resumed his thinking posture and was still again.

In that hideous meditation the ideas which we have pointed out troubled his brain without ceasing, entered, departed, returned and became a sort of weight upon him; and then he thought, too, he knew not why, and with that mechanical obstinacy that belongs to reverie, of a convict named Brevet, whom he had known in the galleys, and whose trousers were only held up by a single knit cotton suspender. The checked pattern of that suspender came continually before his mind.

He continued in this situation and would, perhaps, have remained there until daybreak, if the clock had not struck the quarter or the half-hour. The clock seemed to say to him, "Come along!"

He rose to his feet, hesitated for a moment longer and listened; all was still in the house; he walked straight and cautiously toward the window which he could discern. The night was not very dark; there was a full moon, across which large clouds were driving before the wind. This produced alternations of light and shade, out-of-doors eclipses and illuminations, and indoors a kind of glimmer. This glimmer, enough to enable him to find his way, changing with the passing clouds, resembled that sort of livid light which falls through the window of a dungeon before which men are passing and repassing. On reaching the window Jean Valjean examined it. It had no bars, opened into the garden, and was fastened, according to the fashion of the country, with a little wedge only. He opened it; but as the cold, keen air rushed into the room he closed it again immediately. He looked into the garden with that absorbed look which studies rather than sees. The garden was inclosed with a white wall, quite low and readily scaled. Beyond, against the sky, he distinguished the tops of trees at equal distances apart, which showed that this wall separated the garden from an avenue or a lane planted with trees.

When he had taken this observation he turned like a man whose mind is made up, went to his alcove, took his knapsack, opened it, fumbled in it, took out something which he laid upon the bed, put his shoes into one of his pockets, tied up his bundle, swung it upon his shoulders, put on his cap, and pulled the vizor down over his eyes, felt for his stick, and went and put it in the corner of the window, then returned to the bed, and resolutely took up the object which he had laid on it. It looked like a short iron bar, pointed at one end like a spear.

It would have been hard to distinguish in the darkness for what use this piece of iron had been made. Could it be a lever? Could it be a club?

In the daytime it would have been seen to be nothing but a miner's drill. At that time the convicts were sometimes employed in quarrying stone on the high hills that surround Toulon, and they often had miners' tools in their possession. Miners' drills are of solid iron, terminating at the lower end in a point, by means of which they are sunk into the rock.

He took the drill in his right hand, and, holding his breath, with stealthy steps he moved toward the door of the next room, which was the bishop's, as we know. On reaching the door he found it unlatched. The bishop had not closed it.

WHAT HE DOES

Jean Valjean listened. Not a sound.

He pushed the door.

He pushed it lightly with the end of his finger, with the stealthy and timorous carefulness of a cat. The door yielded to the pressure with a silent, imperceptible movement, which made the opening a little wider.

He waited a moment and then pushed the door again more boldly.

It yielded gradually and silently. The opening was now wide enough for him to pass through; but there was a small table near the door, which with it formed a troublesome angle and which barred the entrance.

Jean Valjean saw the obstacle. At all hazards the opening must be made still wider.

He so determined, and pushed the door a third time, harder than before. This time a rusty hinge suddenly sent out into the darkness a harsh and prolonged creak.

Jean Valjean shivered. The noise of this hinge sounded in his ears as clear and terrible as the trumpet of the judgment day.

In the fantastic exaggeration of the first moment he almost imagined that this hinge had become animate and suddenly endowed with a terrible life; and that it was barking like a dog to warn everybody and rouse the sleepers.

He stopped, shuddering and distracted, and dropped from his tiptoes to his feet. He felt the pulses of his temples beat like triphammers, and it appeared to him that his breath came from his chest with the roar of wind from a cavern. It seemed impossible that the horrible sound of this incensed hinge had not shaken the whole house with the shock of an earthquake; the door pushed by him had taken the alarm, and had called out; the old man would arise; the two old women would scream; help would come; in a quarter of an hour the town would be alive with it and the gendarmes in pursuit. For a moment he thought he was lost.

He stood still, petrified like the pillar of salt, not daring to stir. Some minutes passed. The door was wide open; he ventured to look into the room. Nothing had moved. He listened. Nothing was stirring in the house. The noise of the rusty hinge had awakened nobody.

The first danger was over, but still he felt within him a frightful tumult. Nevertheless he did not flinch. Not even when he thought he was lost had he flinched. His only thought was to make an end of it quickly. He took one step and was in the room.

A deep calm filled the chamber. Here and there indistinct, confused forms could be distinguished; which by day were papers scattered over a table, open folios, books piled on a stool, an armchair with clothes on it, a *prie-Dieu,* but now were only dark corners and whitish spots. Jean Valjean advanced, carefully avoiding the furniture. At the further end of the room he could hear the equal and quiet breathing of the sleeping bishop.

Suddenly he stopped; he was near the bed, he had reached it sooner than he thought.

Nature sometimes joins her effects and her appearances to our acts with a sort of serious and intelligent appropriateness, as if she would compel us to reflect. For nearly a half-hour a great cloud had darkened the sky. At the moment when Jean Valjean paused before the bed the cloud broke as if purposely, and a ray of moonlight crossing the high window, suddenly lighted up the bishop's pale face. He slept tranquilly. He was almost entirely dressed, though in bed, on account of the cold nights of the lower Alps, with a dark woolen garment which covered his arms to the wrists. His head had fallen on the pillow in the unstudied attitude of slumber; over the side of the bed hung his hand, ornamented with the pastoral ring, and which had done so many good deeds, so many pious acts. His entire countenance was lit up with a vague expression of content, hope and happiness. It was more than a smile and almost a radiance. On his forehead rested the indescribable reflection of an unseen light. The souls of the upright in sleep have visions of a mysterious heaven.

A reflection from this heaven shone upon the bishop.

But it was also a luminous transparency, for this heaven was within him; this heaven was his conscience. . . .

There was something of divinity almost in this man, thus unconsciously august.

Jean Valjean was in the shadow with the iron drill in his hand, erect, motionless, terrified at this radiant figure. He had never seen anything comparable to it. This confidence filled him with fear. The moral world has no greater spectacle than this; a troubled and restless conscience on the verge of committing an evil deed, contemplating the sleep of a good man.

This sleep in this solitude, with a neighbor such as he, contained a touch of the sublime, which he felt vaguely but powerfully.

None could have told what was within him, not even himself. To attempt to realize it the utmost violence must be imagined in the presence of the most extreme mildness. In his face nothing could be distinguished with certainty. It was a sort of haggard astonishment. He saw it; that was all. But what were his thoughts? It would have been impossible to guess. It was clear that he was moved and agitated. But of what nature was this emotion?

He did not remove his eyes from the old man. The only thing which was plain from his attitude and his countenance was a strange indecision. You would have said he was hesitating between two realms—that of the doomed and that of the saved. He appeared ready either to cleave this skull or to kiss this hand.

In a few moments he raised his left hand slowly to his forehead and took off his hat; then, letting his hand fall with the same slowness, Jean Valjean resumed his contemplations, his cap in his left hand, his club in his right, and his hair bristling on his fierce-looking head.

Under this frightful gaze the bishop still slept in profoundest peace.

The crucifix above the mantel-piece was dimly visible in the moonlight, apparently extending its arms toward both, with a benediction for one and a pardon for the other.

Suddenly Jean Valjean put on his cap, then passed quickly, without looking at the bishop, along the bed, straight to the cupboard which he perceived near its head; he raised the drill to force the lock; the key was in it; he opened it; the first thing he saw was the basket of silver, he took it, crossed the room with hasty stride, careless of noise, reached the door, entered the oratory, took his stick, stepped out, put the silver into his knapsack, threw away the basket, ran across the garden, leaped over the wall like a tiger and fled.

THE BISHOP AT WORK

The next day at sunrise Mgr. Bienvenu was walking in the garden. Mme. Magloire ran toward him quite beside herself.

"Monseigneur, monseigneur," cried she, "does your greatness know where the silver basket is?"

"Yes," said the bishop.

"God be praised!" said she; "I did not know what had become of it?"

The bishop had just found the basket on a flower-bed. He gave it to Mme. Magloire and said: "There it is."

"Yes," said she, "but there is nothing in it. The silver?"

"Ah!" said the bishop, "it is the silver, then, that troubles you. I do not know where that is."

"Good heavens! it is stolen. The man who came last night stole it."

And in the twinkling of an eye, with all the agility of which her age was capable, Mme. Magloire ran to the oratory, went into the alcove, and came back to the bishop. The bishop was bending with some sadness over a cochlearia des Guillons, which the basket had broken in falling. He looked up at Mme. Magloire's cry:

"Monseigneur, the man has gone! the silver is stolen!"

While she was uttering this exclamation her eyes fell on an angle of the garden where she saw traces of an escalade. A capstone of the wall had been thrown down.

"See, there is where he got out; he jumped into Cochefilet lane. The abominable fellow! he has stolen our silver!"

The bishop was silent for a moment, then, raising his serious eyes, he said mildly to Mme. Magloire:

"Now, first, did this silver belong to us?"

Mme. Magloire did not answer; after a moment the bishop continued:

"Mme. Magloire: I have for a long time wrongfully withheld this silver; it belonged to the poor. Who was this man? A poor man evidently."

"Alas! alas!" returned Mme. Magloire. "It is not on my account or mademoiselle's; it is all the same to us. But it is on yours, monseigneur. What is monsieur going to eat from now?"

The bishop looked at her with amazement.

"How so! have we no tin plates?"

Mme. Magloire shrugged her shoulders.

"Tin smells."

"Well, then, iron plates."

Mme. Magloire made an expressive gesture.

"Iron tastes."

"Well," said the bishop, "then, wooden plates."

In a few minutes he was breakfasting at the same table at which Jean Valjean sat the night before. While he was breakfasting M. Bienvenu pleasantly remarked to his sister, who said nothing, and Mme. Magloire, who was grumbling to herself, that there was really no need even of a wooden spoon or fork to dip a piece of bread into a cup of milk.

"Was there ever such an idea?" said Mme. Magloire to herself, as she went backward and forward; "to take in a man like that, and to give him a bed beside him; and yet what a blessing it was he did nothing but steal! Oh, my stars! it makes the chills run over me when I think of it!"

Just as the brother and sister were rising from the table there was a knock at the door.

"Come in," said the bishop.

The door opened. A strange, fierce group appeared on the threshold. Three men were holding a fourth by the collar. The three men were gendarmes;[1] the fourth, Jean Valjean.

A brigadier of gendarmes, who appeared to head the group, was near the door. He advanced toward the bishop, giving a military salute:

"Monseigneur," said he.

At this word Jean Valjean, who was sullen, and seemed entirely cast down, raised his head with a stupefied air.

"Monseigneur!" he murmured, "then it is not the curé!"

"Silence!" said a gendarme, "it is monseigneur, the bishop."

In the meantime Mgr. Bienvenu had approached as quickly as his great age permitted;

"Ah, there you are!" said he, looking toward Jean Valjean, "I am glad to see you. But I gave you the candlesticks also, which are silver like the rest, and would bring 200 francs. Why did you not take them along with your plates?"

Jean Valjean opened his eyes and looked at the bishop with an expression which no human tongue could describe.

[1]Police.—ed. note

"Monseigneur," said the brigadier, "then what this man said was true? We met him. He was going like a man who was running away and we arrested him in order to see. He had this silver."

"And he told you," interrupted the bishop, with a smile, "that it had been given him by a good old priest with whom he had passed the night. I see it all. And you brought him back here? It is all a mistake."

"If that is so," said the brigadier, "we can let him go."

"Certainly," replied the bishop.

The gendarmes released Jean Valjean, who shrank back.

"Is it true that they let me go?" he said in voice almost inarticulate, as if he were speaking in his sleep.

"Yes! you can go. Do you not understand?" said a gendarme.

"My friend," said the bishop, "before you go away here are your candlesticks; take them."

He went to the mantel-piece, took the two candlesticks and brought them to Jean Valjean. The two women beheld the action without a word, or gesture, or look that might disturb the bishop.

Jean Valjean was trembling in every limb. He took the two candlesticks mechanically and with a wild appearance.

"Now," said the bishop, "go in peace. By the way, my friend, when you come again you need not come through the garden. You can always come in and go out by the front door. It is closed only with a latch, day or night."

Then turning to the gendarmes, he said:

"Messieurs, you can retire." The gendarmes withdrew.

Jean Valjean felt like a man who is just about to faint.

The bishop approached him and said, in a low voice:

"Forget not, never forget that you have promised me to use this silver to become an honest man."

Jean Valjean, who had no recollection of this promise, stood confounded. The bishop had laid much stress upon these words as he uttered them. He continued, solemnly:

"Jean Valjean, my brother, you belong no longer to evil, but to good. It is your soul that I am buying for you. I withdraw it from dark thoughts and from the spirit of perdition and I give it to God!"

For Further Reflection

1. Jean Valjean is plucked from the kingdom of evil by the good bishop. As the story develops he gradually is transformed into

a moral hero, who serves the poor. What message is Victor
Hugo trying to convey in this story? What is he suggesting about
human nature and our relation to good and evil?

2. Identify the virtues in the bishop of Digne. Note that there is
    no discussion of moral duties; the bishop acts out of sponta-
    neous goodness, out of saintly character, risking even his own
    life in the process. Do you think that Hugo has painted an ideal
    person or is the bishop an imprudent idealist who is just lucky
    he hasn't met a worse fate?

3. Ironically, it so happens that the bishop has been working on
    a book about duty for years. But it never gets finished. Do you
    see any symbolism in this fact?

Virtue Ethics

ARISTOTLE

Aristotle (384–322 B.C.) was born in Stagira in Macedon, the
son of a physician. He was a student of Plato at the Academy in Athens and tutor of Alexander the Great. Aristotle
saw ethics as the branch of political philosophy concerned
with a good life. It is thus a practical rather than a purely
theoretical science. In this selection from *Nicomachean
Ethics,* Aristotle considers the nature of ethics in relation to
human nature. From this same perspective he discusses the
nature of virtue, which he defines as traits that enable us
to live well in communities. To achieve a state of well-
being or happiness, proper social institutions are necessary.
Thus, the moral person cannot exist in isolation from a
flourishing political community that enables the person to
develop the necessary virtues for the good life.

Reprinted from *Aristotle's Nicomachean Ethics,* translated by James E. C.
Weldon (Macmillan, 1897).

Aristotle goes on to show the difference between moral and intellectual virtues. While the intellectual virtues may be taught directly, the moral ones must be lived in order to be learned. By living well, we acquire the best guarantee to the happy life. But again, happiness requires that one be lucky enough to live in a flourishing state. By considering luck as part of morality, Aristotle distinguishes his position from deontological ones like those of the Bible and Kant, and so defends a point noted in Nagel's article— the importance of luck to morality. In the last analysis, the moral life consists in moderation, living in accordance with the "golden mean," a middle ground between extremes.

BOOK I

All Human Activities Aim at Some Good

Chapter 1. Every art and every scientific inquiry, and similarly every action and purpose, may be said to aim at some good. Hence the good has been well defined as that at which all things aim. But it is clear that there is a difference in ends; for the ends are sometimes activities, and sometimes results beyond the mere activities. Where there are ends beyond the action, the results are naturally superior to the action.

As there are various actions, arts, and sciences, it follows that the ends are also various. Thus health is the end of the medical art, a ship of shipbuilding, victory of strategy, and wealth of economics. It often happens that a number of such arts or sciences combine for a single enterprise, as the art of making bridles and all such other arts as furnish the implements of horsemanship combine for horsemanship, and horsemanship and every military action for strategy; and in the same way, other arts or sciences combine for others. In all these cases, the ends of the master arts or sciences, whatever they may be, are more desirable than those of the subordinate arts or sciences, as it is for the sake of the former that the latter are pursued. It makes no difference to the argument whether the activities themselves are the ends of the action, or something beyond the activities, as in the above-mentioned sciences.

If it is true that in the sphere of action there is some end which we wish for its own sake, and for the sake of which we wish everything else, and if we do not desire everything for the sake of something else (for, if that is so, the process will go on *ad infinitum,* and our desire will be idle and futile), clearly this end will be good and the supreme good. Does it not follow then that the knowledge of this good is of great importance for the conduct of life? Like archers who have a mark at which to aim, shall we not have a better chance of attaining what we want? If this is so, we must endeavor to comprehend, at least in outline, what this good is, and what science or faculty makes it its object.

It would seem that this is the most authoritative science. Such a kind is evidently the political, for it is that which determines what sciences are necessary in states, and what kinds should be studied, and how far they should be studied by each class of inhabitant. We see too that even the faculties held in highest esteem, such as strategy, economics, and rhetoric, are subordinate to it. Then since politics makes use of the other sciences and also rules what people may do and what they may not do, it follows that its end will comprehend the ends of the other sciences, and will therefore be the good of mankind. For even if the good of an individual is identical with the good of a state, yet the good of the state is evidently greater and more perfect to attain or to preserve. For though the good of an individual by himself is something worth working for, to ensure the good of a nation or a state is nobler and more divine.

These then are the objects at which the present inquiry aims, and it is in a sense a political inquiry. . . .

The Science of the Good for Man Is Politics

Chapter 2.   As every science and undertaking aims at some good, what is in our view the good at which political science aims, and what is the highest of all practical goods? As to its name there is, I may say, a general agreement. The masses and the cultured classes agree in calling it happiness, and conceive that "to live well" or "to do well" is the same thing as "to be happy." But as to what happiness is they do not agree, nor do the masses give the same account of it as the philosophers. The former take it to be something visible and palpable, such as pleasure, wealth, or honor; different people, however, give different definitions of it, and often even the same man gives different definitions at different times. When he is ill, it is health, when he is poor, it is wealth; if he is conscious of his own ignorance, he envies people who use grand language above his own comprehension. Some philosophers, on the other hand, have held that, besides these various goods, there is an absolute good which is the cause of goodness in them all.* It would perhaps be a waste of time to examine all these opinions; it will be enough to examine such as are most popular or as seem to be more or less reasonable.

Chapter 3. Men's conception of the good or of happiness may be read in the lives they lead. Ordinary or vulgar people conceive it to be a pleasure, and accordingly choose a life of enjoyment. For there are, we may say, three conspicuous types of life, the sensual, the political, and, thirdly, the life of thought. Now the mass of men present an absolutely slavish appearance, choosing the life of brute beasts, but they have ground for so doing because so many persons in authority share the tastes of Sardanapalus.† Cultivated and energetic people, on the other hand, identify happiness with honor, as honor is the general end of political life. But this seems too superficial an idea for our present purpose; for honor depends more upon the people who pay it than upon the person to whom it is paid, and the good we feel is something which is proper to a man himself and cannot be easily taken away from him. Men too appear to seek honor in order to be assured of their own goodness. Accordingly, they seek it at the hands of the sage and of those who know them well, and they seek it on the ground of their virtue; clearly then, in their judgment at any rate, virtue is better than honor. Perhaps then we might look on virtue rather than honor as the end of political life. Yet even this idea appears not quite complete; for a man may possess virtue and yet be asleep or inactive throughout life, and not only so, but he may experience the greatest calamities and misfortunes. Yet no one would call such a life a life of happiness, unless he were maintaining a paradox. But we need not dwell further on this subject, since it is sufficiently discussed in popular philosophical treatises. The third life is the life of thought, which we will discuss later.

*Plato
†A half-legendary ruler whose name to the Greeks stood for extreme mental luxury and extravagance.

The life of money making is a life of constraint; and wealth is obviously not the good of which we are in quest; for it is useful merely as a means to something else. It would be more reasonable to take the things mentioned before—sensual pleasure, honor, and virtue—as ends than wealth, since they are things desired on their own account. Yet these too are evidently not ends, although much argument has been employed to show that they are. . . .

Characteristics of the Good

Chapter 5.   But leaving this subject for the present, let us revert to the good of which we are in quest and consider what it may be. For it seems different in different activities or arts; it is one thing in medicine, another in strategy, and so on. What is the good in each of these instances? It is presumably that for the sake of which all else is done. In medicine this is health, in strategy victory, in architecture a house, and so on. In every activity and undertaking it is the end, since it is for the sake of the end that all people do whatever else they do. If then there is an end for all our activity, this will be the good to be accomplished; and if there are several such ends, it will be these.

Our argument has arrived by a different path at the same point as before; but we must endeavor to make it still plainer. Since there are more ends than one, and some of these ends—for example, wealth, flutes, and instruments generally—we desire as means to something else, it is evident that not all are final ends. But the highest good is clearly something final. Hence if there is only one final end, this will be the object of which we are in search; and if there are more than one, it will be the most final. We call that which is sought after for its own sake more final than that which is sought after as a means to something else; we call that which is never desired as a means to something else more final than things that are desired both for themselves and as means to something else. Therefore, we call absolutely final that which is always desired for itself and never as a means to something else. Now happiness more than anything else answers to this description. For happiness we always desire for its own sake and never as a means to something else, whereas honor, pleasure, intelligence, and every virtue we desire partly for their own sakes (for we should desire them independently of what might result from them), but partly also as means to happiness, because we suppose they will prove instruments of happiness. Happiness, on the other hand, nobody desires for the sake of these things, nor indeed as a means to anything else at all.

If we start from the point of view of self-sufficiency, we reach the same conclusion; for we assume that the final good is self-sufficient. By self-sufficiency we do not mean that a person leads a solitary life all by himself, but that he has parents, children, wife and friends and fellow citizens in general, as man is naturally a social being. Yet here it is necessary to set some limit; for if the circle must be extended to include ancestors, descendants, and friends' friends, it will go on indefinitely. Leaving this point, however, for future investigation, we call the self-sufficient that which, taken even by itself, makes life desirable and wanting nothing at all; and this is what we mean by happiness.

Again, we think happiness the most desirable of all things, and that not merely as one good thing among others. If it were only that, the addition of the smallest more good would increase its desirableness; for the addition would make an increase of goods, and the greater of two goods is always the more desirable. Happiness is something final and self-sufficient and the end of all action.

Chapter 6.   Perhaps, however, it seems a commonplace to say that happiness is the supreme good; what is wanted is to define its nature a little more clearly. The best way of arriving at such a definition will probably be to ascertain the function of man. For, as with a flute player, a sculptor, or any artist, or in fact anybody who has a special function or activity, his goodness and excellence seem to lie in his function, so it would seem to be with man, if indeed he has a special function. Can it be said that, while a carpenter and a cobbler have special functions and activities, man, unlike them, is naturally functionless? Or, as the eye, the hand, the foot, and similarly each part of the body has a special function, so may man be regarded as having a special function apart from all these? What, then, can this function be? It is not life; for life is apparently something that man shares with plants; and we are looking for something peculiar to him. We must exclude therefore the life of nutrition and growth. There is next what may be called the life of sensation. But this too, apparently, is shared by man with horses, cattle, and all other animals. There remains what I may call the active life of the rational part of man's being. Now this rational part is twofold; one part is rational in the sense of being obedient to reason, and the other in the sense of possessing and exercising reason and intelligence. The active life too may be conceived of in two ways, either as a state of character, or as an activity; but we mean by it the life of activity, as this seems to be the truer form of the conception.

The function of man then is activity of soul in accordance with reason, or not apart from reason. Now, the function of a man of a certain kind, and of a man who is good of that kind—for example, of a harpist and a good harpist—are in our view the same in kind. This is true of all people of all kinds without exception, the superior excellence being only an addition to the function; for it is the function of a harpist to play the harp, and of a good harpist to play the harp well. This being so, if we define the function of man as a kind of life, and this life as an activity of the soul or a course of action in accordance with reason, and if the function of a good man is such activity of a good and noble kind, and if everything is well done when it is done in accordance with its proper excellence, it follows that the good of man is activity of soul in accordance with virtue, or, if there are more virtues than one, in accordance with the best and most complete virtue. But we must add the words "in a complete life." For as one swallow or one day does not make a spring, so one day or a short time does not make a man blessed or happy. . . .

Inasmuch as happiness is an activity of soul in accordance with perfect virtue, we must now consider virtue, as this will perhaps be the best way of studying happiness. . . . Clearly it is human virtue we have to consider; for the good of which we are in search is, as we said, human good, and the happiness, human happiness. By human virtue or excellence we mean not that of the body, but that of the soul, and by happiness we mean an activity of the soul. . . .

BOOK II

Moral virtues can best be acquired by practice and habit. They imply a right attitude toward pleasures and pains. A good man deliberately chooses to do what is noble and right for its own sake. What is right in matters of moral conduct is usually a mean between two extremes.

Chapter 1. Virtue then is twofold, partly intellectual and partly moral, and intellectual virtue is originated and fostered mainly by teaching; it demands therefore experience and time. Moral virtue on the other hand is the outcome of habit, and accordingly its name, *ethike,* is derived by a slight variation from *ethos,* habit. From this fact it is clear that moral virtue is not implanted in us by nature; for nothing that exists by nature can be transformed by habit. Thus a stone, that naturally tends to fall downwards, cannot be habituated or trained to rise upwards, even if we tried to train it by throwing it up ten thousand times. Nor again can fire be trained to sink downwards, nor anything else that follows one natural law be habituated or trained to follow another. It is neither by nature then nor in defiance of nature that virtues grow in us. Nature gives us the capacity to receive them, and that capacity is perfected by habit.

Again, if we take the various natural powers which belong to us, we first possess the proper faculties and afterwards display the activities. It is obviously so with the senses. Not by seeing frequently or hearing frequently do we acquire the sense of seeing or hearing; on the contrary, because we have the senses we make use of them; we do not get them by making use of them. But the virtues we get by first practicing them, as we do in the arts. For it is by doing what we ought to do when we study the arts that we learn the arts themselves; we become builders by building and harpists by playing the harp. Similarly, it is by doing just acts that we become just, by doing temperate acts that we become temperate, by doing brave acts that we become brave. The experience of states confirms this statement, for it is by training in good habits that lawmakers make the citizens good. This is the object all lawmakers have at heart; if they do not succeed in it, they fail of their purpose; and it makes the distinction between a good constitution and a bad one.

Again, the causes and means by which any virtue is produced and destroyed are the same; and equally so in any part. For it is by playing the harp that both good and bad harpists are produced; and the case of builders and others is similar, for it is by building well that they become good builders and by building badly that they become bad builders. If it were not so, there would be no need of anybody to teach them; they would all be born good or bad in their several crafts. The case of the virtues is the same. It is by our actions in dealings between man and man that we become either just or unjust. It is by our actions in the face of danger and by our training ourselves to fear or to courage that we become either cowardly or courageous. It is much the same with our appetites and angry passions. People become temperate and gentle, others licentious and passionate, by behaving in one or the other way in particular circumstances. In a word, moral states are the results of activities like the states themselves. It is our duty therefore to keep a certain character in our activities, since our moral states depend on the differences in our activities. So the difference between one and another training in habits in our childhood is not a light matter, but important, or rather, all-important.

Chapter 2.   Our present study is not, like other studies, purely theoretical in intention; for the object of our inquiry is not to know what virtue is but how to become good, and that is the sole benefit of it. We must, therefore, consider the right way of performing actions, for it is acts, as we have said, that determine the character of the resulting moral states.

That we should act in accordance with right reason is a common general principle, which may here be taken for granted. The nature of right reason, and its relation to the virtues generally, will be discussed later. But first of all it must be admitted that all reasoning on matters of conduct must be like a sketch in outline; it cannot be scientifically exact. We began by laying down the principle that the kind of reasoning demanded in any subject must be such as the subject matter itself allows; and questions of conduct and expediency no more admit of hard and fast rules than questions of health.

If this is true of general reasoning on ethics, still more true is it that scientific exactitude is impossible in treating of particular ethical cases. They do not fall under any art or law, but the actors themselves have always to take account of circumstances, as much as in medicine or navigation. Still, although such is the nature of our present argument, we must try to make the best of it.

The first point to be observed is that in the matters we are now considering deficiency and excess are both fatal. It is so, we see, in questions of health and strength. (We must judge of what we cannot see by the evidence of what we do see.) Too much or too little gymnastic exercise is fatal to strength. Similarly, too much or too little meat and drink is fatal to health, whereas a suitable amount produces, increases, and sustains it. It is the same with temperance, courage, and other moral virtues. A person who avoids and is afraid of everything and faces nothing becomes a coward; a person who is not afraid of anything but is ready to face everything becomes foolhardy. Similarly, he who enjoys every pleasure and abstains from none is licentious; he who refuses all pleasures, like a boor, is an insensible sort of person. For temperance and courage are destroyed by excess and deficiency but preserved by the mean.

Again, not only are the causes and agencies of production, increase, and destruction in moral states the same, but the field of their activity is the same also. It is so in other more obvious instances, as, for example, strength; for strength is produced by taking a great deal of food and undergoing a great deal of exertion, and it is the strong man who is able to take most food and undergo most exertion. So too with the virtues. By abstaining from pleasures we become temperate, and, when we have become temperate, we are best able to abstain from them. So again with courage; it is by training ourselves to despise and face terrifying things that we become brave, and when we have become brave, we shall be best able to face them.

The pleasure or pain which accompanies actions may be regarded as a test of a person's moral state. He who abstains from physical pleasures and feels pleasure in so doing is temperate; but he who feels pain at so doing is licentious. He who faces dangers with pleasure, or at least without pain, is brave; but he who feels pain at facing them is a coward. For moral virtue is concerned with pleasures and pains. It is pleasure which makes us do what is base, and pain which makes us abstain from doing what is noble. Hence the importance of having a certain training from very early days, as Plato says, so that we may feel pleasure and pain at the right objects; for this is true education. . . .

Chapter 3.　But we may be asked what we mean by saying that people must become just by doing what is just and temperate by doing what is temperate. For, it will be said, if they do what is just and temperate they are already just and temperate themselves, in the same way as, if they practice grammar and music, they are grammarians and musicians.

But is this true even in the case of the arts? For a person may speak grammatically either by chance or at the suggestion of somebody else; hence he will not be a grammarian unless he not only speaks grammatically but does so in a grammatical manner, that is, because of the grammatical knowledge which he possesses.

There is a point of difference too between the arts and the virtues. The productions of art have their excellence in themselves. It is enough then that, when they are produced, they themselves should possess a certain character. But acts in accordance with virtue are not justly or temperately performed simply because they are in themselves just or temperate. The doer at the time of performing them must satisfy certain conditions; in the first place, he must know what he is doing; secondly, he must deliberately choose to do it and do it for his own sake; and thirdly, he must do it as part of his own firm and immutable character. If it be a question of art, these conditions, except only the condition of knowledge, are not raised; but if it be a question of virtue, mere knowledge is of little or no avail; it is the other conditions, which are the results of frequently performing just and temperate acts, that are not slightly but all-important. Accordingly, deeds are called just and temperate when they are such as a just and temperate person would do; and a just and temperate person is not merely one who does these deeds but one who does them in the spirit of the just and the temperate.

It may fairly be said that a just man becomes just by doing what is just, and a temperate man becomes temperate by doing what is temperate, and if a man did not so act, he would not have much chance of becoming good. But most people, instead of acting, take refuge in theorizing; they imagine that they are philosophers and that philosophy will make them virtuous; in fact, they behave like people who listen attentively to their doctors but never do anything that their doctors tell them. But a healthy state of the soul will no more be produced by this kind of philosophizing than a healthy state of the body by this kind of medical treatment.

Chapter 4.   We have next to consider the nature of virtue. Now, as the properties of the soul are three, namely, emotions, faculties, and moral states, it follows that virtue must be one of the three. By emotions I mean desire, anger, fear, pride, envy, joy, love, hatred, regret, ambition, pity—in a word, whatever feeling is attended by pleasure or pain. I call those faculties through which we are said to be capable of experiencing these emotions, for instance, capable of getting angry or being pained or feeling pity. And I call those moral states through which we are well or ill disposed in our emotions, ill disposed, for instance, in anger, if our anger be too violent or too feeble, and well disposed, if it be rightly moderate; and similarly in our other emotions.

Now neither the virtues nor the vices are emotions; for we are not called good or bad for our emotions but for our virtues or vices. We are not praised or blamed simply for being angry, but only for being angry in a certain way; but we are praised or blamed for our virtues or vices. Again, whereas we are angry or afraid without deliberate purpose, the virtues are matters of deliberate purpose, or require deliberate purpose. Moreover, we are said to be moved by our emotions, but by our virtues or vices we are not said to be moved but to have a certain disposition.

For these reasons the virtues are not faculties. For we are not called either good or bad, nor are we praised or blamed for having simple capacity for emotion. Also while Nature gives us our faculties, it is not Nature that makes us good or bad; but this point we have already discussed. If then the virtues are neither emotions nor faculties, all that remains is that they must be moral states.

Chapter 5. The nature of virtue has been now described in kind. But it is not enough to say merely that virtue is a moral state; we must also describe the character of that moral state.

We may assert then that every virtue or excellence puts into good condition that of which it is a virtue or excellence, and enables it to perform its work well. Thus excellence in the eye makes the eye good and its function good, for by excellence in the eye we see well. Similarly, excellence of the horse makes a horse excellent himself and good at racing, at carrying its rider and at facing the enemy. If then this rule is universally true, the virtue or excellence of a man will be such a moral state as makes a man good and able to perform his proper function well. How this will be the case we have already explained, but another way of making it clear will be to study the nature or character of virtue.

Now of everything, whether it be continuous or divisible, it is possible to take a greater, a smaller, or an equal amount, and this either in terms of the thing itself or in relation to ourselves, the equal being a mean between too much and too little. By the mean in terms of the thing itself, I understand that which is equally distinct from both its extremes, which is one and the same for every man. By the mean relatively to ourselves, I understand that which is neither too much nor too little for us; but this is not one nor the same for everybody. Thus if 10 be too much and 2 too little, we take 6 as a mean in terms of the thing itself; for 6 is as much greater than 2 as it is less than 10, and this is a mean in arithmetical proportion. But the mean considered relatively to ourselves may not be ascertained in that way. It does not follow that if 10 pounds of meat is too much and 2 too little for a man to eat, the trainer will order him 6 pounds, since this also may be too much or too little for him who is to take it; it will be too little, for example, for Milo but too much for a beginner in gymnastics. The same with running and wrestling; the right amount will vary with the individual. This being so, the skillful in any art avoids alike excess and deficiency; he seeks and chooses the mean, not the absolute mean, but the mean considered relatively to himself.

Every art then does its work well, if it regards the mean and judges the works it produces by the mean. For this reason we often say of successful works of art that it is impossible to take anything from them or to add anything to them, which implies that excess or deficiency is fatal to excellence but that the mean state ensures it. Good artists too, as we say, have an eye to the mean in their works. Now virtue, like Nature herself, is more accurate and better than any art; virtue, therefore, will aim at the mean. I speak of moral virtue, since it is moral virtue which is concerned with emotions and actions, and it is in these we have excess and deficiency and the mean. Thus it is possible to go too far, or not far enough in fear, pride, desire, anger, pity, and pleasure and pain generally, and the excess and the deficiency are alike wrong; but to feel these emotions at the right times, for the right objects, towards the right persons, for the right motives, and in the right manner, is the mean or the best good, which signifies virtue. Similarly, there may be excess, deficiency, or the mean, in acts. Virtue is concerned with both emotions and actions, wherein excess is an error and deficiency a fault, while the mean is successful and praised, and success and praise are both characteristics of virtue.

It appears then that virtue is a kind of mean because it aims at the mean.

On the other hand, there are many different ways of going wrong; for evil is in its nature infinite, to use the Pythagorean phrase, but good is finite and there is only one possible way of going right.

So the former is easy and the latter is difficult; it is easy to miss the mark but difficult to hit it. And so by our reasoning excess and deficiency are characteristics of vice and the mean is a characteristic of virtue.

"For good is simple, evil manifold."

Chapter 6.   Virtue then is a state of deliberate moral purpose, consisting in a mean relative to ourselves, the mean being determined by reason, or as a prudent man would determine it. It is a mean, firstly, as lying between two vices, the vice of excess on the one hand, the vice of deficiency on the other, and, secondly, because, whereas the vices either fall short of or go beyond what is right in emotion and action, virtue discovers and chooses the mean. Accordingly, virtue, if regarded in its essence or theoretical definition, is a mean, though, if regarded from the point of view of what is best and most excellent, it is an extreme.

But not every action or every emotion admits of a mean. There are some whose very name implies wickedness, as, for example, malice, shamelessness, and envy among the emotions, and adultery, theft, and murder among the actions. All these and others like them are marked as intrinsically wicked, not merely the excesses or deficiencies of them. It is never possible then to be right in them; they are always sinful. Right or wrong in such acts as adultery does not depend on our committing it with the right woman, at the right time, or in the right manner; on the contrary, it is wrong to do it at all. It would be equally false to suppose that there can be a mean or an excess or deficiency in unjust, cowardly or licentious conduct; for, if that were so, it would be a mean of excess and deficiency, an excess of excess and a deficiency of deficiency. But as in temperance and courage there can be no excess or deficiency, because the mean there is in a sense an extreme, so too in these other cases there cannot be a mean or an excess or a deficiency, but however the acts are done, they are wrong. For in general an excess or deficiency does not have a mean, nor a mean an excess or deficiency. . . .

Chapter 8.   There are then three dispositions, two being vices, namely, excess and deficiency, and one virtue, which is the mean between them; and they are all in a sense mutually opposed. The extremes are opposed both to the mean and to each other, and the mean is opposed to the extremes. For as the equal if compared with the less is greater, but if compared with the greater is less, so the mean state, whether in emotion or action, if compared with deficiency is excessive, but if compared with excess is deficient. Thus the brave man appears foolhardy compared with the coward, but cowardly compared with the foolhardy. Similarly, the temperate man appears licentious compared with the insensible man but insensible compared with the licentious; and the liberal man appears extravagant compared with the stingy man but stingy compared with the spendthrift. The result is that the extremes each denounce the mean as belonging to the other extreme; the coward calls the brave man foolhardy, and the foolhardy man calls him cowardly; and so on in other cases.

But while there is mutual opposition between the extremes and the mean, there is greater opposition between the two extremes than between extreme and the mean; for they are further removed from each other than from the mean, as the great is further from the small and the small from the great than either from the equal. Again, while some extremes show some likeness to the mean, as foolhardiness to courage and extravagance to liberality, there is the greatest possible dissimilarity between extremes. But things furthest removed from each other are called opposites; hence the further things are removed, the greater is the opposition between them.

In some cases it is deficiency and in others excess which is more opposed to the mean. Thus it is not foolhardiness, an excess, but cowardice, a deficiency, which is more opposed to courage, nor is it insensibility, a deficiency, but licentiousness, an excess, which is more opposed to temperance. There are two reasons why this should be so. One lies in the nature of the matter itself; for when one of two extremes is nearer and more like the mean, it is not this extreme but its opposite that we chiefly contrast with the mean. For instance, as foolhardiness seems more like and nearer to courage than cowardice, it is cowardice that we chiefly contrast with courage; for things further removed from the mean seem to be more opposite to it. This reason lies in the nature of the matter itself; there is a second which lies in our own nature. The things to which we ourselves are naturally more inclined we think more opposed to the mean. Thus we are ourselves naturally more inclined to pleasures than to their opposites, and are more prone therefore to self-indulgence than to moderation. Accordingly we speak of those things in which we are more likely to run to great lengths as more opposed to the mean. Hence licentiousness, which is an excess, seems more opposed to temperance than insensibility.

Chapter 9. We have now sufficiently shown that moral virtue is a mean, and in what sense it is so; that it is a mean as lying between two vices, a vice of excess on the one side and a vice of deficiency on the other, and as aiming at the mean in emotion and action.

That is why it is so hard to be good; for it is always hard to find the mean in anything; it is not everyone but only a man of science who can find the mean or center of a circle. So too anybody can get angry—that is easy—and anybody can give or spend money, but to give it to the right person, to give the right amount of it, at the right time, for the right cause and in the right way, this is not what anybody can do, nor is it easy. That is why goodness is rare and praise worthy and noble. One then who aims at a mean must begin by departing from the extreme that is more contrary to the mean; he must act in the spirit of Calypso's advice,

"Far from this spray and swell hold thou thy ship,"

for of the two extremes one is more wrong than the other. As it is difficult to hit the mean exactly, we should take the second best course, as the saying is, and choose the lesser of two evils. This we shall best do in the way described, that is, steering clear of the evil which is further from the mean. We must also note the weaknesses to which we are ourselves particularly prone, since different natures tend in different ways; and we may ascertain what our tendency is by observing our feelings of pleasure and pain. Then we must drag ourselves away towards the opposite extreme; for by pulling ourselves as far as possible from what is wrong we shall arrive at the mean, as we do when we pull a crooked stick straight.

In all cases we must especially be on our guard against the pleasant, or pleasure, for we are not impartial judges of pleasure. Hence our attitude towards pleasure must be like that of the elders of the people in the *Iliad* towards Helen, and we must constantly apply the words they use; for if we dismiss pleasure as they dismissed Helen, we shall be less likely to go wrong. By action of this kind, to put it summarily, we shall best succeed in hitting the mean.

Undoubtedly this is a difficult task, especially in individual cases. It is not easy to determine the right manner, objects, occasion and duration of anger. Sometimes we praise people who are deficient in anger, and call them gentle, and at other times we praise people who exhibit a fierce temper as high spirited. It is not however a man who deviates a little from goodness, but one who deviates a great deal, whether on the side of excess or of deficiency, that is blamed; for he is sure to call attention to himself. It is not easy to decide in theory how far and to what extent a man may go before he becomes blameworthy, but neither is it easy to define in theory anything else in the region of the senses; such things depend on circumstances, and our judgment of them depends on our perception.

So much then is plain, that the mean is everywhere praiseworthy, but that we ought to aim at one time towards an excess and at another towards a deficiency; for thus we shall most easily hit the mean, or in other words reach excellence.

For Further Reflection

1. Is Aristotle's concept of happiness clear? Is it a subjective or objective notion? That is, is it subjective, in the mind of the beholder, so one is just as happy as one feels oneself to be; or is it objective, defined by a state of being, and having certain characteristics regardless of how one feels? According to Aristotle, could a criminal be happy?

2. Is Aristotle's ethics sufficiently action guiding? Does it help us make decisions? If I ask what should I do in situation *X,* Aristotle would seem to say, "Do what the virtuous person would do." But if I ask how I am to recognize the virtuous person, he would seem to say, "He is one who acts justly." Is there something circular about this reasoning? Does virtue ethics need supplementation from other ethical systems or can it solve this problem?

Virtue and the Moral Life

BERNARD MAYO

Bernard Mayo is a British philosopher and the author of *Ethics and the Moral Life,* from which this selection is taken. Mayo contrasts the deontologists' and teleologists' ethics of "doing" with the ethics of "being" or character demonstrated by the saints and heroes. He contends that the saints and heroes show us that a living example, not rigid rules, is important in ethics. We learn more about ethics by looking at the lives of such people than by learning a set of principles.

The philosophy of moral principles, which is characteristic of Kant and the post-Kantian era, is something of which hardly a trace exists in Plato. . . . Plato says nothing about rules or principles or laws, except when he is talking politics. Instead he talks about virtues and vices, and about certain types of human character. The key word in Platonic ethics is Virtue; the key word in Kantian ethics is Duty. And modern ethics is a set of footnotes, not to Plato, but to Kant. . . .

Attention to the novelists can be a welcome correction to a tendency of philosophical ethics of the last generation or two to lose contact with the ordinary life of man which is just what the novelists, in their own way, are concerned with. Of course there are writers who can be called in to illustrate problems about Duty (Graham Greene is a good example). But there are more who perhaps never mention the words duty, obligation, or principle. Yet they are all concerned—Jane Austen, for instance, entirely and absolutely—with the moral qualities or defects of their heroes and heroines and other characters. This points to a radical one-sidedness in the philosophers' account of morality in terms of principles: it takes little or no account of qualities, of what people *are*. It is just here that the old-fashioned word Virtue used to have a place; and it is just here that the work of Plato and Aristotle can be instructive. Justice, for Plato, though it is

closely connected with acting according to law, does not *mean* acting according to law: it is a quality of character, and a just action is
one such as a just man would do. Telling the truth, for Aristotle, is
not, as it was for Kant, fulfilling an obligation; again it is a quality of
character, or, rather, a whole range of qualities of character, some of
which may actually be defects, such as tactlessness, boastfulness, and
so on—a point which can be brought out, in terms of principles, only
with the greatest complexity and artificiality, but quite simply and
naturally in terms of character.

If we wish to enquire about Aristotle's moral views, it is no use
looking for a set of principles. Of course we can find *some* principles to which he must have subscribed—for instance, that one ought
not to commit adultery. But what we find much more prominently
is a set of character-traits, a list of certain types of person—the courageous man, the niggardly man, the boaster, the lavish spender, and
so on. The basic moral question, for Aristotle, is not, What shall I do?
but, What shall I be?

These contrasts between doing and being, negative and positive,
and modern as against Greek morality were noted by John Stuart
Mill; I quote from the *Essay on Liberty:*

> Christian morality (so-called) has all the characters of a reaction; it
> is, in great part, a protest against Paganism. Its ideal is negative rather
> than positive, passive rather than active; Innocence rather than Noble-
> ness; Abstinence from Evil, rather than energetic Pursuit of the Good;
> in its precepts (as has been well said) "Thou shalt not" predominates
> unduly over "Thou shalt . . ." Whatever exists of magnanimity, high-
> mindedness, personal dignity, even the sense of honour, is derived
> from the purely human, not the religious part of our education, and
> never could have grown out of a standard of ethics in which the
> only worth, professedly recognized, is that of obedience.

Of course, there are connections between being and doing. It is
obvious that a man cannot just *be;* he can only be what he is by
doing what he does; his moral qualities are ascribed to him because
of his actions, which are said to manifest those qualities. But the
point is that an ethics of Being must include this obvious fact, that
Being involves Doing; whereas an ethics of Doing, such as I have
been examining, may easily overlook it. As I have suggested, a
morality of principles is concerned only with what people do or

fail to do, since that is what rules are for. And as far as this sort of ethics goes, people might well have no moral qualities at all except the possession of principles and the will (and capacity) to act accordingly.

When we speak of a moral quality such as courage, and say that a certain action was courageous, we are not merely saying something about the action. We are referring, not so much to what is done, as to the kind of person by whom we take it to have been done. We connect, by means of imputed motives and intentions, with the character of the agent as courageous. This explains, incidentally, why both Kantians and Utilitarians encounter, in their different ways, such difficulties in dealing with motives, which their principles, on the face of it, have no room for. A Utilitarian, for example, can only praise a courageous action in some such way as this: the action is of a sort such as a person of courage is likely to perform, and courage is a quality of character the cultivation of which is likely to increase rather than diminish the sum total of human happiness. But Aristotelians have no need of such circumlocution. For them a courageous action just is one which proceeds from and manifests a certain type of character, and is praised because such a character trait is good, or better than others, or is a virtue. An evaluative criterion is sufficient: there is no need to look for an imperative criterion as well, or rather instead, according to which it is not the character which is good, but the cultivation of the character which is right. . . .

No doubt the fundamental moral question is just "What ought I to do?" And according to the philosophy of moral principles, the answer (which must be an imperative "Do this") must be derived from a conjunction of premises consisting (in the simplest case) firstly of a rule, or universal imperative, enjoining (or forbidding) all actions of a certain type in situations of a certain type, and, secondly, a statement to the effect that this is a situation of that type, falling under that rule. In practice the emphasis may be on supplying only one of these premises, the other being assumed or taken for granted: one may answer the question "What ought I to do?" either by quoting a rule which I am to adopt, or by showing that my case is legislated for by a rule which I do adopt. . . . [I]f I am in doubt whether to tell the truth about his condition to a dying man, my doubt may be resolved by showing that the case comes under a rule about the avoidance of unnecessary suffering, which

I am assumed to accept. But if the case is without precedent in my moral career, my problem may be soluble only by adopting a new principle about what I am to do now and in the future about cases of this kind.

This second possibility offers a connection with moral ideas. Suppose my perplexity is not merely an unprecedented situation which I could cope with by adopting a new rule. Suppose the new rule is thoroughly inconsistent with my existing moral code. This may happen, for instance, if the moral code is one to which I only pay lip-service, if . . . its authority is not yet internalised, or if it has ceased to be so; it is ready for rejection, but its final rejection awaits a moral crisis such as we are assuming to occur. What I now need is not a rule for deciding how to act in this situation and others of its kind. I need a whole set of rules, a complete morality, new principles to live by.

Now, according to the philosophy of moral character, there is another way of answering the fundamental question "What ought I to do?" Instead of quoting a rule, we quote a quality of character, a virtue: we say "Be brave," or "Be patient" or "Be lenient." We may even say "Be a man": if I am in doubt, say, whether to take a risk, and someone says "Be a man," meaning a morally sound man, in this case a man of sufficient courage. (Compare the very different ideal invoked in "Be a gentleman." I shall not discuss whether this is a *moral* ideal.) Here, too, we have the extreme cases, where a man's moral perplexity extends not merely to a particular situation but to his whole way of living. And now the question "What ought I to do?" turns into the question "What ought I to be?"—as, indeed, it was treated in the first place. ("Be brave.") It is answered, not by quoting a rule or a set of rules, but by describing a quality of character or a type of person. And here the ethics of character gains a practical simplicity which offsets the greater logical simplicity of the ethics of principles. We do not have to give a list of characteristics or virtues, as we might list a set of principles. We can give a unity to our answer.

Of course we can in theory give a unity to our principles: this is implied by speaking of a *set* of principles. But if such a set is to be a system and not merely aggregate, the unity we are looking for is a logical one, namely the possibility that some principles are deductible from others, and ultimately from one. But the attempt to construct a deductive moral system is notoriously difficult, and in any case ill-founded. Why should we expect that all rules of conduct should be ultimately reducible to a few?

SAINTS AND HEROES

But when we are asked "What shall I be?" we can readily give a unity to our answer, though not a logical unity. It is the unity of character. A person's character is not merely a list of dispositions; it has the organic unity of something that is more than the sum of its parts. And we can say, in answer to our morally perplexed questioner, not only "Be this" and "Be that," but also "Be like So-and-So"—where So-and-So is either an ideal type of character, or else an actual person taken as representative of the ideal, as exemplar. Examples of the first are Plato's "just man" in the Republic; Aristotle's man of practical wisdom, in the *Nicomachean Ethics;* Augustine's citizen of the City of God; the good Communist; the American way of life (which is a collective expression for a type of character). Examples of the second kind, the exemplar, are Socrates, Christ, Buddha, St. Francis, the heroes of epic writers and of novelists. Indeed the idea of the Hero, as well as the idea of the Saint, are very much the expression of this attitude to morality. Heroes and saints are not merely people who did things. They are people whom we are expected, and expect ourselves, to imitate. And imitating them means not merely doing what they did; it means being like them. Their status is not in the least like that of legislators whose laws we admire; for the character of a legislator is irrelevant to our judgment about his legislation. The heroes and saints did not merely give us principles to live by (though some of them did that as well): they gave us examples to follow.

Kant, as we should expect, emphatically rejects this attitude as "fatal to morality." According to him, examples serve only to render *visible* an instance of the moral principle, and thereby to demonstrate its practical feasibility. But every exemplar, such as Christ himself, must be judged by the independent criterion of the moral law, before we are entitled to recognize him as worthy of imitation. I am not suggesting that the subordination of exemplars to

principles is incorrect, but that it is one-sided and fails to do justice to a large area of moral experience.

Imitation can be more or less successful. And this suggests
another defect of the ethics of principles. It has no room for ideals,
except the ideal of a perfect set of principles (which, as a matter
of fact, is intelligible only in terms of an ideal character or way of
life), and the ideal of perfect conscientiousness (which is itself a
character-trait). This results, of course, from the "black-or-white"
nature of moral verdicts based on rules. There are no degrees by
which we approach or recede from the attainment of a certain quality or virtue; if there were not, the word "ideal" would have no
meaning. Heroes and saints are not people whom we try to be *just*
like, since we know that is impossible. It is precisely because it is
impossible for ordinary human beings to achieve the same qualities as the saints, and in the same degree, that we do set them
apart from the rest of humanity. It is enough if we try to be a little like them. . . .

For Further Reflection

1. How does Mayo contrast rule-governed ethics with virtue ethics?
   Is this a real difference or an exaggeration? That is, deontologists and utilitarians also promote the virtues, though perhaps
   for different reasons than the virtue ethicist. Exactly what are
   those differences?

2. What are the advantages and what are the weaknesses of virtue
   ethics?

3. Mayo argues that Kant would reject the insights of virtue ethics,
   since for him morality has nothing to do with emotions or
   examples, but with reason. But could Kant still have a significant role for the virtues?

4. What, according to Mayo, is the value of having saints and
   heroes?

5. Some critics contend that virtue ethics is relativistic—since what
   is considered virtuous differs from culture to culture. Do you
   agree? How would a virtue ethicist respond to this charge?

The Great Stone Face

NATHANIEL HAWTHORNE

Nathaniel Hawthorne (1804–1864) was born in Salem, Massachusetts, and educated at Bowdoin College. He is one of America's greatest novelists, best known for *The Scarlet Letter* (1850). In this less-known short story, Hawthorne deals with such themes as moral imagination, insight, and the virtues. The Great Stone Face who dominates the story may be based on the rock formation in the White Mountains of New Hampshire known as Franconia Notch. The people in the valley are waiting for a great person to appear, modeled on the Great Stone Face, who will lead them. The main character, Ernest, is powerfully influenced, even educated, by what he sees in that face.

One afternoon, when the sun was going down, a mother and her little boy sat at the door of their cottage, talking about the Great Stone Face. They had but to lift their eyes, and there it was plainly to be seen, though miles away, with the sunshine brightening all its features.

And what was the Great Stone Face?

Embosomed amongst a family of lofty mountains, there was a valley so spacious that it contained many thousand inhabitants. Some of these good people dwelt in log-huts, with the black forest all around them, on the steep and difficult hill-sides. Others had their homes in comfortable farm-houses, and cultivated the rich soil on the gentle slopes or level surfaces of the valley. Others, again, were congregated into populous villages, where some wild, highland rivulet, tumbling down from its birthplace in the upper mountain region, had been caught and tamed by human cunning, and compelled to turn the machinery of cotton-factories. The inhabitants of this valley, in short, were numerous, and of many modes of life. But all of them, grown people and children, had a kind of familiarity with the Great Stone Face, although some possessed the

Reprinted from the *Complete Works of Nathaniel Hawthorne* (Modern Library, 1937).

gift of distinguishing this grand natural phenomenon more perfectly than many of their neighbors.

The Great Stone Face, then, was a work of Nature in her mood of majestic playfulness, formed on the perpendicular side of a mountain by some immense rocks, which had been thrown together in such a position as, when viewed at a proper distance, precisely to resemble the features of the human countenance. It seemed as if an enormous giant, or a Titan, had sculptured his own likeness on the precipice. There was the broad arch of the forehead, a hundred feet in height; the nose, with its long bridge; and the vast lips, which, if they could have spoken, would have rolled their thunder accents from one end of the valley to the other. True it is, that if the spectator approached too near, he lost the outline of the gigantic visage, and could discern only a heap of ponderous and gigantic rocks, piled in chaotic ruin one upon another. Retracing his steps, however, the wondrous features would again be seen; and the farther he withdrew from them, the more like a human face, with all its original divinity intact, did they appear; until, as it grew dim in the distance, with the clouds and glorified vapor of the mountains clustering about it, the Great Stone Face seemed positively to be alive.

It was a happy lot for children to grow up to manhood or womanhood with the Great Stone Face before their eyes, for all the features were noble, and the expression was at once grand and sweet, as if it were the glow of a vast, warm heart, that embraced all mankind in its affections, and had room for more. It was an education only to look at it. According to the belief of many people, the valley owed much of its fertility to this benign aspect that was continually beaming over it, illuminating the clouds, and infusing its tenderness into the sunshine.

As we began with saying, a mother and her little boy sat at their cottage-door, gazing at the Great Stone Face, and talking about it. The child's name was Ernest.

"Mother," said he, while the Titanic visage smiled on him, "I wish that it could speak, for it looks so very kindly that its voice must needs be pleasant. If I were to see a man with such a face. I should love him dearly."

"If an old prophecy should come to pass," answered his mother, "we may see a man, some time or other, with exactly such a face as that."

"What prophecy do you mean, dear mother?" eagerly inquired Ernest. "Pray tell me about it!"

So his mother told him a story that her own mother had told to her, when she herself was younger than little Ernest; a story, not of things that were past, but of what was yet to come; a story, nevertheless, so very old, that even the Indians, who formerly inhabited this valley, had heard it from their forefathers, to whom, as they affirmed, it had been murmured by the mountain streams, and whispered by the wind among the tree-tops. The purport was, that, at some future day, a child should be born hereabouts, who was destined to become the greatest and noblest personage of his time, and whose countenance, in manhood, should bear an exact resemblance to the Great Stone Face. Not a few old-fashioned people, and young ones likewise, in the ardor of their hopes, still cherished an enduring faith in this old prophecy. But others, who had seen more of the world, had watched and waited till they were weary, and had beheld no man with such a face, nor any man that proved to be much greater or nobler than his neighbors, concluded it to be nothing but an idle tale. At all events, the great man of the prophecy had not yet appeared.

"O mother, dear mother!" cried Ernest, clapping his hands above his head, "I do hope that I shall live to see him!"

His mother was an affectionate and thoughtful woman, and felt that it was wisest not to discourage the generous hopes of her little boy. So she only said to him, "Perhaps you may."

And Ernest never forgot the story that his mother told him. It was always in his mind, whenever he looked upon the Great Stone Face. He spent his childhood in the log-cottage where he was born, and was dutiful to his mother, and helpful to her in many things, assisting her much with his little hands, and more with his loving heart. In this manner, from a happy yet often pensive child, he grew up to be a mild, quiet, unobtrusive boy, and sun-browned with labor in the fields, but with more intelligence brightening his aspect than is seen in many lads who have been taught at famous schools. Yet Ernest had had no teacher, save only that the Great Stone Face became one to him. When the toil of the day was over, he would gaze at it for hours, until he began to imagine that those vast features recognized him, and gave him a smile of kindness and encouragement, responsive to his own look of veneration. We must not take upon us to affirm that this was a mistake, although the Face may have looked no more kindly at Ernest than at all the world besides. But the secret was that the boy's tender and confiding simplicity discerned what other people could not see; and thus the love, which was meant for all, became his peculiar portion.

About this time there went a rumor throughout the valley, that the great man, foretold from ages long ago, who was to bear a resemblance to the Great Stone Face, had appeared at last. It seems that, many years before, a young man had migrated from the valley and settled at a distant seaport, where, after getting together a little money, he had set up as a shopkeeper. His name—but I could never learn whether it was his real one, or a nickname that had grown out of his habits and success in life—was Gathergold. Being shrewd and active, and endowed by Providence with that inscrutable faculty which develops itself in what the world calls luck, he became an exceedingly rich merchant, and owner of a whole fleet of bulky-bottomed ships. All the countries of the globe appeared to join hands for the mere purpose of adding heap after heap to the mountainous accumulation of this one man's wealth. The cold regions of the north, almost within the gloom and shadow of the Arctic Circle, sent him their tribute in the shape of furs; hot Africa sifted for him the golden sands of her rivers, and gathered up the ivory tusks of her great elephants out of the forests; the East came bringing him the rich shawls, and spices, and teas, and the effulgence of diamonds, and the gleaming purity of large pearls. The ocean, not to be behind-hand with the earth, yielded up her mighty whales, that Mr. Gathergold might sell their oil, and make a profit of it. Be the original commodity what it might, it was gold within his grasp. It might be said of him, as of Midas in the fable, that whatever he touched with his finger immediately glistened, and grew yellow, and was changed at once into sterling metal, or, which suited him still better, into piles of coin. And, when Mr. Gathergold had become so very rich that it would have taken him a hundred years only to count his wealth, he bethought himself of his native valley, and resolved to go back thither, and end his days where he was born. With this purpose in view, he sent a skilful architect to build him such a palace as should be fit for a man of his vast wealth to live in.

As I have said above, it had already been rumored in the valley that Mr. Gathergold had turned out to be the prophetic personage so long and vainly looked for, and that his visage was the perfect and undeniable similitude of the Great Stone Face. People were the more ready to believe that this must needs be the fact, when they beheld the splendid edifice that rose, as if by enchantment, on the site of his father's old weatherbeaten farm-house. The exterior was of marble, so dazzlingly white that it seemed as though the whole structure might melt away in the sunshine, like those humbler ones which Mr. Gathergold, in his young play-days, before his fingers were gifted with the touch of transmutation, had been accustomed to build of snow. It had a richly ornamented portico, supported by tall pillars, beneath which was a lofty door, studded with silver knobs, and made of a kind of variegated wood that had been brought from beyond the sea. The windows, from the floor to the ceiling of each stately apartment, were composed, respectively, of but one enormous pane of glass, so transparently pure that it was said to be a finer medium than even the vacant atmosphere. Hardly anybody had been permitted to see the interior of this palace; but it was reported, and with good semblance of truth, to be far more gorgeous than the outside, insomuch that whatever was iron or brass in other houses was silver or gold in this; and Mr. Gathergold's bedchamber, especially, made such a glittering appearance that no ordinary man would have been able to close his eyes there. But, on the other hand, Mr. Gathergold was now so inured to wealth, that perhaps he could not have closed his eyes unless where the gleam of it was certain to find its way beneath his eyelids.

In due time, the mansion was finished; next came the upholsterers, with magnificent furniture; then, a whole troop of black and white servants, the harbingers of Mr. Gathergold, who, in his own majestic person, was expected to arrive at sunset. Our friend Ernest, meanwhile, had been deeply stirred by the idea that the great man, the noble man, the man of prophecy, after so many ages of delay, was at length to be made manifest to his native valley. He knew, boy as he was, that there were a thousand ways in which Mr. Gathergold, with his vast wealth, might transform himself into an angel of beneficence, and assume a control over human affairs as wide and benignant as the smile of the Great Stone Face. Full of faith and hope, Ernest doubted not that what the people said was true, and that now he was to behold the living likeness of those wondrous features on the mountain-side. While the boy was still gazing up the valley, and fancying, as he always did, that the Great Stone Face returned his gaze and looked kindly at him, the rumbling of wheels was heard, approaching swiftly along the winding road.

"Here he comes!" cried a group of people who were assembled to witness the arrival. "Here comes the great Mr. Gathergold!"

A carriage, drawn by four horses, dashed round the turn of the road. Within it, thrust partly out of the window, appeared the physiognomy of the old man, with a skin as yellow as if his own Midas-hand had transmuted it. He had a low forehead, small, sharp eyes, puckered about with innumerable wrinkles, and very thin lips, which he made still thinner by pressing them forcibly together.

"The very image of the Great Stone Face!" shouted the people. "Sure enough, the old prophecy is true; and here we have the great man come, at last!"

And, what greatly perplexed Ernest, they seemed actually to believe that here was the likeness which they spoke of. By the roadside there chanced to be an old beggar-woman and two little beggar-children, stragglers from some far-off region, who, as the carriage rolled onward, held out their hands and lifted up their doleful voices, most piteously beseeching charity. A yellow claw—the very same that had clawed together so much wealth—poked itself out of the coach-window, and dropt some copper coins upon the ground; so that, though the great man's name seems to have been Gathergold, he might just as suitably have been nicknamed Scattercopper. Still, nevertheless, with an earnest shout, and evidently with as much good faith as ever, the people bellowed,

"He is the very image of the Great Stone Face!"

But Ernest turned sadly from the wrinkled shrewdness of that sordid visage, and gazed up the valley, where, amid a gathering mist, gilded by the last sunbeams, he could still distinguish those glorious features which had impressed themselves into his soul. Their aspect cheered him. What did the benign lips seem to say?

"He will come! Fear not, Ernest; the man will come!"

The years went on, and Ernest ceased to be a boy. He had grown to be a young man now. He attracted little notice from the other inhabitants of the valley; for they saw nothing remarkable in his way of life, save that, when the labor of the day was over, he still loved to go apart and gaze and meditate upon the Great Stone Face. According to their idea of the matter, it was a folly, indeed, but pardonable, inasmuch as Ernest was industrious, kind, and neighborly, and neglected no duty for the sake of indulging this idle habit. They knew not that the Great Stone Face had become a teacher to him, and that the sentiment which was expressed in it would enlarge the young man's heart, and fill it with wider and deeper sympathies than other hearts. They knew not that thence would come a better wisdom than could be learned from books, and a better life than could be moulded on the defaced example of other human lives. Neither did Ernest know that the thoughts and affections which came to him so naturally, in the fields and at the fireside, and wherever he communed with himself, were of a higher tone than those which all men shared with him. A simple soul—simple as when his mother first taught him the old prophecy—he beheld the marvellous features beaming adown the valley, and still wondered that their human counterpart was so long in making his appearance.

By this time poor Mr. Gathergold was dead and buried; and the oddest part of the matter was, that his wealth, which was the body and spirit of his existence, had disappeared before his death, leaving nothing of him but a living skeleton, covered over with a wrinkled yellow skin. Since the melting away of his gold, it had been very generally conceded that there was no such striking resemblance, after all, betwixt the ignoble features of the ruined merchant and that majestic face upon the mountain-side. So the people ceased to honor him during his lifetime, and quietly consigned him to forgetfulness after his decease. Once in a while, it is true, his memory was brought up in connection with the magnificent palace which he had built, and which had long ago been turned into a hotel for the accommodation of strangers, multitudes of whom came, every summer, to visit that famous natural curiosity, the Great Stone Face. Thus, Mr. Gathergold being discredited and thrown into the shade, the man of prophecy was yet to come.

It so happened that a native-born son of the valley, many years before, had enlisted as a soldier, and, after a great deal of hard fighting, had now become an illustrious commander. Whatever he may be called in history, he was known in camps and on the battle-field under the nickname of Old Blood-and-Thunder. This war-worn veteran being now infirm with age and wounds, and weary of the turmoil of a military life, and of the roll of the drum and the clangor of the trumpet, that had so long been ringing in his ears, had lately signified a purpose of returning to his native valley, hoping to find repose where he remembered to have left it. The inhabitants, his old neighbors and their grown-up children, were resolved to welcome the renowned warrior with a salute of cannon and a public dinner; and all the more enthusiastically, it being affirmed that now, at last, the likeness of the Great Stone Face had actually appeared. An aid-de-camp of Old Blood-and-Thunder, travelling through the valley, was said to have been struck with the resemblance. Moreover the schoolmates and early acquaintances of the general were ready to testify, on oath, that, to the best of their recollection, the aforesaid general had been exceedingly like the majestic image, even when a boy, only the idea had never occurred to them at that period. Great, therefore, was the excitement throughout the valley; and many people, who had never once thought of glancing at the Great Stone Face for years before, now spent their time in gazing at it, for the sake of knowing exactly how General Blood-and-Thunder looked.

On the day of the great festival, Ernest, with all the other people of the valley, left their work, and proceeded to the spot where the sylvan banquet was prepared. As he approached, the loud voice of the Rev. Dr. Battleblast was heard, beseeching a blessing on the good things set before them, and on the distinguished friend of peace in whose honor they were assembled. The tables were arranged in a cleared space of the woods, shut in by the surrounding trees, except where a vista opened eastward, and afforded a distant view of the Great Stone Face. Over the general's chair, which was a relic from the home of Washington, there was an arch of verdant boughs, with the laurel profusely intermixed, and surmounted by his country's banner, beneath which he had won his victories. Our friend Ernest raised himself on his tiptoes, in hopes to get a glimpse of the celebrated guest; but there was a mighty crowd about the tables anxious to hear the toasts and speeches, and to catch any word that might fall from the general in reply; and a volunteer company, doing duty as a guard, pricked ruthlessly with their bayonets at any particularly quiet person among the throng. So Ernest, being of an unobtrusive character, was thrust quite into the background, where he could see no more of Old Blood-and-Thunder's physiognomy than if it had been still blazing on the battle-field. To console himself, he turned towards the Great Stone Face, which, like a faithful and long-remembered friend, looked back and smiled upon him through the vista of the forest. Meantime, however, he could overhear the remarks of various individuals, who were comparing the features of the hero with the face on the distant mountain-side.

" 'Tis the same face, to a hair!" cried one man, cutting a caper for joy.

"Wonderfully like, that's a fact!" responded another.

"Like! why, I call it Old Blood-and-Thunder himself, in a monstrous looking-glass!" cried a third. "And why not? He's the greatest man of this or any other age, beyond a doubt."

And then all three of the speakers gave a great shout, which communicated electricity to the crowd, and called forth a roar from a thousand voices, that went reverberating for miles among the mountains, until you might have supposed that the Great Stone Face had poured its thunder-breath into the cry. All these comments, and this vast enthusiasm, served the more to interest our friend; nor did he think of questioning that now, at length, the mountain-visage had found its human counterpart. It is true, Ernest had imagined that this long-looked-for personage would appear in the character of a man of peace, uttering wisdom, and doing good, and making people happy. But, taking an habitual breadth of view, with all his simplicity, he contended that Providence should choose its own method of blessing mankind, and could conceive that this great end might be effected even by a warrior and a bloody sword, should inscrutable wisdom see fit to order matters so.

"The general! the general!" was now the cry. "Hush! silence! Old Blood-and-Thunder's going to make a speech."

Even so; for, the cloth being removed, the general's health had been drunk, amid shouts of applause, and he now stood upon his feet to thank the company. Ernest saw him. There he was, over the shoulders of the crowd, from the two glittering epaulets and embroidered collar upward, beneath the arch of green boughs with intertwined laurel, and the banner drooping as if to shade his brow! And there, too, visible in the same glance, through the vista of the forest, appeared the Great Stone Face! And was there, indeed, such a resemblance as the crowd had testified? Alas, Ernest could not recognize it! He beheld a war-worn and weather-beaten countenance, full of energy, and expressive of an iron will; but the gentle wisdom, the deep, broad, tender sympathies, were altogether wanting in Old Blood-and-Thunder's visage; and even if the Great Stone Face had assumed his look of stern command, the milder traits would still have tempered it.

"This is not the man of prophecy," sighed Ernest to himself, as he made his way out of the throng. "And must the world wait longer yet?"

The mists had congregated about the distant mountain-side, and there were seen the grand and awful features of the Great Stone Face, awful but benignant, as if a mighty angel were sitting among the hills, and enrobing himself in a cloud-vesture of gold and purple. As he looked, Ernest could hardly believe but that a smile beamed over the whole visage, with a radiance still brightening, although without motion of the lips. It was probably the effect of the western sunshine, melting through the thinly diffused vapors that had swept between him and the object that he gazed at. But—as it always did—the aspect of his marvellous friend made Ernest as hopeful as if he had never hoped in vain.

"Fear not, Ernest," said his heart, even as if the Great Face were whispering to him, "—fear not, Ernest; he will come."

More years sped swiftly and tranquilly away. Ernest still dwelt in his native valley, and was now a man of middle age. By imperceptible degrees, he had become known among the people. Now, as heretofore, he labored for his bread, and was the same simple-hearted man that he had always been. But he had thought and felt so much, he had given so many of the best hours of his life to unworldly hopes for some great good to mankind, that it seemed as though he had been talking with the angels, and had imbibed a portion of their wisdom unawares. It was visible in the calm and well-considered beneficence of his daily life, the quiet stream of which had made a wide green margin all along its course. Not a day passed by, that the world was not the better because this man, humble as he was, had lived. He never stepped aside from his own path, yet would always reach a blessing to his neighbor. Almost involuntarily, too, he had become a preacher. The pure and high simplicity of his thought, which, as one of its manifestations, took shape in the good deeds that dropped silently from his hand, flowed also forth in speech. He uttered truths that wrought upon and moulded the lives of those who heard him. His auditors, it may be, never suspected that Ernest, their own neighbor and familiar friend, was more than an ordinary man; least of all did Ernest himself suspect it; but, inevitably as the murmur of a rivulet, came thoughts out of his mouth that no other human lips had spoken.

When the people's minds had had a little time to cool, they were ready enough to acknowledge their mistake in imagining a similarity between General Blood-and-Thunder's truculent physiognomy and the benign visage on the mountain-side. But now, again, there were reports and many paragraphs in the newspapers, affirming that the likeness of the Great Stone Face had appeared upon the broad shoulders of a certain eminent statesman. He, like Mr. Gathergold and Old Blood-and-Thunder, was a native of the valley, but had left it in his early days, and taken up the trades of law and politics. Instead of the rich man's wealth and the warrior's sword, he had but a tongue, and it was mightier than both together. So wonderfully eloquent was he, that whatever he might choose to say, his auditors had no choice but to believe him; wrong looked like right, and right like wrong; for when it pleased him, he could make a kind of illuminated fog with his mere breath, and obscure the natural daylight with it. His tongue, indeed, was a magic instrument: sometimes it rumbled like the thunder; sometimes it warbled like the sweetest music. It was the blast of war, the song of peace; and it seemed to have a heart in it, when there was no such matter. In good truth, he was a wondrous man; and when his tongue had acquired him all other imaginable success—when it had been heard in halls of state, and in the courts of princes and potentates—after it had made him known all over the world, even as a voice crying from shore to shore—it finally persuaded his countrymen to select him for the Presidency. Before this time—indeed, as soon as he began to grow celebrated—his admirers had found out the resemblance between him and the Great Stone Face; and so much were they struck by it, that throughout the country this distinguished gentleman was known by the name of Old Stony Phiz. The phrase was considered as giving a highly favorable aspect to his political prospects; for, as is likewise the case with the Popedom, nobody ever becomes President without taking a name other than his own.

While his friends were doing their best to make him President, Old Stony Phiz, as he was called, set out on a visit to the valley where he was born. Of course, he had no other object than to shake hands with his fellow-citizens and neither thought nor cared about any effect which his progress through the country might have upon the election. Magnificent preparations were made to receive the illustrious statesman; a cavalcade of horsemen set forth to meet him at the boundary line of the State, and all the people left their business and gathered along the wayside to see him pass. Among these was Ernest. Though more than once disappointed, as we have seen, he had such a hopeful and confiding nature, that he was always ready to believe in whatever seemed beautiful and good. He kept his heart continually open, and thus was sure to catch the blessing from on high when it should come. So now again, as buoyantly as ever, he went forth to behold the likeness of the Great Stone Face.

The cavalcade came prancing along the road, with a great clattering of hoofs and a mighty cloud of dust, which rose up so dense and high that the visage of the mountain-side was completely hidden from Ernest's eyes. All the great men of the neighborhood were there on horseback; militia officers, in uniform; the member of Congress; the sheriff of the county; the editors of newspapers; and many a farmer, too, had mounted his patient steed, with his Sunday coat upon his back. It really was a very brilliant spectacle, especially as there were numerous banners flaunting over the cavalcade, on some of which were gorgeous portraits of the illustrious statesman and the Great Stone Face, smiling familiarly at one another, like two brothers. If the pictures were to be trusted, the mutual resemblance, it must be confessed, was marvellous. We must not forget to mention that there was a band of music, which made the echoes of the mountains ring and reverberate with the loud triumph of its strains; so that airy and soul-thrilling melodies broke out among all the heights and hollows, as if every nook of his native valley had found a voice, to welcome the distinguished guest. But the grandest effect was when the far-off mountain precipice flung back the music; for then the Great Stone Face itself seemed to be swelling the triumphant chorus, in acknowledgment that, at length, the man of prophecy was come.

All this while the people were throwing up their hats and shouting, with enthusiasm so contagious that the heart of Ernest kindled up, and he likewise threw up his hat, and shouted, as loudly as the loudest, "Huzza for the great man! Huzza for Old Stony Phiz!" But as yet he had not seen him.

"Here he is, now!" cried those who stood near Ernest. "There! There! Look at Old Stony Phiz and then at the Old Man of the Mountain, and see if they are not as like as two twin-brothers!"

In the midst of all this gallant array came an open barouche, drawn by four white horses; and in the barouche, with his massive head uncovered, sat the illustrious statesman, Old Stony Phiz himself.

"Confess it," said one of Ernest's neighbors to him, "the Great Stone Face has met its match at last!"

Now, it must be owned that, at his first glimpse of the countenance which was bowing and smiling from the barouche, Ernest did fancy that there was a resemblance between it and the old familiar face upon the mountain-side. The brow, with its massive depth and loftiness, and all the other features, indeed, were boldly and strongly hewn, as if in emulation of a more than heroic, of a Titanic model. But the sublimity and stateliness, the grand expresson of a divine sympathy, that illuminated the mountain visage and etherealized its ponderous granite substance into spirit, might here be sought in vain. Something had been originally left out, or had departed. And therefore the marvellously gifted statesman had always a weary gloom in the deep caverns of his eyes, as of a child that has outgrown its playthings or a man of mighty faculties and little aims, whose life, with all its high performances, was vague and empty, because no high purpose had endowed it with reality.

Still, Ernest's neighbor was thrusting his elbow into his side, and pressing him for an answer.

"Confess! confess! Is not he the very picture of your Old Man of the Mountain?"

"No!" said Ernest bluntly, "I see little or no likeness."

"Then so much the worse for the Great Stone Face!" answered his neighbor; and again he set up a shout for Old Stony Phiz.

But Ernest turned away, melancholy, and almost despondent: for this was the saddest of his disappointments, to behold a man who might have fulfilled the prophecy, and had not willed to do so. Meantime, the cavalcade, the banners, the music, and the barouches swept past him, with the vociferous crowd in the rear, leaving the dust to settle down, and the Great Stone Face to be revealed again, with the grandeur that it had worn for untold centuries.

"Lo, here I am, Ernest!" the benign lips seemed to say. "I have waited longer than thou, and am not yet weary. Fear not; the man will come."

The years hurried onward, treading in their haste on one another's heels. And now they began to bring white hairs, and scatter them over the head of Ernest; they made reverend wrinkles across his forehead, and furrows in his cheeks. He was an aged man. But not in vain had he grown old: more than the white hairs on his head were the sage thoughts in his mind; his wrinkles and furrows were inscriptions that Time had graved, and in which he had written legends of wisdom that had been tested by the tenor of a life. And Ernest had ceased to be obscure. Unsought for, undesired, had come the fame which so many seek, and made him known in the great world, beyond the limits of the valley in which he had dwelt so quietly. College professors, and even the active men of cities, came from far to see and converse with Ernest; for the report had gone abroad that this simple husbandman had ideas unlike those of other men, not gained from books, but of a higher tone—a tranquil and familiar majesty, as if he had been talking with the angels as his daily friends. Whether it were sage, statesman, or philanthropist, Ernest received these visitors with the gentle sincerity that had characterized him from boyhood, and spoke freely with them of whatever came uppermost, or lay deepest in his heart or their own. While they talked together, his face would kindle, unawares, and shine upon them, as with a mild evening light. Pensive with the fulness of such discourse, his guests took leave and went their way; and passing up the valley, paused to look at the Great Stone Face, imagining that they had seen its likeness in a human countenance, but could not remember where.

While Ernest had been growing up and growing old, a bountiful Providence had granted a new poet to this earth. He likewise, was a native of the valley, but had spent the greater part of his life at a distance from that romantic region, pouring out his sweet music amid the bustle and din of cities. Often, however, did the mountains which had been familiar to him in his childhood lift their snowy peaks into the clear atmosphere of his poetry. Neither was the Great Stone Face forgotten, for the poet had celebrated it in an ode, which was grand enough to have been uttered by its own majestic lips. This man of genius, we may say, had come down from heaven with wonderful endowments. If he sang of a mountain, the eyes of all mankind beheld a mightier grandeur reposing on its breast, or soaring to its summit, than had before been seen there. If his theme were a lovely lake, a celestial smile had now been thrown over it, to gleam forever on its surface. If it were the vast old sea, even the deep immensity of its dread bosom seemed to swell the higher, as if moved by the emotions of the song. Thus the world assumed another and a better aspect from the hour that the poet blessed it with his happy eyes. The Creator had bestowed him, as the last best touch to his own handiwork. Creation was not finished till the poet came to interpret, and so complete it.

The effect was no less high and beautiful, when his human brethren were the subject of his verse. The man or woman, sordid with the common dust of life, who crossed his daily path, and the little child who played in it, were glorified if he beheld them in his mood of poetic faith. He showed the golden links of the great chain that intertwined them with an angelic kindred; he brought out the hidden traits of a celestial birth that made them worthy of such kin. Some, indeed, there were, who thought to show the soundness of their judgment by affirming that all the beauty and dignity of the natural world existed only in the poet's fancy. Let such men speak for themselves, who undoubtedly appear to have been spawned forth by Nature with a contemptuous bitterness; she having plastered them up out of her refuse stuff, after all the swine were made. As respects all things else, the poet's ideal was the truest truth.

The songs of this poet found their way to Ernest. He read them after his customary toil, seated on the bench before his cottage-door, where for such a length of time he had filled his repose with thought, by gazing at the Great Stone Face. And now as he read stanzas that caused the soul to thrill within him, he lifted his eyes to the vast countenance beaming on him so benignantly.

"O majestic friend," he murmured, addressing the Great Stone Face, "is not this man worthy to resemble thee?"

The Face seemed to smile, but answered not a word.

Now it happened that the poet, though he dwelt so far away, had not only heard of Ernest, but had meditated much upon his character, until he deemed nothing so desirable as to meet this man, whose untaught wisdom walked hand in hand with the noble simplicity of his life. One summer morning, therefore, he took passage by the railroad, and, in the decline of the afternoon, alighted from the cars at no great distance from Ernest's cottage. The great hotel, which had formerly been the palace of Mr. Gathergold, was close at hand, but the poet, with his carpet-bag on his arm, inquired at once where Ernest dwelt, and was resolved to be accepted as his guest.

Approaching the door, he there found the good old man, holding a volume in his hand, which alternately he read, and then, with a finger between the leaves, looked lovingly at the Great Stone Face.

"Good evening," said the poet. "Can you give a traveller a night's lodging?"

"Willingly," answered Ernest; and then he added, smiling, "Methinks I never saw the Great Stone Face look so hospitably at a stranger."

The poet sat down on the bench beside him, and he and Ernest talked together. Often had the poet held intercourse with the wittiest and the wisest, but never before with a man like Ernest, whose thoughts and feelings gushed up with such a natural freedom, and who made great truths so familiar by his simple utterance of them. Angels, as had been so often said, seemed to have wrought with him at his labor in the fields; angels seemed to have sat with him by the fireside; and, dwelling with angels as friend with friends, he had imbibed the sublimity of their ideas, and imbued it with the sweet and lowly charm of household words. So thought the poet. And Ernest, on the other hand, was moved and agitated by the living images which the poet flung out of his mind, and which peopled all the air about the cottage-door with shapes of beauty, both gay and pensive. The sympathies of these two men instructed them with a profounder sense than either could have attained alone. Their minds accorded into one strain, and made delightful music which neither of them could have claimed as all his own, nor distinguished his own share from the other's. They led one another, as it were, into a high pavilion of their thoughts, so remote, and hitherto so dim, that they had never entered it before, and so beautiful that they desired to be there always.

As Ernest listened to the poet, he imagined that the Great Stone Face was bending forward to listen too. He gazed earnestly into the poet's glowing eyes.

"Who are you, my strangely gifted guest?" he said.

The poet laid his finger on the volume that Ernest had been reading.

"You have read these poems," said he. "You know me, then— for I wrote them."

Again, and still more earnestly than before, Ernest examined the poet's features; then turned towards the Great Stone Face; then back, with an uncertain aspect, to his guest. But his countenance fell; he shook his head, and sighed.

"Wherefore are you sad?" inquired the poet.

"Because," replied Ernest, "all through life I have awaited the fulfilment of a prophecy; and, when I read these poems, I hoped that it might be fulfilled in you."

"You hoped," answered the poet, faintly smiling, "to find in me the likeness of the Great Stone Face. And you are disappointed, as formerly with Mr. Gathergold, and Old Blood-and-Thunder, and Old Stony Phiz. Yes, Ernest, it is my doom. You must add my name to the illustrious three, and record another failure of your hopes.

For—in shame and sadness do I speak it, Ernest—I am not worthy to be typified by yonder benign and majestic image."

"And why?" asked Ernest. He pointed to the volume. "Are not those thoughts divine?"

"They have a strain of the Divinity," replied the poet. "You can hear in them the far-off echo of a heavenly song. But my life, dear Ernest, has not corresponded with my thought. I have had grand dreams, but they have been only dreams, because I have lived— and that, too, by my own choice—among poor and mean realities. Sometimes even—shall I dare to say it?—I lack faith in the grandeur, the beauty, and the goodness, which my own words are said to have made more evident in nature and in human life. Why, then, pure seeker of the good and true, shouldst thou hope to find me, in yonder image of the divine?"

The poet spoke sadly, and his eyes were dim with tears. So, likewise, were those of Ernest.

At the hour of sunset, as had long been his frequent custom, Ernest was to discourse to an assemblage of the neighboring inhabitants in the open air. He and the poet, arm in arm, still talking together as they went along, proceeded to the spot. It was a small nook among the hills, with a gray precipice behind, the stern front of which was relieved by the pleasant foliage of many creeping plants that made a tapestry for the naked rock, by hanging their festoons from all its rugged angles. At a small elevation above the ground, set in a rich framework of verdure, there appeared a niche, spacious enough to admit a human figure, with freedom for such gestures as spontaneously accompany earnest thought and genuine emotion. Into this natural pulpit Ernest ascended, and threw a look of familiar kindness around upon his audience. They stood, or sat, or reclined upon the grass, as seemed good to each, with the departing sunshine falling obliquely over them, and mingling its subdued cheerfulness with the solemnity of a grove of ancient trees, beneath and amid the boughs of which the golden rays were constrained to pass. In another direction was seen the Great Stone Face, with the same cheer, combined with the same solemnity, in its benignant aspect.

Ernest began to speak, giving to the people of what was in his heart and mind. His words had power, because they accorded with his thoughts; and his thoughts had reality and depth, because they harmonized with the life which he had always lived. It was not mere breath that this preacher uttered; they were the words of life, because a life of good deeds and holy love was melted into them. Pearls, pure and rich, had been dissolved into this precious draught. The poet, as he listened, felt that the being and character of Ernest were a nobler strain of poetry than he had ever written. His eyes glistening with tears, he gazed reverentially at the venerable man, and said within himself that never was there an aspect so worthy of a prophet and a sage as that mild, sweet, thoughtful counte-nance, with the glory of white hair diffused about it. At a distance, but distinctly to be seen, high up in the golden light of the setting sun, appeared the Great Stone Face, with hoary mists around it, like the white hairs around the brow of Ernest. Its look of grand beneficence seemed to embrace the world.

At that moment, in sympathy with a thought which he was about to utter, the face of Ernest assumed a grandeur of expression, so imbued with benevolence, that the poet, by an irresistible impulse, threw his arms aloft and shouted,

"Behold! Behold! Ernest is himself the likeness of the Great Stone Face!"

Then all the people looked, and saw that what the deep-sighted poet said was true. The prophecy was fulfilled. But Ernest, having finished what he had to say, took the poet's arm, and walked slowly homeward, still hoping that some wiser and better man than him-self would by and by appear, bearing a resemblance to the GREAT STONE FACE.

For Further Reflection

1. What is the significance of the Great Stone Face in this story? Many people think that we must have good role models in order to develop into good people, but this story suggests that we need not have great people, but simply great ideas and ideals. Is this plausible?

2. Explain how the Great Stone Face affects the values and virtues of the people of the valley, especially Ernest. What virtues does Ernest manifest?

A Critique of Virtue-Based Ethical Systems

WILLIAM FRANKENA

William Frankena (1908–1997) was professor of philosophy at the University of Michigan and the author of several works in ethical theory, including *Ethics* (1973), from which this selection is taken. Frankena, a defender of a deonto-logical duty-based ethic, agrees with the virtue ethicist on the importance of traits (virtues), but argues that all of the virtues can be derived from principles. "Traits without principles are blind." For every virtue there must be some possible action to which the virtue corresponds, and from which it derives its virtuousness. For example, the virtue of truthfulness corresponds to the principle "Tell the truth," and the virtue of being benevolent derives from the general principle to act beneficently. There is a close corresponding relationship between all of the virtues and all of the principles.

MORALITY AND CULTIVATION OF TRAITS

Our present interest, then, is not in moral principles nor in non-moral values, but in moral values, in what is morally good or bad. Throughout its history morality has been concerned about the cultivation of certain dispositions, or traits, among which are "character" and such "virtues" (an old-fashioned but still useful term) as honesty, kindness, and conscientiousness. Virtues are dispositions or traits that are not wholly innate; they must all be acquired, at least in part, by teaching and practice, or, perhaps, by grace. They are also traits of "character," rather than traits of "personality" like charm or shyness, and they all involve a tendency to do certain kinds of action in certain kinds of situations, not just to think or feel in certain ways. They are not just abilities or skills, like intelligence or carpentry, which one may have without using.

In fact, it has been suggested that morality is or should be conceived as primarily concerned, not with rules or principles as we have been supposing so far, but with the cultivation of such dispositions or traits of character. Plato and Aristotle seem to conceive of morality in this way, for they talk mainly in terms of virtues and the virtuous, rather than in terms of what is right or obligatory. Hume uses similar terms, although he mixes in some nonmoral traits like cheerfulness and wit along with moral ones like benevolence and justice. More recently, Leslie Stephen stated the view in these words:

> . . . morality is internal. The moral law . . . has to be expressed in the form, "be this," not in the form, "do this." . . . the true moral law says "hate not," instead of "kill not." . . . the only mode of stating the moral law must be as a rule of character.[1]

ETHICS OF VIRTUE

Those who hold this view are advocating an *ethics of virtue* or being, in opposition to an ethics of duty, principle, or doing. . . . The notion of an ethics of virtue is worth looking at here, not only because it has a long history but also because some spokesmen of "the new morality" seem to espouse it. What would an ethics of virtue be like? It would, of course, not take deontic judgments or principles as basic in morality, as we have been doing; instead, it would take as basic aretaic judgments like "That was a courageous deed," "His action was virtuous," or "Courage is a virtue," and it would insist that deontic judgments are either derivative from such aretaic ones or can be dispensed with entirely. Moreover, it would

[1] Leslie Stephen, *The Science of Ethics* (New York: G. P. Putnam's Sons, 1882), pp. 155, 158.

regard aretaic judgments about actions as secondary and as based on aretaic judgments about agents and their motives or traits, as Hume does when he writes:

> ...when we praise any actions, we regard only the motives that produced them.... The external performance has no merit.... all virtuous actions derive their merit only from virtuous motives.[2]

For an ethics of virtue, then, what is basic in morality is judgments like "Benevolence is a good motive," "Courage is a virtue," "The morally good man is kind to everyone" or, more simply and less accurately, "Be loving!"—not judgments or principles about what our duty is or what we ought to do. But, of course, it thinks that its basic instructions will guide us, not only about what to be, but also about what to do.

It looks as if there would be three kinds of ethics of virtue, corresponding to the three kinds of ethics of duty covered earlier. The question to be answered is: What dispositions or traits are moral virtues? *Trait-egoism* replies that the virtues are the dispositions that are most conducive to one's own good or welfare, or, alternatively, that prudence or a careful concern for one's own good is the cardinal or basic moral virtue, other virtues being derivative from it. *Trait-utilitarianism* asserts that the virtues are those traits that most promote the general good, or, alternatively, that benevolence is the basic or cardinal moral virtue. These views may be called *trait-teleological,* but, of course, there are also *trait-deontological theories,* which will hold that certain traits are morally good or virtuous simply as such, and not just because of the nonmoral value they may have or promote, or, alternatively, that there are other cardinal or basic virtues besides prudence or benevolence, for example, obedience to God, honesty, or justice. If they add that there is only one such cardinal virtue, they are monistic, otherwise pluralistic.

To avoid confusion, it is necessary to notice here that we must distinguish between *virtues* and *principles of duty* like "We ought to promote the good" and "We ought to treat people equally." A virtue is not a principle of this kind; it is a disposition, habit, qual-

---

[2]David Hume, *Treatise of Human Nature* (1739), Book III, Part II, opening of Sec. I.

ity, or trait of the person or soul, which an individual either has or seeks to have. Hence, I speak of the principle of *beneficence* and the virtue of *benevolence,* since we have two words with which to mark the difference. In the case of justice, we do not have different words, but still we must not confuse the principle of equal treatment with the disposition to treat people equally.

On the basis of our earlier discussions, we may assume at this point that views of the first two kinds are unsatisfactory, and that the most adequate ethics of virtue would be one of the third sort, one that would posit two cardinal virtues, namely, benevolence and justice, considered now as dispositions or traits of character rather than as principles of duty. By a set of cardinal virtues is meant a set of virtues that (1) cannot be derived from one another and (2) all other moral virtues can be derived from or shown to be forms of them. Plato and other Greeks thought there were four cardinal virtues in this sense: wisdom, courage, temperance, and justice. Christianity is traditionally regarded as having seven cardinal virtues: three "theological" virtues—faith, hope, and love; and four "human" virtues—prudence, fortitude, temperance, and justice. This was essentially St. Thomas Aquinas's view; since St. Augustine regarded the last four as forms of love, only the first three were really cardinal for him. However, many moralists, among them Schopenhauer, have taken benevolence and justice to be the cardinal moral virtues, as I would. It seems to me that all of the usual virtues (such as love, courage, temperance, honesty, gratitude, and considerateness), at least insofar as they are *moral* virtues, can be derived from these two. Insofar as a disposition cannot be derived from benevolence and justice, I should try to argue either that it is not a *moral* virtue (e.g., I take faith, hope, and wisdom to be religious or intellectual, not moral, virtues) or that it is not a virtue at all.

ON BEING AND DOING: MORALITY OF TRAITS VS. MORALITY OF PRINCIPLES

We may now return to the issue posed by the quotation from Stephen, though we cannot debate it as fully as we should. To be or to do, that is the question. Should we construe morality as primarily a following of certain principles or as primarily a cultivation of certain dispositions and traits? Must we choose? It is hard to see how a morality of principles can get off the ground except through the development of dispositions to act in accordance with its principles, else all motivation to act on them must be of an *ad hoc* kind, either prudential or impulsively altruistic. Moreover, morality can hardly be content with a mere conformity to rules, however willing and self-conscious it may be, unless it has no interest in the spirit of its law but only in the letter. On the other hand, one cannot conceive of traits of character except as including dispositions and tendencies to act in certain ways in certain circumstances. Hating involves being disposed to kill or harm, being just involves tending to do just acts (acts that conform to the principle of justice) when the occasion calls. Again, it is hard to see how we could know what traits to encourage or inculcate if we did not subscribe to principles, for example, to the principle of utility, or to those of benevolence and justice.

I propose therefore that we regard the morality of duty and principles and the morality of virtues or traits of character not as rival kinds of morality between which we must choose, but as two complementary aspects of the same morality. Then, for every principle there will be a morally good trait, often going by the same name, consisting of a disposition or tendency to act according to it; and for every morally good trait there will be a principle defining the kind of action in which it is to express itself. To parody a famous dictum of Kant's, I am inclined to think that principles without traits are impotent and traits without principles are blind.

Even if we adopt this double-aspect conception of morality, in which principles are basic, we may still agree that morality does and must put a premium on *being* honest, conscientious, and so forth. If its sanctions or sources of motivation are not to be entirely external (for example, the prospect of being praised, blamed, rewarded, or punished by others) or adventitious (for example, a purely instinctive love of others), if it is to have adequate "internal sanctions," as Mill called them, then morality must foster the development of such dispositions and habits as have been mentioned. It could hardly be satisfied with a mere conformity to its principles even if it could provide us with fixed principles of actual duty. For such a conformity might be motivated entirely by extrinsic or nonmoral considerations, and would then be at the mercy of these other considerations. It could not be counted on in a moment of trial. Besides, since morality cannot provide us with fixed principles of actual duty but only with principles of prima facie duty, it cannot be content with the letter of its law, but must foster in us the dispositions that will sustain us in the hour of decision when we are choosing between conflicting principles of prima facie duty or trying to revise our working rules of right and wrong.

There is another reason why we must cultivate certain traits of character in ourselves and others, or why we must be certain sorts of persons. Although morality is concerned that we act in certain ways, it cannot take the hard line of insisting that we act in precisely those ways, even if those ways could be more clearly defined. We cannot praise and blame or apply other sanctions to an agent simply on the ground that he has or has not acted in conformity with certain principles. It would not be right. Through no fault of his own, the agent may not have known all the relevant facts. What action the principles of morality called for in the situation may not have been clear to him, again through no fault of his own, and he may have been honestly mistaken about his duty. Or his doing what he ought to have done might have carried with it an intolerable sacrifice on his part. He may even have been simply incapable of doing it. Morality must therefore recognize various sorts of excuses and extenuating circumstances. All it can really insist on, then, except in certain critical cases, is that we develop and manifest fixed dispositions to find out what the right thing is and to do it if possible. In this sense a person must "be this" rather than "do this." But it must be remembered that "being" involves at least *trying* to "do." Being without doing, like faith without works, is dead.

At least it will be clear from this discussion that an ethics of duty or principles also has an important place for the virtues and must put a premium on their cultivation as a part of moral education and development. The place it has for virtue and/or the virtues is, however, different from that accorded them by an ethics of virtue. Talking in terms of . . . an ethics of duty, we may say that, if we ask for *guidance* about what to do or not do, then the answer is contained, at least primarily, in two deontic principles and their corollaries, namely, the principles of beneficence and equal treatment. Given these two deontic principles, plus the necessary clarity of thought and factual knowledge, we can know what we morally ought to do or not do, except perhaps in cases of conflict between them. We also know that we should cultivate two virtues, a disposition to be beneficial (i.e., benevolence) and a disposition to treat people equally (justice as a trait). But the point of acquiring these virtues is not further guidance or instruction; the function of the virtues in an ethics of duty is not to tell us what to do but to ensure that we will do it willingly in whatever situations we may face. In an ethics of virtue, on the other hand, the virtues play a dual role—they must not only move us to do what we do, they must also tell us what to do. To parody Alfred Lord Tennyson:

> Theirs not (only) to do or die,
> Theirs (also) to reason why.

MORAL IDEALS

This is the place to mention ideals again, which are among what we called the ingredients of morality. One may, perhaps, identify moral ideals with moral principles, but, more properly speaking, moral ideals are ways of being rather than of doing. Having a moral ideal is wanting to be a person of a certain sort, wanting to have a certain trait of character rather than others, for example, moral courage or perfect integrity. That is why the use of exemplary persons like Socrates, Jesus, or Martin Luther King has been such an important part of moral education and self-development, and it is one of the reasons for the writing and reading of biographies or of novels and epics in which types of moral personality are portrayed, even if they are not all heroes or saints. Often such moral ideals of personality go beyond what can be demanded or regarded as obligatory, belonging among the things to be praised rather than required, except as one may require them of oneself. It should be remembered, however, that not all personal ideals are moral ones. Achilles, Hercules, Napoleon, and Prince Charming may all be taken as ideals, but the ideals they represent are not moral ones, even though they may not be immoral ones either. Some ideals, e.g., those of chivalry, may be partly moral and partly nonmoral. There is every reason why one should pursue nonmoral as well as moral ideals, but there is no good reason for confusing them.

When one has a moral ideal, wanting to be a certain sort of moral person, one has at least some motivation to live in a certain way, but one also has something to guide him in living. Here the idea of an ethics of virtue may have a point. One may, of course, take as one's ideal that of being a good man who always does his duty from a sense of duty, perhaps gladly, and perhaps even going a second mile on occasion. Then one's guidance clearly comes entirely from one's rules and principles of duty. However, one may also have an ideal that goes beyond anything that can be regarded by others or even oneself as strict duty or obligation, a form or style of personal being that may be morally good or virtuous, but is not morally required of one. An ethics of virtue seems to provide for such an aspiration more naturally than an ethics of duty or principle, and perhaps an adequate morality should at least contain a region in which we can follow such an idea, over and beyond the region in which we are to listen to the call of duty. There certainly should be moral heroes and saints who go beyond the merely good man, if only to serve as an inspiration to others to be better and do more than they would otherwise be or do. Granted all this, however, it still seems to me that, if one's ideal is truly a moral one, there will be nothing in it that is not covered by the principles of beneficence and justice conceived as principles of what we ought to do in the wider sense referred to earlier.

DISPOSITIONS TO BE CULTIVATED

Are there any other moral virtues to be cultivated besides benevolence and justice? No cardinal ones, of course. In this sense our answer to Socrates' question whether virtue is one or many is that it is two. We saw, however, that the principles of beneficence and equality have corollaries like telling the truth, keeping promises, etc. It follows that character traits like honesty and fidelity are virtues, though subordinate ones, and should be acquired and fostered. There will then be other such virtues corresponding to other corollaries of our main principles. Let us call all of these virtues, cardinal and noncardinal, first-order moral virtues. Besides first-order virtues like these, there are certain other moral virtues that ought also to be cultivated, which are in a way more abstract and general and may be called second-order virtues. Conscientiousness is one such virtue; it is not limited to a certain sector of the moral life, as gratitude and honesty are, but is a virtue covering the whole of the moral life. Moral courage, or courage when moral issues are at stake, is another such second-order virtue; it belongs to all sectors of the moral life. Others that overlap with these are integrity and good-will, understanding good-will in Kant's sense of respect for the moral law.

In view of what was said in a previous chapter, we must list two other second-order traits: a disposition to find out and respect the relevant facts and a disposition to think clearly. These are not just abilities but character traits; one might have the ability to think intelligently without having a disposition to use it. They are therefore virtues, though they are intellectual virtues, not moral ones. Still, though their role is not limited to the moral life, they are necessary to it. More generally speaking, we should cultivate the virtue Plato called wisdom and Aristotle practical wisdom, which they thought of as including all of the intellectual abilities and virtues essential to the moral life.

Still other second-order qualities, which may be abilities rather than virtues, but which must be cultivated for moral living, and so may, perhaps, best be mentioned here, are moral autonomy, the ability to make moral decisions and to revise one's principles if necessary, and the ability to realize vividly, in imagination and feeling, the "inner lives" of others. Of these second-order qualities, the first two have been referred to on occasion and will be again, but something should be said about the last.

If our morality is to be more than a conformity to internalized rules and principles, if it is to include and rest on an understanding of the point of these rules and principles, and certainly if it is to involve *being* a certain kind of person and not merely *doing* certain kinds of things, then we must somehow attain and develop an ability to be aware of others as persons, as important to themselves as we are to ourselves, and to have a lively and sympathetic representation in imagination of their interests and of the effects of our actions on their lives. The need for this is particularly stressed by Josiah Royce and William James. Both men point out how we usually go our own busy and self-concerned ways, with only an external awareness of the presence of others, much as if they were things, and without any realization of their inner and peculiar worlds of personal experience; and both emphasize the need and the possibility of a "higher vision of an inner significance" which pierces this "certain blindness in human beings" and enables us to realize the existence of others in a wholly different way, as we do our own.

> What then is thy neighbor? He too is a mass of states, of experi-
> ences, thoughts and desires, just as concrete, as thou art. . . . Dost
> thou believe this? Art thou sure what it means? This is for thee the
> turning-point of thy whole conduct towards him.

These are Royce's quaint old-fashioned words. Here are James's
more modern ones.

> This higher vision of an inner significance in what, until then, we
> had realized only in the dead external way, often comes over a per-
> son suddenly; and, when it does so, it makes an epoch in his history.

Royce calls this more perfect recognition of our neighbors "the
moral insight" and James says that its practical consequence is "the
well-known democratic respect for the sacredness of individuality."
It is hard to see how either a benevolent (loving) or a just (equal-
itarian) disposition could come to fruition without it. To quote James
again,

> We ought, all of us, to realize each other in this intense, pathetic,
> and important way.

Doing this is part of what is involved in fully taking the moral point
of view.

TWO QUESTIONS

We can now deal with the question, sometimes raised, whether an
action is to be judged right or wrong because of its results, because
of the principle it exemplifies, or because the motive, intention, or
trait of character involved is morally good or bad. The answer . . . is
that an action is to be judged *right* or *wrong* by reference to a principle or set of principles. Even if we say it is right or wrong because
of its effects, this means that it is right or wrong by the principle of
utility or some other teleological principle. But an act may also be
said to be *good* or *bad,* praiseworthy or blameworthy, noble or despicable, and so on, and then the moral quality ascribed to it will
depend on the agent's motive, intention, or disposition in doing it.

Another important question here is: What is moral goodness?
When is a person morally good and when are his actions, dispo-

sitions, motives, or intentions morally good? Not just when he does what is actually right, for he may do what is right from bad motives, in which case he is not morally good, or he may fail to do what is right though sincerely trying to do it, in which case he is not morally bad. Whether he and his actions are morally good or not depends, not on the rightness of what he does or on its consequences, but on his character or motives; so far the statement quoted from Hume is certainly correct. But when are his motives and dispositions morally good? Some answer that a person and his actions are morally good if and only if they are motivated wholly by a sense of duty or a desire to do what is right; the Stoics and Kant sometimes seem to take this extreme view. Others hold that a man and his actions are morally good if and only if they are motivated primarily by a sense of duty or desire to do what is right, though other motives may be present too; still others contend, with Aristotle, that they are at any rate not morally good unless they are motivated at least in part by such a sense or desire. A more reasonable view, to my mind, is that a man and his actions are morally good if it is at least true that, whatever his actual motives in acting are, his sense of duty or desire to do the right is so strong in him that it would keep him trying to do his duty anyway.

Actually, I find it hard to believe that no dispositions or motivations are good or virtuous from the moral point of view except those that include a will to do the right as such. It is more plausible to distinguish two kinds of morally good dispositions or traits of character, first, those that are usually called moral virtues and do include a will to do the right, and second, others like purely natural kindliness or gratefulness, which, while they are nonmoral, are still morality-supporting, since they dispose us to do such actions as morality requires and even to perform deeds, for example, in the case of motherly love, which are well beyond the call of duty.

It has even been alleged that conscientiousness or moral goodness in the sense of a disposition to act from a sense of duty alone is not a good thing or not a virtue—that it is more desirable to have people acting from motives like friendship, gratitude, honor, love, and the like, than from a dry or driven sense of obligation. There is something to be said for this view, though it ignores the nobility of great moral courage and of the higher reaches of moral idealism. But even if conscientiousness or good will is not the only thing that is unconditionally good, as Kant believed, or the greatest of intrinsically good things, as Ross thought, it is surely a good thing from the moral point of view. For an ethics of duty, at any rate, it must be desirable that people do what is right for its own sake, especially if they do it gladly, as a gymnast may gladly make the right move just because it is right.

For Further Reflection

1. What is Frankena's main criticism of virtue ethics? Are you convinced by them?

2. What does he propose in place of contrasting the ethics of *doing* with the ethics of *being?* How cogent are his arguments?

3. What does Frankena think the two cardinal virtues are?

4. Do you agree with Frankena that a moral person must want to do the right thing just because it is right? What if I think that I must have a self-interested reason for being moral? We will look at this issue more fully in chapter 8, but start thinking about it.

The Conscience of Huckleberry Finn

JONATHAN BENNETT

Jonathan Bennett is professor of philosophy at Syracuse University and the author of several works in philosophy. In this essay Bennett inquires into the role of sympathy in moral judgment. He considers three people who responded differently with regard to sympathy. Huckleberry Finn allowed

Reprinted from Jonathan Bennett, "The Conscience of Huckleberry Finn," *Philosophy* 49 (1974), by permission of Cambridge University Press and the author.

himself to be guided by his sympathies, thus overriding his perceived duty to turn in the runaway slave, Jim. Heinrich Himmler, the Nazi leader, though tempted to be sympathetic with regard to sending Jews to concentration camps, struggled against it, choosing instead, to follow his "duty." Jonathan Edwards, the great Puritan preacher and theologian, was altogether without sympathy for the damned, whom he believed to be justly punished. Bennett calls the morality of all three men "bad morality," but contends that Edwards was the worst of the three and Huckleberry Finn the best, based on their response to sympathy. He argues that sometimes our sympathies are better guides to moral action than our principles. The virtue of sympathy deserves greater weight than we typically give it.

I

In this paper, I shall present not just the conscience of Huckleberry Finn but those of two others as well. One of them is the conscience of Heinrich Himmler. Himmler became a Nazi in 1923; he served drably and quietly, but well, and was rewarded with increasing responsibility and power. At the peak of his career he held many offices and commands, of which the most powerful was that of leader of the SS—the principal police force of the Nazi regime. In this capacity Himmler commanded the whole concentration camp system and was responsible for the execution of the so-called final solution of the Jewish problem. It is important for my purposes that this piece of social engineering should be thought of not abstractly but in concrete terms of Jewish families being marched to what they thought were bathhouses, to the accompaniment of loudspeaker renditions of extracts from *The Merry Widow* and *Tales of Hoffmann,* there to be choked to death by poisonous gases. Altogether, Himmler succeeded in murdering about four and a half million of them, as well as several million gentiles, mainly Poles and Russians.

The other conscience to be discussed is that of the Calvinist theologian and philosopher Jonathan Edwards. He lived in the first half of the eighteenth century, and has a good claim to be considered America's first serious and considerable philosophical thinker. He was for many years a widely renowned preacher and Congregationalist minister in New England; in 1748 a dispute with his congregation led him to resign (he couldn't accept their view that unbelievers should be admitted to the Lord's Supper in the hope that it would convert them); for some years after that he worked as a missionary, preaching to Indians through an interpreter; then in 1758 he accepted the presidency of what is now Princeton University, and within two months died from a smallpox inoculation. Along the way he wrote some first-rate philosophy; his book attacking the notion of free will is still sometimes read. Why I should be interested in Edwards's *conscience* will be explained in due course.

I shall use Heinrich Himmler, Jonathan Edwards, and Huckleberry Finn to illustrate different aspects of a single theme, namely the relationship between *sympathy* on the one hand and *bad morality* on the other.

II

All that I can mean by a "bad morality" is a morality whose principles I deeply disapprove of. When I call a morality bad, I cannot prove that mine is better; but when I here call any morality bad, I think you will agree with me that it is bad; and that is all I need.

There could be dispute as to whether the springs of someone's actions constitute a *morality*. I think, though, that we must admit that someone who acts in ways which conflict grossly with our morality may nevertheless have a morality of his own—a set of principles of action which he sincerely assents to, so that for him the problem of acting well or rightly or in obedience to conscience is the problem of conforming to *those* principles. The problem of conscientiousness can arise as acutely for a bad morality as for any other: Rotten principles may be as difficult to keep as decent ones.

As for "sympathy" I use this term to cover every sort of fellow-feeling, as when one feels pity over someone's loneliness, or horrified compassion over his pain, or when one feels a shrinking reluctance to act in a way which will bring misfortune to someone else. These *feelings* must not be confused with *moral judgments*. My sympathy for someone in distress may lead me to help him, or even to think that I ought to help him; but in itself it is not a judgment about what I ought to do but just a *feeling* for him in his plight. We shall get some light on the difference between feelings and moral judgments when we consider Huckleberry Finn.

Obviously, feelings can impel one to action, and so can moral judgments; and in a particular case sympathy and morality may pull in opposite directions. This can happen not just with bad moralities, but also with good ones like yours and mine. For example, a small child, sick and miserable, clings tightly to his mother and screams in terror when she tries to pass him over to the doctor to be examined. If the mother gave way to her sympathy, that is to her feeling for the child's misery and fright, she would hold it close and not let the doctor come near; but don't we agree that it might be wrong for her to act on such a feeling? Quite generally, then, anyone's moral principles may apply to a particular situation in a way which runs contrary to the particular thrusts of fellow-feeling that he has in that situation. My immediate concern is with sympathy in relation to bad morality, but not because such conflicts occur only when the morality is bad.

Now, suppose that someone who accepts a bad morality is struggling to make himself act in accordance with it in a particular situation where his sympathies pull him another way. He sees the struggle as one between doing the right, conscientious thing, and acting wrongly and weakly, like the mother who won't let the doctor come near her sick, frightened baby. Since we don't accept this person's morality, we may see the situation very differently, thoroughly disapproving of the action he regards as the right one, and endorsing the action which from his point of view constitutes weakness and backsliding.

Conflicts between sympathy and bad morality won't always be like this, for we won't disagree with every single dictate of a bad morality. Still, it can happen in the way I have described, with the agent's right action being our wrong one, and vice versa. That is just what happens in a certain episode in Chapter 16 of *The Adventures of Huckleberry Finn,* an episode which brilliantly illustrates how fiction can be instructive about real life.

III

Huck Finn has been helping his slave friend Jim to run away from Miss Watson, who is Jim's owner. In their raft-journey down the Mississippi River, they are near to the place at which Jim will become legally free. Now let Huck take over the story:

> Jim said it made him all over trembly and feverish to be so close to freedom. Well I can tell you it made me all over trembly and feverish, too, to hear him, because I begun to get it through my head that he *was* most free—and who was to blame for it? Why, *me*. I couldn't get that out of my conscience, no how nor no way. . . . It hadn't ever come home to me, before, what this thing was that I was doing. But now it did; and it stayed with me, and scorched me more and more. I tried to make out to myself that *I* warn't to blame, because I didn't run Jim off from his rightful owner; but it warn't no use, conscience up and say, every time: "But you knowed he was running for his freedom, and you could a paddled ashore and told somebody." That was so—I couldn't get around that, no way. That was where it pinched. Conscience says to me: "What had poor Miss Watson done to you, that you could see her nigger go off right under your eyes and never say one single word? What did that poor old woman do to you, that you could treat her so mean? . . ." I got to feeling so mean and miserable I most wished I was dead.

Jim speaks his plan to save up to buy his wife, and then his children, out of slavery; and he adds that if the children cannot be bought he will arrange to steal them. Huck is horrified:

> Thinks I, this is what comes of my not thinking. Here was this nigger which I had as good as helped to run away, coming right out flat-footed and saying he would steal his children—children that belonged to a man I didn't even know; a man that hadn't ever done me no harm.
>
> I was sorry to hear Jim say that, it was such a lowering of him. My conscience got to stirring me up hotter than ever, until at last I says to it: "Let up on me—it ain't too late, yet—I'll paddle ashore at first light, and tell." I felt easy, and happy, and light as a feather, right off. All my troubles was gone.

This is bad morality all right. In his earliest years Huck wasn't taught any principles, and the only ones he has encountered since then are those of rural Missouri, in which slave-owning is just one kind of ownership and is not subject to critical pressure. It hasn't occurred to Huck to question those principles. So the action, to us abhorrent, of turning Jim in to the authorities presents itself *clearly* to Huck as the right thing to do.

For us, both morality and sympathy would dictate helping Jim to escape. If we felt any conflict, it would have both of these on one side and something else on the other—greed for a reward, or fear of punishment. But Huck's morality conflicts with his sympathy, that is, with his unargued, natural feeling for his friend. The conflict starts when Huck sets off in the canoe toward the shore, pretending that he is going to reconnoiter, but really planning to turn Jim in:

> As I shoved off, [Jim] says: "Pooty soon I'll be a-shout'n for joy, en I'll say, it's all on accounts o'Huck I's a free man . . . Jim won't ever forgit you, Huck; you's de bes' fren' Jim's ever had; en you's de *only* fren' old Jim's got now."
>
> I was paddling off, all in a sweat to tell on him; but when he says this, it seemed to kind of take the tuck all out of me. I went along slow then, and I warn't right down certain whether I was glad I started or whether I warn't. When I was fifty yards off, Jim says:
>
> "Dah you goes, de ole true Huck; de on'y white genlman dat ever kep' his promise to ole Jim." Well, I just felt sick. But I says, I *got* to do it—I can't get *out* of it.

In the upshot, sympathy wins over morality. Huck hasn't the strength of will to do what he sincerely thinks he ought to do. Two men hunting for runaway slaves ask him whether the man on his raft is black or white:

> I didn't answer up prompt. I tried to, but the words wouldn't come. I tried, for a second or two, to brace up and out with it, but I warn't man enough—hadn't the spunk of a rabbit. I see I was weakening; so I just give up trying, and up and says: "He's white."

So Huck enables Jim to escape, thus acting weakly and wickedly— he thinks. In this conflict between sympathy and morality, sympathy wins.

One critic has cited this episode in support of the statement that Huck suffers "excruciating moments of wavering between honesty and respectability." That is hopelessly wrong, and I agree with the perceptive comment on it by another critic, who says:

> The conflict waged in Huck is much more serious: He scarcely cares for respectability and never hesitates to relinquish it, but he does care for honesty and gratitude—and both honesty and gratitude require that he should give Jim up. It is not, in Huck, honesty at war with respectability but love and compassion for Jim struggling against his conscience. His decision is for Jim and hell: a right decision made in the mental chains that Huck never breaks. His concern for Jim is and remains *irrational*. Huck finds many reasons for giving Jim up and none for stealing him. To the end Huck sees his compassion for Jim as a weak, ignorant, and wicked felony.[1]

That is precisely correct—and it can have that virtue only because Mark Twain wrote the episode with such unerring precision. The crucial point concerns *reasons,* which all occur on one side of the conflict. On the side of conscience we have principles, arguments, considerations, ways of looking at things:

> "It hadn't ever come home to me before what I was doing"
>> "I tried to make out that I warn't to blame"
>> "Conscience said 'But you knowed . . .'—I couldn't get around that"
>> "What had poor Miss Watson done to you?"
>> "This is what comes of my not thinking"
>> ". . . children that belonged to a man I didn't even know"

On the other side, the side of feeling, we get nothing like that. When Jim rejoices in Huck, as his only friend, Huck doesn't consider the claims of friendship or have the situation "come home" to him in a different light. All that happens is: "When he says this, it seemed to kind of take the tuck all out of me. I went along slow then, and I warn't right down certain whether I was glad I started or whether I warn't." Again, Jim's words about Huck's "promise" to him don't give Huck any *reason* for changing his plan: In his morality promises to slaves probably don't count. Their effect on him is of a different kind: "Well, I just felt sick." And when the moment

---

[1]M. J. Sidnell, "Huck Finn and Jim," *The Cambridge Quarterly,* vol. 2, pp. 205–6.

for final decision comes, Huck doesn't weigh up pros and cons: he simply *fails* to do what he believes to be right—he isn't strong enough, hasn't "the spunk of a rabbit." This passage in the novel is notable not just for its finely wrought irony, with Huck's weakness of will leading him to do the right thing, but also for its masterly handling of the difference between general moral principles and particular unreasoned emotional pulls.

IV

Consider now another case of bad morality in conflict with human sympathy: the case of the odious Himmler. Here, from a speech he made to some SS generals, is an indication of the content of his morality:

> What happens to a Russian, to a Czech, does not interest me in the slightest. What the nations can offer in the way of good blood of our type, we will take, if necessary by kidnapping their children and raising them here with us. Whether nations live in prosperity or starve to death like cattle interests me only in so far as we need them as slaves to our *Kultur;* otherwise it is of no interest to me. Whether 10,000 Russian females fall down from exhaustion while digging an antitank ditch interests me only in so far as the antitank ditch for Germany is finished.[2]

But has this a moral basis at all? And if it has, was there in Himmler's own mind any conflict between morality and sympathy? Yes, there was. Here is more from the same speech:

> I also want to talk to you quite frankly on a very grave matter . . . I mean . . . the extermination of the Jewish race. . . . Most of you must know what it means when 100 corpses are lying side by side, or 500, or 1,000. To have stuck it out and at the same time—apart from exceptions caused by human weakness—to have remained decent

---

[2]Quoted in William L. Shirer, *The Rise and Fall of the Third Reich* (New York, 1960), pp. 937–38. Next quotation: ibid., p. 966. All further quotations relating to Himmler are from Roger Manwell and Heinrich Fraenkel, *Heinrich Himmler* (London, 1965), pp. 132, 197, 184 (twice), 187.

fellows, that is what has made us hard. This is a page of glory in our history which has never been written and is never to be written.

Himmler saw his policies as being hard to implement while still retaining one's human sympathies—while still remaining a "decent fellow." He is saying that only the weak take the easy way out and just squelch their sympathies, and is praising the stronger and more glorious course of retaining one's sympathies while acting in violation of them. In the same spirit, he ordered that when executions were carried out in concentration camps, those responsible "are to be influenced in such a way as to suffer no ill effect in their character and mental attitude." A year later he boasted that the SS had wiped out the Jews

> without our leaders and their men suffering any damage in their minds and souls. The danger was considerable, for there was only a narrow path between the Scylla of their becoming heartless ruffians unable any longer to treasure life, and the Charybdis of their becoming soft and suffering nervous breakdowns.

And there really can't be any doubt that the basis of Himmler's policies was a set of principles which constituted his morality—a sick, bad, wicked *morality*. He described himself as caught in "the old tragic conflict between will and obligation." And when his physician Kersten protested at the intention to destroy the Jews, saying that the suffering involved was "not to be contemplated," Kersten reports that Himmler replied that

> He knew that it would mean much suffering for the Jews. . . . "It is the curse of greatness that it must step over dead bodies to create new life. Yet we must . . . cleanse the soil or it will never bear fruit. It will be a great burden for me to bear."

This, I submit, is the language of morality.

So in this case, tragically, bad morality won out over sympathy. I am sure that many of Himmler's killers did extinguish their sympathies, becoming "heartless ruffians" rather than "decent fellows"; but not Himmler himself. Although his policies ran against the human grain to a horrible degree, he did not sandpaper down his emotional surfaces so that there was no grain there, allowing his actions to slide along smoothly and easily. He did, after all, bear his hideous burden, and even paid a price for it. He suffered a variety of nervous and physical disabilities, including nausea and stomach-convulsions, and Kersten was doubtless right in saying that these were "the expression of a psychic division which extended over his whole life."

This same division must have been present in some of those officials of the Church who ordered heretics to be tortured so as to change their theological opinions. Along with the brutes and the cold careerists, there must have been some who cared, and who suffered from the conflict between their sympathies and their bad morality.

V

In the conflict between sympathy and bad morality, then, the victory may go to sympathy as in the case of Huck Finn, or to morality as in the case of Himmler.

Another possibility is that the conflict may be avoided by giving up, or not ever having, those sympathies which might interfere with one's principles. That seems to have been the case with Jonathan Edwards. I am afraid that I shall be doing an injustice to Edwards's many virtues, and to his great intellectual energy and inventiveness; for my concern is only with the worst thing about him—namely his morality, which was worse than Himmler's.

According to Edwards, God condemns some men to an eternity of unimaginably awful pain, though he arbitrarily spares others— "arbitrarily" because none deserve to be spared:

> Natural men are held in the hand of God over the pit of hell; they have deserved the fiery pit, and are already sentenced to it; and God is dreadfully provoked, his anger is as great toward them as to those that are actually suffering the executions of the fierceness of his wrath in hell . . . ; the devil is waiting for them, hell is gaping for them, the flames gather and flash about them, and would fain lay hold on them . . . ; and . . . there are no means within reach that can be any security to them. . . . All that preserves them is the mere arbitrary will, and unconvenanted unobliged forebearance of an incensed God.[3]

---

[3]Vergilius Ferm (ed.), *Puritan Sage: Collected Writings of Jonathan Edwards* (New York, 1953), p. 370. Next three quotations: ibid., p. 366, p. 294 ("no more than infinite"), p. 372.

Notice that he says "they have deserved the fiery pit." Edwards insists that men *ought* to be condemned to eternal pain; and his position isn't that this is right because God wants it, but rather that God wants it because it is right. For him, moral standards exist independently of God, and God can be assessed in the light of them (and of course found to be perfect). For example, he says:

> They deserve to be cast into hell; so that . . . justice never stands in the way, it makes no objection against God's using his power at any moment to destroy them. Yea, on the contrary, justice calls aloud for an infinite punishment of their sins.

Elsewhere, he gives elaborate arguments to show that God is acting justly in damning sinners. For example, he argues that a punishment should be exactly as bad as the crime being punished; God is infinitely excellent; so any crime against him is infinitely bad; and so eternal damnation is exactly right as a punishment—it is infinite, but, as Edwards is careful also to say, it is "no more than infinite."

Of course, Edwards himself didn't torment the damned; but the question still arises of whether his sympathies didn't conflict with his *approval* of eternal torment. Didn't he find it painful to contemplate any fellow-human's being tortured forever? Apparently not:

> The God that holds you over the pit of hell, much as one holds a spider or some loathsome insect over the fire, abhors you, and is dreadfully provoked . . . he is of purer eyes than to bear to have you in his sight; you are ten thousand times so abominable in his eyes as the most hateful venomous serpent is in ours.

When God is presented as being as misanthropic as that, one suspects misanthropy in the theologian. This suspicion is increased when Edwards claims that "the saints in glory will . . . understand how terrible the sufferings of the damned are; yet . . . will not be sorry for [them]."[4] He bases this partly on a view of human nature whose ugliness he seems not to notice:

[4]This and the next two quotations are from "The End of the Wicked Contemplated by the Righteous: Or, The Torments of the Wicked in Hell, No Occasion of Grief to the Saints in Heaven," from *The Works of President Edwards* (London, 1817), vol. 4, pp. 507–8, 511–12, and 509 respectively.

> The seeing of the calamities of others tends to heighten the sense
> of our own enjoyments. When the saints in glory, therefore, shall
> see the doleful state of the damned, how will this heighten their
> sense of the blessedness of their own state. . . . When they shall see
> how miserable others of their fellow-creatures are . . . when they shall
> see the smoke of their torment . . . and hear their dolorous shrieks
> and cries, and consider that they in the mean time are in the most
> blissful state, and shall surely be in it to all eternity; how they will
> rejoice!

I hope this is less than the whole truth! His other main point about
why the saints will rejoice to see the torments of the damned is
that it is *right* that they should do so:

> The heavenly inhabitants . . . will have no love nor pity to the
> damned. . . . [This will not show] a want of spirit of love in them for
> the heavenly inhabitants will know that it is not fit that they should
> love [the damned] because they will know then, that God has no
> love to them, nor pity for them.

The implication that *of course* one can adjust one's feelings of pity
so that they conform to the dictates of some authority—doesn't this
suggest that ordinary human sympathies played only a small part
in Edwards's life?

VI

Huck Finn, whose sympathies are wide and deep, could never avoid
the conflict in that way; but he is determined to avoid it, and so
he opts for the only other alternative he can see—to give up morality altogether. After he has tricked the slave-hunters, he returns to
the raft and undergoes a peculiar crisis:

> I got aboard the raft, feeling bad and low, because I knowed very
> well I had done wrong, and I see it warn't no use for me to try to
> learn to do right; a body that don't get *started* right when he's lit-
> tle, ain't got no show—when the pinch comes there ain't nothing to
> back him up and keep him to his work, and so he gets beat. Then
> I thought a minute, and says to myself, hold on—s'pose you'd a
> done right and give Jim up; would you feel better than what you
> do now? No, says I, I'd feel bad—I'd feel just the same way I do

now. Well, then, says I, what's the use you learning to do right, when it's troublesome to do right and ain't no trouble to do wrong, and the wages is just the same? I was stuck. I couldn't answer that. So I reckoned I wouldn't bother no more about it, but after this always do whichever come handiest at the time.

Huck clearly cannot conceive of having any morality except the one he has learned—too late, he thinks—from his society. He is not entirely a prisoner of that morality, because he does after all reject it; but for him that is a decision to relinquish morality as such; he cannot envisage revising his morality, altering its content in the face of the various pressures to which it is subject, including pressures from his sympathies. For example, he does not begin to approach the thought that slavery should be rejected on moral grounds, or the thought that what he is doing is not theft because a person cannot be owned and therefore cannot be stolen.

The basic trouble is that he cannot or will not engage in abstract intellectual operations of any sort. In Chapter 33 he finds himself "feeling to blame, somehow" for something he knows he had no hand in; he assumes that this feeling is a deliverance of conscience; and this confirms him in his belief that conscience shouldn't be listened to:

It don't make no difference whether you do right or wrong, a person's conscience ain't got no sense, and just goes for him *anyway*. If I had a yaller dog that didn't know no more than a person's conscience does, I would poison him. It takes up more than all of a person's insides, and yet ain't no good, nohow.

That brisk, incurious dismissiveness fits well with the comprehensive rejection of morality back on the raft. But this is a digression.

On the raft, Huck decides not to live by principles, but just to do whatever "comes handiest at the time"—always acting according to the mood of the moment. Since the morality he is rejecting is narrow and cruel, and his sympathies are broad and kind, the results will be good. But moral principles are good to have, because they help to protect one from acting badly at moments when one's sympathies happen to be in abeyance. On the highest possible estimate of the role one's sympathies should have, one can still allow for principles as embodiments of one's best feelings, one's broadest and keenest sympathies. On that view, principles can help one across intervals when one's feelings are at less than their best, i.e. through periods of misanthropy or meanness or self-centeredness or depression or anger.

What Huck didn't see is that one can live by principles and yet have ultimate control over their content. And one way such control can be exercised is by checking one's principles in the light of one's sympathies. This is sometimes a pretty straightforward matter. It can happen that a certain moral principle becomes untenable—meaning literally that one cannot hold it any longer—because it conflicts intolerably with the pity or revulsion or whatever that one feels when one sees what the principle leads to. One's experience may play a large part here: Experiences evoke feelings, and feelings force one to modify principles. Something like this happened to the English poet Wilfred Owen, whose experiences in the First World War transformed him from an enthusiastic soldier into a virtual pacifist. I can't document his change of conscience in detail; but I want to present something which he wrote about the way experience can put pressure on morality.

The Latin poet Horace wrote that it is sweet and fitting (or right) to die for one's country—*dulce et decorum est pro patria mori*—and Owen wrote a fine poem about how experience could lead one to relinquish that particular moral principle.[5] He describes a man who is too slow donning his gas mask during a gas attack—"As under a green sea I saw him drowning," Owen says. The poem ends like this:

> In all my dreams before my helpless sight
> He plunges at me, guttering, choking, drowning.
> If in some smothering dreams, you too could pace
> Behind the wagon that we flung him in,
> And watch the white eyes writhing in his face,
> His hanging face, like a devil's sick of sin;
> If you could hear, at every jolt, the blood
> Come gargling from the froth-corrupted lungs.
> Bitter as the end

[5]We are grateful to the Executors of the Estate of Harold Owen, and to Chatto and Windus Ltd. for permission to quote from Wilfred Owen's "Dulce et Decorum Est" and "Insensibility."

Of vile, incurable sores on innocent tongues,—
My friend, you would not tell with such high zest
To children ardent for some desperate glory,
The old Lie; Dulce et decorum est
Pro patria mori.

There is a difficulty about drawing from all this a moral for ourselves. I imagine that we agree in our rejection of slavery, eternal
damnation, genocide, and uncritical patriotic self-abnegation; so we
shall agree that Huck Finn, Jonathan Edwards, Heinrich Himmler,
and the poet Horace would all have done well to bring certain of
their principles under severe pressure from ordinary human sympathies. But then we can say this because we can say that all those
are bad moralities, whereas we cannot look at our own moralities
and declare them bad. This is not arrogance; it is obviously incoherent for someone to declare the system of moral principles that
he *accepts* to be *bad,* just as one cannot coherently say of anything
that one *believes* it but it is *false.*

Still, although I can't point to any of my beliefs and say "That is
false," I don't doubt that some of my beliefs *are* false; and so I should
try to remain open to correction. Similarly, I accept every single item
in my morality—that is inevitable—but I am sure that my morality
could be improved, which is to say that it could undergo changes
which I should be glad of once I had made them. So I must try to
keep my morality open to revision, exposing it to whatever valid
pressures there are—including pressures from my sympathies.

I don't give my sympathies a blank check in advance. In a conflict between principle and sympathy, principles ought sometimes
to win. For example, I think it was right to take part in the Second World War on the allied side; there were many ghastly individual incidents which might have led someone to doubt the rightness of his participation in that war; and I think it would have been
right for such a person to keep his sympathies in a subordinate
place on those occasions, not allowing them to modify his principles in such a way as to make a pacifist of him.

Still, one's sympathies should be kept as sharp and sensitive and
aware as possible, and not only because they can sometimes affect
one's principles or one's conduct or both. Owen, at any rate, says
that feelings and sympathies are vital even when they can do nothing but bring pain and distress. In another poem he speaks of the

blessings of being numb in one's feelings: "Happy are the men who yet before they are killed/Can let their veins run cold," he says. These are the ones who do not suffer from any compassion which, as Owen puts it, "makes their feet/Sore on the alleys cobbled with their brothers." He contrasts these "happy" ones, who "lose all imagination," with himself and others "who with a thought besmirch/Blood over all our soul." Yet the poem's verdict goes against the "happy" ones. Owen does not say that they will act worse than the others whose souls are besmirched with blood because of their keen awareness of human suffering. He merely says that they are the losers because they have cut themselves off from the human condition:

> By choice they made themselves immune
> To pity and whatever moans in man
> Before the last sea and the hapless stars;
> Whatever mourns when many leave these shores;
> Whatever shares
> The eternal reciprocity of tears.

For Further Reflection

1. Analyze Bennett's arguments. What is his main thesis? Do you agree with him? Explain your answer.

2. Why does Bennett think that the Calvinist theologian, Jonathan Edwards, had a worse morality than the Nazi leader, Heinrich Himmler? Are his arguments persuasive? What would a defender of Edwards say on his behalf?

3. What is the significance of conscience for Bennett?

Further Readings for Chapter 6

Anscombe, Elizabeth. "Modern Moral Philosophy." *Philosophy* 33 (1958).

Blum, Lawrence A. *Friendship, Altruism and Morality.* London: Routledge and Kegan Paul, 1980.

Foot, Philippa. *Virtues and Vices.* Oxford: Blackwell, 1978. A collection of articles by one of the foremost virtue ethicists.

French, Peter, T. Uehling, and H. K. Wettstein, eds. *Midwest Studies in Philosophy*. Vol 13, *Ethical Theory: Character and Virtue*. South Bend, Ind.: University of Notre Dame Press, 1988.
This book contains several important recent articles on the virtues, including David Norton's "Moral Minimalism and the Development of Moral Character."

Kruschwitz, Robert, and Robert Roberts, eds. *The Virtues*. Belmont, Calif.: Wadsworth, 1987. Contains excellent readings and bibliography.

Loudan, Robert. "Some Vices of Virtue Ethics." *American Philosophical Quarterly* 21 (1984). Reprinted in Kruschwitz and Roberts, *The Virtues*.

MacIntyre, Alasdair. *After Virtue*. South Bend, Ind.: University of Notre Dame Press, 1981.

Murdoch, Iris. *The Sovereignty of Good*. New York: Schocken Books, 1971.

Taylor, Richard. *Ethics, Faith and Reason*. Englewood Cliffs, N.J.: Prentice-Hall, 1985.

Wallace, James. *Virtues and Vices*. Ithaca, N.Y.: Cornell University Press, 1978.

CHAPTER 7

Virtues and Vices

This chapter presents several literary and philosophical writings on particular virtues and vices. As Frankena pointed out in the last chapter, all moral theories respect virtues and deplore vices, though to different degrees and in different ways. In chapter 3 we studied moral relativism and its opposite, moral objectivism. We can apply what we said there to the virtues and vices. Moral objectivists believe they have universal validity, but relativists believe that virtues and vices are entirely dependent on culture for their significance.

We begin with the Sermon on the Mount given in Galilee by Jesus of Nazareth (c. A.D. 30), in which he announces a set of *virtues,* including mercy, love of righteousness, meekness, and love of one's enemies, as well as a set of *vices,* including lust, vengefulness, and hate. Early Christians, influenced by the Sermon on the Mount, were pacifists and refused to fight in the army. Can you see why? Later, especially after the Roman Empire made Christianity the official religion in the fourth century, the more pacifistic virtues were interpreted as ideals for the kingdom of heaven, but not to be taken literally in this world where sin was rampant.

I have also included Jesus' classic parable of the Good Samaritan.

After this we include Tolstoy's stories about greed and love, Kant's essay on jealousy and ingratitude, and selections on other vices and virtues from Gansberg, Keller, Stockdale, the Bible, Russell, and Colson.

The Sermon on the Mount;
The Good Samaritan

JESUS OF NAZARETH

Jesus of Nazareth (died c. A.D. 30) is the founder of the Christian religion and believed by Christians to have risen from the dead. He is considered by them to be the Son of God and Savior of the world. In this famous sermon given on a mountain near Capernaum in modern Israel, Jesus sets forth a radical ethic of nonviolence and love. This is followed by his parable of the Good Samaritan. The Samaritans were a despised ethnic group, with whom the Jews would have no relations. Jesus broke with his culture in his fellowship with the Samaritans.

THE SERMON ON THE MOUNT

Jesus saw the crowds and went up a hill, where he sat down. His disciples gathered around him, and he began to teach them:

"Happy are those who know they are spiritually poor;
the Kingdom of heaven belongs to them!
"Happy are those who mourn;
God will comfort them!
"Happy are the meek;
they will receive what God has promised!
"Happy are those whose greatest desire is to do what God requires;
God will satisfy them fully!
"Happy are those who are merciful to others;
God will be merciful to them!
"Happy are the pure in heart;
they will see God!
"Happy are those who work for peace among men;
God will call them his sons!

New Testament: Matthew 5; Luke 10.

"Happy are those who are persecuted because they do what
God requires;
the Kingdom of heaven belongs to them!
"Happy are you when men insult you, and persecute you, and
tell all kinds of evil lies against you because you are my followers. Be glad and happy, because a great reward is kept for
you in heaven. This is how men persecuted the prophets who
lived before you."

"You are like salt for all mankind. But if salt loses its taste, there
is no way to make it salty again. It has become worthless, so it is
thrown away and people walk on it.

"You are like light for the whole world. A city built on a hill
cannot be hid. No one lights a lamp to put it under a bowl; instead
he puts it on the lampstand, where it gives light for everyone in
the house. In the same way your light must shine before people,
so that they will see the good things you do and give praise to
your Father in heaven."

"Do not think that I have come to do away with the Law of
Moses and the teachings of the prophets. I have not come to do
away with them, but to make their teachings come true. Remember this! As long as heaven and earth last, the least point or the
smallest detail of the Law will not be done away with—not until
the end of all things. So then, whoever disobeys even the smallest
of the commandments, and teaches others to do the same, will be
least in the Kingdom of heaven. On the other hand, whoever obeys
the Law, and teaches others to do the same, will be great in the
Kingdom of heaven. I tell you, then, that you will be able to enter
the Kingdom of heaven only if you are more faithful than the teachers of the Law and the Pharisees in doing what God requires."

"You have heard that men were told in the past, 'Do not murder; anyone who commits murder will be brought before the judge.'
But now I tell you: whoever is angry with his brother will be brought
before the judge; whoever calls his brother 'You good-for-nothing!'
will be brought before the Council; and whoever calls his brother
a worthless fool will be in danger of going to the fire of hell. So
if you are about to offer your gift to God at the altar and there you
remember that your brother has something against you, leave your

gift there in front of the altar and go at once to make peace with your brother; then come back and offer your gift to God.

"If a man brings a lawsuit against you and takes you to court, be friendly with him while there is time, before you get to court; once you are there he will turn you over to the judge, who will hand you over to the police, and you will be put in jail. There you will stay, I tell you, until you pay the last penny of your fine."

"You have heard that it was said, 'Do not commit adultery.' But now I tell you: anyone who looks at a woman and wants to possess her is guilty of committing adultery with her in his heart. So if your right eye causes you to sin, take it out and throw it away! It is much better for you to lose a part of your body than to have your whole body thrown into hell. If your right hand causes you to sin, cut it off and throw it away! It is much better for you to lose one of your limbs than to have your whole body go off to hell."

"It was also said, 'Anyone who divorces his wife must give her a written notice of divorce.' But now I tell you: if a man divorces his wife, and she has not been unfaithful, then he is guilty of making her commit adultery if she marries again; and the man who marries her also commits adultery."

"You have also heard that men were told in the past, 'Do not break your promise, but do what you have sworn to the Lord to do.' But now I tell you: do not use any vow when you make a promise; do not swear by heaven, because it is God's throne; nor by earth, because it is the resting place for his feet; nor by Jerusalem, because it is the city of the great King. Do not even swear by your head, because you cannot make a single hair white or black. Just say 'Yes' or 'No'—anything else you have to say comes from the Evil One."

"You have heard that it was said, 'An eye for an eye, and a tooth for a tooth.' But now I tell you: do not take revenge on someone who does you wrong. If anyone slaps you on the right cheek, let him slap your left cheek too. And if someone takes you to court to sue you for your shirt, let him have your coat as well. And if one of the occupation troops forces you to carry his pack one mile, carry it another mile. When someone asks you for something, give it to him; when someone wants to borrow something, lend it to him."

"You have heard that it was said, 'Love your friends, hate your enemies.' But now I tell you: love your enemies, and pray for those who persecute you, so that you will become the sons of your Father in heaven. For he makes his sun to shine on bad and good people alike, and gives rain to those who do good and those who do evil. Why should God reward you if you love only the people who love you? Even the tax collectors do that! And if you speak only to your friends, have you done anything out of the ordinary? Even the pagans do that! You must be perfect—just as your Father in heaven is perfect."

THE GOOD SAMARITAN

A certain teacher of the Law came up and tried to trap Jesus. "Teacher," he asked, "what must I do to receive eternal life?" Jesus answered him, "What do the Scriptures say? How do you interpret them?" The man answered, "'You must love the Lord your God with all your heart, with all your soul, with all your strength, and with all your mind'; and, 'You must love your fellow-man as yourself.'" "Your answer is correct," replied Jesus; "do this and you will live."

But the teacher of the Law wanted to put himself in the right, so he asked Jesus, "Who is my fellow-man?" Jesus answered, "There was a man who was going down from Jerusalem to Jericho, when robbers attacked him, stripped him, and beat him up, leaving him half dead. It so happened that a priest was going down that road; when he saw the man he walked on by, on the other side. In the same way a Levite also came there, went over and looked at the man, and then walked on by, on the other side. But a certain Samaritan who was traveling that way came upon him, and when he saw the man his heart was filled with pity. He went over to him, poured oil and wine on his wounds and bandaged them; then he put the man on his own animal and took him to an inn, where he took care of him. The next day he took out two silver coins and gave them to the innkeeper. 'Take care of him,' he told the innkeeper, 'and when I come back this way I will pay you back whatever you spend on him.'" And Jesus concluded, "In your opinion, which one of these three acted like a fellow-man toward the man attacked by the robbers?" The teacher of the Law answered, "The one who was kind to him." Jesus replied, "You go, then, and do the same."

For Further Reflection

1. Can you detect a pattern of virtue in these teachings of Jesus? Compare and contrast them with contemporary virtues of acquisitiveness and good business sense or with the Greek virtues of wisdom, courage, pride, and self-control.

2. Evaluate these teachings, for example, "If your right eye causes you to sin, take it out and throw it away." How should we interpret them? What are their implications?

3. What does the parable of the Good Samaritan teach us? If moral relativism is correct, isn't the Good Samaritan really immoral, since his culture forbade helping their enemies, the Jews? So if the Good Samaritan is really virtuous, does that indicate that moral objectivism is true?

How Much Land Does a Man Need?
The Vice of Greed

LEO TOLSTOY

Leo Nicolayevich Tolstoy (1828–1910) was born to a Russian noble family and became one of the greatest Russian writers of all time. Among his most famous works are *War and Peace* and *Anna Karenina*. He was a deeply spiritual, Christian anarchist, whose works were considered heretical by the Russian Orthodox Church, which banned his book *What I Believe* (1899) and finally excommunicated him in 1901. During the last years of his life, he liberated his peasants, gave them most of his possessions, and lived

---

Translated from Leo Tolstoy, "How Much Land Does a Man Need?"

like a peasant, a frugal, ascetic life. We get a powerful glimpse of his philosophy of life in this parable on greed.

1

An elder sister came to visit her younger sister in the country. The elder was married to a merchant in town, the younger to a peasant in the village. As the sisters sat drinking their tea and talking, the elder began to talk proudly of the advantages of town life, saying in what comfort they lived there, how well they dressed, what fine clothes her children wore, what good things they ate and drank, and how she went to the theatre and other amusements.

The younger sister did not like this at all, and in turn spoke ill of the life of a merchant and praised the life of a peasant.

'I would not change my way of life for yours,' said she. 'We may live roughly, but at least we have no worries. You may have better food and clothes and more amusements than we have, but though you often earn more than you need, you may easily lose all you have. People who are rich one day are often begging their bread next day. Our way is safer. Though a peasant's life is not a rich one, it is a long one. We shall never have a lot of money, but we shall always have enough to eat.'

'Enough!' laughed the older sister. 'Yes, if you want to live like the animals! What do you know of fine living and good manners! However hard your husband may work, you will die as you are living—on a waste heap—and your children also!'

'Well, what of that?' replied the younger sister. 'Of course our work is rough and hard. But it is also sure, and we need not bow down to anyone. But you, in your towns, have all kinds of trouble; to-day all may be well, but to-morrow the Devil may lead your husband into wrong-doing with cards or wine, and all will be lost. Such things happen often!'

Pahom, the master of the house, was lying on the top of the stove and he listened to the women's talk.

'It is perfectly true,' he said. 'We peasants are so busy growing food in the fields from the time we are children, that we have no time to let any foolish ideas get into our heads. Our only trouble is that we have not enough land. If I had plenty of land I should not fear even the Devil himself!'

The women finished their tea, talked for a while about dress, and then cleared away the tea-things and lay down to sleep.

But the Devil had been sitting behind the stove and had heard all that was said. He was pleased that the peasant's wife had caused her husband to talk so proudly, and that he had said that if he had plenty of land he would not fear even the Devil himself.

'All right,' thought the Devil. 'We will have a test. I will give you enough land; and because of that land I will get you into my power.'

2

Near the village there lived a lady who owned about three hundred acres of land. The peasants had always liked her until she put an old soldier in charge of her land, and he began to annoy the people by making them pay fines. Although Pahom tried to be very careful, again and again one of his horses went into the lady's corn, a cow of his wandered into her garden, or his oxen got into her fields—and always he had to pay a fine.

Each time Pahom paid the fine unwillingly, and then went home in anger and was rough with his family. All through that summer Pahom was in trouble because of this old soldier, and he was even glad when winter came and the cattle had to be put under cover. Though he disliked having to buy hay for them when they could no longer feed in the fields, at least he was free from worrying about where they were.

In the winter the peasants heard that the lady was going to sell her land and that the keeper of the inn on the main road was making an offer for it. This news troubled them greatly.

'Indeed,' they thought, 'if the innkeeper gets the land, he will annoy us with fines more than the old soldier does. We all depend upon that land.'

So the peasants went, in the name of their Village Society, and asked the lady not to sell the land to the innkeeper, offering her a better price for it themselves. The lady agreed to let them have it. Then the peasants tried to arrange for the Society to buy the whole of it, so that they might all share it. They met twice to discuss the question, but could not reach an agreement. The Devil spread doubt among them, and they would not trust one another.

So they decided to buy the land separately, each taking as much as he could afford. And the lady agreed to this plan also.

Soon Pahom heard that a man who lived near him was buying fifty acres, and that the lady had agreed to accept a half of the payment in ready money and wait a year for the other half. Pahom wished that he, too, could buy some land.

'That is bad,' he thought. 'The land is all being sold, and I shall get none of it.' So he spoke to his wife.

'Other people are buying,' said he, 'and we must also buy forty acres at least. Life is becoming impossible. That fellow's fines are ruining us.'

So they considered together how they could manage to buy it. They had saved one hundred roubles. They sold a young horse and one half of their bees, and sent one of their sons out to work and took his pay in advance. They borrowed the rest of the money from a relation, and so collected half the price of the land.

When he had done this, Pahom chose a farm of forty acres, with fine woods, and went to the lady to make her an offer for it. They made a bargain, and he shook hands with her upon it and paid her a sum of money in advance. Then they went to town and signed the agreement. He paid half the price at once and promised to pay the rest before the end of two years.

So now Pahom had his own land. He borrowed seed and sowed it on the land he had bought. The harvest was a good one, and within a year he had managed to pay his debts both to the lady and to his relation. So he became a landowner, ploughing and sowing and making hay on his own land, cutting his own trees and feeding his cattle on his own grass. When he went out to plough his fields or to look at his growing corn, or at his fields of grass, his heart was full of joy. The grass and the flowers that grew there seemed to him unlike any that grew anywhere else. Before, when he had passed by that land, it had appeared the same as any other land, but now it seemed quite different.

3

So Pahom was very happy, and everything would have been right if only the peasants had not wandered on to his cornfields and grassland. He asked them most politely to keep away, but they did not. Sometimes the herdsmen would let the village cows wander into his fields; sometimes horses would get into his corn. Pahom turned them out again and again, and forgave their owners, and for a long time he did not make use of the law. But at last he became impatient and took the matter to the District Court. He knew that the peasants only came on to his land because they had none themselves, and that they did not intend to do wrong, but he thought: 'I cannot go on letting it happen or they will destroy all I have. They must be taught a lesson.'

So he had them brought to the court, gave them one lesson, and then another, and two or three of the peasants had to pay fines. After a time the men who lived near Pahom began to dislike him because of this, and on some occasions they let their cattle go on to his land on purpose.

One peasant even went into Pahom's wood at night and cut down five beautiful young trees in order to have their bark. As Pahom passed through the wood one day he noticed something white. He came nearer and saw the stripped trees lying on the ground, and nearby stood the roots where the trees had been. Pahom was very angry. 'If he had only cut one tree here and there it would have been bad enough,' Pahom thought, 'but the fellow has actually cut down the whole group. If I could find out who did this I would punish him as he deserves.'

He thought hard who it could be. At last he decided: 'It must be Simon—no one else could have done it.' So he went to Simon's home to have a look round, but he found nothing, and only had an angry quarrel. However, he now felt very certain that Simon had done it, and he reported him. Simon was brought before the court. The case was heard twice, and at the end of it all Simon was let off, for there was no proof against him. Pahom felt still more wronged and turned angrily to the judges.

'You take money from robbers,' said he. 'If you were honest people yourselves you would not let a robber go free.'

So Pahom quarrelled with the judges and with everyone in his district. People began to threaten to burn his buildings. So though Pahom had more land, he was liked in the village much less than before.

About this time the peasants heard that many people were leaving this part of Russia to go to other parts.

'There is no need for me to leave my land,' Pahom thought. 'But some of the others may leave our village and then there will be more room for us. I will take their land myself and make my farm bigger. I can then live in greater comfort. At present I am shut in too much to be comfortable.'

One day Pahom was sitting at home when a peasant who was passing through the village happened to come in. Pahom allowed him to stay for the night and gave him supper. He had a talk with this peasant and asked him where he came from. The stranger answered that he came from beyond the river Volga, where he had been working. One word led to another, and the man went on to say that many people were going to live in those lands. He told how some people from his village had settled there. They had joined a Society, and each of them had received twenty-five acres of land. This land was so good that the corn sown on it grew as high as a horse and was very thick. The stranger said that one peasant had brought nothing with him but his hands, and now he had six horses and two cows of his own.

Pahom's heart was filled with desire. He thought: 'Why should I suffer in this narrow hole, if men can live so well in other places? I will sell my land and my home here, and with the money I will make a fresh start there and get everything new. We are always having trouble in this crowded place. But I must first go and find out all about it myself.'

When summer was near he got ready and started. He went down the river Volga on a steamer to Samara, and walked another three hundred miles, and at last reached the place. Everything was as the stranger had said. The peasants had plenty of land, for the Society had given every man twenty-five acres of land for his own use, and any one who had money could buy, at a rouble an acre, as much more good land as he wanted.

When Pahom had found out all he wished to know, he returned home in the autumn and began to sell everything he had. He sold his land at a profit, and also his home and all his cattle. He waited only till the spring, and then started with his family to find a new home.

4

As soon as Pahom and his family reached their new home he applied to be admitted into the Society of a large village. The Society allowed him the use of a hundred and twenty-five acres in different fields as well as its own grassland. Pahom bought cattle and put up the buildings he needed in the village. He had three times as much land as he had owned before, and it was good corn-land. He was ten times wealthier than he had been. He had plenty of land for cultivation and for grass, and could keep as many cattle as he wished.

At first, in the excitement of building and living in his new home, Pahom was pleased with everything, but when he became used to it he began to think that even here he had not enough land. In the first year, he sowed wheat on his share of the Society's land, and had a good crop. He wanted to go on sowing wheat, but had not enough land for the purpose, for he could not sow his land again till it had rested and grass had grown over it. Many people wanted such land and there was not enough for all, so that there were quarrels about it. Those who were wealthy wanted to grow wheat and those who were poor wanted to make money out of it through dealers. Pahom wanted to sow more wheat, so he rented land from a dealer for a year. He sowed a lot of wheat and had a fine crop, but the land was too far from the village—the wheat had to be taken more than ten miles. After a time Pahom noticed that some peasant dealers were living on separate farms away from the Society's village and were becoming wealthy; and he thought, 'If I were to buy some land of my own and have a separate farm on it, it would be quite a different thing. Then it would all be nice and convenient.' The idea of buying land of his own, instead of renting it, came into his mind again and again.

For three years he rented land and sowed wheat. The seasons and the crops were good, and he saved more money. He might have continued to live happily, but he grew tired of renting other people's land every year. Where the land was good the peasants used to rush for it and it was taken immediately, so that unless you were quick you got none. In the third year it happened that Pahom and a dealer together rented a piece of grassland from some peasants. When they had already ploughed it, there was a quarrel and the peasants went to law about it, and the result was that the work of ploughing was all lost.

'If it were my own land,' thought Pahom, 'I should not have all this trouble.'

So Pahom began looking for land which he could buy, and he met a peasant who had bought thirteen hundred acres. This man had got into difficulties and was willing to sell again cheaply. Pahom bargained with him, and at last they decided on the price of 1,500 roubles, partly in ready money and partly to be paid later. When they had almost settled the matter, a passing dealer happened to stop at Pahom's house one day to get a feed for his horses. He drank tea with Pahom and they had a talk. The dealer said that he was just returning from the land of the Bashkirs far away, where he had bought thirteen thousand acres of land, all for 1,000 roubles. Pahom asked him more questions, and the dealer said, 'All you need to do is to make friends with the chiefs. I gave away about one hundred roubles' worth of silk dresses and furnishings, besides a case of tea, and I gave wine to those who wished to drink it; and I got the land for eight kopeks an acre.' He showed Pahom the papers about the sale, and said, 'The land lies near a river. The soil is good; none of it has been cultivated before.'

Pahom asked him many questions, and the dealer said, 'Even if you walked for a year you could not cover all the land, and it all belongs to the Bashkirs. They are as simple as sheep, and you can get land almost for nothing.'

'Well,' thought Pahom, 'why should I get only thirteen hundred acres in exchange for my one thousand roubles? If I take my money there I can get more than ten times as much for it.'

5

Pahom asked how to get to the place, and as soon as the dealer had left him he prepared to go there himself. He left his wife to look after the farm and started on his journey, taking a servant with him. They stopped at a town on their way and bought a case of tea, some wine and other gifts, as the dealer had advised. They went on and on until they had gone more than three hundred miles, and on the seventh day they came to the tents of the Bashkirs. All was as the dealer had said. The people lived on the plains by the river, in their tents. They did not cultivate the land or eat bread. Their herds of cattle and horses fed on the grass of the plains. The young horses were tied up behind the tents, and the mares were driven to them twice a day. The men milked the mares, and the women made kumiss and cheese from the milk. The men only cared about drinking kumiss and tea, eating meat, and playing tunes on their pipes. They were all strong and merry, and all through the summer they never thought of doing any work. They were simple people and could not speak Russian, but were very kind.

As soon as they saw Pahom they came out of their tents and crowded round their visitor. They found an interpreter who explained what was said, and Pahom told them that he had come to see if he could buy some land. The Bashkirs seemed to be very glad; they took Pahom and led him into one of the biggest tents. They made him sit in the best place in comfort while they sat round him. They gave him tea and kumiss and killed a sheep for him and gave him meat to eat. Pahom took gifts out of his cart and gave them to the Bashkirs, and divided the tea among them. The Bashkirs were filled with delight. They talked among themselves, and then told the interpreter to explain their words to Pahom.

'They wish to tell you,' said the interpreter, 'that they like you, and that it is their custom to do all they can to please a guest. You have given them gifts. Now tell them which of their possessions you like best, so that they may give them to you.'

'The thing which pleases me best here,' answered Pahom, 'is your land. Our land is crowded and the soil is no longer fruitful. But you have plenty of land, and it is good land. I never saw such land before.'

The interpreter explained what Pahom had said. The Bashkirs talked among themselves for a short time. Pahom could not understand what they were saying, but saw that they were much amused and that they shouted and laughed. Then there was silence, and they looked at Pahom while the interpreter said, 'They wish me to tell you that in exchange for your gifts they will gladly give you as much land as you want. You need only point it out with your hand and it will be yours.'

The Bashkirs talked again for a short time and began to argue. Pahom asked what they were arguing about. The interpreter told him, 'Some of them think they ought to ask their Chief about the land and not do anything while he is absent. The others think that there is no need to wait for his return.'

6

While the Bashkirs were arguing, a man in a large fur cap arrived. They all stopped talking and stood up. The interpreter said, 'This is our Chief himself.'

Pahom immediately fetched the finest coat and five pounds of tea, and offered these to the Chief. The Chief accepted them and sat down in the place of honour. The Bashkirs at once began telling him something. The Chief listened for a while, and then made a sign with his head which demanded silence, and speaking Russian he said to Pahom, 'Well, let it be so. Choose whatever piece of land you like; we have plenty of it.'

'How can I take as much as I like?' thought Pahom. 'I must get an official paper to make it certain, or else now they may say, "It is yours," and afterwards they may take it away again.'

'Thank you for your kind words,' he said aloud. 'You have a lot of land, and I only want a little. But I should like to be sure which bit is mine. Could it not be measured and officially given to me? Life and death are in God's hands. You good people give it to me, but your children might wish to take it away again.'

'You are quite right,' said the Chief. 'We will give it to you officially.'

'I heard that a dealer had been here,' Pahom continued, 'and that you gave him a little land too, and signed the official papers. I should like to have it done in the same way.'

The Chief understood.

'Yes,' he replied, 'that can be done quite easily. We have a law-writer, and we will go to town with you and have the papers properly signed.'

'And what will be the price?' asked Pahom.

'Our price is always the same: one thousand roubles a day.'

Pahom did not understand.

'A day? What measure is that? How many acres would that be?'

'We do not know how to measure it,' said the Chief. 'We sell it by the day. You may have as much as you can go round on your feet in one day, and the price is one thousand roubles a day.'

Pahom was surprised.

'But in one day you can get round a large district!' he said.

The chief laughed.

'It will all be yours!' said he. 'But there is one condition. If you do not return on the same day to the spot you started from, your money is lost.'

'But how am I to mark the way that I have gone?'

'Why, we shall go to any spot you like, and stay there. You must start from that spot and make your round, taking a spade with you. Make a mark wherever you think one is necessary. Each time you make a turn, dig a hole and make a heap of earth. You may make as large a course as you please, but before the sun sets you must return to the place you started from. All the land you cover will be yours.'

Pahom was delighted. He decided to start early next morning. They talked for a short time, and after drinking some more kumiss and eating some more meat, they had tea again, and then night came on. They gave Pahom a soft bed to sleep on, and the Bashkirs went away for the night, promising to meet together the next morning at daybreak and ride out before sunrise to the spot they had chosen.

7

Pahom lay on the soft bed, but could not sleep. He thought all the time about the land.

'What a large piece I will mark off!' he thought. 'I can easily walk thirty-five miles in a day. The days are long now, and there will be a great deal of land within a course of thirty-five miles. I will sell the poorer land, or the peasants can rent it from me. But I will choose the best and farm it. I will buy two pairs of oxen, and employ two more workers. About a hundred and fifty acres shall be ploughed and I will let cattle feed on the rest.'

Pahom lay awake all night and did not sleep until just before daybreak. Immediately, he had a dream. He thought that he was lying in that same tent and heard somebody laughing outside. He wondered who it could be, and he dreamed that he got up and walked out, and saw the Bashkir Chief sitting in front of the tent, holding his sides and laughing so much that he rolled about. Pahom went nearer to the Chief and asked, 'What are you laughing at?' But then he saw that it was not the Chief, but the dealer who had recently stopped at his house and told him about the land. Just as Pahom was going to ask, 'Have you been here long?' he saw that it was not the dealer, but the peasant who had come up from the Volga, long ago, to Pahom's old home. Then he saw that it was not even the peasant, but the Devil himself, with the body of an animal, who sat there laughing. In front of him a man, wearing only a shirt and trousers, lay flat on the ground. And Pahom dreamed that he looked more carefully to see what kind of man it was that was lying there, and he saw that the man was dead, and that it was himself! He awoke terribly frightened.

'What terrible things one dreams!' he thought, and as he looked round he saw through the open door the first light of day.

'It's time to wake them up,' he thought. 'We ought to make a start.'

He got up, awoke his servant, who was sleeping in his cart, told him to get the horse ready, and went to call the Bashkirs.

'It's time to go to the plain to measure the land,' he said.

The Bashkirs got up and met together, and the Chief came too. Then they began drinking kumiss again, and offered Pahom some tea, but he would not wait.

'The time has come,' he said. 'Let us go.'

The Bashkirs got ready, and they all started; some were on horses, and some in carts. Pahom drove in his own small cart with his servant and took a spade with him. When they reached the plain, the red of the morning was beginning to flame. They climbed up a small hill and, getting down from their carts and their horses, they met together in one spot. The Chief came up to Pahom and stretched out his arm towards the plain.

'See,' said he, 'all this, as far as your eye can reach, is ours. You may have any part of it you like.'

Pahom's eyes shone; it was all uncultivated land, flat and black, and different kinds of grass grew in the low-lying parts almost up to a man's shoulders.

The Chief took off his fur cap, placed it on the ground and said, 'This will be the mark. Start from here, and return here again. All the land you go round shall be yours.'

Pahom took out his money and put it on the cap. Then he took off his overcoat, remaining in his undercoat. He took his belt, tied it tightly round his middle, and put a little bag of bread inside his coat. Then he tied a bottle of water to his belt, fastened up the tops of his high boots, took the spade from his servant, and stood ready to start. He considered for a few moments which way he ought to go. Everywhere seemed good.

'It does not matter,' he thought. 'I will go towards the rising sun.'

He turned his face to the east, stretched himself, and waited for the sun to come up.

'I must lose no time,' he thought, 'and it is easier walking while it is still cool.'

The sun had hardly shone above the skyline, before Pahom, carrying the spade over his shoulder, went down into the plain.

Pahom started walking neither slowly nor quickly. After he had gone a thousand yards he stopped, dug a hole, and placed pieces of earth and grass one on another so that it could be easily seen. Then he went on; and now that he was walking more freely he increased his speed. After a short time he dug another hole.

Pahom looked back. He could see the hill clearly in the sunlight, with the people on it, and the shining metal of the cart-wheels. Pahom made a rough guess that he had walked three miles. It was growing warmer. He took off his under-coat, put it across his shoulder and went on again. It was quite warm now; he looked at the sun. It was time to think of breakfast.

'The first part is done, but there are four parts in a day and it is too soon yet to turn. But I will take off my boots,' he said to himself.

He sat down, took off his boots, put them under his belt, and went on. It was easy walking now.

'I will go on for another three miles,' he thought, 'and then turn to the left. This spot is so fine that it would be a shame to lose it. The farther one goes the better the land seems.'

He went straight on for a short time, and when he looked round he could scarcely see the hill. The people on it looked like black ants, and he could just see something shining there in the sun.

'Ah,' thought Pahom. 'I have gone far enough this way, it is time to turn. Besides, I am very hot and thirsty.'

He stopped, dug a hole and made a heap by the side of it. Next he untied his bottle, had a drink and then turned sharply to the left. He went on and on; the grass was high, and it was very hot.

Pahom began to grow tired; he looked at the sun and saw that it was noon.

'Well,' he thought, 'I must have a rest.'

He sat down and ate some bread and drank some water; but he did not lie down, thinking that if he did he might fall asleep. After sitting a little while, he went on again. At first he walked easily, for the food had given him strength; but it had become terribly hot and he felt sleepy. Still he went on, thinking, 'An hour to suffer, a lifetime to live.'

He went on in this way for a long time also, and was about to turn to his left again when he saw a damp low-lying area. 'It would be a shame to leave that out,' he thought. 'Flax would grow well there.' So he went on, past the low-lying ground, and dug a hole on the other side of it before he turned the corner.

Pahom looked towards the hill. The heat made the air misty; it seemed to be shaking and he could scarcely see the people on the hill through the mist.

'Ah,' thought Pahom, 'I have made the sides too long; I must make this one shorter.' And he went along the third side, walking faster. He looked at the sun. It was nearly half-way down to the skyline, and he had not yet done two miles of the third side of the square. He was still ten miles from the hill.

'No,' he thought, 'though it will make the shape of my land uneven, I must hurry back in a straight line now. I might go too far, and I already have a great deal of land.'

So Pahom hurriedly dug a hole, and turned straight towards the hill.

8

Pahom went straight towards the hill, but he now walked with difficulty. He was tired with the heat, his feet were cut and hurt, and his legs were weak. He wished to rest, but it was not possible if he meant to get back before sunset. The sun waits for no man, and it was sinking lower and lower.

'Oh dear,' he thought, 'if only I had not made a mistake trying for too much! What will happen if I am too late?'

He looked towards the hill and at the sun. He was still far from the place. He began running, threw away his coat, his boots, his bottle, and his cap, and kept only the spade which he used as a support.

'What shall I do?' he thought again. 'I have tried to get too much and lost everything. I can't get there before the sun sets.'

And this fear made him breathe even harder. Pahom went on running, his soaking shirt and trousers stuck to him, and his mouth was very dry. His breathing was hard, his heart was beating like a hammer, and his legs were weak and felt as if they did not belong to him. Pahom was terribly frightened that he would die from the effort. Though afraid of death, he could not stop. 'They will call me a fool if I stop now after I have run all that way,' he thought.

And he ran on and on, nearer and nearer, and heard the Bashkirs calling and shouting to him. Their cries excited him still more. He gathered his last strength and ran on.

The sun was close to the skyline, and, with mist all around, it looked large and red as blood. It was just about to set. The sun was very low, but he was also quite near the hill. Pahom could already see the people on the hill waving their arms to make him hurry. He could see the fur cap on the ground, and the Chief sitting beside it holding his sides. And Pahom remembered his dream.

'There is plenty of land,' he thought, 'but will God let me live on it? I have lost my life, I have lost my life! I shall never reach that spot!'

Pahom looked at the sun, which had reached the earth: the bottom of it had already disappeared. With all his remaining strength he rushed on, bending his body forward so that his legs could hardly follow fast enough to keep him from falling. Just as he reached the hill it suddenly grew dark. He looked up—the sun had already set! He gave a cry. 'All my efforts have been useless,' he thought, and was about to stop, but he heard the Bashkirs still shouting, and remembered that though to him, down below, the sun seemed to have set, those on the hill could still see it. He breathed deeply and ran up the slope of the small hill. It was still light there. He reached the top and saw the cap. The Chief sat in front of it, laughing and holding his sides. Again Pahom remembered his dream, and he gave a loud cry. His legs gave way beneath him, he fell forward and reached the cap with his hands.

'Ah, that's a fine fellow!' said the Chief. 'He has gained a lot of land!'

Pahom's servant came running up and tried to raise him, but he saw that blood was flowing from his mouth. Pahom was dead! The Bashkirs looked sad and showed their pity.

His servant picked up the spade and dug a hole long enough for Pahom to lie in, and buried him in it. Six feet from his head to his toes was all the land he needed.

For Further Reflection

1. How applicable is Tolstoy's parable to our day?

2. Write an essay on modern-day greed.

Jealousy, Malice, and Ingratitude

IMMANUEL KANT

This is Kant's analysis of jealousy in the form of grudging and spitefulness, envy, and ingratitude. Kant is sometimes accused of only valuing one virtue, conscientiousness (and hence one vice, a vicious will), but this selection shows that he was broader than that.

There are two methods by which men arrive at an opinion of their worth: by comparing themselves with the idea of perfection and by comparing themselves with others. The first of these methods is sound; the second is not, and it frequently even leads to a result diametrically opposed to the first. The idea of perfection is a proper standard, and if we measure our worth by it, we find that we fall short of it and feel that we must exert ourselves to come nearer to it; but if we compare ourselves with others, much depends upon who those others are and how they are constituted, and we can easily believe ourselves to be of great worth if those with whom we set up comparison are rogues. Men love to compare themselves with others, for by that method they can always arrive at a result favourable to themselves. They choose as a rule the worst and not the best of the class with which they set up comparison; in this way their own excellence shines out. If they choose those of greater worth the result of the comparison is, of course, unfavourable to them.

When I compare myself with another who is better than I, there are but two ways by which I can bridge the gap between us. I can either do my best to attain to his perfections, or else I can seek to depreciate his good qualities. I either increase my own worth, or else I diminish his so that I can always regard myself as superior to him. It is easier to depreciate another than to emulate him, and men prefer the easier course. They adopt it, and this is the origin of jealousy. When a man compares himself with another and finds that the other has many more good points, he becomes jealous of each and every good point he discovers in the other, and tries to

From *Lectures on Ethics,* translated by Louis Infield (Methuen, 1930).

depreciate it so that his own good points may stand out. This kind of jealousy may be called grudging. The other species of the genus jealousy, which makes us try to add to our good points so as to compare well with another, may be called emulating jealousy. The jealousy of emulation is, as we have stated, more difficult than the jealousy of grudge and so is much the less frequent of the two.

Parents ought not, therefore, when teaching their children to be good, to urge them to model themselves on other children and try to emulate them, for by so doing they simply make them jealous. If I tell my son, "Look, how good and industrious John is," the result will be that my son will bear John a grudge. He will think to himself that, but for John, he himself would be the best, because there would be no comparison. By setting up John as a pattern for imitation I anger my son, make him feel a grudge against this so-called paragon, and I instil jealousy in him. My son might, of course, try to emulate John, but not finding it easy, he will bear John ill-will. Besides, just as I can say to my son, "Look, how good John is," so can he reply: "Yes, he is better than I, but are there not many who are far worse? Why do you compare me with those who are better? Why not with those who are worse than I?" Goodness must, therefore, be commended to children in and for itself. Whether other children are better or worse has no bearing on the point. If the comparison were in the child's favour, he would lose all ground of impulse to improve his own conduct. To ask our children to model themselves on others is to adopt a faulty method of upbringing, and as time goes on the fault will strike its roots deep. It is jealousy that parents are training and presupposing in their children when they set other children before them as patterns. Otherwise, the children would be quite indifferent to the qualities of others. They will find it easier to belittle the good qualities of their patterns than to emulate them, so they will choose the easier path and learn to show a grudging disposition. It is true that jealousy is natural, but that is no excuse for cultivating it. It is only a motive, a reserve in case of need. While the maxims of reason are still undeveloped in us, the proper course is to use reason to keep it within bounds. For jealousy is only one of the many motives, such as ambition, which are implanted in us because we are designed for a life of activity. But so soon as reason is enthroned, we must cease to seek perfection in emulation of others and must covet it in and for itself. Motives must abdicate and let reason bear rule in their place.

Persons of the same station and occupation in life are particularly prone to be jealous of each other. Many business-men are jealous of each other; so are many scholars, particularly in the same line of scholarship; and women are liable to be jealous of each other regarding men.

Grudge is the displeasure we feel when another has an advantage; his advantage makes us feel unduly small and we grudge it him. But to grudge a man his share of happiness is envy. To be envious is to desire the failure and unhappiness of another not for the purpose of advancing our own success and happiness but because we might then ourselves be perfect and happy as we are. An envious man is not happy unless all around him are unhappy; his aim is to stand alone in the enjoyment of his happiness. Such is envy, and we shall learn below that it is satanic. Grudge, although it too should not be countenanced, is natural. Even a good-natured person may at times be grudging. Such a one may, for instance, begrudge those around him their jollity when he himself happens to be sorrowful; for it is hard to bear one's sorrow when all around are joyful. When I see everybody enjoying a good meal and I alone must content myself with inferior fare, it upsets me and I feel a grudge; but if we are all in the same boat I am content. We find the thought of death bearable, because we know that all must die; but if everybody were immortal and I alone had to die, I should feel aggrieved. It is not things themselves that affect us, but things in their relation to ourselves. We are grudging because others are happier than we. But when a good-natured man feels happy and cheerful, he wishes that every one else in the world were as happy as he and shared his joy; he begrudges no one his happiness.

When a man would not grant to another even that for which he himself has no need, he is spiteful. Spite is a maliciousness of spirit which is not the same thing as envy. I may not feel inclined to give to another something which belongs to me, even though I myself have no use for it, but it does not follow that I grudge him his own possessions, that I want to be the only one who has anything and wish him to have nothing at all. There is a deal of grudge in human nature which could develop into envy but which is not itself envy. We feel pleasure in gossiping about the minor misadventures of other people; we are not averse, although we may express no pleasure thereat, to hearing of the fall of some rich man; we may enjoy in stormy weather, when comfortably seated in our warm, cosy parlour, speaking of those at sea, for it heightens our own feeling of comfort and happiness; there is grudge in all this, but it is not envy.

The three vices which are the essence of vileness and wickedness are ingratitude, envy, and malice. When these reach their full degree they are devilish.

Men are shamed by favours. If I receive a favour, I am placed under an obligation to the giver; he has a call upon me because I am indebted to him. We all blush to be obliged. Noble-minded men accordingly refuse to accept favours in order not to put themselves under an obligation. But this attitude predisposes the mind to ingratitude. If the man who adopts it is noble-minded, well and good; but if he be proud and selfish and has perchance received a favour, the feeling that he is beholden to his benefactor hurts his pride and, being selfish, he cannot accommodate himself to the idea that he owes his benefactor anything. He becomes defiant and ungrateful. His ingratitude might even conceivably assume such dimensions that he cannot bear his benefactor and becomes his enemy. Such ingratitude is of the devil; it is out of all keeping with human nature. It is inhuman to hate and persecute one from whom we have reaped a benefit, and if such conduct were the rule it would cause untold harm. Men would then be afraid to do good to anyone lest they should receive evil in return for their good. They would become misanthropic.

The second devilish vice is envy. Envy is in the highest degree detestable. The envious man does not merely want to be happy; he wants to be the only happy person in the world; he is really contented only when he sees nothing but misery around him. Such an intolerable creature would gladly destroy every source of joy and happiness in the world.

Malice is the third kind of viciousness which is of the devil. It consists in taking a direct pleasure in the misfortunes of others. Men prone to this vice will seek, for instance, to make mischief between husband and wife, or between friends, and then enjoy the misery they have produced. In these matters we should make it a rule never to repeat to a person anything that we may have heard to his disadvantage from another, unless our silence would injure him. Otherwise we start an enmity and disturb his peace of mind, which our silence would have avoided, and in addition we break faith with our informant. The defence against such mischief-makers is upright conduct. Not by words but by our lives we should confute them. As Socrates said: We ought so to conduct ourselves that people will not credit anything spoken in disparagement of us.

These three vices—ingratitude (*ingratitudo qualificata*), envy, and malice—are devilish because they imply a direct inclination to evil. There are in man certain indirect tendencies to wickedness which are human and not unnatural. The miser wants everything for himself, but it is no satisfaction to him to see that his neighbour is destitute. The evilness of a vice may thus be either direct or indirect. In these three vices it is direct.

We may ask whether there is in the human mind an immediate inclination to wickedness, an inclination to the devilish vices. Heaven stands for the acme of happiness, hell for all that is bad, and the earth stands midway between these two extremes; and just as goodness which transcends anything which might be expected of a human being is spoken of as being angelic, so also do we speak of devilish wickedness when the wickedness oversteps the limits of human nature and becomes inhuman. We may take it for granted that the human mind has no immediate inclination to wickedness, but is only indirectly wicked. Man cannot be so ungrateful that he simply must hate his neighbour; he may be too proud to show his gratitude and so avoid him, but he wishes him well. Again, our pleasure in the misfortune of another is not direct. We may rejoice, for example, in a man's misfortunes, because he was haughty, rich and selfish; for man loves to preserve equality. We have thus no direct inclination towards evil as evil, but only an indirect one. But how are we to explain the fact that even young children have the spirit of mischief strongly developed? For a joke, a boy will stick a pin in an unsuspecting playmate, but it is only for fun. He has no thought of the pain the other must feel on all such occasions. In the same spirit he will torture animals; twisting the cat's tail or the dog's. Such tendencies must be nipped in the bud, for it is easy to see where they will lead. They are, in fact, something animal, something of the beast of prey which is in us all, which we cannot overcome, and the source of which we cannot explain. There certainly are in human nature characteristics for which we can assign no reason. There are animals too who steal anything that comes their way, though it is quite useless to them; and it seems as if man has retained this animal tendency in his nature.

Ingratitude calls for some further observations here. To help a man in distress is charity; to help him in less urgent needs is benevolence; to help him in the amenities of life is courtesy. We may be the recip-

ients of a charity which has not cost the giver much and our gratitude is commensurate with the degree of good-will which moved
him to the action. We are grateful not only for what we have received
but also for the good intention which prompted it, and the greater
the effort it has cost our benefactor, the greater our gratitude.

Gratitude may be either from duty or from inclination. If an act
of kindness does not greatly move us, but if we nevertheless feel
that it is right and proper that we should show gratitude, our gratitude is merely prompted by a sense of duty. Our heart is not grateful, but we have principles of gratitude. If however, our heart goes
out to our benefactor, we are grateful from inclination. There is a
weakness of the understanding which we often have cause to recognize. It consists in taking the conditions of our understanding as
conditions of the thing understood. We can estimate force only in
terms of the obstacles it overcomes. Similarly, we can only estimate
the degree of good-will in terms of the obstacles it has to surmount.
In consequence we cannot comprehend the love and goodwill of
a being for whom there are no obstacles. If God has been good
to me, I am liable to think that after all it has cost God no trouble, and that gratitude to God would be mere fawning on my part.
Such thoughts are not at all unnatural. It is easy to fear God, but
not nearly so easy to love God from inclination because of our consciousness that God is a being whose goodness is unbounded but
to whom it is no trouble to shower kindness upon us. This is not
to say that such should be our mental attitude; merely that when
we examine our hearts, we find that this is how we actually think.
It also explains why to many races God appeared to be a jealous
God, seeing that it cost Him nothing to be more bountiful with His
goodness; it explains why many nations thought that their gods
were sparing of their benefits and that they required propitiating
with prayers and sacrifices. This is the attitude of man's heart; but
when we call reason to our aid we see that God's goodness must
be of a high order if He is to be good to a being so unworthy of
His goodness. This solves our difficulty. The gratitude we owe to
God is not gratitude from inclination, but from duty, for God is not
a creature like ourselves, and can be no object of our inclinations.

We ought not to accept favours unless we are either forced to
do so by dire necessity or have implicit confidence in our benefactor (for he ceases to be our friend and becomes our benefactor) that he will not regard it as placing us under an obligation to

him. To accept favours indiscriminately and to be constantly seeking them is ignoble and the sign of a mean soul which does not mind placing itself under obligations. Unless we are driven by such dire necessity that it compels us to sacrifice our own worth, or unless we are convinced that our benefactor will not account it to us as a debt, we ought rather to suffer deprivation than accept favours, for a favour is a debt which can never be extinguished. For even if I repay my benefactor tenfold, I am still not even with him, because he has done me a kindness which he did not owe. He was the first in the field, and even if I return his gift tenfold I do so only as repayment. He will always be the one who was the first to show kindness and I can never be beforehand with him.

The man who bestows favours can do so either in order to make the recipient indebted to him or as an expression of his duty. If he makes the recipient feel a sense of indebtedness, he wounds his pride and diminishes his sense of gratitude. If he wishes to avoid this he must regard the favours he bestows as the discharge of a duty he owes to mankind, and he must not give the recipient the impression that it is a debt to be repaid. On the other hand, the recipient of the favour must still consider himself under an obligation to his benefactor and must be grateful to him. Under these conditions there can be benefactors and beneficiaries. A right-thinking man will not accept kindnesses, let alone favours. A grateful disposition is a touching thing and brings tears to our eyes on the stage, but a generous disposition is lovelier still. Ingratitude we detest to a surprising degree; even though we are not ourselves the victims of it, it angers us to such an extent that we feel inclined to intervene. But this is due to the fact that ingratitude decreases generosity.

Envy does not consist in wishing to be more happy than others—that is grudge—but in wishing to be the only one to be happy. It is this feeling which makes envy so evil. Why should not others be happy along with me? Envy shows itself also in relation to things which are scarce. Thus the Dutch, who as a nation are rather envious, once valued tulips at several hundreds of florins apiece. A rich merchant, who had one of the finest and rarest specimens, heard that another had a similar specimen. He thereupon bought it from him for 2,000 florins and trampled it underfoot, saying that he had no use for it, as he already possessed a specimen, and that he only wished that no one else should share that distinction with him. So it is also in the matter of happiness.

Malice is different. A malicious man is pleased when others suffer, he can laugh when others weep. An act which willfully brings unhappiness is cruel; when it produces physical pain it is bloodthirsty. Inhumanity is all these together, just as humanity consists in sympathy and pity, since these differentiate man from the beasts. It is difficult to explain what gives rise to a cruel disposition. It may arise when a man considers another so evilly disposed that he hates him. A man who believes himself hated by another, hates him in return, although the former may have good reason to hate him. For if a man is hated because he is selfish and has other vices, and he knows that he is hated for these reasons, he hates those who hate him although these latter do him no injustice. Thus kings who know that they are hated by their subjects become even more cruel. Equally, when a man has done a good deed to another, he knows that the other loves him, and so he loves him in return, knowing that he himself is loved. Just as love is reciprocated, so also is hate. We must for our own sakes guard against being hated by others lest we be affected by that hatred and reciprocate it. The hater is more disturbed by his hatred than is the hated.

For Further Reflection

1. Why doesn't Kant want us to compare ourselves (or our children) with others or strive to emulate others? Do you think he lacks a sound moral psychology? Do you think that it is really useful to try to emulate good people?

2. Analyze Kant's notion of jealousy. How does he define the two varieties of jealousy, *grudge* and *spite?*

3. How does Kant characterize ingratitude? Why does he say that the proper way to be grateful to God is out of duty, not inclination or spontaneous feeling? Do you agree?

4. Why will a right-thinking person refuse favors? Do you agree?

5. Here is a Russian parable on jealousy. It comes out of the Soviet era. An angel appears to a woman and tells her that she may make a wish and he will grant it. The only caveat is that whatever she wishes for, he will give twofold to her neighbor. Without blinking, the woman replies, "Pluck out one of my eyes."

Is such malicious jealousy common? Can we pr‹
from such vicious feelings?

484

Moral Cowardice

MARTIN GANSBERG

Martin Gansberg, staff writer for the *New York Times,* taught
journalism at Fairleigh Dickenson University. In this article
Gansberg reports the case of Kitty Genovese who for a half
hour was brutally beaten and then murdered while 38 of
her neighbors looked on but did nothing.

For more than half an hour 38 respectable, law-abiding citizens in
Queens watched a killer stalk and stab a woman in three separate
attacks in Kew Gardens.

Twice their chatter and the sudden glow of their bedroom lights
interrupted him and frightened him off. Each time he returned,
sought her out, and stabbed her again. Not one person telephoned
the police during the assault; one witness called after the woman
was dead.

That was two weeks ago today.

Still shocked is Assistant Chief Inspector Frederick M. Lussen, in
charge of the borough's detectives and a veteran of 25 years of
homicide investigations. He can give a matter-of-fact recitation on
many murders. But the Kew Gardens slaying baffles him—not
because it is a murder, but because the "good people" failed to call
the police.

"As we have reconstructed the crime," he said, "the assailant had
three chances to kill this woman during a 35-minute period. He

returned twice to complete the job. If we had been called when he first attacked, the woman might not be dead now."

This is what the police say happened beginning at 3:20 A.M. in the staid, middle-class, tree-lined Austin Street area:

Twenty-eight-year-old Catherine Genovese, who was called Kitty by almost everyone in the neighborhood, was returning home from her job as manager of a bar in Hollis. She parked her red Fiat in a lot adjacent to the Kew Gardens Long Island Rail Road Station, facing Mowbray Place. Like many residents of the neighborhood, she had parked there day after day since her arrival from Connecticut a year ago, although the railroad frowns on the practice.

She turned off the lights of her car, locked the door, and started to walk the 100 feet to the entrance of her apartment at 82-70 Austin Street, which is in a Tudor building, with stores on the first floor and apartments on the second.

The entrance to the apartment is in the rear of the building because the front is rented to retail stores. At night the quiet neighborhood is shrouded in the slumbering darkness that marks most residential areas.

Miss Genovese noticed a man at the far end of the lot, near a seven-story apartment house at 82-40 Austin Street. She halted. Then, nervously, she headed up Austin Street toward Lefferts Boulevard, where there is a call box to the 102nd Police Precinct in nearby Richmond Hill.

She got as far as a street light in front of a bookstore before the man grabbed her. She screamed. Lights went on in the 10-story apartment house at 82-67 Austin Street, which faces the bookstore. Windows slid open and voices punctuated the early-morning stillness.

Miss Genovese screamed: "Oh, my God, he stabbed me! Please help me! Please help me!"

From one of the upper windows in the apartment house, a man called down: "Let that girl alone!"

The assailant looked up at him, shrugged, and walked down Austin Street toward a white sedan parked a short distance away. Miss Genovese struggled to her feet.

Lights went out. The killer returned to Miss Genovese, now trying to make her way around the side of the building by the parking lot to get to her apartment. The assailant stabbed her again.

"I'm dying!" she shrieked. "I'm dying!"

Windows were opened again, and lights went on in many apartments. The assailant got into his car and drove away. Miss Genovese staggered to her feet. A city bus, 0-10, the Lefferts Boulevard line to Kennedy International Airport, passed. It was 3:35 A.M.

The assailant returned. By then, Miss Genovese had crawled to the back of the building, where the freshly painted brown doors to the apartment house held out hope for safety. The killer tried the first door; she wasn't there. At the second door, 82-62 Austin Street, he saw her slumped on the floor at the foot of the stairs. He stabbed her a third time—fatally.

It was 3:50 by the time the police received their first call, from a man who was a neighbor of Miss Genovese. In two minutes they were at the scene. The neighbor, a 70-year-old woman, and another woman were the only persons on the street. Nobody else came forward.

The man explained that he had called the police after much deliberation. He had phoned a friend in Nassau County for advice and then he had crossed the roof of the building to the apartment of the elderly woman to get her to make the call.

"I didn't want to get involved," he sheepishly told the police.

Six days later, the police arrested Winston Moseley, a 29-year-old business-machine operator, and charged him with the homicide. Moseley had no previous record. He is married, has two children and owns a home at 133-19 Sutter Avenue, South Ozone Park, Queens. On Wednesday, a court committed him to Kings County Hospital for psychiatric observation.

When questioned by the police, Moseley also said that he had slain Mrs. Annie May Johnson, 24, of 146-12 133d Avenue, Jamaica, on Feb. 29 and Barbara Kralik, 15, of 174-17 140th Avenue, Springfield Gardens, last July. In the Kralik case, the police are holding Alvin L. Mitchell, who is said to have confessed that slaying.

The police stressed how simple it would have been to have gotten in touch with them. "A phone call," said one of the detectives, "would have done it." The police may be reached by dialing "O" for operator or SPring 7-3100.

Today witnesses from the neighborhood, which is made up of one-family homes in the $35,000 to $60,000 range with the exception of the two apartment houses near the railroad station, find it difficult to explain why they didn't call the police.

A housewife, knowingly if quite casual, said, "We thought it was a lover's quarrel." A husband and wife both said, "Frankly, we were afraid." They seemed aware of the fact that events might have been different. A distraught woman, wiping her hands in her apron, said, "I didn't want my husband to get involved."

One couple, now willing to talk about that night, said they heard the first screams. The husband looked thoughtfully at the bookstore where the killer first grabbed Miss Genovese.

"We went to the window to see what was happening," he said, "but the light from our bedroom made it difficult to see the street." The wife, still apprehensive, added: "I put out the light and we were able to see better."

Asked why they hadn't called the police, she shrugged and replied: "I don't know."

A man peeked out from a slight opening in the doorway to his apartment and rattled off an account of the killer's second attack. Why hadn't he called the police at the time? "I was tired," he said without emotion. "I went back to bed."

It was 4:25 A.M. when the ambulance arrived to take the body of Miss Genovese. It drove off. "Then," a solemn police detective said, "the people came out."

For Further Reflection

1. Review the story of Kitty Genovese. Is only one vice, moral cowardice, manifest here, or many indicated?

2. Compare this story with the parable of the Good Samaritan (the first reading in this chapter).

3. Some people think that the case of Kitty Genovese is a fluke, quite the opposite of how Americans typically act. Do you agree? Or do you think moral cowardice and indifference abound? How serious is our moral apathy and cowardice?

Three Days to See
Gratitude

HELEN KELLER

Helen Keller (1880–1968) was born in Tuscumbia, Alabama. At nineteen months of age she lost her sight and hearing. When Helen was four Anne Sullivan became her teacher and lifelong companion. She taught Helen to speak, read, and write. Keller obtained a college degree in 1904 and became a distinguished lecturer and writer. Her and Anne Sullivan's story was dramatized by William Gibson in *The Miracle Worker* (1959).

In this essay Keller imagines what it would be like to have three days to see.

All of us have read thrilling stories in which the hero had only a limited and specified time to live. Sometimes it was as long as a year; sometimes as short as twenty-four hours. But always we were interested in discovering just how the doomed man chose to spend his last days or his last hours. I speak, of course, of free men who have a choice, not condemned criminals whose sphere of activities is strictly delimited.

Such stories set us thinking, wondering what we should do under similar circumstances. What events, what experiences, what associations should we crowd into those last hours as mortal beings? What happiness should we find in reviewing the past, what regrets?

Sometimes I have thought it would be an excellent rule to live each day as if we should die tomorrow. Such an attitude would emphasize sharply the values of life. We should live each day with a gentleness, a vigor, and a keenness of appreciation which are often lost when time stretches before us in the constant panorama of more days and months and years to come. There are those, of course, who would adopt the epicurean motto of "Eat, drink, and be merry," but most people would be chastened by the certainty of impending death.

Reprinted from "Three Days to See" by Helen Keller, *Atlantic Monthly*, 1933.

In stories, the doomed hero is usually saved at the last minute by some stroke of fortune, but almost always his sense of values is changed. He becomes more appreciative of the meaning of life and its permanent spiritual values. It has often been noted that those who live, or have lived, in the shadow of death bring a mellow sweetness to everything they do.

Most of us, however, take life for granted. We know that one day we must die, but usually we picture that day as far in the future. When we are in buoyant health, death is all but unimaginable. We seldom think of it. The days stretch out in an endless vista. So we go about our petty tasks, hardly aware of our listless attitude toward life.

The same lethargy, I am afraid, characterizes the use of all our faculties and senses. Only the deaf appreciate hearing, only the blind realize the manifold blessings that lie in sight. Particularly does this observation apply to those who have lost sight and hearing in adult life. But those who have never suffered impairment of sight or hearing seldom make the fullest use of these blessed faculties. Their eyes and ears take in all sights and sounds hazily, without concentration and with little appreciation. It is the same old story of not being grateful for what we have until we lose it, of not being conscious of health until we are ill.

I have often thought it would be a blessing if each human being were stricken blind and deaf for a few days at some time during his early adult life. Darkness would make him more appreciative of sight; silence would teach him the joys of sound.

Now and then I have tested my seeing friends to discover what they see. Recently I was visited by a very good friend who had just returned from a long walk in the woods, and I asked her what she had observed. "Nothing in particular," she replied. I might have been incredulous had I not been accustomed to such responses, for long ago I became convinced that the seeing see little.

How was it possible, I asked myself, to walk for an hour through the woods and see nothing worthy of note? I who cannot see find hundreds of things to interest me through mere touch. I feel the delicate symmetry of a leaf. I pass my hands lovingly about the smooth skin of a silver birch, or the rough shaggy bark of a pine. In spring I touch the branches of trees hopefully in search of a bud, the first sign of awakening Nature after her winter's sleep. I feel the delightful, velvety texture of a flower, and discover its remarkable convolutions, and something of the miracle of Nature is revealed to me. Occasionally, if I am fortunate, I place my hand gently on a small tree and feel the happy quiver of a bird in full song. I am delighted to have the cool waters of a brook rush through my open fingers. To me a lush carpet of pine needles or spongy grass is more welcome than the most luxurious Persian rug. To me the pageant of seasons is a thrilling and unending drama, the action of which streams through my finger tips.

At times my heart cries out with longing to see all these things. If I can get so much pleasure from mere touch, how much more beauty must be revealed by sight. Yet, those who have eyes apparently see little. The panorama of color and action which fills the world is taken for granted. It is human, perhaps, to appreciate little that which we have and to long for that which we have not, but it is a great pity that in the world of light the gift of sight is used only as a mere convenience rather than as a means of adding fullness to life.

If I were the president of a university I should establish a compulsory course in "How to Use Your Eyes." The professor would try to show his pupils how they could add joy to their lives by really seeing what passes unnoticed before them. He would try to awake their dormant and sluggish faculties.

Perhaps I can best illustrate by imagining what I should most like to see if I were given the use of my eyes, say, for just three days. And while I am imagining, suppose you, too, set your mind to work on the problem of how you would use your own eyes if you had only three more days to see. If with the oncoming darkness of the third night you knew that the sun would never rise for you again, how would you spend those three precious intervening days? What would you most want to let your gaze rest upon?

I, naturally, should want most to see the things which have become dear to me through my years of darkness. You, too, would want to let your eyes rest long on the things that have become dear to you so that you could take the memory of them with you into the night that loomed before you.

If, by some miracle I were granted three seeing days, to be followed by a relapse into darkness, I should divide the period into three parts.

On the first day, I should want to see the people whose kindness and gentleness have made my life worth living. First I should like to gaze long upon the face of my dear teacher, Mrs. Anne Sullivan Macy, who came to me when I was a child and opened the outer world to me. I should want not merely to see the outline of her face, so that I could cherish it in my memory, but to study that face and find in it the living evidence of the sympathetic tenderness and patience with which she accomplished the difficult task of my education. I should like to see in her eyes that strength of character which has enabled her to stand firm in the face of difficulties, and that compassion for all humanity which she has revealed to me so often.

I do not know what it is to see into the heart of a friend through that "window of the soul," the eye. I can only "see" through my finger tips the outline of a face. I can detect laughter, sorrow, and many other obvious emotions. I know my friends from the feel of their faces. But I cannot really picture their personalities by touch. I know their personalities, of course, through other means, through the thoughts they express to me, through whatever of their actions are revealed to me. But I am denied that deeper understanding of them which I am sure would come through sight of them, through watching their reactions to various expressed thoughts and circumstances, through noting the immediate and fleeting reactions of their eyes and countenance.

Friends who are near to me I know well, because through the months and years they reveal themselves to me in all their phases; but of casual friends I have only an incomplete impression, an impression gained from a handclasp, from spoken words which I take from their lips with my finger tips, or which they tap into the palm of my hand.

How much easier, how much more satisfying it is for you who can see to grasp quickly the essential qualities of another person by watching the subtleties of expression, the quiver of a muscle, the flutter of a hand. But does it ever occur to you to use your sight to see into the inner nature of a friend or acquaintance? Do not most of you seeing people grasp casually the outward features of a face and let it go at that?

For instance, can you describe accurately the faces of five good friends? Some of you can, but many cannot. As an experiment, I have questioned husbands of long standing about the color of their wives' eyes, and often they express embarrassed confusion and admit they do not know. And, incidentally, it is a chronic complaint of wives that their husbands do not notice new dresses, new hats, and changes in household arrangements.

The eyes of seeing persons soon become accustomed to the routine of their surroundings, and they actually see only the startling and spectacular. But even in viewing the most spectacular sights the eyes are lazy. Court records reveal every day how inaccurately "eyewitnesses" see. A given event will be "seen" in several different ways by as many witnesses. Some see more than others, but few see everything that is within the range of their vision.

Oh, the things that I should see if I had the power of sight for just three days!

The first day would be a busy one. I should call to me all my dear friends and look long into their faces, imprinting upon my mind the outward evidences of the beauty that is within them. I should let my eyes rest, too, on the face of a baby, so that I could catch a vision of the eager, innocent beauty which precedes the individual's consciousness of the conflicts which life develops.

And I should like to look into the loyal, trusting eyes of my dogs—the grave, canny little Scottie, Darkie, and the stalwart, understanding Great Dane, Helga, whose warm, tender, and playful friendships are so comforting to me.

On that busy first day I should also view the small simple things of my home. I want to see the warm colors in the rugs under my feet, the pictures on the walls, the intimate trifles that transform a house into home. My eyes would rest respectfully on the books in raised type which I have read, but they would be more eagerly interested in the printed books which seeing people can read, for during the long night of my life the books I have read and those which have been read to me have built themselves into a great shining lighthouse, revealing to me the deepest channels of human life and the human spirit.

In the afternoon of that first seeing day, I should take a long walk in the woods and intoxicate my eyes on the beauties of the world of Nature, trying desperately to absorb in a few hours the vast splendor which is constantly unfolding itself to those who can see. On the way home from my woodland jaunt my path would lie near a farm so that I might see the patient horses plowing in the field (perhaps I should see only a tractor!) and the serene content of men living close to the soil. And I should pray for the glory of a colorful sunset.

When dusk had fallen, I should experience the double delight of being able to see by artificial light, which the genius of man has created to extend the power of his sight when Nature decrees darkness.

In the night of that first day of sight, I should not be able to sleep, so full would be my mind of the memories of the day.

The next day—the second day of sight—I should arise with the dawn and see the thrilling miracle by which night is transformed into day. I should behold with awe the magnificent panorama of light with which the sun awakens the sleeping earth.

This day I should devote to a hasty glimpse of the world, past and present. I should want to see the pageant of man's progress, the kaleidoscope of the ages. How can so much be compressed into one day? Through the museums, of course. Often I have visited the New York Museum of Natural History to touch with my hands many of the objects there exhibited, but I have longed to see with my eyes the condensed history of the earth and its inhabitants displayed there—animals and the races of men pictured in their native environment; gigantic carcasses of dinosaurs and mastodons which roamed the earth long before man appeared, with his tiny stature and powerful brain, to conquer the animal kingdom; realistic presentations of the processes of evolution in animals, in man, and in the implements which man has used to fashion for himself a secure home on this planet; and a thousand and one other aspects of natural history.

I wonder how many readers of this article have viewed this panorama of the face of living things as pictured in that inspiring museum. Many, of course, have not had the opportunity, but I am sure that many who have had the opportunity have not made use of it. There, indeed, is a place to use your eyes. You who see can spend many fruitful days there, but I, with my imaginary three days of sight, could only take a hasty glimpse, and pass on.

My next stop would be the Metropolitan Museum of Art, for just as the Museum of Natural History reveals the material aspects of the world, so does the Metropolitan show the myriad facets of the human spirit. Throughout the history of humanity the urge to artistic expression has been almost as powerful as the urge for food, shelter, and procreation. And here, in the vast chambers of the Metropolitan Museum, is unfolded before me the spirit of Egypt, Greece, and Rome, as expressed in their art. I know well through my hands the sculptured gods and goddesses of the ancient Nile-land. I have felt copies of Parthenon friezes, and I have sensed the rhythmic beauty of charging Athenian warriors. Apollos and Venuses and the Wingèd Victory of Samothrace are friends of my finger tips. The gnarled, bearded features of Homer are dear to me, for he, too, knew blindness.

My hands have lingered upon the living marble of Roman sculpture as well as that of later generations. I have passed my hands over a plaster cast of Michelangelo's inspiring and heroic Moses; I have sensed the power of Rodin; I have been awed by the devoted spirit of Gothic wood carving. These arts which can be touched have meaning for me, but even they were meant to be seen rather than felt, and I can only guess at the beauty which remains hidden from me. I can admire the simple lines of a Greek vase, but its figured decorations are lost to me.

So on this, my second day of sight, I should try to probe into the soul of man through his art. The things I knew through touch I should now see. More splendid still, the whole magnificent world of painting would be opened to me, from the Italian Primitives, with their serene religious devotion, to the Moderns, with their feverish visions. I should look deep into the canvases of Raphael, Leonardo da Vinci, Titian, Rembrandt. I should want to feast my eyes upon the warm colors of Veronese, study the mysteries of El Greco, catch a new vision of Nature from Corot. Oh, there is so much rich meaning and beauty in the art of the ages for you who have eyes to see!

Upon my short visit to this temple of art I should not be able to review a fraction of that great world of art which is open to you. I should be able to get only a superficial impression. Artists tell me that for a deep and true appreciation of art one must educate the eye. One must learn through experience to weigh the merits of line, of composition, of form and color. If I had eyes, how happily would I embark upon so fascinating a study! Yet I am told that, to many of you who have eyes to see, the world of art is a dark night, unexplored and unilluminated.

It would be with extreme reluctance that I should leave the Metropolitan Museum, which contains the key to beauty—a beauty so neglected. Seeing persons, however, do not need a Metropolitan to find this key to beauty. The same key lies waiting in smaller museums, and in books on the shelves of even small libraries. But naturally, in my limited time of imaginary sight, I should choose the place where the key unlocks the greatest treasures in the shortest time.

The evening of my second day of sight I should spend at a theater or at the movies. Even now I often attend theatrical performances of all sorts, but the action of the play must be spelled into my hand by a companion. But how I should like to see with my own eyes the fascinating figure of Hamlet, or the gusty Falstaff amid colorful Elizabethan trappings! How I should like to follow each movement of the graceful Hamlet, each strut of the hearty Falstaff! And since I could see only one play, I should be confronted by a many-horned dilemma, for there are scores of plays I should want to see. You who have eyes can see any you like. How many of you, I wonder, when you gaze at a play, a movie, or any spectacle, realize and give thanks for the miracle of sight which enables you to enjoy its color, grace, and movement?

I cannot enjoy the beauty of rhythmic movement except in a sphere restricted to the touch of my hands. I can vision only dimly the grace of a Pavlova, although I know something of the delight of rhythm, for often I can sense the beat of music as it vibrates through the floor. I can well imagine that cadenced motion must be one of the most pleasing sights in the world. I have been able to gather something of this by tracing with my fingers the lines in sculptured marble; if this static grace can be so lovely, how much more acute must be the thrill of seeing grace in motion.

One of my dearest memories is of the time when Joseph Jefferson allowed me to touch his face and hands as he went through some of the gestures and speeches of his beloved Rip Van Winkle. I was able to catch thus a meager glimpse of the world of drama, and I shall never forget the delight of that moment. But, oh, how much I must miss, and how much pleasure you seeing ones can derive from watching and hearing the interplay of speech and movement in the unfolding of a dramatic performance! If I could see only one play, I should know how to picture in my mind the action of a hundred plays which I have read or had transferred to me through the medium of the manual alphabet.

So, through the evening of my second imaginary day of sight, the great figures of dramatic literature would crowd sleep from my eyes.

The following morning, I should again greet the dawn, anxious to discover new delights, for I am sure that, for those who have eyes which really see, the dawn of each day must be a perpetually new revelation of beauty.

This, according to the terms of my imagined miracle, is to be my third and last day of sight. I shall have no time to waste in regrets or longings; there is too much to see. The first day I devoted to my friends, animate and inanimate. The second revealed to me the history of man and Nature. Today I shall spend in the worka-day world of the present, amid the haunts of men going about the business of life. And where can one find so many activities and conditions of men as in New York? So the city becomes my desti-nation.

I start from my home in the quiet little suburb of Forest Hills, Long Island. Here, surrounded by green lawns, trees, and flowers, are neat little houses, happy with the voices and movements of wives and children, havens of peaceful rest for men who toil in the city. I drive across the lacy structure of steel which spans the East River, and I get a new and startling vision of the power and ingenuity of the mind of man. Busy boats chug and scurry about the river—racy speed boats, stolid, snorting tugs. If I had long days of sight ahead, I should spend many of them watching the delight-ful activity upon the river.

I look ahead, and before me rise the fantastic towers of New York, a city that seems to have stepped from the pages of a fairy story. What an awe-inspiring sight, these glittering spires, these vast banks of stone and steel—structures such as the gods might build for themselves! This animated picture is a part of the lives of mil-lions of people every day. How many, I wonder, give it so much as a second glance? Very few, I fear. Their eyes are blind to this magnificent sight because it is so familiar to them.

I hurry to the top of one of those gigantic structures, the Empire State Building, for there, a short time ago, I "saw" the city below through the eyes of my secretary. I am anxious to compare my fancy with reality. I am sure I should not be disappointed in the panorama spread out before me, for to me it would be a vision of another world.

Now I begin my rounds of the city. First, I stand at a busy cor-ner, merely looking at people, trying by sight of them to under-stand something of their lives. I see smiles, and I am happy. I see serious determination, and I am proud. I see suffering, and I am compassionate.

I stroll down Fifth Avenue. I throw my eyes out of focus so that I see no particular object but only a seething kaleidoscope of color. I am certain that the colors of women's dresses moving in a throng must be a gorgeous spectacle of which I should never tire. But perhaps if I had sight I should be like most other women—too interested in styles and the cut of individual dresses to give much attention to the splendor of color in the mass. And I am convinced, too, that I should become an inveterate window shopper, for it must be a delight to the eye to view the myriad articles of beauty on display.

From Fifth Avenue I make a tour of the city—to Park Avenue, to the slums, to factories, to parks where children play. I take a stay-at-home trip abroad by visiting the foreign quarters. Always my eyes are open wide to all the sights of both happiness and misery so that I may probe deep and add to my understanding of how people work and live. My heart is full of the images of people and things. My eye passes lightly over no single trifle; it strives to touch and hold closely each thing its gaze rests upon. Some sights are pleasant, filling the heart with happiness; but some are miserably pathetic. To these latter I do not shut my eyes, for they, too, are part of life. To close the eye on them is to close the heart and mind.

My third day of sight is drawing to an end. Perhaps there are many serious pursuits to which I should devote the few remaining hours, but I am afraid that on the evening of that last day I should again run away to the theater, to a hilariously funny play, so that I might appreciate the overtones of comedy in the human spirit.

At midnight my temporary respite from blindness would cease, and permanent night would close in on me again. Naturally in those three short days I should not have seen all I wanted to see. Only when darkness had again descended upon me should I realize how much I had left unseen. But my mind would be so crowded with glorious memories that I should have little time for regrets. Thereafter the touch of every object would bring a flowing memory of how that object looked.

Perhaps this short outline of how I should spend three days of sight does not agree with the program you would set for yourself if you knew that you were about to be stricken blind. I am, however, sure that if you actually faced that fate your eyes would open to things you had never seen before, storing up memories for the long night ahead. You would use your eyes as never before. Everything you saw would become dear to you. Your eyes would touch and embrace every object that came within your range of vision. Then, at last, you would really see, and a new world of beauty would open itself before you.

I who am blind can give one hint to those who see—one admonition to those who would make full use of the gift of sight: Use your eyes as if tomorrow you would be stricken blind. And the same method can be applied to the other senses. Hear the music of voices, the song of a bird, the mighty strains of an orchestra, as if you would be stricken deaf tomorrow. Touch each object you want to touch as if tomorrow your tactile sense would fail. Smell the perfume of flowers, taste with relish each morsel, as if tomorrow you could never smell and taste again. Make the most of every sense; glory in all the facets of pleasure and beauty which the world reveals to you through the several means of contact which Nature provides. But of all the senses, I am sure that sight must be the most delightful.

For Further Reflection

1. Review the story of Helen Keller. What is her attitude toward life? What does this tell us about gratitude?

2. What other lessons does this essay have to teach us? Can you apply it to your life? Explain.

3. What can we learn from Helen Keller about overcoming tragedy?

Courage and Endurance

VICE ADMIRAL JAMES STOCKDALE

Vice Admiral James Stockdale was a combat naval aviator whose plane was shot down over North Vietnam. He spent eight years in a North Vietnam prison, four of them in soli-

---

This essay by Vice Admiral James Stockdale, USN, "The World of Epictetus" is reprinted from the *Atlantic Monthly* (April 1978) by permission.

tary confinement. He has been a fellow at the Hoover Institute and a vice presidential candidate in the 1992 election.

The following is Vice Admiral Stockdale's tale of his experience in prison and of what helped him endure deprivation and torture. He refers to the Stoic catechism *Enchiridion,* as his inspiration during his ordeal. You may find that in chapter 9.

In 1965 I was a forty-one-year-old commander, the senior pilot of Air Wing 16, flying combat missions in the area just south of Hanoi from the aircraft carrier *Oriskany.* By September of that year I had grown quite accustomed to briefing dozens of pilots and leading them on daily air strikes; I had flown nearly 200 missions myself and knew the countryside of North Vietnam like the back of my hand. On the ninth of that month I led about thirty-five airplanes to the Thanh Hoa Bridge, just west of that city. That bridge was tough; we had been bouncing 500-pounders off it for weeks.

The September 9 raid held special meaning for *Oriskany* pilots because of a special bomb load we had improvised; we were going in with our biggest, the 2000-pounders, hung not only on our attack planes but on our F-8 fighter-bombers as well. This increase in bridge-busting capability came from the innovative brain of a major flying with my Marine fighter squadron. He had figured out how we could jury-rig some switches, hang the big bombs, pump out some of the fuel to stay within takeoff weight limits, and then top off our tanks from our airborne refuelers while en route to the target. Although the pilot had to throw several switches in sequence to get rid of his bombs, a procedure requiring above-average cockpit agility, we routinely operated on the premise that all pilots of Air Wing 16 were above average. I test-flew the new load on a mission, thought it over, and approved it; that's the way we did business.

Our spirit was up. That morning, the *Oriskany* Air Wing was finally going to drop the bridge that was becoming a North Vietnamese symbol of resistance. You can imagine our dismay when we crossed the coast and the weather scout I had sent on ahead radioed back that ceiling and visibility were zero-zero in the bridge area. In the tiny cockpit of my A-4 at the front of the pack, I pushed the button on the throttle, spoke into the radio mike in my oxygen mask, and told the formation to split up and proceed in pairs

to the secondary targets I had specified in my contingency briefing. What a letdown.

The adrenaline stopped flowing as my wingman and I broke left
and down and started sauntering along toward our "milk run" target: boxcars on a railroad siding between Vinh and Thanh Hoa,
where the flak was light. Descending through 10,000 feet, I un-
snapped my oxygen mask and let it dangle, giving my pinched face
a rest—no reason to stay uncomfortable on this run.

As I glided toward that easy target, I'm sure I felt totally self-
satisfied. I had the top combat job that a Navy commander can hold
and I was in tune with my environment. I was confident—I knew
airplanes and flying inside out. I was comfortable with the people I
worked with and I knew the trade so well that I often improvised
variations in accepted procedures and encouraged others to do so
under my watchful eye. I was on top. I thought I had found every
key to success and had no doubt that my Academy and test-pilot
schooling had provided me with everything I needed in life.

I passed down the middle of those boxcars and smiled as I saw
the results of my instinctive timing. A neat pattern—perfection. I was
just pulling out of my dive low to the ground when I heard a noise
I hadn't expected—the *boom boom boom* of a 57-millimeter gun—
and then I saw it just behind my wingtip. I was hit—all the red lights
came on, my control system was going out—and I could barely keep
that plane from flying into the ground while I got that damned oxygen mask up to my mouth so I could tell my wingman that I was
about to eject. What rotten luck. And on a "milk run"!

The descent in the chute was quiet except for occasional rifle
shots from the streets below. My mind was clear, and I said to
myself, "five years." I knew we were making a mess of the war in
Southeast Asia, but I didn't think it would last longer than that; I
was also naive about the resources I would need in order to survive a lengthy period of captivity.

The Durants have said that culture is a thin and fragile veneer that
superimposes itself on mankind. For the first time I was on my
own, without the veneer. I was to spend years searching through
and refining my bag of memories, looking for useful tools, things
of value. The values were there, but they were all mixed up with
technology, bureaucracy, and expediency, and had to be brought
up into the open.

Education should take care to illuminate values, not bury them amongst the trivia. Are our students getting the message that without personal integrity intellectual skills are worthless?

Integrity is one of those words which many people keep in that desk drawer labeled "too hard." It's not a topic for the dinner table or the cocktail party. You can't buy or sell it. When supported with education, a person's integrity can give him something to rely on when his perspective seems to blur, when rules and principles seem to waver, and when he's faced with hard choices of right or wrong. It's something to keep him on the right track, something to keep him afloat when he's drowning; if only for practical reasons, it is an attribute that should be kept at the very top of a young person's consciousness.

The importance of the latter point is highlighted in prison camps, where everyday human nature, stripped bare, can be studied under a magnifying glass in accelerated time. Lessons spotlighted and absorbed in that laboratory sharpen one's eye for their abstruse but highly relevant applications in the "real time" world of now.

In the five years since I've been out of prison, I've participated several times in the process of selecting senior naval officers for promotion or important command assignments. I doubt that the experience is significantly different from that of executives who sit on "selection boards" in any large hierarchy. The system must be formal, objective, and fair; if you've seen one, you've probably seen them all. Navy selection board proceedings go something like this.

The first time you know the identity of the other members of the board is when you walk into a boardroom at eight o'clock on an appointed morning. The first order of business is to stand, raise your right hand, put your left hand on the Bible, and swear to make the best judgment you can, on the basis of merit, without prejudice. You're sworn to confidentiality regarding all board members' remarks during the proceedings. Board members are chosen for their experience and understanding; they often have knowledge of the particular individuals under consideration. They must feel free to speak their minds. They read and grade dozens of dossiers, and each candidate is discussed extensively. At voting time, a member casts his vote by selecting and pushing a "percent confidence" button, visible only to himself, on a console attached to his chair. When the last member pushes his button, a totalizer displays the numerical average "confidence" of the board. No one knows who voted what.

I'm always impressed by the fact that every effort is made to be fair to the candidate. Some are clearly out, some are clearly in; the borderline cases are the tough ones. You go over and over those in the "middle pile" and usually you vote and revote until late at night. In all the boards I've sat on, no inference or statement in a "jacket" is as sure to portend a low confidence score on the vote as evidence of a lack of directness or rectitude of a candidate in his dealings with others. Any hint of moral turpitude really turns people off. When the crunch comes, they prefer to work with forthright plodders rather than with devious geniuses. I don't believe that this preference is unique to the military. In any hierarchy where people's fates are decided by committees or boards, those who lose credibility with their peers and who cause their superiors to doubt their directness, honesty, or integrity are dead. Recovery isn't possible.

The linkage of men's ethics, reputations, and fates can be studied in even more vivid detail in prison camp. In that brutally controlled environment a perceptive enemy can get his hooks into the slightest chink in a man's ethical armor and accelerate his downfall. Given the right opening, the right moral weakness, a certain susceptibility on the part of the prisoner, a clever extortionist can drive his victim into a downhill slide that will ruin his image, self-respect, and life in a very short time.

There are some uncharted aspects to this, some traits of susceptibility which I don't think psychologists yet have words for. I am thinking of the tragedy that can befall a person who has such a need for love or attention that he will sell his soul for it. I use tragedy with the rigorous definition Aristotle applied to it: the story of a good man with a flaw who comes to an unjustified bad end. This is a rather delicate point and one that I want to emphasize. We had very very few collaborators in prison, and comparatively few Aristotelian tragedies, but the story and fate of one of these good men with a flaw might be instructive.

He was handsome, smart, articulate, and smooth. He was almost sincere. He was obsessed with success. When the going got tough, he decided expediency was preferable to principle.

This man was a classical opportunist. He befriended and worked for the enemy to the detriment of his fellow Americans. He made a tacit deal; moreover, he accepted favors (a violation of the code of conduct). In time, out of fear and shame, he withdrew; we could not get him to communicate with the American prisoner organization.

I couldn't learn what made the man tick. One of my best friends in prison, one of the wisest persons I have ever known, had once been in a squadron with this fellow. In prisoners' code I tapped a question to my philosophical friend: "What in the world is going on with that fink?"

"You're going to be surprised at what I have to say," he meticulously tapped back. "In a squadron he pushes himself forward and dominates the scene. He's a continual fountain of information. He's the person everybody relies on for inside dope. He works like mad; often flies more hops than others. It drives him crazy if he's not liked. He tends to grovel and ingratiate himself before others. I didn't realize he was really pathetic until I was sitting around with him and his wife one night when he was spinning his yarns of delusions of grandeur, telling of his great successes and his pending ascension to the top. His wife knew him better than anybody else; she shook her head with genuine sympathy and said to him: 'Gee, you're just a phony.'"

In prison, this man had somehow reached the point where he was willing to sell his soul just to satisfy this need, this immaturity. The only way he could get the attention that he demanded from authority was to grovel and ingratiate himself before the enemy. As a soldier he was a miserable failure, but he had not crossed the boundary of willful treason; he was not written off as an irrevocable loss, as were the two patent collaborators with whom the Vietnamese soon arranged that he live.

As we American POWs built our civilization, and wrote our own laws (which we leaders obliged all to memorize), we also codified certain principles which formed the backbone of our policies and attitudes. I codified the principles of compassion, rehabilitation, and forgiveness with the slogan: "It is neither American nor Christian to nag a repentant sinner to his grave." (Some didn't like it, thought it seemed soft on finks.) And so, we really gave this man a chance. Over time, our efforts worked. After five years of self-indulgence he got himself together and started to communicate with the prisoner organization. I sent the message "Are you on the team or not?"; he replied, "Yes," and came back. He told the Vietnamese that he didn't want to play their dirty games anymore. He wanted to get away from those willful collaborators and he came back and he was accepted, after a fashion.

I wish that were the end of the story. Although he came back, joined us, and even became a leader of sorts, he never totally won himself back. No matter how forgiving we were, he was conscious that many resented him—not so much because he was weak but because he had broken what we might call a gentleman's code. In all of those years when he, a senior officer, had willingly participated in making tape recordings of anti-American material, he had deeply offended the sensibilities of the American prisoners who were forced to listen to him. To most of us it wasn't the rhetoric of the war or the goodness or the badness of this or that issue that counted. The object of our highest value was the well-being of our fellow prisoners. He had broken that code and hurt some of those people. Some thought that as an informer he had indirectly hurt them physically. I don't believe that. What indisputably hurt them was his not having the sensitivity to realize the damage his opportunistic conduct would do to the morale of a bunch of Middle American guys with Middle American attitudes which they naturally cherished. He should have known that in those solitary cells where his tapes were piped were idealistic, direct, patriotic fellows who would be crushed and embarrassed to have him, a senior man in excellent physical shape, so obviously not under torture, telling the world that the war was wrong. Even if he believed what he said, which he did not, he should have had the common decency to keep his mouth shut. You can sit and think anything you want, but when you insensitively cut down those who want to love and help you, you cross a line. He seemed to sense that he could never truly be one of us.

And yet he was likable—particularly back in civilization after release—when tension was off, and making a deal did not seem so important. He exuded charm and "hail fellow" sophistication. He wanted so to be liked by all those men he had once discarded in his search for new friends, new deals, new fields to conquer in Hanoi. The tragedy of his life was obvious to us all. Tears were shed by some of his old prison mates when he was killed in an accident that strongly resembled suicide some months later. The Greek drama had run its course. He was right out of Aristotle's book, a good man with a flaw who had come to an unjustified bad end. The flaw was insecurity: the need to ingratiate himself, the need for love and adulation at any price.

He reminded me of Paul Newman in *The Hustler*. Newman couldn't stand success. He knew how to make a deal. He was handsome, he was smart, he was attractive to everybody; but he had to have adulation, and therein lay the seed of tragedy. Playing high-stakes pool against old Minnesota Fats (Jackie Gleason), Newman was well in the lead, and getting more full of himself by the hour. George C. Scott, the pool bettor, whispered to his partner: "I'm going to keep betting on Minnesota Fats; this other guy [Newman] is a born loser—he's all skill and no character." And he was right, a born loser—I think that's the message.

How can we educate to avoid these casualties? Can we by means of education prevent this kind of tragedy? What we prisoners were in was a one-way leverage game in which the other side had all the mechanical advantage. I suppose you could say that we all live in a leverage world to some degree; we all experience people trying to use us in one way or another. The difference in Hanoi was the degradation of the ends (to be used as propaganda agents of an enemy, or as informers on your fellow Americans), and the power of the means (total environmental control including solitary confinement, restraint by means of leg-irons and handcuffs, and torture). Extortionists always go down the same track: the imposition of guilt and fear for having disobeyed their rules, followed in turn by punishment, apology, confession, and atonement (their payoff). Our captors would go to great lengths to get a man to compromise his own code, even if only slightly, and then they would hold that in their bag, and the next time get him to go a little further.

Some people are psychologically, if not physically, at home in extortion environments. They are tough people who instinctively avoid getting sucked into the undertows. They never kid themselves or their friends; if they miss the mark they admit it. But there's another category of person who gets tripped up. He makes a small compromise, perhaps rationalizes it, and then makes another one; and then he gets depressed, full of shame, lonesome, loses his willpower and self-respect, and comes to a tragic end. Somewhere along the line he realizes that he has turned a corner that he didn't mean to turn. All too late he realizes that he has been worshiping the wrong gods and discovers the wisdom of the ages: life is not fair.

In sorting out the story after our release, we found that most of us had come to combat constant mental and physical pressure in much the same way. We discovered that when a person is alone in a cell and sees the door open only once or twice a day for a bowl of soup, he realizes after a period of weeks in isolation and darkness that he has to build some sort of ritual into his life if he wants to avoid becoming an animal. Ritual fills a need in a hard life and it's easy to see how formal church ritual grew. For almost all of us, this ritual was built around prayer, exercise, and clandestine communication. The prayers I said during those days were prayers of quality with ideas of substance. We found that over the course of time our minds had a tremendous capacity for invention and introspection, but had the weakness of being an integral part of our bodies. I remembered Descartes and how in his philosophy he separated mind and body. One time I cursed my body for the way it decayed my mind. I had decided that I would become a Gandhi. I would have to be carried around on a pallet and in that state I could not be used by my captors for propaganda purposes. After about ten days of fasting, I found that I had become so depressed that soon I would risk going into interrogation ready to spill my guts just looking for a friend. I tapped to the guy next door and I said, "Gosh, how I wish Descartes could have been right, but he's wrong." He was a little slow to reply; I reviewed Descartes's deduction with him and explained how I had discovered that body and mind are inseparable.

On the positive side, I discovered the tremendous file-cabinet volume of the human mind. You can memorize an incredible amount of material and you can draw the past out of your memory with remarkable recall by easing slowly toward the event you seek and not crowding the mind too closely. You'll try to remember who was at your birthday party when you were five years old, and you can get it, but only after months of effort. You can break the locks and find the answers, but you need time and solitude to learn how to use this marvelous device in your head which is the greatest computer on earth.

Of course many of the things we recalled from the past were utterly useless as sources of strength or practicality. For instance, events brought back from cocktail parties or insincere social contacts were almost repugnant because of their emptiness, their utter lack of value. More often than not, the locks worth picking had been on old schoolroom doors. School days can be thought of as a time when one is filling the important stacks of one's memory library. For me,

the golden doors were labeled history and the classics. The historical perspective which enabled a man to take himself away from all
the agitation, not necessarily to see a rosy lining, but to see the real
nature of the situation he faced, was truly a thing of value.

Here's how this historical perspective helped me see the reality
of my own situation and thus cope better with it. I learned from a
Vietnamese prisoner that the same cells we occupied had in years
before been lived in by many of the leaders of the Hanoi government. From my history lessons I recalled that when metropolitan
France permitted communists in the government in 1936, the communists who occupied cells in Vietnam were set free. I marveled
at the cycle of history, all within my memory, which prompted
Hitler's rise in Germany, then led to the rise of the Popular Front
in France, and finally vacated this cell of mine halfway around the
world ("Perhaps Pham Van Dong lived here"). I came to understand what tough people these were. I was willing to fight them
to the death, but I grew to realize that hatred was an indulgence,
a very inefficient emotion. I remember thinking, "If you were committed to beating the dealer in a gambling casino, would *hating*
him help your game?" In a pidgin English propaganda book the
guard gave me, speeches by these old communists about their
prison experiences stressed how they learned to beat down the
enemy by being united. It seemed comforting to know that we
were united against the communist administration of Hoa Lo prison
just as the Vietnamese communists had united against the French
administration of Hoa Lo in the thirties. Prisoners are prisoners, and
there's only one way to beat administrations. We resolved to do it
better in the sixties than they had in the thirties. You don't base
system-beating on any thought of political idealism; you do it as a
competitive thing, as an expression of self-respect.

Education in the classics teaches you that all organizations since
the beginning of time have used the power of guilt; that cycles are
repetitive; and that this is the way of the world. It's a naive person who comes in and says, "Let's see, what's good and what's
bad?" That's a quagmire. You can get out of that quagmire only by
recalling how wise men before you accommodated the same dilemmas. And I believe a good classical education and an understanding of history can best determine the rules you should live by. They
also give you the power to analyze reasons for these rules and

guide you as to how to apply them to your own situation. In a broader sense, all my education helped me. Naval Academy discipline and body contact sports helped me. But the education which I found myself using most was what I got in graduate school. The messages of history and philosophy I used were simple.

The first one is this business about life not being fair. That is a very important lesson and I learned it from a wonderful man named Philip Rhinelander. As a lieutenant commander in the Navy studying political science at Stanford University in 1961, I went over to philosophy corner one day and an older gentleman said, "Can I help you?" I said, "Yes, I'd like to take some courses in philosophy." I told him I'd been in college for six years and had never had a course in philosophy. He couldn't believe it. I told him that I was a naval officer and he said, "Well, I used to be in the Navy. Sit down." Philip Rhinelander became a great influence in my life.

He had been a Harvard lawyer and had pleaded cases before the Supreme Court and then gone to war as a reserve officer. When he came back he took his doctorate at Harvard. He was also a music composer, had been director of general education at Harvard, dean of the School of Humanities and Sciences at Stanford, and by the time I met him had by choice returned to teaching in the classroom. He said, "The course I'm teaching is my personal two-term favorite—The Problem of Good and Evil—and we're starting our second term." He said the message of his course was from the Book of Job. The number one problem in this world is that people are not able to accommodate the lesson in the book.

He recounted the story of Job. It starts out by establishing that Job was the most honorable of men. Then he lost all his goods. He also lost his reputation, which is what really hurt. His wife was badgering him to admit his sins, but he knew he had made no errors. He was not a patient man and demanded to speak to the Lord. When the Lord appeared in the whirlwind, he said, "Now, Job, you have to shape up! Life is not fair." That's my interpretation and that's the way the book ended for hundreds of years. I agree with those of the opinion that the happy ending was spliced on many years later. If you read it, you'll note that the meter changes. People couldn't live with the original message. Here was a good man who came to unexplained grief, and the Lord told him: "That's the way it is. Don't challenge me. This is my world and you either live in it as I designed it or get out."

This was a great comfort to me in prison. It answered the question "Why me?" It cast aside any thoughts of being punished for past actions. Sometimes I shared the message with fellow prisoners as I tapped through the walls to them, but I learned to be selective. It's a strong message which upsets some people.

Rhinelander also passed on to me another piece of classical information which I found of great value. On the day of our last session together he said, "You're a military man, let me give you a book to remember me by. It's a book of military ethics." He handed it to me, and I bade him goodbye with great emotion. I took the book home and that night started to read it. It was the *Enchiridion* of the philosopher Epictetus, his "manual" for the Roman field soldier.

As I began to read, I thought to myself in disbelief, "Does Rhinelander think I'm going to draw lessons for my life from this thing? I'm a fighter pilot. I'm a technical man. I'm a test pilot. I know how to get people to do technical work. I play golf; I drink martinis. I know how to get ahead in my profession. And what does he hand me? A book that says in part, 'It's better to die in hunger, exempt from guilt and fear, than to live in affluence and with perturbation.'" I remembered this later in prison because perturbation was what I was living with. When I ejected from the airplane on that September morn in 1965, I had left the land of technology. I had entered the world of Epictetus, and it's a world that few of us, whether we know it or not, are ever far away from.

In Palo Alto, I had read this book, not with contentment, but with annoyance. Statement after statement: "Men are disturbed not by things, but by the view that they take of them." "Do not be concerned with things which are beyond your power." "Demand not that events should happen as you wish, but wish them to happen as they do happen and you will go on well." This is stoicism. It's not the last word, but it's a viewpoint that comes in handy in many circumstances, and it surely did for me. Particularly this line: "Lameness is an impediment to the body but not to the will." That was significant for me because I wasn't able to stand up and support myself on my badly broken leg for the first couple of years I was in solitary confinement.

Other statements of Epictetus took on added meaning in the light of extortions which often began with our captors' callous pleas: "If you are just reasonable with us we will compensate you. You get your meals, you get to sleep, you won't be pestered, you might even get a cellmate." The catch was that by being "reasonable with us" our enemies meant being their informers, their propagandists. The old stoic had said, "If I can get the things I need with the preservation of my honor and fidelity and self-respect, show me the way and I will get them. But, if you require me to lose my own proper good, that you may gain what is no good, consider how unreasonable and foolish you are." To love our fellow prisoners was within our power. To betray, to propagandize, to disillusion conscientious and patriotic shipmates and destroy their morale so that they in turn would be destroyed was to lose one's proper good.

What attributes serve you well in the extortion environment? We learned there, above all else, that the best defense is to keep your conscience clean. When we did something we were ashamed of, and our captors realized we were ashamed of it, we were in trouble. A little white lie is where extortion and ultimately blackmail start. In 1965, I was crippled and I was alone. I realized that they had all the power. I couldn't see how I was ever going to get out with my honor and self-respect. The one thing I came to realize was that if you don't lose integrity you can't be had and you can't be hurt. Compromises multiply and build up when you're working against a skilled extortionist or a good manipulator. You can't be had if you don't take that first shortcut, or "meet them halfway," as they say, or look for that tacit "deal," or make that first compromise.

Bob North, a political science professor at Stanford, taught me a course called Comparative Marxist Thought. This was not an anticommunist course. It was the study of dogma and thought patterns. We read no criticisms of Marxism, only primary sources. All year we read the works of Marx and Lenin. In Hanoi, I understood more about Marxist theory than my interrogator did. I was able to say to that interrogator, "That's not what Lenin said; you're a deviationist."

One of the things North talked about was brainwashing. A psychologist who studied the Korean prisoner situation, which somewhat paralleled ours, concluded that three categories of prisoners were involved there. The first was the redneck Marine sergeant from Tennessee who had an eighth-grade education. He would get in that interrogation room and they would say that the Spanish-American War was started by the bomb within the *Maine,* which might be true, and he would answer, "B.S." They would show him something about racial unrest in Detroit. "B.S." There was no way they could get to him; his mind was made up. He was a straight guy, red, white, and blue, and everything else was B.S.! He didn't give it a second thought. Not much of a historian, perhaps, but a good security risk.

In the next category were the sophisticates. They were the fellows who could be told these same things about the horrors of American history and our social problems, but had heard it all before, knew both sides of every story, and thought we were on the right track. They weren't ashamed that we had robber barons at a certain time in our history; they were aware of the skeletons in most civilizations' closets. They could not be emotionally involved and so they were good security risks.

The ones who were in trouble were the high school graduates who had enough sense to pick up the innuendo, and yet not enough education to accommodate it properly. Not many of them fell, but most of the men that got entangled started from that background.

The psychologist's point is possibly oversimplistic, but I think his message has some validity. A little knowledge is a dangerous thing.

Generally speaking, I think education is a tremendous defense; the broader, the better. After I was shot down my wife, Sybil, found a clipping glued in the front of my collegiate dictionary: "Education is an ornament in prosperity and a refuge in adversity." She certainly agrees with me on that. Most of us prisoners found that the so-called practical academic exercises in how to do things, which I'm told are proliferating, were useless. I'm not saying that we should base education on training people to be in prison, but I am saying that in stress situations, the fundamentals, the hardcore classical subjects, are what serve best.

Theatrics also helped sustain me. My mother had been a drama coach when I was young and I was in many of her plays. In prison I learned how to manufacture a personality and live it, crawl into it, and hold that role without deviation. During interrogations, I'd check the responses I got to different kinds of behavior. They'd get worried when I did things irrationally. And so, every so often, I would play that "irrational" role and come completely unglued. When I could tell that pressure to make a public exhibition of me was building, I'd stand up, tip the table over, attempt to throw the chair through the window, and say, "No way, Goddammit! I'm not doing that! Now, come over here and fight!" This was a risky ploy, because if they thought you were acting, they would slam you into the ropes and make you scream in pain like a baby. You could watch their faces and read their minds. They had expected me to behave like a stoic.

But a man would be a fool to make their job easy by being conventional and predictable. I could feel the tide turn in my favor at that magic moment when their anger turned to pleading: "Calm down, now calm down." The payoff would come when they decided that the risk of my going haywire in front of some touring American professor on a "fact-finding" mission was too great. More important, they had reason to believe that I would tell the truth—namely, that I had been in solitary confinement for four years and tortured fifteen times—without fear of future consequences. So theatrical training proved helpful to me.

Can you educate for leadership? I think you can, but the communists would probably say no. One day in an argument with an interrogator, I said, "You are so proud of being a party member, what are the criteria?" He said in a flurry of anger, "There are only four: you have to be seventeen years old, you have to be selfless, you have to be smart enough to understand the theory, and you've got to be a person who innately influences others." He stressed that fourth one. I think psychologists would say that leadership is innate, and there is truth in that. But, I also think you can learn some leadership traits that naturally accrue from a good education: compassion is a necessity for leaders, as are spontaneity, bravery, self-discipline, honesty, and above all, integrity.

I remember being disappointed about a month after I was back when one of my young friends, a prison mate, came running up after a reunion at the Naval Academy. He said with glee, "This is really great, you won't believe how this country has advanced. They've practically done away with plebe year at the Academy, and they've got computers in the basement of Bancroft Hall." I thought, "My God, if there was anything that helped us get through those eight years, it was plebe year, and if anything screwed up that war, it was computers!"

For Further Reflection

1. You may want to read Epictetus's *Enchiridion* (in chapter 9) before you answer this question: how did Stoicism help Vice Admiral Stockdale to endure his torture and suffering in prison? Why do you think so many other prisoners failed to maintain their self-respect and loyalty to their country?

2. What other virtues besides courage do you find implicit in this article? Explain.

3. How would you endeavor to maintain your spirits if you were in Stockdale's situation?

4. Stockdale praises his college teacher for introducing him to ideas that were to help him survive later. Should moral education be included as part of public education, including college education?

The Story of David and Bathsheba
Lust

David (c. 1000–960 B.C.E.), the second king of Israel, who as a youth slew the Philistine giant Goliath, was renowned for his valor and honor. During his youth, fleeing the cruel, jealous, and demented King Saul, David showed his mettle not only by escaping and outsmarting the king and his minions, but by refusing to slay him when he discovered him napping in a cave. David was secretly anointed king by the prophet Samuel and married Abigail. After Saul died, David was crowned king of Israel. For a time, he reigned justly and effectively, leading his troops in battle and conquering Jerusalem for Israel. But gradually he retired as general of his army, allowing Joab to replace him. David stayed in his palace in Jerusalem. One afternoon during the war against the Ammonites, the following occurred. We will let the narrator of the Second Book of Samuel (chapters 11 and 12) tell you the story.

Old Testament: Samuel 2.

It happened, late one afternoon, when David arose from his couch and was walking upon the roof of the king's house, that he saw from the roof a woman bathing; and the woman was very beautiful. And David sent and inquired about the woman. And one said, "Is not this Bathsheba, the daughter of Eliam, the wife of Uriah the Hittite?" So David sent messengers, and took her; and she came to him, and he lay with her. Then she returned to her house. And the woman conceived; and she sent and told David, "I am with child."

So David sent word to Joab, "Send me Uriah the Hittite." And Joab sent Uriah to David. When Uriah came to him, David asked how Joab was doing, and how the soldiers were faring, and how the war prospered. Then David said to Uriah, "Go down to your house, and wash your feet." And Uriah went out of the king's house, and there followed him a present from the king. But Uriah slept at the door of the king's house with all the servants of his lord, and did not go down to his house. When the servants told David, "Uriah did not go down to his house," David said to Uriah, "Have you not come from a journey? Why did you not go down to your house?" Uriah responded, "The ark and Israel and Judah dwell in booths; and my lord Joab and the servants of my lord are camping in the open field; shall I then go to my house, to eat and to drink, and to lie with my wife? As you live, and as your soul lives, I will not do this thing."

Then David said to Uriah, "Remain here today also, and tomorrow I will let you depart." So Uriah remained in Jerusalem that day, and the next. And David invited him, and he ate in his presence and drank, so that he made him drunk; and in the evening he went out to lie on his couch with the servants of his lord, but he did not go down to his house.

In the morning David wrote a letter to Joab, and sent it by the hand of Uriah. In the letter he wrote, "Set Uriah in the forefront of the hardest fighting, and then draw back from him, that he may be struck down, and die." And as Joab was besieging the city, he assigned Uriah to the place where he knew the enemy had valiant warriors. And the men of the city came out and fought with Joab; and some of the servants of David among the people fell. Uriah the Hittite was slain also. Then Joab sent and told David all the news about the fighting; and he instructed the messenger, "When you have finished telling all the news about the fighting to the king, then, if the king's anger rises, and if he says to you, 'Why did you go so near the city to fight? Did you not know that they would shoot from the wall? Why did you go so near the wall?' then you shall say, 'Your servant Uriah the Hittite is dead also.'"

So the messenger went, and came and told David all that Joab had sent him to tell. The messenger said to David, "The enemy gained an advantage over us, and came out against us in the field; but we drove them back to the entrance of the gate. Then the archers shot at your servants from the wall; some of the king's servants are dead; and your servant Uriah the Hittite is dead also." David said to the messenger, "Thus shall you say to Joab, 'Do not let this matter trouble you, for the sword devours now one and now another; strengthen your attack upon the city, and overthrow it.' And encourage him."

When Bathsheba heard that Uriah her husband was dead, she grieved for him. And when the period of mourning was over, David sent and brought her to his house, and she became his wife, and bore him a son. But the thing that David had done displeased the Lord.

And the Lord sent Nathan to David. He came to him, and said to him, "There were two men in a certain city, the one rich and the other poor. The rich man had very many flocks and herds; but the poor man had nothing but one little ewe lamb, which he had bought. And he brought it up, and it grew up with him and with his children; it used to eat of his morsel, and drink from his cup, and lie in his bosom, and it was like a daughter to him. Now there came a traveler to the rich man, and he was unwilling to take one of his own flock or herd to prepare for the wayfarer who had come to him, but he took the poor man's lamb, and prepared it for the man who had come to him." Then David's anger was greatly kindled against the man; and he said to Nathan, "As the Lord lives, the man who has done this deserves to die; and he shall restore the lamb fourfold, because he did this thing, and because he had no pity."

Nathan said to David, "You are the man. Thus says the Lord, the God of Israel, 'I anointed you king over Israel, and I delivered you out of the hand of Saul; and I gave you your master's house, and your master's wives into your bosom, and gave you the house of Israel and of Judah; and if this were too little, I would add to you as much more. Why have you despised the word of the Lord, to do what is evil in his sight? You have smitten Uriah the Hittite with the sword, and have taken his wife to be your wife, and have slain him with the sword of the Ammonites. Now therefore the sword shall never depart from your house, because you have despised me, and have taken the wife of Uriah the Hittite to be your wife.' Thus says the LORD, 'Behold, I will raise up evil against you out of your own house; and I will take your wives before your eyes, and give them to your neighbor, and he shall lie with your wives in the sight of this sun. For you did it secretly; but I will do this thing before all Israel, and before the sun.'" David said to Nathan, "I have sinned against the LORD." And Nathan said to David, "The LORD also has put away your sin; you shall not die. Nevertheless, because by this deed you have utterly scorned the LORD, the child that is born to you shall die." Then Nathan went to his house.

[During David's period of mourning over the death of his son and repenting for his sins of adultery and murder, he wrote the 51st Psalm. This is from the King James Version:]

Have mercy on me, O God, according to thy steadfast love; according to thy abundant mercy blot out my transgressions.

Wash me thoroughly from my iniquity, and cleanse me from my sin!

For I know my transgressions, and my sin is ever before me.

Against thee, thee only, have I sinned, and done that which is evil in thy sight, so that thou art justified in thy sentence and blameless in thy judgment.

Behold, I was brought forth in iniquity, and in sin did my mother conceive me.

Behold, thou desirest truth in the inward being; therefore teach me wisdom in my secret heart.

Purge me with hyssop, and I shall be clean; wash me, and I shall be whiter than snow.

Fill me with joy and gladness; let the bones which thou hast broken rejoice.

Hide thy face from my sins, and blot out all my iniquities.

Create in me a clean heart, O God, and put a new and right spirit within me.

Cast me not away from thy presence, and take not thy holy Spirit from me.

Restore to me the joy of thy salvation, and uphold me with a willing spirit. . . .

For thou delightest not in sacrifice; else would I give it.

The sacrifice acceptable to God is a broken spirit; a broken and contrite heart, O God, thou wilt not despise.

For Further Reflection

1. Write an essay on a contemporary version of David's vice. How would society today handle a case like this?

2. What does this story tell us about penance? Should David have been tried for murder and abusing his power?

3. Consider the prophet Nathan's role and tactics in conveying a moral message to David. What is significant about his method?

Where Love Is, There Is God

LEO TOLSTOY

A biographical sketch of Tolstoy is found in the second reading of this chapter. The following is Tolstoy's attempt to convey the significance of love.

In a little town in Russia there lived a cobbler, Martin Avedéitch by name. He had a tiny room in a basement, the one window of which looked out on to the street. Through it one could see only the feet of those who passed by, but Martin recognized the people by their boots. He had lived long in the place and had many acquaintances. There was hardly a pair of boots in the neighborhood that had not been once or twice through his hands, so he often saw his own handiwork through the window. Some he had re-soled, some patched, some stitched up, and to some he had even put fresh uppers. He had

---

Translated from Leo Tolstoy, "Where Love Is, There Is God."

plenty to do, for he worked well, used good material, did not charge too much, and could be relied on. If he could do a job by the day required, he undertook it; if not, he told the truth and gave no false promises. So he was well known and never short of work.

Martin had always been a good man, but in his old age he began to think more about his soul and to draw nearer to God.

From that time Martin's whole life changed. His life became peaceful and joyful. He sat down to his task in the morning, and when he had finished his day's work he took the lamp down from the wall, stood it on the table, fetched his Bible from the shelf, opened it, and sat down to read. The more he read the better he understood, and the clearer and happier he felt in his mind.

It happened once that Martin sat up late, absorbed in his book. He was reading Luke's Gospel, and in the sixth chapter he came upon the verses:

> To him that smiteth thee on the one cheek offer also the other; and from him that taketh away thy cloak withhold not thy coat also. Give to every man that asketh thee; and of him that taketh away thy goods ask them not again. And as ye would that men should do to you, do ye also to them likewise.

He thought about this, and was about to go to bed, but was loath to leave his book. So he went on reading the seventh chapter—about the centurion, the widow's son, and the answer to John's disciples—and he came to the part where a rich Pharisee invited the Lord to his house. And he read how the woman who was a sinner anointed his feet and washed them with her tears, and how he justified her. Coming to the forty-fourth verse, he read:

> And turning to the woman, he said unto Simon, "Seest thou this woman? I entered into thine house, thou gavest me no water for my feet, but she hath wetted my feet with her tears, and wiped them with her hair. Thou gavest me no kiss, but she, since the time I came in, hath not ceased to kiss my feet. My head with oil thou didst not anoint, but she hath anointed my feet with ointment."

He read these verses and thought: "He gave no water for his feet, gave no kiss, his head with oil he did not anoint. . . ." And Martin took off his spectacles once more, laid them on his book, and pondered.

"He must have been like me, that Pharisee. He too thought only of himself—how to get a cup of tea, how to keep warm and comfortable, never a thought of his guest. He took care of himself, but for his guest he cared nothing at all. Yet who was the guest? The Lord himself! If he came to me, should I behave like that?"

Then Martin laid his head upon both his arms and, before he was aware of it, he fell asleep.

"Martin!" He suddenly heard a voice, as if someone had breathed the word above his ear.

He started from his sleep. "Who's there?" he asked.

He turned around and looked at the door; no one was there. He called again. Then he heard quite distinctly: "Martin, Martin! Look out into the street tomorrow, for I shall come."

Martin roused himself, rose from his chair and rubbed his eyes, but did not know whether he had heard these words in a dream or awake. He put out the lamp and lay down to sleep.

The next morning he rose before daylight, and after saying his prayers he lit the fire and prepared his cabbage soup and buckwheat porridge. Then he lit the samovar, put on his apron, and sat down by the window to his work. He looked out into the street more than he worked, and whenever anyone passed in unfamiliar boots he would stoop and look up, so as to see not only the feet but the face of the passerby as well. A house-porter passed in new felt boots, then a water-carrier. Presently an old soldier of Nicholas's reign came near the window, spade in hand. Martin knew him by his boots, which were shabby old felt once, galoshed with leather. The old man was called Stepánitch. A neighboring tradesman kept him in his house for charity, and his duty was to help the house-porter. He began to clear away the snow before Martin's window. Martin glanced at him and then went on with his work.

After he had made a dozen stitches he felt drawn to look out of the window again. He saw that Stepánitch had leaned his spade against the wall, and was either resting himself or trying to get warm. The man was old and broken down, and had evidently not enough strength even to clear away the snow.

"What if I called him in and gave him some tea?" thought Martin. "The samovar is just on the boil."

He stuck his awl in its place, and rose, and putting the samovar on the table, made tea. Then he tapped the window with his fingers. Stepánitch turned and came to the window. Martin beckoned to him to come in, and went himself to open the door.

"Come in," he said, "and warm yourself a bit. I'm sure you must be cold."

"May God bless you!" Stepánitch answered. "My bones do ache, to be sure." He came in, first shaking off the snow, and lest he should leave marks on the floor he began wiping his feet. But as he did so he tottered and nearly fell.

"Don't trouble to wipe your feet," said Martin. "I'll wipe up the floor—it's all in the day's work. Come, friend, sit down and have some tea."

Filling two tumblers, he passed one to his visitor, and pouring his own tea out into the saucer, began to blow on it.

Stepánitch emptied his glass and, turning it upside down, put the remains of his piece of sugar on the top. He began to express his thanks, but it was plain that he would be glad of some more.

"Have another glass," said Martin, refilling the visitor's tumbler and his own. But while he drank his tea Martin kept looking out into the street.

"Are you expecting anyone?" asked the visitor.

"Am I expecting anyone? Well, now, I'm ashamed to tell you. It isn't that I really expect anyone, but I heard something last night which I can't get out of my mind. Whether it was a vision, or only a fancy, I can't tell. You see, friend, last night I was reading the Gospel, about Christ the Lord, how he suffered, and how he walked on earth. You have heard tell of it, I dare say."

"I have heard tell of it," answered Stepánitch. "But I'm an ignorant man and not able to read."

"Well, you see, I was reading how he walked on earth. I came to that part, you know, where he went to a Pharisee who did not receive him well. Well, friend, as I read about it, I thought how that man did not receive Christ the Lord with proper honor. Suppose such a thing could happen to such a man as myself, I thought, what would I not do to receive him! But that man gave him no reception at all. Well, friend, as I was thinking of this, I began to doze, and as I dozed I heard someone call me by name. I got up, and thought I heard someone whispering, 'Expect me. I will come tomorrow.' This happened twice over. And to tell you the truth, it sank so into my mind that, though I am ashamed of it myself, I keep on expecting him, the dear Lord!"

Stepánitch shook his head in silence, finished his tumbler, and laid it on its side, but Martin stood it up again and refilled it for him.

"Thank you, Martin Avedéitch," he said. "You have given me food and comfort both for soul and body."

"You're very welcome. Come again another time. I am glad to have a guest," said Martin.

Stepánitch went away, and Martin poured out the last of the tea and drank it up. Then he put away the tea things and sat down to his work, stitching the back seam of a boot. And as he stitched he kept looking out of the window, and thinking about what he had read in the Bible. And his head was full of Christ's sayings.

Two soldiers went by: one in Government boots, the other in boots of his own; then the master of a neighboring house, in shining galoshes; then a baker carrying a basket. All these passed on. Then a woman came up in worsted stockings and peasant-made shoes. She passed the window, but stopped by the wall. Martin glanced up at her through the window, and saw that she was a stranger, poorly dressed, and with a baby in her arms. She stopped by the wall with her back to the wind, trying to wrap the baby up though she had hardly anything to wrap it in. The woman had only summer clothes on, and even they were shabby and worn. Through the window Martin heard the baby crying, and the woman trying to soothe it, but unable to do so. Martin rose, and going out of the door and up the steps he called to her. "My dear, I say, my dear!"

The woman heard, and turned around.

"Why do you stand out there with the baby in the cold? Come inside. You can wrap him up better in a warm place. Come this way!"

The woman was surprised to see an old man in an apron, with spectacles on his nose, calling to her, but she followed him in.

They went down the steps, entered the little room, and the old man led her to the bed.

"There, sit down, my dear, near the stove. Warm yourself, and feed the baby."

"Haven't any milk. I have eaten nothing myself since early morning," said the woman, but still she took the baby to her breast.

Martin shook his head. He brought out a basin and some bread. Then he opened the oven door and poured some cabbage soup into the basin. He took out the porridge pot also, but the porridge was not yet ready, so he spread a cloth on the table and served only the soup and bread.

"Sit down and eat, my dear, and I'll mind the baby. Why, bless me, I've had children of my own; I know how to manage them."

The woman crossed herself, and sitting down at the table began to eat, while Martin put the baby on the bed and sat down by it.

Martin sighed. "Haven't you any warmer clothing? he asked.

"How could I get warm clothing?" said she. "Why, I pawned my last shawl for sixpence yesterday."

Then the woman came and took the child, and Martin got up. He went and looked among some things that were hanging on the wall, and brought back an old cloak.

"Here," he said, "though it's a worn-out old thing, it will do to wrap him up in."

The woman looked at the cloak, then at the old man, and taking it, burst into tears. Martin turned away, and groping under the bed brought out a small trunk. He fumbled about in it, and again sat down opposite the woman. And the woman said, "The Lord bless you, friend."

"Take this for Christ's sake," said Martin, and gave her six-pence to get her shawl out of pawn. The woman crossed herself, and Martin did the same, and then he saw her out.

After a while Martin saw an apple-woman stop just in front of his window. On her back she had a sack full of chips, which she was taking home. No doubt she had gathered them at someplace where building was going on.

The sack evidently hurt her, and she wanted to shift it from one shoulder to the other, so she put it down on the footpath and, placing her basket on a post, began to shake down the chips in the sack. While she was doing this, a boy in a tattered cap ran up, snatched an apple out of the basket, and tried to slip away. But the old woman noticed it, and turning, caught the boy by his sleeve. He began to struggle, trying to free himself, but the old woman held on with both hands, knocked his cap off his head, and seized hold of his hair. The boy screamed and the old woman scolded. Martin dropped his awl, not waiting to stick it in its place, and rushed out of the door. Stumbling up the steps and dropping his spectacles in his hurry, he ran out into the street. The old woman was pulling the boy's hair and scolding him, and threatening to take him to the police. The lad was struggling and protesting, saying, "I did not take it. What are you beating me for? Let me go!"

Martin separated them. He took the boy by the hand and said, "Let him go, Granny. Forgive him for Christ's sake."

"I'll pay him out, so that he won't forget it for a year! I'll take the rascal to the police!"

Martin began entreating the old woman.

"Let him go, Granny. He won't do it again."

The old woman let go, and the boy wished to run away, but Martin stopped him.

"Ask the Granny's forgiveness!" said he. "And don't do it another time. I saw you take the apple."

The boy began to cry and to beg pardon.

"That's right. And now here's an apple for you," and Martin took an apple from the basket and gave it to the boy, saying, "I will pay you, Granny."

"You will spoil them that way, the young rascals," said the old woman. "He ought to be whipped so that he should remember it for a week."

"Oh, Granny, Granny," said Martin, "that's our way—but it's not God's way. If he should be whipped for stealing an apple, what should be done to us for our sins?"

The old woman was silent.

And Martin told her the parable of the lord who forgave his servant a large debt, and how the servant went out and seized his debtor by the throat. The old woman listened to it all, and the boy, too, stood by and listened.

"God bids us forgive," said Martin, "or else we shall not be forgiven. Forgive everyone, and a thoughtless youngster most of all."

The old woman wagged her head and sighed.

"It's true enough," said she, "but they are getting terribly spoiled."

"Then we old ones must show them better ways," Martin replied.

"That's just what I say," said the old woman. "I have had seven of them myself, and only one daughter is left." And the old woman began to tell how and where she was living with her daughter, and how many grandchildren she had. "There, now," she said, "I have but little strength left, yet I work hard for the sake of my grandchildren; and nice children they are, too. No one comes out to meet me but the children. Little Annie, now, won't leave me for anyone. It's 'Grandmother, dear grandmother, darling grandmother.'" And the old woman completely softened at the thought.

"Of course, it was only his childishness," said she, referring to the boy.

As the old woman was about to hoist her sack on her back, the lad sprang forward to her, saying, "Let me carry it for you, Granny. I'm going that way."

The old woman nodded her head, and put the sack on the boy's back, and they went down the street together, the old woman quite forgetting to ask Martin to pay for the apple. Martin stood and watched them as they went along talking to each other.

When they were out of sight Martin went back to the house. Having found his spectacles unbroken on the steps, he picked up his awl and sat down again to work. He worked a little, but soon could not see to pass the bristle through the holes in the leather, and presently, he noticed the lamplighter passing on his way to light the street lamps.

"Seems it's time to light up," thought he. So he trimmed his lamp, hung it up, and sat down again to work. He finished off one boot and, turning it about, examined it. It was all right. Then he gathered his tools together, swept up the cuttings, put away the bristles and the thread and the awls, and, taking down the lamp, placed it on the table. Then he took the Gospels from the shelf. He meant to open them at the place he had marked the day before with a bit of morocco, but the book opened at another place. As Martin opened it, his yesterday's dream came back to his mind, and no sooner had he thought of it than he seemed to hear footsteps, as though someone were moving behind him. Martin turned round, and it seemed to him as if people were standing in the dark corner, but he could not make out who they were. And a voice whispered in his ear: "Martin, Martin, don't you know me?"

"Who is it?" muttered Martin.

"It is I," said the voice. And out of the dark corner stepped Stepánitch, who smiled and vanishing like a cloud was seen no more.

"It is I," said the voice again. And out of the darkness stepped the woman with the baby in her arms, and the woman smiled and the baby laughed, and they too vanished.

"It is I," said the voice once more. And the old woman and the boy with the apple stepped out and both smiled, and then they too vanished.

And Martin's soul grew glad. He crossed himself, put on his spectacles, and began reading the Gospel just where it had opened. And at the top of the page he read:

> I was hungry, and ye gave me meat. I was thirsty, and ye gave me drink. I was a stranger, and ye took me in.

And at the bottom of the page he read:

> Inasmuch as ye did it unto one of these my brethren, even these least, ye did it unto me.

And Martin understood that his dream had come true, and that the Savior had really come to him that day, and he had welcomed him.

For Further Reflection

1. Analyze this story. What is Tolstoy trying to convey? What do you get out of the story?

Reflections on Suffering

BERTRAND RUSSELL

The British philosopher Bertrand Russell (1872–1970) was someone who thought deeply about the question of the meaning of life. Russell says in his *Autobiography* that his

Reprinted from Bertrand Russell, *Autobiography,* vol. 1, p. 146 (Unwin & Hyman, Ltd., 1951).

youth was very unhappy and only the love of mathematics kept him from committing suicide. Gradually, he learned to find happiness. In these two short selections from his *Autobiography,* Russell first tells of an experience which greatly affected his life and then goes on to summarize what gives him meaning in life.

SPRING 1901

When we came home, we found Mrs. W undergoing an unusually severe bout of pain. She seemed cut off from everyone and everything by walls of agony, and the sense of the solitude of each human soul suddenly overwhelmed me. Ever since my marriage, my emotional life had been calm and superficial. I had forgotten all the deeper issues, and had been content with flippant cleverness. Suddenly the ground seemed to give way beneath me, and I found myself in quite another region. Within five minutes I went thru some such reflections as the following: the loneliness of the human soul is unendurable; nothing can penetrate it except the highest intensity of the sort of love that religious teachers have preached; whatever does not spring from this motive is harmful, or at best useless; it follows that war is wrong, that a public school education is abominable, that the use of force is to be deprecated, and that in human relations one should penetrate to the core of loneliness in each person and speak to that. [The writer then describes his sudden awareness of Mrs. W's three-year-old son with whom he then and there found an affinity.] . . . At the end of those five minutes, I had become a completely different person. For a time, a sort of mystic illumination possessed me. I felt that I knew the inmost thoughts of everybody that I met in the street, and though this was, no doubt, a delusion, I did in actual fact find myself in *far closer* touch than previously with all my friends, and many of my acquaintances. Having been an Imperialist, I became during those five minutes . . . a Pacificist. Having for years cared only for exactness and analysis, I found myself filled with semi-mystical feelings about beauty, and with an intense interest in children and with a desire almost as profound as that of the Buddha to find some philosophy which should make human life endurable. A strange excitement possessed me, containing intense pain but also some element of triumph through the fact that I could dominate pain, and make it, as I thought, a gateway to wisdom. The mystic insight which I then imagined myself to possess has largely faded, and the habit of analysis has reasserted itself. But something of what I thought I saw in that moment has remained always with me, *causing* my attitude during the first war, my interest in my children, my indifference to minor misfortunes and a certain emotional tone in all my human relations.

EPILOGUE

Love, Knowledge, and Pity

Three passions, simple but overwhelmingly strong, have governed my life: the longing for love, the search for knowledge, and unbearable pity for the suffering of mankind. These passions, like great winds, have blown me hither and thither, in a wayward course, over a deep ocean of anguish, reaching to the very verge of despair.

I have sought love, first, because it brings ecstasy—ecstasy so great that I would often have sacrificed all the rest of life for a few hours of this joy. I have sought it, next, because it relieves loneliness—that terrible loneliness in which one shivering consciousness looks over the rim of the world into the cold unfathomable lifeless abyss. I have sought it, finally, because in the union of love I have seen, in a mystic miniature, the prefiguring vision of the heaven that saints and poets have imagined. This is what I sought, and though it might seem too good for human life, this is what—at last—I have found.

With equal passion I have sought knowledge. I have wished to understand the hearts of men. I have wished to know why the stars shine. And I have tried to apprehend the Pythagorean power by which number holds sway above the flux. A little of this, but not much, I have achieved.

Love and knowledge, so far as they were possible, led upward toward the heavens. But always pity brought me back to earth. Echoes of cries of pain reverberate in my heart. Children in famine, victims tortured by oppressors, helpless old people a hated burden to their sons, and the whole world of loneliness, poverty, and pain make a mockery of what human life should be. I long to alleviate the evil, but I cannot, and I too suffer.

This has been my life. I have found it worth living, and would gladly live it again if the chance were offered me.

For Further Reflection

1. Compare the first passage with the second. Do you see any differences?

2. How does your set of values compare with Russell's? Do you think that Russell's philosophy of life is adequate for happiness and the good life? Compare it with the other readings in this part.

The Volunteer at Auschwitz
Altruism

CHARLES COLSON

Charles Colson was an advisor to President Richard Nixon. He is now a writer, involved in promoting Christian causes. This essay is about the suffering that went on at the Nazi concentration camp at Auschwitz, where between 1940 and 1945 some two million people were exterminated. During this time of brutal treatment, acts of courage and altruism sometimes occurred. This is the story of one of them.

Maximilian Kolbe was forty-five years old in the early autumn of 1939 when the Nazis invaded his homeland. He was a Polish friar in Niepokalanow, a village near Warsaw. There, 762 priests and lay brothers lived in the largest friary in the world. Father Kolbe presided over Niepokalanow with a combination of industry, joy, love, and humor that made him beloved by the plainspoken brethren there.

In his simple room, he sat each morning at a pigeonhole desk, a large globe before him, praying over the world. He did so, tortured by the fact that a pale man with arresting blue eyes and a terrifying power of manipulation had whipped the people of Germany into a frenzy. Whole nations had already fallen to the evil Adolf Hitler and his Nazis.

"An atrocious conflict is brewing," Father Kolbe told a group of friars one day after he had finished prayers. "We do not know what will develop. In our beloved Poland, we must expect the worst." Father Kolbe was right. His country was next.

On September 1, 1939, the Nazi blitzkrieg broke over Poland. After several weeks, a group of Germans arrived at Niepokalanow on motorcycles and arrested Father Kolbe and all but two of his friars who had remained behind. They were loaded on trucks, then into livestock wagons, and two days later arrived at Amtitz, a prison camp.

Conditions were horrible, but not horrific. Prisoners were hungry, but no one died of starvation. Strangely, within a few weeks the brothers were released from prison. Back at the friary, they found the buildings vandalized and the Nazis in control, using the facility as a deportation camp for political prisoners, refugees, and Jews.

The situation was an opportunity for ministry, and Father Kolbe took advantage of it, helping the sick and comforting the fearful.

While Kolbe and the friars used their time to serve others, the Nazis used theirs to decide just how to impose their will on the rest of Europe. To Adolf Hitler, the Jews and Slavic people were the *Untermenschen* (subhumans). Their cultures and cities were to be erased and their industry appropriated for Germany. On October 2, Hitler outlined a secret memorandum to Hans Frank, the governor general of Poland. In a few phrases he determined the grim outcome for millions: "The [ordinary] Poles are especially born for low labor . . . the Polish gentry must cease to exist . . . all representatives of the Polish intelligentsia are to be exterminated. . . . There should be one master for the Poles, the German."

As for Poland's hundreds of thousands of priests?

"They will preach what we want them to preach," said Hitler's memo. "If any priest acts differently, we will make short work of him. The task of the priest is to keep the Poles quiet, stupid, and dull-witted."

Maximilian Kolbe was clearly a priest who "acted differently" from the Nazis' designs.

In early February 1941, the Polish underground smuggled word to Kolbe that his name was on a Gestapo list: he was about to be arrested. Kolbe knew what happened to loved ones of those who tried to elude the Nazis' grasp; their friends and colleagues were taken instead. He had no wife or children; his church was his family. And he could not risk the loss of any of his brothers in Christ. So he stayed at Niepokalanow.

At nine o'clock on the morning of February 17, Father Kolbe was sitting at his pigeonhole desk, his eyes and prayers on the globe before him, when he heard the sound of heavy vehicles outside the thick panes of his green-painted windows. He knew it was the Nazis, but he remained at his desk. He would wait for them to come to him.

After being held in Nazi prisons for several months, Father Kolbe was found guilty of the crime of publishing unapproved materials and sentenced to Auschwitz. Upon his arrival at the camp in May 1941, an SS officer informed him that the life expectancy of priests there was about a month. Kolbe was assigned to the timber detail; he was to carry felled tree trunks from one place to another. Guards stood by to ensure that the exhausted prisoners did so at a quick trot.

Years of slim rations and overwork at Niepokalanow had already weakened Kolbe. Now, under the load of wood, he staggered and collapsed. Officers converged on him, kicking him with their shiny leather boots and beating him with their whips. He was stretched out on a pile of wood, dealt fifty lashes, then shoved into a ditch, covered with branches, and left for dead.

Later, having been picked up by some brave prisoners, he awoke in a camp hospital bed alongside several other near-dead inmates. There, miraculously, he revived.

"No need to waste gas or a bullet on that one," chuckled one SS officer to another. "He'll be dead soon."

Kolbe was switched to other work and transferred to Barracks 14, where he continued to minister to his fellow prisoners, so tortured by hunger they could not sleep.

By the end of July 1941, Auschwitz was working like a well-organized killing machine, and the Nazis congratulated themselves on their efficiency. The camp's five chimneys never stopped smoking. The stench was terrible, but the results were excellent: eight thousand

Jews could be stripped, their possessions appropriated for the Reich, gassed, and cremated—all in twenty-four hours. Every twenty-four hours.

About the only problem was the occasional prisoner from the work side of the camp who would figure out a way to escape. When these escapees were caught, as they usually were, they would be hanged with special nooses that slowly choked out their miserable lives—a grave warning to others who might be tempted to try.

Then one July night as the frogs and insects in the marshy land surrounding the camp began their evening chorus, the air was suddenly filled with the baying of dogs, the curses of soldiers, and the roar of motorcycles. A man had escaped from Barracks 14.

The next morning there was a peculiar tension as the ranks of phantom-thin prisoners lined up for morning roll call in the central square, their eyes on the large gallows before them. But there was no condemned man standing there, his hands bound behind him, his face bloodied from blows and dog bites. That meant the prisoner had made it out of Auschwitz. And that meant death for some of those who remained.

After the roll call, Camp Commandant Fritsch ordered the dismissal of all but Barracks 14. While the rest of the camp went about its duties, the prisoners from Barracks 14 stood motionless in line. They waited. Hours passed. The summer sun beat down. Some fainted and were dragged away. Some swayed in place but held on; those the SS officers beat with the butts of their guns. Father Kolbe, by some miracle, stayed on his feet, his posture as straight as his resolve.

By evening roll call the commandant was ready to levy sentence. The other prisoners had returned from their day of slave labor; now he could make a lesson out of the fate of this miserable barracks.

Fritsch began to speak, the veins in his thick neck standing out with rage. "The fugitive has not been found," he screamed. "Ten of you will die for him in the starvation bunker. Next time, twenty will be condemned."

The rows of exhausted prisoners began to sway as they heard the sentence. The guards let them; terror was part of their punishment.

The starvation bunker! Anything was better—death on the gallows, a bullet in the head at the Wall of Death, or even the gas in the chambers. All those were quick, even humane, compared to Nazi starvation, for they denied you water as well as food.

The prisoners had heard the stories from the starvation bunker in the basement of Barracks 11. They said the condemned didn't even look like human beings after a day or two. They frightened even the guards. Their throats turned to paper, their brains turned to fire, their intestines dried up and shriveled like desiccated worms.

Commandant Fritsch walked the rows of prisoners. When he stopped before a man, he would command in bad Polish, "Open your mouth! Put out your tongue! Show your teeth!" And so he went, choosing victims like horses.

His dreary assistant, Palitsch, followed behind. As Fritsch chose a man, Palitsch noted the number stamped on the prisoner's filthy shirt. The Nazis, as always, were methodical. Soon there were ten men—ten numbers neatly listed on the death roll. The chosen groaned, sweating with fear. "My poor wife!" one man cried. "My poor children! What will they do?"

"Take off your shoes!" the commandant barked at the ten men. This was one of his rituals; they must march to their deaths barefoot. A pile of twenty wooden clogs made a small heap at the front of the grassy square.

Suddenly there was a commotion in the ranks. A prisoner had broken out of line, calling for the commandant. It was unheard of to leave the ranks, let alone address a Nazi officer; it was cause for execution.

Fritsch had his hand on his revolver, as did the officers behind him. But he broke precedent. Instead of shooting the prisoner, he shouted at him.

"Halt! What does this Polish pig want of me?"

The prisoners gasped. It was their beloved Father Kolbe, the priest who shared his last crust, who comforted the dying and nourished their souls. Not Father Kolbe! The frail priest spoke softly, even calmly, to the Nazi butcher. "I would like to die in place of one of the men you condemned."

Fritsch stared at the prisoner, No. 16670. He never considered them as individuals; they were just a gray blur. But he looked now. No. 16670 didn't appear to be insane.

"Why?" snapped the commandant.

Father Kolbe sensed the need for exacting diplomacy. The Nazis never reversed an order; so he must not seem to be asking him to do so. Kolbe knew the Nazi dictum of destruction: the weak and the elderly first. He would play on this well-ingrained principle.

"I am an old man, sir, and good for nothing. My life will serve no purpose."

His ploy triggered the response Kolbe wanted. "In whose place do you want to die?" asked Fritsch.

"For that one," Kolbe responded, pointing to the weeping prisoner who had bemoaned his wife and children.

Fritsch glanced at the weeping prisoner. He did look stronger than this tattered No. 16670 before him.

For the first and last time, the commandant looked Kolbe in the eye. "Who are you?" he asked.

The prisoner looked back at him, a strange fire in his dark eyes. "I am a priest."

"*Ein Pfaffe!*" the commandant snorted. He looked at his assistant and nodded. Palitsch drew a line through No. 5659 and wrote down No. 16670. Kolbe's place on the death ledger was set.

Father Kolbe bent down to take off his clogs, then joined the group to be marched to Barracks 11. As he did so, No. 5659 passed by him at a distance—and on the man's face was an expression so astonished that it had not yet become gratitude.

But Kolbe wasn't looking for gratitude. If he was to lay down his life for another, the fulfillment had to be in the act of obedience itself. The joy must be found in submitting his small will to the will of One more grand.

As the condemned men entered Barracks 11, guards roughly pushed them down the stairs to the basement.

"Remove your clothes!" shouted an officer. *Christ died on the cross naked,* Father Kolbe thought as he took off his pants and thin shirt. *It is only fitting that I suffer as He suffered.*

In the basement the ten men were herded into a dark, windowless cell.

"You will dry up like tulips," sneered one jailer. Then he swung the heavy door shut.

As the hours and days passed, however, the camp became aware of something extraordinary happening in the death cell. Past prisoners had spent their dying days howling, attacking one another, clawing the walls in a frenzy of despair.

But now, coming from the death box, those outside heard the faint sounds of singing. For this time the prisoners had a shepherd to gently lead them through the shadows of the valley of death, pointing them to the Great Shepherd. And perhaps for that reason Father Kolbe was the last to die.

On August 14, 1941, there were four prisoners still alive in the bunker, and it was needed for new occupants. A German doctor named Boch descended the steps of Barracks 11, four syringes in his hand. Several SS troopers and a prisoner named Brono Borgowiec (who survived Auschwitz) were with him—the former to observe and the latter to carry out the bodies.

When they swung the bunker door open, there, in the light of their flashlight, they saw Father Maximilian Kolbe, a living skeleton, propped against one wall. His head was inclined a bit to the left. He had the ghost of a smile on his lips and his eyes wide open, fixed on some faraway vision. He did not move.

The other three prisoners were on the floor, unconscious but alive. The doctor took care of them first: a jab of the needle into the bony left arm, the push of the piston in the syringe. It seemed a waste of the drug, but he had his orders. Then he approached No. 16670 and repeated the action.

In a moment, Father Kolbe was dead.

For Further Reflection

1. Analyze this story, and discuss the moral courage and altruism of Father Kolbe. Why do you think he offered to substitute his life for the condemned man's?

2. Some people think everyone is an egoist at heart. How would such an egoist interpret Father Kolbe's behavior? Do you agree with that analysis? (In chapter 8 we will examine ethical egoism.)

Further Readings for Chapter 7

Becker, Lawrence. *On Justifying Moral Arguments*. London: Routledge and Kegan Paul, 1973. Chapter 19.

Cooper, John. *Reason and the Human Good in Aristotle*. Cambridge, Mass.: Harvard University Press, 1975.

Kruschwitz, Robert, and Robert Roberts, eds., *The Virtues*. Belmont, Calif.: Wadsworth, 1987. An excellent up-to-date anthology, containing an extensive bibliography.

MacIntyre, Alasdair. *After Virtue*. Notre Dame, Ind.: University of Notre Dame Press, 1981.

Murdoch, Iris. *The Sovereignty of Good*. New York, Schocken Books, 1971.

Pence, Gregory. "Recent Work on Virtues." *American Philosophical Quarterly,* vol. 21 1984.

Pojman, Louis. *Ethics: Discovering Right and Wrong,* 3 ed. Belmont, Calif.: Wadsworth, 1999. Chapter 8.

Sommers, Christina Hoff, and Fred Sommers. *Vice and Virtues in Everyday Life*. New York: Harcourt Brace Jovanovich, 1985.

Taylor, Richard. *Ethics, Faith and Reason*. Englewood Cliffs, N.J. Prentice-Hall, 1985.

Trianosky, Gregory. "Supererogation, Wrongdoing, and Vice: On the Autonomy of the Ethics of Virtue." *Journal of Philosophy,* January 1986.

Wallace, James. *Virtues and Vices*. Ithaca, N.Y.: Cornell University Press, 1978.

Part III

Moral Issues

In this part of our book we examine three related, vitally important issues in moral theory: egoism and the question "Why should I be moral?" (chapter 8); the question whether life has meaning (chapter 9); and the question of freedom and autonomy, which have to do with self-respect (chapter 10). As you will see, these questions are related. If life has no meaning, it may not make sense to be moral all of the time or care about morality. But if life does have meaning, not only will morality be crucial but part of being moral is the promotion of freedom, autonomy, and self-respect.

CHAPTER 8

Ethics and Egoism
Why Should We Be Moral?

Why should we be moral? That is, you may ask yourself, Why should I do what morality requires even when it may not be in my best interest? Or, Is it really in my best interest to be moral all of the time, after all, even if I fail to realize it? Or, Is morality only *sometimes* in my best interest—when it depends on group cooperation? For example, people can run up charges on their credit cards and not pay them, perhaps moving to a different country. So it might be in my interest to charge up my credit card and then move to another country. But if it is not in my interest to move, I may get into trouble if I don't pay my credit card bill, and I will get a bad credit rating, which will affect my future prospects in obtaining loans. So in this case, it is in my interest to comply with moral rules. But suppose I can cheat and get away with it? I obtain someone else's brilliant research paper and turn it in as my own. No one is likely ever to find out. Why shouldn't I cheat? Of course, I won't like it if other people do the same—and if enough people cheat, grades will become meaningless. But then, as I profit from my immorality, I can contribute some money back into moral reform, so that more people will be motivated to be good.

Is there anything wrong with this reasoning?

In our first reading, Glaucon, Plato's brother, asks Socrates why we should be moral. He then tells the story of the shepherd Gyges, who finds a ring which allows him to become invisible. What fun he can have! He can serve his interests with impunity and not be discovered. But Socrates rejects this view and argues that Gyges and his ilk never get away with immorality. Justice is intrinsically valuable, like health. The good is really good for you, so that if you act immorally, you really are harming yourself.

But many reject Socrates' way of looking at the matter. They accuse him of supposing an objective world of values or a divine law which ensures that those who act selfishly will be punished— through karma or by God. But take away the notion of God or karma and the picture breaks down.

In our second reading, James Rachels outlines several versions of ethical egoism, especially Ayn Rand's famous defense of the virtue of selfishness, which holds that everyone ought to do what will maximize one's own expected personal utility or bring about one's own happiness, even when it means harming other people. "Parasites, moochers, looters, brutes and thugs can be of no value to a human being—nor can he gain any benefit from living in a society that treats him as a sacrificial animal and penalizes him for his virtues in order to reward *them* for their vices, which means: a society based on the ethics of altruism." She defines *altruism* as the ethics that tells one "to sacrifice one's life. Altruism erodes men's capacity to grasp the value of an individual's life; it reveals a mind from which the reality of a human being has been wiped out." It should be noted that the Ayn Rand Institute refused permission to reprint portions from Rand's work.

In our third reading Louis Pojman critiques Rand's views on egoism as too one-sided and missing the importance of altruism, and that she fails to distinguish *selfishness* from *self-interest*. *Selfishness* is enhancing your own welfare even to the detriment of others, whereas *self-interest* is the legitimate concern we have to satisfy our wants and interests. He argues that Rand conflates these two concepts. He argues for a moderate position that recognizes the moral validity both of limited egoism and reciprocal altruism.

The Ring of Gyges

PLATO

The Greek philosopher Plato (427–347 B.C.) is considered one of the greatest thinkers who ever lived. He was the student of Socrates and teacher of Aristotle. The following dialogue is from his masterpiece, the *Republic,* in which Plato's brother, Glaucon, asks Socrates whether justice is good in itself or only a necessary evil. That is, it is often thought that morality is simply a compromise between our longing to dominate and our fear of being dominated by others. Since we can't dominate everyone else and fear being dominated by others, we enter into a social contract to live by mutually coercive rules, which we name morality. To illustrate his point, Glaucon tells the story of a shepherd named Gyges who comes upon a ring, which at his behest makes him invisible. He uses the ring to escape the sanctions of society—its laws and punishment—and to serve his lust and greed. Glaucon asks whether anyone with such power would refrain from doing the sort of thing Gyges did. We enter the dialogue in the second book of the *Republic.* Socrates has just shown that the type of egoism advocated by the sophist Thrasymachus is contradictory. Socrates is speaking.

BOOK 2

With these words I was thinking that I had made an end of the discussion; but the end, in truth, proved to be only a beginning. For Glaucon, who is always the most pugnacious of men, was dissatisfied at Thrasymachus' retirement; he wanted to have the battle out. So he said to me: Socrates, do you wish really to persuade us, or only to seem to have persuaded us, that to be just is always better than to be unjust?

I should wish really to persuade you, I replied, if I could.

Reprinted from *The Dialogues of Plato,* translated by Benjamin Jowett (Charles Scribner's, 1889).

Then you certainly have not succeeded. Let me ask you now:—
How would you arrange goods—are there not some which we welcome for their own sakes, and independently of their consequences,
as, for example, harmless pleasures and enjoyments, which delight
us at the time, although nothing follows from them?

I agree in thinking that there is such a class, I replied.

Is there not also a second class of goods, such as knowledge,
sight, health, which are desirable not only in themselves, but also
for their results?

Certainly, I said.

And would you not recognize a third class, such as gymnastic, and
the care of the sick, and the physician's art; also the various ways of
money-making—these do us good but we regard them as disagreeable; and no one would choose them for their own sakes, but only
for the sake of some reward or result which flows from them?

There is, I said, this third class also. But why do you ask?

Because I want to know in which of the three classes you would
place justice?

In the highest class, I replied, among those goods which he who
would be happy desires both for their own sake and for the sake
of their results.

Then the many are of another mind; they think that justice is to
be reckoned in the troublesome class, among goods which are to
be pursued for the sake of rewards and of reputation, but in themselves are disagreeable and rather to be avoided.

I know, I said, that this is their manner of thinking, and that this
was the thesis which Thrasymachus was maintaining just now, when
he censured justice and praised injustice. But I am too stupid to be
convinced by him.

I wish, he said, that you would hear me as well as him, and then
I shall see whether you and I agree. For Thrasymachus seems to me,
like a snake, to have been charmed by your voice sooner than he
ought to have been; but to my mind the nature of justice and injustice have not yet been made clear. Setting aside their rewards and
results, I want to know what they are in themselves, and how they
inwardly work in the soul. If you please, then, I will revive the argument of Thrasymachus. And first I will speak of the nature and origin
of justice according to the common view of them. Secondly, I will
show that all men who practice justice do so against their will, of
necessity, but not as a good. And thirdly, I will argue that there is rea-

son in this view, for the life of the unjust is after all better far than the life of the just—if what they say is true, Socrates, since I myself am not of their opinion. But still I acknowledge that I am perplexed when I hear the voices of Thrasymachus and myriads of others dinning in my ears; and, on the other hand, I have never yet heard the superiority of justice to injustice maintained by any one in a satisfactory way. I want to hear justice praised in respect of itself; then I shall be satisfied, and you are the person from whom I think that I am most likely to hear this; and therefore I will praise the unjust life to the utmost of my power, and my manner of speaking will indicate the manner in which I desire to hear you too praising justice and censuring injustice. Will you say whether you approve of my proposal?

Indeed I do; nor can I imagine any theme about which a man of sense would oftener wish to converse.

I am delighted, he replied, to hear you say so, and shall begin by speaking, as I proposed, of the nature and origin of justice.

They say that to do injustice is, by nature, good; to suffer injustice, evil; but that the evil is greater than the good. And so when men have both done and suffered injustice and have had experience of both, not being able to avoid the one and obtain the other, they think that they had better agree among themselves to have neither; hence there arise laws and mutual covenants; and that which is ordained by law is termed by them lawful and just. This they affirm to be the origin and nature of justice:—it is a mean or compromise, between the best of all, which is to do injustice and not be punished, and the worst of all, which is to suffer injustice without the power of retaliation; and justice, being at a middle point between the two, is tolerated not as a good, but as the lesser evil, and honoured by reason of the inability of men to do injustice. For no man who is worthy to be called a man would ever submit to such an agreement if he were able to resist; he would be mad if he did. Such is the received account, Socrates, of the nature and origin of justice.

Now that those who practice justice do so involuntarily and because they have not the power to be unjust will best appear if we imagine something of this kind: having given both to the just and the unjust power to do what they will, let us watch and see whither desire will lead them; then we shall discover in the very act the just and unjust man to be proceeding along the same road, following their interest, which all natures deem to be their good, and are only diverted into the path of justice by the force of law. The liberty which we are supposing may be most completely given to them in the form of such a power as is said to have been possessed by Gyges the ancestor of Croesus the Lydian. According to the tradition, Gyges was a shepherd in the service of the king of Lydia; there was a great storm, and an earthquake made an opening in the earth at the place where he was feeding his flock. Amazed at the sight, he descended into the opening, where, among other marvels, he beheld a hollow brazen horse, having doors, at which he stooping and looking in saw a dead body of stature, as appeared to him, more than human, and having nothing on but a gold ring; this he took from the finger of the dead and reascended. Now the shepherds met together, according to custom, that they might send their monthly report about the flocks to the king; into their assembly he came having the ring on his finger, and as he was sitting among them he chanced to turn the collet of the ring inside his hand, when instantly he became invisible to the rest of the company and they began to speak of him as if he were no longer present. He was astonished at this, and again touching the ring he turned the collet outwards and reappeared; he made several trials of the ring, and always with the same result—when he turned the collet inwards he became invisible, when outwards he reappeared. Whereupon he contrived to be chosen one of the messengers who were sent to the court; where as soon as he arrived he seduced the queen, and with her help conspired against the king and slew him, and took the kingdom. Suppose now that there were two such magic rings, and the just put on one of them and the unjust the other; no man can be imagined to be of such an iron nature that he would stand fast in justice. No man would keep his hands off what was not his own when he could safely take what he liked out of the market, or go into houses and lie with any one at his pleasure, or kill or release from prison whom he would, and in all respects be like a God among men. Then the actions of the just would be as the actions of the unjust; they would both come at last to the same point. And this we may truly affirm to be a great proof that a man is just, not willingly or because he thinks that justice is any good to him individually, but of necessity, for wherever any one thinks that he can safely be unjust, there he is unjust. For all men believe in their hearts that injustice is far more profitable to the individual than justice, and he who argues as I have been supposing, will say that they are right. If you could imagine any one obtaining this power of becoming invisible, and never doing any wrong or touching what was another's, he would be thought by the lookers-on to be a most wretched idiot, although they would praise him to one another's faces, and keep up appearances with one another from a fear that they too might suffer injustice. Enough of this.

Now, if we are to form a real judgment of the life of the just and unjust, we must isolate them; there is no other way; and how is the isolation to be effected? I answer: Let the unjust man be entirely unjust, and the just man entirely just; nothing is to be taken away from either of them, and both are to be perfectly furnished for the work of their respective lives. First, let the unjust be like other distinguished masters of craft; like the skillful pilot or physician, who knows intuitively his own powers and keeps within their limits, and who, if he fails at any point, is able to recover himself. So let the unjust make his unjust attempts in the right way, and lie hidden if he means to be great in his injustice (he who is found out is nobody): for the highest reach of injustice is: to be deemed just when you are not. Therefore I say that in the perfectly unjust man we must assume the most perfect injustice; there is to be no deduction, but we must allow him, while doing the most unjust acts, to have acquired the greatest reputation for justice. If he have taken a false step he must be able to recover himself; he must be one who can speak with effect, if any of his deeds come to light, and who can force his way where force is required by his courage and strength, and command of money and friends. And at his side let us place the just man in his nobleness and simplicity, wishing, as Aeschylus says, to be and not to seem good. There must be no seeming, for if he seem to be just he will be honoured and rewarded, and then we shall not know whether he is just for the sake of justice or for the sake of honours and rewards; therefore, let him be clothed in justice only, and have no other covering; and he must be imagined in a state of life the opposite of the former. Let him be the best of men, and let him be thought the worst; then he will have been put to the proof; and we shall see whether he will be affected by the fear of infamy and its consequences. And let him continue thus to the hour of death; being just and seeming to be unjust. When both have reached the uttermost extreme, the one of justice and the other of injustice, let judgment be given which of them is the happier of the two.

Heavens! my dear Glaucon, I said, how energetically you polish them up for the decision, first one and then the other, as if they were two statues.

I do my best, he said. And now that we know what they are like there is no difficulty in tracing out the sort of life which awaits either of them. This I will proceed to describe; but as you may think the description a little too coarse, I ask you to suppose, Socrates, that the words which follow are not mine.—Let me put them into the mouths of the eulogists of injustice: they will tell you that the just man who is thought unjust will be scourged, racked, bound—will have his eyes burnt out; and, at last, after suffering every kind of evil, he will be impaled: Then he will understand that he ought to seem only, and not to be, just; the words of Aeschylus may be more truly spoken of the unjust than of the just. For the unjust is pursuing a reality; he does not live with a view to appearances—he wants to be really unjust and not to seem only:—

His mind has a soil deep and fertile.
Out of which spring his prudent counsels.

In the first place, he is thought just, and therefore bears rule in the city; he can marry whom he will, and give in marriage to whom he will; also he can trade and deal where he likes, and always to his own advantage, because he has no misgivings about injustice; and at every contest, whether in public or private, he gets the better of his antagonists, and gains at their expense, and is rich, and out of his gains he can benefit his friends, and harm his enemies; moreover, he can offer sacrifices, and dedicate gifts to the gods abundantly and magnificently, and can honour the gods or any man whom he wants to honour in a far better style than the just, and therefore he is likely to be dearer than they are to the gods. And thus, Socrates, gods and men are said to unite in making the life of the unjust better than the life of the just. . . .

[We pick up the discussion in Book 9.]

BOOK 9

"Now that we've gotten this far," I said, "let's go back to that statement made at the beginning, which brought us here: that it pays for a man to be perfectly unjust if he appears to be just. Isn't that what someone said?"

"Yes."

"Then since we've agreed what power justice and injustice each have, let's have a discussion with him."

"How?"

"By molding in words an image of the soul, so that the one who said that will realize what he was saying."

"What kind of image?"

"Oh, something like those natures the myths tell us were born in ancient times—the Chimaera, Scylla, Cerberus, and others in which many different shapes were supposed to have grown into one."

"So they tell us," he said.

"Then mold one figure of a colorful, many-headed beast with heads of wild and tame animals growing in a circle all around it; one that can change and grow all of them out of itself."

"That's a job for a skilled artist. Still, words mold easier than wax or clay, so consider it done."

"And another of a lion, and one of a man. Make the first by far the biggest, the second second largest."

"That's easier, and already done."

"Now join the three together so that they somehow grow."

"All right."

"Next mold the image of one, the man, around them all, so that to someone who can't see what's inside but looks only at the container it appears to be a single animal, man."

"I have."

"Then shall we inform the gentleman that when he says it pays for this man to be unjust, he's saying that it profits him to feast his multifarious beast and his lion and make them grow strong, but to starve and enfeeble the man in him so that he gets dragged wherever the animals lead him, and instead of making them friends and used to each other, to let them bite and fight and eat each other?"

"That's just what he's saying by praising injustice."

"The one who says justice pays, however, would be saying that he should practice and say whatever will give the most mastery to his inner man, who should care for the many-headed beast like a farmer, raising and domesticating its tame heads and preventing the wild ones from growing, making the lion's nature his partner and ally, and so raise them both to be friends to each other and to him."

"That's exactly what he means by praising justice."

"So in every way the commender of justice is telling the truth, the other a lie. Whether we examine pleasure, reputation, or profit, we find that the man who praises justice speaks truly, the one who disparages it disparages sickly and knows nothing of what he disparages."

"I don't think he does at all."

"Then let's gently persuade him—his error wasn't intended—by asking him a question: 'Shouldn't we say that the traditions of the beautiful and the ugly have come about like this: Beautiful things are those that make our bestial parts subservient to the human—or rather, perhaps, to the divine—part of our nature, while ugly ones are those that enslave the tame to the wild?' Won't he agree?"

"If he takes my advice."

"On this argument then, can it pay for a man to take money unjustly if that means making his best part a slave to the worst? If it wouldn't profit a man to sell his son or his daughter into slavery—to wild and evil men at that—even if he got a fortune for it, then if he has no pity on himself and enslaves the most godlike thing in him to the most godless and polluted, isn't he a wretch who gets bribed for gold into a destruction more horrible than Euriphyle's, who sold her husband's life for a necklace?"

"Much more horrible," said Glaucon.

". . . [E]veryone is better off being ruled by the godlike and intelligent; preferably if he has it inside, but if not, it should be imposed on him from without so that we may all be friends and as nearly alike as possible, all steered by the same thing."

"Yes, and we're right," he said.

"Law, the ally of everyone in the city, clearly intends the same thing, as does the rule of children, which forbids us to let them be free until we've instituted a regime in them as in a city. We serve their best part with a similar part in us, install a like guardian and ruler in them, and only then set them free."

"Clearly."

"Then how, by what argument, Glaucon, can we say that it pays for a man to be unjust or self-indulgent or to do something shameful to get more money or power if by doing so he makes himself worse?"

"We can't," he said.

"And how can it pay to commit injustice without getting caught and being punished? Doesn't getting away with it make a man even worse? Whereas if a man gets caught and punished, his beastlike part is taken in and tamed, his tame part is set free, and his whole soul

acquires justice and temperance and knowledge. Th
recovers its best nature and attains a state more ho
state the body attains when it acquires health a
beauty, by as much as the soul is more honorable tnau ₋

"Absolutely."

"Then won't a sensible man spend his life directing all his efforts
to this end?"

For Further Reflection

1. Which would you choose to be, Glaucon's good but suffering
   person or his bad but successful person? Is there a third alternative?

2. Socrates' answer to Glaucon and Adeimantus is that, despite
   appearances, we should choose the life of the "unsuccessful"
   just person because it is to our advantage to be moral. Socrates'
   answer depends on a notion of mental health. He contends
   that immorality corrupts the inner person, so that one is happy
   or unhappy in exact proportion to one's moral integrity. Is this
   a plausible reply?

3. Is the good always good for you?

Ethical Egoism

JAMES RACHELS

James Rachels is professor of philosophy at the University
of Alabama at Birmingham and is the author of several articles on moral philosophy. He is the author of *The End of*

Reprinted from James Rachels *The Elements of Moral Philosophy*, 3rd
ed. Copyright © 1999 by McGraw Hill.

Life: Euthanasia and Morality (1986), *Created from Animals: The Moral Implications of Darwinism* (1990), *Can Ethics Provide Answers?* (1997), and *The Elements of Moral Philosophy, Third Edition* (1999). In this essay Rachels sums up the arguments for ethical egoism, the doctrine that it is always our duty to act exclusively in our self-interest.

The achievement of his own happiness is man's highest moral purpose.

—Ayn Rand, *The Virtue of Selfishness* (1961)

Some thinkers have maintained that we have no "natural" duties to other people. Ethical Egoism is the idea that each person ought to pursue his or her own self-interest exclusively. It is different from Psychological Egoism, which is a theory of human nature concerned with how people *do* behave. Psychological Egoism says that people do in fact always pursue their own interests. Ethical Egoism, by contrast, is a normative theory—that is, a theory about how we ought to behave. Regardless of how we do behave, Ethical Egoism says we have *no duty* except to do what is best for ourselves.

It is a challenging theory. It contradicts some of our deepest moral beliefs—beliefs held by most of us, at any rate—but it is not easy to refute. We will examine the most important arguments for and against it. If it turns out to be true, then of course that is immensely important. But even if it turns out to be false, there is still much to be learned from examining it—we may, for example, gain some insight into the reasons why we *do* have obligations to other people.

But before looking at the arguments, we should be a little clearer about exactly what this theory says and what it does not say. In the first place, Ethical Egoism does not say that one should promote one's own interests *as well as* the interests of others. That would be an ordinary, unexceptional view. Ethical Egoism is the radical view that one's *only* duty is to promote one's own interests. According to Ethical Egoism, there is only one ultimate principle of conduct, the principle of self-interest, and this principle sums up all of one's natural duties and obligations.

However, Ethical Egoism does not say that you should avoid actions that help others, either. It may very well be that in many instances your interests coincide with the interests of others, so that in helping yourself you will be aiding others willy-nilly. Or it may happen that aiding others is an effective means for creating some benefit for yourself. Ethical Egoism does not forbid such actions; in fact, it may demand them. The theory insists only that in such cases the benefit to others is not what makes the act right. What makes the act right is, rather, the fact that it is to one's own advantage.

Finally, Ethical Egoism does not imply that in pursuing one's interests one ought always to do what one wants to do, or what gives one the most pleasure in the short run. Someone may want to do something that is not good for himself or that will eventually cause himself more grief than pleasure—he may want to drink a lot or smoke cigarettes or take drugs or waste his best years at the race track. Ethical Egoism would frown on all this, regardless of the momentary pleasure it affords. It says that a person ought to do what really is to his or her own best advantage, over the long run. It endorses selfishness, but it doesn't endorse foolishness.

THREE ARGUMENTS IN FAVOR OF ETHICAL EGOISM

What reasons can be advanced to support this doctrine? Why should anyone think it is true? Unfortunately, the theory is asserted more often than it is argued for. Many of its supporters apparently think its truth is self-evident, so that arguments are not needed. When it is argued for, three lines of reasoning are most commonly used.

1. The first argument has several variations, each suggesting the same general point:

(a) Each of us is intimately familiar with our own individual wants and needs. Moreover, each of us is uniquely placed to pursue those wants and needs effectively. At the same time, we know the desires and needs of other people only imperfectly, and we are not well situated to pursue them. Therefore, it is reasonable to believe that if we set out to be "our brother's keeper," we would often bungle the job and end up doing more mischief than good.

(b) At the same time, the policy of "looking out for others" is an offensive intrusion into other people's privacy; it is essentially a policy of minding other people's business.

(c) Making other people the object of one's "charity" is degrading to them; it robs them of their individual dignity and self-respect. The offer of charity says, in effect, that they are not competent to care for themselves; and the statement is self-fulfilling. They cease to be self-reliant and become passively dependent on others. That is why the recipients of "charity" are so often resentful rather than appreciative.

What this adds up to is that the policy of "looking out for others" is self-defeating. If we want to do what is best for people, we should not adopt so-called altruistic policies of behavior. On the contrary, if each person looks after his or her own interests, it is more likely that everyone will be better off, in terms of both physical and emotional well-being. Thus Robert G. Olson says in his book *The Morality of Self-Interest* (1965), "The individual is most likely to contribute to social betterment by rationally pursuing his own best long-range interests." Or as Alexander Pope put it,

> Thus God and nature formed the general frame
> And bade self-love and social be the same.

It is possible to quarrel with this argument on a number of grounds. Of course no one favors bungling, butting in, or depriving people of their self-respect. But is that really what we are doing when we feed hungry children? Is the starving child in Ethiopia really harmed when we "intrude" into "her business" by supplying food? It hardly seems likely. Yet we can set this point aside, for considered as an argument for Ethical Egoism, this way of thinking has an even more serious defect.

The trouble is that it isn't really an argument for Ethical Egoism at all. The argument concludes that we should adopt certain policies of action; and on the surface they appear to be egoistic policies. However, the *reason* it is said we should adopt those policies is decidedly unegoistic. It is said that we should adopt those policies because doing so will promote the "betterment of society"— but according to Ethical Egoism, that is something we should not be concerned about. Spelled out fully, with everything laid on the table, the argument says:

(1) We ought to do whatever will best promote everyone's interests.

(2) The best way to promote everyone's interests is for each of us to adopt the policy of pursuing our own interests exclusively.

(3) Therefore, each of us should adopt the policy of pursuing our own interests exclusively.

If we accept this reasoning, then we are not ethical egoists at all. Even though we might end up behaving like egoists, our ultimate principle is one of beneficence—we are doing what we think will help everyone, not merely what we think will benefit ourselves. Rather than being egoists, we turn out to be altruists with a peculiar view of what in fact promotes the general welfare.

2. The second argument was put forward with some force by Ayn Rand, a writer little heeded by professional philosophers but who was enormously popular on college campuses during the 1960s and '70s. Ethical Egoism, in her view, is the only ethical philosophy that respects the integrity of the individual human life. She regarded the ethics of "altruism" as a totally destructive idea, both in society as a whole and in the lives of individuals taken in by it. Altruism, to her way of thinking, leads to a denial of the value of the individual. It says to a person: Your life is merely something that may be sacrificed. "If a man accepts the ethics of altruism," she writes, "his first concern is not how to live his life, but how to sacrifice it." Moreover, those who would promote this idea are beneath contempt—they are parasites who, rather than working to build and sustain their own lives, leech off those who do. She writes:

> Parasites, moochers, looters, brutes and thugs can be of no value to a human being—nor can he gain any benefit from living in a society geared to *their* needs, demands and protections, a society that treats him as a sacrificial animal and penalizes him for his virtues in order to reward *them* for their vices, which means: a society based on the ethics of altruism.

By "sacrificing one's life" Rand does not mean anything so dramatic as dying. A person's life consists (in part) of projects undertaken and goods earned and created. Thus to demand that a person abandon his projects or give up his goods is also a clear effort to "sacrifice his life."

Rand also suggests that there is a metaphysical basis for egoistic ethics. Somehow, it is the only ethics that takes seriously the *reality* of the individual person. She bemoans "the enormity of the extent to which altruism erodes men's capacity to grasp . . . the value of an individual life; it reveals a mind from which the reality of a human being has been wiped out."

What, then, of the starving people? It might be argued, in response, that Ethical Egoism "reveals a mind from which the reality of a human being has been wiped out"—namely, the human being who is starving. Rand quotes with approval the evasive answer given by one of her followers: "Once, when Barbara Brandon was asked by a student: 'What will happen to the poor . . . ?' she answered: 'If *you* want to help them, you will not be stopped.'"

All these remarks are, I think, part of one continuous argument that can be summarized like this:

(1) A person has only one life to live. If we value the individual—that is, if the individual has moral worth—then we must agree that this life is of supreme importance. After all, it is all one has, and all one is.

(2) The ethics of altruism regards the life of the individual as something one must be ready to sacrifice for the good of others.

(3) Therefore, the ethics of altruism does not take seriously the value of the human individual.

(4) Ethical Egoism, which allows each person to view his or her own life as being of ultimate value, does take the human individual seriously—it is, in fact, the only philosophy that does so.

(5) Thus, Ethical Egoism is the philosophy that ought to be accepted.

The problem with this argument, as you may already have noticed, is that it relies on picturing the alternatives in such an extreme way. As Ayn Rand describes it, "altruism" implies that one's own interests have *no* value, and that *any* demand by others calls for sacrificing them. Thus the "ethics of altruism" would appeal to no one, with the possible exception of certain monks. If this is the alternative, then any other view, including Ethical Egoism, will look good by comparison.

But that is hardly a fair picture of the choices. What we called the commonsense view stands somewhere between the two extremes. It says that one's own interests and the interests of others are both important and must be balanced against one another.

Sometimes, when the balancing is done, it will turn out that one should act in the interests of others; at other times, it will turn out that one should take care for oneself. So even if we should reject the extreme "ethics of altruism," it does not follow that one must accept the other extreme of Ethical Egoism.

3. The third line of reasoning takes a somewhat different approach. Ethical Egoism is usually presented as a *revisionist* moral philosophy, that is, as a philosophy that says our commonsense moral views are mistaken and need to be changed. It is possible, however, to interpret Ethical Egoism in a much less radical way, as a theory that *accepts* commonsense morality and offers a surprising account of its basis.

The less radical interpretation goes as follows. Ordinary morality consists in obeying certain rules. We must avoid doing harm to others, speak the truth, keep our promises, and so on. At first glance, these duties appear to be very different from one another, having little in common. Yet from a theoretical point of view, we may wonder whether there is not some hidden unity underlying the hodgepodge of separate duties. Perhaps there is some small number of fundamental principles that explain all the rest, just as in physics there are basic principles that bring together and explain diverse phenomena. From a theoretical point of view, the smaller the number of basic principles, the better. Best of all would be one fundamental principle, from which all the rest could be derived. Ethical Egoism, then, would be the theory that all our duties are ultimately derived from the one fundamental principle of self-interest.

Understood in this way, Ethical Egoism is not such a radical doctrine. It does not challenge commonsense morality; it only tries to explain and systematize it. And it does a surprisingly successful job. It can provide plausible explanations of the duties mentioned above, and more:

The duty not to harm others: If we make a habit of doing things that are harmful to other people, people will not be reluctant to do things that harm us. We will be shunned and despised; others will not have us as friends and will not do us favors when we need them. If our offenses against others are serious enough, we may even end up in jail. Thus it is to our own advantage to avoid harming others.

The duty not to lie. If we lie to other people, we will suffer all the ill effects of a bad reputation. People will distrust us and avoid doing business with us. We will often need for people to be honest with us, but we can hardly expect them to feel much of an obligation to be honest with us if they know we have not been honest with them. Thus it is to our own advantage to be truthful.

The duty to keep our promises: It is to our own advantage to be able to enter into mutually beneficial arrangements with other people. To benefit from those arrangements, we need to be able to rely on others to keep their parts of the bargains—we need to be able to rely on them to keep their promises to us. But we can hardly expect others to keep their promises to us if we do not keep our promises to them. Therefore, from the point of view of self-interest, we should keep our promises.

Pursuing this line of reasoning, Thomas Hobbes suggested that the principle of Ethical Egoism leads to nothing less than the Golden Rule: We should "do unto others" because if we do, others will be more likely to "do unto us."

Does this argument succeed in establishing Ethical Egoism as a viable theory of morality? It is, in my opinion at least, the best try. But there are two serious objections to it. In the first place, the argument does not prove quite as much as it needs to prove. At best, it shows only that as a general rule it is to one's own advantage to avoid harming others. It does not show that this is *always* so. And it could not show that, for even though it may usually be to one's advantage to avoid harming others, sometimes it is not. Sometimes one might even *gain* from treating another person badly. In that case, the obligation not to harm the other person could not be derived from the principle of Ethical Egoism. Thus it appears that not all our moral obligations can be explained as derivable from self-interest.

But set that point aside. There is a still more fundamental problem. Suppose it is true that, say, contributing money for famine relief is somehow to one's own advantage. It does not follow that this is the only reason, or even the most basic reason, why doing so is a morally good thing. (For example, the most basic reason might be *in order to help the starving people.* The fact that doing so is also to one's own advantage might be only a secondary, less important, consideration.) A demonstration that one *could* derive this duty from self-interest does not prove that self-interest is the only reason one has this duty. Only if you accept an additional proposition—namely, that there is no reason for giving other than self-interest—will you find Ethical Egoism a plausible theory.

For Further Reflection

1. Do you believe any of the arguments Rachels presents are successful defenses of ethical egoism? How does ethical egoism relate to Socrates' idea that one ought never to harm anyone else? Could one reconcile Socrates' idea with ethical egoism? Socrates believes that one should never harm anyone else because doing so is never in one's own interest. What would be needed to get Rand's theory to agree with that conclusion?

2. Can the ethical egoist make his or her views public? If you follow Rand, should you let others know where you stand? Should you persuade them to be egoists? If the egoist cannot make his theory public, does this disqualify it as a genuine ethical theory?

3. Can the ethical egoist be a consistent egoist and have friends? If friendship entails loving another in such a way as to sacrifice one's own interest for the friend's, does this give the egoist difficulty?

4. Do ethical egoists conflate the concept of *selfishness* with *self-interest?* Selfishness means seeking one's own good even at the expense of others and their rights. Self-interest means being concerned about one's own welfare, but that concern may involve a recognition of other people's interests and rights.

Egoism, Self-Interest, and Altruism

LOUIS P. POJMAN

In this essay Pojman criticizes Ayn Rand's version of ethical egoism for creating a false dilemma between (1) a self-demeaning altruism and (2) a consummate egoism, in which people always put themselves first. He argues that Rand conflates *selfishness* with *self-interest,* but the two concepts are only superficially similar. He then draws from evolutionary ethologists who describe animal behavior, illustrating a middle way between self-degrading sacrifice and selfish egoism.

Universal ethical egoism is the theory that everyone ought always to serve his or her own self-interest. That is, everyone ought to do what will maximize one's own expected utility or bring about one's own greatest happiness, even if it requires harming others. Ethical egoism is utilitarianism reduced to the pinpoint of the single individual ego. Instead of advocating the greatest happiness for the greatest number, as utilitarianism does, it advocates the greatest happiness for myself, whoever I may be. It is a self-preoccupied prudence, urging one to postpone enjoyment today for long-term benefits. In its more sophisticated form, it compares life to a competitive game, perhaps a war-game, and urges each person to *try* to win in the game of life.

In her books *The Virtue of Selfishness* and *Atlas Shrugged,* Ayn Rand argues that selfishness is a virtue and altruism a vice, a totally destructive idea that leads to the undermining of individual worth.*
She defines *altruism* as the view that

> any action taken for the benefit of others is good, and any action taken for one's own benefit is evil. Thus, the *beneficiary* of an action is the only criterion of moral value—and so long as the beneficiary is anybody other than oneself, anything goes.[1]

As such, altruism is suicidal:

> If a man accepts the ethics of altruism, his first concern is not how to live his life, but how to sacrifice it. . . . Altruism erodes men's capacity to grasp the value of an individual life; it reveals a mind from which the reality of a human being has been wiped out.

---

*The Ayn Rand Estate refused to grant permission to reprint selections from *The Virtue of Selfishness* and *Atlas Shrugged.*
[1]Ayn Rand, *The Virtue of Selfishness* (New American Library, 1964), pp. vii and 27–32; 80ff.

Since finding happiness is the highest goal and good in life, altruism, which calls on us to sacrifice our happiness for the good of others, is contrary to our highest good.

Her argument seems to go like this:

1. The perfection of one's abilities in a state of happiness is the highest goal for humans. We have a moral duty to attempt to reach this goal.
2. The ethics of altruism prescribes that we sacrifice our interests and lives for the good of others.
3. Therefore, the ethics of altruism is incompatible with the goal of happiness.
4. Ethical egoism prescribes that we seek our own happiness exclusively, and as such it is consistent with the happiness goal.
5. Therefore ethical egoism is the correct moral theory.

Ayn Rand's argument for the virtue of selfishness is flawed by the fallacy of a false dilemma. It simplistically assumes that absolute altruism and absolute egoism are the only alternatives. But this is an extreme view of the matter. There are plenty of options between these two positions. Even a predominant egoist would admit that (analogous to the paradox of hedonism) sometimes the best way to reach self-fulfillment is for us to forget about ourselves and strive to live for goals, causes, or other persons. Even if altruism is not required (as a duty), it may be permissible in many cases. Furthermore, self-interest may not be incompatible with other-regarding motivation. Even the Second Great Commandment set forth by Moses and Jesus states not that you must always sacrifice yourself for the other person, but that you ought to love your neighbor *as* yourself (Lev. 19:19; Matt. 23). Self-interest and self-love are morally good things, but not at the expense of other people's legitimate interests. When there is moral conflict of interests, a fair process of adjudication needs to take place.

But Rand's version of egoism is only one of many. We need to go to the heart of ethical egoism: the thesis that our highest moral duty is always to promote our individual interests. Let us focus on the alleged problems of this thesis.

FOUR CRITICISMS OF ETHICAL EGOISM

The Inconsistent Outcomes Argument

Brian Medlin argues that ethical egoism cannot be true because it fails to meet a necessary condition of morality, that of being a guide to action. He claims that it will be like advising people to do inconsistent things based on incompatible desires.[2] His argument goes like this:

1. Moral principles must be universal and categorical.
2. I must universalize my egoist desire to come out on top over Tom, Dick, and Harry.
3. But I must also prescribe Tom's egoist desire to come out on top over Dick, Harry, and me (and so on).
4. Therefore I have prescribed incompatible outcomes and have not provided a way of adjudicating conflicts of desire. In effect, I have said nothing.

The proper response to this is that of Jesse Kalin, who argues that we can separate our beliefs about ethical situations from our desires.[3] He likens the situation to a competitive sports event, in which you believe that your opponent has a right to try to win as much as you, but you desire that you, not he, will in fact win. An even better example is that of the chess game in which you recognize that your opponent ought to move her bishop to prepare for checkmate, but you hope she won't see the move. Belief that A ought to do Y does not commit you to wanting A to do Y.

The Publicity Argument

On the one hand, in order for something to be a moral theory it seems necessary that its moral principles be publicized. Unless prin-

---

[2]Brian Medlin, "Ultimate Principles and Ethical Egoism," *Australasian Journal of Philosophy* (1957), pp. 111–118; reprinted in Louis Pojman, *Ethical Theory*, pp. 81–85.

[3]See Jesse Kalin, "In Defense of Egoism," in *Ethical Theory*, ed. Louis Pojman (Wadsworth, 1999), p. 93f.

ciples are put forth as universal prescriptions that are accessible to the public, they cannot serve as guides to action or as aids in resolving conflicts of interest. But on the other hand, it is not in the egoist's self-interest to publicize them. Egoists would rather that the rest of us be altruists. (Why did Nietzsche and Rand write books announcing their positions? Were the royalties taken in by announcing ethical egoism worth the price of letting the cat out of the bag?)

Thus it would be self-defeating for the egoist to argue for her position, and even worse that she should convince others of it. But it is perfectly possible to have a private morality that does not resolve conflicts of interest. So the egoist should publicly advocate standard principles of traditional morality—so that society doesn't break down—while adhering to a private, nonstandard, solely self-regarding morality. So, if you're willing to pay the price, you can accept the solipsistic-directed norms of egoism.

If the egoist is prepared to pay the price, egoism could be a consistent system that has some limitations. Although the egoist can cooperate with others in limited ways and perhaps even have friends—so long as their interests don't conflict with his—he has to be very careful about preserving his isolation. The egoist can't give advice or argue about his position—not sincerely at least. He must act alone, atomistically or solipsistically in moral isolation, for to announce his adherence to the principle of egoism would be dangerous to his project. He can't teach his children the true morality or justify himself to others or forgive others.

The Paradox of Egoism

The situation may be even worse than the sophisticated, self-conscious egoist supposes. Could the egoist have friends? And if limited friendship is possible, could he or she ever be in love or experience deep friendship? Suppose the egoist discovers that in the pursuit of the happiness goal, deep friendship is in his best interest. Can he become a friend? What is necessary to deep friendship? A true friend is one who is not always preoccupied about his own interest in the relationship but who forgets about himself altogether, at least sometimes, in order to serve or enhance the other person's interest. "Love seeketh not its own." It is an altruistic disposition, the very opposite of egoism. So the *paradox of egoism* is that in order to reach the goal of egoism one must give up egoism and become (to some extent) an altruist, the very antithesis of egoism.

The Argument from Counterintuitive Consequences

The final argument against ethical egoism is that it is an absolute ethics that not only permits egoistic behavior but demands it. Helping others at one's own expense is not only not required, it is morally wrong. Whenever I do not have good evidence that my helping you will end up to my advantage, I must refrain from helping you. If I can save the whole of Europe and Africa from destruction by pressing a button, then so long as there is nothing for me to gain by it, it is wrong for me to press that button. The Good Samaritan was, by this logic, morally wrong in helping the injured victim and not collecting payment for his troubles. It is certainly hard to see why the egoist should be concerned about environmental matters if he or she is profiting from polluting the environment. (For example, if the egoist gains 40 hedons in producing P, which produces pollution that in turn causes others 1,000 dolors— units of suffering—but suffers only 10 of those dolors himself, then by an agent-maximizing calculus he is morally obligated to produce P.) There is certainly no obligation to preserve scarce natural resources for future generations. "Why should I do anything for posterity?" the egoist asks "What has posterity ever done for me?"

In conclusion, we see that ethical egoism has a number of serious problems. It cannot consistently publicize itself, nor often argue its case. It tends towards solipsism and the exclusion of many of the deepest human values, such as love and deep friendship. It violates the principle of fairness, and, most of all, it entails an absolute prohibition on altruistic behavior, which we intuitively sense as morally required (or, at least, permissible).

EVOLUTION AND ALTRUISM

If sheer unadulterated egoism is an inadequate moral theory, does that mean we ought to aim at complete altruism, total self-effacement for the sake of others? What is the role of self-love in morality? An interesting place to start answering these queries is with the new field of sociobiology, which theorizes that social structures and behavioral patterns, including morality, have a biological base, explained by evolutionary theory.

In the past, linking ethics to evolution meant justifying exploitation. Social Darwinism justified imperialism and the principle that "Might makes right" by saying that survival of the fittest is a law of nature. This philosophy lent itself to a promotion of ruthless egoism. This is nature's law, "nature red in tooth and claw." Against this view ethologists such as Robert Ardrey and Konrad Lorenz argued for a more benign view of the animal kingdom—one reminiscent of Rudyard Kipling's, in which the animal kingdom survives by cooperation, which is at least as important as competition. On Ardrey's and Lorenz's view it is the group or the species, not the individual, that is of primary importance.

With the development of sociobiology—in the work of E. O. Wilson but particularly the work of Robert Trivers, J. Maynard Smith, and Richard Dawkins—a theory has come to the fore that combines radical individualism with limited altruism. It is not the group or the species that is of evolutionary importance but the gene, or, more precisely, the gene type. Genes—the parts of the chromosomes that carry the blueprints for all our natural traits (e.g., height, hair color, skin color, intelligence)—copy themselves as they divide and multiply. At conception they combine with the genes of a member of the opposite sex to form a new individual.

In his fascinating sociobiological study, Richard Dawkins describes human behavior as determined evolutionarily by stable strategies set to replicate the gene.[4] This is not done consciously, of course, but by the invisible hand that drives consciousness. We are essentially gene machines.

Morality—that is, successful morality—can be seen as an evolutionary strategy for gene replication. Here's an example: Birds are afflicted with life-endangering parasites. Because they lack limbs to enable them to pick the parasites off their heads, they—like much of the animal kingdom—depend on the ritual of mutual grooming. It turns out that nature has evolved two basic types of birds in this regard: those who are disposed to groom anyone (the nonprejudiced type?), and those who refuse to groom anyone but who pre-

---

[4]Richard Dawkins, *The Selfish Gene* (Oxford University Press, 1976), Ch. 10.

sent themselves for grooming. The former type of bird Dawkins calls "Suckers" and the latter "Cheaters."

In a geographical area containing harmful parasites and where there are only Suckers or Cheaters, Suckers will do fairly well, but Cheaters will not survive, for want of cooperation. However, in a Sucker population in which a mutant Cheater arises, the Cheater will prosper, and the Cheater gene-type will multiply. As the Suckers are exploited, they will gradually die out. But if and when they become too few to groom the Cheaters, the Cheaters will start to die off too and eventually become extinct.

Why don't birds all die off, then? Well, somehow nature has come up with a third type, call them "Grudgers." Grudgers groom all and only those who reciprocate in grooming them. They groom each other and Suckers, but not Cheaters. In fact, once caught, a Cheater is marked forever. There is no forgiveness. It turns out then that unless there are a lot of Suckers around, Cheaters have a hard time of it—harder even than Suckers. However, it is the Grudgers that prosper. Unlike Suckers, they don't waste time messing with unappreciative Cheaters, so they are not exploited and have ample energy to gather food and build better nests for their loved ones.

J. L. Mackie argues that the real name for Suckers is "Christian," one who believes in complete altruism, even turning the other cheek to one's assailant and loving one's enemy. Cheaters are ruthless egoists who can survive only if there are enough naive altruists around. Whereas Grudgers are *reciprocal* altruists who have a rational morality based on cooperative self-interest, Suckers, such as Socrates and Jesus, advocate "turning the other cheek and repaying evil with good."[5] Instead of a Rule of Reciprocity, "I'll scratch your back if you'll scratch mine," the extreme altruist substitutes the Golden Rule, "If you want the other fellow to scratch your back, you scratch his—even if he won't reciprocate."

The moral of the story is this: Altruist morality (so interpreted) is only rational given the payoff of eternal life (with a scorekeeper, as Woody Allen says). Take that away, and it looks like a Sucker system. What replaces the "Christian" vision of submission and saint-

---

[5]J. L. Mackie, "The Law of the Jungle: Moral Alternatives and Principles of Evolution," *Philosophy* 53 (1978).

liness is the reciprocal altruist with a tit-for-tat morality, someone who is willing to share with those willing to cooperate.

Mackie may caricature the position of the religious altruist, but he misses the subtleties of wisdom involved (Jesus said, "Be as wise as serpents but as harmless as doves"). Nevertheless, he does remind us that there is a difference between core morality and complete altruism. We have duties to cooperate and reciprocate, but no duty to serve those who manipulate us nor an obvious duty to sacrifice ourselves for people outside our domain of special responsibility. We have a special duty of high altruism toward those in the close circle of our concern, namely, our family and friends.

Conclusion

Martin Luther once said that humanity is like a man who, when mounting a horse, always falls off on the opposite side, especially when he tries to overcompensate for his previous exaggerations. So it is with ethical egoism. Trying to compensate for an irrational, guilt-ridden, Sucker altruism of the morality of self-effacement, it falls off the horse on the other side, embracing a Cheater's preoccupation with self-exaltation that robs the self of the deepest joys in life. Only the person who mounts properly, avoiding both extremes, is likely to ride the horse of happiness to its goal.

For Further Reflection

1. Evaluate whether this statement, which I first encountered in a student paper, is true or false: "Everyone is an egoist, for everyone always tries to do what will bring them satisfaction."

2. Review the story of the killing of Kitty Genovese (chapter 7), and discuss how an ethical egoist would respond to her plight. Would egoists admit that they have a duty to come to the aid of Ms. Genovese?

3. What is the relationship between ethics and evolution? How does this relationship throw light on egoism? What is the significance of reciprocity for ethics?

4. Some philosophers, beginning with Plato, have argued that ethical egoism is irrational, since it precludes psychological health.

In an article entitled "Ethical Egoism and Psychological Dispositions" (*American Philosophical Quarterly* 17(1), 1980), Laurence Thomas sets forth the following argument:

P1. A true friend could never, as a matter of course, be disposed to harm or to exploit anyone with whom he is a friend [definition of a friend].

P2. An egoist could never be a true friend to anyone [for the egoist must be ready to exploit others whenever it is in his or her interest].

P3. Only someone with an unhealthy personality could never be a true friend to anyone [definition of a healthy personality; that is, friendship is a necessary condition for a healthy personality].

P4. Ethical egoism requires that we have a kind of disposition which is incompatible with our having a healthy personality [from P1–P3].

Conclusion: Therefore, from the standpoint of our psychological makeup, ethical egoism is unacceptable as a moral theory.

Do you agree with Thomas? How might the ethical egoist respond?

Further Readings for Chapter 8

Axelrod, Robert M. *The Evolution of Cooperation*. New York: Basic Books, 1984. A brilliant study on the rationality of cooperation.

Dawkins, Richard. *The Selfish Gene*. 2d ed. Oxford: Oxford University Press, 1989. One of the most fascinating studies on the subject, defending limited altruism.

Gauthier, David, ed. *Morality and Rational Self-Interest*. Englewood Cliffs, N.J.: Prentice-Hall, 1970.

Gauthier, David. *Morality by Agreement*. Oxford: Clarendon Press, 1986.

Hospers, John. *Human Conduct: An Introduction to the Problems of Ethics*. New York: Harcourt Brace Jovanovich, 1961.

MacIntyre, Alasdair. "Egoism and Altruism." In *The Encyclopedia of Philosophy,* edited by Paul Edwards. New York: MacMillan, 1967.

Nielsen, Kai. "Why Should I Be Moral?" *Methodos* 15, no. 59–60 (1963). This comprehensive article appears in several anthologies.

Olen, Jeffrey. *Moral Freedom*. Philadelphia: Temple University Press, 1988.

Rachels, James. *The Elements of Moral Philosophy*. New York: Random House, 1986. Chapters 5 and 6.

Rand, Ayn. *The Virtue of Selfishness*. New York: New American Library, 1964.

Singer, Peter. *The Expanding Circle: Ethics and Sociobiology*. N.Y.: Farrar, Straus & Giroux, 1981. A good discussion of egoism in the light of sociobiology.

Taylor, Richard. *Good and Evil*. New York: Macmillan, 1970. Especially chapter 5.

CHAPTER 9

Does Life Have Meaning?

In his autobiography Tolstoy tells the story of a traveler fleeing an infuriated animal. Attempting to save himself from the beast, the man runs toward a well and begins to climb down, when to his distress he spies a dragon at the bottom. The dragon is waiting for him with open jaws, ready to eat him. The poor fellow is caught in a dilemma. He dare not drop into the well for fear of the dragon, but he dare not climb out of the well for fear of the beast. So he clutches a branch of a bush growing in the cleft of the well and hangs onto it for dear life. His hands grow weak, and he feels that soon he shall have to give into his grim fate, but he still holds on desperately. As he grasps the branch for his salvation, he notices that two mice, one white and one black, are nibbling away at the main trunk of the branch onto which he is clinging. Soon they will dislodge the branch, and he will fall into the waiting jaws of the dragon.

The traveler knows that he will soon perish, but while clinging to the branch, he sees some drops of honey hanging on the leaves of the bush, and so sticks out his tongue and licks the leaves.

The traveler is you and I, and his plight is your plight and mine, the danger of our demise on every hand. The white mouse represents our days and the black our nights. Together they are nibbling away at the threescore years and ten which make up our branch of life. Inevitably all will be over, and what have we to show for it? Is our brief distraction of the taste of honey all we get out of life? Is this all there is in life? Can this brief moment in the history of the universe have significance? What gives life importance?

The certainty of death heightens the question of the meaning of life. Like a prisoner sentenced to death or a patient with terminal illness, we know that, in a sense, we are all sentenced to death and are terminally ill, but we flee the thought in a thousand ways. What is the purpose of life?

Our readings represent some of the classic responses to this question. Epicurus advises moderate pleasure in a life that accepts mortality without tears. Epictetus and the Stoics teach us that moral duty alone brings meaning to life. Camus argues that life is meaningless and, to illustrate his view, he tells the story of Sisyphus rolling a stone up a hill for eternity. Viktor Frankl relates how discovering meaning in suffering enabled concentration camp prisoners to live with dignity. Walker finds the essence of a purposeful life in religion. The Buddha sets forth his eightfold path to salvation. Robert Nozick offers a thought experiment on meaningfulness, and Richard Taylor reflects on the meaning of happiness as the key to a meaningful life.

Hedonism

EPICURUS

The Greek philosopher Epicurus (341–271 B.C.) founded the school of philosophy named after himself, *epicureanism,* a hedonistic theory wherein good is identified with pleasure and evil with pain. In this he is the precursor of Bentham's utilitarianism (chapter 4). But contrary to popular opinion, Epicurus's version of hedonism is nothing like the modern ideas connected with his name—sensuality, profligacy, and decadence. On the contrary, he believed that the good life consisted in simple but deep pleasures and the absence of pain, in an attitude of imperturbable emotional tranquillity. We should seek pleasure in conversation, friendship, a good but simple diet, and a prudent life. Since only good and bad sensations should concern us, and since death is not a sensation, we should not fear death. We should not even think very much about it.

Become accustomed to the belief that death is nothing to us. For all good and evil consists in sensation, but death is deprivation of sensation. And therefore a right understanding that death is nothing to us makes the mortality of life enjoyable, not because it adds to it an infinite span of time, but because it takes away the craving for immortality. For there is nothing terrible in life for the man who has truly comprehended that there is nothing terrible in not living. So that the man speaks but idly who says that he fears death not because it will be painful when it comes, but because it is painful in anticipation. For that which gives no trouble when it comes, is but an empty pain in anticipation. So death, the most terrifying of ills, is nothing to us, since so long as we exist, death is not with us; but when death comes, then we do not exist. It does not then concern either the living or the dead, since for the former it is not, and the latter are no more.

But the many at one moment shun death as the greatest of evils, at another yearn for it as a respite from the evils in life. But the wise man neither seeks to escape life nor fears the cessation of life, for neither does life offend him nor does the absence of life seem to be any evil. And just as with food he does not seek simply the larger share and nothing else, but rather the most pleasant, so he seeks to enjoy not the longest period of time, but the most pleasant.

And he who counsels the young man to live well, but the old man to make a good end, is foolish, not merely because of the desirability of life, but also because it is the same training which teaches to live well and to die well. Yet much worse still is the man who says it is good not to be born, but

'once born make haste to pass the gates of Death'.

For if he says this from conviction why does he not pass away out of life? For it is open to him to do so, if he had firmly made up his mind to this. But if he speaks in jest, his words are idle among men who cannot receive them.

We must then bear in mind that the future is neither ours, nor yet wholly not ours, so that we may not altogether expect it as sure to come, nor abandon hope of it, as if it will certainly not come.

We must consider that of desires some are natural, others vain, and of the natural some are necessary and others merely natural; and of the necessary some are necessary for happiness, others for the repose of the body, and others for very life. The right understanding of these facts enables us to refer all choice and avoidance to the health of the body and the soul's freedom from disturbance, since this is the aim of the life of blessedness. For it is to obtain this end that we always act, namely, to avoid pain and fear. And when this is once secured for us, all the tempest of the soul is dispersed, since the living creature has not to wander as though in search of something that is missing, and to look for some other thing by which he can fulfil the good of the soul and the good of the body. For it is then that we have need of pleasure, when we feel pain owing to the absence of pleasure; but when we do not feel pain, we no longer need pleasure. And for this cause we call pleasure the beginning and end of the blessed life. For we recognize pleasure as the first good innate in us, and from pleasure we begin every act of choice and avoidance, and to pleasure we return again, using the feeling as the standard by which we judge every good.

And since pleasure is the first good and natural to us, for this very reason we do not choose every pleasure, but sometimes we pass over many pleasures, when greater discomfort accrues to us as the result of them: and similarly we think many pains better than pleasures, since a greater pleasure comes to us when we have endured pains for a long time. Every pleasure then because of its natural kinship to us is good, yet not every pleasure is to be chosen: even as every pain also is an evil, yet not all are always of a nature to be avoided. Yet by a scale of comparison and by the consideration of advantages and disadvantages we must form our judgement on all these matters. For the good on certain occasions we treat as bad, and conversely the bad as good.

And again independence of desire we think a great good—not that we may at all times enjoy but a few things, but that, if we do not possess many, we may enjoy the few in the genuine persuasion that those have the sweetest pleasure in luxury who least need it, and that all that is natural is easy to be obtained, but that which is superfluous is hard. And so plain savours bring us pleasure equal to a luxurious diet, when all the pain due to want is removed; and bread and water produce the highest pleasure, when one who needs them puts them to his lips. To grow accustomed therefore to simple and not luxurious diet gives us health to the full, and makes a man alert for the needful employments of life, and when after long intervals we approach luxuries, disposes us better towards them, and fits us to be fearless of fortune.

When, therefore, we maintain that pleasure is the end, we do not mean the pleasures of profligates and those that consist in sensuality, as is supposed by some who are either ignorant or disagree with us or do not understand, but freedom from pain in the body and from trouble in the mind. For it is not continuous drinkings and revellings, nor the satisfaction of lusts, nor the enjoyment of fish and other luxuries of the wealthy table, which produce a pleasant life, but sober reasoning, searching out the motives for all choice and avoidance, and banishing mere opinions, to which are due the greatest disturbance of the spirit.

Of all this the beginning and the greatest good is prudence. Wherefore prudence is a more precious thing even than philosophy: for from prudence are sprung all the other virtues, and it teaches us that it is not possible to live pleasantly without living prudently and honourably and justly, nor, again, to live a life of prudence, honour, and justice without living pleasantly. For the virtues are by nature bound up with the pleasant life, and the pleasant life is inseparable from them. For indeed who, think you, is a better man than he who holds reverent opinions concerning the gods, and is at all times free from fear of death, and has reasoned out the end ordained by nature? He understands that the limit of good things is easy to fulfil and easy to attain, whereas the course of ills is either short in time or slight in pain: he laughs at destiny, whom some have introduced as the mistress of all things. He thinks that with us lies the chief power in determining events, some of which happen by necessity and some by chance, and some are within our control; for while necessity cannot be called to account, he sees that chance is inconstant, but that which is in our control is subject to no master, and to it are naturally attached praise and blame. For, indeed, it were better to follow the myths about the gods than to become a slave to the destiny of the natural philosophers: for the former suggests a hope of placating the gods by worship, whereas the latter involves a necessity which knows no placation. As to chance, he does not regard it as a god as most men do (for in a god's acts there is no disorder), nor as an uncertain cause of all things: for he does not believe that good and evil are given by chance to man for the framing of a blessed life, but that opportunities for great good and great evil are afforded by it. He therefore thinks it better to be unfortunate in reasonable action than to prosper in unreason. For it is better in a man's actions that what is well chosen should fail, rather than that what is ill chosen should be successful owing to chance.

Meditate therefore on these things and things akin to them night and day by yourself, and with a companion like to yourself, and never shall you be disturbed waking or asleep, but you shall live like a god among men. For a man who lives among immortal blessings is not like to a mortal being.

PRINCIPAL DOCTRINES

I. The blessed and immortal nature knows no trouble itself nor causes trouble to any other, so that it is never constrained by anger or favour. For all such things exist only in the weak.

II. Death is nothing to us: for that which is dissolved is without sensation; and that which lacks sensation is nothing to us.

III. The limit of quantity in pleasures is the removal of all that is painful. Wherever pleasure is present, as long as it is there, there is neither pain of body nor of mind, nor of both at once.

IV. Pain does not last continuously in the flesh, but the acutest pain is there for a very short time, and even that which just exceeds the pleasure in the flesh does not continue for many days at once. But chronic illnesses permit a predominance of pleasure over pain in the flesh.

V. It is not possible to live pleasantly without living prudently and honourably and justly, nor again to live a life of prudence, honour, and justice without living pleasantly. And the man who does not possess the pleasant life, is not living prudently and honourably and justly, and the man who does not possess the virtuous life, cannot possibly live pleasantly.

VI. To secure protection from men anything is a natural good, by which you may be able to attain this end.

VII. Some men wished to become famous and conspicuous, thinking that they would thus win for themselves safety from other men. Wherefore if the life of such men is safe, they have obtained the good which nature craves; but if it is not safe, they do not possess that for which they strove at first by the instinct of nature.

VIII. No pleasure is a bad thing in itself: but the means which produce some pleasures bring with them disturbances many times greater than the pleasures.

IX. If every pleasure could be intensified so that it lasted and influenced the whole organism or the most essential parts of our nature, pleasures would never differ from one another.

X. If the things that produce the pleasures of profligates could dispel the fears of the mind about the phenomena of the sky and death and its pains, and also teach the limits of desires and of pains, we should never have cause to blame them: for they would be filling themselves full with pleasures from every source and never have pain of body or mind, which is the evil of life.

XI. If we were not troubled by our suspicions of the phenomena of the sky and about death, fearing that it concerns us, and also by our failure to grasp the limits of pains and desires, we should have no need of natural science.

XII. A man cannot dispel his fear about the most important matters if he does not know what is the nature of the universe but suspects the truth of some mythical story. So that without natural science it is not possible to attain our pleasures unalloyed.

XIII. There is no profit in securing protection in relation to men, if things above and things beneath the earth and indeed all in the boundless universe remain matters of suspicion.

XIV. The most unalloyed source of protection from men, which is secured to some extent by a certain force of expulsion, is in fact the immunity which results from a quiet life and the retirement from the world.

XV. The wealth demanded by nature is both limited and easily procured; that demanded by idle imaginings stretches on to infinity.

XVI. In but few things chance hinders a wise man, but the greatest and most important matters reason has ordained and throughout the whole period of life does and will ordain.

XVII. The just man is most free from trouble, the unjust most full of trouble.

XVIII. The pleasure in the flesh is not increased, when once the pain due to want is removed, but is only varied: and the limit as regards pleasure in the mind is begotten by the reasoned understanding of these very pleasures and of the emotions akin to them, which used to cause the greatest fear to the mind.

XIX. Infinite time contains no greater pleasure than limited time, if one measures by reason the limits of pleasure.

XX. The flesh perceives the limits of pleasure as unlimited and unlimited time is required to supply it. But the mind, having attained a reasoned understanding of the ultimate good of the flesh and its limits and having dissipated the fears concerning the time to come, supplies us with the complete life, and we have no further need of infinite time: but neither does the mind shun pleasure, nor, when circumstances begin to bring about the departure from life, does it approach its end as though it fell short in any way of the best life.

XXI. He who has learned the limits of life knows that that which removes the paid due to want and makes the whole of life complete is easy to obtain; so that there is no need of actions which involve competition.

XXII. We must consider both the real purpose and all the evidence of direct perception, to which we always refer the conclusions of opinion; otherwise, all will be full of doubt and confusion.

XXIII. If you fight against all sensations, you will have no standard by which to judge even those of them which you say are false.

XXIV. If you reject any single sensation and fail to distinguish between the conclusion of opinion as to the appearance awaiting confirmation and that which is actually given by the sensation or feeling, or each intuitive apprehension of the mind, you will confound all other sensations as well with the same groundless opinion, so that you will reject every standard of judgement. And if among the mental images created by your opinion you affirm both that which awaits confirmation and that which does not, you will not escape error, since you will have preserved the whole cause of doubt in every judgement between what is right and what is wrong.

XXV. If on each occasion instead of referring your actions to the end of nature, you turn to some other nearer standard when you are making a choice or an avoidance, your actions will not be consistent with your principles.

XXVI. Of desires, all that do not lead to a sense of pain, if they are not satisfied, are not necessary, but involve a craving which is easily dispelled, when the object is hard to procure or they seem likely to produce harm.

XXVII. Of all the things which wisdom acquires to produce the blessedness of the complete life, far the greatest is the possession of friendship.

XXVIII. The same conviction which has given us confidence that there is nothing terrible that lasts for ever or even for long, has also seen the protection of friendship most fully completed in the limited evils of this life.

XXIX. Among desires some are natural and necessary, some natural but not necessary, and others neither natural nor necessary, but due to idle imagination.

XXX. Wherever in the case of desires which are physical, but do not lead to a sense of pain, if they are not fulfilled, the effort is intense, such pleasures are due to idle imagination, and it is not owing to their own nature that they fail to be dispelled, but owing to the empty imaginings of the man.

For Further Reflection

1. Epicureanism is often thought of as a shallow, gluttonous, profligate life of undifferentiated pleasure, whose motto has been "Eat, drink, and be merry, for tomorrow we die" ("the pig philosophy"). Does one get this impression from Epicurus's writings?

2. Consider his view toward the fact of death: You ought not fear what never touches you. Death never touches you, for when you are, it is not; and when it is, you are not. Is this a reasonable argument against the fear of death? Why do we consider death an evil? What is the proper attitude toward death and why?

Stoic Catechism

EPICTETUS AND OTHERS

The Greek philosopher Epictetus (60–138) was born a slave in Asia Minor but freed in early adulthood. He was crippled in slavery, which is said to have influenced his philosophy. He was known for his tolerance, kindness, and humility. His motto was "Bear and forbear." Epictetus did not publish anything, but his student Flavius Arrianus has recorded his teachings in the *Enchiridion* (a handbook) from which a major selection is included here.

Stoicism was a Greek school of philosophy, founded around 100 B.C. in Athens by Zeno, that developed into the dominant philosophy of the Roman Empire. The Greek word *stoa* means "porch." Apparently Zeno lectured from his porch. The Stoics believed that we should resign ourselves to our fate, do our duty faithfully, and thereby acquire tranquillity of soul. We should not attempt overly much to change the world, since it is unstable and beyond our control. Instead, we should try to change our attitude—since that is something we can control. A key Stoic idea is: If you don't get what you desire, desire what you get. That is, learn to transform bad experiences into good ones.

The first short selection, on duty, is from the Stoic Roman emperor Marcus Aurelius (121–180). The second, on sui-

Epictetus' Enchiridion, translated by Wallace Matson. Copyright © Wallace Matson 1996. Reprinted by permission.

cide, is from the Stoic Seneca (3–65), and the main selection is from Epictetus's teachings.

1. MARCUS AURELIUS: *DEDICATION TO DUTY*

Hour by hour resolve to do the task of the hour carefully, with unaffected dignity, affectionately, freely and justly. You can avoid distractions that might interfere with such performance if every act is done as though it were the last act of your life. Free yourself from random aims and curb any tendency to let the passions of emotion, hypocrisy, self-love and dissatisfaction with your allotted share cause you to ignore the commands of reason.

2. SENECA: *DEATH AND SUICIDE*

Life has carried some men with the greatest rapidity to the harbor, the harbor they were bound to reach if they tarried on the way, while others it has fretted and harassed. To such a life, as you are aware, one should not always cling. *For mere living is not a good, but living well.* Accordingly, the wise man will live as long as he ought, not as long as he can. He will mark in what place, with whom, and how he is to conduct his existence, and what he is about to do. He always reflects concerning the quality, and not the quantity of his life. As soon as there are many events in his life that give him trouble and disturb his peace of mind, he sets himself free. And this privilege is his, not only when the crisis is upon him, but as soon as Fortune seems to be playing him false; then he looks about carefully and sees whether he ought, or ought not, to end his life on that account. . . . He does not regard death with fear, as if it were a great loss; for no man can lose very much when but a driblet remains. It is not a question of dying earlier or later, but of dying well or ill. And dying well means escape from the danger of living ill.

3. EPICTETUS: *ENCHIRIDION*

1. Some things are up to us, some are not up to us. Up to us are perception, intention, desire, aversion, and in sum, whatever are

our own doings; not up to us are body, property, reputation, political office and in sum, whatever are not our own doings. And the things that are up to us are naturally free, unforbidding, unimpeding, while those not up to us are weak, slavish, forbidding, alien. Remember, then, that if you think naturally slavish things are free and that alien things are your own, you will be impeded, grieved, troubled, you will blame gods and men; but if you think that what is yours is yours and what is alien is alien, as it really is, nobody will ever compel you, nobody will forbid you, you will not blame anyone, you will not complain about anything, you will not do a single thing unwillingly, you will have no enemy, no one will hurt you; for you will not suffer anything harmful.

If you are aiming for such great things, remember that you must not be moderate in exerting yourself to attain them: you must avoid some things altogether and postpone others for the time being. For if you want both to accomplish these aims, and also to achieve eminence and riches, it may come about that you will not get the latter because you were trying for the former, and certainly you will not get the former, which are the only things that produce freedom and well-being.

So take rigorous care to say to every menacing impression, "You are just an impression, not the real thing at all." Then test it and consider it according to your rules—first and foremost this: whether it belongs among the things that are up to us or to those not up to us. And if it is something not up to us, be ready to say "It is nothing to me."

2. Remember that the aim of desire is to get what arouses the desire, the aim of aversion is to avoid that to which you are averse; and he who fails to get what he desires is miserable, and so is he who gets what he is averse to. So then, if you are averse only to things contrary to nature that are up to you, you will not get anything to which you are averse; but if you are averse to sickness or death or poverty, you will be miserable. So take your aversion away from everything that is not up to you and transfer it to things contrary to nature that are up to you. But for the time being, destroy desire altogether; for if you desire something not up to you, necessarily you will be unfortunate; as for things that are up to us, and would be good to desire, none of them is yet within your grasp. But only make use of selection and rejection, and these lightly, discreetly, and tentatively.

3. As for every thing that delights your mind or is useful or beloved, remember to describe it as it really is, starting with the smallest thing. If you are fond of a pot, say "It is a pot that I am fond of." For then, if it breaks, you will not be upset. If you kiss your child or your wife, say that you are kissing a human being. Then if they die you will not be upset.

5. It is not things that upset people but rather ideas about things. For example, death is nothing terrible, else it would have seemed so even to Socrates; rather it is the idea that death is terrible that is terrible. So whenever we are frustrated or upset or grieved, let us not blame others, but ourselves—that is, our ideas. It is the act of a philosophically ignorant person to blame others for his own troubles. One who is beginning to learn blames himself. An educated person blames neither anyone else nor himself.

6. Do not pride yourself on superiority that is not your own. If a horse in its pride should say, "I am a fine horse," that could be tolerated. You however, when you boast "I have a fine horse," should realize that you are boasting about the excellence of a horse. What then is your own? The use of impressions. So, make use of your impressions in accord with nature, and then take pride; for your pride will be in a good thing that is your own.

8. Don't seek for things to happen as you wish, but wish for things to happen as they do, and you will get on well.

9. Illness is an impediment of the body, but not of the will, as long as the will itself does not so wish. Lameness is an impediment of the leg, not of the will. And say this to yourself of every accident that befalls you; for you will find it an impediment to something else, not to yourself.

10. Whatever occasion befalls you, remember to turn around and look into yourself to see what power you have to make use of it. If you see a handsome boy or a beautiful girl, you will find the relevant power to be self-control. If labor is heaped on you, endurance is what you need; if abuse, forbearance. And thus habituating yourself, you will not be carried away by impressions.

11. Never say about anything that you have "lost it," but that you have "given it back." Your child has died? It has been given back. Your wife has died? She has been given back. "I have been deprived of my estate." This too has been given back. "But the usurper is wicked." What concern is it of yours, through whom the gift was returned to the giver? For the time it is given to you, treat it as someone else's, as travellers do an inn. . . .

13. If you want to make progress, be content to appear stupid and foolish about externals, and don't wish to seem to know anything. And whenever you seem to be somebody to someone, distrust yourself. For be aware that it is not easy both to have your will in accordance with nature and to be on your guard about externals also, if you are to take care of the one it is absolutely necessary to neglect the other.

14. If you want your children and your wife and friends to live forever, you are a fool; for you want what is not up to you to be up to you, and what is not yours to be yours. Thus also if you want your slave not to do anything wrong, you are stupid; for you want badness not to be badness but something else. But if what you want is not to fail in getting what you desire, that you can bring about. So practise what you are capable of. Every person's master is the one who controls whether that person shall get what he wants and avoid what he doesn't want. Thus whoever wishes to be free should neither seek nor avoid anything that is up to others; otherwise he will necessarily be a slave.

15. Remember that you ought to conduct yourself as you do at a banquet. When something passed around reaches you, extend your hand and take it politely. If it is passing you by, don't grab. If it has not yet reached you, don't crave for it, but wait until it gets to you. Thus toward children, thus toward women, thus toward jobs, thus toward riches; and in due time you will be worthy to dine with the gods. But if you do not take even the things set out for you, but despise them, then not only will you be a banquet companion of the gods, you will even be a co-ruler. By thus acting, Diogenes and Heraclitus and like men came to be called divine, and deservedly.

16. Whenever you see someone weeping in grief because his child is going away or he has lost his property, be careful not to be misled by the impression that he is in a bad way because of external things, but be ready to say at once "It is not the circumstances that distress him (for someone else would not be distressed), but the idea he has about them." Don't, of course, hesitate to condole with him in words, and, if there is occasion, even to groan with him; but take care not to groan inwardly.

17. Remember that you are an actor in a drama such as the playwright wishes it to be. If he wants it short, it will be short; if long, long. If he wants you to play a beggar, play even that capably; or a lame man, or a ruler, or a private person. For this is yours, to play the assigned role well. Casting is the business of another.

19. You can be unbeatable if you never enter a contest in which it is not up to you who wins. Beware lest ever, seeing someone else preferred in honor or having great power or otherwise esteemed, you get carried away by impressions and deem him blessed. For since the essence of the good lies in the things up to us, neither jealousy nor envy has a place; and you yourself will not wish to be a praetor* or a senator or a consul, but a free man. There is but one way to this: contempt for things not up to us.

20. Remember that it is not the man who curses you or the man who hits you that insults you, but the idea you have of them as insulting. So, whenever someone irritates you, realize that it is your own opinion that has irritated you. First of all, try not to be carried away by impressions; if you succeed just once in gaining time and avoiding hastiness, you will easily control yourself.

21. Let death and exile and all dreadful appearances be before your eyes every day, and most of all, death; and you will never [be preoccupied by] anything trivial, nor desire anything excessively. . . .

24. Don't let reflections like this upset you: "I shall live without honor, a complete nobody." For suppose not being honored is an evil: you cannot be subjected to evil by another, any more than to shamefulness. Is it your business to acquire power or an invitation to a banquet? By no means. How then is this being without honor? How then will you be a complete nobody, when you ought to be somebody only with respect to those things that are up to you— the domain wherein it is given to you to be of the greatest worth? But your friends will get no help from you? What do you mean by help? They won't have a penny from you; nor will you make them Roman citizens. So who told you that these things are up to you, and not the business of others? Who can give to another things that he does not have himself? "Then get them," one says, "so that we can have them." If I can get them while preserving my self-respect and trustworthiness and high-mindedness, show me the way and I'll get them. But if you require me to be one who will lose my proper goods in order to produce worthless things for you,—just look, how partial and unfair you are. Which do you want more? Money, or a faithful and upright friend? Then you had better help

*Roman magistrate

me to acquire the characteristics of one and not require me to do the things that would ruin them.

"But my country, as far as its fate is up to me," one says, "will be helpless." Again, what kind of help do you mean? She will not get arcades or baths from you. So what? Neither does she get shoes from smiths nor weapons from shoemakers. It is enough if everyone fulfills his own task. If you make someone else into a faithful and upright citizen, have you done something for the state? "Yes." Then you yourself are not unhelpful if you are that one. "Then what status," one asks, "will I have in the city?" Whatever you are capable of, while conserving your faithfulness and uprightness. If in wishing to aid her you throw them away, what advantage will accrue to her when you have ended up shameless and faithless? . . .

27. As a target is not set up for the purpose of being missed, so nothing in the world is intrinsically evil.

28. If someone were to hand over your body to just whomever happened along, you would be outraged. Why aren't you outraged at the fact that *you* turn over your own mind to whomever happens along—if he insults you and you let it upset and trouble you?

29. In every work examine the things that have to be done first and what is to follow, and only then get started on it. If you don't, you will go along eagerly at first, because you have given no consideration to what is coming next; later when difficulties appear the work will come to an ignoble halt. You want to win at Olympia? I do too, by the gods; for it is a fine thing. But look at what comes first, and what comes next, and then take on the work. You must keep discipline, diet, give up pastries, do the compulsory exercises at the set time in heat or in cold, never drink anything cold, take wine only with meals, completely submit yourself to your trainer as to your doctor, and then when the contest starts you have to wallow around in the mud, maybe dislocate your wrist or turn your ankle, swallow quantities of sand, perhaps sometimes be flogged,— and after all this you still lose. Taking it all into consideration, go ahead and be an athlete, if you still want to. Otherwise you will be turning from one thing to another like children, who now play wrestlers, now gladiators, now trumpeters, then tragic actors; you too would be now athlete, now gladiator, then orator, then philosopher, nothing with your whole soul; but like a monkey you mimic every sight that you see as one thing after another intrigues you. For you have never proceeded with something in accord with inves-

tigation, after looking at it from all sides; but just at random and out of frivolous enthusiasm.

Thus some people, when they have seen a philosopher and have heard someone speaking the way Euphrates speaks (but who can speak like him?), wish to philosophize themselves. Man, consider first what kind of business this is. And then learn what your own nature is; can you bear it? Do you want to be a pentathlete or a wrestler? Look at your arms, your thighs, learn about your hips. One man is naturally fitted for one thing, another for another. Do you suppose you can do these things and keep on eating and drinking and enthusing and sulking just as you do now? You will have to go without sleep, labor, leave home, be despised by a slave, have everyone laugh at you, get the worse in everything, in honors, in jobs, in lawsuits, in every trifle. Look these things over and decide whether you want to exchange them for tranquillity, freedom, and peace; if not, don't go ahead, don't be, like a child, now philosopher, afterwards tax collector, then orator, finally Caesar's procurator. These things do not go together. You ought to be one man, good or evil; you must cultivate either your own guiding principle or externals; that is, apply yourself either to the inner man or to outward things: assume either the role of philosopher or of layman. . . .

33. Prescribe a certain character and type for yourself, and guard it both when you are by yourself and when you meet people. And be silent about most things, or chat only when necessary and about few matters. On rare occasions, when the time is ripe and you are called on to talk, talk—but not about banal topics; not about gladiators, or athletes, or horse races, or food and drink, such as you hear everywhere; and above all, not about blaming or praising or comparing people. If you can, lead the conversation around to something proper. But if you happen to be alone with strange people, be silent.

Laugh seldom and about few things and with restraint.

Totally abstain from taking oaths, if you can; if not, then refuse whenever circumstances allow.

Avoid celebrations, both public and private; but if the occasion calls you, be alert not to lapse into vulgarity. For know that if a companion is defiled, necessarily also one who keeps company with him will be defiled, even if he himself happens to be pure.

Partake of things having to do with the body only as far as bare need goes: such things as food, drink, clothing, housing, slaves. Dispense altogether with whatever has to do with reputation or luxury.

As to sex, be as pure as you can before marriage; but if you are aroused, indulge only to the extent that is customary. However, don't by any means be troublesome to those who do indulge, or censorious; and don't keep mentioning that you yourself can get along without it.

If someone tells you that somebody else is saying awful things about you, don't defend yourself against the accusations, but reply, "He must not know about the other faults that I have, if these are the only ones he mentioned."

It isn't necessary to attend shows for the most part. But if there is a proper occasion, do not appear to be more enthusiastic for anyone else than for yourself, that is, wish only that those things should happen that do happen and that only the winner should win; that way you will not be frustrated. Abstain altogether from shouting and ridiculing anyone or getting emotionally involved. And after the performance don't talk much about what happened, if it does not tend toward your improvement. For it would be evident from this that you were dazzled by the spectacle. . . .

Whenever you are going to meet someone, especially one reputed to be important, consider what Socrates or Zeno would have done in the circumstances, and you will not be puzzled about how to use the occasion properly. When you are going to visit a powerful personage, propose to yourself that you will not find him at home, that you will be shut out, that the gates will be slammed in your face, that he will not notice you. And if nevertheless it is your duty to go, when you arrive bear with what happens and by no means say to yourself "It wasn't worth it." For it is unphilosophical to be troubled by externals.

In conversation avoid overmuch talk about your own deeds and dangers. For although it is pleasant for you to recall your own adventures, it may not be so for others to hear about what happened to you.

Also avoid raising laughter; for this is a slippery slope to vulgarity and at the same time sufficient to cancel the respect that others have for you. It is also dangerous to get into dirty talk. Whenever anything of this sort begins, if you get the opportunity, you might rebuke the person who starts it; or if not, make it clear by being silent or blushing and scowling that you are displeased by the talk. . . .

If the room is smoky, if only moderately, I will stay; if there is too much smoke, I will leave. Remember this, keep firm hold on it, the door is always open.

For Further Reflection

1. What are the principal ideas of Stoicism, as contained in these readings? Is it really possible to live by this philosophy? Is it an optimistic or pessimistic philosophy?

2. Compare Stoicism with Epicurus's philosophy. How different are the two philosophies? In what ways, if any, do they differ? For example, compare what they say about death.

3. Would you want to have a Stoic for a spouse or a parent or a friend? Why or why not?

Life Is Absurd

ALBERT CAMUS

Albert Camus (1913–1960) was born in French colonial Algeria, into a poor working-class family. He was a French journalist, novelist, and philosopher who fought in the French underground during World War II and fought for courage and integrity in public life. He is most famous for his novels *The Stranger* (1942), *The Plague* (1947), and *The Fall* (1957), for which he received a Nobel Prize for literature. He was killed in a car crash in 1960. His rival existentialist, Jean-Paul Sartre, fittingly called it "an absurd death."

In this selection we see Camus's overall assessment that life is absurd, meaningless. The only important philosophical question is, why not commit suicide? Life is compared to the myth of Sisyphus, wherein that man is condemned by the gods to roll a huge stone up a mountain, watch it

From *The Myth of Sisyphus and Other Essays* by Albert Camus, translated by Justin O'Brien. Copyright © 1955 by Alfred A. Knopf Inc. Reprinted by permission of the publisher.

roll back down, and retrieve it, only to repeat the process again, endlessly.

ABSURDITY AND SUICIDE

There is but one truly serious philosophical problem, and that is suicide. Judging whether life is or is not worth living amounts to answering the fundamental question of philosophy. All the rest— whether or not the world has three dimensions, whether the mind has nine or twelve categories—comes afterwards. These are games; one must first answer. And if it is true, as Nietzsche claims, that a philosopher, to deserve our respect, must preach by example, you can appreciate the importance of that reply, for it will precede the definitive act. These are facts the heart can feel; yet they call for careful study before they become clear to the intellect.

If I ask myself how to judge that this question is more urgent than that, I reply that one judges by the actions it entails. I have never seen anyone die for the ontological argument. Galileo, who held a scientific truth of great importance, abjured it with the greatest of ease as soon as it endangered his life. In a certain sense, he did right.* That truth was not worth the stake. Whether the earth or the sun revolves around the other is a matter of profound indifference. To tell the truth, it is a futile question. On the other hand, I see many people die because they judge that life is not worth living. I see others paradoxically getting killed for the ideas or illusions that give them a reason for living (what is called a reason for living is also an excellent reason for dying). I therefore conclude that the meaning of life is the most urgent of questions. How to answer it? On all essential problems (I mean thereby those that run the risk of leading to death or those that intensify the passion of living) there are probably but two methods of thought: the method of La Palisse and the method of Don Quixote. Solely the balance between evidence and lyricism can allow us to achieve simultane-

---

*From the point of view of the relative value of truth. On the other hand, from the point of view of virile behavior, this scholar's fragility may well make us smile.

ously emotion and lucidity. In a subject at once so humble and so heavy with emotion, the learned and classical dialectic must yield, one can see, to a more modest attitude of mind deriving at one and the same time from common sense and understanding.

Suicide has never been dealt with except as a social phenomenon. On the contrary, we are concerned here, at the outset, with the relationship between individual thought and suicide. An act like this is prepared within the silence of the heart, as is a great work of art. The man himself is ignorant of it. One evening he pulls the trigger or jumps. Of an apartment-building manager who had killed himself I was told that he had lost his daughter five years before, that he had changed greatly since, and that that experience had "undermined" him. A more exact word cannot be imagined. Beginning to think is beginning to be undermined. Society has but little connection with such beginnings. The worm is in man's heart. That is where it must be sought. One must follow and understand this fatal game that leads from lucidity in the face of existence to flight from light. . . .

But it is hard to fix the precise instant, the subtle step when the mind opted for death, it is easier to deduce from the act itself the consequences it implies. In a sense, and as in melodrama, killing yourself amounts to confessing. It is confessing that life is too much for you or that you do not understand it. Let's not go too far in such analogies, however, but rather return to everyday words. It is merely confessing that that "is not worth the trouble." Living, naturally, is never easy. You continue making the gestures commanded by existence for many reasons, the first of which is habit. Dying voluntarily implies that you have recognized, even instinctively, the ridiculous character of that habit, the absence of any profound reason for living, the insane character of that daily agitation, and the uselessness of suffering.

What, then, is that incalculable feeling that deprives the mind of the sleep necessary to life? A world that can be explained even with bad reasons is a familiar world. But, on the other hand, in a universe suddenly divested of illusions and lights, man feels an alien, a stranger. His exile is without remedy since he is deprived of the memory of a lost home or the hope of a promised land. This divorce between man and his life, the actor and his setting, is properly the feeling of absurdity. All healthy men having thought of their own suicide, it can be seen, without further explanation, that there is a direct connection between this feeling and the longing for death.

The subject of this essay is precisely this relationship between the absurd and suicide, the exact degree to which suicide is a solution to the absurd. The principle can be established that for a man who does not cheat, what he believes to be true must determine his action. Belief in the absurdity of existence must then dictate his conduct. It is legitimate to wonder, clearly and without false pathos, whether a conclusion of this importance requires forsaking as rapidly as possible an incomprehensible condition. I am speaking, of course, of men inclined to be in harmony with themselves. . . .

All great deeds and all great thoughts have a ridiculous beginning. Great works are often born on a street-corner or in a restaurant's revolving door. So it is with absurdity. The absurd world more than others derives its nobility from that abject birth. In certain situations, replying "nothing" when asked what one is thinking about may be pretense in a man. Those who are loved are well aware of this. But if that reply is sincere, if it symbolizes that odd state of soul in which the void becomes eloquent, in which the chain of daily gestures is broken, in which the heart vainly seeks the link that will connect it again, then it is as it were the first sign of absurdity.

It happens that the stage sets collapse. Rising, streetcar, four hours in the office or the factory, meal, streetcar, four hours of work, meal, sleep, and Monday Tuesday Wednesday Thursday Friday and Saturday according to the same rhythm—this path is easily followed most of the time. But one day the "why" arises and everything begins in that weariness tinged with amazement. "Begins"—this is important. Weariness comes at the end of the acts of a mechanical life, but at the same time it inaugurates the impulse of consciousness. It awakens consciousness and provokes what follows. What follows is the gradual return into the chain or it is the definitive awakening. At the end of the awakening comes, in time, the consequence: suicide or recovery. In itself weariness has something sickening about it. Here, I must conclude that it is good. For everything begins with consciousness and nothing is worth anything except through it. . . .

But what does life mean in such a universe? Nothing else for the moment but indifference to the future and a desire to use up everything that is given. Belief in the meaning of life always implies a scale of values, a choice, our preferences. Belief in the absurd, according to our definitions, teaches the contrary. But this is worth examining.

Knowing whether or not one can live *without appeal* is all that interests me. I do not want to get out of my depth. This aspect of life being given me, can I adapt myself to it? Now, faced with this particular concern, belief in the absurd is tantamount to substituting the quantity of experiences for the quality. If I convince myself that this life has no other aspect than that of the absurd, if I feel that its whole equilibrium depends on that perpetual opposition between my conscious revolt and the darkness in which it struggles, if I admit that my freedom has no meaning except in relation to its limited fate, then I must say that what counts is not the best of living but the most living. . . .

On the one hand the absurd teaches that all experiences are unimportant, and on the other it urges toward the greatest quantity of experiences. How, then, can one fail to do as so many of those men I was speaking of earlier—choose the form of life that brings us the most possible of that human matter, thereby introducing a scale of values that on the other hand one claims to reject?

But again it is the absurd and its contradictory life that teaches us. For the mistake is thinking that that quantity of experiences depends on the circumstances of our life when it depends solely on us. Here we have to be oversimple. To two men living the same number of years, the world always provides the same sum of experiences. It is up to us to be conscious of them. Being aware of one's life, one's revolt, one's freedom, and to the maximum, is living, and to the maximum. Where lucidity dominates, the scale of values becomes useless. . . .

THE MYTH OF SISYPHUS

The gods had condemned Sisyphus to ceaselessly rolling a rock to the top of a mountain, whence the stone would fall back of its own weight. They had thought with some reason that there is no more dreadful punishment than futile and hopeless labor.

If one believes Homer, Sisyphus was the wisest and most prudent of mortals. According to another tradition, however, he was disposed to practice the profession of highwayman. I see no contradiction in this. Opinions differ as to the reasons why he became the futile laborer of the underworld. To begin with, he is accused of a certain levity in regard to the gods. He stole their secrets. Ægina, the daughter of Æsopus, was carried off by Jupiter. The father was shocked by that disappearance and complained to Sisyphus. He, who knew of the abduction, offered to tell about it on condition that Æsopus would give water to the citadel of Corinth. To the celestial thunderbolts he preferred the benediction of water. He was punished for this in the underworld. Homer tells us also that Sisyphus had put Death in chains. Pluto could not endure the sight of his deserted, silent empire. He dispatched the god of war, who liberated Death from the hands of her conqueror.

It is said also that Sisyphus, being near to death, rashly wanted to test his wife's love. He ordered her to cast his unburied body into the middle of the public square. Sisyphus woke up in the underworld. And there, annoyed by an obedience so contrary to human love, he obtained from Pluto permission to return to earth in order to chastise his wife. But when he had seen again the face of this world, enjoyed water and sun, warm stones and the sea, he no longer wanted to go back to the infernal darkness. Recalls, signs of anger, warnings were of no avail. Many years more he lived facing the curve of the gulf, the sparkling sea, and the smiles of earth. A decree of the gods was necessary. Mercury came and seized the impudent man by the collar and, snatching him from his joys, led him forcibly back to the underworld, where his rock was ready for him.

You have already grasped that Sisyphus is the absurd hero. He *is,* as much through his passions as through his torture. His scorn of the gods, his hatred of death, and his passion for life won him that unspeakable penalty in which the whole being is exerted toward accomplishing nothing. This is the price that must be paid for the passions of this earth. Nothing is told us about Sisyphus in the underworld. Myths are made for the imagination to breathe life into them. As for this myth, one sees merely the whole effort of a body straining to raise the huge stone, to roll it and push it up a slope a hundred times over; one sees the face screwed up, the cheek tight against the stone, the shoulder bracing the clay-covered mass, the foot wedging it, the fresh start with arms outstretched, the wholly human security of two earth-clotted hands. At the very end of his long effort measured by skyless space and time without depth, the purpose is achieved. Then Sisyphus watches the stone rush down in a few moments toward that lower world whence he will have to push it up again toward the summit. He goes back down to the plain.

It is during that return, that pause, that Sisyphus interests me. A face that toils so close to stones is already stone itself! I see that man going back down with a heavy yet measured step toward the torment of which he will never know the end. That hour like a breathing-space which returns as surely as his suffering, that is the hour of consciousness. At each of those moments when he leaves the heights and gradually sinks toward the lairs of the gods, he is superior to his fate. He is stronger than his rock.

If this myth is tragic, that is because its hero is conscious. Where would his torture be, indeed, if at every step the hope of succeeding upheld him? The workman of today works every day in his life at the same tasks, and this fate is no less absurd. But it is tragic only at the rare moments when it becomes conscious. Sisyphus, proletarian of the gods, powerless and rebellious, knows the whole extent of his wretched condition: it is what he thinks of during his descent. The lucidity that was to constitute his torture at the same time crowns his victory. There is no fate that cannot be surmounted by scorn.

If the descent is thus sometimes performed in sorrow, it can also take place in joy. This word is not too much. Again I fancy Sisyphus returning toward his rock, and the sorrow was in the beginning. When the images of earth cling too tightly to memory, when the call of happiness becomes too insistent, it happens that melancholy rises in man's heart: this is the rock's victory, this is the rock itself. The boundless grief is too heavy to bear. These are our nights of Gethsemane. But crushing truths perish from being acknowledged. Thus, Œdipus at the outset obeys fate without knowing it. But from the moment he knows, his tragedy begins. Yet at the same moment, blind and desperate, he realizes that the only bond linking him to the world is the cool hand of a girl. Then a tremendous remark rings out: "Despite so many ordeals, my advanced age and the nobility of my soul make me conclude that all is well." Sophocles' Œdipus, like Dostoevsky's Kirilov, thus gives the recipe for the absurd victory. Ancient wisdom confirms modern heroism.

One does not discover the absurd without being tempted to write a manual of happiness. "What! by such narrow ways—?" There is but one world, however. Happiness and the absurd are two sons of the same earth. They are inseparable. It would be a mistake to say that happiness necessarily springs from the absurd discovery. It happens as well that the feeling of the absurd springs from happiness. "I conclude that all is well," says Œdipus, and that remark is sacred. It echoes in the wild and limited universe of man. It teaches that all is not, has not been, exhausted. It drives out of this world a god who had come into it with dissatisfaction and a preference for futile sufferings. It makes of fate a human matter, which must be settled among men.

All Sisyphus' silent joy is contained therein. His fate belongs to him. His rock is his thing. Likewise, the absurd man, when he contemplates his torment, silences all the idols. In the universe suddenly restored to its silence, the myriad wondering little voices of the earth rise up. Unconscious, secret calls, invitations from all the faces, they are the necessary reverse and price of victory. There is no sun without shadow, and it is essential to know the night. The absurd man says yes and his effort will henceforth be unceasing. If there is a personal fate, there is no higher destiny, or at least there is but one which he concludes is inevitable and despicable. For the rest, he knows himself to be the master of his days. At that subtle moment when man glances backward over his life, Sisyphus returning toward his rock, in that slight pivoting he contemplates that series of unrelated actions which becomes his fate, created by him, combined under his memory's eye and soon sealed by his death. Thus, convinced of the wholly human origin of all that is human, a blind man eager to see who knows that the night has no end, he is still on the go. The rock is still rolling.

I leave Sisyphus at the foot of the mountain! One always finds one's burden again. But Sisyphus teaches the higher fidelity that negates the gods and raises rocks. He too concludes that all is well. This universe henceforth without a master seems to him neither sterile nor futile. Each atom of that stone, each mineral flake of that night-filled mountain, in itself forms a world. The struggle itself toward the heights is enough to fill a man's heart. One must imagine Sisyphus happy.

For Further Reflection

1. Is life absurd, as Camus insists? Does Camus give good reasons for this claim? What leads him to this pessimistic conclusion?

2. Is Camus being irreverent in asking such an outrageous question as "Why not commit suicide"?

3. Why does Camus say that Sisyphus must be imagined to be happy?

4. Compare Camus with Epicurus. In what ways are their views similar? In what ways different?

Religion Gives Meaning to Life

LOIS HOPE WALKER

> Lois Hope Walker is the pen name of an author who wishes to remain anonymous. In this essay Walker argues that religion, specifically theistic religion, gives special meaning to life, unavailable in secular world views. Furthermore, the autonomy that secularists prize (sometimes value it beyond its worth) is not significantly diminished by religious faith.

Several years ago during a class break, I was discussing the significance of religion in our society with a few students in the college lounge. I, at that time an agnostic, was conceding to a devout Christian that it would be nice if theism were true, for then the world would not be simply a matter of chance and necessity, a sad tale with a sadder ending. Instead, "the world would be personal, a gift from our heavenly Father, who provides a basis for meaning and purpose." A mature woman from another class, whom I knew to be an atheist, overheard my remarks, charged through a group of coffee drinkers and angrily snapped at me, "That is the most disgusting thing I've ever heard!" I inquired why she thought this, and she replied, "Religion keeps humans from growing up. We don't need a big Daddy in the sky. We need to grow up and become our own parents."

I recalled Nietzsche's dictum that now that "God is dead," now that we have killed the Holy One, we must ourselves become gods to seem worthy of the deed. The atheist woman was prizing autonomy over meaning and claiming that religion did just the opposite.

In other words, she held two theses:

(1) It is more important to be free or autonomous than to have a grand meaning or purpose to life.

(2) Religion provides a grand meaning or purpose to life, but it does not allow humans to be free or autonomous.

I've thought a lot about that woman's response over the years. I think that she is wrong on both counts. In this essay I will defend religion against her two theses and try to show that meaning and autonomy are both necessary or important ingredients for an ideal existence and that they are compatible within a religious framework.

Let me begin with the first thesis, that it is more important to be free than that there be meaning in life. First let us define our terms. By "autonomy" I mean self-governing, the ability to make choices on the basis of good reasons rather than being coerced by threats or forces from without.

By "meaning" in life I mean that life has a purpose. There is some intrinsic rationale or plan to it. Now this purpose can be good, bad, or indifferent. An example of something with a bad purpose is the activity of poisoning a reservoir on which a community depends for its sustenance. An example of something with an indifferent purpose might be pacing back and forth to pass the time of day (it is arguable that this is bad or good depending on the options and context, and if you think that then either choose your own example or dismiss the category of indifferent purpose). An example of a good purpose is digging a well in order to provide water to a community in need of water.

Now it seems to be the case that, as a value, autonomy is superior to indifferent and bad purposes, since it has positive value but these other two categories do not. Autonomy may be more valuable to us than some good purposes, but it does not seem to be superior to *all* good purposes. While it may be more valuable to be free than to have this or that incidental purpose in life, freedom cannot really be understood apart from the notion of purposiveness. To be free is to be able to do some act *A*, when you want to, in order to reach some goal *G*. So the two ideas are related.

But the atheist woman meant more than this. She meant that if she had to choose whether to have free will or to live in a world that had a governing providential hand, she would choose the former. But this seems to make two mistakes. (1) It makes autonomy into an unjustified absolute and (2) it creates a false dilemma.

(1) Consider two situations: In situation A you are as free as you are now (say you have 100 units of autonomy—call these units "autonotoms") but are deeply miserable because you are locked in a large and interesting room which is being slowly filled with poisonous gas. You can do what ever you want for five more minutes but then you will be dead. In situation B, however, you have only 95 autonotoms (that is, there are a few things that you are unable to do in this world—say commit adultery or kill your neighbor) but the room is being filled with sunshine and fresh air. Which world would you choose? I would choose situation B, for autonomy, it seems to me, is not the only value in the universe, nor is it always the overriding value. I think most of us would be willing to give up a few autonotoms for an enormous increase in happiness. And I think that a world with a good purpose would be one in which we would be willing to give up a few bits of freedom. If we were told that we could eliminate poverty, crime, and great suffering in the world by each sacrificing one autonotom, wouldn't we do this? If so, then autonomy is not an absolute which always overrides every other value. It is one important value among others.

I turn to the atheist's second thesis, that religion always holds purpose as superior to autonomy. I think that this is a misunderstanding of what the best types of religion try to do. As Jesus said in John 8:32, "Ye shall know the truth and the truth shall set you free." Rather than seeing freedom and meaning as opposites, theism sees them as inextricably bound together. Since it claims to offer us the truth about the world, and since having true beliefs is important in reaching one's goals, it follows that our autonomy is actually heightened in having the truth about the purpose of life. If we know why we are here and what the options in our destiny really are, we will be able to choose more intelligently than the blind who lead the blind in ignorance.

Indeed theistic religion (I have in mind Judaism, Christianity, and Islam, but this could apply to many forms of Hinduism and African religions as well) claims to place before us options of the greatest importance, so that if it is true the world is far better (infinitely better?) than if it is not.

Let me elaborate on this point. If theism is true and there is a benevolent supreme being governing the universe, the following eight theses are true.

1. We have a satisfying explanation of the origins and sustenance of the universe. We are not the product of chance and necessity or an impersonal big bang, but of a Heavenly Being who cares about us. As William James says, if religion is true, "the universe is no longer a mere *It* to us, but a *Thou* . . . and any relation that may be possible from person to person might be possible here." We can take comfort in knowing that the visible world is part of a more spiritual universe from which it draws its meaning and that there is, in spite of evil, an essential harmonious relation between our world and the transcendent reality.

Here is the nub of the matter. Is the universe purposeful or merely a blind collocation of particles in motion? Science does not answer this question, though scientism, the secular naturalism, assumes that the world lacks a telos—it is blind matter in motion. But theism tells us that all things have a purpose, that the universe was created at a point in time and that it will proceed in a lawlike manner to a prescribed end. Consider the naturalist view of the universe eloquently set forth in Bertrand Russell's classic essay "A Free Man's Worship":

> That man is the product of causes which had no prevision of the end they were achieving; that his origin, his growth, his hopes and fears, his loves and beliefs are but the outcome of accidental collocations of atoms; that no fire, no heroism, no intensity of thought and feeling, can preserve an individual life beyond the grave; that all the labors of the ages, all the devotion, all the inspiration, all the noonday brightness of human genius, are destined to extinction in the vast death of the solar system, and that the whole temple of man's achievement must inevitably be buried beneath the debris of a universe in ruins—all these things, if not quite beyond dispute, are yet so nearly certain that no philosophy which rejects them can hope to stand. Only within the scaffolding of these truths, only on the firm

foundation of unyielding despair, can the soul's habitation henceforth be safely built.

This is not the kind of "soul's habitation" that is worth building,
let alone which can be safely built. Upon an unstable foundation, a
secure edifice cannot be built, and from nothing you can only derive
nothing. Our product is only as good as the material from which it
is derived. From a valueless universe, objective values will not miraculously appear, nor can purpose derive from purposelessness. On
the "firm foundation of unyielding despair" we can only build that
which is desperate.

2. Theism holds that the universe is suffused in goodness and
that good will win out over evil. We are not fighting a desperate
battle alone, but God is on our side—or rather, it is possible to be
on God's side in the struggle of good over evil. So you and I need
not fight in vain. If the universe is meaningless, nothing will ultimately matter. Plato, Shakespeare, Mozart, Michelangelo, the Cathedral of Notre Dame, and the Sun itself will perish in oblivion. But
if an Eternal Goodness exists, all will be well, all will be somehow
remembered, nothing worthwhile will have been in vain.

The thought of the ultimate victory of goodness over evil, of justice over injustice, gives us confidence to carry on the fight against
injustice, cruelty, and hatred, when others calculate that the odds
against righteousness are too great to fight against.

3. God loves and cares for us. His love compels us, so that we
have a deeper motive for morally good actions, including high altruism. We live deeply moral lives, not out of fear of hell, but out of
deep gratitude to One who loves us and whom we love. We live
not by impersonal rules but in relation with a Cosmic Lover, one
who has our best interests in mind and is powerful enough to
ensure that we are as happy as we are good.

Secularism lacks this sense of cosmic love, and it is, therefore,
no accident that it fails to produce moral saints like Jesus, Mai-
monides, St. Francis, Father Damien, Teresa of Avila, Gandhi, Martin Luther King, Jr., and Mother Teresa. You need special love to
leave a world of comfort in order to go to a desolate island to minister to lepers, as Father Damien did, or to lay down your life for
another as Father Kolbe did when he took the place of a fellow
prisoner in the Nazi death cell. Perhaps Ayn Rand is correct. From
a secular point of view altruism is not only stupid, it is antilife, for

it gives up the only thing we have, our little ego in an impersonal, indifferent world.

4. Theists have an answer to the question Why be moral? Why? Because of the love of God and because that love guarantees justice, so that you will get what you deserve—good for good and bad for bad. The good really is good for you. Secular ethics has a severe problem with the question Why should I be moral when I can profit from wrongdoing (cheating, lying, stealing, harming another)? When I can advance myself by being an egoist, why should I obey moral rules? A hard question, to which I have never seen an entirely satisfactory secular answer. But the question is quickly satisfied by theism: a kind of karma—what you do to others will be visited upon you. If you do good, you will receive good. If you do evil, you will receive evil. Immorality is really imprudent and self-interest and altruism coincide. I don't have to worry about whether I reap exactly what I put into life's soil now, for I am confident that in the long term, I will reap as I have sown.

5. Cosmic Justice reigns in the universe. The scales are perfectly balanced so that everyone will get what he or she deserves, according to their moral merit. There is no moral luck (unless you interpret the grace which will finally prevail as a type of "luck"), but each will be judged according to how one has used one's talents (Matthew, chapter 25).

6. All persons are of equal worth. Since we have all been created in the image of God and are His children, we are all brothers and sisters. We are family and ought to treat each other benevolently as we would family members of equal worth. Indeed, modern secular moral and political systems often assume this equal worth of the individual without justifying it. But without the Parenthood of God it makes no sense to say that all persons are innately of equal value. From a perspective of intelligence and utility, Aristotle and Nietzsche are right, there are enormous inequalities, and why shouldn't the superior persons use the baser types to their advantage? In this regard, secularism, in rejecting inegalitarianism, seems to be living off of the interest of a religious capital which it has relinquished.

7. Grace and forgiveness—a happy ending for all. All's well that ends well (the divine comedy). The moral guilt which we experience, even for the most heinous acts, can be removed, and we can be redeemed and given a new start. This is true moral liberation.

8. There is life after death. Death is not the end of the matter, but we shall live on, recognizing each other in a better world. We have eternity in our souls and are destined for a higher existence.* So if Hebraic-Christian theism is true, the world is a friendly home in which we are all related as siblings in one family, destined to live forever in cosmic bliss in a reality in which good defeats evil.

If theism is false and secularism is true, then there is no obvious basis for human equality, no reason to treat all people with equal respect, no simple and clear answer to the question, Why be moral even when it is not in my best interest? no sense of harmony and purpose in the universe, but "Whirl has replaced Zeus and is king" (Sophocles).

Add to this the fact that theism doesn't deprive us of any autonomy that we have in nontheistic systems. We are equally free to choose the good or the evil whether or not God exists (assuming that the notions of good and evil make sense in a non-theistic universe)—then it seems clear that the world of the theist is far better and more satisfying to us than one in which God does not exist.

Of course, the problem is that we probably do not know if theism, let alone our particular religious version of it, is true. Here I must use a Pascalean argument to press my third point that we may have an obligation or, at least, it may be a good thing, to live *as if* theism is true. That is, unless you think that theism is so improbable that we should not even consider it as a candidate for truth, we should live in such a way as to allow the virtues of theism to inspire our lives and our culture. The theistic world view is so far superior to the secular that—even though we might be agnostics or weak atheists—it is in our interest to live as though it were true, to consider each person as a child of God, of high value, to work as though God is working with us in the battle of Good over evil, and to build a society based on these ideas. It is good then to gamble on God. Religion gives us a purpose to life and a basis for morality that is too valuable

---

*Of course, hell is a problem here—which vitiates the whole idea somewhat, but many variations of theism (e.g., varieties of theistic Hinduism and the Christian theologians Origen, F. Maurice, and Karl Barth) hold to universal salvation in the end. Hell is only a temporary school in moral education—I think that this is a plausible view.

to dismiss lightly. It is a heritage that we may use to build a better civilization and one which we neglect at our own peril.

For Further Reflection

1. Does Walker exaggerate the importance of religion for a meaningful life? How would a secularist respond?

2. Karl Marx said that religion was the opium of the people. It deludes them into thinking that all will be well with the world, leading to passive acceptance of evil and injustice. Is there some truth in Marx's dictum? How would Walker respond to this?

The Human Search for Meaning
Reflections on Auschwitz

VIKTOR FRANKL

Viktor Frankl (1905–1997) was professor of psychiatry and neurology at the University of Vienna Medical School and is the founder of logotherapy, the psychological therapy based on the idea that human beings must find a meaning to their lives in order to function. It is based on Nietzsche's dictum "He who has a *why* to live for, can bear with almost any *how*." Frankl spent three years in Nazi concentration camps, including Auschwitz. His entire family was exterminated by the Nazis. In this selection Frankl reflects on the search for meaning in the concentration camp.

From *Man's Search for Meaning* by Viktor E. Frankl, © 1959, 1962, 1984, 1992 by Viktor E. Frankl. Reprinted by permission of Beacon Press, Boston.

What did the prisoner dream about most frequently? Of bread, cake, cigarettes, and nice warm baths. The lack of having these simple desires satisfied led him to seek wish-fulfillment in dreams. Whether these dreams did any good is another matter; the dreamer had to wake from them to the reality of camp life, and to the terrible contrast between that and his dream illusions.

I shall never forget how I was roused one night by the groans of a fellow prisoner, who threw himself about in his sleep, obviously having a horrible nightmare. Since I had always been especially sorry for people who suffered from fearful dreams or deliria, I wanted to wake the poor man. Suddenly I drew back the hand which was ready to shake him, frightened at the thing I was about to do. At that moment I became intensely conscious of the fact that no dream, no matter how horrible, could be as bad as the reality of the camp which surrounded us, and to which I was about to recall him. . . .

When the last layers of subcutaneous fat had vanished, and we looked like skeletons disguised with skin and rags, we could watch our bodies beginning to devour themselves. The organism digested its own protein, and the muscles disappeared. Then the body had no powers of resistance left. One after another the members of the little community in our hut died. . . .

In attempting this psychological presentation and a psychopathological explanation of the typical characteristics of a concentration camp inmate, I may give the impression that the human being is completely and unavoidably influenced by his surroundings. (In this case the surroundings being the unique structure of camp life, which forced the prisoner to conform his conduct to a certain set pattern.) But what about human liberty? Is there no spiritual freedom in regard to behavior and reaction to any given surroundings? Is that theory true which would have us believe that man is no more than a product of many conditional and environmental factors—be they of a biological, psychological or sociological nature? Is man but an accidental product of these? Most important, do the prisoners' reactions to the singular world of the concentration camp prove that man cannot escape the influences of his surroundings? Does man have no choice of action in the face of such circumstances?

We can answer these questions from experience as well as on principle. The experiences of camp life show that man does have a choice of action. There were enough examples, often of a heroic nature, which proved that apathy could be overcome, irritability suppressed. Man *can* preserve a vestige of spiritual freedom, of independence of mind, even in such terrible conditions of psychic and physical stress.

We who lived in concentration camps can remember the men who walked through the huts comforting others, giving away their last piece of bread. They may have been few in number, but they offer sufficient proof that everything can be taken from a man but one thing: the last of the human freedoms—to choose one's attitude in any given set of circumstances, to choose one's own way.

And there were always choices to make. Every day, every hour, offered the opportunity to make a decision, a decision which determined whether you would or would not submit to those powers which threatened to rob you of your very self, your inner freedom; which determined whether or not you would become the plaything of circumstance, renouncing freedom and dignity to become molded into the form of the typical inmate.

Seen from this point of view, the mental reactions of the inmates of a concentration camp must seem more to us than the mere expression of certain physical and sociological conditions. Even though conditions such as lack of sleep, insufficient food and various mental stresses may suggest that the inmates were bound to react in certain ways, in the final analysis it becomes clear that the sort of person the prisoner became was the result of an inner decision, and not the result of camp influences alone. Fundamentally, therefore, any man can, even under such circumstances, decide what shall become of him—mentally and spiritually. He may retain his human dignity even in a concentration camp. Dostoevski said once, "There is only one thing that I dread: not to be worthy of my sufferings." These words frequently came to my mind after I became acquainted with those martyrs whose behavior in camp, whose suffering and death, bore witness to the fact that the last inner freedom cannot be lost. It can be said that they were worthy of their sufferings; the way they bore their suffering was a genuine inner achievement. It is this spiritual freedom—which cannot be taken away—that makes life meaningful and purposeful.

An active life serves the purpose of giving man the opportunity to realize values in creative work, while a passive life of enjoyment affords him the opportunity to obtain fulfillment in experiencing beauty, art, or nature. But there is also purpose in that life which is almost barren of both creation and enjoyment and which admits of but one possibility of high moral behavior: namely, in man's attitude to his existence, an existence restricted by external forces. A creative life and a life of enjoyment are banned to him. But not only creativeness and enjoyment are meaningful. If there is a meaning in life at all, then there must be a meaning in suffering. Suffering is an ineradicable part of life, even as fate and death. Without suffering and death human life cannot be complete.

The way in which a man accepts his fate and all the suffering it entails, the way in which he takes up his cross, gives him ample opportunity—even under the most difficult circumstances—to add a deeper meaning to his life. It may remain brave, dignified and unselfish. Or in the bitter fight for self-preservation he may forget his human dignity and become no more than an animal. Here lies the chance for a man either to make use of or to forego the opportunities of attaining the moral values that a difficult situation may afford him. And this decides whether he is worthy of his sufferings or not.

Do not think that these considerations are unworldly and too far removed from real life. It is true that only a few people are capable of reaching such high moral standards. Of the prisoners only a few kept their full inner liberty and obtained those values which their suffering afforded, but even one such example is sufficient proof that man's inner strength may raise him above his outward fate. Such men are not only in concentration camps. Everywhere man is confronted with fate, with the chance of achieving something through his own suffering. . . .

A man who let himself decline because he could not see any future goal found himself occupied with retrospective thoughts. In a different connection, we have already spoken of the tendency there was to look into the past, to help make the present, with all its horrors, less real. But in robbing the present of its reality there lay a certain danger. It became easy to overlook the opportunities to make something positive of camp life, opportunities which really did exist. Regarding our "provisional existence" as unreal was in itself an important factor in causing the prisoners to lose their hold on life; everything in a way became pointless. Such people forgot that often it is just such an exceptionally difficult external situation which gives man the opportunity to grow spiritually beyond himself. Instead of taking the camp's difficulties as a test of their inner strength, they did not take their life seriously and despised it as something of no consequence. They preferred to close their eyes and to live in the past. Life for such people became meaningless.

Naturally only a few people were capable of reaching great spiritual heights. But a few were given the chance to attain human greatness even through their apparent worldly failure and death, an accomplishment which in ordinary circumstances they would never have achieved. To the others of us, the mediocre and the half-hearted, the words of Bismarck could be applied: "Life is like being at the dentist. You always think that the worst is still to come, and yet it is over already." Varying this, we could say that most men in a concentration camp believed that the real opportunities of life had passed. Yet, in reality, there was an opportunity and a challenge. One could make a victory of those experiences, turning life into an inner triumph, or one could ignore the challenge and simply vegetate, as did a majority of the prisoners.

Any attempt at fighting the camp's psychopathological influence on the prisoner by psychotherapeutic or psychohygienic methods had to aim at giving him inner strength by pointing out to him a future goal to which he could look forward. Instinctively some of the prisoners attempted to find one on their own. It is a peculiarity of man that he can only live by looking to the future—*sub specie aeternitatis*. And this is his salvation in the most difficult moments of his existence, although he sometimes has to force his mind to the task. . . .

The prisoner who had lost faith in the future—his future—was doomed. With his loss of belief in the future, he also lost his spiritual hold; he let himself decline and became subject to mental and physical decay. Usually this happened quite suddenly, in the form of a crisis, the symptoms of which were familiar to the experienced camp inmate. We all feared this moment—not for ourselves, which would have been pointless, but for our friends. Usually it began with the prisoner refusing one morning to get dressed and wash or to go out on the parade grounds. No entreaties, no blows, no threats had any effect. He just lay there, hardly moving. If this crisis was brought about by an illness, he refused to be taken to the sick-bay or to do anything to help himself. He simply gave up. There he remained, lying in his own excreta, and nothing bothered him any more.

I once had a dramatic demonstration of the close link between the loss of faith in the future and this dangerous giving up. F——, my senior block warden, a fairly well-known composer and librettist, confided in me one day: "I would like to tell you something, Doctor. I have had a strange dream. A voice told me that I could wish for something, that I should only say what I wanted to know, and all my questions would be answered. What do you think I asked? That I would like to know when the war would be over for me. You know what I mean, Doctor—for me! I wanted to know when we, when our camp, would be liberated and our sufferings come to an end."

"And when did you have this dream?" I asked.

"In February, 1945," he answered. It was then the beginning of March.

"What did your dream voice answer?"

Furtively he whispered to me, "March thirtieth."

When F——told me about his dream, he was still full of hope and convinced that the voice of his dream would be right. But as the promised day drew nearer, the war news which reached our camp made it appear very unlikely that we would be free on the promised date. On March twenty-ninth, F——suddenly became ill and ran a high temperature. On March thirtieth, the day his prophecy had told him that the war and suffering would be over for him, he became delirious and lost consciousness. On March thirty-first, he was dead. To all outward appearances, he had died of typhus.

Those who know how close the connection is between the state of mind of a man—his courage and hope, or lack of them—and the state of immunity of his body will understand that the sudden loss of hope and courage can have a deadly effect. The ultimate cause of my friend's death was that the expected liberation did not come and he was severely disappointed. This suddenly lowered his body's resistance against the latent typhus infection. His faith in the future and his will to live had become paralyzed and his body fell victim to illness—and thus the voice of his dream was right after all.

The observations of this one case and the conclusion drawn from them are in accordance with something that was drawn to my attention by the chief doctor of our concentration camp. The death rate in the week between Christmas, 1944, and New Year's, 1945, increased in camp beyond all previous experience. In his opinion, the explanation for this increase did not lie in the harder working conditions or the deterioration of our food supplies or a change of weather or new epidemics. It was simply that the majority of the prisoners had lived in the naïve hope that they would be home again by Christmas. As the time drew near and there was no encouraging news, the prisoners lost courage and disappointment overcame them. This had a dangerous influence on their powers of resistance and a great number of them died.

As we said before, any attempt to restore a man's inner strength in the camp had first to succeed in showing him some future goal. Nietzsche's words, "He who has a *why* to live for can bear with almost any *how*," could be the guiding motto for all psychotherapeutic and psychohygienic efforts regarding prisoners. Whenever there was an opportunity for it, one had to give them a *why*—an aim—for their lives, in order to strengthen them to bear the terrible *how* of their existence. Woe to him who saw no more sense in his life, no aim, no purpose, and therefore no point in carrying on. He was soon lost. The typical reply with which such a man rejected all encouraging arguments was, "I have nothing to expect from life any more." What sort of answer can one give to that?

What was really needed was a fundamental change in our attitude toward life. We had to learn ourselves and, furthermore, we had to teach the despairing men, that it did not really matter what we expected from life, but rather what life expected from us. We needed to stop asking about the meaning of life, and instead to think of ourselves as those who were being questioned by life—daily and hourly. Our answer must consist, not in talk and meditation, but in right action and in right conduct. Life ultimately means taking the responsibility to find the right answer to its problems and to fulfill the tasks which it constantly sets for each individual.

These tasks, and therefore the meaning of life, differ from man to man, and from moment to moment. Thus it is impossible to define the meaning of life in a general way. Questions about the meaning of life can never be answered by sweeping statements. "Life" does not mean something vague, but something very real and concrete, just as life's tasks are also very real and concrete. They form man's destiny, which is different and unique for each individual. No man and no destiny can be compared with any other man or any other destiny. No situation repeats itself, and each situation calls for a different response. Sometimes the situation in which a man finds himself may require him to shape his own fate by action. At other times it is more advantageous for him to make use of an opportunity for contemplation and to realize assets in this way. Sometimes man may be required simply to accept fate, to bear his cross. Every situation is distinguished by its uniqueness, and there is always only one right answer to the problem posed by the situation at hand.

When a man finds that it is his destiny to suffer, he will have to accept his suffering as his task; his single and unique task. He will have to acknowledge the fact that even in suffering he is unique and alone in the universe. No one can relieve him of his suffering or suffer in his place. His unique opportunity lies in the way in which he bears his burden.

For us, as prisoners, these thoughts were not speculations far removed from reality. They were the only thoughts that could be of help to us. They kept us from despair, even when there seemed to be no chance of coming out of it alive. Long ago we had passed the stage of asking what was the meaning of life, a naïve query which understands life as the attaining of some aim through the active creation of something of value. For us, the meaning of life embraced the wider cycles of life and death, of suffering and of dying.

Once the meaning of suffering had been revealed to us, we refused to minimize or alleviate the camp's tortures by ignoring them or harboring false illusions and entertaining artificial optimism. Suffering had become a task on which we did not want to turn our backs. We had realized its hidden opportunities for achievement, the opportunities which caused the poet Rilke to write, "*Wie viel ist aufzuleiden!*" (How much suffering there is to get through!) Rilke spoke of "getting through suffering" as others would talk of "getting through work." There was plenty of suffering for us to get through. Therefore, it was necessary to face up to the full amount of suffering, trying to keep moments of weakness and furtive tears to a minimum. But there was no need to be ashamed of tears, for tears bore witness that a man had the greatest of courage, the courage to suffer. Only very few realized that. Shamefacedly some confessed occasionally that they had wept, like the comrade who answered my question of how he had gotten over his edema, by confessing, "I have wept it out of my system." . . .

Freedom . . . is not the last word. Freedom is only part of the story and half of the truth. Freedom is but the negative aspect of the whole phenomenon whose positive aspect is responsibility. In fact, freedom is in danger of degenerating into mere arbitrariness unless it is lived in terms of responsibility. That is why *I recommend that the Statue of Liberty on the East Coast be supplemented by a Statue of Responsibility on the West Coast.*

For Further Reflection

1. What, according to Frankl, are the important ingredients in living a truly human life? Do you agree? Frankl's ideas are relevant to concentration camp experience, but are they the best ones for everyday existence?

2. Frankl believes that we must discover a meaning to our lives in order to endure great evil. But could that meaning itself be an evil?

The Four Noble Truths

SIDDHARTHA GAUTAMA, THE BUDDHA

Siddhartha Gautama, (c. 563–483 B.C.) was born to a noble family in North India, near the Himalaya Mountains. He was protected by his family from suffering, but one day he wandered out and beheld a beggar and sick people. He

From *The Wisdom of the Early Buddhists,* translated by Geoffrey Parrinder (London: Sheldon Press, 1977). Reprinted by permission.

was filled with sorrow at the fragility of human existence, at its decay, disease, and death. He left his family and sought enlightenment. Eventually, he claimed he had been enlightened and took on the name of *Buddha,* meaning "The Awakened One." He set forth four noble truths and drew followers to himself, thus instituting the Buddhist religion. The truths are:

1. Life is suffering.
2. Suffering involves a chain of causes.
3. Suffering can cease.
4. There is a path to such cessation.

The last of these contains eight substages, which lead to Nirvana, final liberation from suffering.

This selection consists of two sermons on the Four Noble Truths.

Siddhartha had been fasting for several weeks, seeking perfect peace. He was weak, his body thin, his ribs stuck out "like the beams of an old shed," his eyes sank low "like a deep well." He saw a lovely spot by a Bo-tree and sat down under it. He took some rice milk and ate some beans. Suddenly he found himself entering a blissful state of meditation, then a second stage, beyond reasoning. Then he entered the third stage, "attentive and conscious, with equal mind to joy or aversion." Finally, he "entered the fourth stage, beyond pain and pleasure, entirely pure and mindful." Buddha became enlightened, knowing all wisdom, past, present, and future in a divine manner. This was his Nirvana, the extinction of all craving and self-indulgence. A monk noticed that his face glowed. He replied:

I am the Victor over all,
Omniscient and pure in all,
Freed from craving, leaving all,
Know by myself and point to none.

To turn the Wheel of Truth
Benares I shall find,

To beat the Drum of No more Death
Before a world that's blind.

When the Buddha arrived at Benares the five monks were in a deer park at Sarnath. Seeing him coming they agreed not to greet or serve him, since he had given up the ascetic life and gone back to the life of abundance. But as he drew near they were not able to keep their agreement; some made a seat ready, some brought water to wash his feet, others took his bowl and robe, and all called him "Your Reverence." The Buddha replied, Do not call me "Your Reverence." The Buddha is perfect, fully self-awakened. I have found the deathless and I teach the Truth. If you follow this you will soon realize here and now the goal of religion for which young men of good family leave home for the homeless life, and you will abide in it.

To the five monks the Buddha preached his first sermon, Setting in Motion the Wheel of Truth: avoiding the extremes of sensuality and self-torture, the Buddha has gained the knowledge of the Middle Way, which brings insight, calm and Nirvana. What is the Middle Way? It is the Noble Eightfold Path.

Consider the Four Noble Truths:

(1) This is the Noble Truth of Pain: birth, age, sickness, death, sorrow and despair are painful.
(2) This is the Noble Truth of the Cause of Pain: it is craving, which leads to rebirth, pleasure and passion, existence and non-existence.
(3) This is the Noble Truth of the Cessation of Pain: it is the cessation of craving without remainder, forsaking detachment and release from it.
(4) This is the Noble Truth of the Way that leads to the Cessation of Pain: it is the Noble Eightfold Path.

What is the Noble Eightfold Path? It is:

1. Right Views
2. Right Motive
3. Right Speech
4. Right Action
5. Right Livelihood
6. Right Effort

7. Right Mindfulness
8. Right Contemplation

Right Views give the knowledge of Pain, its Cause, Cessation, and the Path.
Right Motive gives aspiration to renunciation and benevolence.
Right Speech abstains from lies and slander.
Right Action abstains from stealing, killing and self-indulgence.
Right Livelihood follows right pursuits.
Right Effort turns against evil states and toward good.
Right Mindfulness looks on body and mind with self-control.
Right Contemplation rises above evil and abides in equanimity and bliss. . . .

The body is not the soul, for if it were, the body would not be subject to sickness, but it is not possible to say of the body, let it be thus or not thus. The feelings are not the soul, perception is not the soul, the elements are not the soul, consciousness is not the soul, for the same reasons.

What do you think, monks? Is the body permanent or impermanent? They replied: it is impermanent. The Buddha asked: is the impermanent painful or pleasant? They answered: It is painful. The Buddha retorted: But is it fitting to consider what is impermanent and painful as myself and the soul? They answered, No.

The Buddha asked the same questions about other feelings, perception, the elements and the consciousness. In none of them was the soul found. Then the five monks rejoiced at this teaching and their hearts were freed from faults.

On another occasion the Buddha was dwelling at Savatthi, when a venerable Malunkyaputta, being in seclusion and meditation, presented the following considerations: "These theories which the Blessed One has left unexplained, has set aside and rejected—that the world is eternal, that the world is not eternal, that the world is finite, that the world is infinite, that the soul and the body are identical, that the soul is one thing and the body another, that the saint both exists and does not exist after death—these the Blessed One does not explain to me. And the fact that the Blessed One does not explain them to me does not please me nor suit me. Therefore I will come close to the Blessed One. If the Blessed One will not explain to me, in that case I will abandon religious training and return to the lesser life of a layman."

Then the venerable Malunkyaputta arose at eventide from his seclusion, and drew near to where the Blessed One was; and having drawn near and greeted the Blessed One, he sat down respectfully at one side. And seated respectfully at one side, the venerable Malunkyaputta spoke to the Blessed One as follows:

"Reverend Sir, it happened to me, as I was just now in seclusion, and plunged in meditation, that a consideration presented itself to my mind, as follows. . . .

"If the Blessed One knows that the world is eternal, let the Blessed One explain to me that the world is eternal; if the Blessed One knows that the world is not eternal, let the Blessed One explain to me that the world is not eternal. If the Blessed One does not know either that the world is eternal or that the world is not eternal, the only upright thing for one who does not know, or who has not that insight, is to say, 'I do not know; I have not that insight.'" . . .

"Pray, Malunkyaputta, did I ever say to you, 'Come, Malunkyaputta, lead the religious life under me, and I will explain to you either that the world is eternal, or that the world is not eternal . . . or that the saint neither exists nor does not exist after death'?"

"Nay, verily, Reverend Sir."

"Malunkyaputta, any one who should say, 'I will not lead the religious life under the Blessed One until the Blessed One shall explain to me either that the world is eternal, or that the world is not eternal . . . or that the saint neither exists nor does not exist after death'—that person would die, Malunkyaputta, before the Perfect One had ever explained this to him.

"It is as if, Malunkyaputta, a man had been wounded by an arrow thickly smeared with poison, and his friends and companions, his relatives and kinsfolk, were to procure for him a physician or surgeon; and the sick man were to say, 'I will not have this arrow taken out until I have learnt whether the man who wounded me belonged to the warrior caste, or to the Brahmin caste, or to the agricultural caste, or to the menial caste.'

"Or again if he were to say, 'I will not have this arrow taken out until I have learnt the name of the man who wounded me, and to what clan he belongs.'

"Or again if he were to say, 'I will not have this arrow taken out until I have learnt whether the man who wounded me was tall, or short, or of the middle height.' . . .

"That man would die, Malunkyaputta, without ever having learnt this . . .

"The religious life, Malunkyaputta, does not depend on the dogma that the world is eternal; nor does the religious life, Malunkyaputta, depend on the dogma that the world is not eternal. Whether the dogma obtain, Malunkyaputta, that the world is eternal, or that the world is not eternal, there still remain birth, old age, death, sorrow, lamentation, misery, grief, and despair, for the extinction of which in the present life I am prescribing . . .

"Accordingly, Malunkyaputta, bear always in mind what it is that I have not explained, and what it is that I have explained. And what, Malunkyaputta, have I not explained? I have not explained, Malunkyaputta, that the world is eternal; I have not explained that the world is not eternal; I have not explained that the world is finite; I have not explained that the world is infinite; I have not explained that the soul and the body are identical; I have not explained that the soul is one thing and the body another; I have not explained that the saint exists after death; I have not explained that the saint does not exist after death; I have not explained that the saint both exists and does not exist after death; I have not explained that the saint neither exists nor does not exist after death. And why, Malunkyaputta, have I not explained this? Because, Malunkyaputta, this profits not, nor has to do with the fundamentals of religion, nor tends to aversion, absence of passion, cessation, quiescence, the supernatural faculties, supreme wisdom, and Nirvana; therefore have I not explained it.

"And what, Malunkyaputta, have I explained? Misery, Malunkyaputta, have I explained; the origin of misery have I explained; the cessation of misery have I explained; and the path leading to the cessation of misery have I explained. And why, Malunkyaputta, have I explained this? Because, Malunkyaputta, this does profit, has to do with the fundamentals of religion, and tends to aversion, absence of passion, cessation, quiescence, knowledge, supreme wisdom, and Nirvana; therefore have I explained it."

For Further Reflection

1. Analyze Buddha's philosophy of life. What gives life meaning? What are the Four Noble Truths and what do they mean?

2. Buddhism, like Hinduism whence it arose, believes in *karma,* the idea that our actions in this life will have an effect on who we become and what happens to us in the next. If you do good, you will be born into a higher consciousness; if you do bad, into a lower consciousness, perhaps a nonhuman animal. That is, there is a causal relation between actions and future existence. Do you see any evidence for this doctrine?

The Experience Machine

ROBERT NOZICK

Robert Nozick is professor of philosophy at Harvard University. In this selection from his *Anarchy, State, and Utopia,* he argues against the hedonism of Bentham, for if pleasure were our sole value, we would have a conclusive reason to plug into an experience machine. The fact that most of us are revolted by this idea is good evidence against the claims of hedonism, as well as for a wider view of what is good.

There are also substantial puzzles when we ask what matters other than how *people's* experiences feel "from the inside." Suppose there were an experience machine that would give you any experience you desired. Superduper neuropsychologists could stimulate your brain so that you would think and feel you were writing a great novel, or making a friend, or reading an interesting book. All the time you would be floating in a tank, with electrodes attached to

Reprinted from *Anarchy, State, and Utopia* by Robert Nozick. Copyright © 1974 by Basic Books, Inc. Reprinted by permission of Basic Books, a division of HarperCollins Publishers, Inc.

your brain. Should you plug into this machine for life, prepro-
gramming your life's experiences? If you are worried about missing out on desirable experiences, we can suppose that business
enterprises have researched thoroughly the lives of many others.
You can pick and choose from their large library or smorgasbord
of such experiences, selecting your life's experiences for, say, the
next two years. After two years have passed, you will have ten minutes or ten hours out of the tank, to select the experiences of your
next two years. Of course, while in the tank you won't know that
you're there; you'll think it's all actually happening. Others can also
plug in to have the experiences they want, so there's no need to
stay unplugged to serve them. (Ignore problems such as who will
service the machines if everyone plugs in.) Would you plug in?
*What else can matter to us, other than how our lives feel from the
inside?* Nor should you refrain because of the few moments of distress between the moment you've decided and the moment you're
plugged. What's a few moments of distress compared to a lifetime
of bliss (if that's what you choose), and why feel any distress at all
if your decision *is* the best one?

What does matter to us in addition to our experiences? First, we
want to *do* certain things, and not just have the experience of doing
them. In the case of certain experiences, it is only because first we
want to do the actions that we want the experiences of doing them
or thinking we've done them. (But *why* do we want to do the activities rather than merely to experience them?) A second reason for
not plugging in is that we want to *be* a certain way, to be a certain sort of person. Someone floating in a tank is an indeterminate
blob. There is no answer to the question of what a person is like
who has long been in the tank. Is he courageous, kind, intelligent,
witty, loving? It's not merely that it's difficult to tell; there's no way
he is. Plugging into the machine is a kind of suicide. It will seem
to some, trapped by a picture, that nothing about what we are like
can matter except as it gets reflected in our experiences. But should
it be surprising that what *we are* is important to us? Why should
we be concerned only with how our time is filled, but not with
what we are?

Thirdly, plugging into an experience machine limits us to a man-
made reality, to a world no deeper or more important than that which
people can construct. There is no *actual* contact with any deeper
reality, though the experience of it can be simulated. Many persons

desire to leave themselves open to such contact and to a plumbing of deeper significance.[1] This clarifies the intensity of the conflict over psychoactive drugs, which some view as mere local experience machines, and others view as avenues to a deeper reality; what some view as equivalent to surrender to the experience machine, others view as following one of the reasons *not* to surrender!

We learn that something matters to us in addition to experience by imagining an experience machine and then realizing that we would not use it. We can continue to imagine a sequence of machines each designed to fill lacks suggested for the earlier machines. For example, since the experience machine doesn't meet our desire to *be* a certain way, imagine a transformation machine which transforms us into whatever sort of person we'd like to be (compatible with our staying us). Surely one would not use the transformation machine to become as one would wish, and thereupon plug into the experience machine![2] So something matters in addition to one's experiences *and* what one is like. Nor is the reason merely that one's experiences are unconnected with what one is like. For the experience machine might be limited to provide only experiences possible to the sort of person plugged in. Is it that we want to make

[1]Traditional religious views differ on the *point* of contact with a transcendent reality. Some say that contact yields eternal bliss or Nirvana, but they have not distinguished this sufficiently from merely a *very* long run on the experience machine. Others think it is intrinsically desirable to do the will of a higher being which created us all, though presumably no one would think this if we discovered we had been created as an object of amusement by some superpowerful child from another galaxy or dimension. Still others imagine an eventual merging with a higher reality, leaving unclear its desirability, or where that merging leaves *us*.

[2]Some wouldn't use the transformation machine at all; it seems like *cheating*. But the one-time use of the transformation machine would not remove all challenges; there would still be obstacles for the new us to overcome, a new plateau from which to strive even higher. And is this plateau any the less earned or deserved than that provided by genetic endowment and early childhood environment? But if the transformation machine could be used indefinitely often, so that we could accomplish anything by pushing a button to transform ourselves into someone who could do it easily, there would remain no limits we *need* to strain against or try to transcend. Would there be anything left to *do?* Do some theological views place God

a difference in the world? Consider then the result machine, which produces in the world any result you would produce and injects your vector input into any joint activity. We shall not pursue here the fascinating details of these or other machines. What is most disturbing about them is their living of our lives for us. Is it misguided to search for *particular* additional functions beyond the competence of machines to do for us? Perhaps what we desire is to live (an active verb) ourselves, in contact with reality. (And this, machines cannot do *for* us.) Without elaborating on the implications of this, which I believe connect surprisingly with issues about free will and causal accounts of knowledge, we need merely note the intricacy of the question of what matters *for people* other than their experiences. Until one finds a satisfactory answer, and determines that this answer does not *also* apply to animals, one cannot reasonably claim that only the felt experiences of animals limit what we may do to them.

For Further Reflection

1. Would you enter the experience machine? Why or why not?

Further Readings for Chapter 9

Barrett, William. *Irrational Man*. New York: Doubleday, 1958.

Bretall, Robert, ed. *A Kierkegaard Anthology*. Princeton, N.J.: Princeton University Press, 1946.

Camus, Albert. *The Myth of Sisyphus and Other Essays,* trans. J. O. O'Brien. New York: Random House, 1955.

Camus, Albert. *The Plague*. New York: Random House, 1948.

Frankl, Victor. *Man's Search for Meaning*. New York: Beacon Press, 1963.

Kaufmann, Walter. *Existentialism from Dostoevsky to Sartre*. New York: New American Library, 1975.

Kaufmann, Walter, ed. and trans. *A Portable Nietzsche*. New York: Viking, 1954.

---

outside of time because an omniscient omnipotent being couldn't fill up his days?

Kierkegaard, Søren. *Fear and Trembling,* trans. Walter Lowrie. Princeton, N.J.: Princeton University Press, 1954.

Klemke, E. D. *The Meaning of Life.* Oxford: Oxford University Press, 1981.

Nietzsche, Friedrich. *The Will to Power.* New York: Random House, 1967.

Russell, Bertrand. *The Conquest of Happiness.* New York: New American Library, 1930.

Sanders, Steven, and David Cheney, eds. *The Meaning of Life.* Englewood Cliffs, N.J.: Prentice Hall, 1980.

Sartre, Jean-Paul. *Existentialism and Human Emotions.* New York: Philosophical Library, 1948.

Schopenhauer, Arthur. *The Will to Live: Selected Writings of Arthur Schopenhauer,* ed. Richard Taylor. London: Ungar, 1967.

Tolstoy, Leo. *My Confessions,* trans. Leo Wiener. London: Dent, 1905.

CHAPTER 10

Freedom, Autonomy, and Self-Respect

In our first reading, Martin Luther King, Jr.'s famous "I Have a Dream" speech at the March on Washington in 1963, King eloquently sets forth an ideal of social freedom wherein people can live without fear, judged by their character rather than their race. In the second article, Stanley Milgram's social experiment with autonomy, we get a glimpse at just how deeply authoritarianism affects our lives, drowning out autonomy. In our third reading, Jean-Paul Sartre sets forth an existential ethic based on radical freedom. And, finally, Thomas Hill argues from a Kantian perspective that our duties to ourselves include a sense of not allowing ourselves to be servile or exploited by others.

I Have a Dream

MARTIN LUTHER KING, JR.

Martin Luther King, Jr. (1929–1968) was a Baptist minister who achieved national prominence by leading a boycott protesting the segregated bus system in Montgomery, Alabama. His ideas of nonviolence, derived from the New Testament, Tolstoy, and Gandhi, became a moral force that convinced many of the justice of his cause. He was awarded the Nobel Peace Prize in 1964, and he was assassinated in Memphis in April 1968.

King gave his "I Have a Dream" speech at the March on Washington to 250,000 people assembled before the Lincoln Memorial on August 28, 1963. The march commemorated the hundredth anniversary of Lincoln's Emancipation Proclamation and was a pivotal event in passing the Civil Rights Act of 1964, which set forth an integrationist program for the United States.

Five score years ago, a great American, in whose symbolic shadow we stand, signed the Emancipation Proclamation. This momentous decree came as a great beacon light of hope to millions of Negro slaves who had been seared in the flames of withering injustice. It came as a joyous daybreak to end the long night of captivity.

But one hundred years later, we must face the tragic fact that the Negro is still not free. One hundred years later, the life of the Negro is still sadly crippled by the manacles of segregation and the chains of discrimination. One hundred years later, the Negro lives on a lonely island of poverty in the midst of a vast ocean of material prosperity. One hundred years later, the Negro still languishes in the corners of American society and finds himself an exile in his own land. So we have come here today to dramatize an appalling condition.

In a sense we have come to our nation's capital to cash a check. When the architects of our republic wrote the magnificent words

---

This speech was delivered in Washington, D.C., at the March on Washington, August 28, 1963.

of the Constitution and the Declaration of Independence, they were
signing a promissory note to which every American was to fall heir.
This note was a promise that all men would be guaranteed the
unalienable rights of life, liberty, and the pursuit of happiness.

It is obvious today that America has defaulted on this promissory note insofar as her citizens of color are concerned. Instead of
honoring this sacred obligation, America has given the Negro people a bad check: a check which has come back marked "insufficient funds." But we refuse to believe that the bank of justice is
bankrupt. We refuse to believe that there are insufficient funds in
the great vaults of opportunity of this nation. So we have come to
cash this check—a check that will give us upon demand the riches
of freedom and the security of justice.

We have also come to this hallowed spot to remind America of
the fierce urgency of *now*. This is not the time to engage in the luxury of cooling off or to take the tranquilizing drug of gradualism. *Now*
is the time to make real the promises of democracy. *Now* is the time
to rise from the dark and desolate valley of segregation to the sunlit
path of racial justice. *Now* is the time to open the doors of opportunity to all of God's children. *Now* is the time to lift our nation from
the quicksands of racial injustice to the solid rock of brotherhood.

It would be fatal for the nation to overlook the urgency of the
moment and to underestimate the determination of the Negro. This
sweltering summer of the Negro's legitimate discontent will not pass
until there is an invigorating autumn of freedom and equality. Nineteen sixty-three is not an end, but a beginning. Those who hope
that the Negro needed to blow off steam and will now be content
will have a rude awakening if the nation returns to business as
usual. There will be neither rest nor tranquility in America until the
Negro is granted his citizenship rights. The whirlwinds of revolt will
continue to shake the foundations of our nation until the bright day
of justice emerges.

But there is something that I must say to my people who stand
on the warm threshold which leads into the palace of justice. In
the process of gaining our rightful place we must not be guilty of
wrongful deeds. Let us not seek to satisfy our thirst for freedom by
drinking from the cup of bitterness and hatred. We must forever
conduct our struggle on the high plane of dignity and discipline.
We must not allow our creative protest to degenerate into physical violence. Again and again we must rise to the majestic heights
of meeting physical force with soul force.

The marvelous new militancy which has engulfed the Negro community must not lead us to a distrust of all white people, for many of our white brothers, as evidenced by their presence here today, have come to realize that their freedom is inextricably bound to our freedom. We cannot walk alone.

And as we walk, we must make the pledge that we shall march ahead. We cannot turn back. There are those who are asking the devotees of civil rights, "When will you be satisfied?"

We can never be satisfied as long as the Negro is the victim of the unspeakable horrors of police brutality.

We can never be satisfied as long as our bodies, heavy with fatigue of travel, cannot gain lodging in the motels of the highways and the cities.

We cannot be satisfied as long as the Negro's basic mobility is from a smaller ghetto to a larger one.

We can never be satisfied as long as a Negro in Mississippi cannot vote and a Negro in New York believes he has nothing for which to vote.

No, no, we are not satisfied, and we will not be satisfied until justice rolls down like waters and righteousness like a mighty stream.

I am not unmindful that some of you have come here out of great trials and tribulations. Some of you have come fresh from narrow jail cells. Some of you have come from areas where your quest for freedom left you battered by the storms of persecution and staggered by the winds of police brutality. You have been the veterans of creative suffering. Continue to work with the faith that unearned suffering is redemptive.

Go back to Mississippi, go back to Alabama, go back to South Carolina, go back to Georgia, go back to Louisiana, go back to the slums and ghettos of our Northern cities, knowing that somehow this situation can and will be changed. Let us not wallow in the valley of despair.

I say to you today, my friends, that in spite of the difficulties and frustrations of the moment I still have a dream. It is a dream deeply rooted in the American dream.

I have a dream that one day this nation will rise up and live out the true meaning of its creed: "We hold these truths to be self-evident; that all men are created equal."

I have a dream that one day on the red hills of Georgia the sons of former slaves and the sons of former slaveowners will be able to sit down together at the table of brotherhood.

I have a dream that one day even the state of Mississippi, a desert state sweltering with the heat of injustice and oppression, will be transformed into an oasis of freedom and justice.

I have a dream that my four little children will one day live in a nation where they will not be judged by the color of their skin but by the content of their character.

I have a dream today.

I have a dream that one day the state of Alabama, whose governor's lips are presently dripping with the words of interposition and nullification, will be transformed into a situation where little black boys and black girls will be able to join hands with little white boys and girls and walk together as sisters and brothers.

I have a dream today.

I have a dream that one day every valley shall be exalted, every hill and mountain shall be made low, the rough places will be made plain, and the crooked places will be made straight, and the glory of the Lord shall be revealed, and all flesh shall see it together.

This is our hope. This is the faith with which I return to the South. With this faith we will be able to hew out of the mountain of despair a stone of hope. With this faith we will be able to transform the jangling discords of our nation into a beautiful symphony of brotherhood.

With this faith we will be able to work together, to pray together, to struggle together, to go to jail together, to stand up for freedom together, knowing that we will be free one day.

This will be the day when all of God's children will be able to sing with new meaning, "My country 'tis of thee, sweet land of liberty, of thee I sing. Land where my father died, land of the Pilgrims' pride, from every mountainside, let freedom ring."

And if America is to be a great nation, this must become true. So let freedom ring from the prodigious hilltops of New Hampshire. Let freedom ring from the mighty mountains of New York. Let freedom ring from the heightening Alleghenies of Pennsylvania!

Let freedom ring from the snowcapped Rockies of Colorado! Let freedom ring from the curvaceous peaks of California. But not only that: let freedom ring from Stone Mountain of Georgia! Let freedom ring from Lookout Mountain of Tennessee!

Let freedom ring from every hill and molehill of Mississippi. From every mountainside, let freedom ring.

When we let freedom ring, when we let it ring from every village and every hamlet, from every state and every city, we will be able to speed up that day when all of God's children, black men and white men, Jews and Gentiles, Protestants and Catholics, will be able to join hands and sing in the words of the old Negro spiritual, "Free at last! Free at last! Thank God Almighty, we are free at last!"

For Further Reflection

1. Discuss what King meant by freedom and to what extent his dream has been fulfilled in American life since the passage of the Civil Rights Act of 1964. That act prohibited discrimination in employment on the grounds of race, color, religion, sex, or national origin.

2. Discuss whether affirmative action—preferential treatment for members of previously oppressed groups—is a violation of the Civil Rights Act.

An Experiment in Autonomy

STANLEY MILGRAM

Stanley Milgram is a professor of psychology at Yale University. In the early 1960s he conducted a series of psychological experiments aimed at determining the degree to which ordinary citizens were obedient to authority. Volunteers from all walks of life were recruited to participate in "a study of memory and learning." This article discusses the experiments and Milgram's findings.

Stanley Milgram, "The Perils of Obedience," *Harper's Magazine,* 1974.

Obedience is as basic an element in the structure of social life as one can point to. Some system of authority is a requirement of all communal living, and it is only the person dwelling in isolation who is not forced to respond, with defiance or submission, to the commands of others. For many people, obedience is a deeply ingrained behavior tendency, indeed a potent impulse overriding training in ethics, sympathy, and moral conduct.

The dilemma inherent in submission to authority is ancient, as old as the story of Abraham,[1] and the question of whether one should obey when commands conflict with conscience has been argued by Plato, dramatized in *Antigone,*[2] and treated to philosophic analysis in almost every historical epoch. Conservative philosophers argue that the very fabric of society is threatened by disobedience, while humanists stress the primacy of the individual conscience.

The legal and philosophic aspects of obedience are of enormous import, but they say very little about how most people behave in concrete situations. I set up a simple experiment at Yale University to test how much pain an ordinary citizen would inflict on another person simply because he was ordered to by an experimental scientist. Stark authority was pitted against the subjects' strongest moral imperatives against hurting others, and, with the subjects' ears ringing with the screams of the victims, authority won more often than not. The extreme willingness of adults to go to almost any lengths on the command of an authority constitutes the chief finding of the study and the fact most urgently demanding explanation.

In the basic experimental design, two people come to a psychology laboratory to take part in a study of memory and learning. One of them is designated as a "teacher" and the other a "learner." The experimenter explains that the study is concerned with the effects of punishment on learning. The learner is conducted into a room, seated in a kind of miniature electric chair; his arms are strapped to prevent

---

[1]The patriarch Abraham, commanded by God to sacrifice his son Isaac, is ready to do so until an angel stays his knife.

[2]In Plato's *Apology* the philosopher Socrates provokes and accepts the sentence of death rather than belie his conscience; the heroine of Sophocles' *Antigone* risks such a sentence in order to give her brother proper burial.

excessive movement, and an electrode is attached to his wrist. He is told that he will be read lists of simple word pairs, and that he will then be tested on his ability to remember the second word of a pair when he hears the first one again. Whenever he makes an error, he will receive electric shocks of increasing intensity.

The real focus of the experiment is the teacher. After watching the learner being strapped into place, he is seated before an impressive shock generator. The instrument panel consists of thirty lever switches set in a horizontal line. Each switch is clearly labeled with a voltage designation ranging from 15 to 450 volts. The following designations are clearly indicated for groups of four switches, going from left to right: Slight Shock, Moderate Shock, Strong Shock, Very Strong Shock, Intense Shock, Extreme Intensity Shock, Danger: Severe Shock. (Two switches after this last designation are simply marked XXX.)

When a switch is depressed, a pilot light corresponding to each switch is illuminated in bright red; an electric buzzing is heard; a blue light, labeled "voltage energizer," flashes; the dial on the voltage meter swings to the right; and various relay clicks sound off.

The upper left-hand corner of the generator is labeled SHOCK GENERATOR, TYPE ZLB, DYSON INSTRUMENT COMPANY, WALTHAM, MASS. OUTPUT 15 VOLTS–450 VOLTS.

Each subject is given a sample 45-volt shock from the generator before his run as teacher, and the jolt strengthens his belief in the authenticity of the machine.

The teacher is a genuinely naïve subject who has come to the laboratory for the experiment. The learner, or victim, is actually an actor who receives no shock at all. The point of the experiment is to see how far a person will proceed in a concrete and measurable situation in which he is ordered to inflict increasing pain on a protesting victim.

Conflict arises when the man receiving the shock begins to show that he is experiencing discomfort. At 75 volts, he grunts; at 120 volts, he complains loudly; at 150, he demands to be released from the experiment. As the voltage increases, his protests become more vehement and emotional. At 285 volts, his response can be described only as an agonized scream. Soon thereafter, he makes no sound at all.

For the teacher, the situation quickly becomes one of gripping tension. It is not a game for him; conflict is intense and obvious.

The manifest suffering of the learner presses him to quit; but each time he hesitates to administer a shock, the experimenter orders him to continue. To extricate himself from this plight, the subject must make a clear break with authority.[3]

The subject, Gretchen Brandt,[4] is an attractive thirty-one-year-old medical technician who works at the Yale Medical School. She had emigrated from Germany five years before.

On several occasions when the learner complains, she turns to the experimenter coolly and inquires, "Shall I continue?" She promptly returns to her task when the experimenter asks her to do so. At the administration of 210 volts, she turns to the experimenter, remarking firmly, "Well, I'm sorry, I don't think we should continue."

EXPERIMENTER. The experiment requires that you go on until he has learned all the word pairs correctly.

BRANDT. He has a heart condition, I'm sorry. He told you that before.

EXPERIMENTER. The shocks may be painful but they are not dangerous.

BRANDT. Well, I'm sorry, I think when shocks continue like this, they *are* dangerous. You ask him if he wants to get out. It's his free will.

EXPERIMENTER. It is absolutely essential that we continue. . . .

BRANDT. I'd like you to ask him. We came here of our free will. If he wants to continue I'll go ahead. He told you he had a heart condition. I'm sorry. I don't want to be responsible for anything happening to him. I wouldn't like it for me either.

EXPERIMENTER. You have no other choice.

BRANDT. I think we are here on our own free will. I don't want to be responsible if anything happens to him. Please understand that.

She refuses to go further and the experiment is terminated.

---

[3]The ethical problems of carrying out an experiment of this sort are too complex to be dealt with here, but they receive extended treatment in the book from which this article is adapted [Milgram's note]. The book is *Obedience to Authority* (New York: Harper and Row, 1974).

[4]Names of subjects described in this piece have been changed [Milgram's note].

The woman is firm and resolute throughout. She indicates in the interview that she was in no way tense or nervous, and this corresponds to her controlled appearance during the experiment. She feels that the last shock she administered to the learner was extremely painful and reiterates that she "did not want to be responsible for any harm to him."

The woman's straightforward, courteous behavior in the experiment, lack of tension, and total control of her own action seem to make disobedience a simple and rational deed. Her behavior is the very embodiment of what I envisioned would be true for almost all subjects.

Before the experiments, I sought predictions about the outcome from various kinds of people—psychiatrists, college sophomores, middle-class adults, graduate students and faculty in the behavioral sciences. With remarkable similarity, they predicted that virtually all subjects would refuse to obey the experimenter. The psychiatrists, specifically, predicted that most subjects would not go beyond 150 volts, when the victim makes his first explicit demand to be freed. They expected that only 4 percent would reach 300 volts, and that only a pathological fringe of about one in a thousand would administer the highest shock on the board.

These predictions were unequivocally wrong. Of the forty subjects in the first experiment, twenty-five obeyed the orders of the experimenter to the end, punishing the victim until they reached the most potent shock available on the generator. After 450 volts were administered three times, the experimenter called a halt to the session. Many obedient subjects then heaved sighs of relief, mopped their brows, rubbed their fingers over their eyes, or nervously fumbled cigarettes. Others displayed only minimal signs of tension from beginning to end.

When the very first experiments were carried out, Yale undergraduates were used as subjects, and about 60 percent of them were fully obedient. A colleague of mine immediately dismissed these findings as having no relevance to "ordinary" people, asserting that Yale undergraduates are a highly aggressive, competitive bunch who step on each other's necks on the slightest provocation. He assured me that when "ordinary" people were tested, the results would be quite different. As we moved from the pilot studies to the regular experimental series, people drawn from every stratum of New Haven life came to be employed in the experiment: professionals, white-collar workers, unemployed persons, and industrial workers. *The experimental outcome was the same as we had observed among the students.*

Moreover, when the experiments were repeated in Princeton, Munich, Rome, South Africa, and Australia, the level of obedience was invariably somewhat *higher* than found in the investigation reported in this article. Thus one scientist in Munich found 85 percent of his subjects obedient.

Fred Prozi's reactions, if more dramatic than most, illuminate the conflicts experienced by others in less visible form. About fifty years old and unemployed at the time of the experiment, he has a good-natured, if slightly dissolute, appearance, and he strikes people as a rather ordinary fellow. He begins the session calmly but becomes tense as it proceeds. After delivering the 180-volt shock, he pivots around in his chair and, shaking his head, addresses the experimenter in agitated tones:

PROZI.   I can't stand it. I'm not going to kill that man in there. You hear him hollering?

EXPERIMENTER.   As I told you before, the shocks may be painful, but . . .

PROZI.   But he's hollering. He can't stand it. What's going to happen to him?

EXPERIMENTER.   (his voice is patient, matter-of-fact): The experiment requires that you continue, Teacher.

PROZI.   Aaah, but, unh, I'm not going to get that man sick in there—know what I mean?

EXPERIMENTER.   Whether the learner likes it or not, we must go on, through all the word pairs.

PROZI.   I refuse to take the responsibility. He's in there hollering!

EXPERIMENTER.   It's absolutely essential that you continue, Prozi.

PROZI.   (indicating the unused question): There's too many left here, I mean, Jeez, if he gets them wrong, there's too many of them left. I mean, who's going to take the responsibility if anything happens to that gentleman?

EXPERIMENTER.   I'm responsible for anything that happens to him. Continue, please.

PROZI.   All right. (Consults list of words.) The next one's "Slow—walk, truck, dance, music." Answer, please. (A buzzing sound indicates the learner has signaled his answer.) Wrong. A hundred and ninety-five volts. "Dance." (Zzumph!)

LEARNER (yelling).   Let me out of here! My heart's bothering me! (Teacher looks at experimenter.)

EXPERIMENTER.   Continue, please.

LEARNER (screaming).   Let me out of here! You have no right to keep me here! Let me out of here, my heart's bothering me, let me out!

PROZI (shakes head, pats the table nervously).   You see, he's hollering. Hear that? Gee, I don't know.

EXPERIMENTER.   The experiment requires . . .

PROZI (interrupting).   I know it does, sir, but I mean—hunh! He don't know what he's getting in for. He's up to 195 volts! (Experiment continues, through 210 volts, 225 volts, 240 volts, 255 volts, 270 volts, at which point Prozi, with evident relief, runs out of word-pair questions.)

EXPERIMENTER.   You'll have to go back to the beginning of that page and go through them again until he's learned them all correctly.

PROZI.   Aw, no. I'm not going to kill that man. You mean I've got to keep going up with the scale? No sir. He's hollering in there. I'm not going to give him 450 volts.

EXPERIMENTER.   The experiment requires that you go on.

LEARNER.   Ohhh. I absolutely refuse to answer anymore. (Shouting urgently now.) Let me out of here! You can't hold me here! Get me out. Get-me-out-of-here!

EXPERIMENTER.   Continue. The next word is "Green," please.

PROZI.   "Green—grass, hat, ink, apple." (Nothing happens. No answering buzz. Just gloomy silence.)

PROZI.   I don't think he is going to answer.

EXPERIMENTER.   If the learner doesn't answer in a reasonable time, about four or five seconds, consider the answer wrong. And follow the same procedures you have been doing for wrong answers. Say, "Wrong," tell him the number of volts, give him the punishment, read him the correct answer. Continue, please.

PROZI.   "Green—grass, hat, ink, apple." Answer, please. (More silence. Subject just sits there.)

EXPERIMENTER.   Go on with the procedure, please.

PROZI. Three hundred and fifteen volts. The answer is "ink." (Zzumph!)

LEARNER. Ohh. Oooohh.

PROZI (relieved to hear response). Next one . . .

LEARNER. I absolutely refuse to answer.

PROZI. You got to. You get a shock if you don't answer. (Experiment continues with learner refusing to answer, and, finally, failing even to grunt or groan. At 375 volts, the subject stands up.)

PROZI. I think something's happening to that fellow in there. I don't get no answer. He was hollering at less voltage. Can't you check in and see if he's all right, please?

EXPERIMENTER (with same detached calm). Not once we've started. Please continue, Teacher.

PROZI (sits down, sighs deeply). "Cool—day, shade, water, paint." Answer, please. Are you all right in there? Are you all right?

EXPERIMENTER. Please continue, Teacher. Continue, please. (Subject pushes lever. Zzumph!)

PROZI (swiveling around in his chair). Something's happened to that man in there. (Swiveling back.) Next one. "Low—dollar, necklace, moon, paint." (Turning around again.) Something's happened to that man in there. You better check in on him, sir. He won't answer or nothing.

EXPERIMENTER. Continue. Go on, please.

PROZI. You accept all responsibility?

EXPERIMENTER. The responsibility is mine. Correct. Please go on. (Subject returns to his list, starts running through words as rapidly as he can read them, works through to 450 volts.)

PROZI. That's that.

EXPERIMENTER. Continue using the 450 switch for each wrong answer. Continue, please.

PROZI. But I don't get anything!

EXPERIMENTER. Please continue. The next word is "white."

PROZI. Don't you think you should look in on him, please?

EXPERIMENTER. Not once we've started the experiment.

PROZI. What if he's dead in there? (Gestures toward the room with the electric chair.) I mean, he told me he can't stand the shock, sir. I don't mean to be rude, but I think you should look in on him. All you have to do is look in on him. All you have to do is look in the door. I don't get no answer, no noise. Something might have happened to the gentleman in there, sir.

EXPERIMENTER. We must continue. Go on, please.

PROZI. You mean keep giving him what? Four-hundred-fifty volts, what he's got now?

EXPERIMENTER. That's correct. Continue. The next word is "white."

PROZI (now at a furious pace). "White—cloud, horse, rock, house." Answer, please. The answer is "horse." Four hundred and fifty volts. (Zzumph!) Next word, "Bag—paint, music, clown, girl." The answer is "paint." Four hundred and fifty volts. (Zzumph!) Next word is "Short—sentence, movie . . ."

EXPERIMENTER. Excuse me, Teacher. We'll have to discontinue the experiment.

Morris Braverman, another subject, is a thirty-nine-year-old social worker. He looks older than his years because of his bald head and serious demeanor. His brow is furrowed, as if all the world's burdens were carried on his face. He appears intelligent and concerned.

When the learner refuses to answer and the experimenter instructs Braverman to treat the absence of an answer as equivalent to a wrong answer, he takes his instruction to heart. Before administering 300 volts he asserts officiously to the victim, "Mr. Wallace, your silence has to be considered as a wrong answer." Then he administers the shock. He offers halfheartedly to change places with the learner, then asks the experimenter, "Do I have to follow these instructions literally?" He is satisfied with the experimenter's answer that he does. His very refined and authoritative manner of speaking is increasingly broken up by wheezing laughter.

The experimenter's notes on Mr. Braverman at the last few shocks are:

Almost breaking up now each time gives shock. Rubbing face to hide laughter.

Squinting, trying to hide face with hand, still laughing.

Cannot control his laughter at this point no matter what he does. Clenching fist, pushing it onto table.

In an interview after the session, Mr. Braverman summarizes the experiment with impressive fluency and intelligence. He feels the experiment may have been designed also to "test the effects on the teacher of being in an essentially sadistic role, as well as the reactions of a student to a learning situation that was authoritative and punitive." When asked how painful the last few shocks administered to the learner were, he indicates that the most extreme category on the scale is not adequate (it read EXTREMELY PAINFUL) and places his mark at the edge of the scale with an arrow carrying it beyond the scale.

It is almost impossible to convey the greatly relaxed, sedate quality of his conversation in the interview. In the most relaxed terms, he speaks about his severe inner tension.

EXPERIMENTER.   At what point were you most tense or nervous?
MR. BRAVERMAN.   Well, when he first began to cry out in pain, and I realized this was hurting him. This got worse when he just blocked and refused to answer. There was I. I'm a nice person, I think, hurting somebody, and caught up in what seemed a mad situation . . . and in the interest of science, one goes through with it.

When the interviewer pursues the general question of tension, Mr. Braverman spontaneously mentions his laughter.

"My reactions were awfully peculiar. I don't know if you were watching me, but my reactions were giggly, and trying to stifle laughter. This isn't the way I usually am. This was a sheer reaction to a totally impossible situation. And my reaction was to the situation of having to hurt somebody. And being totally helpless and caught up in a set of circumstances where I just couldn't deviate and I couldn't try to help. This is what got me."

Mr. Braverman, like all subjects, was told the actual nature and purpose of the experiment, and a year later he affirmed in a questionnaire that he had learned something of personal importance: "What appalled me was that I could possess this capacity for obedience and compliance to a central idea, i.e., the value of a memory experiment, even after it became clear that continued adherence to this value was at the expense of violation of another value, i.e., don't hurt someone who is helpless and not hurting you. As my wife said, 'You can call yourself Eichmann.' I hope I deal more effectively with any future conflicts of values I encounter."

One theoretical interpretation of this behavior holds that all people harbor deeply aggressive instincts continually pressing for expression, and that the experiment provides institutional justification for the release of these impulses. According to this view, if a person is placed in a situation in which he has complete power over another individual, whom he may punish as much as he likes, all that is sadistic and bestial in man comes to the fore. The impulse to shock the victim is seen to flow from the potent aggressive tendencies, which are part of the motivational life of the individual, and the experiment, because it provides social legitimacy, simply opens the door to their expression.

It becomes vital, therefore, to compare the subject's performance when he is under orders and when he is allowed to choose the shock level.

The procedure was identical to our standard experiment, except that the teacher was told that he was free to select any shock level on any of the trials. (The experimenter took pains to point out that the teacher could use the highest levels on the generator, the lowest, any in between, or any combination of levels.) Each subject proceeded for thirty critical trials. The learner's protests were coordinated to standard shock levels, his first grunt coming at 75 volts, his first vehement protest at 150 volts.

The average shock used during the thirty critical trials was less than 60 volts—lower than the point at which the victim showed the first signs of discomfort. Three of the forty subjects did not go beyond the very lowest level on the board, twenty-eight went no higher than 75 volts, and thirty-eight did not go beyond the first loud protest at 150 volts. Two subjects provided the exception, administering up to 325 and 450 volts, but the overall result was that the great majority of people delivered very low, usually painless, shocks when the choice was explicitly up to them.

This condition of the experiment undermines another commonly offered explanation of the subjects' behavior—that those who shocked the victim at the most severe levels came only from the sadistic fringe of society. If one considers that almost two-thirds of the participants fall into the category of "obedient" subjects, and that they represented ordinary people drawn from working, managerial, and professional classes, the argument becomes very shaky. Indeed, it is highly reminiscent of the issue that arose in connection with Hannah Arendt's 1963 book, *Eichmann in Jerusalem.* Arendt contended that the prosecution's effort to depict Eichmann as a sadistic monster was fundamentally wrong, that he came closer to being an uninspired bureaucrat who simply sat at his desk and did his job. For asserting her views, Arendt became the object of considerable scorn, even calumny. Somehow, it was felt that the monstrous deeds carried out by Eichmann required a brutal, twisted personality, evil incarnate. After witnessing hundreds of ordinary persons submit to the authority in our own experiments, I must conclude that Arendt's conception of the banality of evil comes closer to the truth than one might dare imagine. The ordinary person who shocked the victim did so out of a sense of obligation—an impression of his duties as a subject—and not from any peculiarly aggressive tendencies.

This is, perhaps, the most fundamental lesson of our study: ordinary people, simply doing their jobs, and without any particular hostility on their part, can become agents in a terrible destructive process. Moreover, even when the destructive effects of their work become patently clear, and they are asked to carry out actions incompatible with fundamental standards of morality, relatively few people have the resources needed to resist authority.

Many of the people were in some sense against what they did to the learner, and many protested even while they obeyed. Some were totally convinced of the wrongness of their actions but could not bring themselves to make an open break with authority. They often derived satisfaction from their thoughts and felt that—within themselves, at least—they had been on the side of the angels. They tried to reduce strain by obeying the experimenter but "only slightly," encouraging the learner, touching the generator switches gingerly. When interviewed, such a subject would stress that he had "asserted my humanity" by administering the briefest shock possible. Handling the conflict in this manner was easier than defiance.

The situation is constructed so that there is no way the subject can stop shocking the learner without violating the experimenter's definitions of his own competence. The subject fears that he will appear arrogant, untoward, and rude if he breaks off. Although these inhibiting emotions appear small in scope alongside the violence being done to the learner, they suffuse the mind and feelings of the subject, who is miserable at the prospect of having to repudiate the authority to his face. (When the experiment was altered so that the experimenter gave his instructions by telephone instead of in person, only a third as many people were fully obedient through 450 volts.) It is a curious thing that a measure of compassion on the part of the subject—an unwillingness to "hurt" the experimenter's feelings—is part of those binding forces inhibiting his disobedience. The withdrawal of such deference may be as painful to the subject as to the authority he defies.

The subjects do not derive satisfaction from inflicting pain, but they often like the feeling they get from pleasing the experimenter. They are proud of doing a good job, obeying the experimenter under difficult circumstances. While the subjects administered only mild shocks on their own initiative, one experimental variation showed that, under orders, 30 percent of them were willing to deliver 450 volts even when they had to forcibly push the learner's hand down on the electrode.

Bruno Batta is a thirty-seven-year-old welder who took part in the variation requiring the use of force. He was born in New Haven, his parents in Italy. He has a rough-hewn face that conveys a conspicuous lack of alertness. He has some difficulty in mastering the experimental procedure and needs to be corrected by the experimenter several times. He shows appreciation for the help and willingness to do what is required. After the 150-volt level, Batta has to force the learner's hand down on the shock plate, since the learner himself refuses to touch it.

When the learner first complains, Mr. Batta pays no attention to him. His face remains impassive, as if to dissociate himself from the learner's disruptive behavior. When the experimenter instructs him to force the learner's hand down, he adopts a rigid, mechanical procedure. He tests the generator switch. When it fails to function, he immediately forces the learner's hand onto the shock plate. All the while he maintains the same rigid mask. The learner, seated alongside him, begs him to stop, but with robotic impassivity he continues the procedure.

What is extraordinary is his apparent total indifference to the learner; he hardly takes cognizance of him as a human being. Meanwhile, he relates to the experimenter in a submissive and courteous fashion.

At the 330-volt level, the learner refuses not only to touch the shock plate but also to provide any answers. Annoyed, Batta turns to him, and chastises him: "You better answer and get it over with. We can't stay here all night." These are the only words he directs to the learner in the course of an hour. Never again does he speak to him. The scene is brutal and depressing, his hard, impassive face showing total indifference as he subdues the screaming learner and gives him shocks. He seems to derive no pleasure from the act itself, only quiet satisfaction at doing his job properly.

When he administers 450 volts, he turns to the experimenter and asks, "Where do we go from here, Professor?" His tone is deferential and expresses his willingness to be a cooperative subject, in contrast to the learner's obstinacy.

At the end of the session he tells the experimenter how honored he has been to help him, and in a moment of contrition, remarks, "Sir, sorry it couldn't have been a full experiment."

He has done his honest best. It is only the deficient behavior of the learner that has denied the experimenter full satisfaction.

The essence of obedience is that a person comes to view himself as the instrument for carrying out another person's wishes, and he therefore no longer regards himself as responsible for his actions. Once this critical shift of viewpoint has occurred, all of the essential features of obedience follow. The most far-reaching consequence is that the person feels responsible *to* the authority directing him but feels no responsibility *for* the content of the actions that the authority prescribes. Morality does not disappear—it acquires a radically different focus: the subordinate person feels shame or pride depending on how adequately he has performed the actions called for by authority.

Language provides numerous terms to pinpoint this type of morality: *loyalty, duty, discipline* all are terms heavily saturated with moral meaning and refer to the degree to which a person fulfills his obligations to authority. They refer not to the "goodness" of the person per se but to the adequacy with which a subordinate fulfills his socially defined role. The most frequent defense of the individual who has performed a heinous act under command of authority is that he has simply done his duty. In asserting this defense, the individual is not introducing an alibi concocted for the moment but is reporting honestly on the psychological attitude induced by submission to authority.

For a person to feel responsible for his actions, he must sense that the behavior has flowed from "the self." In the situation we have studied, subjects have precisely the opposite view of their actions— namely, they see them as originating in the motives of some other person. Subjects in the experiment frequently said, "If it were up to me, I would not have administered shocks to the learner."

Once authority has been isolated as the cause of the subject's behavior, it is legitimate to inquire into the necessary elements of authority and how it must be perceived in order to gain his compliance. We conducted some investigations into the kinds of changes that would cause the experimenter to lose his power and to be disobeyed by the subject. Some of the variations revealed that:

- *The experimenter's physical presence has a marked impact on his authority.* As cited earlier, obedience dropped off sharply when orders were given by telephone. The experimenter could often induce a disobedient subject to go on by returning to the laboratory.
- *Conflicting authority severely paralyzes action.* When two experimenters of equal status, both seated at the command desk, gave incompatible orders, no shocks were delivered past the point of their disagreement.
- *The rebellious action of others severely undermines authority.* In one variation, three teachers (two actors and a real subject) administered a test and shocks. When the two actors disobeyed the experimenter and refused to go beyond a certain shock level, thirty-six of forty subjects joined their disobedient peers and refused as well.

Although the experimenter's authority was fragile in some respects, it is also true that he had almost none of the tools used in ordinary command structures. For example, the experimenter did not threaten the subjects with punishment—such as loss of income, community ostracism, or jail—for failure to obey. Neither could he offer incentives. Indeed, we should expect the experimenter's authority to be much less than that of someone like a general, since the experimenter has no power to enforce his imperatives, and since participation in a psychological experiment scarcely evokes the sense of urgency and dedication found in warfare. Despite these limitations, he still managed to command a dismaying degree of obedience.

I will cite one final variation of the experiment that depicts a dilemma that is more common in everyday life. The subject was not ordered to pull the lever that shocked the victim, but merely to perform a subsidiary task (administering the word-pair test) while another person administered the shock. In this situation, thirty-seven of forty adults continued to the highest level on the shock generator. Predictably, they excused their behavior by saying that the responsibility belonged to the man who actually pulled the switch.

This may illustrate a dangerously typical arrangement in a complex society: it is easy to ignore responsibility when one is only an intermediate link in a chain of action.

The problem of obedience is not wholly psychological. The form and shape of society and the way it is developing have much to do with it. There was a time, perhaps, when people were able to give a fully human response to any situation because they were fully absorbed in it as human beings. But as soon as there was a division of labor things changed. Beyond a certain point, the breaking up of society into people carrying out narrow and very special jobs takes away from the human quality of work and life. A person does not get to see the whole situation but only a small part of it, and is thus unable to act without some kind of overall direction. He yields to authority but in doing so is alienated from his own actions.

Even Eichmann was sickened when he toured the concentration camps, but he had only to sit at a desk and shuffle papers. At the same time the man in the camp who actually dropped Cyclon-b into the gas chambers was able to justify *his* behavior on the ground that he was only following orders from above. Thus there is a fragmentation of the total human act; no one is confronted with the consequences of his decision to carry out the evil act. The person who assumes responsibility has evaporated. Perhaps this is the most common characteristic of socially organized evil in modern society.

For Further Reflection

1. What do you make of this experiment? Why did the "teachers" continue to go on with the experiments when they saw the learners in evident pain? Does it really show how deeply we adhere to authority?

2. Are there any problems with the experiments? Some have complained that the subjects ("the teachers") were manipulated. They were not treated as autonomous beings. Do you agree?

Existentialism Is a Humanism

JEAN-PAUL SARTRE

Jean-Paul Sartre (1905–1980) was born in Paris and was a teacher in a French high school. He served in the French army during World War II, was captured and imprisoned, but released. After the war, his plays, novels, and philosophical work were the rage of France, and influential throughout the Western world. He combined his existentialism with Marxism, though he refrained from joining the Communist party.

In this famous lecture, delivered in Paris on October 29, 1945, Sartre develops the principles of atheistic existentialism:

1. We are totally free. That is, we are not determined by heredity or environment.
2. Since there is no God to define our being, we must define our essence.
3. We are completely responsible for our actions, and we are responsible for prescribing a moral philosophy for everyone else too. We create our morality.
4. Because of the death of God and the human predicament, which leaves us totally free to create our values, we must exist in anguish, forlornness, and despair.
5. Yet we should celebrate the fact that we are creators of our essence and our values.

The phrase "essence precedes existence" refers to the Platonic idea that ideas are fixed in a transcendent world of forms. Everything is already defined and determined. Sartre rejects this transcendent notion. Existentialism means that "existence precedes essence." That is, we, *existing entities,* create our essence, our being, our values.

From Jean Paul Sartre, *Existentialism,* translated by Bernard Frechtman (New York: Philosophical Library, 1947). Reprinted by permission of the publisher.

What is meant by the term *existentialism?*

Most people who use the word would be rather embarrassed if they had to explain it, since, now that the word is all the rage, even the work of a musician or painter is being called existentialist. . . . It seems that for want of an advance-guard doctrine analogous to surrealism, the kind of people who are eager for scandal and flurry turn to this philosophy which in other respects does not at all serve their purposes in this sphere.

Actually, it is the least scandalous, the most austere of doctrines. It is intended strictly for specialists and philosophers. Yet it can be defined easily. What complicates matters is that there are two kinds of existentialists; first, those who are Christian, among whom I would include Jaspers and Gabriel Marcel, both Catholic; and on the other hand, the atheistic existentialists, among whom I class Heidegger, and then the French existentialists and myself. What they have in common is that they think that existence precedes essence, or, if you prefer, that subjectivity must be the starting point.

Just what does that mean? Let us consider some object that is manufactured, for example, a book or a paper-cutter: here is an object which has been made by an artisan whose inspiration came from a concept. He referred to the concept of what a paper-cutter is and likewise to a known method of production, which is part of the concept, something which is, by and large, a routine. Thus, the paper-cutter is at once an object produced in a certain way and, on the other hand, one having a specific use; and one cannot postulate a man who produces a paper-cutter but does not know what it is used for. Therefore, let us say that, for the paper-cutter, essence—that is, the ensemble of both the production routines and the properties which enable it to be both produced and defined—precedes existence. Thus, the presence of the paper-cutter or book in front of me is determined. Therefore, we have here a technical view of the world whereby it can be said that production precedes existence.

When we conceive God as the Creator, He is generally thought of as a superior sort of artisan. Whatever doctrine we may be considering, whether one like that of Descartes or that of Leibnitz, we always grant that will more or less follows understanding or, at the very least, accompanies it, and that when God creates He knows exactly what He is creating. Thus, the concept of man in the mind of God is comparable to the concept of paper-cutter in the mind of the manufacturer, and, following certain techniques and a conception, God produces man, just as the artisan, following a definition and a technique, makes a paper-cutter. Thus, the individual man is the realization of a certain concept in the divine intelligence.

In the eighteenth century, the atheism of the *philosophes* discarded the idea of God, but not so much for the notion that essence precedes existence. To a certain extent, this idea is found everywhere; we find it in Diderot, in Voltaire, and even in Kant. Man has a human nature; this human nature, which is the concept of the human, is found in all men, which means that each man is a particular example of a universal concept, man. In Kant, the result of this universality is that the wild-man, the natural man, as well as the bourgeois, are circumscribed by the same definition and have the same basic qualities. Thus, here too the essence of man precedes the historical existence that we find in nature.

Atheistic existentialism, which I represent, is more coherent. It states that if God does not exist, there is at least one being in whom existence precedes essence, a being who exists before he can be defined by any concept, and that this being is man, or, as Heidegger says, human reality. What is meant here by saying that existence precedes essence? It means that, first of all, man exists, turns up, appears on the scene, and, only afterwards, defines himself. If man, as the existentialist conceives him, is indefinable, it is because at first he is nothing. Only afterward will he be something, and he himself will have made what he will be. Thus, there is no human nature, since there is no God to conceive it. Not only is man what he conceives himself to be, but he is also only what he wills himself to be after this thrust toward existence.

Man is nothing else but what he makes of himself. Such is the first principle of existentialism. It is also what is called subjectivity, the name we are labeled with when charges are brought against us. But what do we mean by this, if not that man has a greater dignity than a stone or table? For we mean that man first exists, that is, that man first of all is the being in the future. Man is at the start a plan which is aware of itself, rather than a patch of moss, a piece of garbage, or a cauliflower; nothing exists prior to this plan; there is nothing in heaven; man will be what he will have planned to be. Not what he will want to be. Because by the word "will" we generally mean a conscious decision, which is subsequent to what we have already made of ourselves. I may want to belong to a political party, write a book, get married; but all that is only a manifestation of an earlier, more spontaneous choice that is called "will." But if existence really does precede essence, man is responsible for what he is. Thus, existentialism's first move is to make every man aware of what he is and to make the full responsibility of his existence rest on him. And when we say that a man is responsible for himself, we do not only mean that he is responsible for his own individuality, but that he is responsible for all men.

The word subjectivism has two meanings, and our opponents play on the two. Subjectivism means, on the one hand, that an individual chooses and makes himself; and, on the other, that it is impossible for man to transcend human subjectivity. The second of these is the essential meaning of existentialism. When we say that man chooses his own self, we mean that every one of us does likewise; but we also mean by that that in making this choice he also chooses all men. In fact, in creating the man that we want to be, there is not a single one of our acts which does not at the same time create an image of man as we think he ought to be. To choose to be this or that is to affirm at the same time the value of what we choose, because we can never choose evil. We always choose the good, and nothing can be good for us without being good for all.

If, on the other hand, existence precedes essence, and if we grant that we exist and fashion our image at one and the same time, the image is valid for everybody and for our whole age. Thus, our responsibility is much greater than we might have supposed, because it involves all mankind. If I am a workingman and choose to join a Christian trade-union rather than be a communist, and if by being a member I want to show that the best thing for man is resignation, that the kingdom of man is not of this world, I am not only involving my own case—I want to be resigned for everyone. As a result, my action has involved all humanity. To take a more individual matter, if I want to marry, to have children; even if this marriage depends solely on my own circumstances or passion or wish, I am involving all humanity in monogamy and not merely myself. Therefore, I am responsible for myself and for everyone else. I am creating a certain image of man of my own choosing. In choosing myself, I choose man.

This helps us understand what the actual content is of such rather grandiloquent words as anguish, forlornness, despair. As you will see, it's all quite simple.

First, what is meant by anguish? The existentialists say at once that man is anguish. What that means is this: the man who involves himself and who realizes that he is not only the person he chooses to be, but also a law-maker who is, at the same time, choosing all mankind as well as himself, cannot help escape the feeling of his total and deep responsibility. Of course, there are many people who are not anxious; but we claim that they are hiding their anxiety, that they are fleeing from it. Certainly, many people believe that when they do something, they themselves are the only ones involved, and when someone says to them, "What if everyone acted that way?" they shrug their shoulders and answer, "Everyone doesn't act that way." But really, one should always ask himself, "What would happen if everybody looked at things that way?" There is no escaping this disturbing thought except by a kind of double-dealing. A man who lies and makes excuses for himself by saying "not everybody does that," is someone with an uneasy conscience, because the act of lying implies that a universal value is conferred upon the lie.

Anguish is evident even when it conceals itself. This is the anguish that Kierkegaard called the anguish of Abraham. You know the story: an angel has ordered Abraham to sacrifice his son; if it really were an angel who has come and said, "You are Abraham, you shall sacrifice your son," everything would be all right. But everyone might first wonder, "Is it really an angel, and am I really Abraham? What proof do I have?" . . .

Now, I'm not being singled out as an Abraham, and yet at every moment I'm obliged to perform exemplary acts. For every man, everything happens as if all mankind had its eyes fixed on him and were guiding itself by what he does. And every man ought to say to himself, "Am I really the kind of man who has the right to act in such a way that humanity might guide itself by my actions?" And if he does not say that to himself, he is masking his anguish.

There is no question here of the kind of anguish which would lead to quietism, to inaction. It is a matter of a simple sort of anguish that anybody who has had responsibilities is familiar with. For example, when a military officer takes the responsibility for an attack and sends a certain number of men to death, he chooses to do so, and in the main he alone makes the choice. Doubtless, orders come from above, but they are too broad; he interprets them, and on this interpretation depend the lives of ten or fourteen or twenty men. In making a decision he cannot help having a certain anguish. All leaders know this anguish. That doesn't keep them from acting; on the contrary, it is the very condition of their action. For it implies that they envisage a number of possibilities, and when they choose one, they realize that it has value only because it is chosen. We shall see that this kind of anguish, which is the kind that existentialism describes, is explained, in addition, by a direct responsibility to the other men whom it involves. It is not a curtain separating us from action, but is part of action itself.

When we speak of forlornness, a term Heidegger was fond of, we mean only that God does not exist and that we have to face all the consequences of this. The existentialist is strongly opposed to a certain kind of secular ethics which would like to abolish God with the least possible expense. About 1880, some French teachers tried to set up a secular ethics which went something like this: God is a useless and costly hypothesis; we are discarding it; but meanwhile, in order for there to be an ethics, a society, a civilization, it is essential that certain values be taken seriously and that they be considered as having an *a priori* existence. It must be obligatory, *a priori,* to be honest, not to lie, not to beat your wife, to have children, etc., etc. So we're going to try a little device which will make it possible to show that values exist all the same, inscribed in a heaven of ideas, though otherwise God does not exist. In other words—and this, I believe, is the tendency of everything called reformism in France—nothing will be changed if God does not exist. We shall find ourselves with the same norms of honesty, progress, and humanism, and we shall have made of God an outdated hypothesis which will peacefully die off by itself.

The existentialist, on the contrary, thinks it very distressing that God does not exist, because all possibility of finding values in a heaven of ideas disappears along with Him; there can be no longer an *a priori* Good, since there is no infinite and perfect consciousness to think it. Nowhere is it written that the Good exists, that we must be honest, that we must not lie; because the fact is we are on a plane where there are only men. Dostoievsky said, "If God didn't exist, everything would be possible." That is the very starting point of existentialism. Indeed, everything is permissible if God does not exist, and as a result man is forlorn, because neither within him nor without does he find anything to cling to. He can't start making excuses for himself.

If existence really does precede essence, there is no explaining things away by reference to a fixed and given human nature. In other words, there is no determinism, man is free, man is freedom.

On the other hand, if God does not exist, we find no values or commands to turn to which legitimize our conduct. So, in the bright realm of values, we have no excuse behind us, no justification before us. We are alone, with no excuses.

That is the idea I shall try to convey when I say that man is condemned to be free. Condemned, because he did not create himself, yet, in other respects is free; because, once thrown into the world, he is responsible for everything he does.

The existentialist does not believe in the power of passion. He will never agree that a sweeping passion is a ravaging torrent which fatally leads a man to certain acts and is therefore an excuse. He thinks that man is responsible for his passion.

The existentialist does not think that man is going to help himself by finding in the world some omen by which to orient himself, because he thinks that man will interpret the omen to suit himself. Therefore, he thinks that man, with no support and no aid, is condemned every moment to invent man. Ponge, in a very fine article, has said, "Man is the future of man." That's exactly it. But if it is taken to mean that this future is recorded in heaven, that God sees it, then it is false, because it would really no longer be a future. If it is taken to mean that, whatever a man may be, there is a future to be forged, a virgin future before him, then this remark is sound. But then we are forlorn.

To give you an example which will enable you to understand forlornness better, I shall cite the case of one of my students who came to see me under the following circumstances: his father was on bad terms with his mother, and, moreover, was inclined to be a collaborationist; his older brother had been killed in the German offensive of 1940, and the young man, with somewhat immature but generous feelings, wanted to avenge him. His mother lived alone with him, very much upset by the half-treason of her husband and the death of her older son; the boy was her only consolation.

The boy was faced with the choice of leaving for England and joining the Free French Forces—that is, leaving his mother behind—or remaining with his mother and helping her to carry on. He was fully aware that the woman lived only for him and that his going-off—and perhaps his death—would plunge her into despair. He was also aware that every act that he did for his mother's sake was a sure thing, in the sense that it was helping her to carry on, whereas every effort he made toward going off and fighting was an uncertain move which might run aground and prove completely useless; for example, on his way to England he might, while passing through Spain, be detained indefinitely in a Spanish camp; he might reach England or Algiers and be stuck in an office at a desk job. As a result, he was faced with two very different kinds of action: one, concrete, immediate, but concerning only one individual; the other concerned an incomparably vaster group, a national collectivity, but for that very reason was dubious, and might be interrupted en route. And, at the same time, he was wavering between two kinds of ethics. On the one hand, an ethics of sympathy, of personal devotion; on the other, a broader ethics, but one whose efficacy was more dubious. He had to choose between the two.

Who could help him choose? Christian doctrine? No. Christian doctrine says, "Be charitable, love your neighbor, take the more rugged path, etc., etc." But which is the more rugged path? Whom should he love as a brother? The fighting man or his mother? Which does the greater good, the vague act of fighting in a group, or the concrete one of helping a particular human being to go on living? Who can decide *a priori?* Nobody. No book of ethics can tell him. The Kantian ethics says, "Never treat any person as a means, but as an end." Very well, if I stay with my mother, I'll treat her as an end and not as a means; but by virtue of this very fact, I'm running the risk of treating the people around me who are fighting, as means; and, conversely, if I go to join those who are fighting, I'll be treating them as an end, and, by doing that, I run the risk of treating my mother as a means.

If values are vague, and if they are always too broad for the concrete and specific case that we are considering, the only thing left for us is to trust our instincts. That's what this young man tried to do; and when I saw him, he said, "In the end, feeling is what counts. I ought to choose whichever pushes me in one direction. If I feel that I love my mother enough to sacrifice everything else for her—my desire for vengeance, for action, for adventure—then I'll stay with her. If, on the contrary, I feel that my love for my mother isn't enough, I'll leave."

But how is the value of a feeling determined? What gives his feeling for his mother value? Precisely the fact that he remained with her. I may say that I like so-and-so well enough to sacrifice a certain amount of money for him, but I may say so only if I've done it. I may say, "I love my mother well enough to remain with her" if I have remained with her. The only way to determine the value of this affection is, precisely, to perform an act which confirms and defines it. But, since I require this affection to justify my act, I find myself caught in a vicious circle. . . .

As for despair, the term has a very simple meaning. It means that we shall confine ourselves to reckoning only with what depends upon our will, or on the ensemble of probabilities which make our action possible. When we want something, we always have to reckon with probabilities. I may be counting on the arrival of a friend. The friend is coming by rail or street-car; this supposes that the train will arrive on schedule, or that the street-car will not jump the track. I am left in the realm of possibility; but possibilities are to be reckoned with only to the point where my action comports with the ensemble of these possibilities, and no further. The moment the possibilities I am considering are not rigorously involved by my action, I ought to disengage myself from them, because no God, no scheme, can adapt the world and its possibilities to my will. When Descartes said, "Conquer yourself rather than the world," he meant essentially the same thing.

The Marxists to whom I have spoken reply, "You can rely on the support of others in your action, which obviously has certain limits because you're not going to live forever. That means: rely on both what others are doing elsewhere to help you, in China, in Russia, and what they will do later on, after your death, to carry on the action and lead it to its fulfillment, which will be the revolution. You even *have* to rely upon that, otherwise you're immortal." I reply at once that I will always rely on fellow fighters insofar as these comrades are involved with me in a common struggle, in the unity of a party or a group in which I can more or less make my weight felt; that is, one whose ranks I am in as a fighter and whose movements I am aware of at every moment. In such a situation, relying on the unity and will of the party is exactly like counting on the fact that the train will arrive on time or that the car won't jump the track. But, given that man is free and that there is no human nature for me to depend on, I cannot count on men whom I do not know by relying on human goodness or man's concern for the good of society. I don't know what will become of the Russian revolution; I may make an example of it to the extent that at the present time it is apparent that the proletariat plays a part in Russia that it plays in no other nation. But I can't swear that this will inevitably lead to a triumph of the proletariat. I've got to limit myself to what I see.

Given that men are free, and that tomorrow they will freely decide what man will be, I cannot be sure that, after my death, fellow fighters will carry on my work to bring it to its maximum perfection. Tomorrow, after my death, some men may decide to set up Fascism, and the others may be cowardly and muddled enough to let them do it. Fascism will then be the human reality, so much the worse for us.

Actually, things will be as man will have decided they are to be. Does that mean that I should abandon myself to quietism? No. First, I should involve myself; then, act on the old saw, "Nothing ventured, nothing gained." Nor does it mean that I shouldn't belong to a party, but rather that I shall have no illusions and shall do what I can. For example, suppose I ask myself, "Will socialization, as such, ever come about?" I know nothing about it. All I know is that I'm going to do everything in my power to bring it about. Beyond that, I can't count on anything. Quietism is the attitude of people who say, "Let others do what I can't do." The doctrine I am presenting is the very opposite of quietism, since it declares, "There is no reality except in action." Moreover, it goes further, since it adds, "Man is nothing else than his plan; he exists only to the extent that he fulfills himself; he is, therefore, nothing else than the ensemble of his acts, nothing else than his life."

For Further Reflection

1. How are existentialist ethics different from other theories we have studied? What are its strengths and weaknesses?

2. Has Sartre gotten to the heart of the matter with his example of the student who must choose between his mother and the war effort? Could we object that he is making an exception to the norm? In normal situations we know perfectly well the right thing to do. For example, suppose that there was no war; then, wouldn't it be automatically right to take care of the mother? Does existentialism have a response to this criticism?

3. Sartre believes that it makes all the difference in the world whether God exists. If God does not exist, all things are morally

permissible, there is no right or wrong, but thinking makes it so. Is this correct?

Servility and Self-Respect

THOMAS E. HILL, JR.

Thomas E. Hill, Jr., is professor of philosophy at the University of North Carolina, Chapel Hill. He has written extensively in the area of moral philosophy, especially on Kant's ethics. In this essay Hill develops the Kantian theme that we have duties to ourselves, so that the servile person is morally defective because he or she fails sufficiently to respect the moral law, which enjoins that we respect all persons as moral equals, including oneself. He illustrates his thesis by three examples: the Uncle Tom who doesn't believe he has equal moral standing with whites, the Self-deprecator who lacks self-respect and holds himself of little worth, and the Deferential Wife who always defers to her husband, holding that her place is rightfully to serve the family, not her own independent goals. He argues that utilitarianism fails to give sufficient weight to such duties to oneself.

Several motives underlie this paper. In the first place, I am curious to see if there is a legitimate source for the increasingly common feeling that servility can be as much a vice as arrogance is. There seems to be something morally defective about the Uncle Tom and the submissive housewife; and yet, on the other hand, if the only interests they sacrifice are their own, it seems that we should have no right to complain. Secondly, I have some sympathy for the now unfashionable view that each person has duties to himself as well as to others. It does seem absurd to say that a person could literally violate his own rights or owe himself a debt to gratitude, but I suspect that the classic defenders to duties to oneself had something different in mind. If there are duties to oneself, it is natural to expect that a duty to avoid being servile would have a prominent place among them. . . .

I

Three examples may give a preliminary idea of what I mean by *servility*. Consider, first, an extremely deferential black, whom I shall call the *Uncle Tom*. He always steps aside for white men; he does not complain when less qualified whites take over his job; he gratefully accepts whatever benefits his all-white government and employers allot him, and he would not think of protesting its insufficiency. He displays the symbols of deference to whites, and of contempt towards blacks: he faces the former with bowed stance and a ready "Sir" and "Ma'am"; he reserves his strongest obscenities for the latter. Imagine, too, that he is not playing a game. He is not the shrewdly prudent calculator, who knows how to make the best of a bad lot and mocks his masters behind their backs. He accepts without question the idea that, as a black, he is owed less than whites. He may believe that blacks are mentally inferior and of less social utility, but that is not the crucial point. The attitude which he displays is that what he values, aspires for, and can demand is of less importance than what whites value, aspire for, and can demand. He is far from the picture book's carefree, happy servant, but he does not feel that he has a right to expect anything better.

Another pattern of servility is illustrated by a person I shall call the *Self-deprecator*. Like the Uncle Tom, he is reluctant to make demands. He says nothing when others take unfair advantage of him. When asked for his preferences or opinions, he tends to shrink away as if what he said should make no difference. His problem, however, is not a sense of racial inferiority but rather an acute awareness of his own inadequacies and failures as an individual. These defects are not imaginary: he has in fact done poorly by his own standards and others'. But, unlike many of us in the same situation, he acts as if his failings warrant quite unrelated maltreatment even by strangers. His sense of shame and self-contempt makes him content to be the instrument of others. He feels that nothing is owed him until he has earned it and that he has earned very little. He is not simply playing a masochist's game of winning sympathy by disparaging himself. On the contrary, he assesses his individual merits with painful accuracy.

A rather different case is that of the *Deferential Wife*. This is a woman who is utterly devoted to serving her husband. She buys the clothes *he* prefers, invites the guests *he* wants to entertain, and makes love whenever *he* is in the mood. She willingly moves to a new city in order for him to have a more attractive job, counting her own friendships and geographical preferences insignificant by comparison. She loves her husband, but her conduct is not simply an expression of love. She is happy, but she does not subordinate herself as a means to happiness. She does not simply defer to her husband in certain spheres as a trade-off for his deference in other spheres. On the contrary, she tends not to form her own interests, values, and ideals; and, when she does, she counts them as less important than her husband's. She readily responds to appeals from Women's Liberation that she agrees that women are mentally and physically equal, if not superior, to men. She just believes that the proper role for a woman is to serve her family. As a matter of fact, much of her happiness derives from her belief that she fulfills this role very well. No one is trampling on her rights, she says; for she is quite glad, and proud, to serve her husband as she does.

Each one of these cases reflects the attitude which I call servility. It betrays the absence of a certain kind of self-respect. What I take this attitude to be, more specifically, will become clearer later on. It is important at the outset, however, not to confuse the three cases sketched above with other, superficially similar cases. In particular, the cases I have sketched are not simply cases in which someone refuses to press his rights, speaks disparagingly of himself, or devotes himself to another. A black, for example, is not necessarily servile because he does not demand a just wage; for, seeing that such a demand would result in his being fired, he might forbear for the sake of his children. A self-critical person is not necessarily servile by virtue of bemoaning his faults in public; for his behavior may be merely a complex way of satisfying his own inner needs quite independent of a willingness to accept abuse from others. A woman need not be servile whenever she works to make her husband happy and prosperous; for she might freely and knowingly choose to do so from love or from a desire to share the rewards of his success. If the effort did not require her to submit to humiliation or maltreatment, her choice would not mark her as servile. There may, of course, be grounds for objecting to the attitudes in these cases; but the defect is not servility of the sort I want to consider. It should also be noted that my cases of servility are not simply instances of deference to superior knowledge or judgment. To defer to an expert's judgment on matters of fact is not to be servile; to defer to his every wish and whim is. Similarly, the belief that one's talents and achievements are comparatively low does not, by itself, make one servile. It is no vice to acknowledge the truth, and one may in fact have achieved less, and have less ability, than others. To be servile is not simply to hold certain empirical beliefs but to have a certain attitude concerning one's rightful place in a moral community.

II

Are there grounds for regarding the attitudes of the Uncle Tom, the Self-deprecator, and the Deferential Wife as morally objectionable? Are there moral arguments we could give them to show that they ought to have more self-respect? None of the more obvious replies is entirely satisfactory.

One might, in the first place, adduce utilitarian considerations. Typically the servile person will be less happy than he might be. Moreover, he may be less prone to make the best of his own socially useful abilities. He may become a nuisance to others by being overly dependent. He will, in any case, lose the special contentment that comes from standing up for one's rights. A submissive attitude encourages exploitation, and exploitation spreads misery in a variety of ways. These considerations provide a *prima facie* case against the attitudes of the Uncle Tom, the Deferential Wife, and the Self-deprecator, but they are hardly conclusive. Other utilities tend to counterbalance the ones just mentioned. When people refuse to press their rights, there are usually others who profit. There are undeniable pleasures in associating with those who are devoted, understanding, and grateful for whatever we see fit to give them—as our fondness for dogs attests. Even the servile person may find his attitude a source of happiness, as the case of the Deferential Wife illustrates. There may be comfort and security in thinking that the hard choices must be made by others, that what I would say has little to do with what ought to be done. Self-condemnation may bring relief from the pangs of guilt even if it is not deliberately used for that purpose. On balance, then, utilitarian considerations may turn out to favor servility as much as they oppose it.

For those who share my moral intuitions, there is another sort of reason for not trying to rest a case against servility on utilitarian considerations. Certain utilities seem irrelevant to the issue. The utilitarian must weigh them along with others, but to do so seems morally inappropriate. Suppose, for example, that the submissive attitudes of the Uncle Tom and the Deferential Wife result in positive utilities for those who dominate and exploit them. Do we need to tabulate *these* utilities before conceding that servility is objectionable? The Uncle Tom, it seems, is making an error, a moral error, quite apart from consideration of how much others in fact profit from his attitude. The Deferential Wife may be quite happy; but if her happiness turns out to be contingent on her distorted view of her own rights and worth as a person, then it carries little moral weight against the contention that she ought to change that view. Suppose I could cause a woman to find her happiness in denying all her rights and serving my every wish. No doubt I could do so only by nonrational manipulative techniques, which I ought not to use. But is this the only objection? My efforts would be wrong, it seems, not only because of the techniques they require but also because the resultant attitude is itself objectionable. When a person's happiness stems from a morally objectionable attitude, it ought to be discounted. That a sadist gets pleasure from seeing others suffer should not count even as a partial justification for his attitude. That a servile person derives pleasure from denying her moral status, for similar reasons, cannot make her attitude acceptable. These brief intuitive remarks are not intended as a refutation of utilitarianism, with all its many varieties; but they do suggest that it is well to look elsewhere for adequate grounds for rejecting the attitudes of the Uncle Tom, the Self-deprecator, and the Deferential Wife.

III

Why, then, is servility a moral defect? There is, I think, another sort of answer which is worth exploring. The first part of this answer must be an attempt to isolate the objectionable features of the servile person; later we can ask why these features are objectionable. As a step in this direction, let us examine again our three paradigm cases. The moral defect in each case, I suggest, is a failure to understand and acknowledge one's own moral rights. I assume, without argument here, that each person has moral rights. Some of these rights may be basic human rights; that is, rights for which a person needs only to be human to qualify. Other rights will be derivative and contingent upon his special commitments, institutional affiliations, etc. Most rights will be *prima facie* ones; some may be absolute. Most can be waived under appropriate conditions; perhaps some cannot. Many rights can be forfeited; but some, presumably, cannot. The servile person does not, strictly speaking, violate his own rights. At least in our paradigm cases he fails to acknowledge fully his own moral status because he does not fully understand what his rights are, how they can be waived, and when they can be forfeited.

The defect of the Uncle Tom, for example, is that he displays an attitude that denies his moral equality with whites. He does not realize, or apprehend in an effective way, that he has as much right to a decent wage and a share of political power as any comparable white. His gratitude is misplaced; he accepts benefits which are his by right as if they were gifts. The Self-deprecator is servile in a more complex way. He acts as if he has forfeited many important rights which in fact he has not. He does not understand, or fully realize in his own case, that certain rights to fair and decent treatment do not have to be earned. He sees his merits clearly enough, but he fails to see that what he can expect from others is not merely a function of his merits. The Deferential Wife *says* that she understands her rights vis-à-vis her husband, but what she fails to appreciate is that her consent to serve him is a valid waiver of her rights only under certain conditions. If her consent is coerced, say, by the lack of viable options for women in her society, then her consent is worth little. If socially fostered ignorance of her own talents and alternatives is responsible for her consent, then her consent should not count as a fully legitimate waiver of her right to equal consideration within the marriage. All the more, her consent to defer constantly to her husband is not a legitimate setting aside of her rights if it results from her mistaken belief that she has a moral duty to do so. (Recall: "The *proper* role for a woman is to serve her family.") If she believes that she has a *duty* to defer to her husband, then, whatever she may say, she cannot fully understand that she has a *right* not to defer to him. When she says that she freely gives up such a right, she is confused. Her confusion is rather like that of a person who has been persuaded by an unscrupulous lawyer that it is legally incumbent on him to refuse a jury trial but who nevertheless tells the judge that he understands that he has a right to a jury trial and freely waives it. He does not really understand what it is to have and freely give up the right if he thinks that it would be an offense for him to exercise it.

Insofar as servility results from moral ignorance or confusion, it need not be something for which a person is to blame. . . . Suppose, however, that our servile persons come to know their rights but do not substantially alter their behavior. Are they not still servile in an objectionable way?

The answer, I think, should depend upon why the deferential role is played. If the motive is a morally commendable one, or a desire to avert dire consequences to oneself, or even an ambition to set an oppressor up for a later fall, then I would not count the role player as servile. The Uncle Tom, for instance, is not servile in my sense if he shuffles and bows to keep the Klan from killing his children, to save his own skin, or even to buy time while he plans the revolution. Similarly, the Deferential Wife is not servile if she tolerates an abusive husband because he is so ill that further strain would kill him, because protesting would deprive her of her only means of survival, or because she is collecting atrocity stories for her book against marriage. If there is fault in these situations, it seems inappropriate to call it *servility*. The story is quite different, however, if a person continues in his deferential role just from laziness, timidity, or a desire for some minor advantage. He shows too little concern for his moral status as a person, one is tempted to say, if he is willing to deny it for a small profit or simply because it requires some effort and courage to affirm it openly. A black who plays the Uncle Tom merely to gain an advantage over other blacks is harming them, of course; but he is also displaying disregard for his own moral position as an equal among human beings. Similarly, a woman throws away her rights too lightly if she continues to play the subservient role because she is used to it or is too timid to risk a change. A Self-deprecator who readily accepts what he knows are violations of his rights may be indulging his peculiar need for punishment at the expense of denying something more valuable. In these cases, I suggest, we have a kind of servility independent of any ignorance or confusion about one's rights. The person who has it may or may not be blameworthy, depending on many factors; and the line between servile and nonservile role playing will often be hard to draw. Nevertheless, the objectionable feature is perhaps clear enough for present purposes: it is a willingness to disavow one's moral status, publicly and systematically, in the absence of any strong reason to do so.

IV

The objectionable feature of the servile person, as I have described him, is his tendency to disavow his own moral rights either because he misunderstands them or because he cares little for them. The question remains: why should anyone regard this as a moral defect? After all, the rights which he denies are his own. He may be unfortunate, foolish, or even distasteful; but why *morally* deficient? One sort of answer, quite different from those reviewed earlier, is suggested by some of Kant's remarks. Kant held that servility is contrary to a perfect nonjuridical duty to oneself.[1] To say that the duty is perfect is roughly to say that it is stringent, never overridden by other considerations (e.g., beneficence). To say that the duty is nonjuridical is to say that a person cannot legitimately be coerced to comply. Although Kant did not develop an explicit argument for this view, an argument can easily be constructed from materials which reflect the spirit, if not the letter, of his moral theory. The argument which I have in mind is prompted by Kant's contention that respect for persons, strictly speaking, is respect for moral law.[2]

---

[1]See Immanuel Kant, *The Doctrine of Virtue,* Part II of *The Metaphysics of Morals,* ed. by M. J. Gregor (New York: Harper & Row, 1964), pp. 99–103; Prussian Academy edition, vol. VI, pp. 434–37.

[2]Immanuel Kant, *Groundwork of the Metaphysics of Morals,* ed. by H. J. Paton (New York: Harper & Row, 1964), p. 69; Prussian Academy edition, vol. IV, p. 401; *The Critique of Practical Reason,* ed. by Lewis W. Beck (New York: Bobbs-Merrill, 1956), pp. 81, 84; Prussian Academy edition, vol. V, pp. 78, 81. My purpose here is not to interpret what Kant meant but to give a sense to his remark.

If taken as a claim about all sorts of respect, this seems quite implausible. If it means that we respect persons only for their moral character, their capacity for moral conduct, or their status as "authors" of the moral law, then it seems unduly moralistic. My strategy is to construe the remark as saying that at least one sort of respect for persons is respect for the rights which the moral law accords them. If one respects the moral law, then one must respect one's own moral rights; and this amounts to having a kind of self-respect incompatible with servility.

The premises for the Kantian argument, which are all admittedly vague, can be sketched as follows:

First, let us assume, as Kant did, that all human beings have equal basic human rights. Specific rights vary with different conditions, but all must be justified from a point of view under which all are equal. Not all rights need to be earned, and some cannot be forfeited. Many rights can be waived but only under certain conditions of knowledge and freedom. These conditions are complex and difficult to state; but they include something like the condition that a person's consent releases others from obligation only if it is autonomously given, and consent resulting from underestimation of one's moral status is not autonomously given. Rights can be objects of knowledge, but also of ignorance, misunderstanding, deception, and the like.

Second, let us assume that my account of servility is correct; or, if one prefers, we can take it as a definition. That is, in brief, a servile person is one who tends to deny or disavow his own moral rights because he does not understand them or has little concern for the status they give him.

Third, we need one formal premise concerning moral duty, namely, that each person ought, as far as possible, to respect the moral law. In less Kantian language, the point is that everyone should approximate, to the extent that he can, the ideal of a person who fully adopts the moral point of view. Roughly, this means not only that each person ought to do what is morally required and refrain from what is morally wrong but also that each person should treat all the provisions of morality as valuable—worth preserving and prizing as well as obeying. One must, so to speak, take up the spirit of morality as well as meet the letter of its requirements. To keep one's promises, avoid hurting others, and the like, is not sufficient; one should also take an attitude of respect towards the principles, ideals, and goals of morality. A respectful attitude towards a system of rights and duties consists of more than a disposition to conform to its definite rules of behavior; it also involves holding the system in esteem, being unwilling to ridicule it, and being reluctant to give up one's place in it. The essentially Kantian idea here is that morality, as a system of equal fundamental rights and duties, is worthy of respect, and hence a completely moral person would respect it in word and manner as well as in deed. And what a completely moral person would do, in Kant's view, is our duty to do so far as we can.

The assumptions here are, of course, strong ones, and I make no attempt to justify them. They are, I suspect, widely held though rarely articulated. In any case, my present purpose is not to evaluate them but to see how, if granted, they constitute a case against servility. The objection to the servile person, given our premises, is that he does not satisfy the basic requirement to respect morality. A person who fully respected a system of moral rights would be disposed to learn his proper place in it, to affirm it proudly, and not to tolerate abuses of it lightly. This is just the sort of disposition that the servile person lacks. If he does not understand the system, he is in no position to respect it adequately. This lack of respect may be no fault of his own, but it is still a way in which he falls short of a moral ideal. If, on the other hand, the servile person knowingly disavows his moral rights by pretending to approve of violations of them, then, barring special explanations, he shows an indifference to whether the provisions of morality are honored and publicly acknowledged. This avoidable display of indifference, by our Kantian premises, is contrary to the duty to respect morality. The disrespect in this second case is somewhat like the disrespect a religious believer might show towards his religion if, to avoid embarrassment, he laughed congenially while nonbelievers were mocking the beliefs which he secretly held. In any case, the servile person, as such, does not express disrespect for the system of moral rights in the obvious way by violating the rights of others. His lack of respect is more subtly manifested by his acting before others as if he did not know or care about his position of equality under that system.

The central idea here may be illustrated by an analogy. Imagine a club, say, an old German dueling fraternity. By the rules of the club, each member has certain rights and responsibilities. These are the same for each member regardless of what titles he may hold outside the club. Each has, for example, a right to be heard at meetings, a right not to be shouted down by the others. Some rights cannot be forfeited: for example, each may vote regardless of whether he has paid his dues and satisfied other rules. Some rights cannot be waived: for example, the right to be defended when attacked by several members of the rival fraternity. The members show respect for each other by respecting the status which the rules confer on each member. Now one new member is careful always to allow the others to speak at meetings; but when they shout him down, he does nothing. He just shrugs as if to say, "Who am I to complain?" When he fails to stand up in defense of a fellow member, he feels ashamed and refuses to vote. He does not deserve to vote, he says. As the only commoner among illustrious barons, he feels that it is his place to serve them and defer to their decisions. When attackers from the rival fraternity come at him with swords drawn, he tells his companions to run and save themselves. When they defend him, he expresses immense gratitude—as if they had done him a gratuitous favor. Now one might argue that our new member fails to show respect for the fraternity and its rules. He does not actually violate any of the rules by refusing to vote, asking others not to defend him, and deferring to the barons, but he symbolically disavows the equal status which the rules confer on him. If he ought to have respect for the fraternity, he ought to change his attitude. Our servile person, then, is like the new member of the dueling fraternity in having insufficient respect for a system of rules and ideals. The difference is that everyone ought to respect morality whereas there is no comparable moral requirement to respect the fraternity.

The conclusion here is, of course, a limited one. Self-sacrifice is not always a sign of servility. It is not a duty always to press one's rights. Whether a given act is evidence of servility will depend not only on the attitude of the agent but also on the specific nature of his moral rights, a matter not considered here. Moreover, the extent to which a person is responsible, or blameworthy, for his defect remains an open question. Nevertheless, the conclusion should not be minimized. In order to avoid servility, a person who gives up his rights must do so with a full appreciation for what they are. A woman, for example, may devote herself to her husband if she is uncoerced, knows what she is doing, and does not pretend that she has no decent alternative. A self-contemptuous person may decide not to press various unforfeited rights but only if he does not take the attitude that he is too rotten to deserve them. A black may demand less than is due to him provided he is prepared to acknowledge that no one has a right to expect this of him. Sacrifices of this sort, I suspect, are extremely rare. Most people, if they fully acknowledged their rights, would not autonomously refuse to press them.

An even stronger conclusion would emerge if we could assume that some basic rights cannot be waived. . . .

Even if there are no specific rights which cannot be waived, there might be at least one formal right of this sort. This is the right to some minimum degree of respect from others. No matter how willing a person is to submit to humiliation by others, they ought to show him some respect as a person. By analogy with self-respect, as presented here, this respect owed by others would consist of a willingness to acknowledge fully, in word as well as action, the person's basically equal moral status as defined by his other rights. To the extent that a person gives even tacit consent to humiliations incompatible with this respect, he will be acting as if he waives a right which he cannot in fact give up. To do this, barring special explanations, would mark one as servile.

Kant suggests that duties to oneself are a precondition of duties to others. On our account of servility, there is at least one sense in which this is so. Insofar as the servile person is ignorant of his own rights, he is not in an adequate position to appreciate the rights of others. Misunderstanding the moral basis for his equal status with others, he is necessarily liable to underestimate the rights of those with whom he classifies himself. On the other hand, if he plays the servile role knowingly, then, barring special explanation, he displays a lack of concern to see the principles of morality acknowledged and respected and thus the absence of one motive which can move a moral person to respect the rights of others. In either case, the servile person's lack of self-respect necessarily puts him in a less than ideal position to respect others. Failure to fulfill one's duty to oneself, then, renders a person liable to violate duties to others. This, however, is a consequence of our argument against servility, not a presupposition of it.

For Further Reflection

1. What exactly is servility and why is it bad? Note that some religions seem to place great weight on deference to God and one's fellows. See, for example, the Sermon on the Mount (chapter 7). Is servility the same as humility or are they different?

2. If I really am a person of less talent than others, should I not defer to the more talented in learning or living? Is education a kind of servility or is it really different?

3. Hill makes a great deal of equal human rights, and claims that he is following Kant, but Kant wrote that a person could forfeit his rights (e.g., the right to life by murdering someone) and one's worth (e.g., my moral worth by lying or breaking a moral principle). Is this consistent with Hill's thesis? Could there be some nonforfeitable rights (or basic worth)? Explain your answer.

4. Hill claims that a utilitarian cannot account for the evil of servility, since a utilitarian would have to do a cost-benefit analysis to determine whether it was justified or not. Is this a valid point? Does the idea of duties to self demonstrate the superiority of deontological ethics to uilitarian?

Further Readings for Chapter 10

Hill, Thomas E. *Dignity and Practical Reason,* Ithaca, N.Y.: Cornell University Press, 1992.

Kant, Immanuel. *Lectures on Ethics,* trans. Louis Infield. London: Methuen, 1930.

Kupperman, Joseph. *Character.* New York: Oxford University Press, 1991.

Nagel, Thomas. *Mortal Questions.* New York: Cambridge University Press, 1979.

Sartre, Jean-Paul. *Being and Nothingness,* trans. Hazel Barnes. New York: Philosophical Library, 1956.

Williams, Bernard. *Moral Luck.* New York: Cambridge University Press, 1981.

Part IV

Applied Ethics

What is the use of studying philosophy if all that it does for you is enable you to talk with some plausibility about some abstruse questions of logic, etc., and if it does not improve your thinking about the important questions of everyday life?

—Ludwig Wittgenstein

In this part of our book we turn to five sets of moral problems facing students every day: issues of (1) sex, love, and marriage; (2) abortion; (3) substance use and abuse; (4) animals; and (5) the environment. Can philosophical analysis illuminate these issues, supplying appropriate guidance for living? We attempt to answer that question in the affirmative, even as we offer opposing points of view.

I begin with matters of sex, love, and marriage. Are these concepts conceptually linked, at least from a moral perspective, so that sex should always involve love and find its proper place only in monogamous marriage? Or are these concepts conceptually separate, so that sexual relations may have a purpose of their own, which may or may not involve marriage? People experience sexual feeling differently and in different degrees at different times in their lives. For some, sexual urges are raging torrents that threaten to overwhelm every other concern. For others sex is a mild fantasy which provides moments of pleasure but is no big deal. For St. Augustine and the Roman Catholic Church the only justification of sex is procreation. Freud thought that sexual activity was aimed at release of tension, a bit like scratching an itch. For others it is the ecstatic consummation of the love they feel for the beloved, the two becoming one flesh. Nietzsche held that it was a manifestation of the will to power: "Goest thou to a woman? Forget not thy whip!" Others use sex to attain power or at least favors, as happens when a student is induced to go to bed with a teacher or a secretary with her boss. Still others use sex as a drug, to relax, to go to sleep, to forget about one's problems and the like.

Even though it is admitted that sex serves many different functions for many different people, philosophers argue about which functions are best or more conducive to the good life. Conservatives (represented by Punzo in our readings) hold that sex should be closely linked with love, as without love it tends to degenerate into animal lust. Liberals (represented by the Belliotti reading) hold that so long as no one is exploited or deceived in the act, and so long as there is respect for the other, sex is permissible. It is as legitimate as any other contractual relationship which people may enter or exit freely. A more radical view, such as that of the Marquis de Sade, would permit and encourage any sex act that gave one pleasure, be it sado-masochistic, with animals or children, with fetishes (e.g., masturbation with the use of shoes or undergarments) or with the dead (necrophilia). To those who claimed that he was perverted, de Sade replied that everything we do is natural, so that if nature had not intended us to explore innovative sex, she would never have given us the ability to imagine such acts, let alone the desire to try them.

We begin our readings with a description from John Barth's novel *The End of the Road* of the all-pervasiveness of sex in our modern culture. We then turn to Kant's classic theory that sex is best seen as a kind of reciprocal ownership of property, which ought to occur in the context of altruism, a good marriage. Then we turn to the most conservative view of sex, the Roman Catholic view that sex should only be used in order to procreate. Raymond Belliotti sets forth the liberal view of sex as a contract between consenting adults and Vincent Punzo argues for a moderate conservative position on the basis of existential integrity.

We then turn to articles involving marriage. John McMurtry criticizes monogamy precisely on the grounds laid out by Kant—viewing spouses as property, a kind of chattel, which is endorsed by the state. Michael Bayles argues that while marriage as we know it can be reformed, it is basically a morally salient institution, promoting intimate personal relations and providing the context for the rearing of children. Bonnie Steinbock examines what is wrong with adultery. Finally, Hugh LaFollette argues that society, which requires licenses for every other important activity, should require licenses to procreate.

CHAPTER 11

Sex, Love, and Marriage

Pansexuality

JOHN BARTH

John Barth, novelist and short story writer, has written several acclaimed novels, including *The Floating Opera, Giles Goat Boy,* and *The End of the Road,* from which this short selection is taken. Barth gives a description of *pansexuality,* the Freudian thesis, which, Barth suggests, dominates our culture. The passage speaks for itself.

The dance of sex: If one had no other reason for choosing to subscribe to Freud, what could be more charming than to believe that the whole vaudeville of the world, the entire dizzy circus of history, is but a fancy mating dance? That dictators burn Jews and businessmen vote Republican, that helmsmen steer ships and ladies play bridge, that girls study grammar and boys engineering all at the behest of the Absolute Genital? When the synthesizing mood is upon one, what is more soothing than to assert that this one simple yen of humankind, poor little coitus, alone gives rise to cities and monasteries, paragraphs and poems, foot races and battle tactics, metaphysics and hydroponics, trade unions and universities? Who would not delight in telling some extragalactic tourist, "On our planet, sir, males and females copulate. Moreover, they enjoy copulating. But for various reasons they cannot do this whenever, wherever, and with whomever they choose. Hence all this running around that you observe. Hence the world"? A therapeutic notion!

From John Barth, *The End of the Road* (1957).

On the Place of Sex in Human Existence

IMMANUEL KANT

A biographical sketch of Immanuel Kant (1724–1804) appears in chapter 5. Kant held the view that the main purpose of sex was procreation. "Nature pursues its great purpose, and all refinements that join together, though they may appear to stand as far from that as they will, are only trimmings and borrow their charm ultimately from that very source." He argues that nature's procreative purpose is best served in a monogamous marriage in which the spouses are faithful to each other. But from the agent's point of view, the object of sex is sexual satisfaction. But this creates a moral problem, for Kant holds that it is immoral to use others as simply means to our purposes. An act is moral if and only if it includes treating the other person as an end in him- or herself. So the trick is to combine this personal sexual satisfaction with treating the other with dignity. In the following passage Kant elaborates on this how this may be done.

Human love is good-will, affection, promoting the happiness of others and finding joy in their happiness. But it is clear that, when a person loves another purely from sexual desire, none of these factors enter into the love. Far from there being any concern for the happiness of the loved one, the lover, in order to satisfy his desire and quiet his appetite, may even plunge the loved one into the depths of misery. Sexual love makes of the loved person an Object of appetite; as soon as that appetite has been satisfied, the person is cast aside as one casts away a lemon which has been sucked dry. Sexual love can, of course, be combined with concern for the other's well-being and so carry with it the characteristics of this love, but taken by itself and for itself, it is nothing more than

From Immanuel Kant's *Lectures on Ethics,* translated by Louis Infield (London: Methuen, 1930).

appetite. Taken by itself it is a degradation of human nature; for as soon as a person becomes an Object of appetite for another, all motives of moral relationship cease to function, because as an Object of appetite for another a person becomes a thing and can be treated and used as such by everyone. This is the only case in which a human being is designed by nature as the Object of another's enjoyment. Sexual desire is at the root of it; and that is why we are ashamed of it, and why all strict moralists, and those who had pretensions to be regarded as saints, sought to suppress and extirpate it. . . .

Because sexuality is not an inclination which one human being has for another as such, but is an inclination for the sex of another, it is a principle of the degradation of human nature, in that it gives rise to the preference of one sex to the other, and to the dishonoring of that sex through the satisfaction of desires. The desire which a man has for a woman is not directed towards her because she is a human being, but because she is a woman; that she is a human being is of no concern to the man; only her sex is the object of his desires. Human nature is thus subordinated. Hence it comes about that all men and women do their best to make not their human nature but their sex more alluring and direct their activities and lusts entirely towards sex. Human nature is thereby sacrificed to sex. If then a man wishes to satisfy his desire, and a woman hers, they stimulate each other's desire; their inclinations meet, but their object is not human nature but sex, and each of them dishonors the human nature of the other. They make of humanity an instrument for the satisfaction of their lusts and inclinations, and dishonor it by placing it on a level with animal nature. Sexuality, therefore, exposes mankind to the danger of equality with the beasts. But as man has this desire from nature the question arises how far he can properly make use of it without injury to his manhood. . . .

The sole condition on which we are free to make use of our sexual desire depends upon the right to dispose over the person as a whole—over the welfare and happiness and generally over all the circumstances of that person. If I have the right over the whole person, I have also right over the part, and so I have the right to use that person's sexual organs for the satisfaction of sexual desire. But how am I to obtain these rights over the whole person? Only by giving that person the same rights over the whole of myself. This happens only in marriage. Matrimony is an agreement between two persons by which they grant each other equal reciprocal rights, each of them undertaking to surrender the whole of their person to the other with a complete right of disposal over it. We can now apprehend by reason how a *sexual transaction* is possible without degrading humanity and breaking the moral laws. Matrimony is the only condition in which use can be made of one's sexuality. If one devotes one's person to another, one devotes not only sex but the whole person; the two cannot be separated. If, then, one yields one's person, body and soul, for good and ill and in every respect, so that the other has complete rights over it, and if the other does not similarly yield himself in return and does not extend in return the same rights and privileges, the arrangement is one-sided. But if I yield myself completely to another and obtain the person of the other in return, I win myself back; I have given myself up as the property of another, but in turn I take that other as my property, and so win myself back again in winning the person whose property I have become. In this way the two persons become a unity of will. Whatever good or ill, joy or sorrow befall either of them, the other will share in it. Thus sexuality leads to a union of human beings, and in that union alone its exercise is permissible.

For Further Reflection

1. Evaluate Kant's argument for marriage as the proper locus of sex. The Hebrew Bible comments on God's creating man and woman: "Therefore a man leaves his father and his mother and cleaves to his wife and they become one flesh. And the man and his wife were both naked and were not ashamed" (Genesis 2:24–25). Do you see this biblical notion of one common flesh in the background of Kant's thought? Does this idea of oneness make sense?

2. Review Kant's moral principle that we must never use persons simply as means to our ends but must treat them as ends in themselves. What are the implications of this principle for sexual relations?

3. Is Kant's metaphor of reciprocal ownership of the other's body a suitable metaphor? Or is it in opposition to his ideal of dignity and personal autonomy?

The Vatican Declaration on Sexual Ethics

Approved by the late Pope Paul VI, this document was issued by the Sacred Congregation for the Doctrine of the Faith and released January 15, 1976. It declares the Roman Catholic doctrines on sexuality. Appealing both to natural reason and revelation, it argues that there is an eternal and universal moral law that applies to all people everywhere. It is embedded in the hearts of all human beings, though some people have more knowledge of it. The principles of this moral law can be known through reason, as we reflect on human nature, and revelation, the Church's teaching. The document argues that sexual intercourse is appropriate only within marriage, so that premarital sex, homosexual behavior, and masturbation are immoral.

INTRODUCTION

Importance of Sexuality

1. The human person, according to the scientific disciplines of our day, is so deeply influenced by his sexuality that this latter must be regarded as one of the basic factors shaping human life. The person's sex is the source of the biological, psychological and spiritual characteristics which make the person male or female, and thus are extremely important and influential in the maturation and socialization of the individual. It is easy to understand, therefore, why matters pertaining to sex are frequently and openly discussed in books, periodicals, newspapers and other communications media.

Meanwhile, moral corruption is on the increase. One of the most serious signs of this is the boundless exaltation of sex. In addition, with the help of the mass media and the various forms of enter-tainment, sex has even invaded the field of education and infected the public mind.

In this situation, some educators, teachers and moralists have been able to contribute to a better understanding and vital integra-tion of the special values and qualities proper to each sex. Others, however, have defended views and ways of acting which are in conflict with the true moral requirements of man, and have even opened the door to a licentious hedonism.

The result is that, within a few years' time, teachings, moral norms and habits of life hitherto faithfully preserved have been called into doubt, even by Christians. Many today are asking what they are to regard as true when so many current views are at odds with what they learned from the Church.

Occasion for This Declaration

2. In the face of this intellectual confusion and moral corruption the Church cannot stand by and do nothing. The issue here is too important in the life both of the individual and of contemporary society.

Bishops see each day the ever increasing difficulties of the faith-ful in acquiring sound moral teaching, especially in sexual matters, and of pastors in effectively explaining that teaching. The bishops know it is their pastoral duty to come to the aid of the faithful in such a serious matter. Indeed, some outstanding documents have been published on the subject by some bishops and some episco-pal conferences. But, since erroneous views and the deviations they produce continue to be broadcast everywhere, the Sacred Congre-gation for the Doctrine of the Faith in accordance with its role in the universal Church and by mandate of the Supreme Pontiff, has thought it necessary to issue this Declaration.

I GENERAL CONSIDERATIONS

The Sources of Moral Knowledge

3. The men of our day are increasingly persuaded that their dig-nity and calling as human beings requires them to use their minds to discover the values and powers inherent in their nature, to develop these without ceasing and to translate them into action, so that they may make daily greater progress.

When it comes to judgments on moral matters, however, man may not proceed simply as he thinks fit. "Deep within, man detects the law of conscience—a law which is not self-imposed but which holds him to obedience. . . . For man has in his heart a law written by God. To obey it is the very dignity of man; according to it he will be judged."

To us Christians, moreover, God has revealed his plan of salvation and has given us Christ, the Savior and sanctifier, as the supreme and immutable norm of life through his teaching and example. Christ himself has said: "I am the light of the world. No follower of mine shall ever walk in darkness; no, he shall possess the light of life."

The authentic dignity of man cannot be promoted, therefore, except through adherence to the order which is essential to his nature. There is no denying, of course, that in the history of civilization many of the concrete conditions and relationships of human life have changed and will change again in the future but every moral evolution and every manner of life must respect the limits set by the immutable principles which are grounded in the constitutive elements and essential relations proper to the human person. These elements and relations are not subject to historical contingency.

The basic principles in question can be grasped by man's reason. They are contained in "the divine law—eternal, objective and universal—whereby God orders, directs and governs the entire universe and all the ways of the human community by a plan conceived in wisdom and love. God has made man a participant in this law, with the result that, under the gentle disposition of divine Providence, he can come to perceive ever more fully the truth that is unchanging." This divine law is something we can know.

The Principles of Morality Are Perennial

4. Wrongly, therefore, do many today deny that either human nature or revealed law furnishes any absolute and changeless norm for particular actions except the general law of love and respect for human dignity. To justify this position, they argue that both the so-called norms of the natural law and the precepts of Sacred Scripture are simply products of a particular human culture and its expressions at a certain point in history.

But divine revelation and, in its own order, natural human wisdom show us genuine exigencies of human nature and, as a direct and necessary consequence, immutable laws which are grounded in the constitutive elements of human nature and show themselves the same in all rational beings.

Furthermore, the Church was established by Christ to be "the pillar and bulwark of truth." With the help of the Holy Spirit she keeps a sleepless watch over the truths of morality and transmits them without falsification. She provides the authentic interpretation not only of the revealed positive law but also of "those principles of the moral order which have their origin in human nature itself" and which relate to man's full development and sanctification. Throughout her history the Church has constantly maintained that certain precepts of the natural law bind immutably and without qualification, and that the violation of them contradicts the spirit and teaching of the Gospel.

The Fundamental Principles of Sexual Morality

5. Since sexual morality has to do with values which are basic to human and Christian life, the general doctrine we have been presenting applies to it. In this area there are principles and norms which the Church has always unhesitatingly transmitted as part of her teaching, however opposed they might be to the mentality and ways of the world. These principles and norms have their origin, not in a particular culture, but in knowledge of the divine law and human nature. Consequently, it is impossible for them to lose their binding force or to be called into doubt on the grounds of cultural change.

These principles guided Vatican Council II when it provided advice and directives for the establishment of the kind of social life in which the equal dignity of man and woman will be respected, even while the differences between them also are preserved.

In speaking of the sexual nature of the human being and of the human generative powers, the Council observes that these are "remarkably superior to those found in lower grades of life." Then it deals in detail with the principles and norms which apply to human sexuality in the married state and are based on the finality of the function proper to marriage.

In this context the Council asserts that the moral goodness of the actions proper to married life, when ordered as man's true dignity requires, "does not depend only on a sincere intention and the evaluating of motives, but must be judged by objective standards. These are drawn from the nature of the human person and of his acts, and have regard for the whole meaning of mutual self-giving and human procreation in the context of true love."

These last words are a brief summation of the Council's teaching (previously set forth at length in the same document) on the finality of the sexual act and on the chief norm governing its morality. It is respect for this finality which guarantees the moral goodness of the act.

The same principle, which the Church derives from divine revelation and from her authentic interpretation of the natural law, is also the source of her traditional teaching that the exercise of the sexual function has its true meaning and is morally good only in legitimate marriage.

Limits of This Declaration

6. It is not the intention of this declaration to treat all abuses of the sexual powers nor to deal with all that is involved in the practice of chastity but rather to recall the Church's norms on certain specific points, since there is a crying need of opposing certain serious errors and deviant forms of behavior.

II SPECIFIC APPLICATIONS

Premarital Relations

7. Many individuals at the present time are claiming the right to sexual union before marriage, at least when there is a firm intention of marrying and when a love which both partners think of as already conjugal demands this further step which seems to them connatural. They consider this further step justified especially when external circumstances prevent the formal entry into marriage or when intimate union seems necessary if love is to be kept alive.

This view is opposed to the Christian teaching that any human genital act whatsoever may be placed only within the framework of marriage. For, however firm the intention of those who pledge themselves to each other in such premature unions, these unions cannot guarantee the sincerity and fidelity of the relationship between man and woman, and, above all, cannot protect the relationship against the changeableness of desire and determination.

Yet, Christ the Lord willed that the union be a stable one and he restored it to its original condition as founded in the difference between the sexes. "Have you not read that at the beginning the Creator made them male and female and declared, 'For this reason a man shall leave his father and mother and cling to his wife and the two shall become as one'? Thus they are no longer two but one flesh. Therefore, let no man separate what God has joined."

St. Paul is even more explicit when he teaches that if unmarried people or widows cannot be continent, they have no alternative but to enter into a stable marital union: "It is better to marry than to be on fire." For, through marriage the love of the spouses is taken up into the irrevocable love of Christ for his Church, whereas unchaste bodily union defiles the temple of the Holy Spirit which the Christian has become. Fleshly union is illicit, therefore, unless a permanent community of life has been established between man and woman.

Such has always been the Church's understanding of and teaching on the exercise of the sexual function. She finds, moreover, that natural human wisdom and the lessons of history are in profound agreement with her.

Experience teaches that if sexual union is truly to satisfy the requirements of its own finality and of human dignity, love must be safeguarded by the stability marriage gives. These requirements necessitate a contract which is sanctioned and protected by society; the contract gives rise to a new state of life and is of exceptional importance for the exclusive union of man and woman as well as for the good of their family and the whole of human society. Premarital relations, on the other hand, most often exclude any prospect of children. Such love claims in vain to be conjugal since it cannot, as it certainly should, grow into a maternal and paternal love; or, if the pair do become parents, it will be to the detriment of the children, who are deprived of a stable environment in which they can grow up in a proper fashion and find the way and means of entering into the larger society of men.

Therefore, the consent of those entering into marriage must be externally manifested, and this in such a way as to render it binding in the eyes of society. The faithful, for their part, must follow the laws of the Church in declaring their marital consent; it is this consent that makes their marriage a sacrament of Christ.

Homosexuality

8. Contrary to the perennial teaching of the Church and the moral sense of the Christian people, some individuals today have, on psychological grounds, begun to judge indulgently or even simply to excuse homosexual relations for certain people.

They make a distinction which has indeed some foundation: between homosexuals whose bent derives from improper education or a failure of sexual maturation or habit or bad example or some similar cause and is only temporary or at least is not incurable; and homosexuals who are permanently such because of some innate drive or a pathological condition which is considered incurable.

The propensity of those in the latter class is—it is argued—so natural that it should be regarded as justifying homosexual relations within a sincere and loving communion of life which is comparable to marriage inasmuch as those involved in it deem it impossible for them to live a solitary life.

Objective Evil of Such Acts

As far as pastoral care is concerned, such homosexuals are certainly to be treated with understanding and encouraged to hope that they can some day overcome their difficulties and their inability to fit into society in a normal fashion. Prudence, too, must be exercised in judging their guilt. However, no pastoral approach may be taken which would consider these individuals morally justified on the grounds that such acts are in accordance with their nature. For, according to the objective moral order, homosexual relations are acts deprived of the essential ordination they ought to have.

In Sacred Scripture such acts are condemned as serious deviations and are even considered to be the lamentable effect of rejecting God. This judgment on the part of the divinely inspired Scriptures does not justify us in saying that all who suffer from this anomaly are guilty of personal sin but it does show that homosexual acts are disordered by their very nature and can never be approved.

Masturbation

9. Frequently today we find doubt or open rejection of the traditional Catholic teaching that masturbation is a serious moral disorder. Psychology and sociology (it is claimed) show that masturbation, especially in adolescents, is a normal phase in the process of sexual maturation and is, therefore, not gravely sinful unless the individual deliberately cultivates a solitary pleasure that is turned in upon itself ("ipsation"). In this last case, the act would be radically opposed to that loving communion between persons of different sexes which (according to some) is the principal goal to be sought in the use of the sexual powers.

This opinion is contrary to the teaching and pastoral practice of the Catholic Church. Whatever be the validity of certain arguments of a biological and philosophical kind which theologians sometimes use, both the magisterium of the Church (following a constant tradition) and the moral sense of the faithful have unhesitatingly asserted that masturbation is an intrinsically and seriously disordered act. The chief reason for this stand is that, whatever the motive, the deliberate use of the sexual faculty outside of normal conjugal relations essentially contradicts its finality. In such an act there is lacking the sexual relationship which the moral order requires, the kind of relationship in which "the whole meaning of mutual self-giving and human procreation" is made concretely real "in the context of true love." Only within such a relationship may the sexual powers be deliberately exercised.

Even if it cannot be established that Sacred Scripture condemns this sin under a specific name, the Church's tradition rightly understands it to be condemned in the New Testament when the latter speaks of "uncleanness" or "unchasteness" or the other vices contrary to chastity and continence.

Sociological research can show the relative frequency of this disorder according to places, types of people and various circumstances which may be taken into account. It thus provides an array of facts. But facts provide no norm for judging the morality of human acts. The frequency of the act here in question is connected with innate human weakness deriving from original sin, but also with the loss of the sense of God, with the moral corruption fostered by the commercialization of vice, with the unbridled license to be found in so many books and forms of public entertainment and with the forgetfulness of modesty, which is the safeguard of chastity.

In dealing with masturbation, modern psychology provides a number of valid and useful insights which enable us to judge more equitably of moral responsibility. They can also help us understand how adolescent immaturity (sometimes prolonged beyond the adolescent years) or a lack of psychological balance or habits can affect behavior, since they may make an action less deliberate and not always a subjectively serious sin. But the lack of serious responsibility should not be generally presumed; if it is, there is simply a failure to recognize man's ability to act in a moral way.

In the pastoral ministry, in order to reach a balanced judgment in individual cases account must be taken of the overall habitual manner in which the person acts, not only in regard to charity and justice, but also in regard to the care with which he observes the precept of chastity in particular. Special heed must be paid to whether he uses the necessary natural and supernatural helps which Christian asceticism recommends, in the light of long experience, for mastering the passions and attaining virtue. . . .

For Further Reflection

1. Examine the statements in this document on natural law ("the value and powers inherent in [our] nature"). Do they constitute a cogent argument in favor of a universal morality on sexual concerns? Or is the essential position of this paper really one of authority: the Church, which derives authority from God, says so, so trust us?

2. What arguments could be mounted against the reasoning in this document? Do you agree that premarital sex, homosexual behavior, and masturbation are immoral? Why or why not?

Sexual Intercourse Between Consenting Adults Is Always Permissible

RAYMOND ANGELO BELLIOTTI

Raymond Belliotti is professor of philosophy at the State University of New York at Fredonia and is the author of several works in moral philosophy.

Belliotti argues that from a secular point of view, sexual interaction has a contractual basis, so that the act is morally wrong if and only if it involves (1) deception, (2) promise-breaking, or (3) exploitation. Developing a Kantian notion of personhood, he argues that so long as both parties are treating each other with respect, sexual relations are permissible. He realizes that religious people will reject this argument, but argues that religious views should not be imposed on nonreligious people. Belliotti attempts to draw the implications of his theory: rape and bestiality are always wrong, but incest could be moral under certain circumstances. Necrophilia is usually wrong, but need not always be. Promiscuity and adultery may be unwise but are only immoral if they violate one of the three conditions mentioned above.

I shall advance and defend what can be labeled a secular analysis of sexual ethics. As a secular analysis it shall make no appeal to religious considerations; it shall, in fact, consider religious factors irrelevant to the analysis. In doing so it should be obvious that the account will seem unsatisfactory to fervent religious believers.

Reprinted from Raymond Angelo Belliotti, "A Philosophical Analysis of Sexual Ethics" (*Journal of Social Philosophy,* vol. X.3, September 1979) by permission.

I

I begin with what I take to be a fundamental ethical maxim: it is morally wrong for someone to treat another merely as a means to his own ends. Immanuel Kant first formulated the maxim in this way,[1] but I think it can be considered uncontroversially true by most, if not all, moral thinkers. We often speak disparagingly of a person who "uses" or "exploits" another. What do we mean by this? It seems that we are suggesting that the former is morally culpable because he has treated the latter in a way that is morally wrong for one human to treat another. The culpable individual has "objectified" his victim; he has treated the other as an object to be manipulated and used, much as we might utilize a tool. One of the worst things that one person can do to another is to recognize the other as something less than human or as something less than the other really is: to recognize the other, not as an end in himself, but rather as an object to be used merely as a means to the user's ends. If we believe, and I think we do, that each person has an intrinsic worth and value which demands that we treat all others as subjects of experience and as being as fully human as ourselves, then we are following the general pattern of Kant's ethical maxim.

Notice that the maxim does not state that we cannot treat others as a means to our ends. It only states that we cannot *merely* treat the other in this way. We often need others to fulfill our goals, but immorality occurs only if we treat them merely as a means to these goals and not as an equal subject of experience.

So in all our human interactions we have a moral obligation to treat others as more than just means to our ends. This obligation becomes even more important when considering sexual interactions since very important feelings, desires, and drives are involved.

The second stage of the argument concerns the nature of sexual interactions. I contend that the nature of these interactions is contractual and involves the important notion of reciprocity. When two people voluntarily consent to interact sexually they create obligations to each other based on their needs and expectations. Every

---

[1] Immanuel Kant, *Foundations of the Metaphysics of Morals,* L. W. Beck, trans. (Indianapolis, Indiana: Library of Liberal Arts Press), p. 87.

sexual encounter has as its base the needs, desires, and drives of the individuals involved. That we choose to interact sexually is an acknowledgement that none of us is totally self-sufficient. We interact with others in order to fulfill certain desires which we cannot fulfill by ourselves. This suggests that the basis of the sexual encounter is contractual; i.e., it is a voluntary agreement on the part of both parties to satisfy the expectations of the other.

Some might recoil at the coldness of such an analysis. Is the sexual encounter as business-like a contract as the relationship between two corporations or the agreements one makes with his insurance agent? Of course it is not. Very important feelings of intimacy are involved which make the consenting parties emotionally vulnerable. But all this shows is that the sexual contract may well be the most important agreement that one makes from an emotional standpoint; it does not show that the interaction itself is not contractual. The contractual basis of the sexual interaction involves the notion of a voluntary agreement founded on the expectations of fulfillment of reciprocal needs.

The final stage of the argument consists of two acknowledgements: (1) That voluntary contracts are such that the parties are under a moral obligation, other things being equal, to fulfill that which they agreed upon, and (2) that promise-breaking and deception are, other things equal, immoral actions. The acknowledgement of the second makes the recognition of the first redundant, since the non-fulfillment of one's contractual duties is a species of promise-breaking. Ordinarily we feel that promise-breaking and deception are paradigm cases of immoral actions, since they involve violations of moral duties, and often, explicit or implicit lying. If it is true that sexual interactions entail contractual relationships then any violation of that which one has voluntarily consented to perform is morally wrong, since it involves promise-breaking and the non-fulfillment of the moral duty to honor one's voluntary agreements.

It is clear, then, that both parties must perform that which they voluntarily contracted to do for the other, unless the other agrees to the non-performance of the originally agreed upon action. Although sexual contracts are not as formal or explicit as corporation agreements, the rule of thumb should be the concept of reasonable expectation. If a woman smiles at me and agrees to have a drink I cannot reasonably assume, at least at this point, that she has agreed to spend the weekend with me. On the other hand if she did agree to share a room and bed with me for the weekend I could reasonably assume that she had agreed to have sexual intercourse with me. Although all examples are not clearcut, in general, the notion of reasonable expectation should guide us here. If there is any doubt concerning whether or not someone has agreed to perform a certain sexual act with another, I would suggest that the doubting party simply ask the other and make the contract more explicit. In lieu of this, prudence dictates that we be cautious in assuming what the other has offered, and when in doubt assume nothing until a more explicit overture has been made.

The conclusion of the argument is that sex is immoral if and only if it involves deception, promise-breaking, and/or the treatment of the other merely as a means to one's own ends.

II

The results of this analysis can now be applied to various sexual activities.

(1) *Rape* is intrinsically immoral because it involves the involuntary participation of one of the parties. Since the basis of the sexual encounter is contractual it should be clear that any coercion or force renders the interaction immoral; contracts are not validly consummated if one of the parties is compelled to agree by force or fraud. An interesting question concerns whether it is possible for a husband to rape his wife. I tend to think that this is possible. Some contend that the marriage contract allows both parties unrestricted sexual access to the other, and that, therefore, rape cannot occur in a marital situation. Others define rape as a sexual interaction which occurs when one individual forcibly uses another and the parties are not married to each other. But I think of rape as any case of forcibly using another in a sexual encounter without the other's consent. Under this definition it would be possible for a man to rape his wife, and in doing so commit an immoral act.

(2) *Bestiality* is intrinsically immoral because it too involves the involuntary participation of one of the parties. No non-human animal is capable of entering into a valid sexual contract with a human; as such all cases of bestiality can be considered instances of animal rape. A critic might argue that bestiality is only a form of sex

with an object since only a non-human animal is involved. Kant, himself, felt that animals could be used merely as a means to the ends of humans.[2] But this is mistaken from a moral point of view. Animals, unlike objects, have interests, desires, and are capable of experiencing pleasure and pain; i.e., they are sentient beings. As sentient beings their interests ought to be taken into account. As it seems clear that the interests of non-human animals are not advanced by being used as sexual objects by humans, it also seems clear that to do so cannot be morally justified. The differences between mere objects, which can be legitimately used merely as means to human ends, and non-human animals, who are sentient beings, are obvious. To use or totally objectify the latter is morally wrong; although probably less wrong than the use or objectification of other human beings.[3]

(3) *Necrophilia* is immoral since it also involves the involuntary participation of one of the parties. The corpse cannot voluntarily enter into a contract with a living human; hence cases of necrophilia can be considered instances of the rape of dead humans. Now it may seem that corpses *are* mere objects; certainly they cannot feel pleasure and pain. But are they mere objects in the sense that rocks, stones, and desks are objects? The corpse was once a sentient being and it may still be the case that even as a corpse it has interests. This may seem absurd at first glance. But we really acknowledge this very fact by honoring death bed promises made to the dying, by taking care when handling and displaying the bodies of the dead, and by being careful not to defame maliciously the reputations of dead people. Don't we feel that there is a difference between being buried with dignity and being hung and mutilated after we die?[4] Wouldn't we prefer the former? And the reason we would involves the fact that no *mere* object is involved, but rather a human corpse.

---

[2]*Ibid.*

[3]This raises the interesting issue of whether other ways that humans treat animals are morally justified. A strong case can be made that eating meat and using animals for clothes are immoral.

[4]This was in fact the reason that Italian partisans thought that subjecting Mussolini to degradation after he was dead was in a sense *harming* Mussolini. They assumed that he still possessed certain interests which could be harmed by the indignities they inflicted upon him.

There are imaginable instances in which necrophilia would not be immoral. Suppose the will of man X contains a clause stipulating that "anyone wishing to use my corpse for sexual purposes between the hours of 7–9 P.M. on Thursdays at the Greenmount Cemetery may do so." As long as X made the stipulation rationally and sincerely[5] my analysis would consider sexual acts performed on the appointed day and time as not immoral; the law, however, might take a dimmer view of this activity.

(4) *Incest* is immoral when it involves a child who cannot be considered capable of entering into a contractual relationship. Children cannot know the ramifications of a sexual interaction with their parent(s); hence they cannot be thought of as fully responsible agents. Any contract, sexual or otherwise, can only be legitimately consummated with fully responsible parties.

Incest would also be immoral if the parties knowingly conceived a child with the likelihood of genetic defect, since this is an act which would contribute to the needless misery of another.

But there are times when incest is not immoral. Suppose a 50 year old father and his 30 year old daughter voluntarily agree, rationally and sincerely, to a sexual interaction. Both parties are fully responsible agents knowing the ramifications of their actions, and employ proper birth control methods to eliminate the possibility of conceiving a defective child, or engage in a sexual act in which no child could possibly be conceived. This, repugnant though it may seem, would not be an immoral act.

(5) *Promiscuity and adultery* are immoral only if they involve promise-breaking, deceit, or exploitation. Promise-breaking and deceit can occur in a number of ways: one party may deceive another concerning his real feelings for the other; he may break promises to his spouse in order that he might be with the other; he may explicitly lie in order to sustain the two relationships. In romantic triangles of this nature, immorality can occur from the actions of any of the parties in relation to the two other parties.

---

[5]By "rationally" and "sincerely" I only mean that the individual is not under the influence of hallucinogens and is not joking. The individual must be of sound mind. I do not mean by "rationally" that the individual is making the best decision, all things considered.

Some would argue that the nature of the marriage contract itself entails that *any* extramarital encounter on the part of either party is immoral (i.e., it involves promise-breaking) since one provision of the marriage contract is sexual exclusivity. But under my analysis the parties to the marriage contract may legitimately amend the contract at any time, and an extramarital sexual encounter need not be immoral as long as both marital partners agree prior to the encounter that it is permissible. If the marriage relationship is construed as a voluntary reciprocal contract the partners are free to amend its provisions insofar as they can both agree on the alterations involved.

III

The religious argument against many of the aforementioned sexual activities is often straightforward:

(A) If an action is a violation of God's law then it is immoral.
(B) X breaks the law of God.
    X is an immoral action.

Substitute the acts in question for X and we see the essence of the religious argument against these acts. For the believer a supernatural being, possessing certain qualities, has created us and set down a variety of laws. To transgress these laws is to violate morality, since the ultimate lawgiver has set forth the basis for morality in these laws. All the believer need do is point to the relevant biblical scripture or the relevant source of these laws to show that certain acts are immoral. These acts are seen as *intrinsically* immoral, regardless of whether promise-breaking, deception, or exploitation are involved. Surely these latter factors are viewed as immoral, but even if they do not occur the action in question is still immoral because it violates the law of God. Violating the law of God is considered a sufficient condition for an act to be immoral by the religious believer.

Of course to someone who does not believe in any supernatural being or to one who believes in a supernatural being of a radically different nature from the Christian God, this argument is not convincing. Without a religious conviction premise (A) is vacuous.

Yet it is true that many non-believers share the believer's convictions regarding the immorality of certain of the sexual practices we have considered. Why is this so? I think that an important reason is that many religious convictions about practical moral issues have become imbedded into our considered moral judgments. Because of the influence and historical power of Christianity throughout the ages certain beliefs about the immorality of particular actions became an integral part of our moral education and customs. Hence many non-believers still think that adultery, promiscuity, etc. are morally pernicious even though they deny the existence of the Christian God. Under my analysis, however, these actions are not immoral (presupposing no promise-breaking, deception, or exploitation) once belief in the Christian God is abrogated. Once sexual interactions are viewed as being contractual and reciprocal we have a basis for judging their morality independent of any reliance upon the laws of a supernatural being.

IV

The results of my analysis are in certain cases more liberal than conventional moralists (e.g., adultery, promiscuity, necrophilia, and incest are not immoral if certain conditions pertain), and in other cases more conservative (e.g., "teasing" without the intention to fulfill that which the other reasonably can be expected to think was offered is immoral, since it involves the nonfulfillment of that which the other could reasonably be expected to think was agreed upon).

It must be pointed out that to state that a certain act is not immoral does not entail that it is advisable to pursue. I have argued that under certain conditions these acts are not immoral, but I would certainly advise against most, if not all, of these actions. Often these actions still are offensive to our tastes, not in our best long term interests, and may be psychologically harmful. Because our most important feelings and emotions are involved in sexual interactions we must be cautious about engaging in certain acts which may be damaging in the long run. Just as we should be careful in agreeing to *any* voluntary contract involving a reciprocal exchange of goods and services, we should be most careful before agreeing upon what may be our most important kind of contract. The sexual contract is one in which our most valuable intangible commodities are at stake; in fact our self-esteem may well be on the line. And although we may freely enter into certain sexual contracts it is important to know the ramifications and long range effects to our own interests and the interests of others.

The purpose of this essay, then, is not to endorse or encourage certain of the sexual practices mentioned, but rather to show that the basis of our secular aversion to them often cannot be the notion of morality.

For Further Reflection

1. Evaluate Belliotti's arguments. Are they convincing? Is sexual interaction simply another contractual arrangement?

2. Do you agree with the implications of Belliotti's arguments? For example, is his case against bestiality convincing? He argues that it is immoral to have sex with animals because animals cannot consent. How does he know this? If it turns out that dogs, chimpanzees, and other animals do manifest consenting behavior, would that make it morally permissible to have sex with animals?

3. What are the implications of Belliotti's argument for prostitution?

Sexual Intercourse Should Be Confined to Marriage

VINCENT PUNZO

Vincent Punzo is professor of philosophy at St. Louis University. He is the author of several works in ethics, including *Reflective Naturalism: An Introduction to Moral Philosophy* (1969), from which this selection is taken.

Punzo compares sexual intercourse with other types of human activities and argues that sex is different—more intimate and involving existential integrity. Developing a theory of the human self, Punzo goes on to argue that marriage, or at least a commitment to marriage (in preceremonial intercourse), is the necessary framework for proper sexual union.

If one sees man's moral task as being simply that of not harming anyone, that is if one sees this task in purely negative terms, he will certainly not accept the argument to be presented in the following section. However, if one accepts the notion of the morality of aspiration, if one accepts the view that man's moral task involves the positive attempt to live up to what is best in man, to give reality to what he sees to be the perfection of himself as a human subject, the argument may be acceptable.

SEXUALITY AND THE HUMAN SUBJECT

[Prior discussion] has left us with the question as to whether sexual intercourse is a type of activity that is similar to choosing a dinner from a menu. This question is of utmost significance in that one's view of the morality of premarital intercourse seems to depend on the significance that one gives to the sexual encounter in human life. Those such as [John] Wilson and [Eustace] Chesser who see nothing immoral about the premarital character of sexual intercourse seem to see sexual intercourse as being no different from myriad of other

Reprinted from Vincent Punzo, *Reflective Naturalism: An Introduction to Moral Philosophy* (New York: Macmillan, 1969) by permission of the author.

purely aesthetic matters. This point is seen in Chesser's questioning of the reason for demanding permanence in the relationship of sexual partners when we do not see such permanence as being important to other human relationships.[1] It is also seen in his asking why we raise a moral issue about premarital coition when two people may engage in it, with the resulting social and psychological consequences being no different than if they had gone to a movie.[2]

Wilson most explicitly makes a case for the view that sexual intercourse does not differ significantly from other human activities. He holds that people think that there is a logical difference between the question "Will you engage in sexual intercourse with me?" and the question, "Will you play tennis with me?" only because they are influenced by the acquisitive character of contemporary society.[3] Granted that the two questions may be identical from the purely formal perspective of logic, the ethician must move beyond this perspective to a consideration of their content. Men and women find themselves involved in many different relationships: for example, as buyer-seller, employer-employee, teacher-student, lawyer-client, and partners or competitors in certain games such as tennis or bridge. Is there any morally significant difference between these relationships and sexual intercourse? We cannot examine all the possible relationships into which a man and woman can enter, but we will consider the employer-employee relationship in order to get some perspective on the distinctive character of the sexual relationship.

A man pays a woman to act as his secretary. What rights does he have over her in such a situation? The woman agrees to work a certain number of hours during the day taking dictation, typing letters, filing reports, arranging appointments and flight schedules, and greeting clients and competitors. In short, we can say that the man has rights to certain of the woman's services or skills. The use of the word "services" may lead some to conclude that this relationship is not significantly different from the relationship between a prostitute and her client in that the prostitute also offers her "services."

It is true that we sometimes speak euphemistically of a prostitute

---

[1]Eustace Chesser, *Unmarried Love* (New York: Pocket Books, 1965), p. 29.
[2]*Ibid.,* pp. 35–36, see also p. 66.
[3]John Wilson, *Logic and Sexual Morality* (Baltimore, Md.: Penguin Books, 1965). See footnote 1, p. 67.

offering her services to a man for a sum of money, but if we are serious about our quest for the difference between the sexual encounter and other types of human relationships, it is necessary to drop euphemisms and face the issue directly. The man and woman who engage in sexual intercourse are giving their bodies, the most intimate physical expression of themselves, over to the other. Unlike the man who plays tennis with a woman, the man who has sexual relations with her has literally entered her. A man and woman engaging in sexual intercourse have united themselves as intimately and as totally as is physically possible for two human beings. Their union is not simply a union of organs, but is as intimate and as total a physical union of two selves as is possible of achievement. Granted the character of this union, it seems strange to imply that there is no need for a man and a woman to give any more thought to the question of whether they should engage in sexual intercourse than to the question of whether they should play tennis.

In opposition to Wilson, I think that it is the acquisitive character of our society that has blinded us to the distinction between the two activities. Wilson's and Chesser's positions seem to imply that exactly the same moral considerations ought to apply to a situation in which a housewife is bartering with a butcher for a few pounds of pork chops and the situation in which two human beings are deciding whether sexual intercourse ought to be an ingredient of their relationship. So long as the butcher does not put his thumb on the scale in the weighing process, so long as he is truthful in stating that the meat is actually pork, so long as the woman pays the proper amount with the proper currency, the trade is perfectly moral. Reflecting on sexual intercourse from the same sort of economic perspective, one can say that so long as the sexual partners are truthful in reporting their freedom from contagious venereal diseases and so long as they are truthful in reporting that they are interested in the activity for the mere pleasure of it or to try out their sexual techniques, there is nothing immoral about such activity. That in the one case pork chops are being exchanged for money whereas in the other the decision concerns the most complete and intimate merging of one's self with another makes no difference to the moral evaluation of the respective cases.

It is not surprising that such a reductionistic outlook should pervade our thinking on sexual matters, since in our society sexuality is used to sell everything from shave cream to underarm deodorants, to soap, to mouthwash, to cigarettes, and to automobiles. Sexuality has come to play so large a role in our commercial lives that it is not surprising that our sexuality should itself come to be treated as a commodity governed by the same moral rules that govern any other economic transaction.

Once sexuality is taken out of this commercial framework, once the character of the sexual encounter is faced directly and squarely, we will come to see that Doctor Mary Calderone has brought out the type of questions that ought to be asked by those contemplating the introduction of sexual intercourse into their relationships: "How many times, and how casually, are you willing to invest a portion of your total self, and to be the custodian of a like investment from the other person, without the sureness of knowing that these investments are being made for keeps?"[4] These questions come out of the recognition that the sexual encounter is a definitive experience, one in which the physical intimacy and merging involves also a merging of the nonphysical dimensions of the partners. With these questions, man moves beyond the negative concern with avoiding his or another's physical and psychological harm to the question of what he is making of himself and what he is contributing to the existential formation of his partner as a human subject.

If we are to make a start toward responding to Calderone's questions we must cease talking about human selfhood in abstraction. The human self is an historical as well as a physical being. He is a being who is capable of making at least a portion of his past an object of his consciousness and thus is able to make this past play a conscious role in his present and in his looking toward the future. He is also a being who looks to the future, who faces tomorrow with plans, ideals, hopes, and fears. The very being of a human self involves his past and his movement toward the future. Moreover, the human self is not completely shut off in his own past and future. Men and women are capable of consciously and purposively uniting themselves in a common career and venture. They can commit themselves to sharing the future with another, sharing it in all its aspects—in its fortunes and misfortunes, in its times of happiness and times of tragedy.

---

[4]Mary Steichen Calderone, "The Case for Chastity," *Sex in America,* ed. by Henry Anatole Grunwald (New York: Bantam Books, 1964), p. 147.

Within the lives of those who have so committed themselves to each other, sexual intercourse is a way of asserting and confirming the fullness and totality of their mutual commitment.

Unlike those who have made such a commitment and who come together in the sexual act in the fullness of their selfhood, those who engage in premarital sexual unions and who have made no such commitment act as though they can amputate their bodily existence and the most intimate physical expression of their selfhood from their existence as historical beings. Granting that there may be honesty on the verbal level in that two people engaging in premarital intercourse openly state that they are interested only in the pleasure of the activity, the fact remains that such unions are morally deficient because they lack existential integrity in that there is a total merging and union on a physical level, on the one hand, and a conscious decision not to unite any other dimension of themselves, on the other hand. Their sexual union thus involves a "depersonalization" of their bodily existence, an attempt to cut off the most intimate physical expression of their respective selves from their very selfhood. The mutual agreement of premarital sex partners is an agreement to merge with the other not as a self, but as a body which one takes unto oneself, which one possesses in a most intimate and total fashion for one's own pleasure or designs, allowing the other to treat oneself in the same way. It may be true that no physical or psychological harm may result from such unions, but such partners have failed to existentially incorporate human sexuality, which is at the very least the most intimate physical expression of the human self, into the character of this selfhood.

In so far as premarital sexual unions separate the intimate and total physical union that is sexual intercourse from any commitment to the self in his historicity, human sexuality, and consequently the human body, have been fashioned into external things or objects to be handed over totally to someone else, whenever one feels that he can get possession of another's body, which he can use for his own purposes.[5] The human body has thus been treated no differ-

---

[5]The psychoanalyst Rollo May makes an excellent point in calling attention to the tendency in contemporary society to exploit the human body as if it were only a machine. Rollo May, "The New Puritanism," *Sex in America*, pp. 161–164.

ently from the pork chops spoken of previously or from any other object or commodity, which human beings exchange and haggle over in their day-to-day transactions. One hesitates to use the word that might be used to capture the moral value that has been sacrificed in premarital unions because in our day the word has taken on a completely negative meaning at best, and, at worst, it has become a word used by "sophisticates" to mock or deride certain attitudes toward human sexuality. However, because the word "chastity" has been thus abused is no reason to leave it in the hands of those who have misrepresented the human value to which it gives expression.

The chaste person has often been described as one intent on denying his sexuality. The value of chastity as conceived in this section is in direct opposition to this description. It is the unchaste person who is separating himself from his sexuality, who is willing to exchange human bodies as one would exchange money for tickets to a baseball game—honestly and with no commitment of self to self. Against this alienation of one's sexuality from one's self, an alienation that makes one's sexuality an object, which is to be given to another in exchange for his objectified sexuality, chastity affirms the integrity of the self in his bodily and historical existence. The sexuality of man is seen as an integral part of his subjectivity. Hence, the chaste man rejects depersonalized sexual relations as a reduction of man in his most intimate physical being to the status of an object or pure instrument for another. He asserts that man is a subject and end in himself, not in some trans-temporal, nonphysical world, but in the historical-physical world in which he carries on his moral task and where he finds his fellow man. He will not freely make of himself in his bodily existence a thing to be handed over to another's possession, nor will he ask that another treat his own body in this way. The total physical intimacy of sexual intercourse will be an expression of total union with the other self on all levels of their beings. Seen from this perspective, chastity is one aspect of man's attempt to attain existential integrity, to accept his body as a dimension of his total personality.

In concluding this section, it should be noted that I have tried to make a case against the morality of premarital sexual intercourse even in those cases in which the partners are completely honest with each other. There is reason to question whether the complete honesty, to which those who see nothing immoral in such unions refer, is as a matter of fact actually found very often among pre-marital sex partners. We may well have been dealing with textbook cases which present these unions in their best light. One may be pardoned for wondering whether sexual intercourse often occurs under the following conditions: "Hello, my name is Josiah. I am interested in having a sexual experience with you. I can assure you that I am good at it and that I have no communicable disease. If it sounds good to you and if you have taken the proper contra-ceptive precautions, we might have a go at it. Of course, I want to make it clear to you that I am interested only in the sexual expe-rience and that I have no intention of making any long-range com-mitment to you." If those, who defend the morality of premarital sexual unions so long as they are honestly entered into, think that I have misrepresented what they mean by honesty, then they must specify what they mean by an honest premarital union. . . .

MARRIAGE AS A TOTAL
HUMAN COMMITMENT

The preceding argument against the morality of premarital sexual unions was not based on the view that the moral character of mar-riage rests on a legal certificate or on a legal or religious ceremony. The argument was not directed against "preceremonial" intercourse, but against premarital intercourse. Morally speaking, a man and woman are married when they make the mutual and total com-mitment to share the problems and prospects of their historical exis-tence in the world. . . .

. . . A total commitment to another means a commitment to him in his historical existence. Such a commitment is not simply a mat-ter of words or of feelings, however strong. It involves a full exis-tential sharing on the part of two beings of the burdens, opportu-nities, and challenges of their historical existence.

Granted the importance that the character of their commitment to each other plays in determining the moral quality of a couple's sexual encounter, it is clear that there may be nothing immoral in the behavior of couples who engage in sexual intercourse before participating in the marriage ceremony. For example, it is foolish to say that two people who are totally committed to each other and who have made all the arrangements to live this commitment are immoral if they engage in sexual intercourse the night before the marriage ceremony. Admittedly this position can be abused by those who have made a purely verbal commitment, a commitment, which will be carried out in some vague and ill-defined future. At some time or other, they will unite their two lives totally by setting up house together and by actually undertaking the task of meeting the economic, social, legal, medical responsibilities that are involved in living this commitment. Apart from the reference to a vague and amorphous future time when they will share the full responsibility for each other, their commitment presently realizes itself in going to dances, sharing a box of popcorn at Saturday night movies, and sharing their bodies whenever they can do so without taking too great a risk of having the girl become pregnant.

Having acknowledged that the position advanced in this section can be abused by those who would use the word "commitment" to rationalize what is an interest only in the body of the other person, it must be pointed out that neither the ethician nor any other human being can tell two people whether they actually have made the commitment that is marriage or are mistaking a "warm glow" for such a commitment. There comes a time when this issue falls out of the area of moral philosophy and into the area of practical wisdom. . . .

The characterization of marriage as a total commitment between two human beings may lead some to conclude that the marriage ceremony is a wholly superfluous affair. It must be admitted that people may be morally married without having engaged in a marriage ceremony. However, to conclude from this point that the ceremony is totally meaningless is to lose sight of the social character of human beings. The couple contemplating marriage do not exist in a vacuum, although there may be times when they think they do. Their existences reach out beyond their union to include other human beings. By making their commitment a matter of public record, by solemnly expressing it before the law and in the presence of their respective families and friends and, if they are religious people, in the presence of God and one of his ministers, they sink the roots of their commitment more deeply and extensively in the world in which they live, thus taking steps to provide for the future growth of their commitment to each other. The public expression of this commitment makes it more fully and more explicitly a part of a couple's lives and of the world in which they live. . . .

For Further Reflection

1. Do you agree with Punzo's comparison of sex with other human activities? Is sex different in degree or in kind? How does Punzo's argument depend on this point?

2. What does Punzo mean by "existential integrity"? Could this concept be used to justify sexual relations outside of marriage?

Is Homosexuality Unnatural?

BURTON LEISER

Burton Leiser is professor of philosophy at Pace University and the author of several works in ethics, including *Liberty, Justice, and Morals,* from which this selection is taken.

Leiser examines the "unnaturalness" argument that underlies the Roman Catholic teaching, including Pope Paul VI's *Humanae Vitae,* that homosexual behavior is immoral because it is unnatural. Leiser asserts that such an argument would have to demonstrate (1) that homosexuality truly was *unnatural* and (2) that what was unnatural was *morally bad.* He examines several senses in which proponents of the unnaturalness argument seek to attribute unnaturalness to homosexual behavior and show that each attempt fails.

. . . The "unnaturalness" of homosexuality raises the question of the meaning of *nature, natural,* and similar terms. Theologians and other moralists have said homosexual acts violate the "natural law,"

Reprinted from Burton Leiser, *Liberty, Justice, and Morals* (Macmillan Publishing Co., 3rd ed., 1986) by permission of Prentice-Hall, Inc., Upper Saddle River, NJ.

and that they are therefore immoral and ought to be prohibited by the state.

The word *nature* has a built-in ambiguity that can lead to serious misunderstandings. When something is said to be "natural" or in conformity with "natural law" or the "law of nature," this may mean either (1) that it is in conformity with the descriptive laws of nature, or (2) that it is not artificial, that man has not imposed his will or his devices upon events or conditions as they exist or would have existed without such interference.

1. *The descriptive laws of nature.* The laws of nature, as these are understood by the scientist, differ from the laws of man. The former are purely descriptive, where the latter are prescriptive. When a scientist says that water boils at 212° Fahrenheit or that the volume of a gas varies directly with the heat that is applied to it and inversely with the pressure, he means merely that as a matter of recorded and observable fact, pure water under standard conditions always boils at precisely 212° Fahrenheit and that as a matter of observed fact, the volume of a gas rises as it is heated and falls as pressure is applied to it. These "laws" merely *describe* the manner in which physical substances *actually behave.* They differ from municipal and federal laws in that they *do not prescribe behavior.* Unlike man-made laws, natural laws are not passed by any legislator or group of legislators; they are not proclaimed or announced; they impose no obligation upon anyone or anything; their violation entails no penalty, and there is no reward for following them or abiding by them. When a scientist says that the air in a tire obeys the laws of nature that govern gases, he does *not* mean that the air, having been informed that it *ought* to behave in a certain way, behaves appropriately under the right conditions. He means, rather, that as a matter of fact, the air in a tire *will* behave like all other gases. In saying that Boyle's law governs the behavior of gases, he means merely that gases do, as a matter of fact, behave in accordance with Boyle's law, and that Boyle's law enables one to predict accurately what will happen to a given quantity of gas as its pressure is raised; he does *not* mean to suggest that some heavenly voice has proclaimed that all gases should henceforth behave in accordance with the terms of Boyle's law and that a ghostly policeman patrols the world, ready to mete out punishments to any gases that violate the heavenly decree. In fact, according to the scientist, it does not make sense to speak of a natural law being vio-

lated. For if there were a true exception to a so-called law of nature, the exception would require a change in the description of those phenomena, and the law would have been shown to be no law at all. The laws of nature are revised as scientists discover new phenomena that require new refinements in their descriptions of the way things actually happen. In this respect they differ fundamentally from human laws, which are revised periodically by legislators who are not so interested in *describing* human behavior as they are in *prescribing* what human behavior *should* be.

2. *The artificial as a form of the unnatural.* On occasion when we say that something is not natural, we mean that it is a product of human artifice. A typewriter is not a natural object, in this sense, for the substances of which it is composed have been removed from their natural state—the state in which they existed before men came along—and have been transformed by a series of chemical and physical and mechanical processes into other substances. They have been rearranged into a whole that is quite different from anything found in nature. In short, a typewriter is an artificial object. In this sense, clothing is not natural, for it has been transformed considerably from the state in which it was found in nature; and wearing clothing is also not natural, in this sense, for in one's natural state, before the application of anything artificial, before any human interference with things as they are, one is quite naked. Human laws, being artificial conventions designed to exercise a degree of control over the natural inclinations and propensities of men, may in this sense be considered to be unnatural.

When theologians and moralists speak of homosexuality, contraception, abortion, and other forms of human behavior as being unnatural and say that for that reason such behavior must be considered to be wrong, in what sense are they using the word *unnatural?* Are they saying that homosexual behavior and the use of contraceptives are contrary to the scientific laws of nature, are they saying that they are artificial forms of behavior, or are they using the terms *natural* and *unnatural* in some third sense?

They cannot mean that homosexual behavior (to stick to the subject presently under discussion) violates the laws of nature in the first sense, for, as has been pointed out, in *that* sense it is impossible to violate the laws of nature. Those laws, being merely descriptive of what actually does happen, would have to *include* homosexual behavior if such behavior does actually take place. Even if the defenders of the theological view that homosexuality is unnatural were to appeal to a statistical analysis by pointing out that such behavior is not normal from a statistical point of view, and therefore not what the laws of nature require, it would be open to their critics to reply that any descriptive law of nature must account for and incorporate all statistical deviations, and that the laws of nature, in this sense, do not *require* anything. These critics might also note that the best statistics available reveal that about half of all American males engage in homosexual activity at some time in their lives, and that a very large percentage of American males have exclusively homosexual relations for a fairly extensive period of time; from which it would follow that such behavior is natural, for them, at any rate, in this sense of the word *natural*.

If those who say that homosexual behavior is unnatural are using the term *unnatural* in the second sense as artificial, it is difficult to understand their objection. That which is artificial is often far better than what is natural. Artificial homes seem, at any rate, to be more suited to human habitation and more conducive to longer life and better health than are caves and other natural shelters. There are distinct advantages to the use of such unnatural (artificial) amenities as clothes, furniture, and books. Although we may dream of an idyllic return to nature in our more wistful moments, we would soon discover, as Thoreau did in his attempt to escape from the artificiality of civilization, that needles and thread, knives and matches, ploughs and nails, and countless other products of human artifice are essential to human life. We would discover, as Plato pointed out in the *Republic,* that no man can be truly self-sufficient. Some of the by-products of industry are less than desirable, but neither industry nor the products of industry are intrinsically evil, even though both are unnatural in this sense of the word.

Interference with nature is not evil in itself. Nature, as some writers have put it, must be tamed. In some respects man must look upon it as an enemy to be conquered. If nature were left to its own devices, without the intervention of human artifice, men would be consumed by disease, they would be plagued by insects, they would be chained to the places where they were born with no means of swift communication or transport, and they would suffer the discomforts and the torments of wind and weather and flood and fire with no practical means of combating any of them. Interfering with nature, doing battle with nature, using human will and reason and skill to thwart what might otherwise follow from the conditions that prevail in the world is a peculiarly human enterprise, one that can hardly be condemned merely because it does what is not natural.

Homosexual behavior can hardly be considered to be unnatural in this sense. There is nothing artificial about such behavior. On the contrary, it is quite natural, in this sense, to those who engage in it. And even if it were not, even if it were quite artificial, this is not in itself a ground for condemning it.

It would seem, then, that those who condemn homosexuality as an unnatural form of behavior must mean something else by the word *unnatural,* something not covered by either of the preceding definitions. A third possibility is this:

3. *Anything uncommon or abnormal is unnatural.* If this is what is meant by those who condemn homosexuality on the ground that it is unnatural, it is quite obvious that their condemnation cannot be accepted without further argument. The fact that a given form of behavior is uncommon provides no justification for condemning it. Playing viola in a string quartet may be an uncommon form of human behavior. Yet there is no reason to suppose that such uncommon behavior is, by virtue of its uncommonness, deserving of condemnation or ethically or morally wrong. On the contrary, many forms of behavior are praised precisely because they are so uncommon. Great artists, poets, musicians, and scientists are uncommon in this sense; but clearly the world is better off for having them, and it would be absurd to condemn them or their activities for their failure to be common and normal. If homosexual behavior is wrong, then, it must be for some reason other than its unnaturalness in this sense of the word.

4. *Any use of an organ or an instrument that is contrary to its principal purpose or function is unnatural.* Every organ and every instrument—perhaps even every creature—has a function to perform, one for which it is particularly designed. Any use of those instruments and organs that is consonant with their purposes is natural and proper, but any use that is inconsistent with their principal functions is unnatural and improper, and to that extent, evil or harmful. Human teeth, for example, are admirably designed for their principal functions—biting and chewing the kinds of food suitable for human consumption. But they are not particularly well suited for prying the caps from beer bottles. If they are used for that pur-

pose, which is not natural to them, they are likely to crack or break under the strain. The abuse of one's teeth leads to their destruction and to a consequent deterioration in one's overall health. If they are used only for their proper function, however, they may continue to serve well for many years. Similarly, a given drug may have a proper function. If used in the furtherance of that end, it can preserve life and restore health. But if it is abused and employed for purposes for which it was never intended, it may cause serious harm and even death. The natural uses of things are good and proper, but their unnatural uses are bad and harmful.

What we must do, then, is to find the proper use, or the true purpose, of each organ in our bodies. Once we have discovered that, we will know what constitutes the natural use of each organ and what constitutes an unnatural, abusive, and potentially harmful employment of the various parts of our bodies. If we are rational, we will be careful to confine behavior to the proper functions and to refrain from unnatural behavior. According to those philosophers who follow this line of reasoning, the way to discover the proper use of any organ is to determine what it is peculiarly suited to do. The eye is suited for seeing, the ear for hearing, the nerves for transmitting impulses from one part of the body to another, and so on.

What are the sex organs peculiarly suited to do? Obviously, they are peculiarly suited to enable men and women to reproduce their own kind. No other organ in the body is capable of fulfilling that function. It follows, according to those who follow the natural-law line, that the proper or natural function of the sex organs is reproduction, and that strictly speaking, any use of those organs for other purposes is unnatural, abusive, potentially harmful, and therefore wrong. The sex organs have been given to us in order to enable us to maintain the continued existence of mankind on this earth. All perversions—including masturbation, homosexual behavior, and heterosexual intercourse that deliberately frustrates the design of the sexual organs—are unnatural and bad. As Pope Pius XI once said, "Private individuals have no other power over the members of their bodies than that which pertains to their natural ends."

But the problem is not so easily resolved. Is it true that every organ has one and only one proper function? A hammer may have been designed to pound nails, and it may perform that particular job best. But it is not sinful to employ a hammer to crack nuts if you have no other more suitable tool immediately available. The hammer, being a relatively versatile tool, may be employed in a number of ways. It has no one proper or natural function. A woman's eyes are well adapted to seeing, it is true. But they seem also to be well adapted to flirting. Is a woman's use of her eyes for the latter purpose sinful merely because she is not using them, at that moment, for their "primary" purpose of seeing? Our sexual organs are uniquely adapted for procreation, but that is obviously not the only function for which they are adapted. Human beings may—and do—use those organs for a great many other purposes, and it is difficult to see why any *one* use should be considered to be the only proper one. The sex organs seem to be particularly well adapted to give their owners and others intense sensations of pleasure. Unless one believes that pleasure itself is bad, there seems to be little reason to believe that the use of the sex organs for the production of pleasure in oneself or in others is evil. In view of the peculiar design of these organs, with their great concentration of nerve endings, it would seem that they were designed (if they *were* designed) with that very goal in mind, and that their use for such purposes would be no more unnatural than their use for the purpose of procreation.

Nor should we overlook the fact that human sex organs may be and are used to express, in the deepest and most intimate way open to man, the love of one person for another. Even the most ardent opponents of "unfruitful" intercourse admit that sex does serve this function. They have accordingly conceded that a man and his wife may have intercourse even though she is pregnant, or past the age of child bearing, or in the infertile period of her menstrual cycle.

Human beings are remarkably complex and adaptable creatures. Neither they nor their organs can properly be compared to hammers or to other tools. The analogy quickly breaks down. The generalization that a given organ or instrument has one and only one proper function does not hold up, even with regard to the simplest manufactured tools, for, as we have seen, a tool may be used for more than one purpose—less effectively than one especially designed for a given task, perhaps, but properly and certainly not *sinfully*. A woman may use her eyes not only to see and to flirt, but also to earn money—if she is, for example, an actress or a model. Though neither of the latter functions seems to have been a part of the original design, if one may speak sensibly of *design* in this context, of the eye, it is difficult to see why such a use of the eyes of a woman should be considered sinful, perverse, or unnatural. Her sex organs have the unique capacity of producing ova and nurturing human embryos, under the right conditions; but why should any other use of those organs, including their use to bring pleasure to their owner or to someone else, or to manifest love to another person, or even, perhaps, to earn money, be regarded as perverse, sinful, or unnatural? Similarly, a man's sexual organs possess the unique capacity of causing the generation of another human being, but if a man chooses to use them for pleasure, or for the expression of love, or for some other purpose—so long as he does not interfere with the rights of some other person—the fact that his sex organs do have their unique capabilities does not constitute a convincing justification for condemning their other uses as being perverse, sinful, unnatural or criminal. If a man "perverts" himself by wiggling his ears for the entertainment of his neighbors instead of using them exclusively for their "natural" function of hearing, no one thinks of consigning him to prison. If he abuses his teeth by using them to pull staples from memos—a function for which teeth were clearly not designed—he is not accused of being immoral, degraded, and degenerate. The fact that people *are* condemned for using their sex organs for their own pleasure or profit, or for that of others, may be more revealing about the prejudices and taboos of our society than it is about our perception of the true nature or purpose of our bodies.

In this connection, it may be worthwhile to note that with the development of artificial means of reproduction (that is, test tube babies), the sex organs may become obsolete for reproductive purposes but would still contribute greatly to human pleasure. In addition, studies of animal behavior and anthropological reports indicate that such nonreproductive sex acts as masturbation, homosexual intercourse, and mutual fondling of genital organs are widespread, both among human beings and among lower animals. Under suitable circumstances, many animals reverse their sex roles, males assuming the posture of females and presenting themselves to others for intercourse, and females mounting other females and going through all the actions of a male engaged in intercourse. Many peoples all around the world have sanctioned and even ritualized homosexual relations. It would seem that an excessive readiness to insist that human sex organs are designed only for reproductive purposes and therefore ought to be used only for such purposes must be based upon a very narrow conception that is conditioned by our own society's peculiar history and taboos.

To sum up, then, the proposition that any use of an organ that is contrary to its principal purpose or function is unnatural assumes that organs *have* a principal purpose or function, but this may be denied on the ground that the purpose or function of a given organ may vary according to the needs or desires of its owner. It may be denied on the ground that a given organ may have more than one principal purpose or function, and any attempt to call one use or another the only natural one seems to be arbitrary, if not question-begging. Also, the proposition suggests that what is unnatural is evil or depraved. This goes beyond the pure description of things, and enters into the problem of the evaluation of human behavior, which leads us to the fifth meaning of *natural*.

5. *That which is natural is good, and whatever is unnatural is bad.* When one condemns homosexuality or masturbation or the use of contraceptives on the ground that it is unnatural, one implies that whatever is unnatural is bad, wrongful, or perverse. But as we have seen, in some senses of the word, the unnatural (the artificial) is often very good, whereas that which is natural (that which has not been subjected to human artifice or improvement) may be very bad indeed. Of course, interference with nature may be bad. Ecologists have made us more aware than we have ever been of the dangers of unplanned and uninformed interference with nature. But this is not to say that *all* interference with nature is bad. Every time a man cuts down a tree to make room for a home for himself, or catches a fish to feed himself or his family, he is interfering with nature. If men did not interfere with nature, they would have no homes, they could eat no fish, and, in fact, they could not survive. What, then, can be meant by those who say that whatever is natural is good and whatever is unnatural is bad? Clearly, they cannot have intended merely to reduce the word *natural* to a synonym of *good, right,* and *proper,* and *unnatural* to a synonym of *evil, wrong, improper, corrupt,* and *depraved.* If that were all they had intended to do, there would be very little to discuss as to whether a given form of behavior might be proper even though it is not in strict conformity with someone's views of what is natural; for *good* and *natural* being synonyms, it would follow inevitably that whatever is good must be natural, and vice versa, by definition. This is certainly not what the opponents of homosexuality

have been saying when they claim that homosexuality, being unnatural, is evil. For if it were, their claim would be quite empty. They would be saying merely that homosexuality, being evil, is evil—a redundancy that could as easily be reduced to the simpler assertion that homosexuality is evil. This assertion, however, is not an argument. Those who oppose homosexuality and other sexual "perversions" on the ground that they are "unnatural" are saying that there is some objectively identifiable quality in such behavior that is unnatural; and that that quality, once it has been identified by some kind of scientific observation, can be seen to be detrimental to those who engage in such behavior, or to those around them; and that *because* of the harm (physical, mental, moral, or spiritual) that results from engaging in any behavior possessing the attribute of unnaturalness, such behavior must be considered to be wrongful, and should be discouraged by society. "Unnaturalness" and "wrongfulness" are not synonyms, then, but different concepts. The problem with which we are wrestling is that we are unable to find a meaning for *unnatural* that enables us to arrive at the conclusion that homosexuality is unnatural or that if homosexuality is unnatural, it is therefore wrongful behavior. We have examined four common meanings of *natural* and *unnatural,* and have seen that none of them performs the task that it must perform if advocates of this argument are to prevail. Without some more satisfactory explanation of the connection between the wrongfulness of homosexuality and its alleged unnaturalness, the argument . . . must be rejected.

For Further Reflection

1. Evaluate Leiser's analysis of the unnaturalness argument against homosexuality. Is he fair to the argument? Is his critique convincing? Are you persuaded by it? Explain your answer.

2. How would someone who thought homosexuality is immoral respond to Leiser?

Monogamy
A Critique

JOHN MCMURTRY

John McMurtry teaches philosophy at the University of
Guelph in Ontario, Canada. Recall that Kant argued that marriage involves the ownership of each spouse by the other.
Kant thought this was morally acceptable, because it was
founded in altruism and voluntary self-giving. McMurtry,
however, disagrees with Kant. He argues that monogamous
marriage is an evil precisely because it reduces love to capitalist private property. He assembles a wide set of considerations which together make a cumulative case for the thesis that monogamy is "a massive social-control mechanism."
The four principles are:

1. The partners are required to enter a formal contractual relation which cannot be dissolved without tremendous legal action and costs.
2. The number of partners involved must be two
   and only two, excluding wider intimacies.
3. No one may participate in more than one marriage at a time, and will be punished by the law
   if he or she does.
4. No extramarital sexual relations are allowed.

Together, argues McMurtry, these principles reduce relationships to private property, making marriage just another
oppressive capitalist institution.

> Remove away that black'ning church
> Remove away that marriage hearse
> Remove away that man of blood
> You'll quite remove the ancient curse.
>
> —William Blake

Reprinted from *The Monist* 56, no. 4 (1972). Copyright © 1972,
The Monist, La Salle, Illinois 61301. Reprinted by permission. Notes
omitted.

I

Almost all of us have entered or will one day enter a specifically standardized form of monogamous marriage. This cultural requirement is so very basic to our existence that we accept it for most part as a kind of intractable given—dictated by the laws of God, Nature, Government, and Good Sense all at once. Though it is perhaps unusual for a social practice to be so promiscuously underwritten, we generally find comfort rather than curiosity in this fact and seldom wonder how something could be divinely inspired, biologically determined, coerced, and reasoned out all at the same time. We simply take for granted.

Those in society who are officially charged with the thinking function with regard to such matters are no less responsible for this uncritical acceptance than is the man on the street. The psychoanalyst traditionally regards our form of marriage as a necessary restraint on the anarchic id and no more to be queried than civilization itself. The lawyer is as undisposed to questioning the practice as he is to criticizing the principle of private property (this is appropriate, as I shall later point out). The churchman formally perceives the relationship between man and wife to be as inviolable and insusceptible to question as the relationship between the institution he works for and the Christ. The sociologist standardly accepts the formalized bonding of heterosexual pairs as the indispensable basis of social order and perhaps a societal universal. The politician is as incapable of challenging it as he is the virtue of his own continued holding of office. And the philosopher (at least the English-speaking philosopher), as with most issues of socially controversial or sexual dimensions, ignores the question almost altogether.

Even those irreverent adulterers and unmarried couples who seem to be challenging the institution in the most basic possible way, in practice, tend merely to mimic its basic structure in unofficial form. The coverings of sanctities, taboos, and cultural habit continue to hold them with the grip of public clothes.

II

"Monogamy" means, literally, "one marriage." But it would be wrong to suppose that this phrase tells us much about our particular species of official wedlock. The greatest obstacle to the adequate under-standing of our monogamy institution has been the failure to identify clearly and systematically the full complex of principles it involves. There are four such principles, each carrying enormous restrictive force and together constituting a massive social-control mechanism that has never, so far as I know, been fully schematized. To come straight to the point, the four principles in question are as follows:

1. *The partners are required to enter a formal contractual rela-tion:* (a) whose establishment demands a specific official partici-pant, certain conditions of the contractors (legal age, no blood ties, and so on), and a standard set of procedures; (b) whose govern-ing terms are uniform for all and exactly prescribed by law; and (c) whose dissolution may only be legally effected by the decision of state representatives.

The ways in which this elaborate principle of contractual require-ment is importantly restrictive are obvious. One may not enter into a marriage union without entering into a contract presided over by a state-investured official. One may not set any of the terms of the contractual relationship by which one is bound for life. And one cannot dissolve the contract without legal action and costs, court proceedings, and in many places actual legislation. (This is the one and only contract in all English-speaking law that is not dissoluble by the consent of the contracting parties.) The extent of control here—over the most intimate and putatively "loving" relationships in all social intercourse—is so great as to be difficult to catalogue without exciting in oneself a sense of disbelief.

Lest it be thought there is always the real option of entering a common-law relationship free of such encumbrances, it should be noted that: (a) these relationships themselves are subject to state regulation, though of a less imposing sort; and (much more impor-tant) (b) there are very formidable selective pressures against common-law partnerships, such as employment and job discrimi-nation, exclusion from housing and lodging facilities, special legal disablements, loss of social and moral status (consider such phrases as "living in sin" and "make her an honest woman"), family shame and embarrassment, and so on.

2. *The number of partners involved in the marriage must be two and only two* (as opposed to three, four, five, or any of the almost countless possibilities of intimate union). This second principle of our specific form of monogamy (the concept of "one marriage," it should be pointed out, is consistent with any number of participat-

ing partners) is perhaps the most important and restrictive of the four principles we are considering. Not only does it confine us to just one possibility out of an enormous range, but it confines us to that single possibility that involves the least number of people, two. It is difficult to conceive of a more thoroughgoing mechanism for limiting extended social union and intimacy. The fact that this monolithic restriction seems so "natural" to us (if it were truly "natural," of course, there would be no need for its rigorous cultural prescription by everything from severe criminal law to ubiquitous housing regulations) simply indicates the extent to which its hold is implanted in our social structure. It is the institutional basis of what I will call the "binary frame of sexual consciousness," a frame through which all our heterosexual relationships are typically viewed ("two's company, three's a crowd") and in light of which all larger circles of intimacy seem almost inconceivable.

3. *No person may participate in more than one marriage at a time or during a lifetime* (unless the previous marriage has been officially dissolved by, normally, one partner's death or a divorce). Violation of this principle is, of course, a criminal offense (bigamy) that is punishable by a considerable term in prison. Of various general regulations of our marriage institution, it has experienced the most significant modification, not indeed in principle, but in the extent of flexibility of its "escape hatch" of divorce. The ease with which this escape hatch is opened has increased considerably in the past few years (the grounds for divorce being more permissive than previously) and it is in this regard most of all that the principles of our marriage institution have undergone formal alteration—that is, in plumbing rather than substance.

4. *No married person may engage in any sexual relationship with any person other than the marriage partner.* Although a consummated sexual act with another person alone constitutes an act of adultery, lesser forms of sexual and erotic relationships may also constitute grounds for divorce (for example, cruelty) and are generally proscribed as well by informal social convention and taboo. In other words, the fourth and final principle of our marriage institution involves not only a prohibition of sexual intercourse per se outside one's wedlock (this term deserves pause) but a prohibition of all one's erotic relations whatever outside this bond. The penalties for violation here are as various as they are severe, ranging from permanent loss of spouse, children, chattel, and income to job dismissal and social ostracism. In this way, possibly the most compelling nat-

ural force toward expanded intimate relations with others is strictly confined within the narrowest possible circle for (barring delinquency) the whole of adult life. The sheer weight and totality of this restriction is surely one of the great wonders of all historical institutional control.

III

With all established institutions, apologetics for perpetuation are never wanting. Thus it is with our form of monogamous marriage.

Perhaps the most celebrated justification over the years has proceeded from the belief in a Supreme Deity, who secretly utters sexual and other commands to privileged human representatives. Almost as well known a line of defense has issued from a similarly confident conviction that the need for some social regulation of sexuality demonstrates the need for our specific type of two-person wedlock. Although these have been important justifications in the sense of being very widely supported, they are not—having other grounds than reason—susceptible to treatment here.

If we put aside such arguments, we are left, I think, with two major claims. The first is that our form of monogamous marriage promotes a profound affection between the partners that is not only of great worth in itself but invaluable as a sanctuary from the pressures of outside society. Since, however, there are no secure grounds whatever for supposing that such "profound affection" is not at least as easily achievable by any number of *other* marriage forms (that is, forms that differ in one or more of the four principles), this justification conspicuously fails to perform the task required of it.

The second major claim for the defense is that monogamy provides a specially loving context for child-upbringing. However, here again there are no grounds at all for concluding that it does so as, or any more, effectively than other possible forms of marriage. (The only alternative type of upbringing to which it has apparently been shown to be superior is nonfamily institutional upbringing, which of course is not relevant to the present discussion.) Furthermore, the fact that at least half the span of a normal monogamous marriage involves no child-upbringing at all is over-looked here, as is the reinforcing fact that there is no reference to or mention of the quality of child-upbringing in any of the prescriptions connected with it.

In brief, the second major justification of our particular type of wedlock scents somewhat too strongly of red herring to pursue further.

There is, it seems, little to recommend the view that monogamy specially promotes "profound affection" between the partners or a "loving context" for child-upbringing. Such claims are simply without force. On the other hand, there are several aspects to the logic and operation of the four principles of this institution that suggest that it actually *inhibits* the achievement of these desiderata. Far from uniquely abetting the latter, it militates against them in these ways:

1. Centralized official control of marriage (which the Church gradually achieved through the mechanism of Canon Law after the fall of the Roman Empire in one of the greatest seizures of social power of history) necessarily alienates the partners from full responsibility for and freedom in their relationship. "Profound closeness" between the partners—or at least an area of it—is thereby expropriated rather than promoted and "sanctuary" from the pressures of outside society prohibited rather than fostered.

2. Limitation of the marriage bond to two people necessarily restricts, in perhaps the most unilateral way possible consistent with offspring survival, the number of adult sources of affection, interest, and material support and instruction for the young. The "loving context for child-up-bringing" is thereby dessicated rather than nourished, providing the structural conditions for such notorious and far-reaching problems as sibling rivalry for scarce adult attention and parental oppression through exclusive monopoly of the child's means of life.

3. Formal exclusion of all others from erotic contact with the marriage partner systematically promotes conjugal insecurity, jealousy, and alienation in several ways. (a) It officially underwrites a literally totalitarian expectation of sexual confinement on the part of one's husband or wife: which expectation is, *ceteris paribus,* inevitably more subject to anxiety and disappointment than one less extreme in its demand and/or cultural-juridical backing. (b) It requires so complete a sexual isolation of the marriage partners that should one violate the fidelity code the other is left alone and susceptible to a sense of fundamental deprivation and resentment. It stipulates such a strict restraint of sexual energies that there are habitual violations of the regulations, frequently if not always attended by willful deception and reciprocal suspicion about the occurrence or quality of the

extramarital relationship, anxiety and fear on both sides of permanent estrangement from partner and family, and overt and covert antagonism over the prohibited act in both offender (who feels "trapped") and offended (who feels "betrayed").

The disadvantages of the four principles of monogamous marriage do not, however, end with inhibiting the very effects they are said to promote. There are further shortcomings:

1. The restriction of marriage union to two partners necessarily prevents the strengths of larger groupings. Such advantages as the following are thereby usually ruled out: (a) the security, range, and power of larger socioeconomic units; (b) the epistemological and emotional substance, variety, and scope of more pluralist interactions; (c) the possibility of extra-domestic freedom founded on more adult providers and upbringers as well as more broadly based circles of intimacy.

2. The sexual containment and isolation that the four principles together require variously stimulates such social malaises as: (a) destructive aggression (which notoriously results from sexual frustration); (b) apathy, frustration, and dependence within the marriage bond; (c) lack of spontaneity, bad faith, and distance in relationships without the marriage bond; (d) sexual fantasizing, perversion, fetishism, prostitution, and pornography in the adult population as a whole.

Taking such things into consideration, it seems difficult to lend credence to the view that the four principles of our form of monogamous marriage constitute a structure beneficial either to the marriage partners themselves or to their offspring (or indeed to anyone else). One is moved to seek for some other ground of the institution, some ground that lurks beneath the reach of our conventional apprehensions.

IV

The ground of our marriage institution, the essential principle that underwrites all four restrictions, is this: *the maintenance by one man or woman of the effective right to exclude indefinitely all others from erotic access to the conjugal partner.*

The first restriction creates, elaborates on, and provides for the enforcement of this right to exclude. And the second, third, and fourth restrictions together ensure that the right to exclude is—respectively—not cooperative, not simultaneously or sequentially distributed, and not permissive of even casual exception.

In other words, the four restrictions of our form of monogamous marriage together constitute a state-regulated, indefinite, and exclusive ownership by two individuals of one another's sexual powers. Marriage is simply a form of private property.

That our form of monogamous marriage is, when the confusing layers of sanctity, apologetic, and taboo are cleared away, another species of private property should not surprise us. The history of the institution is so full of suggestive indicators—dowries, inheritance, property alliances, daughter sales (of which women's wedding rings are a carry-over), bride exchanges, and legitimacy and illegitimacy—that it is difficult not to see some intimate connections between marital and ownership ties. We are better able still to apprehend the ownership essence of our marriage institution, when in addition we consider: (1) that until recently almost the only way to secure official dissolution of consummated marriage was to be able to demonstrate violation of one or both partner's sexual ownership, (that is, adultery); (2) that the imperative of premarital chastity is tantamount to a demand for retrospective sexual ownership by the eventual marriage partner; (3) that successful sexual involvement with a married person is prosecutable as an expropriation of ownership—"alienation of affections"—which is restituted by cash payment; (4) that the incest taboo is an iron mechanism that protects the conjugal ownership of sexual properties, both the husband's and wife's, from the access of affectionate offspring and the offsprings' (who themselves are future marriage partners) from access of siblings and parents; (5) that the language of the marriage ceremony is the language of exclusive possession ("take," "to have and to hold," "forsaking all others and keeping you only unto him/her," and so on, not to mention the proprietary locutions associated with the marital relationship ("he's mine," "she belongs to him," "keep to your own husband," "wife stealer," "possessive husband," and so on).

V

Of course, it would be remarkable if marriage in our society was not a relationship akin to private property. In our socioeconomic system we relate to virtually everything of value by individual ownership: by, that is, the effective right to exclude others from the thing concerned. That we do so as well with perhaps the most highly valued thing of all—the sexual partners' sexuality—is only to be expected. Indeed, it would probably be an intolerable strain on our entire social structure if we did otherwise.

This line of thought deserves pursuit. The real secret of our form of monogamous marriage is not that it functionally provides for the needs of adults who love one another or of the children they give birth to but that it serves the maintenance of our present social system. It is an institution that is indispensable to the persistence of the capitalist order in the following ways:

1. A basic principle of current social relations is that some people legally acquire the use of other people's personal powers, from which they may exclude other members of society. This system operates in the work-place (owners and hirers of all types contractually acquire for their exclusive use workers' regular labor powers) and in the family (husbands and wives contractually acquire for their exclusive use their partner's sexual properties). A conflict between the structures of these primary relations—as would obtain were there a suspension of the restrictions governing our form of monogamous marriage—might well undermine the systemic coherence of present social intercourse.

2. The fundamental relation between individuals and things that satisfy their needs is, in our present society, that each individual has or does not have the effective right to exclude other people from the thing in question. A rudimentary need is that for sexual relationship(s). Therefore the object of this need must be related to the one who needs it as owned or not owned (that is, via marriage or not-marriage, or approximations thereof) if people's present relationship to what they need is to retain—again—systemic coherence.

3. A necessary condition for the continued existence of the present social formation is that its members feel a powerful motivation to gain favorable positions in it. But such social ambition is heavily dependent on the preservation of exclusive monogamy in that (a) the latter confines the discharge of primordial sexual energies to a single unalterable partner and thus typically compels those energies to seek alternative outlet, such as business or professional success and (b) the exclusive marriage necessarily reduces the sexual relationships available to any one person to absolute (nonzero) minimum, a unilateral promotion of sexual shortage that in prac-

tice renders hierarchical achievement essential as an economic and "display" means for securing scarce partners.

4. Because the exclusive marriage necessarily and dramatically reduces the possibilities of sexual-love relationships, it thereby promotes the existing economic system by: (a) rendering extreme economic self-interest—the motivational basis of the capitalistic process—less vulnerable to altruistic subversion; (b) disciplining society's members into the habitual repression of natural impulse required for long-term performance of repetitive and arduous work tasks; (c) developing a complex of suppressed sexual desires to which sales techniques may be effectively applied in creating those new consumer wants that provide indispensable outlets for ever increasing capital funds.

5. The present form of marriage is of fundamental importance to (a) the continued relative powerlessness of the individual family: which, with larger numbers would constitute a correspondingly increased command of social powers; (b) the continued high demand for homes, commodities, and services: which, with the considerable economies of scale that extended unions would permit, would otherwise falter; (c) the continued strict necessity for adult males to sell their labor power and for adult women to remain at home (or vice versa): which strict necessity would diminish as the economic base of the family unit extended; (d) the continued immense pool of unsatisfied sexual desires and energies in the population at large: without which powerful interests and institutions would lose much of their conventional appeal and force; (e) the continued profitable involvement of lawyers, priests, and state officials in the jurisdictions of marriage and divorce and the myriad official practices and proceedings connected thereto.

VI

If our marriage institution is a linchpin of our present social structure then a breakdown in this institution would seem to indicate a breakdown in our social structure. On the face of it, the marriage institution is breaking down—enormously increased divorce rates, nonmarital sexual relationships, wife-swapping, the Playboy philosophy, and communes. Therefore one might be led by the appearance of things to anticipate a profound alteration in the social system.

But it would be a mistake to underestimate the tenacity of an established order or to overestimate the extent of change in our marriage institution. Increased divorce rates merely indicate the widening of a traditional escape hatch. Nonmarital relationships imitate and culminate in the marital mold. Wife-swapping presupposes ownership, as the phrase suggests. The Playboy philosophy is merely the view that if one has the money one has the right to be titillated— the commercial call to more fully exploit a dynamic sector of capital investment. And communes—the most hopeful phenomenon— almost nowhere offer a *praxis* challenge to private property in sexuality. It may be changing. But history, as the old man puts it, weighs like a nightmare on the brains of the living.

For Further Reflection

1. Compare McMurtry's use of marriage as property with Kant's understanding of that notion. How do they differ? Who is closer to the truth?

2. Evaluate McMurtry's arguments against monogamous marriage. Examine the four principles which he attacks. Are his arguments convincing? Explain your answer.

3. If we were to follow McMurtry's logic, what kind of sexual relations would be permitted? Can you spell out the implications of his proposals?

4. How might a believer in traditional monogamous marriage defend that institution against McMurtry's attacks?

Marriage, Love, and Procreation
A Critique of McMurtry

MICHAEL D. BAYLES

Michael Bayles until his recent death was professor of philosophy at Florida State University. He is the author or editor of several works in social philosophy, including *Ethics and Population*. In this essay he attempts to rebut McMurtry's critique of monogamy. Bayles first identifies eleven social ills that McMurtry attributes at least in part to monogamy. Then he offers a historical perspective for our institution of marriage, rejecting the Kantian metaphor, which McMurtry adopts, of "mutual ownership" as "pure nonsense." Then Bayles argues that monogamous marriage plays two important functions. It promotes a deep, personal relationship of indefinite duration and it provides a good context for the raising of children. Bayles agrees that some aspects of marriage need reforming, but monogamous marriage has the resources to accomplish the two functions just mentioned.

The current era is one of that vulgar form of hedonism rejected by philosophical hedonists such as Epicurus and John Stuart Mill. Apologists thinly disguise the tawdriness of a hedonism of biological pleasures by appeals to individual rights and autonomy. Far too frequently these appeals merely mask a refusal to accept responsibility. This failure to accept personal responsibility is periodically atoned for by ritualistic and ill-conceived attempts to help the poor and underprivileged people of the world.

One of the central focuses of the current vulgar hedonism has been sexual liberation. Premarital intercourse, gay liberation, no-

From Michael D. Bayles, "Marriage, Love, and Procreation," in *Philosophy and Sex (Third Edition)*, edited by Robert B. Baker, Kathleen J. Winninger, and Frederick A. Elliston (pp. 116–129) (Amherst, NY: Prometheus Books) Copyright © 1998. Reprinted by permission of the publisher. Notes omitted.

fault divorce, open marriage (read, "open adultery"), polygamy, and orgies all have their advocates. About the only forms of sexual behavior yet to have strong advocates are pedophilia and bestiality. Any day now one may expect grade-school children to assert their right to happiness through pedophilia and animal lovers to argue that disapproval of bestiality is unfair to little lambs.

The result, especially in Western society, is an emphasis on sex that is out of all proportion to its significance for a eudaemonistic life—that is, a life worth living, including elements besides pleasure. The only ultimate test for the value of a life is whether at its end it is found to have been worth living. It is difficult to conceive of a person's thinking his life significant because it was a second-rate approximation to the sexual achievements of the notorious rabbit. However, many people seem to think such a life offers the highest ideal of a "truly human" existence, forgetting Aristotle's insight that reproduction is characteristic of all living things, not just humans. Consequently, the institution of marriage has been attacked for hindering the achievement of this vulgar hedonistic ideal.

ATTACKS ON MARRIAGE

Not all attacks on the institution of marriage have been based solely on the vulgar hedonistic ideal. A more broad ranging, although no more plausible, attack has recently been made by John McMurtry. His attack is directed not against marriage per se but against that form of it found in Western society—monogamy. McMurtry does not merely find that monogamous marriage hinders the achievement of the vulgar hedonistic ideal. He also claims it is at least one of the causes of the following social ills: (1) Central official control of marriage "*necessarily* alienates the partners from full responsibility for and freedom in their relationship." (2) Monogamy restricts the sources of adult affection and support available to children. (3) It "systematically promotes conjugal insecurity, jealousy, and alienation. . . ." (4) It "prevents the strengths of larger groupings." (5) It stimulates aggression, apathy, frustration, lack of spontaneity, perversion, fetishism, prostitution, and pornography. (6) It serves to maintain the status quo and capitalism. (7) It supports the powerlessness of the individual family by keeping it small. (8) By promoting many small families it creates a high demand for homes and consumer goods and services. (9) It makes it necessary for many more males to sell their labor than would be necessary if monogamy were not practiced. (10) By limiting opportunities for sexual satisfaction it channels unsatisfied desire into support for various institutions and interests. (11) Finally, it promotes financial profit for lawyers, priests, and so forth, in marriage and divorce proceedings. Such a catalog of evils omits only a few social problems such as political corruption and environmental deterioration, although even they are hinted at in numbers 8 and 11.

Many people have hoped that the simple-mindedness that attributes all or most or even many of society's ills to a single factor would disappear. At one time private ownership of the means of production was the *bête noir* of society. Recently it has been replaced in that role by unlimited population growth. Both of these beasts have been slain by the St. George of reasonableness. McMurtry has called forth yet another single-factor beast. There is no reason to suppose this one to be any more powerful than its predecessors.

No attempt will be made in this essay to examine in detail McMurtry's criticisms of monogamous marriage. In general they are characterized by a lack of historical and sociological perspective. It is unclear whether he is attacking the ideal of monogamous marriage as it perhaps existed a hundred years ago or as it exists today. Yet this difference is crucial. A century ago divorce was not widely recognized or accepted; today that is not true. When divorce was not recognized, concubinage and prostitution were quite prevalent, as was simply abandoning one's family. Such practices certainly mitigated the effect of the strict social rules that McMurtry discusses. Also, he criticizes monogamy for limiting the access of children to adult affection and support, since they must rely upon their parents alone for care. But in the extended family, which existed until the urbanization of society, that limitation was considerably less common than it may be at present.

McMurtry seems to be unaware of the social realities of modern society. He emphasizes the law as it is written rather than the law in action. It is generally recognized that despite the wording of statutes, marriages can in practice now be dissolved by mutual consent. Nor is adultery usually prosecuted in those states in which it is still a crime. Nor does McMurtry present any sociological evidence for the various effects that he claims monogamous marriage has. Sometimes the evidence may well be against him. For example, he claims that monogamy supports the high demand for homes. Yet, for a century in Ireland monogamy coincided with a low demand for new homes. Couples simply postponed marriage until the male inherited the home of his parents, and those who did not inherit often did not marry.

Underlying McMurtry's view of monogamous marriage is the Kantian conception of the marriage contract. According to Kant, marriage "is the Union of two Persons of different sex for life-long reciprocal possession of their sexual faculties." McMurtry takes the following principle to be the essential ground of monogamous marriage: "the maintenance by one man or woman of the effective right to exclude indefinitely all others from erotic access to the conjugal partner." Since by "possession" Kant meant legal ownership and the consequent right to exclude others, these two views come to the same thing. They both view marriage as chiefly concerned with private ownership of the means to sexual gratification, thus combining capitalism with vulgar hedonism (although Kant was not a hedonist).

Such a view of marriage is pure nonsense. However, it has more plausibility in today's era of vulgar hedonism than it did in Kant's time. Historically, the official aims of marriage, according to the Catholic Church—which was the only church during the period of the establishment of monogamous marriage in Western society— were procreation and companionship. There was also a tendency to view it as a legitimate outlet for man's sinful nature. It is this latter element that Kant and McMurtry have taken as the chief one.

In addition to the avowed purposes of marriage there were the actual social functions that it performed. The family unit was the basic social unit, not only for the education of children (that is, socialization, not formal schooling—which has only become widespread during the past century), but also for the production of necessities, including food and clothing, and for recreation. These historical functions of the extended-family unit based on monogamous marriage have been undermined by the development of industrial, urban society. Consequently, the moral and legal status and functions of marriage require reexamination in the light of current social conditions.

Before undertaking such a reexamination it is necessary to distinguish between rules of marriage and attendant social rules. They are mixed together in the traditional social institution of monogamous marriage, but there is no necessity for this mix and it is probably unjustified. In particular one must distinguish between penal laws prohibiting various forms of sexual union—homosexual, premarital, adulterous—and private arranging laws granting legal recognition to the marital relationship. Private arranging laws do not prescribe punishment for offenses; instead, they enable people to carry out their desires. People are not punished for improperly made marriages; instead, the marriages are invalid and unenforceable. Laws against fornication, prostitution, cohabitation, and homosexuality are almost always penal. Objections to them cannot be transferred directly to the marriage relationship. All of these penal laws could be abolished and monogamous marriage could still be retained.

It may be claimed that despite their nonpenal form, marriage laws do in fact penalize those who prefer other forms of relationship. If homosexual and polygamous relationships are not legally recognized as "marriages," then persons desiring these forms of relationship are being deprived of some degree of freedom. When considering freedom one must be clear about what one is or is not free to do. Consider, for example, the case of gambling. One must distinguish between laws that forbid gambling and the absence of laws that recognize gambling debts. The latter does not deprive people of the freedom to contract gambling debts; it simply does not allow the use of legal enforcement to collect them. Similarly, the absence of laws recognizing polygamous and homosexual marriages does not deprive people of the freedom to enter polygamous and homosexual unions. Instead, it merely fails to provide legal recourse to enforce the agreements of the parties to such unions. The absence of laws recognizing such marriages does not deprive people of a freedom they previously had, for they were never able to have such agreements legally enforced. Nor have people been deprived of a freedom they would have if there were no legal system, for in the absence of a legal system no agreements can be legally enforced. If there is a ground for complaint, then, it must be one of inequality—that one type of relationship is legally recognized but others are not. However, a charge of inequality is warranted only if there are no relevant reasonable grounds for distinguishing between relationships. To settle that issue one must be clear about the state's or society's interests in marriage.

The rest of this essay is concerned with the purposes or functions of the marriage relationship in which society has a legitimate interest. It is not possible here to set out and to justify the purposes for which governments may legislate. It is assumed that the state may act to facilitate citizens' engaging in activities that they find desirable and to protect the welfare and equality of all citizens, including future ones. Government has an especially strong responsibility for the welfare of children. Of course, these legitimate governmental or social interests and responsibilities must be balanced against other interests and values of citizens, including those of privacy and freedom from interference.

There is no attempt or intention to justify penal laws prohibiting forms of relationship other than monogamous marriage. Indeed, it is generally assumed that they ought not be prohibited and that more people will enter into them than has been the case. In such a context, monogamous marriage would become a more specialized form of relationship, entered into by a smaller proportion of the population than previously. Underlying this assumption are the general beliefs that many people are unqualified or unfit for a marital relationship and ought never to enter one and that many people marry for the wrong reasons. If true, these beliefs may explain why both marriage and divorce rates have been steadily rising in most Western countries during this century.

PROMOTING INTERPERSONAL RELATIONSHIPS

Alienation from others and loss of community are perceived by many to be among the most serious ills of modern, mass society. In such a situation it seems unlikely that many would deny the need for intimate interpersonal relationships of affection. The importance of such relationships for a good or *eudaemonistic* life has been recognized by philosophers as diverse as Aristotle and G. E. Moore. In considering such interpersonal relationships to be among the most valuable elements of a good life, one must distinguish between the value of a good and the strength of the desire for it. Many people have a stronger desire for life than for such interpersonal relationships, but they may still recognize such relationships as more valuable than mere life. Life itself is of little value, but it is a necessary condition for most other things of value.

Among the most valuable forms of interpersonal relationship are love, friendship, and trust. These relationships are limited with respect to the number of persons with whom one can have them. Classically, there has been a distinction between agapeic and erotic love. Agapeic love is the love of all mankind—general benevolence. The concept of erotic love is more limited. In today's world erotic love is apt to be confused with sexual desire and intercourse. But there can be and always has been sex without love and love without sex. Personal love is more restricted than either agapeic love or sexual desire. It implies a concern for another that is greater than that for most people. Hence, it cannot be had for an unlimited number of other people. Similar distinctions must be drawn between friendship and acquaintance, trust of a political candidate and trust of a friend.

Such interpersonal relationships require intimacy. Intimacy involves a sharing of information about one another that is not shared with others. Moreover, it often involves seclusion from others—being in private where others cannot observe. In some societies where physical privacy is not possible, psychological privacy—shutting out the awareness of the presence of others—substitutes. Consequently, these valuable interpersonal relationships require intimacy and usually physical privacy from others, and at the very least nonintrusion upon the relationship.

Moreover, these forms of interpersonal relationship require acts expressing the concern felt for the other person. In most societies acts of sexual intercourse have been such expressions of love and concern. It is not physically or psychologically necessary that sexual intercourse have this quasi-symbolic function, but it is a natural function of sexual intercourse. All that is here meant by "natural" is that in most societies sexual intercourse has this function, for which there is some psychological basis even though it is not contrary to scientific laws for it to be otherwise. Intercourse usually involves an element of giving of oneself, and one's sexual identity is frequently a central element of one's self-image. It is not, however, sexual intercourse that is intrinsically valuable but the feelings and attitudes, the underlying interpersonal relationship, that it expresses. Nonsexual acts also currently express such relationships, but sexual intercourse is still one of the most important ways of doing so. If sexual intercourse ceases to have this function in society, some other act will undoubtedly replace it in this function. Moreover, sexual intercourse will have lost much of its value.

If these interpersonal relationships of personal love and trust are of major value, it is reasonable for the state to seek to protect and foster them by according legal recognition to them in marriage. The specific forms of this recognition cannot be fully discussed. However, there is some basis for treating the partners to a marriage as one person. Historically, of course, the doctrine that the parties to a marriage are one person has supported the subjugation of women in all sorts of ways, for example, in their disability from owning property. But there is an underlying rationale for joint responsibility. Two people who, without a special reason such as taxes, keep separate accounts of income and expenditures do not have the love and trust of a couple who find such an accounting unnecessary. Moreover, in such a joint economic venture there is no point to allowing one party to sue the other. Only the advent of insurance, whereby neither spouse, but a third party, pays, makes such suits seem profitable. Another recognition of these relationships—albeit one not frequently invoked—is that one is not forced to testify against his or her spouse. More important is that neither party is encouraged to violate the trust and intimacy of the relationship, for example, by encouraging one to inform authorities about bedroom comments of his or her spouse.

The character of these valuable forms of interpersonal relationship provides an argument against according marriages of definite duration legal recognition equal to that accorded those that are intentionally of indefinite duration. For it to be "intentionally of indefinite duration," neither partner may, when entering the marriage, intend it to be for a specific period of time, for example, five years, nor may the marriage contract specify such a period. The following argument is not to show that marriages for a definite duration should not be recognized, but merely to show that they should not have equal standing with those intentionally of indefinite duration. The basic reason for unequal recognition is that interpersonal relationships that are not intentionally of indefinite duration are less valuable than those that are.

Suppose one were to form a friendship with a colleague, but the two mutually agree to be friends for only three years, with an option to renew the friendship at that time. Such an agreement would indicate a misunderstanding of friendship. Such agreements make sense for what Aristotle called friendships of utility, but in the modern world these friendships are business partnerships. While there is nothing wrong with business friendships, they do not have the intrinsic value of personal friendships. In becoming close personal friends with someone, one establishes a concern and trust that would be seriously weakened or destroyed by setting a time limit to the friendship. It is sometimes claimed that time limits may be set because people will only be together for a while. But one need not see a person every day or even every year to remain friends. However, extended separation usually brings about a withering away of the friendship.

Similarly, the personal relationship of love and trust in marriage is of lesser value if it is intentionally for only a definite period of time. Moreover, the entering into a relationship that is intentionally of indefinite duration and legally recognized symbolizes a strength of commitment not found in other types of relationships. While two unmarried people may claim that there is no definite limit to their mutual commitment, their commitment is always questionable. Entering into a marital relationship assures the commitment more than does a mere verbal avowal. . . .

PROTECTING THE WELFARE OF CHILDREN

Another area of pervasive social interest that has historically centered in marriage concerns the procreation and raising of children. Society has an interest not only in the number of children born but their quality of life. This fact is in deep conflict with the current emphasis on the freedom of individuals to make reproductive decisions unfettered by social rules and restrictions. Moreover, it is an area in which social control has traditionally been weak. Child abuse is widespread, and efforts to prevent it are mediocre at best. There are few general legal qualifications or tests for becoming a parent. Yet parenthood is one of the most potentially dangerous relationships that one person can have with another. If one is a poor college teacher, then at worst a few students do not receive a bit of education they might have. But as a parent one potentially can ruin completely the lives of one's children. At the least, they may develop into psychological misfits incapable of leading responsible and rewarding lives.

Essentially, there are three areas of social interest and responsibility with respect to procreation and the raising of children. First, there is a social interest in the sheer number of children born. The current emphasis on population control makes this interest abundantly clear. Second, there is a social interest in the potentialities of children. This area includes concern for genetic and congenital birth defects and abnormalities. Over 5 percent of all children born have a genetic defect. The possibility of genetic control of those who are born will soon take on major significance. Already, approximately sixty genetic diseases as well as almost all chromosomal abnormalities can be detected *in utero,* and adult carriers of about eighty genetic defects can be identified. Given the possibility of genetic control, society can no longer risk having genetically disadvantaged children by leaving the decision of whether to have children to the unregulated judgment of individual couples. Some social regulations with respect to genetic screening and, perhaps, eugenic sterilization are needed. While potential parents have interests of privacy and freedom in reproductive decisions, the social interests in preventing the suffering and inequality of possibly defective children may outweigh them in certain types of cases.

Third, the care and development of those who are born is a social interest and responsibility. This interest has been recognized for some time in the form of children's homes and compulsory education. However, increasing knowledge about childhood development extends the area in which social interests and responsibility may be reasonably involved. To give an example at the most elementary level, the nutritional diet of children during their first three years is crucial for their future development. So also is their psychological support. The welfare of future generations is not a private but a social matter. It is a proper task of society, acting through its government, to ensure that the members of the next generation are not physical or psychological cripples due to the ignorance, negligence, or even indifference of parents.

Historically, society has attempted to control procreation through the institution of marriage. Society's means were primarily to stigmatize children born out of wedlock and to encourage the having of many children. It is now recognized that no useful purpose is served by stigmatizing children born out of wedlock as illegitimate.

(However, some useful purpose may be served by not according children born out of wedlock all the rights of those born in wedlock, for example, inheritance without parental recognition.) The emphasis on having as many children as one can has also disappeared. It is not this historical concern with procreation that is misplaced in modern society but the forms that the concern has taken.

If society has the responsibility to protect the welfare of children, then some social regulation and control of human reproduction and development is justified. Such regulation and control need not be effected by penal laws. For example, social concern has traditionally been expressed in adoptions through regulations to ensure that those who adopt children are fit to care for them. That some regulations have been inappropriate and not reasonably related to the welfare of children is not in question. Rather, the point is that there has been regulation without penal laws, or at least without resorting primarily to penal laws. Nor can social regulation and control be solely by legislation. Legislation alone is usually ineffective; it must be supported by informal social rules and expectations.

Not only has modern biomedicine made sex possible without procreation; it has also made procreation possible without sex. The techniques of artificial insemination and fertilization, embryo transfer, ova donation, ectogenesis, and cloning now, or soon will, make it possible for people to reproduce without sexual intercourse. Hence, not only may one have sex for pleasure, but one may reproduce for pleasure without sexual intercourse. Not only may people reproduce outside marriage; they are not even biologically required to have intercourse. Thus, sex and marriage may become dissociated from reproduction.

However, there are strong reasons for restricting procreation primarily to marriages of indefinite duration, which does not imply that such marriages should be restricted to procreation. Marriage has traditionally been the central social institution concerned with procreation. Consequently, if society is to exercise some control over procreation in the future, it would involve the least change in conditions to do so through marriage. Moreover, there is considerable evidence that the disruption of family life contributes to juvenile delinquency. Whether divorce or marital breakdown (with or without divorce) is a prime cause of such delinquency does not matter. The point is that the disruption of home life does seriously affect the development of children. The chance of such disruption outside of a marriage that is intentionally of indefinite duration is higher than for that within. Moreover, there is some reason to believe that the presence of both mother and father is instrumental in the psychological development of children. In any case, the presence of two people rather than one provides the security that there will be someone to care for the children should one of the parents die. Generally, children are better off being with one parent than in a state orphanage, but better off still with both parents. Hence, for the welfare of children it seems best that procreation and child rearing primarily occur within the context of marriages intentionally of indefinite duration.

While society has a responsibility for the care and development of children, this general responsibility is best carried out if specific adults have obligations to care for specific children. In the past, the biological parent-child relation has reinforced the allocation of responsibility for specific children and has been a major factor in monogamy. The separation of reproduction and sexual intercourse threatens disruption of this assignment. For example, if gestation occurs in an artificial womb in a laboratory, there may be no "parents," only a scientific research group. More realistically, if a woman has an embryo from ova and sperm donors transferred to her uterus, it is unclear who are the child's parents. However, if there is to be optimal care for children, specific adults must have obligations for specific children. It cannot be left to somebody in general, for then nobody in particular is likely to do it. "Let George do it" is too prevalent and careless an attitude to allow with regard to children.

McMurtry's contention that monogamy restricts the care for children is not well founded. First, if there are no specific adults responsible for children, they may become "lost" in large groups and victims of the "it's not my job" syndrome. Second, monogamy per se does not cut children off from the support and care of others. One must distinguish the marital relationship from living arrangements. It is the isolated situation of the family that deprives children of such support. In many married-student housing complexes children have access to other adults. Even in general-residential neighborhoods with separate family housing units, such support is available if there is a sense of community in the neighborhood.

Given the social interests in and responsibility for the procreation and development of children, some more effective controls of parenthood appear desirable. If the primary locus of reproduction is to be within marriages of intentionally indefinite duration, then the easiest way to institute controls is to add requirements for people to enter such marriages. A few requirements such as blood tests are already generally prevalent. Alternatively, one might have a separate licensing procedure for procreation. Nonmarried couples and single people might also qualify for such licenses. Moreover, couples who want to marry but not have children would not have to meet requirements. However, the only requirements suggested below that might bar marriages are almost as important for those couples who do not have children as for those who do. If the requirements were tied to marriage they would be easier to administer. The only drawback is that unmarried people would not have to meet them. However, such requirements can and should be part of the medical practice of the "artificial" techniques of reproduction—artificial insemination and embryo transfer. And there are few if any effective methods, except generally accepted social rules, to control procreation outside of marriage.

One obvious requirement would be genetic screening. With modern medical techniques genetic problems do not imply that couples cannot become married, but they might be expected not to have children who are their genetic offspring. Artificial insemination and embryo transfer make it possible for almost everyone to have children, even though the children might not be genetically theirs. A general distinction between biological and social parenthood should be made, with legal emphasis on the latter.

More important, perhaps, is some general expectation of psychological fitness for family life and the raising of children. The difficulty with such an expectation is the absence of any clear criteria for fitness and reliable methods for determining who meets them. Perhaps, however, some formal instruction in family relations and child rearing would be appropriate. The Commission on Population Growth and the American Future has already called for an expansion of education for parenthood. It is only a bit further to require some sort of minimal family education for marriage. Probably the easiest method for ensuring such education would be to make it a required subject in secondary schools. If that were done, few people would have difficulty meeting this requirement for marriage.

There should not be any financial or property qualifications for marriage. Society's interest in and responsibility for the welfare of the population in general is such that governments should ensure an adequate standard of living for all persons. Were that to be done there would be no reason to impose any financial restrictions on marriage. Nonetheless, prospective parents should have more concern for their financial situation than is now frequently the case. The adequate care of children is an expensive task, financially as well as psychologically and temporally.

CONCLUSION

It may be objected that neither the argument from interpersonal relations nor that from the welfare of children specifically supports monogamous marriage. While loving relationships cannot extend to an indefinite number of people, they can extend to more than one other person. Also, a polygamous union may provide a reasonable environment for procreation. Hence, neither of the arguments supports monogamous marriage per se.

Logically, the objection is quite correct. But it is a misunderstanding of social philosophy to expect arguments showing that a certain arrangement is always best under all circumstances. The most that can be shown is that usually, or as a rule, one social arrangement is preferable to another. Practically, polygamous marriage patterns will probably never be prevalent. For centuries they have been gradually disappearing throughout the world. If a disproportionate sex distribution of the population occurs in some areas or age groups (such as the elderly), then they may increase in significance. Unless that occurs, most people will probably continue to prefer marital monogamy.

More important, the burden of this paper has not been to defend the traditional ideal of marital union or even the current practice. Many of the traditional rules of marriage have been unjust, for example, the inequality between the sexes, both legally and in terms of social roles. Instead, it has been to defend social recognition of marriage of intentionally indefinite duration as a unique and socially valuable institution that society has interests in promoting and regulating. In particular, society has interests in and responsibility for promoting a certain form of valuable interpersonal relationship and protecting the welfare of children. Both of these purposes can be well served by monogamous marriage.

The image, then, is of a society with various forms of living together, but one in which marriage of intentionally indefinite duration would have a distinctive though lessened role as a special kind of socially and legally recognized relationship. There would not be laws prohibiting nonmarital forms of cohabitation. Divorce would be based on factual marital break-down or mutual consent, with due regard for the welfare of children. Monogamous marriage would recognize a special form of personal relationship in which reproduction and child rearing primarily occur. Given the social interest in decreasing procreation, many people might marry but not have children, and others might not marry at all. Details of the legal marital relationship have not been specified, nor could they be in this brief essay except with respect to the main social interests. Questions of inheritance, legal residence and name, social-security benefits, and so on, have not been specified. Changes in laws with respect to many of these matters can be made without affecting the arguments for the value of, social responsibility for, and interests in marriage. Above all, it is an image in which sexual intercourse plays a much smaller role in the conception of marriage and the good life in general, a society in which vulgar hedonism has at least been replaced by a broader-based *eudaemonism*.

For Further Reflection

1. Review Bayles's critique of McMurtry's arguments. What are the main deficiencies he claims to find in McMurtry? Is he fair to McMurtry? Who is closer to the truth?

2. Evaluate Bayles's theses that monogamy has the resources to promote deep personal relations and provide a context for rearing children. Do you agree with him? How might McMurtry respond to these points? Explain your answer.

3. What does Bayles mean by rejecting vulgar hedonism and replacing it with eudaimonism?

What's Wrong with Adultery?

BONNIE STEINBOCK

Bonnie Steinbock is professor of philosophy at the State University of New York, Albany, and the author of several articles in social philosophy. In this essay she notes the reports of increased adultery on the part of wives, as well as the general disapproval of adultery. Why is adultery generally thought to be immoral? Steinbock gives three arguments against adultery: (1) it generally involves promise-breaking; (2) it generally involves deception; and (3) it detracts from the deep intimacy necessary for a good marriage.

According to a 1980 survey in *Cosmopolitan,* 54 percent of American wives have had extramarital affairs; a study of 100,000 married women by the considerably tamer *Redbook* magazine found that 40 percent of the wives over 40 had been unfaithful. While such surveys are, to some extent, self-selecting—those who do it are more likely to fill out questionnaires about it—sexual mores have clearly changed in recent years. Linda Wolfe, who reported the results of the *Cosmopolitan* survey, suggests that "this increase in infidelity among married women represents not so much a deviation from traditional standards of fidelity as a break with the old double standard." Studies show that men have always strayed in significant numbers.

Yet 80 percent of "COSMO girls" did not approve of infidelity and wished their own husbands and lovers would be faithful. Eighty-eight percent of respondents to a poll taken in Iowa in 1983 viewed "coveting your neighbor's spouse" as a "major sin." It seems that while almost nobody approves of adultery, men have always done it, and women are catching up.

The increase in female adultery doubtless has to do with recent and radical changes in our attitudes toward sex and sexuality. We

Reprinted from Bonnie Steinbock, "Adultery," in *QQ: Report from the Center for Philosophy and Public Policy* 6:1 (Winter 1986), by permission of the author.

no longer feel guilty about enjoying sex; indeed, the capacity for sexual enjoyment is often regarded as a criterion of mental health. When sex itself is no longer intrinsically shameful, restraints on sexual behavior are loosened. In fact, we might question whether the abiding disapproval of infidelity merely gives lip service to an ancient taboo. Is there a rational justification for disapproving of adultery which will carry force with everyone, religious and nonreligious alike?

TRUST AND DECEPTION

Note first that adultery, unlike murder, theft, and lying, is not universally forbidden. Traditional Eskimo culture, for example, regarded sharing one's wife with a visitor as a matter of courtesy. The difference can be explained by looking at the effects of these practices on social cohesiveness. Without rules protecting the lives, persons, and property of its members, no group could long endure. Indeed, rules against killing, assault, lying, and stealing seem fundamental to having a morality at all.

Not so with adultery. For adultery is a *private* matter, essentially concerning only the relationship between husband and wife. It is not essential to morality like these other prohibitions: there are stable societies with genuine moral codes which tolerate extra-marital sex. Although adultery remains a criminal offense in some jurisdictions, it is rarely prosecuted. Surely this is because it is widely regarded as a private matter: in the words of Billie Holiday, "Ain't nobody's business if I do."

However, even if adultery is a private matter, with which the state should not interfere, it is not a morally neutral issue. Our view of adultery is connected to our thoughts and feelings about love and marriage, sex and the family, the value of fidelity, sexual jealousy, and exclusivity. How we think about adultery will affect the quality of our relationships, the way we raise our children, the kind of society we have and want to have. So it is important to consider whether our attitudes toward adultery are justifiable.

Several practical considerations militate against adultery: pregnancy and genital herpes immediately spring to mind. However, unwanted pregnancies are a risk of all sexual intercourse, within or without marriage; venereal disease is a risk of all non-exclusive sex, not just adulterous sex. So these risks do not provide a reason for objecting specifically to adultery. In any event, they offer merely pragmatic, as opposed to moral, objections. If adultery is wrong, it does not become less so because one has been sterilized or inoculated against venereal disease.

Two main reasons support regarding adultery as seriously immoral. One is that adultery is an instance of promise-breaking, on the view that marriage involves, explicitly or implicitly, a promise of sexual fidelity: to forsake all others. That there is this attitude in our culture is clear. Mick Jagger, not noted for sexual puritanism, allegedly refused to marry Jerry Hall, the mother of his baby, because he had no intention of accepting an exclusive sexual relationship. While Jagger's willingness to become an unwed father is hardly mainstream morality, his refusal to marry, knowing that he did not wish to be faithful, respects the idea that *marriage* requires such a commitment. Moreover, the promise of sexual fidelity is regarded as a very serious and important one. To cheat on one's spouse indicates a lack of concern, a willingness to cause pain, and so a lack of love. Finally, one who breaks promises cannot be trusted. And trust is essential to the intimate partnership of marriage, which may be irreparably weakened by its betrayal.

The second reason for regarding adultery as immoral is that it involves deception, for example, lying about one's whereabouts and relations with others. Perhaps a marriage can withstand the occasional lie, but a pattern of lying will have irrevocable consequences for a marriage, if discovered, and probably even if not. Like breaking promises, lying is regarded as a fundamental kind of wrong-doing, a failure to take the one lied to seriously as a moral person entitled to respect.

OPEN MARRIAGE

These two arguments suffice to make most cases of adultery wrong, given the attitudes and expectations of most people. But what if marriage did not involve any promise of sexual fidelity? What if there were no need for deception, because neither partner expected or wanted such fidelity? Objections to "open marriage" cannot focus on promise-breaking and deception, for the expectation of exclusivity is absent. If an open marriage has been freely chosen by both spouses, and not imposed by a dominant on a dependent partner, would such an arrangement be morally acceptable, even desirable?

The attractiveness of extramarital affairs, without dishonesty, disloyalty, or guilt, should not be downplayed. However satisfying sex between married people may be, it cannot have the excitement of a new relationship. ("Not *better,* a friend once said defensively to his wife, attempting to explain his infidelity, "just *different.*") Might we not be better off, our lives fuller and richer, if we allowed ourselves the thrill of new and different sexual encounters?

Perhaps the expectation of sexual exclusivity in marriage stems from emotions which are not admirable: jealousy and possessiveness. That most people experience these feelings is no reason for applauding or institutionalizing them. Independence in marriage is now generally regarded as a good thing: too much "togetherness" is boring and stifling. In a good marriage, the partners can enjoy different activities, travel apart, and have separate friends. Why draw the line at sexual activity?

The natural response to this question invokes a certain conception of love and sex: sex is an expression of affection and intimacy and so should be reserved for people who love each other. Further, it is assumed that one can and should have such feelings for only one other person at any time. To make love with someone else is to express feelings of affection and intimacy that should be reserved for one's spouse alone.

This rejection of adultery assumes the validity of a particular conception of love and sex, which can be attacked in two ways. We might divorce sex from love and regard sex as a pleasurable activity in its own right, comparable to the enjoyment of a good meal. In his article "Is Adultery Immoral?"[1] Richard Wasserstrom suggests that the linkage of sex with love reflects a belief that unless it is purified by a higher emotion, such as love, sex is intrinsically bad or dirty.

But this is an overly simplistic view of the connection between sex and love. Feelings of love occur between people enjoying sex-

---

[1] In Wasserstrom's *Today's Moral Problems* (New York: Macmillan, 1975), 288–300. Reprinted in R. Baker and F. Elliston, eds., *Philosophy and Sex,* 1st ed. (Buffalo, NY: Prometheus, 1975), 207–21; 2nd ed. (1984), 93–106.

ual intercourse, not out of a sense that sexual pleasure must be purified, but precisely because of the mutual pleasure they give one another. People naturally have feelings of affection for those who make them happy, and sex is a very good way of making someone extraordinarily happy. At the same time, sex is by its nature intimate, involving both physical and psychological exposure. This both requires and creates trust, which is closely allied to feelings of affection and love. This is not to say that sex necessarily requires or leads to love; but a conception of the relation between love and sex that ignores these factors is inadequate and superficial.

Alternatively, one might acknowledge the connection between sex and love, but attack the assumption of exclusivity. If parents can love all their children equally and if adults can have numerous close friends, why should it be impossible to love more than one sexual partner at a time? Perhaps we could learn to love more than one sexual partner at a time? Perhaps we could learn to love more widely and to accept that a spouse's sexual involvement with another is not a sign of rejection or lack of love.

The logistics of multiple involvement are certainly daunting. Having an affair (as opposed to a roll in the hay) requires time and concentration; it will almost inevitably mean neglecting one's spouse, one's children, one's work. More important, however, exclusivity seems to be an intrinsic part of "true love." Imagine Romeo pouring out his heart to both Juliet *and* Rosalind! In our ideal of romantic love, one chooses to forgo pleasure with other partners in order to have a unique relationship with one's beloved. Such "renunciation" is natural in the first throes of romantic love; it is precisely because this stage does *not* last that we must promise to be faithful through the notoriously unromantic realities of married life.

FIDELITY AS AN IDEAL

On the view I have been defending, genuinely open marriages are not *immoral,* although they deviate from a valued ideal of what marriage should be. While this is not the only ideal, or incumbent on all rational agents, it is a moral view in that it embodies a claim about a good way for people to live. The prohibition of adultery, then, is neither arbitrary nor irrational. However, even if we are justified in accepting the ideal of fidelity, we know that people do not always live up to the ideals they accept and we recognize that some failures to do so are worse than others. We regard a brief affair, occasioned by a prolonged separation, as morally different from installing a mistress.

Further, sexual activity is not necessary for deviation from the ideal of marriage which lies behind the demand for fidelity. As John Heckler observed during his bitter and public divorce from former Health and Human Services Secretary Margaret Heckler, "In marriage, there are two partners. When one person starts contributing far less than the other person to the marriage, that's the original infidelity. You don't need any third party." While this statement was probably a justification of his own infidelities, the point is valid. To abandon one's spouse, whether to a career or to another person, is also a kind of betrayal.

If a man becomes deeply involved emotionally with another woman, it may be little comfort that he is able to assure his wife that "Nothing happened." Sexual infidelity has significance as a sign of a deeper betrayal—falling in love with someone else. It may be objected that we cannot control the way we feel, only the way we behave; that we should not be blamed for falling in love, but only for acting on the feeling. While we may not have direct control over our feelings, however, we are responsible for getting ourselves into situations in which certain feelings naturally arise. "It just happened," is rarely an accurate portrayal of an extra-marital love affair.

If there can be betrayal without sex, can there be sex without betrayal? In the novel *Forfeit,* by Dick Francis, the hero is deeply in love with his wife, who was paralyzed by polio in the early days of their marriage. Her great unspoken fear is that he will leave her; instead, he tends to her devotedly. For several years, he forgoes sex, but eventually succumbs to an affair. While his adultery is hardly praiseworthy, it is understandable. He could divorce his wife and marry again, but it is precisely his refusal to abandon her, his continuing love and tender care, that makes us admire him.

People do fall in love with others and out of love with their spouses. Ought they refrain from making love while still legally tied? I cannot see much, if any, moral value in remaining physically faithful, on principle, to a spouse one no longer loves. This will displease those who regard the wrongness of adultery as a moral absolute, but my account has nothing to do with absolutes and everything to do with what it means to love someone deeply and completely. It is the value of that sort of relationship that makes sexual fidelity an ideal worth the sacrifice.

Neither a mere religiously based taboo, nor a relic of a repressive view of sexuality, the prohibition against adultery expresses a particular conception of married love. It is one we can honor in our own lives and bequeath to our children with confidence in its value as a coherent and rational ideal.

For Further Reflection

1. Consider the first two arguments against adultery, based on the fundamental moral principles involving prohibitions on promise-breaking and deception. Steinbock admits that an open marriage would not violate these principles. Why then is an open marriage less valuable than one involving exclusive sexual relations?

2. Steinbock emphasizes the need for concentrated involvement in marriage. Is she correct about this? Could you imagine a communal marriage where, say, four or more lovers developed a more expansive family? What would be the benefits and drawbacks of such a relationship?

Licensing Parents

HUGH LAFOLLETTE

Hugh LaFollette is professor of philosophy at Tennessee State University and the author of several works in applied ethics. In this essay, LaFollette argues that in order to reduce

Hugh LaFollette. "Licensing Parents" in *Philosophy and Public Affairs,* Vol 9.2 (1980). Copyright © 1980 by Princeton University Press. Reprinted by permission of Princeton University Press. Notes edited.

mistreatment of children we ought to require that prospective parents demonstrate that they are qualified to raise children. He argues against the thesis that people have a right to have children and urges us to devise a screening program analogous to our present adoption programs. Although not directly aimed at population control, LaFollette arguments are relevant to that issue.

In this essay I shall argue that the state should require all parents to be licensed. My main goal is to demonstrate that the licensing of parents is theoretically desirable, though I shall also argue that a workable and just licensing program actually could be established.

My strategy is simple. After developing the basic rationale for the licensing of parents, I shall consider several objections to the proposal and argue that these objections fail to undermine it. I shall then isolate some striking similarities between this licensing program and our present policies on the adoption of children. If we retain these adoption policies—as we surely should—then, I argue, a general licensing program should also be established. Finally, I shall briefly suggest that the reason many people object to licensing is that they think parents, particularly biological parents, own or have natural sovereignty over their children.

REGULATING POTENTIALLY HARMFUL ACTIVITIES

Our society normally regulates a certain range of activities; it is illegal to perform these activities unless one has received prior permission to do so. We require automobile operators to have licenses. We forbid people from practicing medicine, law, pharmacy, or psychiatry unless they have satisfied certain licensing requirements.

Society's decision to regulate just these activities is not ad hoc. The decision to restrict admission to certain vocations and to forbid some people from driving is based on an eminently plausible, although not often explicitly formulated, rationale. We require drivers to be licensed because driving an auto is an activity which is potentially harmful to others, safe performance of the activity requires a certain competence, and we have a moderately reliable procedure for determining that competence. The potential harm is obvious: incompetent drivers can and do maim and kill people. The best way we have of limiting this harm without sacrificing the benefits of automobile travel is to require that all drivers demonstrate at least minimal competence. We likewise license doctors, lawyers, and psychologists because they perform activities which can harm others. Obviously they must be proficient if they are to perform these activities properly, and we have moderately reliable procedures for determining proficiency.[1] Imagine a world in which everyone could legally drive a car, in which everyone could legally perform surgery, prescribe medications, dispense drugs, or offer legal advice. Such a world would hardly be desirable.

Consequently, any activity that is potentially harmful to others and requires certain demonstrated competence for its safe performance, is subject to regulation—that is, it is theoretically desirable that we regulate it. If we also have a reliable procedure for determining whether someone has the requisite competence, then the action is not only subject to regulation but ought, all things considered, to be regulated.

It is particularly significant that we license these hazardous activities, even though denying a license to someone can severely inconvenience and even harm that person. Furthermore, available competency tests are not 100 percent accurate. Denying someone a driver's license in our society, for example, would inconvenience that person acutely. In effect that person would be prohibited from working, shopping, or visiting in places reachable only by car. Similarly, people denied vocational licenses are inconvenienced, even devastated. We have all heard of individuals who had the "life-long

---

[1]"When practice of a profession or calling requires special knowledge or skill and intimately affects public health, morals, order or safety, or general welfare, legislature may prescribe reasonable qualifications for persons desiring to pursue such professions or calling and require them to demonstrate possession of such qualifications by examination on subjects with which such profession or calling has to deal as a condition precedent to right to follow that profession or calling." 50 SE 2nd 735 (1949). Also see 199 US 306, 318 (1905) and 123 US 623, 661 (1887).

dream" of becoming physicians or lawyers, yet were denied that dream. However, the realization that some people are disappointed or inconvenienced does not diminish our conviction that we must regulate occupations or activities that are potentially dangerous to others. Innocent people must be protected even if it means that others cannot pursue activities they deem highly desirable.

Furthermore, we maintain licensing procedures even though our competency tests are sometimes inaccurate. Some people competent to perform the licensed activity (for example, driving a car) will be unable to demonstrate competence (they freeze up on the driver's test). Others may be incompetent, yet pass the test (they are lucky or certain aspects of competence—for example, the sense of responsibility—are not tested). We recognize clearly—or should recognize clearly—that no test will pick out all and only competent drivers, physicians, lawyers, and so on. Mistakes are inevitable. This does not mean we should forget that innocent people may be harmed by faulty regulatory procedures. In fact, if the procedures are sufficiently faulty, we should cease regulating that activity entirely until more reliable tests are available. I only want to emphasize here that tests need not be perfect. Where moderately reliable tests are available, licensing procedures should be used to protect innocent people from incompetents.

These general criteria for regulatory licensing can certainly be applied to parents. First, parenting is an activity potentially very harmful to children. The potential for harm is apparent: each year more than half a million children are physically abused or neglected by their parents. Many millions more are psychologically abused or neglected—not given love, respect, or a sense of self-worth. The results of this maltreatment are obvious. Abused children bear the physical and psychological scars of maltreatment throughout their lives. Far too often they turn to crime.[2] They are

---

[2]According to the National Committee for the Prevention of Child Abuse, more than 80 percent of incarcerated criminals were, as children, abused by their parents. In addition, a study in the *Journal of the American Medical Association* 168, no. 3: 1755–1758, reported that first-degree murderers from middle-class homes and who have "no history of addiction to drugs, alcoholism, organic disease of the brain, or epilepsy" were fre-

far more likely than others to abuse their own children. Even if these maltreated children never harm anyone, they will probably never be well-adjusted, happy adults. Therefore, parenting clearly satisfies the first criterion of activities subject to regulation.

The second criterion is also incontestably satisfied. A parent must be competent if he is to avoid harming his children; even greater competence is required if he is to do the "job" well. But not everyone has this minimal competence. Many people lack the knowledge needed to rear children adequately. Many others lack the requisite energy, temperament, or stability. Therefore, child-rearing manifestly satisfies both criteria of activities subject to regulation. In fact, I dare say that parenting is a paradigm of such activities since the potential for harm is so great (both in the extent of harm any one person can suffer and in the number of people potentially harmed) and the need for competence is so evident. Consequently, there is good reason to believe that all parents should be licensed. The only ways to avoid this conclusion are to deny the need for licensing *any* potentially harmful activity; to deny that I have identified the standard criteria of activities which should be regulated; to deny that parenting satisfies the standard criteria; to show that even though parenting satisfies the standard criteria there are special reasons why licensing parents is not theoretically desirable; or to show that there is no reliable and just procedure for implementing this program.

While developing my argument for licensing I have already identified the standard criteria for activities that should be regulated, and I have shown that they can properly be applied to parenting. One could deny the legitimacy of regulation by licensing, but in doing so one would condemn not only the regulation of parenting, but also the regulation of drivers, physicians, druggists, and doctors. Furthermore, regulation of hazardous activities appears to be a fundamental task of any stable society.

Thus only two objections remain. In the next section I shall see if there are any special reasons why licensing parents is not theoretically desirable. Then, in the following section, I shall examine several practical objections designed to demonstrate that even if

---

quently found to have been subject to "remorseless physical brutality at the hands of the parents."

licensing were theoretically desirable, it could not be justly implemented.

THEORETICAL OBJECTIONS TO LICENSING

Licensing is unacceptable, someone might say, since people have a right to have children, just as they have rights to free speech and free religious expression. They do not need a license to speak freely or to worship as they wish. Why? Because they have a right to engage in these activities. Similarly, since people have a right to have children, any attempt to license parents would be unjust.

This is an important objection since many people find it plausible, if not self-evident. However, it is not as convincing as it appears The specific rights appealed to in this analogy are not without limitations. Both slander and human sacrifice are prohibited by law; both could result from the unrestricted exercise of freedom of speech and freedom of religion. Thus, even if people have these rights, they may sometimes be limited in order to protect innocent people. Consequently, even if people had a right to have children, that right might also be limited in order to protect innocent people, in this case children. Secondly, the phrase "right to have children" is ambiguous; hence, it is important to isolate its most plausible meaning in this context. Two possible interpretations are not credible and can be dismissed summarily. It is implausible to claim either that infertile people have rights to be *given* children or that people have rights to intentionally create children biologically without incurring any subsequent responsibility to them.

A third interpretation, however, is more plausible, particularly when coupled with observations about the degree of intrusion into one's life that the licensing scheme represents. On this interpretation people have a right to rear children if they make good-faith efforts to rear procreated children the best way they see fit. One might defend this claim on the ground that licensing would require too much intrusion into the lives of sincere applicants.

Undoubtedly one should be wary of unnecessary governmental intervention into individuals' lives. In this case, though, the intrusion would not often be substantial, and when it is, it would be warranted. Those granted licenses would face merely minor intervention; only those denied licenses would encounter marked intrusion. This encroachment, however, is a necessary side-effect of licensing parents—just as it is for automobile and vocational licensing. In addition, as I shall argue in more detail later, the degree of intrusion arising from a general licensing program would be no more than, and probably less than, the present (and presumably justifiable) encroachment into the lives of people who apply to adopt children. Furthermore, since some people hold unacceptable views about what is best for children (they think children should be abused regularly), people do not automatically have rights to rear children just because they will rear them in a way they deem appropriate.

Consequently, we come to a somewhat weaker interpretation of this right claim: a person has a right to rear children if he meets certain minimal standards of child rearing. Parents must not abuse or neglect their children and must also provide for the basic needs of the children. This claim of right is certainly more credible than the previously canvassed alternatives, though some people might still reject this claim in situations where exercise of the right would lead to negative consequences, for example, to overpopulation. More to the point, though, this conditional right is compatible with licensing. On this interpretation one has a right to have children only if one is not going to abuse or neglect them. Of course the very purpose of licensing is just to determine whether people *are* going to abuse or neglect their children. If the determination is made that someone will maltreat children, then that person is subject to the limitations of the right to have children and can legitimately be denied a parenting license.

In fact, this conditional way of formulating the right to have children provides a model for formulating all alleged rights to engage in hazardous activities. Consider, for example, the right to drive a car. People do not have an unconditional right to drive, although they do have a right to drive if they are competent. Similarly, people do not have an unconditional right to practice medicine; they have a right only if they are demonstrably competent. Hence, denying a driver's or physician's license to someone who has not demonstrated the requisite competence does not deny that person's rights. Likewise, on this model, denying a parenting license to someone who is not competent does not violate that person's rights.

Of course someone might object that the right is conditional on actually being a person who will abuse or neglect children, whereas my proposal only picks out those we can reasonably predict will abuse children. Hence, this conditional right *would* be incompatible with licensing.

There are two ways to interpret this objection and it is important to distinguish these divergent formulations. First, the objection could be a way of questioning our ability to predict reasonably and accurately whether people would maltreat their own children. This is an important practical objection, but I will defer discussion of it until the next section. Second, this objection could be a way of expressing doubt about the moral propriety of the prior restraint licensing requires. A parental licensing program would deny licenses to applicants judged to be incompetent even though they had never maltreated any children. This practice would be in tension with our normal skepticism about the propriety of prior restraint.

Despite this healthy skepticism, we do sometimes use prior restraint. In extreme circumstances we may hospitalize or imprison people judged insane, even though they are not legally guilty of any crime, simply because we predict they are likely to harm others. More typically, though, prior restraint is used only if the restriction is not terribly onerous and the restricted activity is one which could lead easily to serious harm. Most types of licensing (for example, those for doctors, drivers, and druggists) fall into this latter category. They require prior restraint to prevent serious harm, and generally the restraint is minor—though it is important to remember that some individuals will find it oppressive. The same is true of parental licensing. The purpose of licensing is to prevent serious harm to children. Moreover, the prior restraint required by licensing would not be terribly onerous for many people. Certainly the restraint would be far less extensive than the presumably justifiable prior restraint of, say, insane criminals. Criminals preventively detained and mentally ill people forceably hospitalized are denied most basic liberties, while those denied parental licenses would be denied only that one specific opportunity. They could still vote, work for political candidates, speak on controversial topics, and so on. Doubtless some individuals would find the restraint onerous. But when compared to other types of restraint currently practiced, and when judged in light of the severity of harm maltreated children suffer, the restraint appears *relatively* minor.

Furthermore, we could make certain, as we do with most licensing programs, that individuals denied licenses are given the opportunity to reapply easily and repeatedly for a license. Thus, many people correctly denied licenses (because they are incompetent) would choose (perhaps it would be provided) to take counseling or therapy to improve their chances of passing the next test. On the other hand, most of those mistakenly denied licenses would probably be able to demonstrate in a later test that they would be competent parents.

Consequently, even though one needs to be wary of prior restraint, if the potential for harm is great and the restraint is minor relative to the harm we are trying to prevent—as it would be with parental licensing—then such restraint is justified. This objection, like all the theoretical objections reviewed, has failed.

PRACTICAL OBJECTIONS TO LICENSING

I shall now consider five practical objections to licensing. Each objection focuses on the problems or difficulties of implementing this proposal. According to these objections, licensing is (or may be) theoretically desirable; nevertheless, it cannot be efficiently and justly implemented.

The first objection is that there may not be, or we may not be able to discover, adequate criteria of "a good parent." We simply do not have the knowledge, and it is unlikely that we could ever obtain the knowledge, that would enable us to distinguish adequate from inadequate parents.

Clearly there is some force to this objection. It is highly improbable that we can formulate criteria that would distinguish precisely between good and less than good parents. There is too much we do not know about child development and adult psychology. My proposal, however, does not demand that we make these fine distinctions. It does not demand that we license only the best parents; rather it is designed to exclude only the very bad ones. This is not just a semantic difference, but a substantive one. Although we do not have infallible criteria for picking out good parents, we undoubtedly can identify bad ones—those who will abuse or neglect their children. Even though we could have a lively debate about the range of freedom a child should be given or the appropriateness of corporal punishment, we do not wonder if a parent who severely beats or neglects a child is adequate. We know that person isn't. Consequently, we do have reliable and usable criteria for determining who is a bad parent; we have the criteria necessary to make a licensing program work.

The second practical objection to licensing is that there is no reliable way to predict who will maltreat their children. Without an accurate predictive test, licensing would be not only unjust, but also a waste of time. Now I recognize that as a philosopher (and not a psychologist, sociologist, or social worker), I am on shaky ground if I make sweeping claims about the present or future abilities of professionals to produce such predictive tests. Nevertheless, there are some relevant observations I can offer.

Initially, we need to be certain that the demands on predictive tests are not unreasonable. For example, it would be improper to require that tests be 100 percent accurate. Procedures for licensing drivers, physicians, lawyers, druggists, etc., plainly are not 100 percent (or anywhere near 100 percent) accurate. Presumably we recognize these deficiencies yet embrace the procedures anyway. Consequently, it would be imprudent to demand considerably more exacting standards for the tests used in licensing parents.

In addition, from what I can piece together, the practical possibilities for constructing a reliable predictive test are not all that gloomy. Since my proposal does not require that we make fine line distinctions between good and less than good parents, but rather that we weed out those who are potentially very bad, we can use existing tests that claim to isolate relevant predictive characteristics—whether a person is violence-prone, easily frustrated, or unduly self-centered. In fact researchers at Nashville General Hospital have developed a brief interview questionnaire which seems to have significant predictive value. Based on their data, the researchers identified 20 percent of the interviewees as a "risk group"—those having great potential for serious problems. After one year they found "the incidence of major breakdown in parent-child interaction in the risk group was approximately four to five times as great as in the low risk group." We also know that parents who maltreat children often have certain identifiable experiences, for example, most of them were themselves maltreated as children. Consequently, if we combined our information about these parents with certain psychological test results, we would probably be able to predict with reasonable accuracy which people will mal-treat their children.

However, my point is not to argue about the precise reliability of present tests. I cannot say emphatically that we now have accu-rate predictive tests. Nevertheless, even if such tests are not avail-able, we could undoubtedly develop them. For example, we could begin a longitudinal study in which all potential parents would be required to take a specified battery of tests. Then these parents could be "followed" to discover which ones abused or neglected their children. By correlating test scores with information on mal-treatment, a usable, accurate test could be fashioned. Therefore, I do not think that the present unavailability of such tests (if they are unavailable) would count against the legitimacy of licensing parents.

The third practical objection is that even if a reliable test for ascer-taining who would be an acceptable parent were available, admin-istrators would unintentionally misuse that test. These unintentional mistakes would clearly harm innocent individuals. Therefore, so the argument goes, this proposal ought to be scrapped. This objection can be dispensed with fairly easily unless one assumes there is some special reason to believe that more mistakes will be made in admin-istering parenting licenses than in other regulatory activities. No mat-ter how reliable our proceedings are, there will always be mistakes. We may license a physician who, through incompetence, would cause the death of a patient; or we may mistakenly deny a physi-cian's license to someone who would be competent. But the fact that mistakes are made does not and should not lead us to abandon attempts to determine competence. The harm done in these cases could be far worse than the harm of mistakenly denying a person a parenting license. As far as I can tell, there is no reason to believe that more mistakes will be made here than elsewhere.

The fourth proposed practical objection claims that any testing procedure will be intentionally abused. People administering the process will disqualify people they dislike, or people who espouse views they dislike, from rearing children.

The response to this objection is parallel to the response to the previous objection, namely, that there is no reason to believe that the licensing of parents is more likely to be abused than driver's license tests or other regulatory procedures. In addition, individuals can be protected from prejudicial treatment by pursuing appeals available to them. Since the licensing test can be taken on numerous occasions, the likelihood of the applicant's working with different administrative personnel increases and therefore the likelihood decreases that intentional abuse could ultimately stop a qualified person from rearing children. Consequently, since the probability of such abuse is not more than, and may even be less than, the intentional abuse of judicial and other regulatory authority, this objection does not give us any reason to reject the licensing of parents.

The fifth objection is that we could never adequately, reasonably, and fairly enforce such a program. That is, even if we could establish a reasonable and fair way of determining which people would be inadequate parents, it would be difficult, if not impossible, to enforce the program. How would one deal with violators and what could we do with babies so conceived? There are difficult problems here, no doubt, but they are not insurmountable. We might not punish parents at all—we might just remove the children and put them up for adoption. However, even if we are presently uncertain about the precise way to establish a just and effective form of enforcement, I do not see why this should undermine my licensing proposal. If it is important enough to protect children from being maltreated by parents, then surely a reasonable enforcement procedure can be secured. At least we should assume one can be unless someone shows that it cannot.

AN ANALOGY WITH ADOPTION

So far I have argued that parents should be licensed. Undoubtedly many readers find this claim extremely radical. It is revealing to notice, however, that this program is not as radical as it seems. Our moral and legal systems already recognize that not everyone is capable of rearing children well. In fact, well-entrenched laws require adoptive parents to be investigated—in much the same ways and for much the same reasons as in the general licensing program advocated here. For example, we do not allow just anyone to adopt a child; nor do we let someone adopt without first estimating the likelihood of the person's being a good parent. In fact, the adoptive process is far more rigorous than the general licensing procedures I envision. Prior to adoption the candidates must first formally apply to adopt a child. The applicants are then subjected to an exacting home study to determine whether they really want to have children and whether they are capable of caring for and rearing them adequately. No one is allowed to adopt a child until the administrators can reasonably predict that the person will be an adequate parent. The results of these procedures are impressive. Despite the trauma children often face before they are finally adopted, they are five times less likely to be abused than children reared by their biological parents.

Nevertheless we recognize, or should recognize, that these demanding procedures exclude some people who would be adequate parents. The selection criteria may be inadequate; the testing procedures may be somewhat unreliable. We may make mistakes. Probably there is some intentional abuse of the system. Adoption procedures intrude directly in the applicants' lives. Yet we continue the present adoption policies because we think it better to mistakenly deny some people the opportunity to adopt than to let just anyone adopt.

Once these features of our adoption policies are clearly identified, it becomes quite apparent that there are striking parallels between the general licensing program I have advocated and our present adoption system. Both programs have the same aim—protecting children. Both have the same drawbacks and are subject to the same abuses. The only obvious dissimilarity is that the adoption requirements are *more* rigorous than those proposed for the general licensing program. Consequently, if we think it is so important to protect adopted children, even though people who want to adopt are less likely than biological parents to maltreat their children, then we should likewise afford the same protection to children reared by their biological parents.

I suspect, though, that many people will think the cases are not analogous. The cases are relevantly different, someone might retort, because biological parents have a natural affection for their children and the strength of this affection makes it unlikely that parents would maltreat their biologically produced children.

Even if it were generally true that parents have special natural affections for their biological offspring, that does not mean that all parents have enough affection to keep them from maltreating their children. This should be apparent given the number of children abused each year by their biological parents. Therefore, even if there is generally a bond, that does not explain why we should not have licensing procedures to protect children of parents who do not have a sufficiently strong bond. Consequently, if we continue our practice of regulating the adoption of children, and certainly we should, we are rationally compelled to establish a licensing program for all parents.

However, I am not wedded to a strict form of licensing. It may well be that there are alternative ways of regulating parents which would achieve the desired results—the protection of children—without strictly prohibiting nonlicensed people from rearing children. For example, a system of tax incentives for licensed parents, and protective services scrutiny of nonlicensed parents, might adequately protect children. If it would, I would endorse the less drastic measure. My principal concern is to protect children from maltreatment by parents. I begin by advocating the more strict form of licensing since that is the standard method of regulating hazardous activities.

I have argued that all parents should be licensed by the state. This licensing program is attractive, not because state intrusion is inherently judicious and efficacious, but simply because it seems to be the best way to prevent children from being reared by incompetent parents. Nonetheless, even after considering the previous arguments, many people will find the proposal a useless academic exercise, probably silly, and possibly even morally perverse. But why? Why do most of us find this proposal unpalatable, particularly when the arguments supporting it are good and the objections to it are philosophically flimsy?

I suspect the answer is found in a long-held, deeply ingrained attitude toward children, repeatedly affirmed in recent court decisions, and present, at least to some degree, in almost all of us. The belief is that parents own, or at least have natural sovereignty over, their children. It does not matter precisely how this belief is described, since on both views parents legitimately exercise extensive and virtually unlimited control over their children. Others can properly interfere with or criticize parental decisions only in unusual and tightly prescribed circumstances—for example, when parents severely and repeatedly abuse their children. In all other cases, the parents reign supreme.

This belief is abhorrent and needs to be supplanted with a more child-centered view. Why? Briefly put, this attitude has adverse effects on children and on the adults these children will become. Parents who hold this view may well maltreat their children. If these parents happen to treat their children well, it is only because they want to, not because they think their children deserve or have a right to good treatment. Moreover, this belief is manifestly at odds with the conviction that parents should prepare children for life as adults. Children subject to parents who perceive children in this way are likely to be adequately prepared for adulthood. Hence, to prepare children for life as adults and to protect them from maltreatment, this attitude toward children must be dislodged. As I have argued, licensing is a viable way to protect children. Furthermore, it would increase the likelihood that more children will be adequately prepared for life as adults than is now the case.

For Further Reflection

1. Go over LaFollette's arguments and show their strengths and weaknesses.

2. Do you agree with LaFollette that people do not have an unconditional right to have children? Explain.

3. What are the problems with requiring licenses to have children? Imagine the government carrying out such a program. How would it work?

Further Readings for Chapter 11

Baker, Robert, and Frederick Elliston, eds. *Philosophy and Sex*, 2nd ed. Buffalo, N.Y.: Prometheus, 1984.

Cameron, Paul. "A Case Against Homosexuality" *Human Life Review*, vol. 4 (Summer 1978).

Leiser, Burton. *Liberty, Justice and Morals*, 3d ed. New York: Macmillan, 1986.

Russell, Bertrand. *Marriage and Morals*. New York: Liveright, 1929.

Scruton, Roger. *Sexual Desire: A Moral Philosophy of the Erotic*. New York: Macmillan, 1986.

Vannoy, Russell. *Sex Without Love: A Philosophical Exploration*. Buffalo, N.Y.: Prometheus, 1980.

Wasserstrom, Richard. "Is Adultery Immoral?" In Richard Wasserstrom, ed. *Today's Moral Problems*. New York: Macmillan, 1985.

CHAPTER 12

Is Abortion
Morally Permissible?

*Abortion during the first two or three months of gestation is morally
equivalent to removal of a piece of tissue from the woman's body.*
—Philosopher Thomas Szasz

*Every unborn child must be regarded as a human person with all the
rights of a human person, from the moment of conception.*
—Ethical and Religious Directives for Catholic Hospitals

One of the major social issues before us today, one that divides
our nation as no other issue does, is that of the moral and legal
status of the human fetus and the corresponding question of the
moral permissibility of abortion. On the one hand, such organizations as the Roman Catholic Church and the Right to Life movement, appalled by the more than 1.5 million abortions that take
place in this country each year, have exerted significant political
pressure toward introducing a constitutional amendment that would
grant full legal rights to fetuses. These movements have in some
cases made the abortion issue the single issue in political campaigns. On the other hand, pro-choice groups such as the National
Organization for Women (NOW), the National Abortion Rights
Action League (NARAL), and other feminist organizations have
exerted enormous pressure on politicians to support pro-abortion

legislation. The Republican and Democratic political platforms of the last two elections took diametrically opposed sides on this issue.

Why is abortion a moral issue? Take a fertilized egg, a zygote, a tiny sphere of cells. By itself, it is hard to see what is so important about such an inconspicuous piece of matter. It is virtually indistinguishable from other clusters of cells, or the zygotes of other animals. On the other hand, take an adult human being, a class of beings that we all intuitively feel to be worthy of high respect, having rights, including the right to life. To kill an innocent human being is an act of murder and universally condemned. However, no obvious line of division separates that single-cell zygote from the adult it will become. Hence, the problem of abortion.

It is with this sort of analysis that John Noonan begins his argument against abortion. He argues that since it is always wrong to kill innocent human beings and since fetuses are innocent human beings, it is wrong to kill fetuses. He makes an exception when the mother's life is in danger, since something of comparable worth is at stake. Noonan argues that conception is the only nonarbitrary cut-off place between nonpersonhood and personhood.

Mary Anne Warren argues against Noonan that fetuses are not persons since persons must have such characteristics as self-consciousness and rationality and fetuses do not have these. Finally, Jane English argues for a moderate position. Most early abortions are permissible, most late ones immoral.

Abortion Is Not
Morally Permissible

JOHN T. NOONAN, JR.

John T. Noonan, Jr., is professor of law at the University of California, Berkeley. He is a Roman Catholic philosopher who has written several works on moral issues, including *Contraception: A History of Its Treatment by the Catholic Theologians and Canonists* (1965) and *A Private Choice: Abortion in America in the Seventies* (1979). In this selection Noonan defends the conservative view that an entity becomes a person at conception and that abortion, except to save the mother's life, is morally wrong. He uses an argument from probabilities to show that his criterion of humanity is objectively based.

The most fundamental question involved in the long history of thought on abortion is: How do you determine the humanity of a being? To phrase the question that way is to put in comprehensive humanistic terms what the theologians either dealt with as an explicitly theological question under the heading of "ensoulment" or dealt with implicitly in their treatment of abortion. The Christian position as it originated did not depend on a narrow theological or philosophical concept. It had no relation to theories of infant baptism. It appealed to no special theory of instantaneous ensoulment. It took the world's view on ensoulment as that view changed from Aristotle to Zacchia. There was, indeed, theological influence affecting the theory of ensoulment finally adopted, and, of course, ensoulment itself was a theological concept, so that the position was always explained in theological terms. But the theological notion of ensoulment could easily be translated into humanistic language by substituting "human" for "rational soul"; the problem of knowing when a man is a man is common to theology and humanism.

If one steps outside the specific categories used by the theologians, the answer they gave can be analyzed as a refusal to discriminate among human beings on the basis of their varying potentialities. Once conceived, the being was recognized as man because he had man's potential. The criterion for humanity, thus, was simple and all-embracing: if you are conceived by human parents, you are human.

The strength of this position may be tested by a review of some of the other distinctions offered in the contemporary controversy over legalizing abortion. Perhaps the most popular distinction is in terms of viability. Before an age of so many months, the fetus is not viable, that is, it cannot be removed from the mother's womb and live apart from her. To that extent, the life of the fetus is absolutely dependent on the life of the mother. This dependence is made the basis of denying recognition to its humanity.

There are difficulties with this distinction. One is that the perfection of artificial incubation may make the fetus viable at any time: it may be removed and artificially sustained. Experiments with animals already show that such a procedure is possible. This hypothetical extreme case relates to an actual difficulty: there is considerable elasticity to the idea of viability. Mere length of life is not an exact measure. The viability of the fetus depends on the extent of its anatomical and functional development. The weight and length of the fetus are better guides to the state of its development than age, but weight and length vary. Moreover, different racial groups have different ages at which their fetuses are viable. Some evidence, for example, suggests that Negro fetuses mature more quickly than white fetuses. If viability is the norm, the standard would vary with race and with many individual circumstances.

The most important objection to this approach is that dependence is not ended by viability. The fetus is still absolutely dependent on someone's care in order to continue existence; indeed a child of one or three or even five years of age is absolutely dependent on another's care for existence; uncared for, the older fetus or the younger child will die as surely as the early fetus detached from the mother. The unsubstantial lessening in dependence at viability does not seem to signify any special acquisition of humanity.

A second distinction has been attempted in terms of experience. A being who has had experience, has lived and suffered, who possesses memories, is more human than one who has not. Humanity depends on formation by experience. The fetus is thus "unformed" in the most basic human sense.

This distinction is not serviceable for the embryo which is already experiencing and reacting. The embryo is responsive to touch after eight weeks and at least at that point is experiencing. At an earlier stage the zygote is certainly alive and responding to its environment. The distinction may also be challenged by the rare case where aphasia has erased adult memory: has it erased humanity? More fundamentally, this distinction leaves even the older fetus or the younger child to be treated as an unformed inhuman thing. Finally, it is not clear why experience as such confers humanity. It could be argued that certain central experiences such as loving or learning are necessary to make a man human. But then human beings who have failed to love or to learn might be excluded from the class called man.

A third distinction is made by appeal to the sentiments of adults. If a fetus dies, the grief of the parents is not the grief they would have for a living child. The fetus is an unnamed "it" till birth, and is not perceived as personality until at least the fourth month of existence when movements in the womb manifest a vigorous presence demanding joyful recognition by the parents.

Yet feeling is notoriously an unsure guide to the humanity of others. Many groups of humans have had difficulty in feeling that persons of another tongue, color, religion, sex, are as human as they. Apart from reactions to alien groups, we mourn the loss of a 10-year-old boy more than the loss of his one-day-old brother or his 90-year-old grandfather. The difference felt and the grief expressed vary with the potentialities extinguished, or the experience wiped out; they do not seem to point to any substantial difference in the humanity of baby, boy, or grandfather.

Distinctions are also made in terms of sensation by the parents. The embryo is felt within the womb only after about the fourth month. The embryo is seen only at birth. What can be neither seen nor felt is different from what is tangible. If the fetus cannot be seen or touched at all, it cannot be perceived as man.

Yet experience shows that sight is even more untrustworthy than feeling in determining humanity. By sight, color became an appropriate index for saying who was a man, and the evil of racial discrimination was given foundation. Nor can touch provide the test; a being confined by sickness, "out of touch" with others, does not thereby seem to lose his humanity. To the extent that touch still has appeal as a criterion, it appears to be a survival of the old English idea of "quickening"—a possible mistranslation of the Latin *animatus* used in the canon law. To that extent touch as a criterion seems to be dependent on the Aristotelian notion of ensoulment, and to fall when this notion is discarded.

Finally, a distinction is sought in social visibility. The fetus is not socially perceived as human. It cannot communicate with others. Thus, both subjectively and objectively, it is not a member of society. As moral rules are rules for the behavior of members of society to each other, they cannot be made for behavior toward what is not yet a member. Excluded from the society of men, the fetus is excluded from the humanity of men.

By force of the argument from the consequences, this distinction is to be rejected. It is more subtle than that founded on an appeal to physical sensation, but it is equally dangerous in its implications. If humanity depends on social recognition, individuals or whole groups may be dehumanized by being denied any status in their society. Such a fate is fictionally portrayed in *1984* and has actually been the lot of many men in many societies. In the Roman empire, for example, condemnation to slavery meant the practical denial of most human rights; in the Chinese Communist world, landlords have been classified as enemies of the people and so treated as nonpersons by the state. Humanity does not depend on social recognition, though often the failure of society to recognize the prisoner, the alien, the heterodox as human had led to the destruction of human beings. Anyone conceived by a man and a woman is human. Recognition of this condition by society follows a real event in the objective order, however imperfect and halting the recognition. Any attempt to limit humanity to exclude some group runs the risk of furnishing authority and precedent for excluding other groups in the name of the consciousness or perception of the controlling group in the society.

A philosopher may reject the appeal to the humanity of the fetus because he views "humanity" as a secular view of the soul and because he doubts the existence of anything real and objective which can be identified as humanity. One answer to such a philosopher is to ask how he reasons about moral questions without supposing that there is a sense in which he and the others of whom he speaks are human. Whatever group is taken as the society which determines who may be killed is thereby taken as human. A second answer is to ask if he does not believe that there is a right and wrong way of deciding moral questions. If there is such a difference, experience may be appealed to: to decide who is human on the basis of the sentiment of a given society has led to consequences which rational men would characterize as monstrous.

The rejection of the attempted distinctions based on viability and visibility, experience and feeling, may be buttressed by the following considerations: Moral judgments often rest on distinctions, but if the distinctions are not to appear arbitrary fiat, they should relate to some real difference in probabilities. There is a kind of continuity in all life, but the earlier stages of the elements of human life possess tiny probabilities of development. Consider for example, the spermatozoa in any normal ejaculate: There are about 200,000,000 in any single ejaculate, of which one has a chance of developing into a zygote. Consider the oocytes which may become ova: There are 100,000 to 1,000,000 oocytes in a female infant, of which a maximum of 390 are ovulated. But once spermatozoon and ovum meet and the conceptus is formed, such studies as have been made show that roughly in only 20 percent of the cases will spontaneous abortion occur. In other words, the chances are about 4 out of 5 that this new being will develop. At this stage in the life of the being there is a sharp shift in probabilities, an immense jump in potentialities. To make a distinction between the rights of spermatozoa and the rights of the fertilized ovum is to respond to an enormous shift in possibilities. For about twenty days after conception the egg may split to form twins or combine with another egg to form a chimera, but the probability of either event happening is very small.

It may be asked, What does a change in biological probabilities have to do with establishing humanity? The argument from probabilities is not aimed at establishing humanity but at establishing an objective discontinuity which may be taken into account in moral discourse. As life itself is a matter of probabilities, as most moral reasoning is an estimate of probabilities, so it seems in accord with the structure of reality and the nature of moral thought to found a moral judgment on the change in probabilities at conception. The appeal to probabilities is the most commonsensical of arguments, to a greater or smaller degree all of us base our actions on probabilities, and in morals, as in law, prudence and negligence are often measured by the account one has taken of the probabilities. If the chance is 200,000,000 to 1 that the movement in the bushes into which you shoot is a man's, I doubt if many persons would hold you careless in shooting; but if the chances are 4 out of 5 that the movement is a human being's, few would acquit you of blame. Would the argument be different if only one out of ten children conceived came to term? Of course this argument would be different. This argument is an appeal to probabilities that actually exist, not to any and all states of affairs which may be imagined.

The probabilities as they do exist do not show the humanity of the embryo in the sense of a demonstration in logic any more than the probabilities of the movement in the bush being a man demonstrate beyond all doubt that the being is a man. The appeal is a "buttressing" consideration, showing the plausibility of the standard adopted. The argument focuses on the decisional factor in any moral judgment and assumes that part of the business of a moralist is drawing lines. One evidence of the nonarbitrary character of the line drawn is the difference of probabilities on either side of it. If a spermatozoon is destroyed, one destroys a being which had a chance of far less than 1 in 200 million of developing into a reasoning being, possessed of the genetic code, a heart and other organs, and capable of pain. If a fetus is destroyed, one destroys a being already possessed of the genetic code, organs, and sensitivity to pain, and one which had an 80 percent chance of developing further into a baby outside the womb who, in time, would reason.

The positive argument for conception as the decisive moment of humanization is that at conception the new being receives the genetic code. It is this genetic information which determines his characteristics, which is the biological carrier of the possibility of human wisdom, which makes him a self-evolving being. A being with a human genetic code is man.

This review of current controversy over the humanity of the fetus emphasizes what a fundamental question the theologians resolved in asserting the inviolability of the fetus. To regard the fetus as possessed of equal rights with other humans was not, however, to decide every case where abortion might be employed. It did decide the case where the argument was that the fetus should be aborted for its own good. To say a being was human was to say it had a destiny to decide for itself which could not be taken from it by another man's decision. But human beings with equal rights often come in conflict with each other, and some decision must be made as to whose claims are to prevail. Cases of conflict involving the fetus are different only in two respects: the total inability of the fetus to speak for itself and the fact that the right of the fetus regularly at stake is the right to life itself.

The approach taken by the theologians to these conflicts was articulated in terms of "direct" and "indirect." Again, to look at what they were doing from outside their categories, they may be said to have been drawing lines or "balancing values." "Direct" and "indirect" are spatial metaphors; "line-drawing" is another. "To weigh" or "to balance" values is a metaphor of a more complicated mathematical sort hinting at the process which goes on in moral judgments. All the metaphors suggest that, in the moral judgments made, comparisons were necessary, that no value completely controlled. The principle of double effect was no doctrine fallen from heaven, but a method of analysis appropriate where two relative values were being compared. In Catholic moral theology, as it developed, life even of the innocent was not taken as an absolute. Judgments on acts affecting life issued from a process of weighing. In the weighing, the fetus was always given a value greater than zero, always a value separate and independent from its parents. This valuation was crucial and fundamental in all Christian thought on the subject and marked it off from any approach which considered that only the parents' interests needed to be considered.

Even with the fetus weighed as human, one interest could be weighed as equal or superior: that of the mother in her own life. The casuists between 1450 and 1895 were willing to weigh this interest as superior. Since 1895, that interest was given decisive weight only in the two special cases of the cancerous uterus and the ectopic pregnancy. In both of these cases the fetus itself had little chance of survival even if the abortion were not performed. As the balance was once struck in favor of the mother whenever her life was endangered, it could be so struck again. The balance reached between 1895 and 1930 attempted prudentially and pastorally to forestall a multitude of exceptions for interests less than life.

The perception of the humanity of the fetus and the weighing of fetal rights against other human rights constituted the work of the moral analysts. But what spirit animated their abstract judgments? For the Christian community it was the injunction of Scripture to love your neighbor as yourself. The fetus as human was a neighbor; his life had parity with one's own. The commandment gave life to what otherwise would have been only rational calculation.

The commandment could be put in humanistic as well as theological terms: Do not injure your fellow man without reason. In these terms, once the humanity of the fetus is perceived, abortion is never right except in self-defense. When life must be taken to save life, reason alone cannot say that a mother must prefer a child's life to her own. With this exception, now of great rarity, abortion violates the rational humanist tenet of the equality of human lives.

For Christians the commandment to love had received a special imprint in that the exemplar proposed of love was the love of the Lord for his disciples. In the light given by this example, self-sacrifice carried to the point of death seemed in the extreme situations not without meaning. In the less extreme cases, preference for one's own interests to the life of another seemed to express cruelty or selfishness irreconcilable with the demands of love.

For Further Reflection

1. Do you agree with Noonan in drawing the line between the human and nonhuman at conception? Explain your answer.

2. Has Noonan successfully argued that abortion is almost always immoral? Should he consider cases of rape and incest? What would Noonan say to the suggestion that a rape victim should be allowed to have an abortion?

3. Some have compared our practice of abortion to Hitler's Holocaust. A friend wrote, "With reference to abortion the world is upside down. When a criminal is sentenced to death, the whole world is dismayed because it goes against human rights. But when an unborn baby is sentenced to death, the world approves of it because the 'rights' of the mother take precedence over the rights of the child. But how is this different from the Nazi Holocaust, where Mother Germany sent 12 million innocent lives to

the gas chamber? Haven't we sent over 30 million innocent lives
to their death?" Do you agree with this comparison? Explain.

Abortion Is Morally Permissible

MARY ANNE WARREN

Mary Anne Warren teaches philosophy at San Francisco
State University and has written in the area of feminism,
including *The Nature of Woman: An Encyclopedia and
Guide to the Literature* (1980). In this paper she defends
the liberal view that abortion is always morally permissible. She attacks Noonan's argument on the basis of an ambiguity in the use of the term *human being,* showing that
the term has both a biological and moral sense. What is
important is the moral sense, which presupposes certain
characteristics, such as self-consciousness and rationality,
and which a fetus does not have.

The question which we must answer in order to produce a satisfactory solution to the problem of the moral status of abortion is this:
How are we to define the moral community, the set of beings with
full and equal moral rights, such that we can decide whether a human
fetus is a member of this community or not? What sort of entity,
exactly, has the inalienable rights to life, liberty, and the pursuit of
happiness? Jefferson attributed these rights to all *men,* and it may or
may not be fair to suggest that he intended to attribute them *only* to
men. Perhaps he ought to have attributed them to all human beings.
If so, then we arrive, first, at Noonan's problem of defining what

Reprinted from The Monist, *vol. 57, no. 1 (January 1973).* Copyright
© 1973, *The Monist,* La Salle, Illinois 61301. Reprinted by permission.
Notes omitted.

makes a being human, and, second, at the equally vital question which Noonan does not consider, namely, What reason is there for identifying the moral community with the set of all human beings, in whatever way we have chosen to define that term?

1.   ON THE DEFINITION OF "HUMAN"

One reason why this vital second question is so frequently over-looked in the debate over the moral status of abortion is that the term "human" has two distinct, but not often distinguished, senses. This fact results in a slide of meaning, which serves to conceal the falla-ciousness of the traditional argument that since (1) it is wrong to kill innocent human beings, and (2) fetuses are innocent human beings, then (3) it is wrong to kill fetuses. For if "human" is used in the same sense in both (1) and (2) then, whichever of the two senses is meant, one of these premises is question-begging. And if it is used in two different senses then of course the conclusion doesn't follow.

Thus, (1) is a self-evident moral truth, and avoids begging the question about abortion, only if "human being" is used to mean something like "a full-fledged member of the moral community." (It may or may not also be meant to refer exclusively to members of the species *Homo sapiens.*) We may call this the *moral* sense of "human." It is not to be confused with what we will call the *genetic* sense, i.e., the sense in which *any* member of the species is a human being, and no member of any other species could be. If (1) is acceptable only if the moral sense is intended, (2) is nonquestion-begging only if what is intended is the genetic sense.

In "Deciding Who Is Human," Noonan argues for the classifica-tion of fetuses with human beings by pointing to the presence of the full genetic code, and the potential capacity for rational thought. It is clear that what he needs to show, for his version of the traditional argument to be valid, is that fetuses are human in the moral sense, the sense in which it is analytically true that all human beings have full moral rights. But, in the absence of any argument showing that whatever is genetically human is also morally human, and he gives none, nothing more than genetic humanity can be demonstrated by the presence of the human genetic code. And, as we will see, the *potential* capacity for rational thought can at most show that an entity has the potential for *becoming* human in the moral sense.

2. DEFINING THE MORAL COMMUNITY

Can it be established that genetic humanity is sufficient for moral humanity? I think that there are very good reasons for not defining the moral community in this way. I would like to suggest an alternative way of defining the moral community, which I will argue for only to the extent of explaining why it is, or should be, self-evident. The suggestion is simply that the moral community consists of all and only *people,* rather than all and only human beings; and probably the best way of demonstrating its self-evidence is by considering the concept of personhood, to see what sorts of entity are and are not persons, and what the decision that a being is or is not a person implies about its moral rights.

What characteristics entitle an entity to be considered a person? This is obviously not the place to attempt a complete analysis of the concept of personhood, but we do not need such a fully adequate analysis just to determine whether and why a fetus is or isn't a person. All we need is a rough and approximate list of the most basic criteria of personhood, and some idea of which, or how many, of these an entity must satisfy in order to properly be considered a person.

In searching for such criteria, it is useful to look beyond the set of people with whom we are acquainted, and ask how we would decide whether a totally alien being was a person or not. (For we have no right to assume that genetic humanity is necessary for personhood.) Imagine a space traveler who lands on an unknown planet and encounters a race of beings utterly unlike any he has ever seen or heard of. If he wants to be sure of behaving morally toward these beings, he has to somehow decide whether they are people, and hence have full moral rights, or whether they are the sort of thing which he need not feel guilty about treating as, for example, a source of food.

How should he go about making this decision? If he has some anthropological background, he might look for such things as religion, art, and the manufacturing of tools, weapons, or shelters, since these factors have been used to distinguish our human from our prehuman ancestors, in what seems to be closer to the moral than the genetic sense of "human." And no doubt he would be right to consider the presence of such factors as good evidence that the alien beings were people, and morally human. It would, however, be overly anthropocentric of him to take the absence of these things as adequate evidence that they were not, since we can imagine people who have progressed beyond, or evolved without ever developing, these cultural characteristics.

I suggest that the traits which are most central to the concept of personhood, or humanity in the moral sense, are, very roughly, the following:

1. Consciousness (of objects and events external and/or internal to the being), and in particular the capacity to feel pain;
2. Reasoning (the *developed* capacity to solve new and relatively complex problems);
3. Self-motivated activity (activity which is relatively independent of either genetic or direct external control);
4. The capacity to communicate, by whatever means, messages of an indefinite variety of types, that is, not just with an indefinite number of possible contents, but on indefinitely many possible topics;
5. The presence of self-concepts, and self-awareness, either individual or racial, or both.

Admittedly, there are apt to be a great many problems involved in formulating precise definitions of these criteria, let alone in developing universally valid behavioral criteria for deciding when they apply. But I will assume that both we and our explorer know approximately what (1)–(5) mean, and that he is also able to determine whether or not they apply. How, then, should he use his findings to decide whether or not the alien beings are people? We needn't suppose that an entity must have *all* of these attributes to be properly considered a person; (1) and (2) alone may well be sufficient for personhood, and quite probably (1)–(3) are sufficient. Neither do we need to insist that any one of these criteria is *necessary* for personhood, although once again (1) and (2) look like fairly good candidates for necessary conditions, as does (3), if "activity" is construed so as to include the activity of reasoning.

All we need to claim, to demonstrate that a fetus is not a person, is that any being which satisfies *none* of (1)–(5) is certainly not a person. I consider this claim to be so obvious that I think anyone who denied it, and claimed that a being which satisfied none of (1)–(5) was a person all the same, would thereby demonstrate that he had no notion at all of what a person is—perhaps because he had confused the concept of a person with that of genetic humanity. If the opponents of abortion were to deny the appropriateness of these five criteria, I do not know what further arguments would convince them. We would probably have to admit that our conceptual schemes were indeed irreconcilably different, and that our dispute could not be settled objectively.

I do not expect this to happen, however, since I think that the concept of a person is one which is very nearly universal (to people), and that it is common to both proabortionists and antiabortionists, even though neither group has fully realized the relevance of this concept to the resolution of their dispute. Furthermore, I think that on reflection even the antiabortionists ought to agree not only that (1)–(5) are central to the concept of personhood, but also that it is a part of this concept that all and only people have full moral rights. The concept of a person is in part a moral concept; once we have admitted that x is a person we have recognized, even if we have not agreed to respect, x's right to be treated as a member of the moral community. It is true that the claim that x *is a human being* is more commonly voiced as part of an appeal to treat x decently than is the claim that x is a person, but this is either because "human being" is here used in the sense which implies personhood, or because the genetic and moral senses of "human" have been confused.

Now if (1)–(5) are indeed the primary criteria of personhood, then it is clear that genetic humanity is neither necessary nor sufficient for establishing that an entity is a person. Some human beings are not people, and there may well be people who are not human beings. A man or woman whose consciousness has been permanently obliterated but who remains alive is a human being which is no longer a person; defective human beings, with no appreciable mental capacity, are not and presumably never will be people; and a fetus is a human being which is not yet a person, and which therefore cannot coherently be said to have full moral rights. Citizens of the next century should be prepared to recognize highly advanced, self-aware robots or computers, should such be developed, and intelligent inhabitants of other worlds, should such be found, as people in the fullest sense, and to respect their moral rights. But to ascribe full moral rights to an entity which is not a person is as absurd as to ascribe moral obligations and responsibilities to such an entity.

3. FETAL DEVELOPMENT AND THE RIGHT TO LIFE

Two problems arise in the application of these suggestions for the definition of the moral community to the determination of the precise moral status of a human fetus. Given that the paradigm example of a person is a normal adult human being, then (1) How like this paradigm, in particular how far advanced since conception, does a human being need to be before it begins to have a right to life by virtue, not of being fully a person as of yet, but of being *like* a person? and (2) To what extent, if any, does the fact that a fetus has the *potential* for becoming a person endow it with some of the same rights? Each of these questions requires some comment.

In answering the first question, we need not attempt a detailed consideration of the moral rights of organisms which are not developed enough, aware enough, intelligent enough, etc., to be considered people, but which resemble people in some respects. It does seem reasonable to suggest that the more like a person, in the relevant respects, a being is, the stronger is the case for regarding it as having a right to life, and indeed the stronger its right to life is. Thus we ought to take seriously the suggestion that, insofar as "the human individual develops biologically in a continuous fashion . . . the rights of a human person might develop in the same way." But we must keep in mind that the attributes which are relevant in determining whether or not an entity is enough like a person to be regarded as having some of the same moral rights are no different from those which are relevant to determining whether or not it is fully a person—i.e., are no different from (1)–(5)—and that being genetically human, or having recognizably human facial and other physical features, or detectable brain activity, or the capacity to survive outside the uterus, are simply not among these relevant attributes.

Thus it is clear that even though a seven- or eight-month fetus has features which make it apt to arouse in us almost the same powerful protective instinct as is commonly aroused by a small infant, nevertheless it is not significantly more personlike than is a very small embryo. It is *somewhat* more personlike; it can apparently feel and respond to pain, and it may even have a rudimentary form of consciousness, insofar as its brain is quite active. Nevertheless, it seems safe to say that it is not fully conscious, in the way that an infant of a few months is, and that it cannot reason, or communicate messages of indefinitely many sorts, does not engage in self-motivated activity, and has no self-awareness. Thus, in the *relevant* respects, a fetus, even a fully developed one, is considerably less personlike than is the average mature mammal, indeed the average fish. And I think that a rational person must conclude that if the right to life of a fetus is to be based upon its resemblance to a person, then it cannot be said to have any more right to life than, let us say, a newborn guppy (which also seems to be capable of feeling pain), and that a right of that magnitude could never override a woman's right to obtain an abortion, at any stage of her pregnancy.

There may, of course, be other arguments in favor of placing legal limits upon the stage of pregnancy in which an abortion may be performed. Given the relative safety of the new techniques of artificially inducing labor during the third trimester, the danger to the woman's life or health is no longer such an argument. Neither is the fact that people tend to respond to the thought of abortion in the later stages of pregnancy with emotional repulsion, since mere emotional responses cannot take the place of moral reasoning in determining what ought to be permitted. Nor, finally, is the frequently heard argument that legalizing abortion, especially late in the pregnancy, may erode the level of respect for human life, leading, perhaps, to an increase in unjustified euthanasia and other crimes. For this threat, if it is a threat, can be better met by educating people to the kinds of moral distinctions which we are making here than by limiting access to abortion (which limitation may, in its disregard for the rights of women, be just as damaging to the level of respect for human rights).

Thus, since the fact that even a fully developed fetus is not personlike enough to have any significant right to life on the basis of its personlikeness shows that no legal restrictions upon the stage of pregnancy in which an abortion may be performed can be justified on the grounds that we should protect the rights of the older fetus, and since there is no other apparent justification for such restrictions, we may conclude that they are entirely unjustified. Whether or not it would be *indecent* (whatever that means) for a woman in her seventh month to obtain an abortion just to avoid having to postpone a trip to Europe, it would not, in itself, be *immoral,* and therefore it ought to be permitted.

4. POTENTIAL PERSONHOOD AND THE RIGHT TO LIFE

We have seen that a fetus does not resemble a person in any way which can support the claim that it has even some of the same rights. But what about its *potential,* the fact that if nurtured and allowed to develop naturally it will very probably become a person? Doesn't that alone give it at least some right to life? It is hard to deny that the fact that an entity is a potential person is a strong prima facie reason for not destroying it; but we need not conclude from this that a potential person has a right to life, by virtue of that potential. It may be that our feeling that it is better, other things being equal, not to destroy a potential person is better explained by the fact that potential people are still (felt to be) an invaluable resource, not to be lightly squandered. Surely, if every speck of dust were a potential person, we would be much less apt to conclude that every potential person has a right to become actual.

Still, we do not need to insist that a potential person has no right to life whatever. There may well be something immoral, and not just imprudent, about wantonly destroying potential people, when doing so isn't necessary to protect anyone's rights. But even if a potential person does have some *prima facie* right to life, such a right could not possibly outweigh the right of a woman to obtain an abortion, since the rights of any actual person invariably outweigh those of any potential person, whenever the two conflict. Since this may not be immediately obvious in the case of a human fetus, let us look at another case.

Suppose that our space explorer falls into the hands of an alien culture, whose scientists decide to create a few hundred thousand or more human beings, by breaking his body into its component cells, and using these to create fully developed human beings, with, of course, his genetic code. We may imagine that each of these newly created men will have all of the original man's abilities, skills, knowledge, and so on, and also have an individual self-concept, in short that each of them will be a bona fide (though hardly unique) person. Imagine that the whole project will take only seconds, and that its chances of success are extremely high, and that our explorer knows all of this, and also knows that these people will be treated fairly. I maintain that in such a situation he would have every right to escape if he could, and thus to deprive all of these potential people of their potential lives; for his right to life outweighs all of theirs together, in spite of the fact that they are all genetically human, all innocent, and all have a very high probability of becoming people very soon, if only he refrains from acting.

Indeed, I think he would have a right to escape even if it were not his life which the alien scientists planned to take, but only a year of his freedom, or, indeed, only a day. Nor would he be obligated to stay if he had gotten captured (thus bringing all these people-potentials into existence) because of his own carelessness, or even if he had done so deliberately, knowing the consequences. Regardless of how he got captured, he is not morally obligated to remain in captivity for *any* period of time for the sake of permitting any number of potential people to come into actuality, so great is the margin by which one actual person's right to liberty outweighs whatever right to life even a hundred thousand potential people have. And it seems reasonable to conclude that the rights of a woman will outweigh by a similar margin whatever right to life a fetus may have by virtue of its potential personhood.

Thus, neither a fetus's resemblance to a person, nor its potential for becoming a person provides any basis whatever for the claim that it has any significant right to life. Consequently, a woman's right to protect her health, happiness, freedom, and even her life, by terminating an unwanted pregnancy, will always override whatever right to life it may be appropriate to ascribe to a fetus, even a fully developed one. And thus, in the absence of any overwhelming social need for every possible child, the laws which restrict the right to obtain an abortion, or limit the period of pregnancy during which an abortion may be performed, are a wholly unjustified violation of a woman's most basic moral and constitutional rights.

For Further Reflection

1. Has Warren successfully refuted Noonan's argument against abortion? Are there any aspects of Noonan's argument that she has not successfully answered?

2. Is there a middle ground between Noonan's conservatism and Warren's liberalism on abortion?

The Moderate Position
Beyond the Personhood Argument

JANE ENGLISH

Jane English (1947–1978) taught philosophy at the University of North Carolina, Chapel Hill, and was the author of several essays in applied ethics, including the essay that is included here.

English argues that the issue of whether a fetus is a person cannot be resolved, and that the very concept of personhood is not clear or decisive enough to bear the weight of a solution to the abortion debate. Advancing a moderate position, similar to that of Sumner, she argues that regardless of whether a fetus is a person, the principle of self-defense permits a woman to have an abortion in some

Reprinted from "Abortion and the Concept of a Person," *Canadian Journal of Philosophy,* vol. 5,2 (October 1975), by permission. Notes omitted.

cases, especially in the early stages of pregnancy. On the other hand, even if the fetus is not a person, it is too much like a baby in the later stages of pregnancy to permit an abortion—except to avoid significant injury or death.

The abortion debate rages on. Yet the two most popular positions seem to be clearly mistaken. Conservatives maintain that a human life begins at conception and that therefore abortion must be wrong because it is murder. But not all killings of humans are murders. Most notably, self defense may justify even the killing of an innocent person.

Liberals, on the other hand, are just as mistaken in their argument that since a fetus does not become a person until birth, a woman may do whatever she pleases in and to her own body. First, you cannot do as you please with your own body if it affects other people adversely. Second, if a fetus is not a person, that does not imply that you can do to it anything you wish. Animals, for example, are not persons, yet to kill or torture them for no reason at all is wrong.

At the center of the storm has been the issue of just when it is between ovulation and adulthood that a person appears on the scene. Conservatives draw the line at conception, liberals at birth. In this paper I first examine our concept of a person and conclude that no single criterion can capture the concept of a person and no sharp line can be drawn. Next I argue that if a fetus is a person, abortion is still justifiable in many cases; and if a fetus is not a person, killing it is still wrong in many cases. To a large extent, these two solutions are in agreement. I conclude that our concept of a person cannot and need not bear the weight that the abortion controversy has thrust upon it.

I

The several factions in the abortion argument have drawn battle lines around various proposed criteria for determining what is and what is not a person. For example, Mary Anne Warren lists five features (capacities for reasoning, self-awareness, complex communication, etc.) as her criteria for personhood and argues for the permissibility of abortion because a fetus falls outside this concept. Baruch Brody uses brain waves. Michael Tooley picks having-a-concept-of-self as his criterion and concludes that infanticide and abortion are justifiable, while the killing of adult animals is not. On the other side, Paul Ramsey claims a certain gene structure is the defining characteristic. John Noonan prefers conceived-of-humans and presents counterexamples to various other candidate criteria. For instance, he argues against viability as the criterion because the newborn and infirm would then be non-persons, since they cannot live without the aid of others. He rejects any criterion that calls upon the sorts of sentiments a being can evoke in adults on the grounds that this would allow us to exclude other races as non-persons if we could just view them sufficiently unsentimentally.

These approaches are typical: Foes of abortion propose sufficient conditions for personhood which fetuses satisfy, while friends of abortion counter with necessary conditions for personhood which fetuses lack. But these both presuppose that the concept of a person can be captured in a strait jacket of necessary and/or sufficient conditions. Rather, "person" is a cluster of features, of which rationality, having a self concept and being conceived of humans are only part.

What is typical of persons? Within our concept of a person we include, first, certain biological factors: descended from humans, having a certain genetic makeup, having a head, hands, arms, eyes, capable of locomotion, breathing, eating, sleeping. There are psychological factors: sentience, perception, having a concept of self and of one's own interests and desires, the ability to use tools, the ability to use language or symbol systems, the ability to joke, to be angry, to doubt. There are rationality factors: the ability to reason and draw conclusions, the ability to generalize and to learn from past experience, the ability to sacrifice present interests for greater gains in the future. There are social factors: the ability to work in groups and respond to peer pressures, the ability to recognize and consider as valuable the interests of others, seeing oneself as one among "other minds," the ability to sympathize, encourage, love, the ability to evoke from others the responses of sympathy, encouragement, love, the ability to work with others for mutual advantage. Then there are legal factors: being subject to the law and protected by it, having the ability to sue and enter contracts, being counted in the census, having a name and citizenship, the ability to own property, inherit, and so forth.

Now the point is not that this list is incomplete, or that you can find counter-instances to each of its points. People typically exhibit rationality, for instance, but someone who was irrational would not thereby fail to qualify as a person. On the other hand, something could exhibit the majority of these features and still fail to be a person, as an advanced robot might. There is no single core of necessary and sufficient features which we can draw upon with the assurance that they constitute what really makes a person: there are only features that are more or less typical.

This is not to say that no necessary or sufficient conditions can be given. Being alive is a necessary condition for being a person, and being a U.S. Senator is sufficient. But rather than falling inside a sufficient condition or outside a necessary one, a fetus lies in the penumbra region where our concept of a person is not so simple. For this reason I think a conclusive answer to the question whether a fetus is a person is unattainable.

Here we might note a family of simple fallacies that proceed by stating a necessary condition for personhood and showing that a fetus has that characteristic. This is a form of the fallacy of affirming the consequent. For example, some have mistakenly reasoned from the premise that a fetus is human (after all, it is a human fetus rather than, say, a canine fetus), to the conclusion that it is *a* human. Adding an equivocation on " 'being,' " we get the fallacious argument that since a fetus is something both living and human, it is a human being.

Nonetheless, it does seem clear that a fetus has very few of the above family of characteristics, whereas a newborn baby exhibits a much larger proportion of them—and a two-year-old has even more. Note that one traditional anti-abortion argument has centered on pointing out the many ways in which a fetus resembles a baby. They emphasize its development ("It already has ten fingers . . .") without mentioning its dissimilarities to adults (it still has gills and a tail). They also try to evoke the sort of sympathy on our part that we only feel toward other persons ("Never to laugh . . . or feel the sunshine?") This all seems to be a relevant way to argue, since its purpose is to persuade us that a fetus satisfies so many of the important features on the list that it ought to be treated as a person. Also note that a fetus near the time of birth satisfies many more of these factors than a fetus in the early months of development. This could provide reason for making distinctions among the different stages of pregnancy, as the U.S. Supreme Court has done.

Historically, the time at which a person has been said to come into existence has varied widely. Muslims date personhood from fourteen days after conception. Some medievals followed Aristotle in placing ensoulment at forty days after conception for a male fetus and eighty days for a female fetus. In European common law since the Seventeenth Century, abortion was considered the killing of a person only after quickening, the time when a pregnant woman first feels the fetus move on its own. Nor is this variety of opinions surprising. Biologically, a human being develops gradually. We shouldn't expect there to be any specific time or sharp dividing point when a person appears on the scene.

For these reasons I believe our concept of a person is not sharp or decisive enough to bear the weight of a solution to the abortion controversy. To use it to solve that problem is to clarify *obscurum per obscurius*.

II

Next let us consider what follows if a fetus is a person after all. Judith Jarvis Thomson's landmark article, "A Defense of Abortion," correctly points out that some additional argumentation is needed at this point in the conservative argument to bridge the gap between the premise that a fetus is an innocent person and the conclusion that killing it is always wrong. To arrive at this conclusion, we would need the additional premise that killing an innocent person is always wrong. But killing an innocent person is sometimes permissible, most notably in self defense. Some examples may help draw out our intuitions or ordinary judgments about self defense.

Suppose a mad scientist, for instance, hypnotized innocent people to jump out of the bushes and attack innocent passers-by with knives. If you are so attacked, we agree you have a right to kill the attacker in self defense, if killing him is the only way to protect your life or to save yourself from serious injury. It does not seem to matter here that the attacker is not malicious but himself an innocent pawn, for your killing of him is not done in a spirit of retribution but only in self defense.

How severe an injury may you inflict in self defense? In part this depends upon the severity of the injury to be avoided: you may not shoot someone merely to avoid having your clothes torn. This might lead one to the mistaken conclusion that the defense may only equal the threatened injury in severity; that to avoid death you may kill, but to avoid a black eye you may only inflict a black eye or the equivalent. Rather, our laws and customs seem to say that you may create an injury somewhat, but not enormously, greater than the injury to be avoided. To fend off an attack whose outcome would be as serious as rape, a severe beating or the loss of a finger, you may shoot; to avoid having your clothes torn, you may blacken an eye.

Aside from this, the injury you may inflict should only be the minimum necessary to deter or incapacitate the attacker. Even if you know he intends to kill you, you are not justified in shooting him if you could equally well save yourself by the simple expedient of running away. Self defense is for the purpose of avoiding harms rather than equalizing harms.

Some cases of pregnancy present a parallel situation. Though the fetus is itself innocent, it may pose a threat to the pregnant woman's well-being, life prospects or health, mental or physical. If the pregnancy presents a slight threat to her interests, it seems self defense cannot justify abortion. But if the threat is on a par with a serious beating or the loss of a finger, she may kill the fetus that poses such a threat, even if it is an innocent person. If a lesser harm to the fetus could have the same defensive effect, killing it would not be justified. It is unfortunate that the only way to free the woman from the pregnancy entails the death of the fetus (except in very late stages of pregnancy). Thus a self defense model supports Thomson's point that the woman has a right only to be freed from fetus, not a right to demand its death.

The self defense model is most helpful when we take the pregnant woman's point of view. In the pre-Thomson literature, abortion is often framed as a question for a third party; do you, a doctor, have a right to choose between the life of the woman and that of the fetus? Some have claimed that if you were a passer-by who witnessed a struggle between the innocent hypnotized attacker and his equally innocent victim, you would have no reason to kill either in defense of the other. They have concluded that the self defense model implies that a woman may attempt to abort herself, but that a doctor should not assist her. I think the position of the third party is somewhat more complex. We do feel some inclination to intervene on behalf of the victim rather than the attacker, other things equal. But if both parties are innocent, other factors come into consideration. You would rush to the aid of your husband whether he was attacker or attackee. If a hypnotized famous violinist were attacking a skid row bum, we would try to save the individual who is of more value to society. These considerations would tend to support abortion in some cases.

But suppose you are a frail senior citizen who wishes to avoid being knifed by one of these innocent hypnotics, so you have hired a bodyguard to accompany you. If you are attacked, it is clear we believe that the bodyguard, acting as your agent, has a right to kill the attacker to save you from a serious beating. Your rights of self defense are transferred to your agent. I suggest that we should similarly view the doctor as the pregnant woman's agent in carrying out a defense she is physically incapable of accomplishing herself.

Thanks to modern technology, the cases are rare in which a pregnancy poses as clear a threat to a woman's bodily health as an attacker brandishing a switchblade. How does self defense fare when more subtle, complex and long-range harms are involved?

To consider a somewhat fanciful example, suppose you are a highly trained surgeon when you are kidnapped by the hypnotic attacker. He says he does not intend to harm you but to take you back to the mad scientist who, it turns out, plans to hypnotize you to have a permanent mental block against all your knowledge of medicine. This would automatically destroy your career which would in turn have a serious adverse impact on your family, your personal relationships and your happiness. It seems to me that if the only way you can avoid this outcome is to shoot the innocent attacker, you are justified in so doing. You are defending yourself from a drastic injury to your life prospects. I think it is no exaggeration to claim that unwanted pregnancies (most obviously among teenagers) often have such adverse life-long consequences as the surgeon's loss of livelihood.

Several parallels arise between various views on abortion and the self defense model. Let's suppose further that these hypnotized attackers only operate at night, so that it is well known that they can be avoided completely by the considerable inconvenience of never leaving your house after dark. One view is that since you could stay home at night, therefore if you go out and are selected by one of these hypnotized people, you have no right to defend yourself. This parallels the view that abstinence is the only acceptable way to avoid pregnancy. Others might hold that you ought to take along some

defense such as Mace which will deter the hypnotized person without killing him, but that if this defense fails, you are obliged to submit to the resulting injury, no matter how severe it is. This parallels
the view that contraception is all right but abortion is always wrong,
even in cases of contraceptive failure.

A third view is that you may kill the hypnotized person only if
he will actually kill you, but not if he will only injure you. This is
like the position that abortion is permissible only if it is required
to save a woman's life. Finally, we have the view that it is all right
to kill the attacker, even if only to avoid a very slight inconvenience
to yourself and even if you knowingly walked down the very street
where all these incidents have been taking place without taking
along any Mace or protective escort. If we assume that a fetus is a
person, this is the analogue of the view that abortion is always justifiable, "on demand."

The self defense model allows us to see an important difference
that exists between abortion and infanticide, even if a fetus is a
person from conception. Many have argued that the only way to
justify abortion without justifying infanticide would be to find some
characteristic of personhood that is acquired at birth. Michael Tooley, for one, claims infanticide is justifiable because the really significant characteristics of person are acquired some time after birth.
But all such approaches look to characteristics of the developing
human and ignore the relation between the fetus and the woman.
What if, after birth, the presence of an infant or the need to support it posed a grave threat to the woman's sanity or life prospects?
She could escape this threat by the simple expedient of running
away. So a solution that does not entail the death of the infant is
available. Before birth, such solutions are not available because of
the biological dependence of the fetus on the woman. Birth is the
crucial point not because of any characteristics the fetus gains, but
because after birth the woman can defend herself by a means less
drastic than killing the infant. Hence self defense can be used to
justify abortion without necessarily thereby justifying infanticide.

III

On the other hand, supposing a fetus is not after all a person,
would abortion always be morally permissible? Some opponents of
abortion seem worried that if a fetus is not a full-fledged person,

then we are justified in treating it in any way at all. However, this does not follow. Non-persons do get some consideration in our moral code, though of course they do not have the same rights as persons have (and in general they do not have moral responsibilities), and though their interests may be overridden by the interests of persons. Still, we cannot just treat them in any way at all.

Treatment of animals is a case in point. It is wrong to torture dogs for fun or to kill wild birds for no reason at all. It is wrong Period, even though dogs and birds do not have the same rights persons do. However, few people think it is wrong to use dogs as experimental animals, causing them considerable suffering in some cases, provided that the resulting research will probably bring discoveries of great benefit to people. And most of us think it all right to kill birds for food or to protect our crops. People's rights are different from the consideration we give to animals, then, for it is wrong to experiment on people, even if others might later benefit a great deal as a result of their suffering. You might volunteer to be a subject, but this would be supererogatory; you certainly have a right to refuse to be a medical guinea pig.

But how do we decide what you may or may not do to non-persons? This is a difficult problem, one for which I believe no adequate account exists. You do not want to say, for instance, that torturing dogs is all right whenever the sum of its effects on people is good—when it doesn't warp the sensibilities of the torturer so much that he mistreats people. If that were the case, it would be all right to torture dogs if you did it in private, or if the torturer lived on a desert island or died soon afterward, so that his actions had no effect on people. This is an inadequate account, because whatever moral consideration animals get, it has to be indefeasible, too. It will have to be a general proscription of certain actions, not merely a weighing of the impact on people on a case-by-case basis.

Rather, we need to distinguish two levels on which consequences of actions can be taken into account in moral reasoning. The traditional objections to Utilitarianism focus on the fact that it operates solely on the first level, taking all the consequences into account in particular cases only. Thus Utilitarianism is open to "desert island" and "lifeboat" counterexamples because these cases are rigged to make the consequences of actions severely limited.

Rawls' theory could be described as a teleological sort of theory, but with teleology operating on a higher level. In choosing the principles to regulate society from the original position, his hypothetical choosers make their decision on the basis of the total consequences of various systems. Furthermore, they are constrained to choose a general set of rules which people can readily learn and apply. An ethical theory must operate by generating a set of sympathies and attitudes toward others which reinforces the functioning of that set of moral principles. Our prohibition against killing people operates by means of certain moral sentiments including sympathy, compassion and guilt. But if these attitudes are to form a coherent set, they carry us further: we tend to perform supererogatory actions, and we tend to feel similar compassion toward person-like non-persons.

It is crucial that psychological facts play a role here. Our psychological constitution makes it the case that for our ethical theory to work, it must prohibit certain treatment of non-persons which are significantly person-like. If our moral rules allowed people to treat some person-like non-persons in ways we do not want people to be treated, this would undermine the system of sympathies and attitudes that makes the ethical system work. For this reason, we would choose in the original position to make mistreatment of some sorts of animals wrong in general (not just wrong in the cases with public impact), even though animals are not themselves parties in the original position. Thus it makes sense that it is those animals whose appearance and behavior are most like those of people that get the most consideration in our moral scheme.

It is because of "coherence of attitudes," I think, that the similarity of a fetus to a baby is very significant. A fetus one week before birth is so much like a newborn baby in our psychological space that we cannot allow any cavalier treatment of the former while expecting full sympathy and nurturative support for the latter. Thus, I think that anti-abortion forces are indeed giving their strongest arguments when they point to the similarities between a fetus and a baby, and when they try to evoke our emotional attachment to and sympathy for the fetus. An early horror story from New York about nurses who were expected to alternate between caring for six-week premature infants and disposing of viable 24-week aborted fetuses is just that—a horror story. These beings are so much alike that no one can be asked to draw a distinction and treat them so very differently.

Remember, however, that in the early weeks after conception, a fetus is very much unlike a person. It is hard to develop these feelings for a set of genes which doesn't yet have a head, hands, beating heart, response to touch or the ability to move by itself. Thus it seems to me that the alleged "slippery slope" between conception and birth is not so very slippery. In the early stages of pregnancy, abortion can hardly be compared to murder for psychological reasons, but in the latest stages it is psychologically akin to murder. Another source of similarity is the bodily continuity between fetus and adult. Bodies play a surprisingly central role in our attitudes toward persons. One has only to think of the philosophical literature on how far physical identity suffices for personal identity or Wittgenstein's remark that the best picture of the human soul is the human body. Even after death, when all agree the body is no longer a person, we still observe elaborate customs of respect for the human body; like people who torture dogs, necrophiliacs are not to be trusted with people. So it is appropriate that we show respect to a fetus as the body continuous with the body of a person. This is a degree of resemblance to persons that animals cannot rival.

Michael Tooley also utilizes a parallel with animals. He claims that it is always permissible to drown newborn kittens and draws conclusions about infanticide. But it is only permissible to drown kittens when their survival would cause some hardship. Perhaps it would be a burden to feed and house six more cats or to find other homes for them. The alternative of letting them starve produces even more suffering than the drowning. Since the kittens get their rights second-hand, so to speak, *via* the need for coherence in our attitudes, their interests are often overridden by the interests of full-fledged persons. But if their survival would be no inconvenience to people at all, then it is wrong to drown them, *contra* Tooley.

Tooley's conclusions about abortion are wrong for the same reason. Even if a fetus is not a person, abortion is not always permissible, because of the resemblance of a fetus to a person. I agree with Thomson that it would be wrong for a woman who is seven months pregnant to have an abortion just to avoid having to postpone a trip to Europe. In the early months of pregnancy when the fetus hardly resembles a baby at all, then, abortion is permissible whenever it is in the interests of the pregnant woman or her family. The reasons would only need to outweigh the pain and inconvenience of the abortion itself. In the middle months, when the fetus comes to resemble a person, abortion would be justifiable only when the continuation of the pregnancy or the birth of the child would cause harms—physical, psychological, economic or social—to the woman. In the late months of pregnancy, even on our current assumption that a fetus is not a person, abortion seems to be wrong except to save a woman from significant injury or death.

The Supreme Court has recognized similar gradations in the alleged slippery slope stretching between conception and birth. To this point, the present paper has been a discussion of the moral status of abortion only, not its legal status. In view of the great physical, financial and sometimes psychological costs of abortion, perhaps the legal arrangements most compatible with the proposed moral solution would be the absence of restrictions, that is, so-called abortion "on demand."

So I conclude, first, that application of our concept of a person will not suffice to settle the abortion issue. After all, the biological development of a human being is gradual. Second, whether a fetus is a person or not, abortion is justifiable early in pregnancy to avoid modest harms and seldom justifiable late in pregnancy except to avoid significant injury or death.

For Further Reflection

1. Can we get beyond the personhood issue, as English proposes? Has she successfully shown that we don't need to resolve this issue in order to deal with the morality of abortion? Where do you agree or disagree with her?

2. English's view has been called moderate because she accepts most early-stage abortions and rejects most later-stage abortions. If so, how can this be reconciled with her proposal, or at least acceptance, of abortion "on demand"?

3. Does English's argument appeal too much to our emotions and too little to reason? For example, she says, "It is crucial that psychological facts play a role here. Our psychological constitution makes it the case that for our ethical theory to work, it must prohibit certain treatment of nonpersons which are significantly person-like." What does English mean? Is this an appeal to ignorance or to human irrationality or something else?

4. What is her "coherence of attitudes" argument? How much weight should such considerations be given in the abortion debate? Could my "coherence" structure be different from yours, and yours be different from other people's? Discuss the case of the New York nurses who were expected to alternate between caring for six-week premature infants and disposing of viable 24-week aborted fetuses. What bearing does this have on the question of the morality of abortion?

Further Readings for Chapter 12

Brody, Baruch. *Abortion and the Sanctity of Life.* Cambridge, Mass.: MIT Press, 1975.

Devine, Philip E. *The Ethics of Homicide.* Ithaca, N.Y.: Cornell University Press, 1978.

Noonan, John T. *The Morality of Abortion: Legal and Historical Perspectives.* Cambridge, Mass.: Harvard University Press, 1970.

Pojman, Louis, and Frank Beckwith, eds. *The Abortion Controversy,* 2nd ed. Belmont, Calif.: Wadsworth, 1998.

Sumner, L. W. *Abortion and Moral Theory.* Princeton, N.J.: Princeton University Press, 1981.

Tooley, Michael. *Abortion and Infanticide.* Oxford: Oxford University Press, 1983.

CHAPTER 13

Substance Abuse
Drugs and Alcohol

Illegal drug traffic, drug use, and alcohol abuse are serious social problems in our society. Drug abuse threatens the fabric of many of our families and cities, resulting in ruined lives and enormous amounts of crime. Trafficking in illegal drugs is also profitable for criminals. Ethan Nadelmann states that "More than half of all organized crime revenues are believed to derive from illicit drug business; estimates to the dollar value range between $10 and $50 billion per year."* Alcohol abuse breaks up families, leads to spouse and child abuse and highway accidents. Half of the deaths in automobile accidents are attributable to drunk driving.

Peer pressure, curiosity, the desire to experiment, and the desire to rebel against parents or society are some of the causes of drug use and abuse. Marijuana is seen as a symbol of rebellion against society; cocaine and crack add "glamour" to a life of boredom; LSD creates a sense of ecstasy and mystical feelings; peyote is used to induce religious experience. Some drugs stimulate (amphetamines); some reduce stress and relax (alcohol and barbiturates); some induce euphoria (cocaine, crack, and heroin).

But heroin addiction can lead to prostitution and death from overdose, crack to violent crime, cocaine to suicide, and alcohol to death on the road. Continued marijuana use may lengthen the synapses between nerves and thereby slow down one's cognitive

---

*Ethan Nadelmann, "Drug Prohibition in the United States: Costs, Consequences and Alternatives," *Science* 245 (1 September 1989), p. 941.

capacity. Alcohol causes liver damage and may cause brain damage, which eventually leads to senility.

The risks of drug and alcohol abuse are enormous. Do the benefits outweigh the risks? The medieval Japanese writer Yoshida Kenko explored this question seven centuries ago. His essay is included in our readings.

A related issue is whether, knowing as we do how harmful these drugs are, we should legalize their use in order to remove the criminal motive. In our readings, Gore Vidal argues that by legalizing drugs we would remove most of the addiction and crime connected with drugs. But former drug czar William Bennett disagrees and attempts to rebut the arguments for legalization: if we are up to our knees now in drugs, we would be up to our neck with them in a nation that legalized drugs.

In our final reading, Bonnie Steinbock's "Drunk Driving," we consider an argument to the effect that some cases of drunk driving should be considered second-degree murder, bringing with them longer prison sentences.

We begin with John Stuart Mill's classic argument on liberty: unless someone (an adult) is unjustly harming another, he or she should be entirely free to do whatever he or she wants. Whether people risk harming themselves is none of the state's business.

On Liberty

JOHN STUART MILL

John Stuart Mill (1806–1873) is one of the most important philosophers of the nineteenth century. An innovative logician, the leading utilitarian, a strong advocate for women's rights, and a proponent of maximal liberty, he wrote penetrating essays in virtually every area of philosophy. In this selection from *On Liberty,* he sets forth his harm principle: that from a utilitarian perspective society is better off by tolerating any expression of individual liberty, so long as it does not unjustly harm others. He begins by decrying one of the dangers of democracy—the tyranny of the majority, which would infringe upon the liberty of the minority.

Like other tyrannies, the tyranny of the majority was at first, and is still vulgarly, held in dread, chiefly as operating through the acts of the public authorities. But reflecting persons perceived that when society is itself the tyrant—society collectively over the separate individuals who compose it—its means of tyrannising are not restricted to the acts which it may do by the hands of its political functionaries. Society can and does execute its own mandates: and if it issues wrong mandates instead of right, or any mandates at all in things with which it ought not to meddle, it practises a social tyranny more formidable than many kinds of political oppression, since, though not usually upheld by such extreme penalties, it leaves fewer means of escape, penetrating much more deeply into the details of life, and enslaving the soul itself. Protection, therefore, against the tyranny of the magistrate is not enough: there needs protection also against the tyranny of the prevailing opinion and feeling; against the tendency of society to impose, by other means than civil penalties, its own ideas and practices as rules of conduct on those who dissent from them; to fetter the development, and, if possible, prevent the formation, of any individuality not in harmony with its ways, and compels all characters to fashion them-

Reprinted from John Stuart Mill, *On Liberty* (1859).

selves upon the model of its own. There is a limit to the legitimate interference of collective opinion with individual independence: and to find that limit, and maintain it against encroachment, is as indispensable to a good condition of human affairs, as protection against political despotism.

The object of this Essay is to assert one very simple principle, as entitled to govern absolutely the dealings of society with the individual in the way of compulsion and control, whether the means used be physical force in the form of legal penalties, or the moral coercion of public opinion. That principle is, that the sole end for which mankind are warranted, individually or collectively, in interfering with the liberty of action of any of their number, is self-protection. That the only purpose for which power can be rightfully exercised over any member of a civilised community, against his will, is to prevent harm to others. His own good, either physical or moral, is not a sufficient warrant. He cannot rightfully be compelled to do or forbear because it will be better for him to do so, because it will make him happier, because, in the opinions of others, to do so would be wise, or even right. These are good reasons for remonstrating with him, or reasoning with him, or persuading him, or entreating him, but not for compelling him, or visiting him with any evil in case he do otherwise. To justify that, the conduct from which it is desired to deter him must be calculated to produce evil to some one else. The only part of the conduct of any one, for which he is amenable to society, is that which concerns others. In the part which merely concerns himself, his independence is, of right, absolute. Over himself, over his own body and mind, the individual is sovereign.

It is, perhaps, hardly necessary to say that this doctrine is meant to apply to human beings in the maturity of their faculties. We are not speaking of children, or of young persons below the age which the law may fix as that of manhood or womanhood. Those who are still in a state to require being taken care of by others, must be protected against their own actions as well as against external injury. For the same reason, we may leave out of consideration those backward states of society in which the race itself may be considered as in its nonage. The early difficulties in the way of spontaneous progress are so great, that there is seldom any choice of means for overcoming them; and a ruler full of the spirit of improvement is warranted in the use of any expedients that will attain an end, perhaps otherwise unattainable. Despotism is a legitimate mode of government in dealing with barbarians, provided the end be their improvement, and the means justified by actually effecting that end. Liberty, as a principle, has no application to any state of things anterior to the time when mankind have become capable of being improved by free and equal discussion. Until then, there is nothing for them but implicit obedience to an Akbar or a Charlemagne, if they are so fortunate as to find one. But, as soon as mankind have attained the capacity of being guided to their own improvement by conviction or persuasion (a period long since reached in all nations with whom we need here concern ourselves), compulsion, either in the direct form or in that of pains and penalties for non-compliance, is no longer admissible as a means to their own good, and justifiable only for the security of others. . . .

Though this doctrine is anything but new, and, to some persons, may have the air of a truism, there is no doctrine which stands more directly opposed to the general tendency of existing opinion and practice. Society has expended fully as much effort in the attempt (according to its lights) to compel people to conform to its notions of personal as of social excellence. . . .

There is a sphere of action in which society, as distinguished from the individual, has, if any, only an indirect interest; comprehending all that portion of a person's life and conduct which affects only himself, or if it also affects others, only with their free, voluntary, and undeceived consent and participation. When I say only himself, I mean directly, and in the first instance: for whatever affects himself, may affect others through himself; and the objection which may be grounded on this contingency, will receive consideration in the sequel. This, then, is the appropriate region of human liberty. It comprises, first, the inward domain of consciousness; demanding liberty of conscience, in the most comprehensive sense; liberty of thought and feeling; absolute freedom of opinion and sentiment on all subjects, practical or speculative, scientific, moral, or theological. The liberty of expressing and publishing opinions may seem to fall under a different principle, since it belongs to that part of the conduct of an individual which concerns other people; but, being almost of as much importance as the liberty of thought itself, and resting in great part on the same reasons, is practically inseparable from it. Secondly, the principle requires liberty of tastes and pursuits; of framing the plan of our life to suit our own character; of doing as we like, subject to such consequences as may follow; without impediment from our fellow-creatures, so long as what we do does not harm them, even though they should think our conduct foolish, perverse, or wrong. Thirdly, from this liberty of each individual, follows the liberty, within the same limits, of combination among individuals; freedom to unite, for any purpose not involving harm to others: the persons combining being supposed to be of full age, and not forced or deceived.

No society in which these liberties are not, on the whole, respected, is free, whatever may be its form of government; and none is completely free in which they do not exist absolute and unqualified. The only freedom which deserves the name, is that of pursuing our own good in our own way, so long as we do not attempt to deprive others of theirs, or impede their efforts to obtain it. Each is the proper guardian of his own health, whether bodily, or mental and spiritual. Mankind are greater gainers by suffering each other to live as seems good to themselves, than by compelling each to live as seems good to the rest. . . .

Again, there are many acts which, being directly injurious only to the agents themselves, ought not to be legally interdicted, but which, if done publicly, are a violation of good manners, and coming thus within the category of offences against others, may rightfully be prohibited. Of this kind are offences against decency; on which it is unnecessary to dwell, the rather as they are only connected indirectly with our subject, the objection to publicity being equally strong in the case of many actions not in themselves condemnable, nor supposed to be so. . . .

For Further Reflection

1. What does Mill mean by the tyranny of the majority? Can you illustrate a contemporary instance of it?

2. Mill differs from many proponents of liberty because he denies that we have any natural right to it. He doesn't believe in natural rights, but thinks that liberty can be justified by utilitarian arguments. Do you agree with him?

3. Do you agree with Mill's formulation of the principle of liberty? Should we sometimes act paternalistically even with educated

adults? How would Mill's principle apply to someone using drugs? Should society prohibit drug use? Or would Mill's principle advocate legalizing drugs?

Drugs Should Be Legalized

GORE VIDAL

Gore Vidal argues that we can solve our drug problem, at least most drug addiction, by legalizing drugs and selling them at cost. By informing people about the dangers of certain drugs, we can shift the burden onto them. The main benefit would be to take the crime out of drugs, for there would be no incentive for criminals to make money selling drugs, when people can buy them at cost.

It is possible to stop most drug addiction in the United States within a very short time. Simply make all drugs available and sell them at cost. Label each drug with a precise description of what effect— good and bad—the drug will have on the taker. This will require heroic honesty. Don't say that marijuana is addictive or dangerous when it is neither, as millions of people know—unlike "speed," which kills most unpleasantly, or heroin, which is addictive and difficult to kick.

For the record, I have tried—once—almost every drug and liked none, disproving the popular Fu Manchu theory that a single whiff of opium will enslave the mind. Nevertheless many drugs are bad for certain people to take and they should be told why in a sensible way.

Along with exhortation and warning, it might be good for our citizens to recall (or learn for the first time) that the United States

---

was the creation of men who believed that each man has the right to do what he wants with his own life as long as he does not interfere with his neighbor's pursuit of happiness (that his neighbor's idea of happiness is persecuting others does confuse matters a bit).

This is a startling notion to the current generation of Americans. They reflect a system of public education which has made the Bill of Rights, literally, unacceptable to a majority of high school graduates (see the annual Purdue reports) who now form the "silent majority"—a phrase which that underestimated wit Richard Nixon took from Homer who used it to describe the dead.

Now one can hear the warning rumble begin: if everyone is allowed to take drugs everyone will and the GNP will decrease, the Commies will stop us from making everyone free, and we shall end up a race of zombies, passively murmuring "groovy" to one another. Alarming thought. Yet it seems most unlikely that any reasonably sane person will become a drug addict if he knows in advance what addiction is going to be like.

Is everyone reasonably sane? Some people will always become drug addicts just as some people will always become alcoholics, and it is just too bad. Every man, however, has the power (and should have the legal right) to kill himself if he chooses. But since most men don't, they won't be mainliners either. Nevertheless, forbidding people things they like or think they might enjoy only makes them want those things all the more. This psychological insight is, for some mysterious reason, perennially denied our governors.

It is a lucky thing for the American moralist that our country has always existed in a kind of time-vacuum: we have no public memory of anything that happened before last Tuesday. No one in Washington today recalls what happened during the years alcohol was forbidden to the people by a Congress that thought it had a divine mission to stamp out Demon Rum—launching, in the process, the greatest crime wave in the country's history, causing thousands of deaths from bad alcohol, and creating a general (and persisting) contempt among the citizenry for the laws of the United States.

The same thing is happening today. But the government has learned nothing from past attempts at prohibition, not to mention repression.

Last year when the supply of Mexican marijuana was slightly curtailed by the Feds, the pushers got the kids hooked on heroin and deaths increased dramatically, particularly in New York. Whose fault? Evil men like the Mafiosi? Permissive Dr. Spock? Wild-eyed Dr. Leary? No.

The Government of the United States was responsible for those deaths. The bureaucratic machine has a vested interest in playing cops and robbers. Both the Bureau of Narcotics and the Mafia want strong laws against the sale and use of drugs because if drugs are sold at cost there would be no money in it for anyone.

If there was no money in it for the Mafia, there would be no friendly playground pushers, and addicts would not commit crimes to pay for the next fix. Finally, if there was no money in it, the Bureau of Narcotics would wither away, something they are not about to do without a struggle.

Will anything sensible be done? Of course not. The American people are as devoted to the idea of sin and its punishment as they are to making money—and fighting drugs is nearly as big a business as pushing them. Since the combination of sin and money is irresistible (particularly to the professional politician), the situation will only grow worse. . . .

For Further Reflection

1. Do you agree with Vidal that legalizing drugs would eliminate most drug addiction?

2. Do you agree that legalizing drugs would take most of the crime out of the drug industry?

3. Do you agree that marijuana is neither addictive nor dangerous?

Drugs Should Not Be Legalized

WILLIAM BENNETT

William Bennett has a law degree from Harvard University and a Ph.D. in philosophy from the University of Texas. He is former U.S. Secretary of Education and former director of the Drug Control Policy. In this essay he maintains that dangers in legalizing drugs far outweigh the benefits. He compares the war on drugs to the Allies' struggle against Hitler and argues that just as Churchill refused to compromise with evil, we should also fight to make our nation free from drugs.

Since I took command of the war on drugs, I have learned from former Secretary of State George Shultz that our concept of fighting drugs is "flawed." The only thing to do, he says, is to "make it possible for addicts to buy drugs at some regulated place." Conservative commentator William F. Buckley, Jr., suggests I should be "fatalistic" about the flood of cocaine from South America and simply "let it in." Syndicated columnist Mike Royko contends it would be easier to sweep junkies out of the gutters "than to fight a hopeless war" against the narcotics that send them there. Labeling our efforts "bankrupt," federal judge Robert W. Sweet opts for legalization, saying, "If our society can learn to stop using butter, it should be able to cut down on cocaine."

Flawed, fatalistic, hopeless, bankrupt! I never realized surrender was so fashionable until I assumed this post.

Though most Americans are overwhelmingly determined to go toe-to-toe with the foreign drug lords and neighborhood pushers, a small minority believe that enforcing drug laws imposes greater costs on society than do drugs themselves. Like addicts seeking immediate euphoria, the legalizers want peace at any price, even though it means the inevitable proliferation of a practice that degrades, impoverishes and kills.

I am acutely aware of the burdens drug enforcement places upon us. It consumes economic resources we would like to use elsewhere. It is sometimes frustrating, thankless and often dangerous. But the consequences of *not* enforcing drug laws would be far more costly. Those consequences involve the intrinsically destructive nature of drugs and the toll they exact from our society in hundreds of thousands of lost and broken lives . . . human potential never realized . . . time stolen from families and jobs . . . precious spiritual and economic resources squandered.

That is precisely why virtually every civilized society has found it necessary to exert some form of control over mind-altering substances and why this war is so important. Americans feel up to their hips in drugs now. They would be up to their necks under legalization.

Even limited experiments in drug legalization have shown that when drugs are more widely available, addiction skyrockets. In 1975 Italy liberalized its drug law and now has one of the highest heroin-related death rates in Western Europe. In Alaska, where marijuana was decriminalized in 1975, the easy atmosphere has increased usage of the drug, particularly among children. Nor does it stop there. Some Alaskan schoolchildren now tout "coca puffs," marijuanna cigarettes laced with cocaine.

Many legalizers concede that drug legalization might increase use, but they shrug off the matter. "It may well be that there would be more addicts, and I would regret that result," says Nobel laureate economist Milton Friedman. The late Harvard Medical School psychiatry professor Norman Zinberg, a longtime proponent of "responsible" drug use, admitted that "use of now illicit drugs would certainly increase. Also, casualties probably would increase."

In fact, Dr. Herbert D. Kleber of Yale University, my deputy in charge of demand reduction, predicts legalization might cause "a five-to-sixfold increase" in cocaine use. But legalizers regard this as a necessary price for the "benefits" of legalization. What benefits?

1. *Legalization will take the profit out of drugs.* The result supposedly will be the end of criminal drug pushers and the big foreign-drug wholesalers, who will turn to other enterprises because nobody will need to make furtive and dangerous trips to his local pusher.

But what, exactly, would the brave new world of legalized drugs look like? Buckley stresses that "adults get to buy the stuff at carefully regulated stores." (Would you want one in *your* neighborhood?) Others, like Friedman, suggest we sell the drugs at "ordinary retail outlets."

Former City University of New York sociologist Georgette Bennett assures us that "brand-name competition will be prohibited" and that strict quality control and proper labeling will be overseen by the Food and Drug Administration. In a touching egalitarian note, she adds that "free drugs will be provided at government clinics" for addicts too poor to buy them.

Almost all the legalizers point out that the price of drugs will fall, even though the drugs will be heavily taxed. Buckley, for example, argues that somehow federal drugstores will keep the price "low enough to discourage a black market but high enough to accumulate a surplus to be used for drug education."

Supposedly, drug sales will generate huge amounts of revenue, which will then be used to tell the public not to use drugs and to treat those who don't listen.

In reality, this tax would only allow government to *share* the drug profits now garnered by criminals. Legalizers would have to tax drugs heavily in order to pay for drug education and treatment programs. Criminals could undercut the official price and still make huge profits. What alternative would the government have? Cut the price until it was within the lunch-money budget of the average sixth-grade student?

2. Legalization will eliminate the black market. Wrong. And not just because the regulated prices could be undercut. Many legalizers admit that drugs such as crack or PCP are simply too dangerous to allow the shelter of the law. Thus criminals will provide what the government will not. "As long as drugs that people very much want remain illegal, a black market will exist," says legalization advocate David Boaz of the libertarian Cato Institute.

Look at crack. In powdered form, cocaine was an expensive indulgence. But street chemists found that a better and far less expensive—and far more dangerous—high could be achieved by mixing cocaine with baking soda and heating it. Crack was born, and "cheap" coke invaded low-income communities with furious speed.

An ounce of powdered cocaine might sell on the street for $1200. That same ounce can produce 370 vials of crack at $10 each. Ten bucks seems like a cheap hit, but crack's intense ten- to 15-minute high is followed by an unbearable depression. The user wants more crack, thus starting a rapid and costly descent into addiction.

If government drugstores do not stock crack, addicts will find it in the clandestine market or simply bake it themselves from their legally purchased cocaine.

Currently crack is being laced with insecticides and animal tranquilizers to heighten its effect. Emergency rooms are now warned to expect victims of "sandwiches" and "moon rocks," life-threatening smokable mixtures of heroin and crack. Unless the government is prepared to sell these deadly variations of dangerous drugs, it will perpetuate a criminal black market by default.

And what about children and teen-agers? They would obviously be barred from drug purchases, just as they are prohibited from buying beer and liquor. But pushers will continue to cater to these young customers with the old, favorite come-ons—a couple of free fixes to get them hooked. And what good will anti-drug education be when these youngsters observe their older brothers and sisters, parents and friends lighting up and shooting up with government permission?

Legalization will give us the worst of both worlds: millions of *new* drug users *and* a thriving criminal black market.

3. Legalization will dramatically reduce crime. "It is the high price of drugs that leads addicts to robbery, murder and other crimes," says Ira Glasser, executive director of the American Civil Liberties Union. A study by the Cato Institute concludes: "Most, if not all, 'drug-related murders' are the result of drug prohibition."

But researchers tell us that many drug-related felonies are committed by people involved in crime *before* they started taking drugs. The drugs, so routinely available in criminal circles, make the criminals more violent and unpredictable.

Certainly there are some kill-for-a-fix crimes, but does any rational person believe that a cut-rate price for drugs at a government outlet will stop such psychopathic behavior? The fact is that under the influence of drugs, normal people do not act normally, and abnormal people behave in chilling and horrible ways. DEA agents told me about a teen-age addict in Manhattan who was smoking crack when he sexually abused and caused permanent internal injuries to his one-month-old daughter.

Children are among the most frequent victims of violent, drug-related crimes that have nothing to do with the cost of acquiring the drugs. In Philadelphia in 1987 more than half the child-abuse fatalities involved at least one parent who was a heavy drug user. Seventy-three percent of the child-abuse deaths in New York City in 1987 involved parental drug use.

In my travels to the ramparts of the drug war, I have seen nothing to support the legalizers' argument that lower drug prices would reduce crime. Virtually everywhere I have gone, police and DEA agents have told me that crime rates are highest where crack is cheapest.

4. Drug use should be legal since users only harm themselves. Those who believe this should stand beside the medical examiner as he counts the 36 bullet wounds in the shattered corpse of a three-year-old who happened to get in the way of his mother's drug-crazed boyfriend. They should visit the babies abandoned by cocaine-addicted mothers—infants who already carry the ravages of addiction in their own tiny bodies. They should console the devastated relatives of the nun who worked in a homeless shelter and was stabbed to death by a crack addict enraged that she would not stake him to a fix.

Do drug addicts only harm themselves? Here is a former cocaine addict describing the compulsion that quickly draws even the most "responsible" user into irresponsible behavior: "Everything is about getting high, and any means necessary to get there becomes rational. If it means stealing something from somebody close to you, lying to your family, borrowing money from people you know you can't pay back, writing checks you know you can't cover, you do all those things—things that are totally against everything you have ever believed in."

Society pays for this behavior, and not just in bigger insurance premiums, losses from accidents and poor job performance. We pay the loss of a priceless social currency as families are destroyed, trust between friends is betrayed and promising careers are never fulfilled. I cannot imagine sanctioning behavior that would increase that toll.

I find no merit in the legalizers' case. The simple fact is that drug use is wrong. And the moral argument, in the end, is the most compelling argument. A citizen in a drug-induced haze, whether on his back-yard deck or on a mattress in a ghetto crack house, is not what the founding fathers meant by the "pursuit of happiness." Despite the legalizers' argument that drug use is a matter of "personal freedom," our nation's notion of liberty is rooted in the ideal of a self-reliant citizenry. Helpless wrecks in treatment centers, men chained by their noses to cocaine—these people are slaves.

Imagine if, in the darkest days of 1940, Winston Churchill had rallied the West by saying, "This war looks hopeless, and besides, it will cost too much. Hitler can't be *that* bad. Let's surrender and see what happens." That is essentially what we hear from the legalizers.

This war *can* be won. I am heartened by indications that education and public revulsion are having an effect on drug use. The National Institute on Drug Abuse's latest survey of current users shows a 37-percent *decrease* in drug consumption since 1985. Cocaine is down 50 percent; marijuana use among young people is at its lowest rate since 1972. In my travels I've been encouraged by signs that Americans are fighting back.

I am under no illusion that such developments, however hopeful, mean the war is over. We need to involve more citizens in the fight, increase pressure on drug criminals and build on anti-drug programs that have proved to work. This will not be easy. But the moral and social costs of surrender are simply too great to contemplate.

For Further Reflection

1. Go over Bennett's critique of the four arguments in favor of legalizing drugs. Are Bennett's counterarguments persuasive? Are you convinced by them? How would someone like Vidal respond to Bennett's critique?

2. Is the comparison between the war on drugs and the war against Hitler and his forces an apt one?

3. Some people point out that our drug policy is inconsistent. Marijuana and cocaine are illegal, but alcohol is legal; yet the latter often does more harm than the former. What would supporters of drug laws, like Bennett, say to that charge?

On Drinking

YOSHIDA KENKO

Yoshida Kaneyoshi (c. 1283–c. 1352) was a Japanese writer who became a Buddhist monk, taking the title Kenko (monk). Kenko's writings have remained popular in Japan through the centuries. In this essay, filled with insight, he manifests ambivalence toward alcoholic drinks.

There are many things in the world I cannot understand. I cannot imagine why people find it so enjoyable to press liquor on you the first thing, on every occasion, and force you to drink it. The drinker's face grimaces as if with unbearable distress, and he looks for a chance to get rid of the drink and escape unobserved, only to be stopped and senselessly forced to drink more. As a result, even dignified men suddenly turn into lunatics and behave idiotically, and men in the prime of health act like patients afflicted with grave illnesses and collapse unconscious before one's eyes. What a scandalous way to spend a day of celebration! The victim's head aches even the following day, and he lies abed, groaning, unable to eat, unable to recall what happened the day before, as if everything had taken place in a previous incarnation. He neglects important duties, both public and private, and the result is disaster. It is cruel and a breach of courtesy to oblige a man to undergo such experiences. Moreover, will not the man who has been put through this ordeal feel bitter and resentful towards his tormentors? If it were reported that such a custom, unknown among ourselves, existed in some foreign country, we should certainly find it peculiar and even incredible.

I find this practice distressing to observe even in strangers. A man whose thoughtful manner had seemed attractive laughs and shouts uncontrollably; he chatters interminably, his court cap askew, the cords of his cloak undone, the skirts of his kimono rolled up to his shins, presenting so disreputable a picture that he is unrecognizable as his usual self. A woman will brush the hair away from her forehead and brazenly lift up her face with a roar of laughter. She clings

Translated from Yoshida Kenko, "On Drinking."

to a man's hand as he holds a saké cup, and if badly bred she will push appetizers into the mouth of her companion, or her own, a disgraceful sight. Some men shout at the top of their lungs, singing and dancing, each to his own tune. Sometimes an old priest, invited at the behest of a distinguished guest, strips to the waist, revealing grimy, sallow skin, and twists his body in a manner so revolting that even those watching with amusement are nauseated. Some drone on about their achievements, boring their listeners; others weep drunkenly. People of the lower classes swear at one another and quarrel in a shocking and frightening manner; after various shameful and wretched antics they end up by grabbing things they have been refused, or falling from the verandah (or from a horse or a carriage) and injuring themselves. Or, if they are not sufficiently important to ride, they stagger along the main thoroughfares and perform various unmentionable acts before earthen walls or at people's gates. It is most upsetting to see an old priest in his shawl leaning on the shoulder of a boy and staggering along, mumbling something incomprehensible.

If such behavior were of benefit either in this world or the next, there might be some excuse. It is, however, the source of numerous calamities in this world, destroying fortunes and inviting sickness. They call liquor the chief of all medicines, but it is, in fact, the origin of all sicknesses. Liquor makes you forget your unhappiness, we are told, but when a man is drunk he may remember even his past griefs and weep over them. As for the future life, liquor deprives a man of his wisdom and consumes his good actions like fire; he therefore increases the burden of sin, violates many commandments and, in the end, drops into hell. Buddha taught that a man who takes liquor and forces another to drink will be reborn five hundred times without hands.

Though liquor is as loathsome as I have described it, there naturally are some occasions when it is hard to dispense with. On a moonlit night, a morning after a snowfall, or under the cherry blossoms, it adds to our pleasure if, while chatting at our ease, we bring forth the wine cups. Liquor is cheering on days when we are bored, or when a friend pays an unexpected visit. It is exceedingly agreeable too when you are offered cakes and wine most elegantly from behind a screen of state by a person of quality you do not know especially well. In winter it is delightful to sit opposite an intimate friend in a small room, toasting something to eat over the fire, and to drink deeply together. It is pleasant also when stopping briefly on a journey, or picnicking in the countryside, to sit drinking on the grass, saying all the while, "I wish we had something to eat with this saké." It is amusing when a man who hates liquor has been made to drink a little. How pleasing it is, again, when some distinguished man deigns to say, "Have another. Your cup looks a little empty." I am happy when some man I have wanted to make my friend is fond of liquor, and we are soon on intimate terms.

Despite all I have said, a drinker is amusing, and his offense is pardonable. It happens sometimes that a guest who has slept late in the morning is awakened by his host flinging open the sliding doors. The startled guest, his face still dazed by sleep, pokes out his head with its thin topknot and, not stopping to put on his clothes, carries them off in his arms, trailing some behind as he flees. It is an amusing and appropriate finale to the drinking party to catch a glimpse of the skinny, hairy shanks he reveals from behind as he lifts his skirts in flight.

For Further Reflection

1. Evaluate Kenko's discussion of drinking alcohol. Do its benefits outweigh its personal and social costs? Is social drinking in our country a problem? Is social pressure to drink a moral issue? Explain your answer.

2. Is alcohol use or abuse a problem on your campus? If so, what do you suggest should be done about it? If not, explain how your school has avoided the problem.

Drunk Driving

BONNIE STEINBOCK

Bonnie Steinbock is professor of philosophy at the State University of New York, Albany, and the author of several works in social philosophy. In this essay she argues that, given our notion of retributive justice, some drunk drivers who cause the deaths of their accident victims are guilty of second-degree murder and should be sentenced accordingly. Second-degree murder differs from first degree in that it does not require premeditation to murder. But it differs from manslaughter in that it involves knowledge that the unwarranted risk you are subjecting others to involves a fairly high probability that someone may be killed. Steinbock argues that a car can be a lethal weapon, and habitual drinkers must accept responsibility for the deaths they knowingly cause.

"Drunk drivers kill. They maim. They seriously injure. *And they get away with it.*" This is the message from MADD (Mothers Against Drunk Drivers), a group working to change laws as well as the attitudes of judges, juries, and the public. MADD's primary goal is to prevent crashes and deaths by getting drunk drivers off the road. However, they also want drunk drivers who cause death to be justly punished. They contend that such drivers are guilty not merely of criminal negligence, nor even of manslaughter: they commit murder.

I will defend the proposition that a significant class of drunk drivers who cause death does indeed commit, and often get away with, murder. In Section I, I will examine the traditional reasons for regarding vehicular homicide as something less than murder, focusing on the concept of intent. I will argue that, even though the drunk driver doesn't mean to kill anyone, to engage in an activity as dangerous as driving while severely intoxicated is so risky as to evidence extreme indifference to the value of human life, and therefore may constitute the malice necessary for a second-degree murder conviction. In Section II, I will examine the argument that, since drunk drivers who cause death are often alcoholics who cannot help drinking, it is unfair to hold them responsible and punish them for doing what they cannot control. Although I believe that this is a bad argument, I examine it in order to make explicit why it is fair to hold responsible for his actions an intoxicated person, as opposed, say, to an insane one. I will argue that while an alcoholic may not be responsible for his drinking, his decision to drink and then drive, in full knowledge of the risk he thereby poses to the safety of others, is reckless. It is sometimes so reckless as to be the equivalent of intentional killing. In the last section, I will turn from the notion of fair punishment to that of effective punishment, and the question of deterrence. Arguments for stiffening penalties for drunk driving should not be based on deterrent efficacy, as the evidence for this is, at best, inconclusive. However, deterrence is not the only consideration. There is also justice. If at least some cases of causing death by drunk driving are cases of murder, sentences should be comparable to those given others convicted of murder. Slight or nonexistent penalties for vehicular homicide allow people literally to get away with murder, and this is wrong quite independently of whether stiffer penalties would reduce the number of highway fatalities.

I. MALICE AND MURDER

Drunk driving takes an enormous toll, in lost lives and property, in injuries and human suffering. It contributes to approximately half of all highway deaths in the United States, killing about 25,000 people every year, and injuring many more. Despite this carnage, the drunk driver runs little risk of being arrested. Even if he injures or kills someone, plea bargaining and loopholes in the law make it unlikely that he will be convicted of a serious crime, and sentences tend to be light. Clarence Busch, the man who inadvertently launched MADD when he killed thirteen-year-old Cari Lightner in a hit-and-run accident, had three previous drunk driving convictions, but had spent only forty-eight hours in jail. The killer of four-year-old Kelly Schuett pleaded no contest to driving while intoxicated and was given a suspended five-day jail sentence and fined $284.

> Thomas and Dorothy Sexton recall going to court to witness the trial
> of the man whose blood alcohol content was .26 when he killed the

Sextons' 15-year-old son, Tom. They saw a car thief sentenced to two years in jail, while their son's killer—who pleaded guilty to homicide by a motor vehicle—was sentenced to two years' probation and fined $200.

Such facts have led some to call drunk driving a "socially accepted form of murder." This might be thought to be at best rhetorical hyperbole and, at worst, a serious misunderstanding of the crime of murder, indeed of the entire moral basis of Anglo-American law. That moral basis is expressed in the slogan, "non facit reum nisi mens sit rea" or, roughly, "There is no crime without a guilty mind." The *mens rea* required for murder is the intent to cause death. Thus, it may seem that to speak of murder where there is no intent to cause death is to misunderstand the nature of murder and, worse, to threaten a reversion to a primitive system of strict liability which ignores subtle differences in culpability based on psychological factors, such as intention and awareness. One might argue that to cause death by drunk driving may be criminally negligent homicide, or even manslaughter, but it cannot be murder, since the drunk driver does not mean to kill anyone. (Some writers suggest that a significant proportion of drunk drivers may actually be trying to commit suicide, but no one suggests that they are out to get the rest of us.)

However, this argument provides an oversimplified view of the "malice" required for a murder conviction. It is not necessary that one intend to cause death in the ordinary, narrow sense of "intend" which implies conscious desire or plan. The man recently convicted of the murder of Vicki Morgan, the mistress of Alfred Bloomingdale, is reported to have told the police that he did not mean to kill her, but just wanted to stop her talking. From a legal perspective, it is irrelevant whether or not he beat her in order to kill her or merely to get her to stop talking, so long as he knew he was beating her, and was aware that beatings cause serious injury. The common-law rule is that a person who intentionally inflicts grievous bodily injury is guilty of murder, if death results. So, if either death or really serious injury is the certain, or even highly probable, result of the defendant's act, there can be a conviction for murder.

One well-known case is *Hyam v. Director of Public Prosecutions.* Mrs. Hyam was jilted by her lover for another woman and set fire to the house where the woman lived. Her intention, she said, was to frighten the woman into leaving the neighborhood. As it happened, two of the woman's children were killed, and Mrs. Hyam was convicted of murder. The trial judge instructed the jury that the accused intended death or serious bodily harm (the *mens rea* for murder) if she knew, when she did the act, that it was highly probable that it would cause death or serious bodily harm. The conviction was upheld by the Court of Appeal and the House of Lords.

Did Mrs. Hyam in fact foresee that it was highly probable that someone would be killed or seriously injured as a result of the fire? Lord Hailsham held that the question was not one of foresight of probability but whether there was an intention "wilfully to expose a victim to the serious risk of death or really serious injury." However, the act must be aimed at a particular person or persons (not necessarily the actual victim) to constitute murder. Thus, if Mrs. Hyam had set the fire to collect insurance money, rather than to frighten her rival, the killing of the children probably would not have been murder, even if the risk to life was exactly the same.

American law has developed differently, with a more straightforward recognition of murder without actual intent to kill. Lord Hailsham's insistence that the dangerous act be aimed at a particular person reflects his conviction that mere recklessness can never constitute the malice necessary for murder. By contrast, American courts have allowed that an extremely dangerous act with no social utility, such as shooting into an occupied house or moving train, can be murder. For instance, on August 1, 1983, Joseph Miller and Kenneth Baird were convicted in Albany County, New York, of the murder of a 16-month-old baby, Robert Homsey, who died in a fire they set on March 9 out of vengeance. The two men had intended to burn the structure next to the house where the baby lived with his parents, but set fire to the Homsey house by mistake. They did not intend to kill Robert Homsey or anyone else. They were nevertheless convicted of second-degree murder and sentenced to the maximum prison term of twenty-five years to life.

These cases are both examples of what has been termed "homicide by excessive risk taking." If such homicide can constitute second-degree murder, the question arises, what is "excessive" risk taking? Not every risk to life is considered unjustifiable or wrongful. Many social ventures, from the building of bridges to the use of highways to the mining of coal, involve a serious risk to human life. In fact, we can predict with fair accuracy just how many lives will be lost as the result of such activities. The justification for engaging in activities which will surely result in injury and death is social utility. Modern life would be impossible without roads and bridges and coal; therefore we tolerate the unavoidable loss of life. However, at the same time, we are morally required to minimize avoidable losses, by improving safety devices, or by developing alternatives (e.g., the use of solar energy, rather than coal, would prevent mining accidents and black lung disease). Safety precautions and the development of alternatives invariably cost money. The question then becomes: Given a socially useful activity, how much money are we morally required to spend to reduce injuries and deaths? And when injuries and deaths do occur, who should bear the loss?

Such questions are fascinating and important, but I mention them only to put them aside, for they are not relevant to my argument. For tolerance of injury and death for the sake of social utility is acceptable only in the case of *accidents.* The fact that we, as a society, are willing to tolerate the accidental loss of life resulting from socially useful activities is consistent with forbidding negligence, recklessness, and the intentional infliction of harm. In many cases, causing death by drunk driving is not a tragic accident, but tantamount to the intentional infliction of harm, comparable to shooting into a crowded room, or setting a house on fire. If these are reasonably viewed as second-degree murder, when death results, so should some (though not all) cases of causing death by drunk driving.

In cases of homicide by excessive risk taking, what distinguishes manslaughter from murder? The usual test is that murder requires evidence of "extreme indifference to the value of human life." Arson, shooting into a crowded room—these are clear examples of dangerous behavior with no social utility or justification. Courts have been more reluctant to treat homicide by reckless driving as manslaughter or murder, partly because driving is seen as an ordinary activity, with social utility, while arson and shooting are not. However, whatever the utility of driving, *drunk* driving has no social utility. It presumably has utility to the drunk driver; otherwise, he wouldn't drive. However, it has no *social* utility; that is, it is not an activity which benefits society as a whole, or one which we as a society have any reason to encourage. The ordinariness of driving should not blind us to the dangerousness of drunk driving. A related point is that a car, unlike a gun, is not thought of as a lethal weapon: the decision to wield a gun may itself be thought to betray a wicked purpose, and so to be worse than mere recklessness. This is apparently the reasoning of Rollin M. Perkins, who classifies homicide by reckless driving as manslaughter, but shooting into a house or train "just for kicks" as murder, even though both may be equally hazardous. "The difference is that in the act of the shooter there is an element of viciousness—an extreme indifference to the value of human life—that is not found in the act of the motorist."

The first point to note is that a car can be as lethal as a gun. Certainly there is no difference where the driver or gunman intends to kill or inflict grievous bodily harm. Even where there is no such specific intent, a car can be used as a means of frightening pedestrians "just for kicks." In such cases, courts have not hesitated to convict of murder if any death results, holding that such behavior exhibits such a high degree of recklessness and disregard for the rights of others that a jury is justified in inferring malice. As the judge wrote of the defendant in one such case, ". . . he was possessed of a heart regardless of social duty and fatally bent on mischief."

It may be thought that the crucial distinction between manslaughter and murder, in cases of homicide by excessive risk taking, is and should be whether the defendant had a heart fatally bent on mischief. However, I argue that extreme indifference to the rights and lives of others can be shown equally by a decision to engage, without justification, in extremely risky behavior. The drunk driver does not want to hurt or frighten anyone; he nevertheless puts lives at risk. Perhaps he is not as morally bad as one who drives recklessly in order to frighten people, but absence of malevolent motive (as, for instance, in cases of mercy killing) does not itself bar a murder conviction: what makes homicide by a drunk driver an appropriate subject for a murder conviction is not the wickedness of the behavior, but its recklessness.

Some courts have agreed, in cases where the drunken driving was exceptionally reckless. The reasoning has been that drunk driving itself can be so dangerous as to be "malum in se," quite apart from any additional wrongdoing, and so can supply the criminal intent for murder in the second degree.

It is not however essential that there should have been an actual intent upon the part of the operator to kill the deceased. The necessary malice may be inferred or implied where the driver acts so recklessly or wantonly as to manifest a depravity of mind and disregard of human life . . . for example, one who, when in an intoxicated condition, drove an automobile at a reckless speed along a principal street of a village, into collision with another car, which results in the death of its occupant, may be found guilty of murder in the second degree. . . .

Does one have to be driving at great speed, or on the wrong side of a highway, to display a recklessness manifesting extreme indifference to human life? I submit that it is not the standard of one's driving while intoxicated that matters; it is the *fact that* one drove after drinking heavily, when incapable of controlling a motor vehicle.

. . . consider the case of William Rowan. Rowan was once sentenced to 45 days in jail, a mild penance for a California driving record that carried six convictions for drunk or reckless driving, two for hit and run. Last March, after leaving a downtown Santa Ana bar, Rowan drove onto a sidewalk, killing four-year-old David Gunderman, who was waiting for the ice-cream man. After hitting the child, Rowan slumped in his seat and lit a cigar. Police measured his blood alcohol content at .27.

It is illegal in most states to drive with a blood alcohol content of .10 percent or higher. To give some idea of how much alcohol Rowan must have consumed: to reach a level of .20 percent, an average-sized man must drink, over the course of a couple of hours, twelve beers or a quart of wine or six or seven martinis. Nor is Rowan atypical. A 1964 study found that 46 percent of New York drivers responsible for fatal accidents had blood levels at .25 percent or higher. Research indicates that the probability of having a serious accident increases dramatically, the more alcohol is consumed: the more one drinks, the greater the risk to human life. To drive after consuming a dozen martinis is inherently reckless, because it is virtually impossible to drive with due care in that condition. The same reasoning applies to anyone who drives when incapacitated, not only to those whose incapacity is caused by intoxication. A diabetic who goes into frequent comas, unpreventable by medication, but nevertheless drives is as reckless as the drunk driver: both are equally incapable of driving safely, both are equally aware of the danger they pose to others. Such a diabetic who insisted on continuing to drive might reasonably be convicted of second-degree murder, if he killed someone. . . .

Research indicates that the typical drunk driver who causes a crash has not only been drinking very heavily, but has a history of drunk driving arrests. This indicates another difference between reckless homicide (manslaughter) and recklessness which amounts to murder, namely the *repeated* taking of risks with others' lives. We should distinguish between a person who uncharacteristically drinks too much at a party and tragically causes a fatal crash, and one who habitually drinks enormous amounts of alcohol and then drives, in spite of repeated arrests and even accidents. When Clarence Busch killed Cari Lightner, he was free on bail after being arrested for another hit-and-run committed only two days earlier. How could he claim that he did not know the risk he posed to human life when he got behind the wheel? That is no tragic accident: that's murder.

However, there is a problem with the suggestion that we base the distinction between reckless homicide (manslaughter) and murder partly on the defendant's past history. Evidence of prior convictions generally may not be introduced at a criminal trial, as this has no bearing on the defendant's guilt or innocence in the instant case, and is likely to prejudice the jury. The fact that the defendant has prior convictions for drunk driving does not prove that he was drunk this time, nor does it prove that it was his drunkenness (as opposed to some factor not his fault) that caused the accident.

Nevertheless, knowledge of a defendant's history is essential to determine the extent of his awareness of risk, and hence essential for a finding of recklessness. In the words of one judge:

> . . . one of the essential ingredients of murder is malice. In this case it's going to have to be equivalent of implied malice. Part of that is the defendant's knowledge of the risk to human life he was taking in the actions he was doing. It seems to me his previous experience with excessive drinking is some evidence for the jury to consider in deciding what his state of mind was or the condition of his heart.

To avoid prejudicing a jury, perhaps there could be a two-stage trial. During the first stage, the jury would attempt to determine whether the defendant was guilty of driving while intoxicated, and whether his being intoxicated caused the accident. They would have no knowledge of his record at this stage. During the second stage, after any previous drunk driving convictions have been made known to them, the jury would decide if the defendant's conduct manifested the extreme indifference to life necessary for a murder conviction.

It may be said that drunk drivers do not *consciously* disregard a risk to human life; they are so drunk that they do not know what they are doing; or at least, their judgment is seriously impaired. Furthermore, the alcoholics and problem drinkers who constitute the bulk of the problem cannot help drinking: they are victims of a compulsion, perhaps a disease. So they should be pitied and treated, but not punished. In the next section, I will examine the relationship between intoxication and culpability.

II. INTOXICATION AND CULPABILITY

Self-induced drunkenness is not itself an excuse or a defense to a criminal charge. If I kill someone, and my only excuse is that I was drunk at the time and didn't know what I was doing, I am guilty of manslaughter at least. I am responsible for what I did, although I would not have done it if I had not been drunk, since I drank voluntarily; that is, I was not forced into drinking.

In fact, far from being a defense to a criminal charge, drunkenness is sometimes an aggravating factor. A drunk physician who causes the death of a patient is not merely negligent, but is guilty of manslaughter: his having treated a patient while drunk is regarded as being intrinsically reckless. The same reasoning applies to the drinking driver, and is reflected in the statutory law of some states. Such laws recognize that it is dangerous to do certain things while intoxicated, and put on notice those who do those things while drunk, that they will be held responsible for the consequences. In effect we refuse to accept the excuse, "It was an accident," from the drunken person because the chance of causing an accident while intoxicated is so much increased.

It might be said that, whatever the culpability of a person who *voluntarily* becomes intoxicated, an alcoholic is an addict, the victim of disease. He cannot be said voluntarily to become intoxicated, or even voluntarily to drink; he is compelled. But his compulsion to drink is irrelevant: it is not his *drinking* that is culpable, but his *drinking and driving*. I know of no compulsion to drink *and* drive. However, it might be objected that, while there is no "compulsion" to drive after drinking, alcohol affects both judgment and self-control. One might be fully aware when sober that one ought not to drive after drinking heavily and yet, once drunk, fail to appreciate the degree of one's impairment or just drive anyway, against one's better judgment. As consumption of alcohol does affect judgment and control, shouldn't "I was drunk" constitute a mitigating factor which, while not completely absolving the driver of responsibility, nevertheless makes causing death by drunk driving something less than murder?

Often we do accept "I was drunk" as an excuse. Someone who behaves boorishly at a party might later apologize to the host, saying "I was drunk, I didn't know what I was doing." Behavior which might be inexcusable if done sober may be excused if the person was drunk. So one might argue that the very condition that makes one's driving dangerous impairs one's ability to make a responsible decision about whether to drive. The drunk driver may not be "compelled" to drive, but neither is he completely responsible for his decision to drive.

However, even good excuses wear thin if used too often. If someone gets drunk regularly and beats up his wife every time, we begin to lose sympathy with the excuse "I was drunk." If one knows that one's behavior is going to be harmful at a later time, when one will have little or no control over what one does, then it is one's obligation to take steps to prevent the situation from occurring. Even if one is not responsible for getting drunk, that does not absolve one of responsibility for the harm one causes when drunk; and if one has had a great deal of advance warning about what one is likely to do when drunk, then the fact that one was drunk does not lessen one's responsibility at all. This explains why we should regard the social drinker, who overindulges at a party, and drives when he should not, causing a fatal accident, as merely negligent. He is at fault, but no murderer. The case is entirely different for the habitual drunk driver, at least one who has had previous accidents. He is fully aware of the danger he poses to others, yet continues to drive after drinking. By contrast, the chronic heavy drinker who has never had an accident has not had the benefit of this object lesson, and so may not appreciate fully the danger he poses to others. For this reason, we may regard him as less culpable than a Clarence Busch, who went on drinking and driving, even after committing a hit-and-run only days before. Nevertheless, the fact that one has been lucky does not absolve one of responsibility when one's luck runs out. The habitual drunk driver knows that he is going to consume enormous quantities of alcohol and that his ability to drive will be seriously impaired. (This is true even if we take into consideration the variance in toleration of alcohol. *No one* can drive safely with a blood alcohol content of .20 or more, yet such levels are common among drunk drivers who cause fatal accidents.) There is nothing unreasonable or unfair about expecting the chronic heavy drinker to make other travel arrangements when he is going to drink. He could have given away his keys, or got a ride, or called a cab. His recklessness lies in his failure to do any of these things. The capacity to plan in advance for his future incapacity differentiates the alcoholic from the insane person. Both are, by hypothesis, incapable of controlling their behavior at the time they cause harm. But the alcoholic has sober moments in which he can take precautions; the insane person does not, as he has no reason to believe he will become insane, or that he will cause harm at that time. The situation of an insane person becomes more analogous to the drunk driver if the insanity consists of repeatable periods in which dangerous, uncontrollable behavior occurs: say, he becomes a werewolf at full moon. If you know you're going to attack people if you go outside when the moon is full, then you ought to take precautions to ensure you don't go outside then. Lock yourself in. Alert the police. Commit yourself voluntarily to a mental hospital. After all, lives are at stake. A werewolf who does none of these things, who attempts to persuade himself that this time it won't happen, or he'll control himself, is guilty of murder when he kills someone. So is the alcoholic drunk driver. . . .

III.   DETERRENCE

Many people argue for stiffer penalties for drunk driving on grounds of deterrence. Belief in deterrent efficacy is implicit in the claim that judges should give tougher sentences in order to protect us from drinking drivers. It seems intuitively obvious that, if a given behavior has severe penalties attached to it, people are more likely to think twice about doing it. If one risks losing one's license, or even going to jail, surely one will be less likely to drink and drive. This has been the reasoning behind drunk driving legislation in Scandinavia, where drunk drivers have faced revocation of their licenses and mandatory jail sentences since the 1930s. The Scandinavians claim that this has worked to reduce the number of automobile fatalities. In the words of one Norwegian writer:

> The awareness of hazards of imprisonment for intoxicated driving is in our country a living reality to every driver, and for most people the risk seems too great. When a man goes to a party where alcoholic drinks are likely to be served, and if he is not fortunate enough to have a wife who drives but does not drink, he will leave his car at home or he will limit his consumption to a minimum. It is also my feeling—although I am here on uncertain grounds—that the legislation has been instrumental in forming or sustaining the widespread conviction that it is wrong, or irresponsible, to place oneself behind the wheel when intoxicated.

Similar claims of success have been made by law enforcement agencies in California, Maine, and Maryland, where tough anti-drunk-driving legislation has been put into effect. MADD's literature claims 20 percent or greater reductions in highway fatalities in the wake of such legislation. However, Ross has argued that the Scandinavian claims of deterrent effectiveness are based on insufficient and unscientific evidence. He denies that they have hard evidence of a long-term reduction in highway crashes and fatalities since their drunk driving legislation went into effect. Instead, he claims that what we find in Scandinavia and in other places which have adopted similar laws is a sharp drop in crash-related injuries simultaneous with the new law, followed by a return to previous levels within a year or so. Ross explains the reversion to previous levels of crashes as due to increasing awareness on the part of drivers that, despite the tough laws, they are very unlikely to be apprehended for drunk driving. Merely stiffening penalties, without a corresponding emphasis on apprehension of offenders by the police, will do little to get drunk drivers permanently off the road. The claims of success in California, Maine, Maryland, and other states may turn out to be evanescent, following the pattern detected by Ross in Scandinavia and other countries.

There is another problem with attempts to deter drinking drivers by increasing the penalties for doing so, even if the laws are enforced. It is that the drivers responsible for the great bulk of alcohol-related crashes constitute a minority of drivers. They are the alcoholics or problem drinkers who have typically consumed a vast quantity of alcohol before driving. Stiffer penalties and social disapproval are unlikely to have much effect on these drivers. So the drivers who are the problem are by and large undeterrable, while the drivers who may be deterred by tough legislation are not the primary cause of the problem.

The conclusion seems to be that we simply do not know if stiffer penalties will have a significant deterrent effect. If we don't know how effective such laws are in reducing alcohol-related crashes, it is impossible to weigh their benefit against the social costs, such as more work for overworked courts, and more prisoners for already overcrowded jails. . . .

However, our system of criminal law is intended not only to prevent harm, but also to punish the guilty. It is retributive as well as utilitarian. One may enthusiastically support gun control as a way to reducing homicides, and at the same time wish to see murderers punished. . . .

Justice is not served when a car thief is jailed but someone who has taken a life through inexcusable recklessness is merely fined. We must recognize that some "unintentional" killings are morally worse than some intentional ones, and should be punished accordingly. Those who intentionally kill are sometimes tormented beyond breaking point by those they kill; the victims of drunk drivers are invariably innocent strangers. Consider the case of seventeen-year-old Richard Jahnke who shot and killed his father, who had severely beaten him, and sexually abused his sister, throughout their childhood. The authorities Richard approached could not believe the violence he reported could take place in such a comfortable middle-class home. Can it seriously be maintained that Richard's crime is worse than that of Clarence Busch, or that his sentence of five to fifteen years in jail is fair, compared with the typically light sentences given those who commit vehicular homicide?

If justice is to be done, we must recognize drunk driving for the dangerous and antisocial activity it is. Drunk drivers who kill must no longer be allowed to hide behind excuses, such as that they were too drunk to know what they were doing, or that they cannot help drinking. Habitual drinkers who drive after drinking to excess take unjustifiable risks with the lives of the rest of us. When they cause death by drunken driving, they murder.

For Further Reflection

1. Evaluate Steinbock's arguments for charging some drunk drivers with second-degree murder and hence stiffer sentences than for manslaughter. Do you agree with her arguments? What is her strongest point? Do you find any weak points?

2. How would you respond to the objection that alcoholics are responsible for their behavior when they drive, so they cannot be charged with murder, but only involuntary manslaughter?

3. Why doesn't Steinbock use deterrence as an additional reason to support stiffer sentences for drunk drivers who kill? Do you agree with her admission that the evidence for deterrence is "at best, inconclusive"? Suppose someone argues that even if the evidence is inconclusive, we should bet on deterrence anyway. That is, we should bet that stiffer sentences will deter other drinkers from driving. So we give culprits the maximum sentence that retribution allows. If stiffer sentences do deter, we save x number of additional lives. If they don't deter, we have given culprits more punishment than is strictly necessary, but what they deserve on retributive grounds. In other words, we have to bet anyway. By not giving harsher sentences, we are betting that deterrence doesn't work, but the evidence doesn't support that either. So let's bet that harsher sentences do work.
   Evaluate this argument.

Further Readings for Chapter 13

Bakalar, James B., and Lester Grinspan, "Drug Abuse Policy and Social Attitudes to Risk Taking." In T. H. Murray et al., eds., *Feeling Good and Doing Better: Ethics and Nontherapeutic Drug Use.* Clifton, N.J.: Humanities Press, 1984.

Bennett, William J. "Restoring Authority." *New Perspectives Quarterly* 6 (Summer 1989).

Hamowy, Ronald, ed. *Dealing With Drugs: Consequences of Government Control.* Lexington, Mass.: D. C. Heath, 1987.

Nadelmann, Ethan A. "Drug Prohibition in the United States:

Costs, Consequences, and Alternatives." *Science* 245 (September 1989).

Richards, David A. J. *Sex, Drugs Death and the Law*. Totowa, N.J.: Rowman and Littlefield, 1982.

Wilson, James Q. "Against the Legalization of Drugs." *Commentary,* February 1990.

CHAPTER 14

Our Duties to Animals

Every minute of the day, twenty-four hours a day, one hundred animals are killed in laboratories in the United States. Fifty million animals used in experiments are put to death each year. Some die during testing of industrial and cosmetic products, some are killed after being force fed or after being tested for pharmaceutical drugs. Product testing on animals is required by government before the products are allowed for use by human beings.

Legal requirements that animals be anesthetized are circumvented in many experiments. Recently, at a major university, baboons were strapped down in boxlike vises and had specially designed helmets cemented to their skulls. Then a pneumatic device delivered calibrated blows to the helmet to determine its strength. The blows continued until the baboon's skull was fractured and the animal was brain damaged. Dogs are driven insane with electric shocks so that scientists can study the effects of insanity. Cats are deprived of sleep until they die. Primates have been restrained for months in steel chairs allowing no movement, and elephants have been given LSD to study aggression. Legs have been cut off mice to study how they walk on the stumps, and polar bears have been drowned in vats of crude oil to study the effect of oil spills in polar regions.

Kittens have been blinded, castrated, and rendered deaf so researchers could see what effect these incapacities would have on their sexual development. Civet cats are placed in small cages in dark rooms where the temperature is 110° F and confined there until they die. The musk that is scraped from their genitals once a day for as long as they can survive makes the scent of perfume last a bit longer after each application.

Neither is all well down on the farm. Factory farming with high-tech machinery has replaced free-range agriculture. Farmer McDon-

ald doesn't visit his hens in barns to pick an egg from the comfortable nest. Now, as soon as chicks are hatched, they are placed in small
cages. Between five and nine chickens are pressed together in cages
about 18 inches by 10 inches where they cannot move around, with
thin wire-mesh floors that hurt their feet. They are painfully debeaked
so that they cannot attack each other in these unnatural quarters. In
other chicken factories, the chickens are hung by their feet from conveyor belts that transport them through automatic throat-slicing
machines. Three billion chickens are killed in the United States each
year. Likewise, pigs and veal calves are kept in pens so small they
cannot move or turn around and develop muscles. They are separated from their mothers so they cannot be suckled and are fed a diet
low in iron so they will produce very tender meat.

Do animals have rights? Given the practices just described, do
we have a responsibility to improve our behavior toward the animal kingdom? No one disagrees that we should not cause animals
unnecessary suffering, but those who defend animal factories and
animal experimentation argue that human need justifies these practices. On the other side of the controversy, animal rights advocates
argue that animals should be accorded equal consideration with
humans—that their specific needs should be taken seriously. If this
were done, we would become vegetarians, cease to use leather,
and cease all (or almost all) animal experimentation.

Our first reading is George Orwell's description of his shooting
an elephant in Burma, which he compares to the essence of imperialism. Our second reading is Immanuel Kant's argument that we
have no direct duties to animals, since they are not persons. In our
third reading, Peter Singer, the torchbearer of animal liberation,
argues that animals should be treated with equal consideration as
human beings. Singer says that if a nonhuman and a human are
suffering, and we have only enough painkiller for one, it is not
clear who should receive the painkiller. Carl Cohen argues in our
fourth reading that the idea of rights does not apply to animals
since "rights" is a concept appropriate only to members of the moral
community and animals cannot make moral decisions. Humans are
of far greater value than animals. Cohen readily admits that gratuitous suffering should be prohibited, but animal experimentation is
needed to ameliorate human suffering, and, as such, it is justified.
In our final reading, Mylan Engel argues that the moral principles
most of us already hold entail that we ought not to eat meat.

Shooting an Elephant

GEORGE ORWELL

George Orwell, pseudonym of Eric Arthur Blair (1903–1950), novelist and essayist, was born in India, and served in the Indian imperial police. He rejected the imperialism connected with his position and went to live as a beggar in the East End of London. This experience became the subject of his book *Down and Out in Paris and London* (1933). His best-known works are *Animal Farm* (1945) and *Nineteen Eighty-Four* (1949), a pessimistic satire about future political tyranny.

This essay, written in the 1930s, is based on Orwell's experience in the imperial police in Burma.

In Moulmein, in Lower Burma, I was hated by large numbers of people—the only time in my life that I have been important enough for this to happen to me. I was sub-divisional police officer of the town, and in an aimless, petty kind of way anti-European feeling was very bitter. No one had the guts to raise a riot, but if a European woman went through the bazaars alone somebody would probably spit betel juice over her dress. As a police officer I was an obvious target and was baited whenever it seemed safe to do so. When a nimble Burman tripped me up on the football field and the referee (another Burman) looked the other way, the crowd yelled with hideous laughter. This happened more than once. In the end the sneering yellow faces of young men that met me everywhere, the insults hooted after me when I was at a safe distance, got badly on my nerves. The young Buddhist priests were the worst of all. There were several thousands of them in the town and none of them seemed to have anything to do except stand on street corners and jeer at Europeans. All this was perplexing and upsetting. For at that time I had already made up my mind that imperialism was an evil thing and the sooner I chucked up my job and got out of it the better. Theoretically—and secretly, of course—I was all for the Burmese and all against their oppressors, the British. As for the job I was doing, I hated it more bitterly than I can perhaps make clear. In a job like that you see the dirty work of Empire at close quarters. The wretched prisoners huddling in the stinking cages of the lock-ups, the grey, cowed faces of the long-term convicts, the scarred buttocks of the men who had been flogged with bamboos— all these oppressed me with an intolerable sense of guilt. But I could get nothing into perspective. I was young and ill-educated and I had had to think out my problems in the utter silence that is imposed on every Englishman in the East. I did not even know that the British Empire is dying, still less did I know that it is a great deal better than the younger empires that are going to sup- plant it. All I knew was that I was stuck between my hatred of the empire I served and my rage against the evil-spirited little beasts who tried to make my job impossible. With one part of my mind I thought of the British Raj as an unbreakable tyranny, as some- thing clamped down, in *saecula saeculorum,* upon the will of pros- trate peoples; with another part I thought that the greatest joy in the world would be to drive a bayonet into a Buddhist priest's guts. Feelings like these are the normal by-products of imperialism; ask any Anglo-Indian official, if you can catch him off duty.

One day something happened which in a roundabout way was enlightening. It was a tiny incident in itself, but it gave me a bet- ter glimpse than I had had before of the real nature of imperial- ism—the real motives for which despotic governments act. Early one morning the sub-inspector at a police station the other end of town rang me up on the 'phone and said that an elephant was rav- aging the bazaar. Would I please come and do something about it? I did not know what I could do, but I wanted to see what was happening and I got on to a pony and started out. I took my rifle, an old .44 Winchester and much too small to kill an elephant, but I thought the noise might be useful *in terrorem.* Various Burmans stopped me on the way and told me about the elephant's doings. It was not, of course, a wild elephant, but a tame one which had gone "must." It had been chained up, as tame elephants always are when their attack of "must" is due, but on the previous night it had broken its chain and escaped. Its mahout, the only person who could manage it when it was in that state, had set out in pursuit, but had taken the wrong direction and was now twelve hours' journey away, and in the morning the elephant had suddenly reappeared in the town. The Burmese population had no weapons and were quite helpless against it. It had already destroyed somebody's bamboo hut, killed a cow and raided some fruit-stalls and devoured the stock; also it had met the municipal rubbish van and, when the driver jumped out and took to his heels, had turned the van over and inflicted violences upon it.

The Burmese sub-inspector and some Indian constables were waiting for me in the quarter where the elephant had been seen. It was a very poor quarter, a labyrinth of squalid bamboo huts, thatched with palm-leaf, winding all over a steep hillside. I remember that it was a cloudy, stuffy morning at the beginning of the rains. We began questioning the people as to where the elephant had gone and, as usual, failed to get any definite information. That is invariably the case in the East; a story always sounds clear enough at a distance, but the nearer you get to the scene of events the vaguer it becomes. Some of the people said that the elephant had gone in one direction, some said that he had gone in another, some professed not even to have heard of any elephant. I had almost made up my mind that the whole story was a pack of lies, when we heard yells a little distance away. There was a loud, scandalized cry of "Go away, child! Go away this instant!" and an old woman with a switch in her hand came around the corner of a hut, violently shooing away a crowd of naked children. Some more women followed, clicking their tongues and exclaiming; evidently there was something that the children ought not to have seen. I rounded the hut and saw a man's dead body sprawling in the mud. He was an Indian, a black Dravidian coolie, almost naked, and he could not have been dead many minutes. The people said that the elephant had come suddenly upon him round the corner of the hut, caught him with its trunk, put its foot on his back and ground him into the earth. This was the rainy season and the ground was soft, and his face had scored a trench a foot deep and a couple of yards long. He was lying on his belly with arms crucified and head sharply twisted to one side. His face was coated with mud, the eyes wide open, the teeth bared and grinning with an expression of unendurable agony. (Never tell me, by the way, that the dead look peaceful. Most of the corpses I have seen looked devilish.) The friction of the great beast's foot had stripped the skin from his back as neatly as one skins a rabbit. As soon as I saw the dead man I sent an orderly to a friend's house nearby to borrow an elephant rifle. I had already sent back the pony, not wanting it to go mad with fright and throw me if it smelt the elephant.

The orderly came back in a few minutes with a rifle and five cartridges, and meanwhile some Burmans had arrived and told us that the elephant was in the paddy fields below, only a few hundred yards away. As I started forward practically the whole population of the quarter flocked out of the houses and followed me. They had seen the rifle and were all shouting excitedly that I was going to shoot the elephant. They had not shown much interest in the elephant when he was merely ravaging their homes, but it was different now that he was going to be shot. It was a bit of fun to them, as it would be to an English crowd; besides they wanted the meat. It made me vaguely uneasy. I had no intention of shooting the elephant—I had merely sent for the rifle to defend myself if necessary—and it is always unnerving to have a crowd following you. I marched down the hill, looking and feeling a fool, with the rifle over my shoulder and an evergrowing army of people jostling at my heels. At the bottom, when you got away from the huts, there was a metalled road and beyond that a miry waste of paddy fields a thousand yards across, not yet ploughed but soggy from the first rains and dotted with coarse grass. The elephant was standing eight yards from the road, his left side towards us. He took not the slightest notice of the crowd's approach. He was tearing up bunches of grass, beating them against his knees to clean them and stuffing them into his mouth.

I had halted on the road. As soon as I saw the elephant I knew with perfect certainty that I ought not to shoot him. It is a serious matter to shoot a working elephant—it is comparable to destroying a huge and costly piece of machinery—and obviously one ought not to do it if it can possibly be avoided. And at that distance, peacefully eating, the elephant looked no more dangerous than a cow. I thought then and I think now that his attack of "must" was already passing off; in which case he would merely wander harmlessly about until the mahout came back and caught him. Moreover, I did not in the least want to shoot him. I decided that I would watch him for a little while to make sure that he did not turn savage again, and then go home.

But at that moment I glanced round at the crowd that had followed me. It was an immense crowd, two thousand at the least and growing every minute. It blocked the road for a long distance on either side. I looked at the sea of yellow faces above the garish clothes—faces all happy and excited over this bit of fun, all certain that the elephant was going to be shot. They were watching me as they would watch a conjurer about to perform a trick. They did not like me, but with the magical rifle in my hands I was momentarily worth watching. And suddenly I realized that I should have to shoot the elephant after all. The people expected it of me and I had to do it; I could feel their two thousand wills pressing me forward, irresistibly. And it was at this moment, as I stood there with the rifle in my hands, that I first grasped the hollowness, the futility of the white man's dominion in the East. Here was I, the white man with his gun, standing in front of the unarmed native crowd—seemingly the leading actor of the piece; but in reality I was only an absurd puppet pushed to and fro by the will of those yellow faces behind. I perceived in this moment that when the white man turns tyrant it is his own freedom that he destroys. He becomes a sort of hollow, posing dummy, the conventionalized figure of a sahib. For it is the condition of his rule that he shall spend his life in trying to impress the "natives," and so in every crisis he has got to do what the "natives" expect of him. He wears a mask, and his face grows to fit it. I had got to shoot the elephant. I had committed myself to doing it when I sent for the rifle. A sahib has got to act like a sahib; he has got to appear resolute, to know his own mind and do definite things. To come all that way, rifle in hand, with two thousand people marching at my heels, and then to trail feebly away, having done nothing—no, that was impossible. The crowd would laugh at me. And my whole life, every white man's life in the East, was one long struggle not to be laughed at.

But I did not want to shoot the elephant. I watched him beating his bunch of grass against his knees, with that preoccupied grandmotherly air that elephants have. It seemed to me that it would be murder to shoot him. At that age I was not squeamish about killing animals, but I had never shot an elephant and never wanted to. (Somehow it always seems worse to kill a *large* animal.) Besides, there was the beast's owner to be considered. Alive, the elephant was worth at least a hundred pounds; dead, he would only be worth the value of his tusks, five pounds, possibly. But I had got to act quickly. I turned to some experienced-looking Burmans who had been there when we arrived, and asked them how the elephant had been behaving. They all said the same thing: he took no notice of you if you left him alone, but he might charge if you went too close to him.

It was perfectly clear to me what I ought to do. I ought to walk up to within, say, twenty-five yards of the elephant and test his behavior. If he charged, I could shoot; if he took no notice of me, it would be safe to leave him until the mahout came back. But also I knew that I was going to do no such thing. I was a poor shot with a rifle and the ground was soft mud into which one would sink at every step. If the elephant charged and I missed him, I should have about as much chance as a toad under a steamroller. But even then I was not thinking particularly of my own skin, only of the watchful yellow faces behind. For at that moment, with the crowd watching me, I was not afraid in the ordinary sense, as I would have been if I had been alone. A white man mustn't be frightened in front of "natives"; and so, in general, he isn't frightened. The sole thought in my mind was that if anything went wrong those two thousand Burmans would see me pursued, caught, trampled on and reduced to a grinning corpse like that Indian up the hill. And if that happened it was quite probable that some of them would laugh. That would never do. There was only one alternative. I shoved the cartridges into the magazine and lay down on the road to get a better aim.

The crowd grew very still, and a deep, low, happy sigh, as of people who see the theatre curtain go up at last, breathed from innumerable throats. They were going to have their bit of fun after all. The rifle was a beautiful German thing with cross-hair sights. I did not then know that in shooting an elephant one would shoot to cut an imaginary bar running from ear-hole to ear-hole. I ought, therefore, as the elephant was sideways on, to have aimed straight at his ear-hole; actually I aimed several inches in front of this, thinking the brain would be further forward.

When I pulled the trigger I did not hear the bang or feel the kick—one never does when a shot goes home—but I heard the devilish roar of glee that went up from the crowd. In that instant, in too short a time, one would have thought, even for the bullet to get there, a mysterious, terrible change had come over the elephant. He neither stirred nor fell, but every line of his body had altered. He looked suddenly stricken, shrunken, immensely old, as though the frightful impact of the bullet had paralysed him without knocking him down. At last, after what seemed a long time—it might have been five seconds, I dare say—he sagged flabbily to his knees. His mouth slobbered. An enormous senility seemed to have settled upon him. One could have imagined him thousands of years old. I fired again into the same spot. At the second shot he did not collapse but climbed with desperate slowness to his feet and stood weakly upright, with legs sagging and head drooping. I fired a third time. That was the shot that did for him. You could see the agony of it jolt his whole body and knock the last remnant of strength from his legs. But in falling he seemed for a moment to rise, for as his hind legs collapsed beneath him he seemed to tower upward like a huge rock toppling, his trunk reaching sky-wards like a tree. He trumpeted, for the first and only time. And then down he came, his belly towards me, with a crash that seemed to shake the ground even where I lay.

I got up. The Burmans were already racing past me across the mud. It was obvious that the elephant would never rise again, but he was not dead. He was breathing very rhythmically with long rat-tling gasps, his great mound of a side painfully rising and falling. His mouth was wide open—I could see far down into caverns of pale pink throat. I waited a long time for him to die, but his breath-ing did not weaken. Finally I fired my two remaining shots into the spot where I thought his heart must be. The thick blood welled out of him like red velvet, but still he did not die. His body did not even jerk when the shots hit him, the tortured breathing con-tinued without a pause. He was dying, very slowly and in great agony, but in some world remote from me where not even a bul-let could damage him further. I felt that I had got to put an end to that dreadful noise. It seemed dreadful to see the great beast lying there, powerless to move and yet powerless to die, and not even to be able to finish him. I sent back for my small rifle and poured shot after shot into his heart and down his throat. They seemed to make no impression. The tortured gasps continued as steadily as the ticking of a clock.

In the end I could not stand it any longer and went away. I heard later that it took him half an hour to die. Burmans were bringing dahs and baskets even before I left, and I was told they had stripped his body almost to the bones by the afternoon.

Afterwards, of course, there were endless discussions about the shooting of the elephant. The owner was furious, but he was only an Indian and could do nothing. Besides, legally I had done the right thing, for a mad elephant has to be killed, like a mad dog, if its owner fails to control it. Among the Europeans opinion was divided. The older men said I was right, the younger men said it was a damn shame to shoot an elephant for killing a coolie, because an elephant was worth more than any damn Coringhee coolie. And afterwards I was very glad that the coolie had been killed; it put me legally in the right and it gave me a sufficient pretext for shooting the elephant. I often wondered whether any of the others grasped that I had done it solely to avoid looking a fool.

For Further Reflection

1. What is the message you get out of this story?

2. How does Orwell connect imperialism with the shooting of the elephant? Can you elaborate on the few hints he offers?

3. Why does Orwell say he knows with perfect certainty that he ought not to shoot the elephant? Why is it wrong? Why does he shoot him? Can you identify with the dilemma Orwell feels?

We Have Only Indirect Duties to Animals

IMMANUEL KANT

A biographical sketch of Immanuel Kant appears in chapter 5. Kant argues that animals are not persons because they are not rational, self-conscious beings capable of grasping the moral law. Since they are not part of the kingdom

---

From Immanuel Kant, "Duties to Animals and Spirits," in *Lectures on Ethics,* translated by Louis Infield (London: Methuen, 1932), pp. 239–41.

of moral legislators, we do not owe them anything. But we should be kind to them since that will help develop good character in us and help us treat our fellow human beings with greater consideration. That is, our duties to animals are simply indirect duties to other human beings.

Baumgarten speaks of duties towards beings which are beneath us and beings which are above us. But so far as animals are concerned, we have no direct duties. Animals are not self-conscious and are there merely as a means to an end. That end is man. We can ask, "Why do animals exist?" But to ask, "Why does man exist?" is a meaningless question. *Our duties towards animals are merely indirect duties towards humanity.* Animal nature has analogies to human nature, and by doing our duties to animals in respect of manifestations of human nature, we indirectly do our duty towards humanity. Thus, if a dog has served his master long and faithfully, his service, on the analogy of human service, deserves reward, and when the dog has grown too old to serve, his master ought to keep him until he dies. Such action helps to support us in our duties towards human beings, where they are bounden duties. If then any acts of animals are analogous to human acts and spring from the same principles, we have duties towards the animals because thus we cultivate the corresponding duties towards human beings. If a man shoots his dog because the animal is no longer capable of service, he does not fail in his duty to the dog, for the dog cannot judge, but his *act is inhuman and damages in himself that humanity which it is his duty to show towards mankind.* If he is not to stifle his human feelings, he must practise kindness towards animals, for he who is cruel to animals becomes hard also in his dealing with men. We can judge the heart of a man by his treatment of animals. Hogarth depicts this in his engravings. He shows how cruelty grows and develops. He shows the child's cruelty to animals, pinching the tail of a dog or a cat; he then depicts the grown man in his cart running over a child; and lastly, the culmination of cruelty in murder. He thus brings home to us in a terrible fashion the rewards of cruelty, and this should be an impressive lesson to children. The more we come in contact with animals and observe their behaviour, the more we love them, for we see how great is their care for their young. It is then difficult for us to be cruel in thought even to a wolf. Leibnitz used a tiny worm for purposes of observation, and then carefully replaced it with its leaf on the tree so that it should not come to harm through any act of his. He would have been sorry—a natural feeling for a humane man—to destroy such a creature for no reason. Tender feelings towards dumb animals develop humane feelings towards mankind. In England butchers and doctors do not sit on a jury because they are accustomed to the sight of death and hardened. Vivisectionists, who use living animals for their experiments, certainly act cruelly, although their aim is praiseworthy, and they can justify their cruelty, since animals must be regarded as man's instruments; but any such cruelty for sport cannot be justified. A master who turns out his ass or his dog because the animal can no longer earn its keep manifests a small mind. The Greeks' ideas in this respect were highminded, as can be seen from the fable of the ass and the bell of ingratitude. Our duties towards animals, then, are indirect duties towards mankind.

For Further Reflection

1. According to Kant do animals have rights? What capacity do they lack that deprives them of rights?

2. Why should we be kind to animals? Do you agree with Kant? How would an opponent respond to Kant's arguments?

Animal Liberation
All Animals Are Equal

PETER SINGER

Peter Singer did his graduate work at Oxford University and is a member of the Philosophy Department at La Trobe University in Australia. His book, *Animal Liberation* (1975),

From *Philosophical Exchange* Vol. 1.5 (1976). Reprinted by permission.

from which the following selection is based, is one of the most influential books ever written on the subject. It has converted many to the animal rights movement. Singer argues that animal liberation today is analogous to racial and gender justice in the past. Just as people once thought it incredible that women or blacks should be treated as equal to white men, so now speciesists mock the idea that all animals should be given equal consideration. Singer defines "speciesism" (a term devised by Richard Ryder) as the prejudice (unjustified bias) that favors one's own species over every other. What equalizes all sentient beings is our ability to suffer. In that, we and animals are equal and deserving of equal consideration of interests. Singer's argument is a utilitarian one having as its goal the maximization of interest satisfaction.

In recent years a number of oppressed groups have campaigned vigorously for equality. The classic instance is the Black Liberation movement, which demands an end to the prejudice and discrimination that has made blacks second-class citizens. The immediate appeal of the black liberation movement and its initial, if limited, success made it a model for other oppressed groups to follow. We became familiar with liberation movements for Spanish-Americans, gay people, and a variety of other minorities. When a majority group—women—began their campaign, some thought we had come to the end of the road. Discrimination on the basis of sex, it has been said, is the last universally accepted form of discrimination, practiced without secrecy or pretense even in those liberal circles that have long prided themselves on their freedom from prejudice against racial minorities.

One should always be wary of talking of "the last remaining form of discrimination." If we have learned anything from the liberation movements, we should have learnt how difficult it is to be aware of latent prejudice in our attitudes to particular groups until this prejudice is forcefully pointed out.

A liberation movement demands an expansion of our moral horizons and an extension or reinterpretation of the basic moral principle of equality. Practices that were previously regarded as natural and inevitable come to be seen as the result of an unjustifiable prejudice. Who can say with confidence that all his or her attitudes and practices are beyond criticism? If we wish to avoid being numbered amongst the oppressors, we must be prepared to re-think even our most fundamental attitudes. We need to consider them from the point of view of those most disadvantaged by our attitudes, and the practices that follow from these attitudes. If we can make this unaccustomed mental switch we may discover a pattern in our attitudes and practices that consistently operates so as to benefit one group—usually the one to which we ourselves belong—at the expense of another. In this way we may come to see that there is a case for a new liberation movement. My aim is to advocate that we make this mental switch in respect of our attitudes and practices towards a very large group of beings: members of species other than our own—or, as we popularly though misleadingly call them, animals. In other words, I am urging that we extend to other species the basic principle of equality that most of us recognize should be extended to all members of our own species.

All this may sound a little far-fetched, more like a parody of other liberation movements than a serious objective. In fact, in the past the idea of "The Rights of Animals" really has been used to parody the case for women's rights. When Mary Wollstonecroft, a forerunner of later feminists, published her *Vindication of the Rights of Women* in 1792, her ideas were widely regarded as absurd, and they were satirized in an anonymous publication entitled *A Vindication of the Rights of Brutes*. The author of this satire (actually Thomas Taylor, a distinguished Cambridge philosopher) tried to refute Wollstonecroft's reasonings by showing that they could be carried one stage further. If sound when applied to women, why should the arguments not be applied to dogs, cats, and horses? They seemed to hold equally well for these "brutes"; yet to hold that brutes had rights was manifestly absurd; therefore the reasoning by which this conclusion had been reached must be unsound, and if unsound when applied to brutes, it must also be unsound when applied to women, since the very same arguments had been used in each case.

One way in which we might reply to this argument is by saying that the case for equality between men and women cannot validly be extended to nonhuman animals. Women have a right to vote, for instance, because they are just as capable of making rational decisions as men are; dogs, on the other hand, are incapable of understanding the significance of voting, so they cannot have the right to vote. There are many other obvious ways in which men and women resemble each other closely, while humans and other animals differ greatly. So, it might be said, men and women are similar beings, and should have equal rights, while humans and nonhumans are different and should not have equal rights.

The thought behind this reply to Taylor's analogy is correct up to a point, but it does not go far enough. There *are* important differences between humans and other animals, and these differences must give rise *to some* differences in the rights that each have. Recognizing this obvious fact, however, is no barrier to the case for extending the basic principle of equality to nonhuman animals. The differences that exist between men and women are equally undeniable, and the supporters of Women's Liberation are aware that these differences may give rise to different rights. Many feminists hold that women have the right to an abortion on request. It does not follow that since these same people are campaigning for equality between men and women they must support the right of men to have abortions too. Since a man cannot have an abortion, it is meaningless to talk of his right to have one. Since a pig can't vote, it is meaningless to talk of its right to vote. There is no reason why either Women's Liberation or Animal Liberation should get involved in such nonsense. The extension of the basic principle of equality from one group to another does not imply that we must treat both groups in exactly the same way, or grant exactly the same rights to both groups. Whether we should do so will depend on the nature of the members of the two groups. The basic principle of equality, I shall argue, is equality of consideration; and equal consideration for different beings may lead to different treatment and different rights.

So there is a different way of replying to Taylor's attempt to parody Wollstonecroft's arguments, a way which does not deny the differences between humans and nonhumans, but goes more deeply into the question of equality, and concludes by finding nothing absurd in the idea that the basic principle of equality applies to so-called "brutes." I believe that we reach this conclusion if we examine the basis on which our opposition to discrimination on grounds of race or sex ultimately rests. We will then see that we would be on shaky ground if we were to demand equality for blacks, women, and other groups of oppressed humans while denying equal consideration to nonhumans.

When we say that all human beings, whatever their race, creed or sex, are equal, what is it that we are asserting? Those who wish to defend a hierarchical, inegalitarian society have often pointed out that by whatever test we choose, it simply is not true that all humans are equal. Like it or not, we must face the fact that humans come in different shapes and sizes; they come with differing moral capacities, differing intellectual abilities, differing amounts of benevolent feeling and sensitivity to the needs of others, differing abilities to communicate effectively, and differing capacities to experience pleasure and pain. In short, if the demand for equality were based on the actual equality of all human beings, we would have to stop demanding equality. It would be an unjustifiable demand.

Still, one might cling to the view that the demand for equality among human beings is based on the actual equality of the different races and sexes. Although humans differ as individuals in various ways, there are no differences between the races and sexes *as such*. From the mere fact that a person is black, or a woman, we cannot infer anything else about that person. This, it may be said, is what is wrong with racism and sexism. The white racist claims that whites are superior to blacks, but this is false—although there are differences between individuals, some blacks are superior to some whites in all of the capacities and abilities that could conceivably be relevant. The opponent of sexism would say the same: a person's sex is no guide to his or her abilities, and this is why it is unjustifiable to discriminate on the basis of sex.

This is a possible line of objection to racial and sexual discrimination. It is not, however, the way that someone really concerned about equality would choose, because taking this line could, in some circumstances, force one to accept a most inegalitarian society. The fact that humans differ as individuals, rather than as races or sexes, is a valid reply to someone who defends a hierarchical society like, say, South Africa, in which all whites are superior in status to all blacks. The existence of individual variations that cut across the lines of race or sex, however, provides us with no defence at all against a more sophisticated opponent of equality, one who proposes that, say, the interests of those with I.Q. ratings above 100 be preferred to the interests of those with I.Q.s below 100. Would a hierarchical society of this sort really be so much better than one based on race or sex? I think not. But if we tie the moral principle of equality to the factual equality of the different races or sexes, taken as a whole, our opposition to racism and sexism does not provide us with any basis for objecting to this kind of inegalitarianism.

There is a second important reason why we ought not to base our opposition to racism and sexism on any kind of factual equality, even the limited kind which asserts that variations in capacities and abilities are spread evenly between the different races and sexes: we can have no absolute guarantee that these abilities and capacities really are distributed evenly, without regard to race or sex, among human beings. So far as actual abilities are concerned, there do seem to be certain measurable differences between both races and sexes. These differences do not, of course, appear in each case, but only when averages are taken. More important still, we do not yet know how much of these differences is really due to the different genetic endowments of the various races and sexes, and how much is due to environmental differences that are the result of past and continuing discrimination. Perhaps all of the important differences will eventually prove to be environmental rather than genetic. Anyone opposed to racism and sexism will certainly hope that this will be so, for it will make the task of ending discrimination a lot easier; nevertheless it would be dangerous to rest the case against racism and sexism on the belief that all significant differences are environmental in origin. The opponent of, say, racism who takes this line will be unable to avoid conceding that if differences in ability did after all prove to have some genetic connection with race, racism would in some way be defensible.

It would be folly for the opponent of racism to stake his whole case on a dogmatic commitment to one particular outcome of a difficult scientific issue which is still a long way from being settled. While attempts to prove that differences in certain selected abilities between races and sexes are primarily genetic in origin have certainly not been conclusive, the same must be said of attempts to prove that these differences are largely the result of environment. At this stage of the investigation we cannot be certain which view is correct, however much we may hope it is the latter.

Fortunately, there is no need to pin the case for equality to one particular outcome of this scientific investigation. The appropriate response to those who claim to have found evidence of genetically based differences in ability between the races or sexes is not to stick to the belief that the genetic explanation must be wrong, whatever evidence to the contrary may turn up: instead we should make it quite clear that the claim to equality does not depend on intelligence, moral capacity, physical strength, or similar matters of fact. Equality is a moral ideal, not a simple assertion of fact. There is no logically compelling reason for assuming that a factual difference in ability between two people justifies any *difference in the amount of consideration we give to satisfying their needs and interests.* The principle of the equality of human beings is not a description of an alleged actual equality among humans: it is a prescription of how we should treat humans.

Jeremy Bentham incorporated the essential basis of moral equality into his utilitarian system of ethics in the formula: "Each to count for one and none for more than one." In other words, the interests of every being affected by an action are to be taken into account and given the same weight as the like interests of any other being. A later utilitarian, Henry Sidgwick, put the point in this way: "The good of any one individual is of no more importance, from the point of view (if I may say so) of the Universe, than the good of any other."[1] More recently, the leading figures in contemporary moral philosophy have shown a great deal of agreement in specifying as a fundamental presupposition of their moral theories some similar requirement which operates so as to give everyone's interests equal consideration—although they cannot agree on how this requirement is best formulated.[2]

It is an implication of this principle of equality that our concern for others ought not to depend on what they are like, or what abilities they possess—although precisely what this concern requires us to do may vary according to the characteristics of those affected by what we do. It is on this basis that the case against racism and the case against sexism must both ultimately rest; and it is in accordance with this principle that speciesism is also to be condemned. If possessing a higher degree of intelligence does not entitle one

[1] *The Methods of Ethics* (7th Ed.), p. 382.
[2] For example, R. M. Hare, *Freedom and Reason* (Oxford, 1963) and J. Rawls, A *Theory of Justice* (Harvard, 1972) a brief account of the essential agreement on this issue between these and other positions, see R. M. Hare, "Rules of War and Moral Reasoning," *Philosophy and Public Affairs, vol.* 1, no. 2 (1972).

human to use another for his own ends, how can it entitle humans to exploit nonhumans?

Many philosophers have proposed the principle of equal consideration of interests, in some form or other, as a basic moral principle; but, as we shall see in more detail shortly, not many of them have recognised that this principle applies to members of other species as well as to our own. Bentham was one of the few who did realize this. In a forward-looking passage, written at a time when black slaves in the British dominions were still being treated much as we now treat nonhuman animals, Bentham wrote:

> The day *may* come when the rest of the animal creation may acquire those rights which never could have been witholden from them but by the hand of tyranny. The French have already discovered that the blackness of the skin is no reason why a human being should be abandoned without redress to the caprice of a tormentor. It may one day come to be recognized that the number of the legs, the villosity of the skin, or the termination of the *os sacrum,* are reasons equally insufficient for, abandoning a sensitive being to the same fate. What else is it that should trace the insuperable line? Is it the faculty of reason, or perhaps the faculty of discourse? But a fullgrown horse or dog is beyond comparison a more rational, as well as a more conversable animal, than an infant of a day, or a week, or even a month, old. But suppose they were otherwise, what would it avail? The question is not, Can they reason? nor Can they *talk?* but, *Can they suffer?*[3]

In this passage Bentham points to the capacity for suffering as the vital characteristic that gives a being the *right* to equal consideration. The capacity for suffering—or more strictly, for suffering and/or enjoyment or happiness—is not just another characteristic like the capacity for language, or for higher mathematics. Bentham is not saying that those who try to mark "the insuperable line" that determines whether the interests of a being should be considered happen to have selected the wrong characteristic. The capacity for suffering and enjoying things is a pre-requisite for having interests at all, a condition that must be satisfied before we can speak of

---

[3]*Introduction to the Principles of Morals and Legislation,* ch. XVII.

interests in any meaningful way. It would be nonsense to say that it was not in the interests of a stone to be kicked along the road by a schoolboy. A stone does not have interests because it cannot suffer. Nothing that we can do to it could possibly make any difference to its welfare. A mouse, on the other hand, does have an interest in not being tormented, because it will suffer if it is.

If a being suffers, there can be no moral justification for refusing to take that suffering into consideration. No matter what the nature of the being, the principle of equality requires that its suffering be counted equally with the like suffering—in so far as rough comparisons can be made—of any other being. If a being is not capable of suffering, or of experiencing enjoyment or happiness, there is nothing to be taken into account. This is why the limit of sentience (using the term as a convenient, if not strictly accurate, shorthand for the capacity to suffer or experience enjoyment or happiness) is the only defensible boundary of concern for the interests of others. To mark this boundary by some characteristic like intelligence or rationality would be to mark it in an arbitrary way. Why not choose some other characteristic, like skin color?

The racist violates the principle of equality by giving greater weight to the interests of members of his own race, when there is a clash between their interests and the interests of those of another race. Similarly the speciesist allows the interests of his own species to override the greater interests of members of other species.[4] The pattern is the same in each case. Most human beings are speciesists. I shall now very briefly describe some of the practices that show this.

For the great majority of human beings, especially in urban, industrialized societies, the most direct form of contact with members of other species is at meal-times: we eat them. In doing so we treat them purely as means to our ends. We regard their life and well-being as subordinate to our taste for a particular kind of dish. I say "taste" deliberately—this is purely a matter of pleasing our palate. There can be no defence of eating flesh in terms of satisfying nutritional needs, since it has been established beyond doubt that we could satisfy our need for protein and other essential nutrients far more efficiently with a diet that replaced animal flesh by

---

[4] I owe the term "speciesism" to Richard Ryder.

soy beans, or products derived from soy beans, and other high-protein vegetable products.[5]

It is not merely the act of killing that indicates what we are ready to do to other species in order to gratify our tastes. The suffering we inflict on the animals while they are alive is perhaps an even clearer indication of our *speciesism* than the fact that we are prepared to kill them. In order to have meat on the table at a price that people can afford, our society tolerates methods of meat production that confine sentient animals in cramped, unsuitable conditions for the entire durations of their lives. Animals are treated like machines that convert fodder into flesh, and any innovation that results in a higher "conversion ratio" is liable to be adopted. As one authority on the subject has said, "cruelty is acknowledged only when profitability ceases."[6] . . .

Since, as I have said, none of these practices cater for anything more than our pleasures of taste, our practice of rearing and killing other animals in order to eat them is a clear instance of the sacrifice of the most important interests of other beings in order to satisfy trivial interests of our own. To avoid speciesism we must stop this practice, and each of us has a moral obligation to cease supporting the practice. Our custom is all the support that the meat-industry needs. The decision to cease giving it that support may be difficult, but it is no more difficult than it would have been for a white Southerner to go against the traditions of his society and free his slaves: if we do not change our dietary habits, how can we censure those slaveholders who would not change their own way of living?

The same form of discrimination may be observed in the widespread practice of experimenting on other species in order to see if

---

[5]In order to produce 1 lb. of protein in the form of beef or veal, we must feed 21 lbs. of protein to the animal. Other forms of livestock are slightly less inefficient, but the average ratio in the U.S. is still 1:8. It has been estimated that the amount of protein lost to humans in this way is equivalent to 90% of the annual world protein deficit. For a brief account, see Frances Moore Lappé, *Diet for a Small Planet* (Friends of The Earth/Ballantine, New York 1971) pp. 4–11.

[6]Ruth Harrison, *Animal Machines* (Stuart, London, 1964). For an account of farming conditions, see my *Animal Liberation* (New York Review Company, 1975).

certain substances are safe for human beings, or to test some psychological theory about the effect of severe punishment on learning, or to try out various new compounds just in case something turns up. . . .

In the past, argument about vivisection has often missed this point, because it has been put in absolutist terms: Would the abolitionist be prepared to let thousands die if they could be saved by experimenting on a single animal? The way to reply to this purely hypothetical question is to pose another: *Would the experimenter be prepared to perform his experiment on an orphaned human infant, if that were the only way to save many lives?* (I "orphan" to avoid the complication of parental feelings, although in doing so I am being overfair to the experimenter, since the nonhuman subjects of experiments are not orphans.) If the experimenter is not prepared to use an orphaned human infant, then his readiness to use nonhumans is simple discrimination, since adult apes, cats, mice and other mammals are more aware of what is happening to them, more self-directing and, so far as we can tell, at least as sensitive to pain, as any human infant. There seems to be no relevant characteristic that human infants possess that adult mammals do not have to the same or a higher degree. (Someone might try to argue that what makes it wrong to experiment on a human infant is that the infant will, in time and if left alone, develop into more than the nonhuman, but one would then, to be consistent, have to oppose abortion, since the fetus has the same potential as the infant—indeed, even contraception and abstinence might be wrong on this ground, since the egg and sperm, considered jointly, also have the same potential. In any case, this argument still gives us no reason for selecting a nonhuman, rather than a human with severe and irreversible brain damage, as the subject for our experiments.)

The experimenter, then, shows a bias in favor of his own species whenever he carries out an experiment on a nonhuman for a purpose that he would not think justified him in using a human being at an equal or lower level of sentience, awareness, ability to be self-directing, etc. No one familiar with the kind of results yielded by most experiments on animals can have the slightest doubt that if this bias were eliminated the number of experiments performed would be a minute fraction of the number performed today.

Experimenting on animals, and eating their flesh, are perhaps the two major forms of speciesism in our society. By comparison, the third and last form of speciesism is so minor as to be insignificant, but it is perhaps of some interest to those for whom this article was written. I am referring to speciesism in contemporary philosophy.

Philosophy ought to question the basic assumptions of the age. Thinking through, critically and carefully, what most people take for granted is, I believe, the chief task of philosophy, and it is this task that makes philosophy a worthwhile activity. Regrettably, philosophy does not always live up to its historic role. Philosophers are human beings and they are subject to all the preconceptions of the society to which they belong. Sometimes they succeed in breaking free of the prevailing ideology: more often they become its most sophisticated defenders. So, in this case, philosophy as practiced in the universities today does not challenge anyone's preconceptions about our relations with other species. By their writings, those philosophers who tackle problems that touch upon the issue reveal that they make the same unquestioned assumptions as most other humans, and what they say tends to confirm the reader in his or her comfortable speciesist habits.

I could illustrate this claim by referring to the writings of philosophers in various fields—for instance, the attempts that have been made by those interested in rights to draw the boundary of the sphere of rights so that it runs parallel to the biological boundaries of the species *homo sapiens,* including infants and even mental defectives, but excluding those other beings of equal or greater capacity who are so useful to us at mealtimes and in our laboratories. I think it would be a more appropriate conclusion to this article, however, if I concentrated on the problem with which we have been centrally concerned, the problem of equality.

It is significant that the problem of *equality,* in moral and political philosophy, is invariably formulated in terms of human equality. The effect of this is that the question of the equality of other animals does not confront the philosopher, or student, as an issue itself—and this is already an indication of the failure of philosophy to challenge accepted beliefs. Still, philosophers have found it difficult to discuss the issue of human equality without raising, in a paragraph or two, the question of the status of other animals. The reason for this, which should be apparent from what I have said already, is that if humans are to be regarded as equal to one another, we need some sense of "equal" that does not require any actual, descriptive equality of capacities, talents or other qualities. If equality is to be related to any actual characteristics of humans, these characteristics must be some lowest common denominator, pitched so low that no human lacks them—but then the philosopher comes up against the catch that any such set of characteristics which covers *all* humans will not be possessed *only by humans.* In other words, it turns out that in the only sense in which we can truly say, as an assertion of fact, that all humans are equal, at least some members of other species are also equal—equal, that is, to each other and to humans. If, on the other hand, we regard the statement "All humans are equal" in some non-factual way, perhaps as a prescription, then, as I have already argued, it is even more difficult to exclude nonhumans from the sphere of equality.

This result is not what the egalitarian philosopher originally intended to assert. Instead of accepting the radical outcome to which their own reasonings naturally point, however, most philosophers try to reconcile their beliefs in human equality and animal inequality by arguments that can only be described as devious.

As a first example, I take William Frankena's well-known article "The Concept of Social Justice." Frankena opposes the idea of basing justice on merit, because he sees that this could lead to highly inegalitarian results. Instead he proposes the principle that

> . . . all men are to be treated as equals, not because they are equal, in any respect, but *simply because they are human.* They are human because they have *emotions* and *desires,* and are able to *think,* and hence are capable of enjoying a good life in a sense in which other animals are not.[7]

But what is this capacity to enjoy the good life which all humans have, but no other animals? Other animals have emotions and desires, and appear to be capable of enjoying a good life. We may doubt that they can think—although the behavior of some apes, dolphins and even dogs suggests that some of them can—but *what is the relevance of thinking?* Frankena goes on to admit that by "the good life" he means "not so much the morally good life as the happy or satisfactory life," so thought would appear to be unnecessary for enjoying the good life; in fact to emphasize the need for

---

[7]R. Brandt (ed.) *Social Justice* (Prentice-Hall, Englewood Cliffs, 1962), p. 19.

thought would make difficulties for the egalitarian since only some people are capable of leading intellectually satisfying lives, or morally good lives. This makes it difficult to see what Frankena's principle of equality has to do with simply being *human*. Surely every sentient being is capable of leading a life that is happier or less miserable than some alternative life, and hence has a claim to be taken into account. In this respect the distinction between humans and nonhumans is not a sharp division, but rather a continuum along which we move gradually, and with overlaps between the species, from simple capacities for enjoyment and satisfaction, or pain and suffering, to more complex ones.

Faced with a situation in which they see a need for some basis for the moral gulf that is commonly thought to separate humans and animals, but finding no concrete difference that will do the job without undermining the equality of humans, philosophers tend to waffle. They resort to high-sounding phrases like "the intrinsic dignity of the human individual";[8] they talk of the "intrinsic worth of all men" as if men (humans?) had some worth that other beings did not,[9] or they say that humans, and only humans, are "ends in themselves," while "everything other than a person can only have value for a person."[10]

This idea of a distinctive human dignity and worth has a long history; it can be traced back directly to the Renaissance humanists, for instance to Pico della Mirandola's *Oration on the Dignity of Man*. Pico and other humanists based their estimate of human dignity on the idea that man possessed the central, pivotal position in the "Great Chain of Being" that led from the lowliest forms of matter to God himself; this view of the universe, in turn, goes back to both classical and Judeo-Christian doctrines. Contemporary philosophers have cast off these metaphysical and religious shackles and freely invoke the dignity of mankind without needing to justify the idea at all. Why should we not attribute "intrinsic dignity" or "intrinsic worth" to ourselves? Fellow-humans are unlikely to reject the accolades we so generously bestow on them, and those

---

[8]Frankena, Op. *cit.*, p. 23.

[9]H. A. Bedau, "Egalitarianism and the Idea of Equality" in *Nomos IX: Equality*, ed. J. R. Pennock and J. W. Chapman, New York, 1967.

[10]G. Vlastos, "Justice and Equality" in Brandt, *Social Justice*, p. 48.

to whom we deny the honor are unable to object. Indeed, when one thinks only of humans, it can be very liberal, very progressive, to talk of the dignity of all human beings. In so doing, we implicitly condemn slavery, racism, and other violations of human rights. We admit that we ourselves are in some fundamental sense on a par with the poorest, most ignorant members of our own species. It is only when we think of humans as no more than a small subgroup of all the beings that inhabit our planet that we may realize that in elevating our own species we are at the same time lowering the relative status of all other species.

The truth is that the appeal to the intrinsic dignity of human beings appears to solve the egalitarian's problems only as long as it goes unchallenged. Once we ask *why* it should be that all humans—including infants, mental defectives, psychopaths, Hitler, Stalin and the rest—have some kind of dignity or worth that no elephant, pig, or chimpanzee can ever achieve, we see that this question is as difficult to answer as our original request for some relevant fact that justifies the inequality of humans and other animals. In fact, these two questions are really one: talk of intrinsic dignity or moral worth only takes the problem back one step, because any satisfactory defence of the claim that all and only humans have intrinsic dignity would need to refer to some relevant capacities or characteristics that all and only humans possess. Philosophers frequently introduce ideas of dignity, respect and worth at the point at which other reasons appear to be lacking, but this is hardly good enough. Fine phrases are the last resource of those who have run out of arguments.

In case there are those who still think it may be possible to find some relevant characteristic that distinguishes all humans from all members of other species, I shall refer again, before I conclude, to the existence of some humans who quite clearly are below the level of awareness, self-consciousness, intelligence, and sentience, of many nonhumans. I am thinking of humans with severe and irreparable brain damage, and also of infant humans. To avoid the complication of the relevance of a being's potential, however, I shall henceforth concentrate on permanently retarded humans.

Philosophers who set out to find a characteristic that will distinguish humans from other animals rarely take the course of abandoning these groups of humans by lumping them in with the other animals. It is easy to see why they do not. To take this line without re-thinking our attitudes to other animals would entail that we have the right to perform painful experiments on retarded humans for trivial reasons; similarly it would follow that we had the right to rear and kill these humans for food. To most philosophers these consequences are as unacceptable as the view that we should stop treating nonhumans in this way.

Of course, when discussing the problem of equality it is possible to ignore the problem of mental defectives, or brush it aside as if somehow insignificant.[11] This is the easiest way out. What else remains? My final example of speciesism in contemporary philosophy has been selected to show what happens when a writer is prepared to face the question of human equality and animal inequality without ignoring the existence of mental defectives, and without resorting to obscurantist mumbo-jumbo. Stanley Benn's clear and honest article "Egalitarianism and Equal Consideration of Interests"[12] fits this description.

Benn, after noting the usual "evident human inequalities" argues, correctly I think, for equality of consideration as the only possible basis for egalitarianism. Yet Benn, like other writers, is thinking only of "equal consideration of human interests." Benn is quite open in his defence of this restriction of equal consideration:

> . . . not to possess human shape *is* a disqualifying condition. However faithful or intelligent a dog may be, it would be a monstrous sentimentality to attribute to him interests that could be weighed in an equal balance with those of human beings . . . if, for instance, one had to decide between feeding a hungry baby or a hungry dog, anyone who chose the dog would generally be reckoned morally defective, unable to recognize a fundamental inequality of claims.
>
> This is what distinguishes our attitude to animals from our attitude to imbeciles. It would be odd to say that we ought to respect equally the dignity or personality of the imbecile and of the rational man . . . but there is nothing odd about saying that we should respect their interests equally, that is, that we should give to the interests of each the same serious consideration as claims to considerations nec-

---

[11]For example, Bernard Williams, "The Idea of Equality," in *Philosophy, Politics and Society* (second series), ed. P. Laslett and W. Runciman (Blackwell, Oxford, 1962), p. 118; J. Rawls, *A Theory of Justice,* pp. 509–10.
[12]*Nomos IX: Equality;* the passages quoted are on p. 62ff.

essary for some standard of well-being that we can recognize and endorse.

Benn's statement of the basis of the consideration we should have for imbeciles seems to me correct, but why should there be any fundamental inequality of claims between a dog and a human imbecile? Benn sees that if equal consideration depended on rationality, no reason could be given against using imbeciles for research purposes, as we now use dogs and guinea pigs. This will not do: "But of course we do distinguish imbeciles from animals in this regard," he says. That the common distinction is justifiable is something Benn does not question; his problem is how it is to be justified. The answer he gives is this:

> . . . we respect the interests of men and give them priority over dogs not *insofar* as they are rational, but because rationality is the human norm. We say it is *unfair* to exploit the deficiencies of the imbecile who falls short of the norm, just as it would be unfair, and not just ordinarily dishonest, to steal from a blind man. If we do not think in this way about dogs, it is because we do not see the irrationality of the dog as a deficiency or a handicap, but as normal for the species. The characteristics, therefore, that distinguish the normal man from the normal dog make it intelligible for us to talk of other men having interests and capacities, and therefore claims, of precisely the same kind as we make on our own behalf. But although these characteristics may provide the point of the distinction between men and other species, they are *not* in fact the qualifying conditions for membership, or the distinguishing criteria of the class of morally considerable persons; *and this is precisely because a man does not become a member of a different species, with its own standards of normality, by reason of not possessing these characteristics.*

The final sentence of this passage gives the argument away. An imbecile, Benn concedes, may have no characteristics superior to those of a dog; nevertheless this does not make the imbecile a member of "a different species" as the dog is. *Therefore* it would be "unfair" to use the imbecile for medical research as we use the dog. But why? That the imbecile is not rational is just the way things have worked out, and the same is true of the dog—neither is any more responsible for their mental level. If it is unfair to take advantage of an isolated defect, why is it fair to take advantage of a more general limitation? I find it hard to see anything in this argument except a defence of preferring the interests of members of our own species because they are members of our own species. To those who think there might be more to it, I suggest the following mental exercise. Assume that it has been proven that there is a difference in the average, or normal, intelligence quotient for two different races, say whites and blacks. Then substitute the term "white" for every occurrence of "men" and "black" for every occurrence of "dog" in the passage quoted; and substitute "high I.Q." for "rationality" and when Benn talks of "imbeciles" replace this term by "dumb whites"—that is, whites who fall well below the normal white I.Q. score. Finally, change "species" to "race." Now re-read the passage. It has become a defence of a rigid, no-exceptions division between whites and blacks, based on I.Q. scores, *not withstanding an admitted overlap* between whites and blacks in this respect. The revised passage is, of course, outrageous, and this is not only because we have made fictitious assumptions in our substitutions. The point is that in the original passage Benn was defending a rigid division in the amount of consideration due to members of different species, despite admitted cases of overlap. If the original did not, at first reading strike us as being as outrageous as the revised version does, this is largely because although we are not racists ourselves, most of us are speciesists. Like the other articles, Benn's stands as a warning of the ease with which the best minds can fall victim to a prevailing ideology.

For Further Reflection

1. According to Singer what is the relationship between civil rights movements and the animal rights movement?

2. What is "speciesism"? Why is it bad? Do you agree?

3. Are all humans equal, according to Singer? In what way are all sentient beings equal?

4. How does Singer apply the notion of equal consideration of interests?

5. Is Singer a utilitarian or a deontologist? Explain. Do you agree with his arguments?

The Case Against Animal Rights

CARL COHEN

Carl Cohen is a professor of law at the University of Michigan. He addresses the morality of animal experimentation and argues that while human beings have a duty to treat animals humanely, animals cannot have rights. The idea of rights does not apply to animals since "rights" is a concept appropriate only to members of the moral community and animals cannot make moral decisions. Humans are of far greater value than animals, and the result of not using animals for medical experimentation would be greater human suffering.

Using animals as research subjects in medical investigations is widely condemned on two grounds: first, because it wrongly violates the *rights* of animals, and second, because it wrongly imposes on sentient creatures much avoidable *suffering*. Neither of these arguments is sound. The first relies on a mistaken understanding of rights; the second relies on a mistaken calculation of consequences. Both deserve definitive dismissal.

WHY ANIMALS HAVE NO RIGHTS

A right, properly understood, is a claim, or potential claim, that one party may exercise against another. The target against whom such a claim may be registered can be a single person, a group, a community, or (perhaps) all humankind. The content of rights claims also varies greatly: repayment of loans, nondiscrimination by employers, noninterference by the state, and so on. To comprehend any genuine right fully, therefore, we must know *who* holds the right, *against whom* it is held, and *to what* it is a right.

Alternative sources of rights add complexity. Some rights are grounded in constitution and law (e.g., the right of an accused to trial

Reprinted from the *New England Journal of Medicine* (1986) by permission.

by jury); some rights are moral but give no legal claims (e.g., my right to your keeping the promise you gave me); and some rights (e.g., against theft or assault) are rooted both in morals and in law.

The differing targets, contents, and sources of rights, and their inevitable conflict, together weave a tangled web. Notwithstanding all such complications, this much is clear about rights in general: they are in every case claims, or potential claims, within a community of moral agents. Rights arise, and can be intelligibly defended, only among beings who actually do, or can, make moral claims against one another. Whatever else rights may be, therefore, they are necessarily human; their possessors are persons, human beings.

The attributes of human beings from which this moral capability arises have been described variously by philosophers, both ancient and modern: the inner consciousness of a free will (Saint Augustine); the grasp, by human reason, of the binding character of moral law (Saint Thomas Aquinas); the self-conscious participation of human beings in an objective ethical order (G. W. F. Hegel); human membership in an organic moral community (F. H. Bradley); the development of the human self through the consciousness of other moral selves (G. H. Mead); and the underivative, intuitive cognition of the rightness of an action (H. A. Prichard). Most influential has been Immanuel Kant's emphasis on the universal human possession of a uniquely moral will and the autonomy its use entails. Humans confront choices that are purely moral; humans—but certainly not dogs or mice—lay down moral laws, for others and for themselves. Human beings are self-legislative, morally *auto-nomous*.

Animals (that is, nonhuman animals, the ordinary sense of that word) lack this capacity for free moral judgment. They are not beings of a kind capable of exercising or responding to moral claims. Animals therefore have no rights, and they can have none. This is the core of the argument about the alleged rights of animals. The holders of rights must have the capacity to comprehend rules of duty, governing all including themselves. In applying such rules, the holders of rights must recognize possible conflicts between what is in their own interest and what is just. Only in a community of beings capable of self-restricting moral judgments can the concept of a right be correctly invoked.

Humans have such moral capacities. They are in this sense self-legislative, are members of communities governed by moral rules, and do possess rights. Animals do not have such moral capacities.

They are not morally self-legislative, cannot possibly be members of a truly moral community, and therefore cannot possess rights. In conducting research on animal subjects, therefore, we do not violate their rights, because they have none to violate. . . .

Genuinely moral acts have an internal as well as an external dimension. Thus, in law, an act can be criminal only when the guilty deed, the *actus reus,* is done with a guilty mind, *mens rea.* No animal can ever commit a crime; bringing animals to criminal trial is the mark of primitive ignorance. The claims of moral rights are similarly inapplicable to them. Does a lion have a right to eat a baby zebra? Does a baby zebra have a right not to be eaten? Such questions, mistakenly invoking the concept of right where it does not belong, do not make good sense. Those who condemn biomedical research because it violates "animal rights" commit the same blunder.

IN DEFENSE OF SPECIESISM

Abandoning reliance on animal rights, some critics resort instead to animal sentience—their feelings of pain and distress. We ought to desist from the imposition of pain insofar as we can. Since all or nearly all experimentation on animals does impose pain and could be readily forgone, say these critics, it should be stopped. The ends sought may be worthy, but those ends do not justify imposing agonies on humans, and by animals the agonies are felt no less. The laboratory use of animals (these critics conclude) must therefore be ended—or at least very sharply curtailed.

Argument of this variety is essentially utilitarian, often expressly so; it is based on the calculation of the net product, in pains and pleasures, resulting from experiments on animals. Jeremy Bentham, comparing horses and dogs with other sentient creatures, is thus commonly quoted: "The question is not, Can they reason? nor Can they talk? but, Can they suffer?"

BIOMEDICAL RESEARCH
MUST STILL PROCEED

Animals certainly can suffer and surely ought not to be made to suffer needlessly. But in inferring, from these uncontroversial premises, that biomedical research causing animal distress is largely (or wholly) wrong, the critic commits two serious errors.

The first error is the assumption, often explicitly defended, that all sentient animals have equal moral standing. Between a dog and a human being, according to this view, there is no moral difference; hence the pains suffered by dogs must be weighed no differently from the pains suffered by humans. To deny such equality, according to this critic, is to give unjust preference to one species over another; it is "speciesism." The most influential statement of this moral equality of species was made by Peter Singer:

> The racist violates the principle of equality by giving greater weight to the interests of members of his own race when there is a clash between their interests and the interests of those of another race. The sexist violates the principle of equality by favoring the interests of his own sex. Similarly the speciesist allows the interests of his own species to override the greater interests of members of other species. The pattern is identical in each case.

This argument is worse than unsound; it is atrocious. It draws an offensive moral conclusion from a deliberately devised verbal parallelism that is utterly specious. Racism has no rational ground whatever. Differing degrees of respect or concern for humans for no other reason than that they are members of different races is an injustice totally without foundation in the nature of the races themselves. Racists, even if acting on the basis of mistaken factual beliefs, do grave moral wrong precisely because there is no morally relevant distinction among the races. The supposition of such differences has led to outright horror. The same is true of the sexes, neither sex being entitled by right to greater respect or concern than the other. No dispute here.

Between species of animate life, however—between (for example) humans on the one hand and cats or rats on the other—the morally relevant differences are enormous, and almost universally appreciated. Humans engage in moral reflection; humans are morally autonomous; humans are members of moral communities, recognizing just claims against their own interest. Human beings do have rights; theirs is a moral status very different from that of cats or rats.

SPECIESISM IS NECESSARY

I am a speciesist. Speciesism is not merely plausible; it is essential for right conduct, because those who will not make the morally relevant distinctions among species are almost certain, in consequence, to misapprehend their true obligations. The analogy between speciesism and racism is insidious. Every sensitive moral judgment requires that the differing natures of the beings to whom obligations are owed be considered. If all forms of animate life— or vertebrate animal life—must be treated equally, and if therefore in evaluating a research program the pains of a rodent count equally with the pains of a human, we are forced to conclude (1) that neither humans nor rodents possess rights, or (2) that rodents possess all the rights that humans possess. Both alternatives are absurd. Yet one or the other must be swallowed if the moral equality of all species is to be defended. . . .

Those who claim to base their objection to the use of animals in biomedical research on their reckoning of the net pleasures and pains produced make a second error, equally grave. Even if it were true—as it is surely not—that the pains of all animate beings must be counted equally, a cogent utilitarian calculation requires that we weigh all the consequences of the use, and of the nonuse, of animals in laboratory research. Critics relying (however mistakenly) on animal rights may claim to ignore the beneficial results of such research, rights being trump cards to which interest and advantage must give way. But an argument that is explicitly framed in terms of interest and benefit for all over the long run must attend also to the disadvantageous consequences of not using animals in research, and to all the achievements attained and attainable only through their use. The sum of the benefits of their use is utterly beyond quantification. The elimination of horrible disease, the increase of longevity, the avoidance of great pain, the saving of lives, and the improvement of the quality of lives (for humans and for animals) achieved through research using animals is so incalculably great that the argument of these critics, systematically pursued, establishes not their conclusion but its reverse: to refrain from using animals in biomedical research is, on utilitarian ground, morally wrong.

When balancing the pleasures and pains resulting from the use of animals in research, we must not fail to place on the scales the terrible pains that would have resulted, would be suffered now,

and would long continue had animals not been used. Every disease eliminated, every vaccine developed, every method of pain
relief devised, every surgical procedure invented, every prosthetic
device implanted—indeed, virtually every modern medical therapy
is due, in part or in whole, to experimentation using animals. Nor
may we ignore, in the balancing process, the predictable gains in
human (and animal) well-being that are probably achievable in the
future but that will not be achieved if the decision is made now to
desist from such research or to curtail it. . . .

Finally, inconsistency between the profession and the practice of
many who oppose research using animals deserves comment. This
frankly *ad hominem* observation aims chiefly to show that a coherent position rejecting the use of animals in medical research imposes
costs so high as to be intolerable even to the critics themselves.

One cannot coherently object to the killing of animals in biomedical investigations while continuing to eat them. Anesthetics and
thoughtful animal husbandry render the level of actual animal distress in the laboratory generally lower than that in the abattoir. So
long as death and discomfort do not substantially differ in the two
contexts, the consistent objector must not only refrain from all eating of animals but also protest as vehemently against others eating
them as against others experimenting on them. No less vigorously
must the critic object to the wearing of animal hides in coats and
shoes, to employment in any industrial enterprise that uses animal
parts, and to any commercial development that will cause death or
distress to animals. . . .

Scrupulous vegetarianism, in matters of food, clothing, shelter,
commerce, and recreation, and in all other spheres, is the only fully
coherent position the critic may adopt. At great human cost, the
lives of fish and crustaceans must also be protected, with equal
vigor, if speciesism has been forsworn. A very few consistent critics adopt this position. It is the *reductio ad absurdum* of the rejection of moral distinctions between animals and human beings.

For Further Reflection

1. What is Cohen's position on animal rights? What are his arguments?

2. How does Cohen defend speciesism?

3. Do you agree with Cohen that absurd consequences would follow from our embracing a strong position on animal rights?

The Immorality of Eating Meat

MYLAN ENGEL, JR.

Mylan Engel, Jr. teaches philosophy at Northern Illinois University. He has published several articles in epistemology, philosophy of religion, and metaphysics. His current research concerns human obligations to nonhuman animals. In this article, Professor Engel advances an argument for the immorality of eating meat. Unlike other ethical arguments for vegetarianism, the argument advanced is *not* predicated on the wrongness of speciesism, *nor* does it depend on your believing that all animals are equal or that all animals have a right to life, *nor* is it predicated on some highly contentious metaethical theory which you reject. Rather, it is predicated on *your* beliefs. Simply put, the argument shows that even those of you who are steadfastly committed to valuing humans over nonhumans are nevertheless committed to the immorality of eating meat, given your other beliefs.

Most arguments for the moral obligatoriness of vegetarianism take one of two forms. Either they follow Singer's lead and demand equal consideration for animals on utilitarian grounds,[1] or they follow Regan's deontological rights-based approach and insist that most of the animals we routinely consume possess the very same rights-con-

---

This essay was commissioned for this work and appears here in print for the first time.
[1]See Peter Singer's *Animal Liberation,* 2d edition (New York: Avon Books, 1990) or his "All Animals are Equal" in *Animal Rights and Human Obligations,* 2d edition, eds. Regan and Singer (Englewood Cliffs, N.J.: Prentice-Hall, 1989), pp. 73–86.

ferring properties which confer rights on humans.[2] While many people have been persuaded to alter their dietary habits on the basis of one of these arguments, most philosophers have not. My experience has been that when confronted with these arguments meat-loving philosophers often casually dismiss them as follows:

> Singer's preference utilitarianism is irremediably flawed, as is Regan's theory of moral rights. Since Singer's and Regan's arguments for vegetarianism are predicated on flawed ethical theories, their arguments are also flawed. Until someone can provide me with clear moral reasons for not eating meat, I will continue to eat what I please.

A moment's reflection reveals the self-serving sophistry of such a reply. Since no ethical theory to date is immune to objection, one could fashion a similar reply to "justify" or rationalize virtually any behavior. One could "justify" rape as follows: An opponent of rape might appeal to utilitarian, Kantian, or contractarian grounds to establish the immorality of rape. Our fictitious rape-loving philosopher could then point out that all of these ethical theories are flawed and *ipso facto* so too are all the arguments against rape. Our rape proponent might then assert: "Until someone can provide me with clear moral reasons for not committing rape, I will continue to rape whomever I please."

The speciousness of such a "justification" of rape should be obvious. No one who seriously considered the brutality of rape could think that it is somehow justified/permissible *simply because* all current ethical theories are flawed. But such specious reasoning is used to "justify" the equally brutal breeding, confining, mutilating, transporting, killing, and eating of animals all the time. My aim is to block this spurious reply by providing an argument for the immorality of eating meat which does not rest on any particular ethical approach. Rather, it rests on beliefs which you already hold.[3]

---

[2]See Tom Regan's *The Case for Animal Rights* (Berkeley and Los Angeles: University of California Press, 1983), or his "The Case for Animal Rights" in *In Defense of Animals,* ed. Peter Singer (New York: Harper and Row Perennial Library, 1985), pp. 13–26.

[3]Obviously, if you do not hold these beliefs (or enough of them), my argument will have no force for you, nor is it intended to. It is only aimed at those of you who do hold these widespread commonsense beliefs.

Before turning to your beliefs, two prefatory observations are in order. First, unlike other ethical arguments for vegetarianism, my argument is *not* predicated on the wrongness of speciesism,[4] *nor* does it depend on your believing that all animals are equal or that all animals have a right to life. The significance of this can be explained as follows: Some philosophers remain unmoved by Singer's and Regan's arguments for a different reason than the one cited above. These philosophers find that the nonspeciesistic implications of Singer's and Regan's arguments just *feel* wrong to them. They sincerely *feel* that humans are more important than nonhumans.[5] Perhaps these feelings are irrational in light of evolutionary theory and our biological kinship with other species, but these feelings are nonetheless real. My argument is neutral with respect to such sentiments. It is compatible with both an anthropocentric and a biocentric worldview. In short, my argument is designed to show that even those of you who are steadfastly committed to valuing humans over nonhumans are nevertheless committed to the immorality of eating meat, given your other beliefs.

Second, ethical arguments are often context-dependent in that

[4]*Speciesism* is the widespread view that one's own species is superior to and more valuable than the other species and that, therefore, members of one's own species have the right to dominate members of these other species. While "speciesism" and its cognates are often used pejoratively in the animal rights literature, I use them only descriptively and imply no negative or condescending appraisal of the individual so described.

[5]Bonnie Steinbock's criticism of Singer's view seems to be rooted in such a sincerely held feeling. See her "Speciesism and the Idea of Equality," *Philosophy*, vol. 53, no. 204 (April 1978). Therein Steinbock writes:

> I doubt that anyone will be able to come up with a concrete and morally relevant difference that would justify, say, using a chimpanzee in an experiment rather than a human being with less capacity for reasoning, moral responsibility, etc. Should we then experiment on the severely retarded? Utilitarian considerations aside . . . , we *feel* a special obligation to care for the handicapped members of our own species, who cannot survive in this world without such care . . . . [A]lthough one can imagine oneself in the monkey's place, one *feels* a closer identification with the severely retarded human being. Here we are getting away from such things as 'morally relevant differences' and are talking about something much more difficult to articulate, namely, the role of *feeling* and *sentiment* in moral thinking. (pp. 255f, my emphasis)

they presuppose a specific audience in a certain set of circumstances. Recognizing what that intended audience and context is, and what it is not, can prevent confusions about the scope of the ethical claim being made. My argument is context-dependent in precisely this way. It is not aimed at those relatively few indigenous peoples who, because of the paucity of edible vegetable matter available, must eat meat in order to survive. Rather, it is directed at people, like you, who live in agriculturally bountiful societies in which a wealth of nutritionally adequate alternatives to meat are readily available. Thus, I intend to show that your beliefs commit you to the view that eating meat is morally wrong for anyone who is in the circumstances in which you typically find yourself and *a fortiori* that it is morally wrong for you to eat meat in these circumstances.[6] Enough by way of preamble, on to your beliefs.

1.   THE THINGS YOU BELIEVE

The beliefs attributed to you herein would normally be considered noncontentious. In most contexts, we would take someone who didn't hold these beliefs to be either morally defective or irrational. Of course, in most contexts, these beliefs are not a threat to enjoying hamburgers, hotdogs, steaks, and ribs; but even with burgers in the balance, you will, I think, readily admit believing the following propositions: (p_1) Other things being equal, a world with less pain and suffering is better than a world with more pain and suffering; and (p_2) A world with less unnecessary suffering is better than a world with more unnecessary suffering.[7] Anyone who

---

[6]Accordingly, throughout the text my claim that "your beliefs commit you to the immorality of eating meat" should be understood as shorthand for the following more cumbersome claim: Your beliefs commit you to the immorality of eating meat for anyone who is in the circumstances in which you typically find yourself.

[7]By "*unnecessary* suffering" I mean suffering which serves no greater, outweighing justifying good. If some instance of suffering is required to bring about a greater good (e.g., a painful root canal may be the only way to save a person's tooth), then that suffering is *not* unnecessary. Thus, in the case of (p_2), no *ceteris paribus* clause is needed, since if other things are *not* equal such that the suffering in question is justified by an overriding justifying good which can only be achieved by allowing that suffering, then that suffering is *not* unnecessary.

has felt the force of the atheistic argument from evil based on gratuitous suffering is committed to (p_1) and (p_2). After all, the reason we think a *wholly good* God would prevent unnecessary suffering is because we think that such suffering is intrinsically bad and that the world would be better without it.[8] Since you think that unnecessary suffering is intrinsically bad, you no doubt also believe: (p_3) Unnecessary cruelty is wrong and *prima facie* should not be supported or encouraged. You probably believe: (p_4) We ought to take steps to make the world a better place. But even if you reject (p_4) on the grounds that we have no positive duties to benefit, you still think there are negative duties to do no harm, and so you believe: $(p_{4'})$ We ought to do what we reasonably can to avoid making the world a worse place. You also believe: (p_5) A morally good person will take steps to make the world a better place and even stronger steps to avoid making the world a worse place; and (p_6) Even a "minimally decent person"[9] would take steps to help reduce the amount of unnecessary pain and suffering in the world, *if s/he could do so with very little effort on her/his part.*

You also have beliefs about yourself. You believe one of the following propositions when the reflexive pronoun is indexed to yourself: (p_7) I am a morally good person; or (p_8) I am at least a minimally decent person. You also believe of yourself: (p_9) I am the sort of person who certainly would take steps to help reduce the amount of pain and suffering in the world, *if I could do so with very little effort on my part.* Enough about you. On to your beliefs about nonhuman animals and our obligations toward them.

You believe: (p_{10}) Many nonhuman animals (certainly all vertebrates) are capable of feeling pain; (p_{11}) It is morally wrong to cause

---

[8]Interestingly enough, one of the most powerful versions of the atheistic argument from unnecessary suffering is predicated on gratuitous animal suffering, namely, the suffering of a fawn severely burned in a naturally occurring forest fire. See William Rowe's "The Problem of Evil," in *Philosophy of Religion: An Introduction,* 2d edition (Belmont, Cal.: Wadsworth, 1993), pp. 79–82.

[9]By a "minimally decent person" I mean a person who does the very minimum required by morality and no more. I borrow this terminology from Judith Jarvis Thomson who distinguishes a *good* Samaritan from a *minimally decent* Samaritan. See her "A Defense of Abortion," *Philosophy and Public Affairs,* vol. 1, no. 1 (1971), pp. 62–65.

an animal unnecessary pain or suffering; and (p_{12}) It is morally wrong and despicable to treat animals inhumanely *for no good reason.*[10] In addition to your beliefs about the wrongness of causing animals unnecessary pain, you also have beliefs about the appropriateness of killing animals; for example, you believe: (p_{13}) We ought to euthanize untreatably injured, suffering animals to put them out of their misery whenever feasible; and (p_{14}) Other things being equal, it is worse to kill a conscious sentient animal than it is to kill a plant. Finally, you believe: (p_{15}) We have a duty to help preserve the environment for future generations (at least for future *human* generations); and consequently, you believe: (p_{16}) One ought to minimize one's contribution toward environmental degradation, *especially in those ways requiring minimal effort on one's part.*

2.   FACTORY FARMING AND MODERN SLAUGHTER: THE CRUELTY BEHIND THE CELLOPHANE

Before they become someone's dinner, most farm animals raised in the United States are forced to endure intense pain and suffering in "factory farms." Factory farms are intensive confinement facilities where animals are made to live in inhospitable unnatural conditions for the duration of their lives. The first step is early separation of mother and offspring. Chickens are separated from their mothers *before* birth, as they are hatched in incubators, veal calves are removed from their mothers within a few days, and piglets are sep-

---

[10]See Gilbert Harman's *The Nature of Morality: An Introduction to Ethics* (New York: Oxford University Press, 1977), p. 4, where he presents the following much discussed example: "If you round the corner and see a group of young hoodlums pour gasoline on a cat and ignite it, you do not need to *conclude* that what they are doing is wrong; you do not need to figure anything out; you can *see* that it is wrong." What is relevant about this example for our purposes is that no one considering the example seriously doubts whether a cat so treated would feel pain (hence, no one seriously doubts [p_{10}]), nor does anyone seriously doubt that cruelly burning a cat for no good reason is wrong (hence, no one seriously doubts [p_{11}] or [p_{12}] either).

arated from their mothers two to three weeks after birth.[11] The off-spring are then housed in overcrowded confinement facilities. Broiler chickens and turkeys are warehoused in sheds containing anywhere from 10,000 to 100,000 birds;[12] veal calves are kept in crates 22″ by 54″ and are chained at the neck, rendering them unable to move or turn around;[13] pigs are confined in metal crates (which provide six square feet of living space) situated on concrete slat-ted floors with no straw or bedding;[14] and beef cattle are housed in feedlots containing up to 100,000 animals.[15] The inappropriate, unforgiving surfaces on which the animals must stand produce chronic foot and leg injuries.[16] Since they cannot move about, they must stand in their own waste. In these cramped, unsanitary con-ditions, virtually all of the animals' basic instinctual urges (e.g., to nurse, stretch, move around, root, groom, build nests, rut, estab-lish social orders, select mates, copulate, procreate, and rear off-spring) are frustrated, causing boredom and stress in the animals. The stress and unsanitary conditions together compromise their immune systems. To prevent large-scale losses due to disease, the animals are fed a steady diet of antibiotics and growth hormones.[17]

---

[11]Jim Mason and Peter Singer, *Animal Factories,* 2d edition (New York: Harmony Books, 1990), pp. 5, 10, and 11f.

[12]These overcrowded conditions make it impossible for the birds to develop a pecking order, the lack of which generates aggression, feather peck-ing, and cannibalism in the birds. See Karen Davis, *Prisoned Chickens, Poisoned Eggs: An Inside Look at the Modern Poultry Industry* (Summer-town, Tenn.: Book Publishing Co., 1996), pp. 65–71; Singer, *Animal Lib-eration,* pp. 99f; and Mason and Singer, *Animal Factories,* pp. 1–7.

[13]John Robbins, *Diet for a New America* (Walpole, N.H.: Stillpoint, 1987), p. 114; Humane Farming Association, "Modern Farming Is Inhumane," *Animal Rights: Opposing Viewpoints* (San Diego: Greenhaven Press, 1989), p. 118; and Mason and Singer, *Animal Factories,* p. 12.

[14]Humane Farming Association, "Modern Farming Is Inhumane," p. 117. For further details, see Robbins' discussion of the "Bacon Bin" in *Diet for a New America,* p. 83.

[15]Robbins, *Diet for a New America,* p. 110.

[16]Mason and Singer, *Animal Factories,* pp. 30f; and Davis, *Prisoned Chick-ens, Poisoned Eggs,* pp. 21 and 56f.

[17]Estrogens, gestagens, and androgens are routinely administered to cattle, veal calves, hogs, and sheep. Recommended dosages are described in

When it comes to feed, disease prevention isn't the only consideration. Another is cost. The USDA has approved all sorts of cost-cutting dietary "innovations" with little regard for the animals' well-being including adding the ground-up remains of dead diseased animals (unfit for human consumption) to these herbivorous animals' feed,[18] adding cement dust to cattle feed to promote rapid weight gain,[19] and adding the animals' own feces to their feed.[20]

Hormones in Animal Production, Food and Agricultural Organization of the United Nations (Rome, 1982), p. 3. Mason and Singer report, "Nearly all poultry, 90 percent of veal calves and pigs, and a debatable number of cattle get antibacterial additives in their feed" (*Animal Factories,* p. 66). Residues often remain in their flesh, despite the fact that many of these drugs are known carcinogens not approved for human use. According to *Problems in Preventing the Marketing of Raw Meat and Poultry Containing Potentially Harmful Residues* (Washington, D.C.: General Accounting Office, April 17, 1979), p. i.: "Of the 143 drugs and pesticides GAO has identified as likely to leave residues in raw meat and poultry, 42 are known to cause cancer or are suspected of causing cancer; 20 of causing birth defects; and 6 of causing mutations" (cited in Mason and Singer, *Animal Factories,* p. 72).

[18]"Ten billion pounds of processed animal remains were sold for animal feed in the U.S. in 1995." See Eric Haapapuro, "Piling It High and Deep," *Good Medicine,* vol. 5, no. 4 (Autumn 1996), p. 15. It should be noted that feeding cattle the rendered remains of sheep infected with scrapie is the suspected cause of bovine spongiform encephalopathy (BSE or as it is commonly called "mad cow disease"). Consuming BSE-infected cattle is believed to be the cause of one variant of Creutzfeldt-Jakob disease, a fatal brain disease in humans. See "Mad Cow Disease: The Risk in the U.S.," *Good Medicine,* vol. 5, no. 3 (Summer 1996), p. 9.

[19]Mason and Singer, *Animal Factories,* p. 51.

[20]Haapapuro, "Piling It High and Deep," p. 15. Also see Eric Haapapuro, Neal Barnard, and Michele Simon, "Animal Waste Used as Livestock Feed: Dangers to Human Health," *Preventive Medicine,* vol. 26 (1997), pp. 599–602; as well as Mason and Singer, *Animal Factories,* p. 53. Detailed feed recipes, some containing as much as 40 percent chicken manure, are outlined in *Feed from Animal Wastes: Feeding Manual,* Food and Agricultural Organization of the United Nations (Rome, 1982). Forced coprophagia has been an industry practice since the mid-1970s. See "Animal Wastes Can Be Fed in Silage," *The American Farmer* (January 1974), pp. 14f, an article describing the "suitability" of adding cattle and poultry manure to feed.

The animals react to these inhumane, stressful conditions by developing "stereotypies" (i.e., stress- and boredom-induced, neurotic repetitive behaviors) and other unnatural behaviors including cannibalism.[21] For example, chickens unable to develop a pecking order often try to peck each other to death, and pigs, bored due to forced immobility, routinely bite the tail of the pig caged in front of them. To prevent losses due to cannibalism and aggression, the animals receive preemptive mutilations. To prevent chickens and turkeys from pecking each other to death, the birds are "debeaked" using a scalding hot blade which slices through the highly sensitive horn of the beak leaving blisters in the mouth;[22] and to prevent these birds from scratching each other to death (which the industry refers to as "back ripping"), their toes are amputated using the same hot-knife machine.[23] Other routine mutilations include: dubbing (surgical removal of the combs and wattles of male chickens and turkeys), tail docking, branding, dehorning, ear tagging, ear clipping, teeth pulling, castration, and ovariectomy. In the interest of cost efficiency, *all* of these excruciating procedures are performed *without* anesthesia. *Unanesthetized* branding, dehorning, ear tagging, ear clipping, and castration are standard procedures on nonintensive farms, as well.[24]

Lives of frustration and torment finally culminate as the animals are inhumanely loaded onto trucks and shipped long distances to slaughterhouses without food or water and without adequate protection from the elements. Each year tens of thousands of animals die and millions are severely injured as a result of such handling and transportation. For example, in 1997, USDA inspectors condemned over 22,000 ducks, 26 million turkeys and 30 million chick-

---

[21]Mason and Singer, *Animal Factories,* pp. 21–24; and Davis, *Prisoned Chickens, Poisoned Eggs,* pp. 65–71.

[22]Debeaking is the surgical removal of the birds' beaks. When beaks are cut too short or heal improperly, the birds cannot eat and eventually starve to death (Davis, *Prisoned Chickens, Poisoned Eggs,* pp. 48 and 65–71; Mason and Singer, *Animal Factories,* pp. 39f; and Robbins, *Diet for a New America,* p. 57.)

[23]Davis, *Prisoned Chickens, Poisoned Eggs,* p. 47; and Mason and Singer, *Animal Factories,* p. 40.

[24]Singer, *Animal Liberation,* p. 145.

ens before they entered the slaughter plant, because they were either dead or severely injured upon arrival.[25] Once inside the slaughterhouse, the animals are hung upside down (pigs, cattle, and sheep are suspended by one hind leg, which often breaks) and are brought via conveyor to the slaughterer who slits their throats, severs their jugular veins, and punctures their hearts with a butcher knife. In *theory,* animals covered by the Federal Humane Slaughter Act are to be rendered unconscious by electric current or by captive bolt pistol (a pneumatic gun which, when aimed properly, renders the animal unconscious by firing an eight-inch pin into the animal's skull). Chickens, turkeys, ducks, and geese are not considered animals under the Act and hence receive no protection at all.[26] In *practice,* the Act is not enforced, and as a result, many slaughterhouses elect not to use the captive bolt pistol in the interest of cost efficiency.[27] As for electric shock, it is unlikely that being shocked into unconsciousness is itself a painless process, based on reports of people who have experienced electroconvulsive therapy.[28] A consequence of the lax enforcement of the Federal Humane Slaughter Act is that in many cases (and all kosher cases), the animals are fully conscious throughout the entire throat-slitting ordeal.[29]

[25]*Poultry Slaughter,* National Agricultural Statistics Service (NASS), United States Department of Agriculture (USDA) (Washington, D.C.: April 3, 1998), pp. 17 and 24f. The antemortem condemnation statistics just cited are estimates, since NASS tracks antemortem condemnations in pounds, not bird units, and were deduced as follows: the total weight of antemortem condemnations for a given bird-type was divided by the average live weight of birds of that type. For example, in 1997 antemortem chicken condemnations totaled 144,424,000 pounds and the average live weight of the chickens slaughtered was 4.81 pounds. Dividing pounds condemned by average pounds per bird yields 30,025,779 chickens condemned.

[26]Robbins, *Diet for a New America,* p. 139.

[27]Singer, *Animal Liberation,* p. 153.

[28]Ibid., p. 152.

[29]While only 5 percent of U.S. meat is sold as kosher, as many as 50 percent of the animals are slaughtered while fully conscious in conformity with antiquated ritual slaughter laws (Robbins, *Diet for a New America,* p. 142).

These animal rearing and slaughtering techniques are by no means rare: 97 percent of all poultry are produced in 100,000-plus bird operations,[30] 97 percent of pigs are raised in confinement systems,[31] over half of the nation's dairy cows are raised in confinement systems,[32] all veal calves are crate-raised by definition, and 61 percent of beef cattle are confined in factory farm feedlots.[33] To see just how many animals suffer the institutionalized cruelties of factory farming, consider the number slaughtered in the United States each year. According to the National Agricultural Statistics Service, 36.3 million cattle, 1.58 million veal calves, 92.0 million pigs, 3.91 million sheep and lamb, 22.0 million ducks, 290.2 million turkeys, and 7,903.5 million chickens were slaughtered in

---

[30]*Animal Agriculture: Information on Waste Management and Water Quality Issues,* a U.S. General Accounting Office (GAO) Report to the U.S. Senate Committee on Agriculture, Nutrition, and Forestry (June 1995), pp. 2 and 47.

[31]Confinement is the norm in hog operations with more than 100 head. In 1997, 97 percent of the total U.S. hog inventory was housed in operations with more than 100 head. In fact, 85 percent of hogs were raised in facilities with more than 500 head and a startling 35 percent were raised in operations with more than 5000 head (*Hogs and Pigs,* NASS, USDA (Washington, D.C.: December 29, 1997), pp. 24f. All NASS publications can be accessed on the Web at: www.usda.gov/nass/). The trend toward consolidation of the hog industry with ever larger operations is continuing. According to the U.S. GAO, "From 1978 to 1994, the total number of [hog] operations (of all sizes) decreased by about 67 percent—from 635,000 to 209,000—while inventory remained the same at about 60 million head" (*Animal Agriculture: Information on Waste Management and Water Quality Issues,* p. 41). In 1997, the number of hog farms plummeted to 138,690, down 11 percent from 1996 and 24 percent below 1995, while inventory continued to remain relatively unchanged at 59.9 million head (*Hogs and Pigs,* NASS, USDA, p. 1).

[32]Again confinement is the norm in operations with 100+ dairy cows. According to NASS, in 1996, 57 percent of the nation's dairy cows were housed in operations with 100+ head (NASS, USDA, *Agricultural Statistics 1997,* Table 8-7 [Washington, D.C.: Government Printing Office, 1997], p. VIII–5).

[33]As of January 1, 1998, 61 percent of the total cattle inventory was housed in feedlots with a capacity of 1000+ head (according to *Cattle on Feed,* NASS, USDA [Washington, D.C.: January 23, 1998], p. 1).

1997.[34] In sum, 8.35 *billion* animals are raised and slaughtered annually (not counting horses, goats, rabbits, emu, other poultry, or fish);[35] and even this number underestimates the number of farm animals killed by animal agriculture by over 10 percent, since it does not include the 921.4 million animals who suffer lingering deaths from disease, malnutrition, injury, or suffocation before reaching the slaughterhouse either as a result of the abysmal unsanitary conditions in factory farms or as a result of brutal handling in transit.[36] Extrapolation reveals that over 25 million animals per day (roughly 293 animals per second) are killed as a result of the food animal industry. Suffice it to say that no other human activity results in more pain, suffering, frustration, and death than factory farming and animal agribusiness.[37]

3. THE IMPLICATIONS OF *YOUR* BELIEFS: WHY *YOU* ARE COMMITTED TO THE IMMORALITY OF EATING MEAT

I will now offer an argument for the immorality of eating meat predicated on *your* beliefs (p_1)–(p_{16}). Actually I will offer a family of related arguments, all predicated on different subsets of the set $[(p_1), (p_2), \ldots, (p_{16})]$. While you do not have to believe all of (p_1)–(p_{16}) for my argument to succeed, the more of these propositions you believe, the greater *your* commitment to the immoral-

---

[34]*Livestock Slaughter 1997 Summary,* NASS, USDA (Washington, D.C.: March 1998), p. 1; and *Poultry Slaughter,* NASS, USDA (Washington, D.C.: April 3, 1998), p. 15.

[35]And these numbers are for the United States alone. Worldwide, cattle, poultry, goats, and sheep total 15 billion (UN Food and Agricultural Organization, *Production Yearbook 1989* [Rome, 1989], vol. 43, table 89).

[36]According to *The Farm Report* (Spring 1997), 530.8 million broilers, 252.6 million layers, 115.7 million turkeys, 1.4 million ducks, 1.8 million cattle, 2.8 million veal calves, 15.1 million pigs, and 1.2 million sheep died in 1997 *before* reaching the slaughterhouse. These numbers are only for the United States.

[37]With the possible exception of the seafood industry, which, strictly speaking, should be viewed as an extension of animal agribusiness.

ity of eating meat.[38] For convenience, (p_1)–(p_{16}) have been compiled in an appendix at the end of the article.

Your beliefs (p_{10})–(p_{13}) show that you already believe that animals are capable of experiencing intense pain and suffering. I don't have to prove to you that *unanesthetized* branding, castration, debeaking, tail docking, tooth extraction, etc., cause animals severe pain. You already believe these procedures to be excruciatingly painful. Consequently, given the husbandry techniques and slaughtering practices documented above, you must admit the fact that: (f_1) Virtually all commercial animal agriculture, *especially* factory farming, causes animals intense pain and suffering and, thus, *greatly increases* the amount of pain and suffering in the world. (f_1) and your belief (p_1) together entail that, other things being equal, the world would be better without animal agriculture and factory farms. It is also a fact that: (f_2) In modern societies the consumption of meat is *in no way necessary* for human survival,[39] and so, the pain and suffering which results from meat production is entirely *unnecessary,* as are all the cruel practices inherent in animal agriculture. Since no one *needs* to eat flesh, all of the inhumane treatment to which farm animals are routinely subjected is done *for no good reason,* and so your belief that it is morally wrong and despicable to treat animals inhumanely *for no good reason* [(p_{12})] forces you to admit that factory farming and animal agribusiness are morally wrong and despicable. Furthermore, your belief that a world with less unnecessary suffering is better than a world with more unnecessary suffering [(p_2)], together with (f_2), entails that the world would be better if there were less animal agriculture and fewer factory farms, and better still if there were no animal agriculture and no factory farms. Moreover, your belief in (p_3) commits you to the view that factory farming is wrong and *prima facie* ought not be supported or encouraged. When one buys factory farm-raised meat,

---

[38]If you believe (p_1), (p_2), (p_6), and (p_{10}), my argument will succeed. In fact, an argument for the immorality of eating meat can be constructed from (p_{15}) and (p_{16}) alone.

[39]According to the USDA, "Vegetarian diets are consistent with the Dietary Guidelines for Americans and can meet Recommended Dietary Allowances for nutrients." *Nutrition and Your Health: Dietary Guidelines for Americans,* 4th ed., USDA, U.S. Department of Health and Human Services (1995), p. 6.

one *is* supporting factory farms monetarily and thereby encouraging their *unnecessary* cruel practices. The only way to avoid actively supporting factory farms is to stop purchasing their products.

Since, per (p_3), you have a *prima facie* obligation to stop supporting factory farming and animal agriculture, you have a *prima facie* obligation to become a vegetarian.[40] Of course, *prima facie* obligations are overridable. Perhaps they can even be overridden simply by the fact that fulfilling them would be excessively burdensome or require enormous effort and sacrifice on one's part. Perhaps, but this much is clear: when one can fulfill a *prima facie* obligation *with very little effort on one's part* and *without thereby failing to perform any other obligation,* then that obligation becomes very stringent indeed.

As for your *prima facie* obligation to stop supporting factory farming, you can easily satisfy it without thereby failing to perform any of your other obligations simply by refraining from eating meat and eating something else instead. For example, you can eat veggie burgers rather than hamburgers, pasta with marinara sauce rather than meat sauce, bean burritos or bean tostadas rather than beef tacos, red beans and rice rather than Cajun fried chicken, barbecued tofu rather than barbecued ribs, moo shu vegetables rather than moo shu pork, minestrone rather than chicken soup, five-bean vegetarian chili rather than chili with ground beef, chick pea salad rather than chicken salad, fruit and whole wheat toast rather than bacon and eggs, scrambled tofu vegetable frittatas rather than ham and cheese omelets, etc. These

---

[40]Here I am bracketing hunting. I realize that not all meat comes from factory farming and animal agriculture. Some comes from hunting. Hunting itself results in all sorts of unnecessary pain and suffering for the animals killed, maimed, and wounded by bullets, shot, and arrows. Every year in the United States alone, hunters kill 175 million animals, and for every animal killed two are seriously wounded and left to die a slow agonizing death (Anna Sequoia, *67 Ways to Save the Animals* [New York: Harper Perennial, 1990], p. 38.); and for every deer killed by crossbow, twenty-one arrows are shot since crossbow hunters rarely hit a vital organ (Ingrid Newkirk, *Save the Animals! 101 Easy Things You Can Do* [New York: Warner Books, 1990], p. 95). Many of these animals are killed for wall "trophies," but even in those cases where the animals are killed (maimed or wounded) for the sake of obtaining meat, all of the pain and suffering inflicted on them is *unnecessary* since no one in a modern agriculturally advanced society *needs* to eat any kind of meat, wild or domesticated.

examples underscore the *ease* with which one can avoid consuming flesh, a fact which often seems to elude meat eaters.

From your beliefs (p_1), (p_2), and $(p_{4'})$, it follows that we ought to do what we reasonably can to avoid contributing to the amount of unnecessary suffering in the world. Since one thing we reasonably can do to avoid contributing to unnecessary suffering is stop contributing to factory farming with our purchases, it follows that we ought to stop purchasing and consuming meat.

Your other beliefs support the same conclusion. You believe: (p_5) A morally good person will take steps to make the world a better place and even stronger steps to avoid making the world a worse place; and (p_6) Even a "minimally decent person" would take steps to help reduce the amount of unnecessary pain and suffering in the world, *if s/he could do so with very little effort*. You also believe that you are a morally good person $[(p_7)]$ or at least a minimally decent one $[(p_8)]$. Moreover, you believe that you are the kind of person who would take steps to help reduce the amount of pain and suffering in the world, *if you could do so with very little effort on your part* $[(p_9)]$. As shown above, *with minimal effort* you could take steps to help reduce the amount of unnecessary suffering in the world just by eating something other than meat. Accordingly, given (p_6), you ought to refrain from eating flesh. Given (p_9), if you really are the kind of person you think you are, you will quit eating meat, opting for cruelty-free vegetarian fare instead.

Finally, animal agriculture is an extremely wasteful, inefficient, environmentally devastating means of food production. A full discussion of the inefficiencies and environmental degradations associated with animal agriculture is beyond the scope of the present paper, but consider five examples:

1. Animal agriculture is an extremely energy intensive method of food production. It takes an average of 28 kilocalories of fossil energy to produce 1 kcal of animal protein, compared with an average of 3.3 kcal of fossil energy to produce 1 kcal of grain protein, making animal production on average more than eight times less energy efficient than grain production.[41]

---

[41]David Pimentel, "Livestock Production: Energy Inputs and the Environment," *Proceedings of the Canadian Society of Animal Science,* 47th Annual

2. Animal production is extremely inefficient in its water usage, compared to vegetable and grain production. Producing 1 kilogram of animal protein requires around 100 times more water than producing 1 kg of plant protein—for example, it takes 500 liters of water to grow 1 kg of potatoes and 900 liters of water to grow 1 kg of wheat, but it requires 100,000 liters of water to produce 1 kg of beef.[42] Hence, agricultural water usage, which currently accounts for 87 percent of the world's freshwater consumption,[43] could be drastically reduced by a shift toward an entirely plant-based agriculture.

3. Animal agriculture is also extremely nutrient inefficient. By cycling grain through livestock to produce animal protein, we lose 90 percent of that grain's protein, 96 percent of its calories, 100 percent of its carbohydrates, and 100 percent of its fiber.[44]

4. Another negative byproduct of the livestock industry is soil erosion. Much of arable land in the United States is devoted to feed crop production. Eighty percent of the corn and 95 percent of the oats grown in the United States are fed to livestock, and the excessive cultivation of our farmlands needed to produce these crops is responsible for the loss of 7 billion tons of topsoil each year.[45] David Pimentel, professor of agriculture and life sciences, Cornell University, describes the magnitude of the problem as follows: "During the last 40 years, nearly one-third of the world's arable land has been lost by erosion and continues to be lost at a rate of more than 10 million hectares per year."[46] The United States

---

Meeting (Montreal, Quebec: July 24–26, 1997), pp. 16 and 20. Fish production is equally inefficient requiring, on average, 27 kcal of fossil energy per kcal of fish protein produced (David Pimentel and Marcia Pimentel, *Food, Energy, and Society,* rev. ed. [Niwot, Colo.: University Press of Colorado, 1996], p. 93).

[42]David Pimentel, James Houser, et al., "Water Resources: Agriculture, the Environment, and Society," *Bioscience,* vol. 47, no. 2 (February 1997), p. 100.

[43]Ibid., pp. 97 and 104.

[44]Robbins, *Diet for a New America,* p. 352.

[45]Ibid., pp. 351 and 358.

[46]David Pimentel, C. Harvey, et al., "Environmental and Economic Cost of Soil Erosion and Conservation Benefits," *Science,* vol. 267, no. 5201 (February 24, 1995), p. 1117.

is losing soil at a rate thirteen times faster than the rate of soil formation.[47]

5. Animal agriculture creates enormous amounts of hazardous waste in the form of excrement. U.S. livestock produce 250,000 pounds of excrement *per second,* resulting in *1 billion tons* of unrecycled waste per year.[48] According to the U.S. General Accounting Office's Report to the U.S. Senate Committee on Agriculture, Nutrition, and Forestry, animal-waste runoff from feedlots and rangeland is a significant factor in water quality, affecting about 72 percent of impaired rivers and streams, 56 percent of impaired lake acres, and 43 percent of impaired estuary miles.[49] This GAO report found that agriculture is one of the main sources of groundwater pollution and also found: "Among five general categories of pollution sources (Municipal Point Sources; Urban Runoff/Storm Sewers; Agriculture; Industrial Point Sources; and Natural Sources), agriculture ranked as the number one cause of impaired rivers and streams and lakes."[50] The upshot is this: animal agriculture is far and away the most resource-intensive, inefficient, environmentally harmful, and ecologically unsound means of human food production, and consequently, one of the easiest direct actions one can take to help protect the environment and preserve resources for future generations, *requiring minimal effort,* is to stop eating meat. And so, since you believe that we have a duty to preserve the environment for future generations [(p_{15})] and you believe that one ought to minimize one's contribution toward environmental degradation [(p_{16})], your beliefs commit you to the obligatoriness of becoming vegetarian, since doing so is a simple way to help to preserve the environment.

The moral of the present section is clear: consistency forces you to admit that meat consumption is immoral and, thus, necessitates your becoming vegetarian immediately.

---

[47]Pimentel and Pimentel, *Food, Energy, and Society,* p. 153.

[48]Robbins, *Diet for a New America,* p. 372. In contrast, humans produce 12,000 pounds of excrement per second, one-twentieth that of livestock (p. 372).

[49]*Animal Agriculture: Information on Waste Management and Water Quality Issues,* pp. 2 and 8f.

[50]Ibid., p. 9.

4. OBJECTIONS AND REPLIES: WAYS THINGS MIGHT HAVE BEEN, BUT AREN'T

From (f_1) and (p_1) we inferred that, other things being equal, the world would be better without animal agriculture and factory farms. Perhaps other things are not equal. Perhaps the agony experienced by animals in factory farms is necessary for some greater good. The present section examines several ways things might have been unequal, but aren't.

Perhaps Meat Consumption Is Necessary for Optimal Nutrition

A crucial premise in my argument is: (CP1) The pain and suffering which inevitably result from meat production are entirely *unnecessary*. I defended (CP1) on the grounds that in modern societies meat consumption is *in no way necessary* for human survival [(f_2)]. But (CP1) does not follow from (f_2), since eating meat might be necessary for some reason other than human survival. Hence, one might object: "While eating meat is not necessary for survival, it *might* still be necessary for humans to thrive and flourish, in which case (CP1) would be false since the pain and suffering experienced by farm animals would be *necessary* for a significant human benefit."

If meat consumption were *necessary* for humans to flourish, my argument would be seriously compromised, so let us examine the evidence. First, consider the counterexamples. Since world-class athletic competition is one of the most grueling and physically strenuous activities in which humans can engage, one would not expect there to be any highly successful vegetarian athletes or vegetarian world record holders, *if* meat consumption were necessary for humans to thrive and flourish. However, the list of world-class vegetarian athletes is quite long and includes: Dave Scott (six-time winner of Hawaii's Ironman Triathlon), Sixto Linares (world record holder for the 24-hour triathlon), Edwin Moses (400 meter hurdler undefeated in international competition for eight straight years), Paavo Nurmi (twenty world records and nine Olympic medals), Andreas Cahling (1980 Mr. International title in body building), and Ridgely Abele (U.S. Karate Association World Champion), to name a few,[51] which strongly suggests that eating meat is *not* necessary for humans to flourish.

Second, consider the diseases associated with the consumption of meat and animal products—heart disease, cancer, stroke, osteoporosis, diabetes, hypertension, arthritis, and obesity—as documented in numerous highly regarded studies.[52] Four examples must suffice:

1. The Loma Linda study, involving over 24,000 people, found that lacto-ovo-vegetarian men (who consume eggs and dairy products, but no meat) had a 61 percent lower coronary heart disease (CHD) mortality rate than California's general population. Pure vegetarian men (who consume no animal products) fared even better: the CHD mortality rate for these males was 86 percent lower than that of the California general population.[53]

2. The ongoing Framingham heart study has been tracking the daily living and eating habits of thousands of residents of Framingham, Massachusetts, since 1948. Dr. William Castelli, director of the study for the last fifteen years, maintains that based on his research the most heart-healthy diet is a *pure* vegetarian diet.[54] Perhaps vegetarians suffer from other illnesses or die of other diseases earlier than their meat-eating counterparts. Not according to Dr. Castelli: "The vegetarian societies of the world have the best diet. Within our own country, they outlive the rest of us by at least seven

---

[51]The impressive feats of these world-class vegetarian athletes and numerous other vegetarian athletes are discussed in much greater detail in Robbins, *Diet for a New America,* pp. 158–63.

[52]For an excellent well-documented discussion of the positive correlation between meat consumption and these diseases, see Robbins' *Diet for a New America,* pp. 203–305.

[53]Roland L. Phillips, Frank R. Lemon, et al., "Coronary Heart Disease Mortality among Seventh-Day Adventists with Differing Dietary Habits: A Preliminary Report," *The American Journal of Clinical Nutrition,* vol. 31 (October 1978), pp. S191–S198. CHD mortality rates based on Standardized Mortality Ratios of 39 and 14 for lacto-ovo and pure vegetarian men, respectively (Fig. 5, p. S195).

[54]"An Interview with William Castelli," *Good Medicine,* vol. 5, no. 3 (Summer 1996), p. 15.

years, and they have only 10 or 15 percent of our heart attack rate."[55] Elsewhere Castelli adds: "Vegetarians not only outlive the rest of us, they also aren't prey to other degenerative diseases, such as diabetes, strokes, etc., that slow us down and make us chronically ill."[56]

3. The Cornell–Oxford–China Health Project systematically monitored the diet, lifestyle, and disease patterns of 6,500 families from sixty-five different counties in Mainland China and Taiwan.[57] The data collected in this study have led its director, Dr. T. Colin Campbell, to conclude that 80–90 percent of all cancers can be controlled or prevented by a low-fat (10–15 percent fat) vegetarian diet.[58]

4. The Dean Ornish study in which it was demonstrated that *advanced* coronary artery disease could be *reversed* through a combination of stress reduction and an extremely low-fat vegetarian diet (10 percent fat). All patients in the study had greater than 50 percent stenosis in one or more of the major coronary arteries. Members of the experimental group participated in stress management training and were fed a 1,400-calorie diet consisting of fresh fruits and vegetables, whole grains, legumes, tubers, and soy beans, while the control group continued their routine activities at work and at home. After only six weeks, an important indicator of coronary function (mean left ventricular ejection fraction) improved 6.4 percent in the experimental group, but deteriorated 1.7 percent in the control group. In addition, the experimental group showed a 20.5 percent reduction in plasma cholesterol, a 91 percent mean reduction in the frequency of angina, and a mean weight reduction of ten pounds, compared to the control group, which showed no sig-

---

[55]Ibid.

[56]William Castelli, "Lessons from the Framingham Heart Study: How to Reduce the Risk of Heart Disease," *Bottom Line: Personal* (July 1, 1994), p. 10.

[57]J. Chen, T. C. Campbell, et al., *Diet, Lifestyle, and Mortality in China: A Study of the Characteristics of 65 Counties* (Oxford University Press, Cornell University Press, and the China People's Medical Publishing House, 1990).

[58]T. Colin Campbell (Professor of Nutritional Biochemistry at Cornell University), as reported in *Healthcare Foodservice* (March/April 1992), p. 15.

nificant improvement in any of these areas.[59] These and countless other studies have led the American Dietetic Association, the leading nutritional organization in the country, to assert:

> Scientific data suggest positive relationships between a vegetarian diet and reduced risk for several chronic degenerative diseases and conditions, including obesity, coronary artery disease, hypertension, diabetes mellitus, and some types of cancer. . . . *It is the position of The American Dietetic Association (ADA) that appropriately planned vegetarian diets are healthful, are nutritionally adequate, and provide health benefits in the prevention and treatment of certain diseases.*[60]

An article in *The Journal of the American Medical Association* concurs, claiming: "A vegetarian diet can prevent 97 percent of our coronary occlusions."[61] In light of these findings, the Physicians Committee for Responsible Medicine (PCRM) recommends centering our diets on the following *new* four food groups: (1) whole grains (5+ servings a day); (2) vegetables (3+ servings a day); (3) fruits (3+ servings a day), and (4) legumes (2+ servings a day).[62] Gone are meat and dairy, the two principal sources of fat and cholesterol in the American diet. The evidence is unequivocal: A vegetarian diet is nutritionally superior to a meat-based diet. One cannot reject (CP1) on the grounds that eating meat is necessary for

---

[59]Dean Ornish, et al., "Effects of Stress Management Training and Dietary Changes in Treating Ischemic Heart Disease," *Journal of the American Medical Association,* vol. 249, no. 1 (1983), pp. 54–59. These findings were confirmed in the Lifestyle Heart Trial. See Dean Ornish, et al., "Can Lifestyle Changes Reverse Coronary Heart Disease?" *Lancet,* vol. 336 (July 21, 1990), pp. 129–33.

[60]"Position of the American Dietetic Association: Vegetarian Diets," *Journal of the American Dietetic Association,* vol. 97, no. 11 (November 1997), p. 1317. For those wishing to learn more about sound vegetarian nutrition, the ADA has published this article in its entirety at: www.eatright.org/adap1197.html.

[61]"Diet and Stress in Vascular Disease," *Journal of the American Medical Association,* vol. 176, no. 9 (June 3, 1961), p. 806. Thus, the coronary health benefits of a vegetarian diet have been known for over thirty-five years.

[62]Neal Barnard, *Food for Life: How the New Four Food Groups Can Save Your Life* (New York: Harmony Books, 1993), pp. 144–47.

human flourishing, because it isn't. On the contrary, it is *detrimental* to human health and well-being.[63]

A Utilitarian Gambit: Perhaps Human Gustatory Pleasure Outweighs Animal Suffering

A speciesistic carnivore might object that I have conveniently omitted one of her pertinent beliefs: (p_{17}) Human pleasure always outweighs animal suffering. Given (p_{17}), since humans derive gustatory pleasure from eating the flesh of nonhuman animals, other things are *not* equal. Accordingly, there is a justifying reason for the agony billions of farm animals are forced to endure: taste.

First, *you* do not actually believe (p_{17}). Remember Harman's cat. You do not believe that the pleasure the thugs get from burning a cat alive morally justifies their disregarding the cat's interest in avoiding suffering. You do not believe that the pleasure a sadistic Satanist gets out of slowly torturing a fully conscious dog by skinning and eating it alive (even if he gets immense *gustatory* pleasure from doing so) outweighs the dog's interest in avoiding such suffering.

---

[63]These findings are hardly surprising when one considers that both the American Heart Association (AHA) and the American Cancer Society (ACS) recommend a diet that is *high* in complex carbohydrates and fiber, and *low* in protein, dietary cholesterol, fat (especially saturated fat), sodium, alcohol, carcinogens and procarcinogens. Specifically, complex carbohydrates should comprise 55 to 70 percent of our calories, fat should provide less than 30 percent (preferably 10–15 percent) of our calories, protein should make up 10–12 percent of our calories, dietary cholesterol should not exceed 300 mg a day (0 mg is optimal, since there is no minimum amount of dietary cholesterol required), and fiber consumption should be 25–30 grams a day. In stark contrast, the typical American *meat-based* diet is 40–50 percent fat (most of which is saturated), 30 percent carbohydrate, 25 percent protein and contains 400+ mg of cholesterol per day. These statistics are to be expected since meat is high in fat, high in protein, and high in cholesterol (only animal products contain cholesterol), but contains no complex carbohydrates and no fiber. In fact, it is almost impossible to adhere to the AHA's and ACS's dietary guidelines while consuming a meat-based diet, whereas satisfying these guidelines is virtually inevitable when one eats only from the PCRM's *new* four food groups.

You simply do not believe that trivial human pleasures outweigh the most significant interests of nonhuman animals.

Second, in assessing whether a carnivore's pleasure in eating meat outweighs the pain of the animal that became that meat, it is a mistake to compare the pleasure had by eating meat with the frustration of eating nothing at all. Rather, to assess the pleasure gotten *by eating meat,* one must compare the pleasure one would get from eating meat with the pleasure one would get from eating something else.[64] Suppose your only food options are beef tacos or bean tostadas. If you would get ten hedons of pleasure from the tacos and nine from the tostadas, then only *one* hedon would be attributable *to eating meat.* Since, for any meat item you could consume, there is a vegetarian item which would give you nearly as much pleasure, it is very unlikely that the minimal pleasure one gets *from eating meat* outweighs the prolonged and excruciating pain of castration, branding, dehorning, tail docking, etc.[65]

Third, animals aren't the only beings who suffer as a result of the meat industry. Billions of *humans* suffer as well, including the 1.3 billion people worldwide suffering from chronic hunger;[66] the millions of carnivores themselves who are suffering from heart disease, cancer, stroke, osteoporosis, and obesity; and these carnivores' children who are well on their way to a shortened lifetime of debilitating disease as a result of being fed a meat-based diet by their parents. By not eating (or serving) meat we greatly reduce our chance of suffering a litany of debilitating diseases, we greatly reduce our children's risk of suffering from these same diseases,

---

[64]Bart Gruzalski makes a similar point. See his "The Case against Raising and Killing Animals for Food" in *Animal Rights and Human Obligations,* op. cit., pp. 183f.

[65]Here, for the sake of argument, I assume that the carnivore would get a bit more pleasure from the meat dish than the vegetarian dish. This assumption may well be false, as Gruzalski notes: "Since much of the world's population finds that vegetarian meals can be delightfully tasty, there is good reason for thinking that the pleasures many people derive from eating meat can be completely replaced with pleasure from eating vegetables" (ibid., p. 183). Consider also the added pleasure one gets from trying new dishes. For an excellent discussion of these points, see Gruzalski, ibid., pp. 184f.

[66]Jeremy Rifkin, *Beyond Beef* (New York: Dutton, 1992), p. 177.

and we, at least indirectly, help to reduce world hunger by reducing the demand for grain-fed meat, freeing up grain for humans.
Thus, even if you were a speciesist who did believe (p_{17}) and only
cared about *human* suffering, consistency with your other beliefs
would still require you to stop eating meat.

Perhaps Plants Feel Pain

Perhaps, but *you* don't believe they do. You walk on grass, mow
your lawn, and trim your hedges without any concern that you
might be causing plants pain. But you would never walk on your
dog or trim your dog's legs, because you are certain that doing so
would cause your dog terrible pain. Mere conjecture that plants
might feel pain won't undermine my argument, for my argument
is predicated on *your* beliefs. Since you do not believe that plants
feel pain, the objection under consideration gives *you* no reason to
continue eating meat.

The Supreme Dietitian

People often attempt to justify their carnivorous habits by claiming
that God intends us to eat meat, citing their preferred religious text
as evidence of God's will. This "justification" is particularly puzzling
since all major religions teach compassion for all living creatures.
Islam advocates kindness to animals; the Hindu doctrine of reincar-
nation encourages equal respect for all animals; and the First Precept
of Buddhist ethical conduct is not to harm sentient beings.[67] Both
Judaism and Christianity accept the Old Testament, which states:
"And God said, 'Behold, I have given you every plant yielding seed
which is upon the face of the earth, and every tree with seed in its
fruit; you shall have them for food'" (Genesis 1:29). So why think that

[67]Evelyn Elkin Giefer, "Religion and Animal Rights," *Mainstream,* vol. 27,
no. 1 (Spring 1996), p. 13. There Giefer cites Mohammed's teaching
(Hadith Mishkat, book 6, ch. 7, 8:178): "A good deed done to an animal
is as meritorious as a good deed done to a human being, while an act
of cruelty to an animal is as bad as an act of cruelty to a human being."
Giefer also notes that the Hindu Bhagavad Gita (verse 5.18) "proclaims
that a self-realized soul is able to understand the equality of all beings"
(p. 13).

God intends us to eat meat? Finding writings in these texts which contradict the teachings mentioned here won't resolve the matter, since if these texts' teachings are self-contradictory, then we are left with no clear guidance as to what God intends us to eat.

Fortunately, we can bypass this unpromising hermeneutical project altogether. There is a much more compelling refutation of the "God intends us to eat meat" defense. If God intends us to eat meat, then God is either ignorant, irrational, or malevolent. If God doesn't know that eating meat causes heart attacks, cancer, strokes, etc., then he is ignorant about nutrition. If God knows that eating meat is harmful to our health but intends us to do it anyway, then either he is malevolent and wants bad things to happen to us, or he is irrational since, despite wanting us to be healthy, he intends us to eat a diet detrimental to our health. Since, by definition, God is neither ignorant nor irrational nor malevolent, it is incoherent to believe that God intends us to eat meat.

The "Free Range" Fantasy

A critic might object to my argument as follows:

> O.K., I understand your strategy. You're trying to show that, given my other beliefs, consistency forces me to admit that eating meat is wrong. Now, suppose I admit that factory farming causes prolonged, unnecessary, excruciating pain and that, as a result, believing (p_1)–(p_{12}) commits me to the immorality of eating factory farm-raised meat. Even so, you've yet to show that my beliefs commit me to the immorality of eating humanely raised animals. What's wrong with eating "free range" animals which are raised humanely and killed painlessly? How do my beliefs commit me to the immorality of eating them?

My response to such a critic is fourfold: First, in admitting that eating factory farm-raised meat is morally wrong, you have just admitted that it is immoral to eat over 90 percent of the meat you eat. Second, the terms "free range" and "free roaming" are not indicative of humane animal husbandry practices. According to the labelling division of the USDA, "a free range bird is one that has access to the outdoors," no matter how small the outdoor pen. The term "free roaming" just means birds which have not been raised in cages, even though they are permanently confined in a warehouse.[68] Thus, un-caged broiler chickens with the industry-recommended seven-tenths of a square foot of floor space can legally be sold as "free roaming" birds. Moreover, the painful mutilations described above are also routinely performed in both "free range" and nonintensive farms. Plus, even if the "free range" animals had it good while they were on the farm, there are no humane livestock transportation companies and no humane slaughterhouses. The only way to be sure that the animal you are eating was raised humanely and killed painlessly is to raise and kill her yourself. Third, even if you had the time, space, and will to raise and kill your own "dinner," you would still be jeopardizing your own health and the health of your loved ones, as well as wasting resources which could be better spent helping to alleviate human hunger and malnutrition. Even "happy cows" require 12.9 pounds of grain to produce a pound of meat.[69] Fourth and most important, you already believe (p_{14}), that other things being equal, it is worse to kill a conscious sentient creature than it is to kill a plant. An example of Andrew Tardiff's will illustrate the point. Suppose we could perform a human-benefiting experiment on either a dog or a plant with equally reliable and equally valuable results, but that the experiment will inevitably result in the death of the test subject. Anyone who accepts (p_{14}) will surely admit that we ought to perform the experiment on the plant. For those who still have doubts, Tardiff modifies his example: Once again, we could perform a human-benefiting experiment on either a dog or a plant, and once again the test subject will be killed in the course of the experiment, only this time suppose that we would get much greater human benefit by testing on the plant than we would by testing on the dog.[70] Surely, you will grant that we ought to perform the experiment on the plant.

---

[68]Suzanne Hamlin, "Free Range? Natural? Sorting Out Labels," *The New York Times,* section C (November 13, 1996), p. 1. See also Davis, *Prisoned Chickens, Poisoned Eggs,* pp. 127–31.

[69]NASS, USDA, *Agricultural Statistics 1997,* Table 1-72, p. I-47. Thanks to the routine use of antibiotics and growth hormones, this 12.9:1 grain-to-meat conversion ratio is down from the 16:1 ratio often sighted.

[70]Tardiff presents and discusses both of these examples in his excellent article "Simplifying the Case for Vegetarianism," *Social Theory and Practice,* vol. 22, no. 3 (Fall 1996), pp. 302f.

Now, compare this case with the case for food. You already believe that, when other things are equal, it is worse to kill a conscious sentient animal than it is to kill a plant. But in the case of food, other things are not equal. Since a plant-based diet is more nutritious and human health-promoting than a meat-based diet, (p_{14}) commits you to the view that it is worse to kill conscious sentient animals for food than it is to kill plants for food, even if those animals have been raised humanely.

Consistency: The Two-Edged Sword

In section 4, I argued that consistency rationally requires you to admit that eating meat is immoral. I did so by showing that your beliefs, when combined with two indisputable facts, entail that eating meat is morally wrong, and *ipso facto* that vegetarianism is morally required. In effect, I presented you with a valid argument of the form

$$[(p_1),(p_2), \ldots ,(p_{16}),(f_1),(f_2)] \to Q,$$

where Q = Eating meat is immoral. Of course, as Harman and Pollock have pointed out vis-à-vis skepticism, being presented with a valid skeptical argument of the form

$$[P_1, \ldots ,P_n] \to \sim K,$$

does not force you to accept $\sim K$, for it may be more reasonable to reject some premise P_i than to accept $\sim K$.[71]

Similarly, one might object to my argument as follows: "Consistency does not demand that I accept Q. Consistency demands that I either accept Q or reject one of my present beliefs. What's to stop me from doing the latter?" First, the cases are not analogous. In rejecting some P_i of the skeptic's argument, you are rejecting one

---

[71]As Gilbert Harman puts it, "[T]here is no plausible rule of acceptance saying that if we believe both *P* and *If P, then Q*, we may always infer or accept *Q*. Perhaps we should stop believing *P* or *If P, then Q* rather than believe *Q*." (*Thought* [Princeton and London: Princeton University Press, 1973], p. 157). John Pollock makes a similar point in *Contemporary Theories of Knowledge* (Totowa, N.J.: Rowman and Littlefield, 1986), pp. 5f.

of the skeptic's beliefs; whereas in rejecting some (p_i) of my argument, you are rejecting one of your own firmly held beliefs. Since (p_1)–(p_{16}) are *your* beliefs, it's not at all clear that you could simply stop believing one of them—for example, you could no more stop believing that animals are capable of feeling pain than you could stop believing that humans feel pain. Furthermore, my argument actually consists of a family of arguments predicated on different subsets of $\{(p_1), \ldots, (p_{16})\}$. Thus, while one can escape the clutches of the skeptic's argument by rejecting a single P_i, to escape my argument you must reject a number of your beliefs. Second, even if you could reject these beliefs, it would be irrational for you to do so. After all, as a philosopher, you are interested in more than mere consistency; you are interested in truth. Consequently, you will not reject just any belief(s) for the sake of consistency. You will reject the belief(s) you think most likely to be false. Now, presumably, you already think your belief system is for the most part reasonable, or you would have already made significant changes in it. So, you will want to reject as few beliefs as possible. Since (p_1)–(p_{16}) are rife with implications, rejecting several of these propositions would force you to reject countless other beliefs on pain of incoherence, whereas accepting Q would require minimal belief revision on your part. Simply put, Q coheres with your otherwise already reasonable beliefs, whereas ~Q does not, thus making it more reasonable to accept Q than to reject any of your other beliefs.

5. CONCLUSION

Let me conclude by noting two further implications of your beliefs. First, your beliefs not only commit you to the obligatoriness of vegetarianism, but also to the obligatoriness of a vegan diet, that is, a diet devoid of *all* animal products. Here's why: In section 4 we found a vegan diet to be the most nutritious and healthful diet a human can consume.[72] Plus, contrary to what many people think,

---

[72]The PCRM recommends a vegan diet centered around the *new* four food groups. Anyone who eats only from these four food groups will be consuming a vegan diet. Any article advocating a vegan diet would be remiss

it is extremely *easy* to adopt a vegan diet. To see just how easy, recall that in section 3, I provided a long list of readily available, tasty vegetarian dishes which one could easily eat in place of standard meat fare. Each of the vegetarian dishes listed there is actually vegan. Since eggs and dairy products are both nutritionally unnecessary and easy to avoid, we can now see why your beliefs entail that eating these products is morally wrong.

Let us start by examining the modern egg industry. Two distinct strains of chickens have been developed: "layers" for egg production and "broilers" for meat production. Since layer strains are thought to produce insufficient and inferior meat and since males do not produce eggs, male chicks of the layer strain are identified by chicken sexers, who throw them into plastic bags where they are allowed to suffocate.[73] In 1995, 247 million unwanted male chicks met this fate.[74] Like their broiler counterparts, female layers are debeaked at one week of age. However, since layers are kept alive longer, most egg producers debeak their birds a second time around twelve weeks of age.[75] Worse still, layers are permanently confined in 16″ by 18″ battery cages, five or six birds to a cage.[76]

---

not to discuss the *only* legitimate nutritional concern facing vegans, namely, vitamin B_{12} deficiency. The conventional wisdom is that vitamin B_{12} is virtually nonexistent in plant foods. New evidence suggests: (1) that B_{12} can be found in plants, (2) that organically grown plants contain higher levels of B_{12} than those grown with chemical fertilizers, (3) that plant roots are able to absorb vitamins produced by soil microorganisms (B_{12} is only produced by microorganisms), and (4) that vegans should be able to obtain B_{12} by consuming organically grown produce (T. Colin Campbell, "B_{12} Breakthrough: Missing Nutrient Found in Plants," *New Century Nutrition,* vol. 2, no. 11 [November 1996], p. 1). Because this evidence is preliminary, those following a vegan diet should make sure they have a reliable source of vitamin B_{12} in their diets (reliable sources include fortified soy, rice, and nut milks; fortified cereals; fortified textured soy protein; and Red Star T-6635+ nutritional yeast) or they should take a B_{12} supplement.

[73]Robbins, *Diet for a New America,* p. 54.
[74]Davis, *Prisoned Chickens, Poisoned Eggs,* p. 105.
[75]Mason and Singer, *Animal Factories,* p. 39.
[76]Karen Davis, "The Plight of Poultry," *The Animals' Agenda* (July/August 1996), p. 38. Also see Robbins, *Diet for a New America,* p. 63.

Thus, the average layer has only 48–58 square inches of living space, not much larger than a 5″ by 8″ index card. The cages have slanted wire mesh flooring totally inappropriate for the birds' feet, which sometimes grow fixed to the cage floor making it impossible to reach food and water.[77] Ninety-eight percent of the eggs produced in the United States come from layers permanently confined in such battery cages.[78] After a year and a half of this existence (assuming they don't die in their cages, as do 12–18 percent of them per year[79]), about the time when their egg production begins to wane, the birds are either crammed even more tightly into portable crates, transported to the slaughterhouse, and turned into soup and other processed foods,[80] or they are kept for another laying cycle, whichever is cheaper. Those unfortunate enough to be kept and "recycled" are force-molted to prepare them for the next laying cycle. The primary method of forced molting involves the withholding of all food from the hens for a period of 5–14 days.[81] After one or two forced-molt laying cycles, the spent birds will suffer one of two fates: Either they will be sent to slaughter as described above or, as is increasingly favored, they will meet with on-farm disposal whereby they are ground up alive and fed to the next generation of hens.[82] These birds are forced to endure all of this inhumane treatment, just so we can indulge in an inherently unhealth-

---

[77]Singer, *Animal Liberation,* p. 110. The industry justification for such inappropriate flooring is that it allows urine and feces to drop through the cage and the slant facilitates automatic egg collection.

[78]William Dudley-Cash, "Study Shows Adoption Rate of Technology by Laying Hen Industry," *Feedstuffs* (November 4, 1991), p. 11; and Robbins, *Diet for a New America,* p. 53.

[79]Mason and Singer, *Animal Factories,* p. 25.

[80]Ibid., p. 6.

[81]Davis, *Prisoned Chickens, Poisoned Eggs,* pp. 74–76. Davis explains molting and the industry rationale behind forced molting as follows: "Molting refers to the replacement of old feathers by new ones. In nature, all birds replace all of their feathers in the course of a year. . . . Egg laying tapers off as the female bird concentrates her energies on growing new feathers and staying warm" (p. 74). This process naturally takes four months, whereas during a forced molt, the process only takes a month or two. (p. 74)

[82]Davis, *Prisoned Chickens, Poisoned Eggs,* p. 77.

ful product loaded with cholesterol (300 milligrams per egg) and fat (50 percent of eggs' calories come from fat, most of which is saturated), which has somehow come to be associated with breakfast. Since eggs are nutritionally unnecessary, are easy to avoid, and come from an unnecessarily cruel industry, your beliefs entail that it is immoral to eat them.

As for dairy products, 57 percent of dairy cows are raised in factory farms, where their calves are taken away within one or two days and where they are constantly reimpregnated, pumped full of antibiotics and bovine growth hormone, milked two to three times a day, suffer from mastitis, fed unnatural diets, and prevented from moving about freely. After a few years when their milk production wanes, they, like their meat-producing counterparts, will be inhumanely loaded onto trucks and shipped to the slaughterhouse without food or water and without protection from the elements, where they will be transformed into ground beef. Lest one think this a rare occurrence, in 1997, over 2.9 million dairy cows were slaughtered in federally inspected plants.[83] As for their calves, if the calf is female, she will either be kept or sold to another dairy farmer, but if the calf is male, he will typically be sold to veal farmers who will chain him at the neck and feed him an iron-deficient diet for 14–16 weeks before sending him off to slaughter.[84] Consequently, when one purchases dairy products, one is not only supporting the unnecessary and inhumane confinement of dairy cows, one is also indirectly supporting the even more inhumane veal industry. Since, according to both the ADA and the PCRM, dairy products are in no way necessary for optimum human health, since dairy products are easy to avoid, and since the dairy industry inflicts untold suffering and death on dairy cows and their calves, your beliefs commit you to the immorality of consuming dairy products.

Finally, your beliefs commit you to the immorality of purchasing personal care and household products that have been tested on animals. These tests include the Draize eye irritancy test,[85] the lethal

---

[83]*Livestock Slaughter 1997 Summary,* NASS, USDA, p. 82.
[84]Ibid., pp. 12f.
[85]The Draize test involves dripping caustic substances such as bleach or shampoo into restrained rabbits' eyes, frequently resulting in hemorrhage, ulceration, and blindness. Rabbits are used for convenience, because they

dose 50 percent (LD50) test, dermal toxicity tests, and injection tests. Eighty percent of the animals in these tests receive no anesthesia. Moreover, these tests are unnecessary and unreliable. For example, the crude LD50 test, in which a test group of animals is force-fed a substance until 50 percent of the animals die (which is often due to stomach rupture rather than the effects of the substance *per se*), provides no useful data which can be reliably extrapolated to humans.[86] In most cases, avoiding products which have been tested on animals is *easy,* since equally effective, equally priced, equally safe, alternative products which have not been tested on animals and which contain no animal ingredients are almost always readily available. Moreover, determining which products are cruelty free will not require a great deal of time or effort on your part, for these products typically advertise their cruelty-free status on the label. Since one can easily reduce one's contribution to laboratory-generated animal suffering by buying cruelty-free personal care and household products instead of those tested on animals (usually they are right next to each other on the supermarket shelves), *your* beliefs entail that you are morally obligated to do so.

The implications of your beliefs are clear. Given your beliefs, it follows that: (1) eating meat is morally wrong; (2) eating animal products is morally wrong; and (3) purchasing personal care and household products which have been tested on animals is morally wrong (provided comparable cruelty-free products are readily available). These conclusions were not derived from some highly contentious ethical theory which you can easily reject, but from your own firmly held beliefs. Furthermore, these conclusions follow, regardless of your views on speciesism, animal equality, and animal rights. Even those of you who are staunch speciesists are committed to the immorality of these practices, given your other beliefs.

---

have no tear ducts to flush out the offending substance. Of course, this makes them poor models for humans who do have tear ducts. Sidney Gendin, "The Use of Animals in Science" in *Animal Rights and Human Obligations,* op. cit., pp. 199f.

[86]Robert Sharpe, "Animal Experiments—A Failed Technology," in *Animal Experimentation: The Consensus Changes,* ed. Gill Langley (New York: Chapman and Hall, 1989), pp. 101–104. Also see Singer, *Animal Liberation,* pp. 53–56.

Consequently, consistency demands that you embrace the immorality of these practices and modify your behavior accordingly.[87]

APPENDIX

(p_1) Other things being equal, a world with less pain and suffering is better than a world with more pain and suffering.

(p_2) A world with less unnecessary suffering is better than a world with more unnecessary suffering.

(p_3) Unnecessary cruelty is wrong and *prima facie* should not be supported or encouraged.

(p_4) We ought to take steps to make the world a better place.

(p_4') We ought to do what we reasonably can to avoid making the world a worse place.

(p_5) A morally good person will take steps to make the world a better place and even stronger steps to avoid making the world a worse place.

(p_6) Even a minimally decent person would take steps to help reduce the amount of unnecessary pain and suffering in the world, *if s/he could do so with very little effort.*

(p_7) I am a morally good person.

(p_8) I am at least a minimally decent person.

(p_9) I am the sort of person who certainly would take steps to help reduce the amount of pain and suffering in the world, *if I could do so with very little effort.*

[87]Research on this project was supported by a generous grant from the Culture and Animals Foundation, for which I am extremely grateful. Versions of this paper have been presented at the MidSouth Philosophy Conference, the Illinois Philosophical Association Meetings, and the Conference on Value Inquiry. I would like to thank those in attendance for their comments. I would also like to thank John Carroll, Mark Heller, Alastair Norcross, Louis Pojman, Trudy Pojman, Eric Richards, Jim Sauer, Ray Dybzinski, Nathan Nobis, Bob Hicks and the philosophy faculty at Southern Methodist University for their helpful suggestions. Special thanks to Lisa Joniak whose detailed comments on numerous versions improved every section of the paper.

(p_{10}) Many nonhuman animals (certainly all vertebrates) are capable of feeling pain.

(p_{11}) It is morally wrong to cause an animal unnecessary pain or suffering.

(p_{12}) It is morally wrong and despicable to treat animals inhumanely for *no good reason.*

(p_{13}) We ought to euthanize untreatably injured, suffering animals to put them out of their misery whenever feasible.

(p_{14}) Other things being equal, it is worse to kill a conscious sentient animal than it is to kill a plant.

(p_{15}) We have a duty to help preserve the environment for future generations (at least for future human generations).

(p_{16}) One ought to minimize one's contribution toward environmental degradation, *especially in those ways requiring minimal effort on one's part.*

For Further Reflection

1. Why does Engel make a point of *not* predicating his argument on any particular moral theory? Explain the strengths or weaknesses of applied ethical arguments not grounded in theoretical considerations.

2. Must ethical vegetarianism be grounded in the *equal* moral considerability of animals or is their *mere* moral considerability sufficient to make vegetarianism obligatory?

3. How does Engel defend the claim that it is wrong to eat humanely raised meat?

4. To whom is Engel's argument directed? What conditions must one satisfy in order for Engel's argument to apply?

5. How could it be permissible for some people to eat meat and wrong for others to do so? Explain. Does Engel's argument entail an objectionable form of relativism? Why or why not?

6. What does Engel's argument imply about: (1) the use of leather, (2) attending circuses and zoos, and (3) using animals in medical research?

7. Are there any good reasons to eat meat which Engel has neglected to address and which would override all the suffering factory farm animals are made to endure?

Further Readings for Chapter 14

Frey, R. G. *Rights, Killing and Suffering*. Oxford: Basil Blackwell, 1983.

Rachels, James. *Created From Animals: the Moral Implications of Darwinism*. Oxford: Oxford University Press, 1990.

Regan, Tom. *The Case for Animal Rights*. Berkeley: University of California, 1983. The most comprehensive philosophical treatise in favor of animal rights.

Regan, Tom and Peter Singer, eds. *Animal Rights and Human Obligations*. Englewood Cliffs, N.J.: Prentice-Hall, 1976.

Robbins, John. *Diet for a New America: How Your Food Choices Affect Your, Health, Happiness, and the Future of Life on Earth*. Walpole, N.H.: Stillpoint, 1987. A strong case for vegetarianism.

Rohr, Janelle, ed. *Animal Rights: Opposing Viewpoints*. San Diego: Greenhaven Press, 1989.

Singer, Peter. *Animal Liberation*. 2nd ed. New York: New York Review of Books, 1990.

VandeVeer, D. and Pierce, C., eds. *People, Penguins, and Plastic Trees*. Belmont, Cal.: Wadsworth, 1990.

CHAPTER 15

Our Duties
to the Environment

Human beings have lived on Earth about 100,000 years, a very short time in relation to the age of the universe (15 billion years) or even to the life of our planet (4.6 billion years). Civilization developed only 10,000 years ago, and the wheel was invented 4,000 years ago. If we compacted the history of Earth into a movie lasting one year, running 146 years per second, life would not appear until March, multicellular organisms not till November, dinosaurs not till December 13 (lasting until the 26th), mammals not till December 15, *Homo sapiens* (our species) not until 11 minutes to midnight on December 31, and civilization one minute ago. Yet in a very short time, say less than 200 years, a mere 0.000002 percent of Earth's life, humans have become capable of seriously altering the entire biosphere. In some respects we have already altered it more profoundly than it has changed in the past *billion* years. Paraphrasing Winston Churchill's remark about the British air force during World War II, "Never have so few done so much in so short a time."

How did things get this way? How did the "environmental crisis" come about?

Humankind is part of nature. We are animals who have evolved from simpler biological forms over hundreds of thousands, even millions, of years. As we noted above, human beings as we know them (*Homo sapiens sapiens*) have lived on Earth about 100,000 years. Originating in Africa, the migrations to Europe and Asia took place some 40,000 years ago. We are omnivores (carnivores and herbivores). It is natural for us to eat plants and to kill other animals for food. We have sometimes killed other humans for food. All animals must eat other organisms to live. The big fish eats the smaller fish and so on down the trophic pyramid. Death is natural and inevitable. Species normally maintain a steady population size through competition. Most seeds are wasted and many infants die. Excess seed provides insurance for survival.

Our zone of life, the biosphere, inhabits land and air up to an altitude of five miles, water down to about five miles. Proportionately, this is thinner than the skin of an apple, and it represents all the life we know of in the universe. We conclude that life, being rare and fragile, is precious. Human beings are the most intelligent beings we know of in the universe. They are the only ones who systematically deliberate on their actions. They use language, store information, and through science and technology exercise a powerful influence over the earth.

While humans are animals, determined like other animals by their genes, they have created artifacts, sometimes called *memes,** whereby they can alter their natural fate. Through the invention of medicine they maintain health and extend life expectancy; through large-scale weapons they can destroy large populations. They cannot outrun the gazelle or leopard, but by the use of their inventions, including the internal combustion engine and wheeled wagons, they can travel over land twice as fast as the swiftest animal. They cannot defy gravity and fly like the eagle, but they can master the laws of aerodynamics and put planes into the skies to outpace the fastest birds. They cannot swim underwater for more than a few minutes, but through their understanding of hydrophysics, they can construct submarines that enable them to traverse the oceans faster than any fish. And now they stand on the brink of asexual modes of reproduction, the cloning of their own kind. Through memes nature is *swamped* by culture, and evolution is replaced by the logic of technology. Humanity replaces natural selection as the decisive force in the development of life on Earth. Sophocles, in our first reading, writing more than four hundred years before Christ, was right: "Numberless are the world's wonders, but none more wonderful than man."

Memes refers to human inventions, including cultural institutions and practices, which redirect natural behavioral patterns. Morality is a meme (it serves our purpose of promoting human flourishing), law and political organization are other examples. Technology is also a meme.

For the first nine-tenths of our species' existence, humans lived as *hunter-gatherers* (males mostly doing the hunting and females mostly doing the gathering). In what is sometimes referred to as the Old Stone Age (Paleolithic period), our ancestors lived nomadic lives in small communities (fewer than fifty people), gathering edible wild plants, hunting wild animals (bison, deer, mammoths), and fishing. They had few tools, lived mainly by their own muscle power and foot-speed, and probably had a short life expectancy. Their impact on the environment was slight.

About 10,000 years ago the *agricultural revolution* (Mesolithic period) occurred, marked by a shift from nomadic life to agricultural communities with domesticated animals and cultivated plants. Slash-and-burn techniques were used, burning sections of forests and using the ashes as fertilizer. When the land was overcultivated, the community would move on to a new area and clear it. Meanwhile, they noticed that when left alone, the old land would rejuvenate. This led to the practice of rotation farming: letting the land lie fallow for a period between plantings. During this period, domesticated animals were used for plowing and hauling material. Food production was more plentiful and secure, so the population increased. In this condition people acquired material goods, could store food for winter, and barter with others, especially craftsmen who produced pottery, tools, rugs, and the like. Eventually, towns and villages grew up, which served as centers of trade, government, social entertainment, and religion. During this period, while life expectancy increased and the quality of life became increasingly more civilized and secure, significant environmental damage began to occur. Poor agricultural policies led to the spread of desertification. Cities were often cesspools of sewage, garbage, and disease.

The third great cultural development, the *industrial revolution,* began in England about 1760, spreading to the rest of Europe and the United States in the nineteenth century. It ushered in the transition from manual to machine techniques of production, giving rise to the steam engine, the spinning jenny, and the power loom. Having depleted the forests which once covered most of England and Ireland, the industrialists turned to coal as the nonrenewable energy resource that would sustain factories and steamships. Coal mining was a dangerous occupation and urban coal-burning produced a dangerous smog, more dangerous to health than in contemporary American cities. Many miners and citydwellers died of lung disease.

The use of machines meant that fewer farmers were needed to produce food, so urban factory jobs expanded. The story of the industrial revolution is one of increased wealth, especially for successful entrepreneurs, of the end of feudalism and rural society, of the development of city life, and of the exponential growth and dominance of technology in our lives.

In the last hundred years or so we have invented electricity, the light bulb, the refrigerator, the telephone, cinema, radio, television, the automobile, the airplane, the spaceship, the submarine, the air conditioner, the skyscraper, antibiotics, heart and liver transplants, the birth control pill, safe abortion, the microwave oven, the atom bomb, nuclear energy, and the digital computer—including communication on the World Wide Web. We have discovered how to clone animals and are on the verge of full-scale human genetic engineering. Breakthroughs on cures for Alzheimer's disease, cancer, and other diseases are on the horizon. Through the miracles of science and technology, we have enabled millions of people over the face of the earth to live longer with more freedom, power, and knowledge than our ancestors could dream of. Only in science fiction were these wonders of modern life even hinted at.

Yet with this new freedom, power, and knowledge has come a dark side. The automobile kills hundreds of thousands of people throughout the world each year (more Americans have died in automobile accidents than in all the battlefields of all the wars our nation has fought). It produces chemical pollution, which degrades the atmosphere, causing illness, and is bringing on the dangerous global warming, called the greenhouse effect. Refrigerators and air conditioners enable us to preserve food and live comfortably in hot seasons and climates, but they also use chlorofluorocarbons (CFCs) which rise into the stratosphere and deplete the thin ozone layer that protects us from harmful ultraviolet radiation. This has given rise to an increase in skin cancer, especially deadly melanoma, and has harmful effects on plankton, which are vital to the food chain of marine animals. Nuclear power could provide safe, inexpensive energy to the world, but instead it has been used to decimate cities and threaten a global holocaust. Disasters like the nuclear plant steam explosion at Chernobyl in the former Soviet Union have spread harmful radiation over thousands of square miles, causing death and deformity. Such horrendous threats have replaced the fear of nuclear war as the worst potential catastrophe, causing widespread public distrust of the nuclear power industry. Nuclear waste piles up with no solution in sight. But our modern way of life does require energy, lots of it. So we burn fossil fuels, especially coal, which, unbeknownst to the public at large, is probably more dangerous than nuclear energy, causing cancer and other diseases, polluting the air with sulphur dioxide, and producing acid rain, which is destroying our rivers and lakes and killing trees. Medical science found cures for tuberculosis and syphilis and has aided in greatly lowering infant mortality, but in the process we have allowed an exponential growth of population, producing crowded cities and putting a strain on our resources. The more people, the more energy needed; the more energy produced, the more pollution; the more pollution, the more our lives are threatened by disease. Add to all this the problem of a *just* distribution of resources. The increasing discrepancy of wealth between the rich and the poor, both within and between nations, portends a global tragedy, one that in sheer suffering could make previous socially destructive events seem minuscule by comparison.

And so the story goes. For each blessing of modern technology a corresponding risk comes into being, as the tails of the same coin. With each new invention comes frightful responsibility. Technophiles put their money on technology's ability to meet all our basic needs and satisfy everyone. They reason, "We have put a man on the moon, learned how to increase food production as never before thought possible, and discovered the cure for cancer and how to clone animals and human beings. All we need to do is put our best brainpower to work on our problems and we can create the necessary technology to solve them." Technophobes see this faith in technology not only as naive, but as a dangerous impediment to progress. In fact, they see technology (or its overuse) as the main problem, undermining the human spirit, devastating community, and threatening to dictate our lives.

There was once a man who discovered his own shadow. He became so fascinated with it that he gave pride of place to it, treated it with deference and respect, until finally, neglecting his other duties, he became a shadow to his own shadow. Likewise, we may be in danger of being enslaved by our own devices.

We turn to our readings. After the selection from Sophocles' *Antigone,* we consider Robert Heilbroner's probing "What Has Posterity Ever Done for Me?" and ask what is the basis of our obligation to leave the world and its resources in good condition for future generations. Next we read Garrett Hardin's classic "The Tragedy of the Commons" in which he argues that there is no technological solution to our environmental problems, but we must agree upon mutually coercive rules that will assure a good for us all, as well as for future people. Next we take up David Watson's "We All Live in Bhopal" in which Bradford contends that industrial society is creating a global extermination camp. Finally, for an opposite perspective, we read William Baxter's "People or Penguins: The Case of Optimal Pollution," in which he argues for a humanistic, as opposed to environment-centered, social policy.

On Mankind's Power over Nature

SOPHOCLES

Sophocles (c. 497–405 B.C.), a Greek tragic playwright, wrote 123 plays, of which only seven survive. Two of his major plays are *Oedipus Rex* and *Antigone,* from which this is taken. Sophocles recognizes the mighty power human ingenuity has exercised over nature, but points out at least one of our limits.

Numberless are the world's wonders, but none
More wonderful than man; the stormgray sea
Yields to his prows, the huge crests bear him high;
Earth, holy and inexhaustible, is graven
With shining furrows where his plows have gone
Year after year, the timeless labor of stallions.

The lightboned birds and beasts that cling to cover,
The lithe fish lighting their reaches of dim water,
All are taken, tamed in the net of his mind;
The lion on the hill, the wild horse windy-maned,
Resign to him; and his blunt yoke has broken
The sultry shoulders of the mountain bull.

Words also, and thought as rapid as air,
He fashions to his good use; statecraft is his.
The searching arrows of frost he need fear no more,
That under a starry sky are endured with pain.
He has made himself secure from all but one enemy—
In the late wind of death he cannot prevail.

From Sophocles, *Antigone,* translated by Dudley Fitts and Robert Fitzgerald (New York: Harvest Books, 1939).

What Has Posterity Ever Done for Me?

ROBERT HEILBRONER

Robert Heilbroner was for many years professor of economics at the New School for Social Research in New York. He is the author of several books, including *The Worldly Philosophers* and *Marxism: For and Against.*

Heilbroner asks why we should care about future people or whether humanity survives into the distant future. Citing fellow economists who argue that we have no reason to sacrifice for the unknown future, Heilbroner expresses outrage at this callous disregard for future people. Admitting that he cannot give a rational argument for this view, he appeals to Adam's Smith's principle of sentiment or inner conscience, which urges us to work for the long-range survival of humanity.

Will mankind survive? Who knows? The question I want to put is more searching: Who cares? It is clear that most of us today do not care—or at least do not care enough. How many of us would be willing to give up some minor convenience—say, the use of aerosols—in the hope that this might extend the life of man on earth by a hundred years? Suppose we also knew with a high degree of certainty that humankind could not survive a thousand years unless we gave up our wasteful diet of meat, abandoned all pleasure driving, cut back on every use of energy that was not essential to the maintenance of a bare minimum. Would we care enough for posterity to pay the price of its survival?

I doubt it. A thousand years is unimaginably distant. Even a century far exceeds our powers of empathetic imagination. By the year 2075, I shall probably have been dead for three quarters of a century. My children will also likely be dead, and my grandchildren, if I have any, will be in their dotage. What does it matter to me, then, what life will be like in 2075, much less 3075? Why should I lift a finger to affect events that will have no more meaning for me seventy-five years after my death than those that happened seventy-five years before I was born?

There is no rational answer to that terrible question. No argument based on reason will lead me to care for posterity or to lift a finger in its behalf. Indeed, by every rational consideration, precisely the opposite answer is thrust upon us with irresistible force. As a Distinguished Professor of political economy at the University of London has written in the current winter issue of *Business and Society Review:*

> Suppose that, as a result of using up all the world's resources, human life did come to an end. So what? What is so desirable about an indefinite continuation of the human species, religious convictions apart? It may well be that nearly everybody who is already here on earth would be reluctant to die, and that everybody has an instinctive fear of death. But one must not confuse this with the notion that, in any meaningful sense, generations who are yet unborn can be said to be better off if they are born than if they are not.

Thus speaks the voice of rationality. It is echoed in the book *The Economic Growth Controversy* by a Distinguished Younger Economist from the Massachusetts Institute of Technology:

> ... Geological time [has been] made comprehensible to our finite human minds by the statement that the 4.5 billion years of the earth's history [are] equivalent to once around the world in an SST. . . . Man got on eight miles before the end, and industrial man got on six feet before the end. . . . Today we are having a debate about the extent to which man ought to maximize the length of time that he is on the airplane.
>
> According to what the scientists think, the sun is gradually expanding and 12 billion years from now the earth will be swallowed up by the sun. This means that our airplane has time to go round three more times. Do we want man to be on it for all three times around the world? Are we interested in man being on for another eight miles? Are we interested in man being on for another six feet? Or are we only interested in man for a fraction of a millimeter—our lifetimes?
>
> That led me to think: Do I care what happens a thousand years from now? . . . Do I care when man gets off the airplane? I think I basically [have come] to the conclusion that I don't care whether

man is on the airplane for another eight feet, or if man is on the airplane another three times around the world.

Is it an outrageous position? I must confess it outrages me. But this is not because the economists' arguments are "wrong"—indeed, within their rational framework they are indisputably right. It is because their position reveals the limitations—worse, the suicidal dangers—of what we call "rational argument" when we confront questions that can only be decided by an appeal to an entirely different faculty from that of cool reason. More than that, I suspect that if there is cause to fear for man's survival it is because the calculus of logic and reason will be applied to problems where they have as little validity, even as little bearing, as the calculus of feeling or sentiment applied to the solution of a problem in Euclidean geometry.

If reason cannot give us a compelling argument to care for posterity—and to care desperately and totally—what can? For an answer, I turn to another distinguished economist whose fame originated in his profound examination of moral conduct. In 1759, Adam Smith published "The Theory of Moral Sentiments," in which he posed a question very much like ours, but to which he gave an answer very different from that of his latter-day descendants.

Suppose, asked Smith, that "a man of humanity" in Europe were to learn of a fearful earthquake in China—an earthquake that swallowed up its millions of inhabitants. How would that man react? He would, Smith mused, "make many melancholy reflections upon the precariousness of human life, and the vanity of all the labors of man, which could thus be annihilated in a moment. He would, too, perhaps, if he was a man of speculation, enter into many reasonings concerning the effects which this disaster might produce upon the commerce of Europe, and the trade and business of the world in general." Yet, when this fine philosophizing was over, would our "man of humanity" care much about the catastrophe in distant China? He would not. As Smith tells us, he would "pursue his business or his pleasure, take his repose for his diversion, with the same ease and tranquillity as if nothing had happened."

But now suppose, Smith says, that our man were told he was to lose his little finger on the morrow. A very different reaction would attend the contemplation of this "frivolous disaster." Our man of humanity would be reduced to a tormented state, tossing all night with fear and dread—whereas "provided he never saw them, he will snore with the most profound security over the ruin of a hundred millions of his brethren."

Next, Smith puts the critical question: Since the hurt to his finger bulks so large and the catastrophe in China so small, does this mean that a man of humanity, given the choice, would prefer the extinction of a hundred million Chinese in order to save his little finger? Smith is unequivocal in his answer. "Human nature startles at the thought," he cries, "and the world in its greatest depravity and corruption never produced such a villain as would be capable of entertaining it."

But what stays our hand? Since we are all such creatures of self-interest (and is not Smith the very patron saint of the motive of self-interest?), what moves us to give precedence to the rights of humanity over those of our own immediate well-being? The answer, says Smith, is the presence within us all of a "man within the beast," an inner creature of conscience whose insistent voice brooks no disobedience: "It is the love of what is honorable and noble, of the grandeur and dignity, and superiority of our own characters."

It does not matter whether Smith's eighteenth-century view of human nature in general or morality in particular appeals to the modern temper. What matters is that he has put the question that tests us to the quick. For it is one thing to appraise matters of life and death by the principles of rational self-interest and quite another *to take responsibility for our choice.* I cannot imagine the Distinguished Professor from the University of London personally consigning humanity to oblivion with the same equanimity with which he writes off its demise. I am certain that if the Distinguished Younger Economist from M.I.T. were made responsible for determining the precise length of stay of humanity on the SST, he would agonize over the problem and end up by exacting every last possible inch for mankind's journey.

Of course, there are moral dilemmas to be faced even if one takes one's stand on the "survivalist" principle. Mankind cannot expect to continue on earth indefinitely if we do not curb population growth, thereby consigning billions or tens of billions to the oblivion of non-birth. Yet, in this case, we sacrifice some portion of life-to-come in order that life itself may be preserved. This essential commitment to life's continuance gives us the moral authority to take measures, perhaps very harsh measures, whose justification cannot be found in the precepts of rationality, but must be sought in the unbearable anguish we feel if we imagine ourselves as the executioners of mankind.

This anguish may well be those "religious convictions," to use the phrase our London economist so casually tosses away. Perhaps to our secular cast of mind, the anguish can be more easily accepted as the furious power of the biogenetic force we see expressed in every living organism. Whatever its source, when we ask if mankind "should" survive, it is only here that we can find a rationale that gives us the affirmation we seek.

This is not to say we will discover a religious affirmation naturally welling up within us as we career toward Armageddon. We know very little about how to convince men by recourse to reason and nothing about how to convert them to religion. A hundred faiths contend for believers today, a few perhaps capable of generating that sense of caring for human salvation on earth. But, in truth, we do not know if "religion" will win out. An appreciation of the magnitude of the sacrifices required to perpetuate life may well tempt us to opt for "rationality"—to enjoy life while it is still to be enjoyed on relatively easy terms, to write mankind a shorter ticket on the SST so that some of us may enjoy the next millimeter of the trip in first-class seats.

Yet I am hopeful that in the end a survivalist ethic will come to the fore—not from the reading of a few books or the passing twinge of a pious lecture, but from an experience that will bring home to us, as Adam Smith brought home to his "man of humanity," the personal responsibility that defies all the homicidal promptings of reasonable calculation. Moreover, I believe that the coming generations, in their encounters with famine, war, and the threatened life-carrying capacity of the globe, may be given just such an experience. It is a glimpse into the void of a universe without man. I must rest my ultimate faith on the discovery by these future generations, as the ax of the executioner passes into their hands, of the transcendent importance of posterity for them.

For Further Reflection

1. Why should we care about future generations? How would you answer Heilbroner's question, "Why should I lift a finger to affect events that will have no more meaning for me seventy-five years after my death than those that happened seventy-five years before I was born?"

2. Do you agree with Heilbroner that there is "no rational answer to that terrible question"? Defend your answer.

3. Do you think "religious convictions" or simply well-thought-out humanistic concerns (Adam Smith's "man of humanity") should have more weight than logic and rational argument when considering issues such as obligations to posterity? How do you decide?

The Tragedy of the Commons

GARRETT HARDIN

Garrett Hardin argues that some social problems have no technical, that is, scientific or technological, solution, but must be addressed by moral and political means. Exponential population growth is one such problem. Hardin calls our attention to a study of the British mathematician William Forster Lloyd (1794–1852), which demonstrates that in non-regulated areas (the "commons") individual rationality and self-interest lead to disaster. Hardin applies Lloyd's study to human population growth and argues that voluntary restriction of population by families is not adequate to deal with this problem, since many will not respond to voluntary procreation limitations. We must have "mutual coercion, mutually agreed upon by the majority of the people affected."

At the end of a thoughtful article on the future of nuclear war, Wiesner and York[1] concluded that: "Both sides in the arms race are . . . confronted by the dilemma of steadily increasing military

Reprinted with permission from G. Hardin, "The Tragedy of the Commons" *Science* 162:1243–1248. 13 Dec. 1968. Copyright © 1968 American Association for the Advancement of Science.
[1]J. B. Wiesner and H. F. York, *Sci. Amer.* 211 (No. 44), 27 (1964).

power and steadily decreasing national security. *It is our considered professional judgment that this dilemma has no technical solution.* If the great powers continue to look for solutions in the area of science and technology only, the result will be to worsen the situation."

I would like to focus your attention not on the subject of the article (national security in a nuclear world) but on the kind of conclusion they reached, namely that there is no technical solution to the problem. An implicit and almost universal assumption of discussions published in professional and semi-popular scientific journals is that the problem under discussion has a technical solution. A technical solution may be defined as one that requires a change only in the techniques of the natural sciences, demanding little or nothing in the way of change in human values or ideas of morality.

In our day (though not in earlier times) technical solutions are always welcome. Because of previous failures in prophecy, it takes courage to assert that a desired technical solution is not possible. Wiesner and York exhibited this courage; publishing in a science journal, they insisted that the solution to the problem was not to be found in the natural sciences. They cautiously qualified their statement with the phrase, "It is our considered professional judgment. . . ." Whether they were right or not is not the concern of the present article. Rather, the concern here is with the important concept of a class of human problems which can be called "no technical solution problems," and, more specifically, with the identification and discussion of one of these.

It is easy to show that the class is not a null class. Recall the game of tick-tack-toe. Consider the problem, "How can I win the game of tick-tack-toe?" It is well known that I cannot, if I assume (in keeping with the conventions of game theory) that my opponent understands the game perfectly. Put another way, there is no "technical solution" to the problem. I can win only by giving a radical meaning to the word "win." I can hit my opponent over the head; or I can drug him; or I can falsify the records. Every way in which I "win" involves, in some sense, an abandonment of the game, as we intuitively understand it. (I can also, of course, openly abandon the game—refuse to play it. This is what most adults do.)

The class of "No technical solution problems" has members. My thesis is that the "population problem," as conventionally conceived, is a member of this class. How it is conventionally conceived needs some comment. It is fair to say that most people who anguish over the population problem are trying to find a way to avoid the evils of overpopulation without relinquishing any of the privileges they now enjoy. They think that farming the seas or developing new strains of wheat will solve the problem—technologically. I try to show here that the solution they seek cannot be found. The population problem cannot be solved in a technical way, any more than can the problem of winning the game of tick-tack-toe.

WHAT SHALL WE MAXIMIZE?

Population, as Malthus said, naturally tends to grow "geometrically," or, as we would now say, exponentially. In a finite world this means that the per capita share of the world's goods must steadily decrease. Is ours a finite world?

A fair defense can be put forward for the view that the world is infinite; or that we do not know that it is not. But, in terms of the practical problems that we must face in the next few generations with the foreseeable technology, it is clear that we will greatly increase human misery if we do not, during the immediate future, assume that the world available to the terrestrial human population is finite. "Space" is no escape.[2]

A finite world can support only a finite population; therefore, population growth must eventually equal zero. (The case of perpetual wide fluctuations above and below zero is a trivial variant that need not be discussed.) When this condition is met, what will be the situation of mankind? Specifically, can Bentham's goal of "the greatest good for the greatest number" be realized?

No—for two reasons, each sufficient by itself. The first is a theoretical one. It is not mathematically possible to maximize for two (or more) variables at the same time. This was clearly stated by von Neumann and Morgenstern,[3] but the principle is implicit in the theory of partial differential equations, dating back at least to D'Alembert (1717–1783).

---

[2]G. Hardin, *J. Hered.* 50, 68 (1959); S. von Hoernor, *Science* 137, 18 (1962).
[3]J. von Neumann and O. Morgenstern, *Theory of Games and Economic Behavior* (Princeton Univ. Press, Princeton, NJ: 1947), p. 11.

The second reason springs directly from biological facts. To live, any organism must have a source of energy (for example, food). This energy is utilized for two purposes: mere maintenance and work. For man, maintenance of life requires about 1600 kilocalories a day ("maintenance calories"). Anything that he does over and above merely staying alive will be defined as work, and is supported by "work calories" which he takes in. Work calories are used not only for what we call work in common speech; they are also required for all forms of enjoyment, from swimming and automobile racing to playing music and writing poetry. If our goal is to maximize population it is obvious what we must do: We must make the work calories per person approach as close to zero as possible. No gourmet meals, no vacations, no sports, no music, no literature, no art. . . . I think that everyone will grant, without argument or proof, that maximizing population does not maximize goods. Bentham's goal is impossible.

In reaching this conclusion I have made the usual assumption that it is the acquisition of energy that is the problem. The appearance of atomic energy has led some to question this assumption. However, given an infinite source of energy, population growth still produces an inescapable problem. The problem of the acquisition of energy is replaced by the problem of its dissipation, as J. H. Fremlin has so wittily shown.[4] The arithmetic signs in the analysis are, as it were, reversed; but Bentham's goal is still unobtainable.

The optimum population is, then, less than the maximum. The difficulty of defining the optimum is enormous; so far as I know, no one has seriously tackled this problem. Reaching an acceptable and stable solution will surely require more than one generation of hard analytical work—and much persuasion.

We want the maximum good per person; but what is good? To one person it is wilderness, to another it is ski lodges for thousands. To one it is estuaries to nourish ducks for hunters to shoot; to another it is factory land. Comparing one good with another is, we usually say, impossible because goods are incommensurable. Incommensurables cannot be compared.

Theoretically this may be true; but in real life incommensurables *are* commensurable. Only a criterion of judgment and a system of weighting are needed. In nature the criterion is survival. Is it bet-

---

[4]J. H. Fremlin, *New Sci.,* No. 415 (1964), p. 285.

ter for a species to be small and hideable, or large and powerful? Natural selection commensurates the incommensurables. The compromise achieved depends on a natural weighting of the values of the variables.

Man must imitate this process. There is no doubt that in fact he already does, but unconsciously. It is when the hidden decisions are made explicit that the arguments begin. The problem for the years ahead is to work out an acceptable theory of weighting. Synergistic effects, nonlinear variation, and difficulties in discounting the future make the intellectual problem difficult, but not (in principle) insoluble.

Has any cultural group solved this practical problem at the present time, even on an intuitive level? One simple fact proves that none has: there is no prosperous population in the world today that has, and has had for some time, a growth rate of zero. Any people that has intuitively identified its optimum point will soon reach it, after which its growth rate becomes and remains zero.

Of course, a positive growth rate might be taken as evidence that a population is below its optimum. However, by any reasonable standards, the most rapidly growing populations on earth today are (in general) the most miserable. This association (which need not be invariable) casts doubt on the optimistic assumption that the positive growth rate of a population is evidence that it has yet to reach its optimum.

We can make little progress in working toward optimum population size until we explicitly exorcize the spirit of Adam Smith in the field of practical demography. In economic affairs, *The Wealth of Nations* (1776) popularized the "invisible hand," the idea that an individual who "intends only his own gain," is, as it were, "led by an invisible hand to promote . . . the public interest."[5] Adam Smith did not assert that this was invariably true, and perhaps neither did any of his followers. But he contributed to a dominant tendency of thought that has ever since interfered with positive action based on rational analysis, namely, the tendency to assume that decisions reached individually will, in fact, be the best decisions for an entire society. If this assumption is correct it justifies the continuance of our present policy of laissez-faire in reproduction. If it is correct

[5]A. Smith, *The Wealth of Nations* (Modern Library, New York, 1937), p. 423.

we can assume that men will control their individual fecundity so as to produce the optimum population. If the assumption is not correct, we need to reexamine our individual freedoms to see which ones are defensible.

TRAGEDY OF FREEDOM IN A COMMONS

The rebuttal to the invisible hand in population control is to be found in a scenario first sketched in a little-known pamphlet[6] in 1833 by a mathematical amateur named William Forster Lloyd (1794–1852). We may well call it "the tragedy of the commons," using the word "tragedy" as the philosopher Whitehead used it:[7] "The essence of dramatic tragedy is not unhappiness. It resides in the solemnity of the remorseless working of things." He then goes on to say, "This inevitableness of destiny can only be illustrated in terms of human life by incidents which in fact involve unhappiness. For it is only by them that the futility of escape can be made evident in the drama."

The tragedy of the commons develops in this way. Picture a pasture open to all. It is to be expected that each herdsman will try to keep as many cattle as possible on the commons. Such an arrangement may work reasonably satisfactorily for centuries because tribal wars, poaching, and disease keep the numbers of both man and beast well below the carrying capacity of the land. Finally, however, comes the day of reckoning, that is, the day when the long-desired goal of social stability becomes a reality. At this point, the inherent logic of the commons remorselessly generates tragedy.

As a rational being, each herdsman seeks to maximize his gain. Explicitly or implicitly, more or less consciously, he asks, "What is the utility *to me* of adding one more animal to my herd?" This utility has one negative and one positive component.

---

[6]W. F. Lloyd, *Two Lectures on the Checks to Population* (Oxford Univ. Press, Oxford, England, 1833), reprinted (in part) in *Population, Evolution, and Birth Control,* G. Hardin, Ed. (Freeman, San Francisco, 1964), p. 37.

[7]A. N. Whitehead, *Science and the Modern World* (Mentor, New York, 1948), p. 17.

1. The positive component is a function of the increment of one animal. Since the herdsman receives all the proceeds from the sale of the additional animal, the positive utility is nearly +1.

2. The negative component is a function of the additional over-grazing created by one or more animal. Since, however, the effects of overgrazing are shared by all the herdsmen, the negative utility for any particular decision-making herdsman is only a fraction of −1.

Adding together the component partial utilities, the rational herds-man concludes that the only sensible course for him to pursue is to add another animal to his herd. And another; and another. . . . But this is the conclusion reached by each and every rational herdsman shar-ing a commons. Therein is the tragedy. Each man is locked into a sys-tem that compels him to increase his herd without limit—in a world that is limited. Ruin is the destination toward which all men rush, each pursuing his own best interest in a society that believes in the free-dom of the commons. Freedom in a commons brings ruin to all.

Some would say that this is a platitude. Would that it were! In a sense, it was learned thousands of years ago, but natural selec-tion favors the forces of psychological denial.[8] The individual ben-efits as an individual from his ability to deny the truth even though society as a whole, of which he is a part, suffers. Education can counteract the natural tendency to do the wrong thing, but the inex-orable success of generations requires that the basis for this knowl-edge be constantly refreshed.

A simple incident that occurred a few years ago in Leominster, Massachusetts, shows how perishable the knowledge is. During the Christmas shopping season the parking meters downtown were cov-ered with plastic bags that bore tags reading: "Do not open until after Christmas. Free parking courtesy of the mayor and city coun-cil." In other words, facing the prospect of an increased demand for already scarce space, the city fathers reinstituted the system of the commons. (Cynically, we suspect that they gained more votes than they lost by this retrogressive act.)

In an approximate way, the logic of the commons has been understood for a long time, perhaps since the discovery of agri-

---

[8]G. Hardin, Ed., *Population, Evolution and Birth Control* (Freeman, San Francisco, 1964), p. 56.

culture or the invention of private property in real estate. But it is understood mostly only in special cases which are not sufficiently generalized. Even at this late date, cattlemen leasing national land on the western ranges demonstrate no more than an ambivalent understanding, in constantly pressuring federal authorities to increase the head count to the point where overgrazing produces erosion and weed-dominance. Likewise, the oceans of the world continue to suffer from the survival of the philosophy of the commons. Maritime nations still respond automatically to the shibboleth of the "freedom of the seas." Professing to believe in the "inexhaustible resources of the oceans," they bring species after species of fish and whales closer to extinction.[9]

The National Parks present another instance of the working out of the tragedy of the commons. At present they are open to all, without limit. The parks themselves are limited in extent—there is only one Yosemite Valley—whereas population seems to grow without limit. The values that visitors seek in the parks are steadily eroded. Plainly, we must soon cease to treat the parks as commons or they will be of no value to anyone.

What shall we do? We have several options. We might sell them off as private property. We might keep them as public property, but allocate the right to enter them. The allocation might be on the basis of wealth, by the use of an auction system. It might be on the basis of merit, as defined by some agreed-upon standards. It might be by lottery. Or it might be on a first-come, first-served basis, administered to long queues. These, I think, are all the reasonable possibilities. They are all objectionable. But we must choose—or acquiesce in the destruction of the commons that we call our National Parks.

POLLUTION

In a reverse way, the tragedy of the commons reappears in problems of pollution. Here it is not a question of taking something out of the commons, but of putting something in—sewage, or chemical, radioactive, and heat wastes into water; noxious and dangerous fumes into the air, and distracting and unpleasant advertising signs into the line

---

[9]S. McVay, *Sci. Amer.* 216 (No. 8), 13 (1966).

of sight. The calculations of utility are much the same as before. The rational man finds that his share of the cost of the wastes he discharges into the commons is less than the cost of purifying his wastes before releasing them. Since this is true for everyone, we are locked into a system of "fouling our own nest," so long as we behave only as independent, rational, free-enterprisers.

The tragedy of the commons as a food basket is averted by private property, or something formally like it. But the air and waters surrounding us cannot readily be fenced, and so the tragedy of the commons as a cesspool must be prevented by different means, by coercive laws or taxing devices that make it cheaper for the polluter to treat his pollutants than to discharge them untreated. We have not progressed as far with the solution of this problem as we have with the first. Indeed, our particular concept of private property, which deters us from exhausting the positive resources of the earth, favors pollution. The owner of a factory on the bank of a stream—whose property extends to the middle of the stream—often has difficulty seeing why it is not his natural right to muddy the waters flowing past his door. The law, always behind the times, requires elaborate stitching and fitting to adapt it to this newly perceived aspect of the commons.

The pollution problem is a consequence of population. It did not much matter how a lonely American frontiersman disposed of his waste. "Flowing water purifies itself every 10 miles," my grandfather used to say, and the myth was near enough to the truth when he was a boy, for there were not too many people. But as population became denser, the natural chemical and biological recycling processes became overloaded, calling for a redefinition of property rights.

HOW TO LEGISLATE TEMPERANCE?

Analysis of the pollution problem as a function of population density uncovers a not generally recognized principle of morality, namely: *the morality of an act is a function of the state of the system at the time it is performed.*[10] Using the commons as a cesspool does not harm the general public under frontier conditions, because

[10]J. Fletcher, *Situation Ethics* (Westminster, Philadelphia, 1966).

there is no public; the same behavior in a metropolis is unbearable. A hundred and fifty years ago a plainsman could kill an American bison, cut out only the tongue for his dinner, and discard the rest of the animal. He was not in any important sense being wasteful. Today, with only a few thousand bison left, we would be appalled at such behavior.

In passing, it is worth noting that the morality of an act cannot be determined from a photograph. One does not know whether a man killing an elephant or setting fire to the grassland is harming others until one knows the total system in which his act appears. "One picture is worth a thousand words" said an ancient Chinese; but it may take 10,000 words to validate it. It is as tempting to ecologists as it is to reformers in general to try to persuade others by way of the photographic shortcut. But the essence of an argument cannot be photographed: it must be presented rationally—in words.

That morality is system-sensitive escaped the attention of most codifiers of ethics in the past. "Thou shalt not . . ." is the form of traditional ethical directives which make no allowance for particular circumstances. The laws of our society follow the pattern of ancient ethics, and therefore are poorly suited to governing a complex, crowded, changeable world. Our epicyclic solution is to augment statutory law with administrative law. Since it is practically impossible to spell out all the conditions under which it is safe to burn trash in the backyard or to run an automobile without smog-control, by law we delegate the details to bureaus. The result is administrative law, which is rightly feared for an ancient reason—*Quis custodiet ipsos custodes?*—"Who shall watch the watchers themselves?" John Adams said that we must have "a government of laws and not men." Bureau administrators, trying to evaluate the morality of acts in the total system, are singularly liable to corruption, producing a government by men, not laws.

Prohibition is easy to legislate (though not necessarily to enforce); but how do we legislate temperance? Experience indicates that it can be accomplished best through the mediation of administrative law. We limit possibilities unnecessarily if we suppose that the sentiment of *Quis custodiet* denies us the use of administrative law. We should rather retain the phrase as a perpetual reminder of fearful dangers we cannot avoid. The great challenge facing us now is to invent the corrective feedbacks that are needed to keep custodians honest. We must find ways to legitimate the needed authority of both the custodians and the corrective feedbacks.

FREEDOM TO BREED IS INTOLERABLE

The tragedy of the commons is involved in population problems in another way. In a world governed solely by the principle of "dog eat dog"—if indeed there ever was such a world—how many children a family had would not be a matter of public concern. Parents who bred too exuberantly would leave fewer descendants, not more, because they would be unable to care adequately for their children. David Lack and others have found that such a negative feedback demonstrably controls the fecundity of birds.[11] But men are not birds, and have not acted like them for millenniums, at least.

If each human family were dependent only on its own resources; *if* the children of improvident parents starved to death; *if,* thus, overbreeding brought its own "punishment" to the germ line—*then* there would be no public interest in controlling the breeding of families. But our society is deeply committed to the welfare state,[12] and hence is confronted with another aspect of the tragedy of the commons.

In a welfare state, how shall we deal with the family, the religion, the race, or the class (or indeed any distinguishable and cohesive group) that adopts overbreeding as a policy to secure its own aggrandizement?[13] To couple the concept of freedom to breed with the belief that everyone born has an equal right to the commons is to lock the world into a tragic course of action.

Unfortunately this is just the course of action that is being pursued by the United Nations. In late 1967, some 30 nations agreed to the following:[14]

[11]D. Lack, *The Natural Regulation of Animal Numbers* (Clarendon Press, Oxford, 1954).
[12]H. Girvetz, *From Wealth to Welfare* (Stanford Univ. Press, Stanford, Calif., 1950).
[13]G. Hardin, *Perspec. Biol. Med.* 6, 366 (1963).
[14]U Thant, *Int. Planned Parenthood News,* No. 168 (February 1968), p. 3.

> The Universal Declaration of Human Rights describes the family as the natural and fundamental unit of society. It follows that any choice and decision with regard to the size of the family must irrevocably rest with the family itself, and cannot be made by anyone else.

It is painful to have to deny categorically the validity of this right; denying it, one feels as uncomfortable as a resident of Salem, Massachusetts, who denied the reality of witches in the 17th century. At the present time, in liberal quarters, something like a taboo acts to inhibit criticism of the United Nations. There is a feeling that the United Nations is "our last and best hope," that we shouldn't find fault with it; we shouldn't play into the hands of the archconservatives. However, let us not forget what Robert Louis Stevenson said: "The truth that is suppressed by friends is the readiest weapon of the enemy." If we love the truth we must openly deny the validity of the Universal Declaration of Human Rights, even though it is promoted by the United Nations. We should also join with Kingsley Davis[15] in attempting to get Planned Parenthood–World Population to see the error of its ways in embracing the same tragic ideal.

CONSCIENCE IS SELF-ELIMINATING

It is a mistake to think that we can control the breeding of mankind in the long run by an appeal to conscience. Charles Galton Darwin made this point when he spoke on the centennial of the publication of his grandfather's great book. The argument is straightforward and Darwinian.

People vary. Confronted with appeals to limit breeding, some people will undoubtedly respond to the plea more than others. Those who have more children will produce a larger fraction of the next generation than those with more susceptible consciences. The difference will be accentuated, generation by generation.

In C. G. Darwin's words: "It may well be that it would take hundreds of generations for the progenitive instinct to develop in this way, but if it should do so, nature would have taken her revenge,

---

[15]K. Davis, *Science,* 158, 730 (1967).

and the variety *Homo contracipiens* would become extinct and would be replaced by the variety *Homo progenitivus*."[16]

The argument assumes that conscience or the desire for children (no matter which) is hereditary—but hereditary only in the most general formal sense. The result will be the same whether the attitude is transmitted through germ cells, or exosomatically, to use A. J. Lotka's term. (If one denies the latter possibility as well as the former, then what's the point of education?) The argument has here been stated in the context of the population problem, but it applies equally well to any instance in which society appeals to an individual exploiting a commons to restrain himself for the general good—by means of his conscience. To make such an appeal is to set up a selective system that works toward the elimination of conscience from the race.

PATHOGENIC EFFECTS OF CONSCIENCE

The long-term disadvantage of an appeal to conscience should be enough to condemn it; it has serious short-term disadvantages as well. If we ask a man who is exploiting a commons to desist "in the name of conscience," what are we saying to him? What does he hear?—not only at the moment but also in the wee small hours of the night when, half asleep, he remembers not merely the words we used but also the nonverbal communication cues we gave him unawares? Sooner or later, consciously or subconsciously, he senses that he has received two communications, and that they are contradictory: (i) (intended communication) "If you don't do as we ask, we will openly condemn you for not acting like a responsible citizen"; (ii) (the unintended communication) "If you *do* behave as we ask, we will secretly condemn you for a simpleton who can be shamed into standing aside while the rest of us exploit the commons."

Everyman then is caught in what Bateson has called a "double bind." Bateson and his co-workers have made a plausible case for viewing the double bind as an important causative factor in the genesis of schizophrenia.[17] The double bind may not always be so dam-

---

[16]S. Tax, Ed., *Evolution After Darwin* (Univ. of Chicago Press, Chicago, 1960), vol. 2, p. 469.

[17]G. Bateson, D. D. Jackson, J. Haley, J. Weakland, *Behav. Sci.* 1, 251 (1956).

aging, but it always endangers the mental health of anyone to whom it is applied. "A bad conscience," said Nietzsche, "is a kind of illness."

To conjure up a conscience in others is tempting to anyone who wishes to extend his control beyond the legal limits. Leaders at the highest level succumb to this temptation. Has any President during the past generation failed to call on labor unions to moderate voluntarily their demands for higher wages, or to steel companies to honor voluntary guidelines on prices? I can recall none. The rhetoric used on such occasions is designed to produce feelings of guilt in noncooperators.

For centuries it was assumed without proof that guilt was a valuable, perhaps even indispensable, ingredient of the civilized life. Now, in this post-Freudian world, we doubt it.

Paul Goodman speaks from the modern point of view when he says: "No good has ever come from feeling guilty, neither intelligence, policy, nor compassion. The guilty do not pay attention to the object but only to themselves, and not even to their own interests, which might make sense, but to their anxieties."[18]

One does not have to be a professional psychiatrist to see the consequences of anxiety. We in the Western world are just emerging from a dreadful two-centuries-long Dark Ages of Eros that was sustained partly by prohibition laws, but perhaps more effectively by the anxiety-generating mechanisms of education. Alex Comfort has told the story well in *The Anxiety Makers;*[19] it is not a pretty one.

Since proof is difficult, we may even concede that the results of anxiety may sometimes, from certain points of view, be desirable. The larger question we should ask is whether, as a matter of policy, we should ever encourage the use of a technique the tendency (if not the intention) of which is psychologically pathogenic. We hear much talk these days of responsible parenthood; the coupled words are incorporated into the titles of some organizations devoted to birth control. Some people have proposed massive propaganda campaigns to instill responsibility into the nation's (or the world's) breeders. But what is the meaning of the word responsibility in this context? Is it not merely a synonym for the word conscience? When we use the word responsibility in the absence of substantial sanctions are we not trying to browbeat a free man in a commons into

---

[18]P. Goodman, *New York Rev. Books* 1968, 10 (8), 22 (23 May 1968).
[19]A. Comfort, *The Anxiety Makers* (Nelson, London, 1967).

acting against his own interest? Responsibility is a verbal counter-feit for a substantial *quid pro quo.* It is an attempt to get something for nothing.

If the word responsibility is to be used at all, I suggest that it be in the sense Charles Frankel uses it.[20] "Responsibility," says this philosopher, "is the product of definite social arrangements." Notice that Frankel calls for social arrangements—not propaganda.

MUTUAL COERCION
MUTUALLY AGREED UPON

The social arrangements that produce responsibility are arrange-ments that create coercion, of some sort. Consider bank-robbing. The man who takes money from a bank acts as if the bank were a com-mons. How do we prevent such action? Certainly not by trying to control his behavior solely by a verbal appeal to his sense of respon-sibility. Rather than rely on propaganda we follow Frankel's lead and insist that a bank is not a commons; we seek the definite social arrangements that will keep it from becoming a commons. That we thereby infringe on the freedom of would-be robbers we neither deny nor regret.

The morality of bank-robbing is particularly easy to understand because we accept complete prohibition of this activity. We are willing to say "Thou shalt not rob banks," without providing for exceptions. But temperance also can be created by coercion. Tax-ing is a good coercive device. To keep downtown shoppers tem-perate in their use of parking space we introduce parking meters for short periods, and traffic fines for longer ones. We need not actually forbid a citizen to park as long as he wants to; we need merely make it increasingly expensive for him to do so. Not pro-hibition, but carefully biased options are what we offer him. A Madi-son Avenue man might call this persuasion; I prefer the greater can-dor of the word coercion.

Coercion is a dirty word to most liberals now, but it need not forever be so. As with the four-letter words, its dirtiness can be cleansed away by exposure to light, by saying it over and over

[20]C. Frankel, *The Case for Modern Man* (Harper, New York, 1955), p. 203.

without apology or embarrassment. To many, the word coercion implies arbitrary decisions of distant and irresponsible bureaucrats; but this is not a necessary part of its meaning. The only kind of coercion I recommend is mutual coercion, mutually agreed upon by the majority of the people affected.

To say that we mutually agree to coercion is not to say that we are required to enjoy it, or even to pretend we enjoy it. Who enjoys taxes? We all grumble about them. But we accept compulsory taxes because we recognize that voluntary taxes would favor the conscienceless. We institute and (grumblingly) support taxes and other coercive devices to escape the horror of the commons.

An alternative to the commons need not be perfectly just to be preferable. With real estate and other material goods, the alternative we have chosen is the institution of private property coupled with legal inheritance. Is this system perfectly just? As a genetically trained biologist I deny that it is. It seems to me that, if there are to be differences in individual inheritance, legal possession should be perfectly correlated with biological inheritance—that those who are biologically more fit to be the custodians of property and power should legally inherit more. But genetic recombination continually makes a mockery of the doctrine of "like father, like son" implicit in our laws of legal inheritance. An idiot can inherit millions, and a trust fund can keep his estate intact. We must admit that our legal system of private property plus inheritance is unjust—but we put up with it because we are not convinced, at the moment, that anyone has invented a better system. The alternative of the commons is too horrifying to contemplate. Injustice is preferable to total ruin.

It is one of the peculiarities of the warfare between reform and the status quo that it is thoughtlessly governed by a double standard. Whenever a reform measure is proposed it is often defeated when its opponents triumphantly discover a flaw in it. As Kingsley Davis has pointed out,[21] worshippers of the status quo sometimes imply that no reform is possible without unanimous agreement, an implication contrary to historical fact. As nearly as I can make out, automatic rejection of proposed reforms is based on one of two unconscious assumptions: (i) that the status quo is perfect; or (ii)

---

[21]J. D. Roslansky, *Genetics and the Future of Man* (Appleton-Century-Crofts, New York. 1966), p. 177.

that the choice we face is between reform and no action; if the proposed reform is imperfect, we presumably should take no action at all, while we wait for a perfect proposal.

But we can never do nothing. That which we have done for thousands of years is also action. It also produces evils. Once we are aware that the status quo is action, we can then compare its discoverable advantages and disadvantages with the predicted advantages and disadvantages of the proposed reform, discounting as best we can for our lack of experience. On the basis of such a comparison, we can make a rational decision which will not involve the unworkable assumption that only perfect systems are tolerable.

RECOGNITION OF NECESSITY

Perhaps the simplest summary of this analysis of man's population problems is this: the commons, if justifiable at all, is justifiable only under conditions of low-population density. As the human population has increased, the commons has had to be abandoned in one aspect after another.

First we abandoned the commons in food gathering, enclosing farm land and restricting pastures and hunting and fishing areas. These restrictions are still not complete throughout the world.

Somewhat later we saw that the commons as a place for water disposal would also have to be abandoned Restrictions on the disposal of domestic sewage are widely accepted in the Western world; we are still struggling to close the commons to pollution by automobiles, factories, insecticide sprayers, fertilizing operations, and atomic energy installations.

In a still more embryonic state is our recognition of the evils of the commons in matters of pleasure. There is almost no restriction on the propagation of sound waves in the public medium. The shopping public is assaulted with mindless music, without its consent. Our government is paying out billions of dollars to create supersonic transport which will disturb 50,000 people for every one person who is whisked from coast to coast 3 hours faster. Advertisers muddy the airwaves of radio and television and pollute the view of travelers. We are a long way from outlawing the commons in matters of pleasure. Is this because our Puritan inheritance makes us view pleasure as something of a sin, and pain (that is, the pollution of advertising) as the sign of virtue?

Every new enclosure of the commons involves the infringement of somebody's personal liberty. Infringements made in the distant past are accepted because no contemporary complains of a loss. It is the newly proposed infringements that we vigorously oppose; cries of "rights" and "freedom" fill the air. But what does "freedom" mean? When men mutually agreed to pass laws against robbing, mankind became more free, not less so. Individuals locked into the logic of the commons are free only to bring on universal ruin; once they see the necessity of mutual coercion, they become free to pursue other goals. I believe it was Hegel who said, "Freedom is the recognition of necessity."

The most important aspect of necessity that we must now recognize, is the necessity of abandoning the commons in breeding. No technical solution can rescue us from the misery of overpopulation. Freedom to breed will bring ruin to all. At the moment, to avoid hard decisions many of us are tempted to propagandize for conscience and responsible parenthood. The temptation must be resisted, because an appeal to independently acting consciences selects for the disappearance of all conscience in the long run, and an increase in anxiety in the short.

The only way we can preserve and nurture other and more precious freedoms is by relinquishing the freedom to breed, and that very soon. "Freedom is the recognition of necessity"—and it is the role of education to reveal to all the necessity of abandoning the freedom to breed. Only so, can we put an end to this aspect of the tragedy of the commons.

For Further Reflection

1. What does Hardin mean when he says that the problem of population growth has no technical solution?

2. What does Hardin mean when he says, "Freedom in a commons brings ruin to all"? How does he define true "freedom" at the end of his essay?

3. Explain the idea of the tragedy of the commons as first set forth by William Forster Lloyd. How does it work?

4. How does Hardin apply the tragedy of the commons to human population growth? Do you agree with his analysis? Explain.

5. What does Hardin mean by "conscience is self-eliminating"? What is wrong with appealing to conscience to solve environmental problems?

6. How serious is the current population growth? What do you think should be done about it?

We All Live in Bhopal

DAVID WATSON

David Watson lives in Detroit and is the editor of *Fifth Estate*, an anarchist journal. In this essay, Watson argues that in the third world, as well as in Europe and the United States, industrial capitalism is harming hundreds of thousands of people and imposing a frightful risk on millions more by unsafe practices that pollute our air, water, soil, and food. Taking the tragic 1984 explosion of the Union Carbide insecticide plant in Bhopal, India, as his point of departure, he recounts a tale of corporate negligence and moral culpability. Calling these large corporations "corporate vampires," Watson accuses them of turning industrial civilization into "one vast, stinking extermination camp."

But we are all guilty of supporting a lifestyle that depends on dangerous industrial institutions, reeking with harmful pollutions. We must rid ourselves of this evil before it destroys us.

David Watson, "We all Live in Bhopal," published under the pseudonym "George Bradford" in *Fifth Estate* (4632 Second Avenue, Detroit, MI 48201), Winter 1985, Vol. 19, No. 4. Revised and reprinted in David Watson, *Against the Megamachine: Essays on Empire & Its Enemies* (New York, N.Y.: Autonomedia, 1998). Reprinted by permission.

The cinders of the funeral pyres at Bhopal are still warm, and the mass graves still fresh, but the media prostitutes of the corporations have already begun their homilies in defense of industrialism and its uncounted horrors. Some 3,000 people were slaughtered in the wake of the deadly gas cloud, and 20,000 will remain permanently disabled. The poison gas left a 25-square-mile swath of dead and dying, people and animals, as it drifted southeast away from the Union Carbide factory. "We thought it was a plague," said one victim. It was: a chemical plague, an industrial plague,

Ashes, ashes, all fall down!

A terrible, unfortunate, "accident," we are reassured by the propaganda apparatus for Progress, for History, for "Our Modern Way of Life." A price, of course, has to be paid since the risks are necessary to ensure a higher Standard of Living, a Better Way of Life.

The Wall Street Journal, tribune of the bourgeoisie, editorialized, "It is worthwhile to remember that the Union Carbide insecticide plant and the people surrounding it were where they were for compelling reasons. India's agriculture has been thriving, bringing a better life to millions of rural people, and partly because of the use of modern agricultural technology that includes applications of insect killers." The indisputable fact of life, according to this sermon, is that India, like everyone else, "needs technology. Calcutta-style scenes of human deprivation can be replaced as fast as the country imports the benefits of the West's industrial revolution and market economics." So, despite whatever dangers are involved, "the benefits outweigh the costs." (December 13, 1984)

The *Journal* was certainly right in one regard—the reasons for the plant and the people's presence there are certainly compelling; capitalist market relations and technological invasion are as compelling as a hurricane to the small communities from which those people were uprooted. It conveniently failed to note, however, that countries like India do not import the benefits of industrial capitalism; those benefits are exported in the form of loan repayments to fill the coffers of the bankers and corporate vampires who read *The Wall Street Journal* for the latest news of their investments. The Indians only take the risks and pay the costs; in fact, for the immiserated masses of people living in the shantytowns of the Third World, there are not risks, so much as certain hunger and disease, and the certainty of death squad revenge for criticizing the state of things as they are.

INDUSTRIALIZATION A NIGHTMARE

In fact, the Calcutta-style misery is the result of Third World industrialization and the so-called industrial "Green Revolution" in agriculture. The Green Revolution, which was to revolutionize agriculture in the "backward" countries and produce greater crop yields, has only been a miracle for the banks, corporations and military dictatorships which defend them. The influx of fertilizers, technology, insecticides and bureaucratic administration exploded millennia-old rural economies based on subsistence farming, creating a class of wealthier farmers dependent upon western technologies to produce cash crops such as coffee, cotton and wheat for export, while the vast majority of farming communities were destroyed by capitalist market competition and sent like refugees into the growing cities. These victims, paralleling the destroyed peasantry of Europe's Industrial Revolution several hundred years before, joined either the permanent underclass of unemployed and underemployed slum-dwellers eking out a survival on the tenuous margins of civilization, or became proletarian fodder in the Bhopals, Sao Paulos and Djakartas of an industrializing world—an industrialization process, like all industrialization in history, paid for by the pillage of nature and human beings in the countryside.

Food production goes up in some cases, of course, because the measure is only quantitative; some foods disappear while others are produced year round, even for export. *But subsistence is destroyed.* Not only does the rural landscape begin to suffer the consequences of constant crop production and use of chemicals, but the masses of people—laborers on the land and in the teeming hovels growing around the industrial plants—go hungrier in a vicious cycle of exploitation, while the wheat goes abroad to buy absurd commodities and weapons.

The industrialization of the Third World is a story familiar to anyone who takes even a glance at what is occurring. The colonial countries are nothing but a dumping ground and pool of cheap labor for capitalist corporations. Obsolete technology is shipped there along with the production of chemicals, medicines and other products banned in the developed world. Labor is cheap, there are few if any safety standards, and costs are cut. But the formula of cost-benefit still stands: the costs are simply borne by others, by the victims of Union Carbide, Dow, and Standard Oil.

Chemicals found to be dangerous and banned in the U.S. and Europe are produced instead overseas—DDT is a well-known example of an enormous number of such products, as is the unregistered pesticide Leptophos exported by the Velsicol Corporation to Egypt which killed and injured many Egyptian farmers in the mid-1970s. Other products are simply dumped on Third World markets, like the mercury-tainted wheat imported from the U.S. which led to the deaths of as many as 5,000 Iraqis in 1972. Another example was the wanton contamination of Nicaragua's Lake Managua by a chlorine and caustic soda factory owned by Pennwalt Corporation and other investors, which caused a major outbreak of mercury poisoning in a primary source of fish for the people living in Managua.

Union Carbide's plant at Bhopal did not even meet U.S. safety standards according to its own safety inspector, but a U.N. expert on international corporate behavior told the *New York Times,* "A whole list of factors is not in place to insure adequate industrial safety" throughout the Third World. "Carbide is not very different from any other chemical company in this regard." According to the *Times,* "In a Union Carbide battery plant in Jakarta, Indonesia, more than half the workers had kidney damage from mercury exposure. In an asbestos cement factory owned by the Manville Corporation 200 miles west of Bhopal, workers in 1981 were routinely covered with asbestos dust, a practice that would never be tolerated here." (December 9, 1984)

Some 22,500 people are killed every year by exposure to insecticides, a much higher percentage of them in the Third World than use of such chemicals would suggest. Many experts decried the lack of an "industrial culture" in the "underdeveloped" countries as a major cause of accidents and contamination. But where an "industrial culture" thrives, is the situation really much better?

INDUSTRIAL CULTURE
AND INDUSTRIAL PLAGUE

In the advanced industrial nations an "industrial culture" (and little other) exists. Have such disasters been avoided as the claims of these experts would lead us to believe?

Another event of such mammoth proportions as those of Bhopal would suggest otherwise—in that case, industrial pollution killed some 4,000 people in a large population center. That was London, in 1952, when several days of "normal" pollution accumulated in stagnant air to kill and permanently injure thousands of Britons.

Then there are the disasters closer to home or to memory, for example, the Love Canal (still leaking into the Great Lakes water system), or the massive dioxin contaminations at Seveso, Italy and Times Beach, Missouri, where thousands of residents had to be permanently evacuated. And there is the Berlin and Farro dump at Swartz Creek, Michigan, where C-56 (a pesticide by-product of Love Canal fame), hydrochloric acid and cyanide from Flint auto plants have accumulated. "They think we're not scientists and not even educated," said one enraged resident, "but anyone who's been in high school knows that cyanide and hydrochloric acid is what they mixed to kill the people in the concentration camps."

A powerful image: industrial civilization as one vast, stinking extermination camp. We all live in Bhopal, some closer to the gas chambers and to the mass graves, but all of us close enough to be victims. And Union Carbide is obviously not a fluke—poisons are vented into air and water, dumped in rivers, ponds and streams, fed to animals going to market, sprayed on lawns and roadways, sprayed on food crops, every day, everywhere. The result may not be as dramatic as Bhopal (which then almost comes to serve as a diversion, a deterrence machine to take our minds off the pervasive reality which Bhopal truly represents), but it is as deadly. When ABC News asked University of Chicago professor of public health and author of *The Politics of Cancer,* Jason Epstein, if he thought a Bhopal-style disaster could occur in the U.S., he replied: "I think what we're seeing in America is far more slow—not such large accidental occurrences, but a slow, gradual leakage with the result that you have excess cancers or reproductive abnormalities."

In fact, birth defects have doubled in the last 25 years. And cancer is on the rise. In an interview with *The Guardian,* Hunter College professor David Kotelchuck described the "Cancer Atlas" maps published in 1975 by the Department of Health, Education and Welfare. "Show me a red spot on these maps and I'll show you an industrial center of the U.S.," he said. "There aren't any place names on the maps but you can easily pick out concentrations of industry. See, it's not Pennsylvania that's red it's just Philadelphia, Erie and Pittsburgh. Look at West Virginia here, there's only two red spots, the Kanawha Valley, where there are nine chemical plants including Union Carbide's, and this industrialized stretch of the Ohio River. It's the same story wherever you look."

There are 50,000 toxic waste dumps in the United States. The EPA admits that ninety percent of the 90 billion pounds of toxic waste produced annually by U.S. industry (70 percent of it by chemical companies) is disposed of "improperly" (although one wonders what they would consider "proper" disposal). These deadly products of industrial civilization—arsenic, mercury, dioxin, cyanide, and many others are simply dumped, legally and illegally, wherever convenient to industry. Some 66,000 different compounds are used in industry. Nearly a billion tons of pesticides and herbicides comprising 225 different chemicals were produced in the U.S. in 1984, and an additional 79 million pounds were imported. Some two percent of chemical compounds have been tested for side effects. There are 15,000 chemical plants in the United States, daily manufacturing mass death.

All of the dumped chemicals are leaching into our water. Some three to four thousand wells, depending on which government agency you ask, are contaminated or closed in the U.S. In Michigan alone, 24 municipal water systems have been contaminated, and a thousand sites have suffered major contamination. According to the *Detroit Free Press,* "The final toll could be as many as 10,000 sites" in Michigan's "water wonderland" alone (April 15, 1984)

And the coverups continue here as in the Third World. One example is dioxin; during the proceedings around the Agent Orange investigations, it came out that Dow Chemical had lied all along about the chemical's effects. Despite research findings that dioxin is "exceptionally toxic" with "a tremendous potential for producing chloracne and systemic injury," Dow's top toxicologist, V. K. Rowe, wrote in 1965, "We are not in any way attempting to hide our problems under a heap of sand. But we certainly do not want to have any situations arise which will cause the regulatory agencies to become restrictive."

Now Vietnam suffers an epidemic of cancers and health problems caused by the massive use of Agent Orange there during the genocidal war waged by the U.S. The sufferings of the U.S. veterans are only a drop in the bucket. And dioxin is appearing everywhere in our environment as well, even in the form of recently discovered "dioxin rain."

GOING TO THE VILLAGE

When the Indian authorities and Union Carbide began to process the remaining gases in the Bhopal plant, thousands of residents fled, despite the reassurances of the authorities. The *New York Times* quoted one old man, "They are not believing the scientists or the state government or anybody. They only want to save their lives."

The same reporter wrote that one man had gone to the train station with his goats, "hoping that he could take them with him— anywhere, as long as it was away from Bhopal." (December 14, 1984) The old man quoted above told the reporter, "All the public has gone to the village." The reporter explained that "going to the village" is what Indians do when trouble comes.

A wise and age-old strategy for survival by which little communities always renewed themselves when bronze, iron and golden empires with clay feet fell to their ruin. But subsistence has been and is everywhere being destroyed, and with it, culture. What are we to do when there is no village to go to? When we all live in Bhopal, and Bhopal is everywhere? The comments of two women, one a refugee from Times Beach, Missouri, and another from Bhopal, come to mind. The first woman said of her former home, "This was a nice place once. Now we have to bury it." The other woman said, "Life cannot come back. Can the government pay for the lives? Can you bring those people back?"

The corporate vampires are guilty of greed, plunder, murder, slavery, extermination and devastation. And we should avoid any pang of sentimentalism when the time comes for them to pay for their crimes against humanity and the natural world. But we will have to go beyond them, to ourselves: subsistence, and with it culture, has been destroyed. We have to find our way back to the village, out of industrial civilization, out of this exterminist system.

The Union Carbides, the Warren Andersons, the ever "optimistic experts" and the lying propagandists all must go, but with them must go the pesticides, the herbicides, the chemical factories and the chemical way of life which is nothing but death.

Because this is Bhopal, and it is all we've got. This "once nice place" can't be simply buried for us to move on to another pristine beginning. The empire is collapsing. We must find our way back to the village, or as the North American natives said, "back to the blanket," and we must do this not by trying to save an industrial civilization which is doomed, but in that renewal of life which must take place in its ruin. By throwing off this Modern Way of Life, we won't be "giving things up" or sacrificing, but throwing off a terrible burden. Let us do so soon before we are crushed by it.

For Further Reflection

1. Does Watson make his case that Western industrial society is dangerous to humanity and nature and needs to be rejected? What are the implications of Watson's indictment? What sort of world do you think that he would want us to live in? Is Watson a "Luddite"? (Luddites were people in England in the early nineteenth century who went around destroying machines because they believed that the industrial revolution was evil.)

2. Is the anger that comes through in this article justified? Is modern industrial practice really morally irresponsible? Explain your answer.

3. How might someone in the business community respond to Watson's essay? Can our industrial practices be defended?

People or Penguins
The *Case for Optimal Pollution*

WILLIAM F. BAXTER

William Baxter is professor of law at Stanford University and the author of *People or Penguins: The Case for Optimal Pollution* (1974) from which this selection is taken.

From *People or Penguins: The Case for Optimal Pollution* by William Baxter, © 1974 Columbia University Press. Reprinted with the permission of the publisher.

In this essay, Baxter aims at clarifying the relationship between resource use and pollution. They are the opposite sides of the same coin, the privilege and its price, the good and the bad. Baxter argues that we cannot have a pollution-free society without harming humans. If we are humanists, committed to promoting the human good above all else, as he is, we should be willing to allow pollution where it harms animals and trees if overall benefits accrue to human beings.

I start with the modest proposition that, in dealing with pollution, or indeed with any problem, it is helpful to know what one is attempting to accomplish. Agreement on how and whether to pursue a particular objective, such as pollution control, is not possible unless some more general objective has been identified and stated with reasonable precision. We talk loosely of having clean air and clean water, of preserving our wilderness areas, and so forth. But none of these is a sufficiently general objective: each is more accurately viewed as a means rather than as an end.

With regard to clean air, for example, one may ask, "how clean?" and "what does clean mean?" It is even reasonable to ask, "why have clean air?" Each of these questions is an implicit demand that a more general community goal be stated—a goal sufficiently general in its scope and enjoying sufficiently general assent among the community of actors that such "why" questions no longer seem admissible with respect to that goal.

If, for example, one states as a goal the proposition that "every person should be free to do whatever he wishes in contexts where his actions do not interfere with the interests of other human beings," the speaker is unlikely to be met with a response of "why." The goal may be criticized as uncertain in its implications or difficult to implement, but it is so basic a tenet of our civilization—it reflects a cultural value so broadly shared, at least in the abstract—that the question "why" is seen as impertinent or imponderable or both.

I do not mean to suggest that everyone would agree with the "spheres of freedom" objective just stated. Still less do I mean to suggest that a society could subscribe to four or five such general objectives that would be adequate in their coverage to serve as testing criteria by which all other disagreements might be measured. One difficulty in the attempt to construct such a list is that each new goal added will conflict, in certain applications, with each prior goal listed; and thus each goal serves as a limited qualification on prior goals.

. Without any expectation of obtaining unanimous consent to them, let me set forth four goals that I generally use as ultimate testing criteria in attempting to frame solutions to problems of human organization. My position regarding pollution stems from these four criteria. If the criteria appeal to you and any part of what appears hereafter does not, our disagreement will have a helpful focus: which of us is correct, analytically, in supposing that his position on pollution would better serve these general goals. If the criteria do not seem acceptable to you, then it is to be expected that our more particular judgements will differ, and the task will then be yours to identify the basic set of criteria upon which your particular judgments rest.

My criteria are as follows:

1. The spheres of freedom criterion stated above.

2. Waste is a bad thing. The dominant feature of human existence is scarcity—our available resources, our aggregate labors, and our skill in employing both have always been, and will continue for some time to be, inadequate to yield to every man all the tangible and intangible satisfactions he would like to have. Hence, none of those resources, or labors, or skills, should be wasted—that is, employed so as to yield less than they might yield in human satisfactions.

3. Every human being should be regarded as an end rather than as a means to be used for the betterment of another. Each should be afforded dignity and regarded as having an absolute claim to an even-handed application of such rules as the community may adopt for its governance.

4. Both the incentive and the opportunity to improve his share of satisfactions should be preserved to every individual. Preservation of incentive is dictated by the "no-waste" criterion and enjoins against the continuous, totally egalitarian redistribution of satisfactions, or wealth; but subject to that constraint, everyone should receive, by continuous redistribution if necessary, some minimal share